How to Use This Book

Welcome to the world of programming! If you want to learn QBasic programming in just 21 days, you've come to the right book. This book is aimed at the readers who regularly use computers for common applications such as word processors, databases, or spreadsheets. As a computer user, you should be familiar with the basic operations of a computer (how to turn it on), its hardware (your screen, monitor, and disk drive), and some basic concepts (such as filenames, directories, and drive names).

I assume that you have no programming experience. Therefore, this book teaches you how to program in QBasic (which is bundled with MS-DOS, versions 5.0 and later) as your first programming language. The book contains 21 chapters, and you should be able to cover one chapter a day. At the end of each week I present a review session—a longer program that uses most of the week's topics.

Special Features of This Book

The book contains some special features to guide you on your QBasic journey. Syntax boxes help you master a specific QBasic topic. Each box provides concrete examples and a full explanation of the QBasic concept. To get a feel for the style of the syntax boxes, look at the following example. (Don't try to understand the material; you haven't even reached Day 1!)

Syntax

The INPUT$ Function

The general syntax for the INPUT$ function is

```
INPUT$(count)
```

The parameter *count* specifies the number of characters to read from the keyboard. The typical value for this parameter is 1. You don't need to press the Return key to end your input. The INPUT$ function does not automatically display your input—you need to use PRINT statements to echo the input on the screen. Figure 8.2 shows how the INPUT$(1) function call works.

Example:

```
DO
    PRINT "More calculations? (Y/N) ";
    aChar = INPUT$(1)
    PRINT aChar
    aChar = UCASE$(aChar)
LOOP UNTIL aChar = "Y" OR aChar = "N"
```

Another feature of this book is DO/DON'T boxes, which give you tips on what to do and what not to do.

DO read the rest of this section. It provides an explanation of the workshop section at the end of each day.

DON'T skip any of the quiz questions or exercises. If you can finish the day's workshop, you are ready to move on to new material.

I provide numerous examples with explanations to help you learn how to program. Each day ends with a Q&A section containing answers to common questions relating to that day's material. There is also a workshop at the end of each day. The workshop contains quiz questions and exercises. The quiz tests your knowledge of the concepts presented that day. If you want to check your responses, or in case you're stumped, the answers are in Appendix B, "Answers."

You won't learn QBasic by just reading this book, however. If you want to be a programmer, you've got to write programs. Following each set of quiz questions is a set of exercises. I recommend that you attempt each exercise. Writing QBasic code is the best way to learn the QBasic programming language.

Conventions Used in This Book

This book uses different typefaces to help you differentiate between QBasic code and regular English, and also to help you identify important concepts. Actual QBasic code is typeset in a special monospace font. Placeholders—terms used to represent what you actually type within the code—are typeset in an *italic monospace* font. New or important terms are typeset in *italic*.

Sometimes, I type a line that is too long to print in the book. When I need to split a line, I preface the second line with the ➥ character. When you see two lines like this, type them in as one line.

New Term Also, I have highlighted some new key terms with the New Term icon. I also have included a glossary at the end of the book if you need to look up any confusing computer terms.

One last note: I have made the listings in this book available to readers who want to save the time of typing them. Please use the form in the back of the book to order your disk copy.

I hope that this book enables you to make the bold step into the world of programming. It is an exciting world that gives you more control over what your machine does. Finally, I wish you happy programming!

Namir Clement Shammas

Teach Yourself QBasic™
in 21 Days

Teach Yourself
QBasic™ in 21 Days

Namir Clement Shammas

SAMS
PUBLISHING

A Division of Prentice Hall Computer Publishing
11711 North College, Carmel, Indiana 46032 USA

To my son Joseph, the youngest "QBaskick" user!

International Standard Book Number: 0-672-30324-8
Library of Congress Catalog Card Number: 93-83432

96   4   3

Interpretation of the printing code: the rightmost double-digit number is the year of the book's printing; the rightmost single-digit, the number of the book's printing. For example, a printing code of 93-1 shows that the first printing of the book occurred in 1993.

Trademarks

Composed in AGaramond and MCPdigital by Prentice Hall Computer Publishing

Printed in the United States of America

Publisher
Richard K. Swadley

Acquisitions Manager
Jordan Gold

Acquisitions Editor
Stacy Hiquet

**Development and Production
Editor**
Dean Miller

Senior Editor
Tad Ringo

Copy Editor
Keith Davenport

Editorial Coordinators
Rebecca S. Freeman
Bill Whitmer

Editorial Assistants
Sharon Cox
Rosemarie Graham

Technical Editor
Greg Guntle

Cover Designer
Dan Armstrong

**Director of Production
and Manufacturing**
Jeff Valler

Production Manager
Corinne Walls

Imprint Manager
Matthew Morrill

Book Designer
Michele Laseau

Production Analyst
Mary Beth Wakefield

**Proofreading/Indexing
Coordinator**
Joelynn Gifford

Graphics Image Specialists
Dennis Sheehan
Sue VandeWalle

Production
Jeff Baker, Claudia Bell,
Katy Bodenmiller,
Jodie Cantwell, Brad Chinn,
Christine Cook, Lisa Daugherty,
Terri Edwards, Mark Enock,
Brook Farling, Howard Jones,
John Kane, Heather Kaufman,
Sean Medlock, Juli Pavey,
Angela M. Pozdol, Linda Quigley,
Susan Shepard, Angie Trzepacz,
Suzanne Tully, Linda Seifert,
Greg Simsic, Alyssa Yesh

Indexer
Loren Malloy

Overview

Contents

Acknowledgments

I would like to thank the many people at Sams Publishing for encouraging me and working with me on this project. I would like to thank publisher Richard Swadley and acquisitions manager Jordan Gold for their vital support. Many thanks to editor Stacy Hiquet for sharing the vision for this book project. My special thanks to editor Dean Miller who gave 100 percent and bent over backward to accommodate the tight schedule and to manage the book size. My appreciation to technical reviewer Greg Guntle for his valuable comments. Finally, I want to thank all those at Sams Publishing who participated in producing this book.

About the Author

Namir Clement Shammas is a software engineer and an expert in object-oriented programming. He has written many articles for leading computer magazines and is responsible for many books on computer programming, including *Turbo Pascal 6 Object-Oriented Programming* and *Windows Programmer's Guide to ObjectWindows Library*.

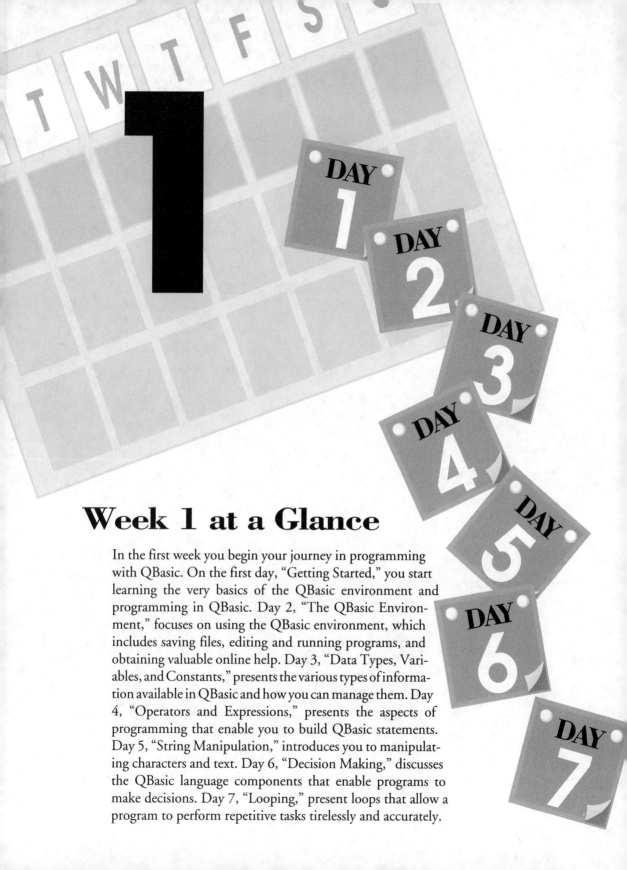

Week 1 at a Glance

In the first week you begin your journey in programming with QBasic. On the first day, "Getting Started," you start learning the very basics of the QBasic environment and programming in QBasic. Day 2, "The QBasic Environment," focuses on using the QBasic environment, which includes saving files, editing and running programs, and obtaining valuable online help. Day 3, "Data Types, Variables, and Constants," presents the various types of information available in QBasic and how you can manage them. Day 4, "Operators and Expressions," presents the aspects of programming that enable you to build QBasic statements. Day 5, "String Manipulation," introduces you to manipulating characters and text. Day 6, "Decision Making," discusses the QBasic language components that enable programs to make decisions. Day 7, "Looping," present loops that allow a program to perform repetitive tasks tirelessly and accurately.

DAY 1

Getting Started

Welcome to the world of programming! It's an exciting world that I hope will open new doors for you. Today you'll learn about the following topics:

☐ What is a program?

☐ Loading QBasic

☐ Overviewing the QBasic environment

☐ Entering simple QBasic programs

☐ Running QBasic programs

☐ Saving your work

☐ Commenting programs

☐ Exiting the QBasic environment

What is a Program?

When you hear the word "program" in general, you might think of an ordered sequence of events or tasks. This definition also fits for programming a computer. Consider programming a VCR to tape a specific television show (a task only slightly more complex than computer programming). To program my VCR, for example, I perform the following tasks:

1. Select the channel for the show I need to tape.

2. Press the start button.

3. Enter the time when the show begins.

4. Press the end button.

5. Enter the time when the show ends.

6. Press the timer button. (This action gives the timer control over the VCR, enabling it to start and stop taping at the designated times.)

The six tasks are very specific and must occur in a particular order. If I leave out any task, or swap the sequence of steps, I might end up with a tape of *Casablanca*—the Dudley Moore version (not the desired result). The same notion is true for programming computers. So what's a computer program? The answer is a sequence of instructions that processes and manipulates information.

Typically, a program contains three kinds of tasks: input, p
output. The program must obtain meaningful data before it
with that data. This is the input task. The processing task invo
altering, and even creating additional data. All these subtasks happen
computer's memory. However, once the computer has finished processing
information it must save or reveal this information. This is the output. Programs
typically output to the screen, printer, and data files stored on disks.

Loading QBasic

QBasic combines a *programming environment* with a *programming language*. (If
these terms confuse you, see the following box.) QBasic is Microsoft's latest
implementation of a BASIC *interpreter*. It succeeds the popular GW-BASIC
and BASICA implementations, also created by Microsoft. The main advantages
of QBasic over the previous BASIC implementation are its superior environment, its support for structured programming, and its extensive on-line help.

TECHNO-JARGON

> **programming environment:** a special program that enables you
> to write, edit, run, and manage a program.
>
> **programming language:** how a programmer communicates with a
> computer to teach it a set of instructions.
>
> **interpreter:** one of two essential ways programs run. An inter-
> preter examines your program one statement at a time and ex-
> ecutes that statement. Once the interpreter performs this task, it
> moves on to the next statement.

QBasic is bundled with DOS 5.0 and later versions, and it's located in the
DOS directory. On most computers, the DOS PATH includes the DOS
directory. This means that you can load QBasic from any other directory. If you
aren't sure about your DOS PATH, type **SET** from the DOS prompt. DOS
responds by showing your various environment variables, including one named
PATH. On my machine, the DOS PATH looks like this:

```
PATH=C:\;C:\DOS;\C:\WINDOWS;
```

As long as you see the DOS directory in your DOS PATH, you are fine. Otherwise, the DOS PATH needs to be modified to include the DOS directory.

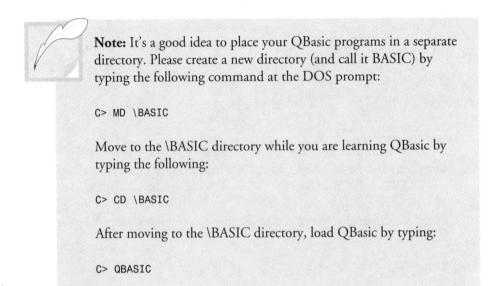

Note: It's a good idea to place your QBasic programs in a separate directory. Please create a new directory (and call it BASIC) by typing the following command at the DOS prompt:

```
C> MD \BASIC
```

Move to the \BASIC directory while you are learning QBasic by typing the following:

```
C> CD \BASIC
```

After moving to the \BASIC directory, load QBasic by typing:

```
C> QBASIC
```

Figure 1.1 shows the QBasic screen when it loads. Press the Esc key to bypass the online help screen. Figure 1.2 shows the current screen.

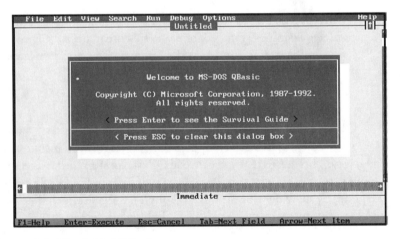

Figure 1.1. The initial QBasic screen.

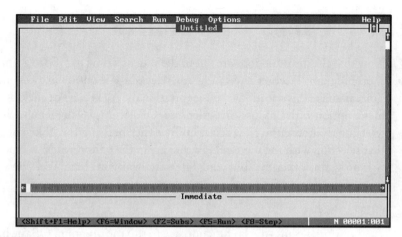

Figure 1.2. The blank QBasic editor screen.

The QBasic Environment

The QBasic environment has the following components, shown in Figure 1.2:

1. The **Program editing window** occupies most of the screen (by default).
   This is the part of the QBasic environment where you type in programs. Notice that the Program editing window has a title at the center
   of the top window edge. The window title is also the name of the file
   that stores the current program. Initially, the window title is **Untitled**.

2. The **Immediate execution window** enables you to execute one-line
   QBasic statements and test program components you build. You easily
   can alter the size of this window by using your mouse to drag the
   upper window edge.

3. The **Main menu bar**. This component is located at the top of the
   screen and shows the main menu options. These options are File, Edit,
   View, Search, Run, Debug, Options, and Help. In Day 2, I explain in
   more detail what these options do.

4. The **Status bar**. This component is located at the bottom screen line
   and shows the shortcut keys and the location of the cursor.

Your First Program

Now that the introductions are out of the way, it's time to type in a simple and short program. To enter a new program, select the File option in the main menu. You can make this selection by either pressing the Alt+F keys or clicking the File menu option with a mouse. In either case, QBasic displays a menu with various selections. Choose the New selection by either pressing the N key or clicking that selection with the mouse. Now you are in the editor, ready to type in your first program. Enter the following line exactly as you see it. You don't have to press Enter when you finish typing:

```
PRINT "Hello World!"
```

Now press Shift+the F5 function key to run the program. QBasic hides the environment and displays the text **Hello World!** in the screen from which you launched QBasic. Figure 1.3 shows the sample output from my computer. Notice that QBasic displays a message at the bottom of the output screen asking you to press any key to return to the QBasic environment. Press the space bar to return to the editor.

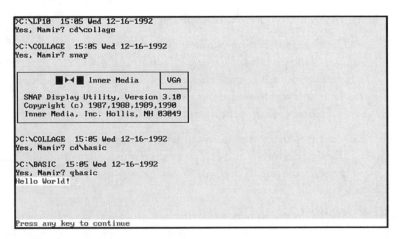

```
>C:\LP10  15:05 Wed 12-16-1992
Yes, Namir? cd\collage

>C:\COLLAGE  15:05 Wed 12-16-1992
Yes, Namir? snap


     ■ ►◄ ■  Inner Media      VGA

  SNAP Display Utility, Version 3.10
  Copyright (c) 1987,1988,1989,1990
  Inner Media, Inc. Hollis, NH 03049


>C:\COLLAGE  15:05 Wed 12-16-1992
Yes, Namir? cd\basic

>C:\BASIC  15:05 Wed 12-16-1992
Yes, Namir? qbasic
Hello World!



Press any key to continue
```

Figure 1.3. A sample output generated by the simple greeting program.

Look at the one-line program that you typed. The program's one statement contains two parts: the PRINT keyword and the quoted text "Hello World!". PRINT is a QBasic command that displays on the screen the item (or items) that

follows it. In this case, the item after PRINT is the quoted text. Although QBasic requires that you correctly type the PRINT keyword, it does not concern itself with the contents of quoted text. This means, if I typed the following line:

```
PRINT "Hellow WOrld!"
```

QBasic will not be upset about the poor spelling and errant capitalization; the above one-line program also will run, displaying the text Hellow WOrld!, exactly as it appears in the quoted text.

Although QBasic does not care whether you type keywords in uppercase or lowercase, it does require correct spelling of keywords. Otherwise, you will produce an error. For example, if I type the following line:

```
PRIN "Hello World!"
```

and omit the trailing T in the keyword PRINT, I get an error message box (shown in Figure 1.4) when I press the Shift+F5 key to run the program.

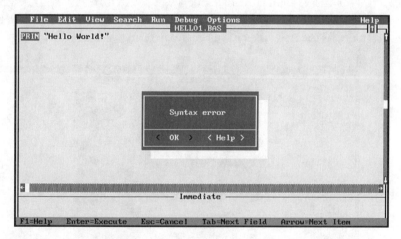

Figure 1.4. A sample QBasic error message.

 Note: Quoted text is commonly called a **string**, which is short for **string of characters**.

A QBasic statement must appear on a single program line. QBasic allows you to include multiple statements in a line. In this case, you must separate each neighboring statement with a colon.

Saving Your Work

To save a program you are currently editing, select the File option in the main menu (just like you did when you created a new window). This time, however, you need to choose the Save As... selection, either by pressing the A key or clicking that selection with your mouse. The QBasic environment responds by popping up a dialog box, shown in Figure 1.5, that permits you to specify the filename and the target directory. Because you are in the \BASIC directory already, you only have to specify the filename. Type **HELLO1**. You can include the .BAS file extension name, but if you omit it, QBasic is nice enough to add it for you. After typing the filename, press the Return key. Your first program is now stored in the file HELLO1.BAS. The QBasic environment also uses this filename as the new title of the Program editing window.

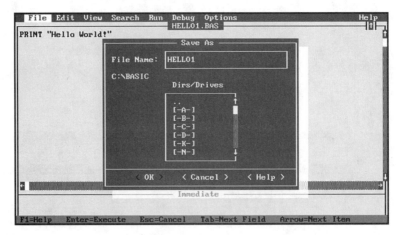

Figure 1.5. The Save As dialog box.

To update your work by saving it in the same file, QBasic provides a shortcut menu selection. First invoke the File option, and then choose the Save selection. This selection writes the current contents of the edited program to the filename that appears as the window title.

Your Second Program

The first program you typed is an example of a minimal QBasic program. The program displays text. It performs neither input nor processing. The following is another simple program that offers a little more flavor of QBasic programming.

Note: Listing 1.1 shows the new program. Notice that the listing is numbered. This numbering is NOT part of the program; it serves only for reference. The rest of the programs in this book are numbered. Type in the listing (without the numbers) and save it in file DICE1.BAS.

The program in Listing 1.1 performs the following tasks:

1. Clears the output screen. This task enables you to display the output of the current program on a clean screen. Everything else is erased.

2. Prompts you to enter a number between -32768 and 32676. The program uses this number as a seed for generating a random number.

3. Displays the text Dice throw is followed by a number between 1 and 6. This random value of the output emulates a dice throw.

These tasks cover all three basic components of a computer program: input, processing, and output.

Listing 1.1. The simple dice-throwing program DICE1.BAS.

```
1: CLS
2: RANDOMIZE
3: PRINT "Dice throw is"; INT(RND * 6) + 1
4: END
```

1

Here is a sample output generated by the program in Listing 1.1 (the output does not include the systematic QBasic prompt that appears at the bottom of the screen):

```
Random-number seed (-32768 to 32767)? 45
Dice throw is 5
```

Let's look at the lines of Listing 1.1. Each line contains a QBasic statement. Statements are to programs what sentences are to people. The single phrase on line 1 is CLS, the QBasic clear screen command. This command erases the screen and places the cursor at the top left corner of the screen. Line 2 uses the QBasic command RANDOMIZE to provide the random-number generating function RND with a new seed. A seed is a value used to generate subsequent random numbers. The RANDOMIZE command prompts you to enter a seed. This is the input part of the program. Line 3 contains a PRINT command that outputs a result. Notice that this command is followed by two items separated by a semicolon: a string and a value. The PRINT statement displays the string followed by the integer value. The RND keyword is a predefined QBasic function that generates a number greater than or equal to zero and less than 1. Multiplying RND by 6 yields a floating-point number (a number with decimals) greater than or equal to 0 and less than 6. The INT keyword is another predefined QBasic function that chops off the decimal part and retains the integer part of a number. The INT function in line 3 yields a number between 0 and 5. Because the result of dice throw is between 1 and 6, line 3 adds 1 to the number. Consequently, the PRINT statement displays a number between 1 and 6. On line 4 of the program the END statement declares a formal end to the program. Although the END statement is not required for simple programs, it is needed in more structured programs (such as the ones you will learn about on Day 10, "Subroutines and Procedures").

Commenting Programs

A good programming habit to learn early is adding comments to your programs. There are two kinds of comments that you can add. The first kind incorporates background information about the program. Such information includes program purpose, version number, date of creation, date of last update, programmer name, and so on. The second kind of comment clarifies the tasks of the various program statements.

QBasic offers two syntaxes for inserting comments. The first syntax uses the keyword **REM** (short for REMARK). **REM** comments must appear in separate lines. QBasic ignores the text that comes after the **REM**. The second, and more flexible, syntax for the QBasic comments uses the single quotation mark ('). You can place this kind of comment either on a separate line or following a statement.

Listing 1.2 presents a commented version of Listing 1.1. It includes both kinds of comments and uses the **REM** and single quotation mark comments. The program in Listing 1.2 performs the same tasks as the program in Listing 1.1. Type in the listing and save it in the file DICE2.BAS. Once again, remember that the line numbers are not part of the program—don't type them in.

Listing 1.2. The modified dice-throwing program DICE2.BAS.

```
1: REM Program that throws a dice
2: REM Version 1.0
3: REM Created 12/16/1992    Last Update 12/18/1992
4: REM
5: CLS ' clear the screen
6: RANDOMIZE ' randomize the seed
7: ' output number between 1 and 6
8: PRINT "Dice throw is"; INT(RND * 6) + 1
9: END
```

```
Random-number seed (-32768 to 32767)? 777
Dice throw is 3
```

Lines 1–3 use REM comments to state the purpose of the program, its version number, and the dates of creation and last update. Line 4 throws in a blank REM comment that I use for separating the program information comments from the program statements. Lines 5 and 6 use the single-quotation mark comment, placing them after each QBasic statement. Use this type of comment when your comment text is short. Line 7 shows a single-quotation mark comment on a separate line.

Exiting QBasic

To exit QBasic, select the File option in the main menu and then choose the Exit selection either by pressing the keys Alt+F and X or clicking Exit with the mouse. If you haven't saved your most recent changes in the current program and you attempt to exit, QBasic prompts you with a dialog box to save the changes.

Summary

This chapter introduces you to programming in general and using QBasic in particular. The chapter covered the following topics:

☐ A program is a sequence of instructions that processes and manipulates information. Typically, programs perform input, processing of data, and output.

☐ To load QBasic from DOS, type QBASIC at the DOS prompt.

☐ The QBasic environment is made of the Program editing window, the Immediate execution window, the main menu bar, and the status bar. The main menu offers the options File, Edit, View, Search, Run, Debug, Options, and Help.

☐ How to type in and run simple QBasic programs.

☐ How to save your work by choosing the Save As or Save selections in the File menu option. The shortcut keys for Save As are Alt+F and A. The shortcut keys for the Save selection are Alt+F and S.

☐ How to comment your programs, which enables you to add background information and clarify the tasks of various program statements. QBasic supports using the REM keyword and the single quotation mark (') to specify a comment. Qbasic ignores the text that comes after the REM or single quotation mark.

☐ How to exit the QBasic environment by invoking the Exit selection in the File menu option. The shortcut keys for the Exit selection are Alt+F and X.

On Day 2, "The QBasic Environment," you will learn about using the various menu options in the QBasic environment.

Q&A

Q. Does QBasic use line numbers?

A. No. Unlike its predecessors (GW-BASIC and BASICA), QBasic needs no line numbers. You can type in line numbers in a QBasic program, but QBasic will regard them as labels (you learn more about labels on Day 6, "Decision Making"). This feature allows QBasic to run many GW-BASIC programs with little or no modifications.

Q. Does the QBasic environment monitor what I type?

A. Yes. In fact, when you press Return or move the cursor away from a line, the QBasic editor quickly scans the line and makes sure that QBasic keywords appear in uppercase.

Q. What happens if I forget to type the second double-quote in the first program?

A. The QBasic editor is smart enough to insert the trailing double-quote for you. Consequently, you can still press the Shift+F5 function key and run the program.

Workshop

The Workshop provides quiz questions to help you solidify your understanding of the material covered and exercises to provide you with experience in using what you've learned. Try to understand the quiz and exercise answers before continuing on to the next chapter. Answers are provided in Appendix B, "Answers."

Quiz

1. What is the output of the following program?

```
1: REM Program that throws a dice
2: REM Version 1.0
3: REM Created 12/16/1992   Last Update 12/18/1992
4: REM
```

```
5: CLS ' clear the screen
6: RANDOMIZE ' randomize the seed
7: ' output number between 1 and 6
8: REM PRINT "Dice throw is"; INT(RND * 6) + 1
9: END
```

2. How different is the final output screen of the following program from the one in Listing 1.3?

```
1: REM Program that throws a dice
2: REM Version 1.0
3: REM Created 12/16/1992   Last Update 12/18/1992
4: REM
5: RANDOMIZE ' randomize the seed
6: CLS ' clear the screen
7: ' output number between 1 and 6
8: PRINT "Dice throw is"; INT(RND * 6) + 1
9: END
```

Exercises

1. Write a program that displays the message **I am a QBasic Programmer**.

2. Modify Listing 1.3 to create a program that generates a random day of the month. The program should display the appropriate text and a value that ranges between 1 and 31.

DAY 2

The QBasic Environment

This chapter looks at the options in Qbasic's main menu. The focus in this chapter is on the mechanics of using the QBasic environment, not programming in QBasic. You will learn about the following:

☐ Options for loading QBasic

☐ Choosing menu selections

☐ The **File** option

☐ The **Edit** option

☐ The **View** option

☐ The **Search** option

☐ The **Run** option

☐ The **Debug** option

☐ The **Options** option

☐ The **Help** option

☐ The menu shortcut keys

☐ The QBasic editing keys

Options for Loading QBasic

On Day 1, "Getting Started," you learned you can load QBasic by typing the word QBASIC (and pressing the Return key) at the DOS prompt. QBasic enables you to specify options at the DOS prompt to fine tune its performance and display. Table 2.1 lists the various options for loading QBasic. The general syntax for specifying an option is

```
QBASIC option1 option2 ...
```

Table 2.1. Options for loading QBasic from the DOS prompt.

Option	Purpose
/?	Displays the options available at the DOS prompt. This option does **not** load QBasic.
/B	Allows a better display for a computer that has a color graphics adapter connected to a monochrome monitor, or a laptop/notepad computer with an LCD display.
/EDITOR	Invokes QBasic as the MS-DOS editor. You get the same result if you type EDIT at the DOS prompt.
/ED	Offers an abbreviated form of the /EDITOR option.
/G	Cures the snow-like flickering that you might experience with your CGA monitor.
/H	Automatically sets the number of lines to the maximum available for the video adapter in your system. The default (based on CGA adapters) is 25 lines. If you have an EGA screen, the maximum number of lines is 43. If you have a VGA screen, the maximum number of lines is 50.
/MBF	Uses a special format developed by Microsoft to convert and store numeric data. The default is a numeric format that complies with the IEEE specifications. This option enables you to switch to the numeric format Microsoft had developed earlier for BASICA and GW-BASIC.
/NOHI	Indicates that your screen does not support high-intensity text.
/RUN filename	Loads and runs the program in **filename**. This file must be a text file with the .BAS file extension.
filename	Loads the file **filename**. This file must be a text file with the .BAS file extension.

Options
For Loading
QBasic

2

Choosing Menu Selections

To choose a menu selection in any QBasic menu option, you can perform one of the following tasks:

1. Using your mouse, move the mouse cursor to the desired selection and click the left mouse button.

2. Press the shortcut key for the targeted menu selection. The shortcut key corresponds to the highlighted letter of that selection. In this book, shortcut keys are highlighted in bold. For example, to choose the Save As selection, press A. Shortcut keys are case-insensitive—you don't have to press the Shift key with the shortcut key.

3. Using the up or down arrow key, move from one selection to another. The QBasic menu selections work as a circular list. This feature enables you to wrap around the menu selection by using either the up or down arrow keys. To invoke the currently chosen menu selection, press the Return key.

The File Option

The **F**ile option enables you to create, store, recall, and print your programs. Figure 2.1 shows the menu selections in the **F**ile option. The shortcut key for **F**ile is Alt+F. The **F**ile menu contains the selections **N**ew, **O**pen, Save **A**s, **S**ave, **P**rint, and E**x**it. Notice that the **O**pen, Save **A**s, and **P**rint selections are followed by three dots. These dots indicate that the menu selection invokes a dialog box. Using dots to indicate a dialog box has become the industry standard in menus. For further proof, just open your favorite word processor or spreadsheet and check the menus.

The **N**ew selection enables you to start typing in a new program. If the Program editing window contains an updated listing, QBasic will prompt you to save that listing first.

The **O**pen selection allows you to load text files from either the current directory or any other directory. As a default, the dialog box lists only the files with the .BAS extension. Figure 2.2 shows the dialog box for the **O**pen selection. Use this option to load the program DICE2.BAS, which I presented in Listing 1.2.

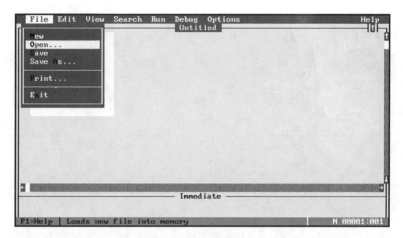

Figure 2.1. The menu selections in the File option.

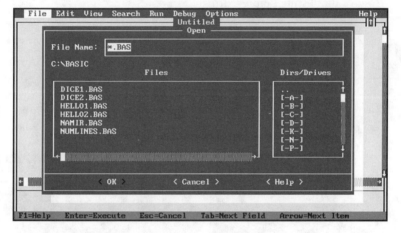

Figure 2.2. The dialog box for the Open selection.

Click the Save **A**s selection to store the program you currently are editing in a new file. If you want to modify and experiment with a program, you can use this selection to create extra copies of the program—a safe copy and an experimental copy. If you attempt to write to an existing file, QBasic will warn you and give you the options of overwriting the existing file. The **S**ave selection quickly and systematically saves the currently edited program in the associated file.

DO save your programs in the BASIC directory you created on Day 1. Keeping your programs in a common directory will make it easier to find them later.

DON'T forget to save your work periodically using the **S**ave selection.

The **P**rint selection pops up a dialog box that offers you the choice of printing either the entire program, the selected text, or the text that appears in the Program editing window.

The E**x**it selection enables you to leave the QBasic environment. If the Program editing window contains an updated listing, QBasic will prompt you to save that listing before exiting.

The Edit Option

The **E**dit option, shown in Figure 2.3, contains two groups of selections. The first group of functions manipulate the currently edited text. The second group enables you to spawn new program components, a topic covered on Day 10.

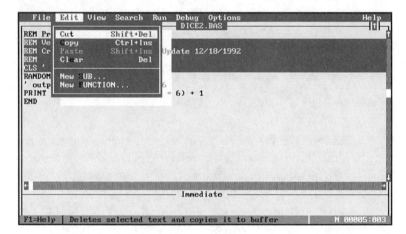

Figure 2.3. The menu selections in Edit option.

The text-manipulating selections include Cut, Copy, Paste, and Clear. These selections manipulate the visible text in the Program editing window and the invisible text located in a special memory block, called the *clipboard*. The Cut selection, which has the Shift+Del shortcut key, deletes the selected text and copies it to the clipboard. The Copy selection, which has the Ctrl+Ins shortcut keys, copies the selected text to the clipboard. The Paste selection, which has the shortcut keys Shift+Ins, copies text from the clipboard to the current cursor location. The Clear selection, which has the shortcut key Del, deletes the selected text. If you haven't selected text, the Cut, Copy, and Clear options are not available, so they are grayed out. If there is no text in the clipboard, the Paste selection is not available. so it is grayed out.

The View Option

The View option has three selections—SUBs, Split, and Output Screen. The SUBs selection, which uses the F2 function key as its shortcut key, enables you to view the hierarchy of a program and all of its semi-independent programs (you learn more about this option on Day 10). The Split selection toggles splitting the Program editing window into two smaller windows. Splitting the windows enables you to view, compare, and edit two portions of the same program—a useful feature when you are dealing with a long listing. Figure 2.4 shows a split Program editing window. The Output Screen selection, which has the F4 function key as its shortcut key, enables you to look at the last program's output screen. This selection is useful with programs that require a long time to output results. If this selection was not available, you would have to rerun a program to take a second look at its output.

The Search Option

The Search option offers selections that enable you to find and change text in the currently edited program. The three selections in this option are Find, Repeat Last Find, and Change.

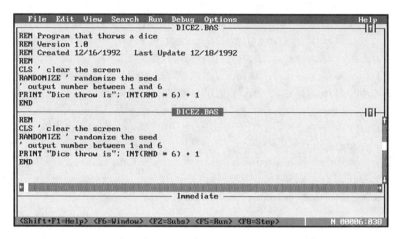

Figure 2.4. A sample split editing screen.

The **F**ind selection pops up the Find dialog box, shown in Figure 2.5. This dialog box contains the following components:

☐ An input text box labeled **Find What:** that permits you to enter the text you want to find.

☐ A check box labeled **Match Upper/Lowercase** that enables you to specify the case-sensitivity of the text search.

☐ A check box labeled **Whole Word** that enables you to specify whether the matching text has to be a whole word.

☐ The button labeled **OK**. When you click this button or press Return, you accept your input in the text box and trigger the text search.

☐ The button labeled **Cancel**. When you click this button, you cancel the text search and close the dialog box. If you do not have a mouse, you can use the Tab key to select this button. When the button is selected, press Return to invoke the Cancel button.

☐ The button labeled **Help**. Clicking this button, or selecting it and pressing Return invokes online help that explains the use of the Find dialog box.

When Find locates matching text, it highlights it.

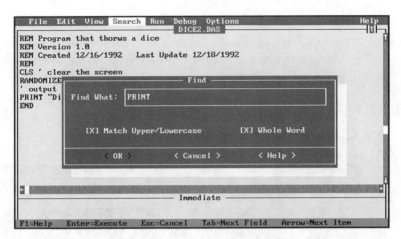

Figure 2.5. A sample session with the Find dialog box.

The **R**epeat Last Find selection searches for the next occurrence of the search text. The search uses the same states of the check boxes that you set when you last invoked the **F**ind selection.

The **C**hange selection pops up the Change dialog box, shown in Figure 2.6. This dialog box contains the following components:

☐ An input text box labeled **Find What:** that enables you to enter the text you want to find.

☐ An input text box labeled **Change to:** that enables you to enter the replacement text.

☐ A check box labeled **Match Upper/Lowercase** that permits you to specify the case-sensitivity of the text change.

☐ A check box labeled **Whole Word** that enables you to specify whether the matching text has to be a whole word.

☐ The button labeled **Find and Verify**. When you click this button or press Return, you accept your input in the text box and trigger the text change. A dialog box prompts you to confirm changing the various occurrences of the matching text before the replacement.

☐ The button labeled **Change All**. When you click this button or press Return, you accept your input in the text box and trigger the text change without prompting you for confirmation.

☐ The button labeled **Cancel**. When you click this button, you cancel the text-changing process. If you do not have a mouse, you can use the Tab key to select this button. Once selected, press Return to invoke the Cancel button.

☐ The button labeled **Help**. Clicking on this button, or selecting it and then pressing Return invokes online help that explains the use of the Change dialog box.

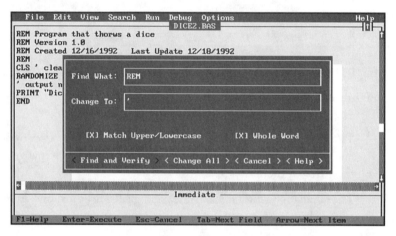

Figure 2.6. A sample session with the Change dialog box.

The Run Option

The **R**un option has three selections that handle program execution. These selections are **S**tart, **R**estart, and **C**ontinue. The **S**tart selection, which uses the Shift+F5 shortcut key, begins execution of a QBasic program. The **C**ontinue selection, which uses the F5 shortcut key, enables you to resume program execution when the program reaches the STOP statement. (The STOP command, which I do not use in this book, enables you to temporarily halt a program.) This statement acts like a temporary END statement, making the program dormant until you invoke the **C**ontinue selection. The **R**estart selection enables you to reset the program after you fix an error in your listing. This selection ensures that the program execution starts at the beginning of the program, not where the runtime error occurred.

The Debug Option

The selections in the **D**ebug option enable you to examine more closely the execution of a program and its data. I will introduce you to the various aspects of debugging throughout the book. For now, it's too early to discuss the topics of debugging and using the debugger.

The Options Option

The **O**ptions option enables you to fine-tune the operations of the QBasic environment. This option offers three selections: **D**isplay, Help **P**ath, and **S**yntax Checking. The **D**isplay selection pops up a dialog box (shown in Figure 2.7) that enables you to choose the foreground and background colors for the normal text, current statement, and breakpoint lines in a QBasic program. The Help **P**ath selection pops up a dialog box that enables you to specify the directory that contains QBASIC.HLP—the file containing the online help for QBasic. You need to use the Help **P**ath selection only if QBASIC.HLP is located in a directory other than \DOS. The **S**yntax Checking selection enables you to toggle the syntax-checking feature of the QBasic editor. I suggest that you set or leave the syntax checking on (which should be the default setting) while you are using this book.

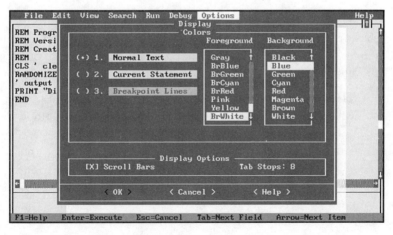

Figure 2.7. The Display selection dialog box.

The Help Option

The **Help** option offers powerful, context-sensitive online help. Using the QBasic help system is like having an electronic reference manual. The power of the help system comes from its use of hypertext technology. This technology uses special keywords that are part of the text to jump from one location in the help system to another. The system is excellent for checking the syntax of predefined commands, functions, and various language components. The **Help** option has five selections: **I**ndex, **C**ontents, **T**opic:, Using **H**elp, and **A**bout.

TECHNO-JARGON

> **hypertext technology:** a method for creating documents with special words and phrases that link different parts of the document. These links appear either in special and distinctive colors or (as in the case of the QBasic Help system) are enclosed in special characters. To activate a hypertext link and jump to the related topics, move the cursor to a hypertext link, or click it with the mouse. As a result, the hypertext document editor displays another part of the document that is related to the hypertext link you just activated.

The **I**ndex selection displays an index of the QBasic keywords. Figure 2.8 shows a sample screen produced by invoking **I**ndex. The QBasic keywords are grouped alphabetically. You can jump to a particular group of keywords by pressing the first letter of the grouped keywords.

The **C**ontents selection invokes a help screen that displays a table of contents, shown in Figure 2.9. There are four topics and subtopics:

1. The Orientation topic contains the following subtopics:

   ☐ Using Help

   ☐ Using Menus and Commands

   ☐ Using a Dialog Box

   ☐ Syntax Conventions

2. The Using QBasic topic contains the following subtopics:

☐ QBasic Command Line

☐ Basic Character Set

☐ Keywords by Programming Task

☐ QBasic Environment Limits

☐ Version Differences

☐ Converting BASICA Programs

☐ Beyond QBasic

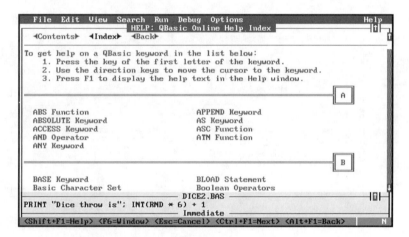

Figure 2.8. A sample screen produced by invoking the Index selection.

3. The Keys topic includes the following subtopics:

☐ Shortcut Keys Summary

☐ Editing Keys

☐ View and Search Keys

☐ Run and Debug Keys

☐ Help Keys

4. The Quick Reference topic contains the following subtopics:

- ☐ ASCII Character Codes

- ☐ Keyboard Scan Codes

- ☐ Run-Time Error Codes

- ☐ Copyright and Trademarks

To select any subtopic, move the mouse to the desired subtopic and click the mouse button. You also can use the Tab key or the cursor keys to traverse the various subtopics. Press the Return key to obtain help on the currently selected subtopic.

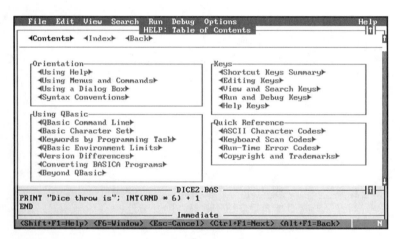

Figure 2.9. The Contents selection help screen.

The **T**opic: selection is context-sensitive. When you press the F1 key, you invoke a selection guided by the word where the cursor is located. Figure 2.10 shows using the **T**opic: selection to explain the PRINT statement.

The Using **H**elp selection enables you to obtain online information regarding the help system—help with using help! This feature is useful if you find yourself somewhat overwhelmed by the help system.

The **A**bout selection pops up a simple dialog box that contains the copyright notice for QBasic and its version number. Using the **A**bout selection helps you determine the exact version of QBasic that you are using.

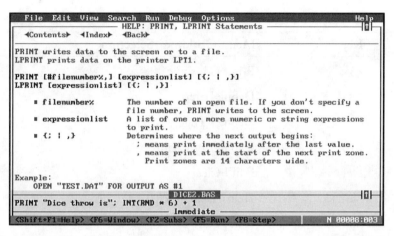

```
  File  Edit  View  Search  Run  Debug  Options                    Help
 ┌─────────────── HELP: PRINT, LPRINT Statements ──────────────────┤↑├
 │ ◄Contents► ◄Index► ◄Back►                                         │
 │                                                                   │
 │ PRINT writes data to the screen or to a file.                     │
 │ LPRINT prints data on the printer LPT1.                           │
 │                                                                   │
 │ PRINT [#filenumber%,] [expressionlist] [{; │ ,}]                   │
 │ LPRINT [expressionlist] [{; │ ,}]                                 │
 │                                                                   │
 │   ▪ filenumber%        The number of an open file. If you don't specify a │
 │                        file number, PRINT writes to the screen.   │
 │   ▪ expressionlist     A list of one or more numeric or string expressions │
 │                        to print.                                  │
 │   ▪ {; │ ,}            Determines where the next output begins:    │
 │                           ; means print immediately after the last value. │
 │                           , means print at the start of the next print zone. │
 │                           Print zones are 14 characters wide.     │
 │                                                                   │
 │ Example:                                                          │
 │    OPEN "TEST.DAT" FOR OUTPUT AS #1                               │
 ├──────────────────────── DICE2.BAS ────────────────────────┤▣├───┤
 │ PRINT "Dice throw is"; INT(RND * 6) + 1                           │
 └──────────────────────── Immediate ───────────────────────────────┘
  <Shift+F1=Help> <F6=Window> <F2=Subs> <F5=Run> <F8=Step>    │ N 00008:003
```

Figure 2.10. The Topic: selection invoking the help system to explain the PRINT statement.

The Menu Shortcut Keys

As I've mentioned throughout the chapter, the QBasic environment supports a set of shortcut keys for the menus. Learning these shortcut keys enables you to quickly invoke important menu selections. Table 2.2 lists the menu shortcut keys. The table uses the bar character (|) to specify the selection and its parent menu option. For example, the F5 function key is the shortcut key for the **C**ontinue selection in the **R**un menu option. Table 2.2 uses **R**un | **C**ontinue to indicate that relationship between the selection and its parent menu option.

Table 2.2. **The menu shortcut keys for the QBasic environment.**

Key	Menu Option or Selection
F1	**H**elp
F2	**S**UBs...
F3	**R**epeat Last Find
F4	**V**iew	**O**utput Screen

continues

Table 2.2. continued

Key	Menu Option or Selection
F5	**R**un	**C**ontinue
F8	**D**ebug	**S**tep
F9	**D**ebug	**T**oggle Breakpoint
F10	**D**ebug	**P**rocedure Step
Del	**E**dit	**C**lear
Shift+F1	**H**elp	**U**sing **H**elp
Shift+F5	**R**un	**S**tart
Shift+Del	**E**dit	Cu**t**
Shift+Ins	**E**dit	**P**aste
Ctrl+Ins	**E**dit	**C**opy

DO use shortcut keys—they can make your programming life much easier.

DON'T forget the online help if you get stuck.

The QBasic Editing Keys

The QBasic environment incorporates a versatile text editor. Because I assume that as a PC user you have used a text editor or a word processor, I will not go into the details of how to edit text. Nevertheless, you might find it useful to learn about the various types of commands and their keystrokes. Table 2.3 lists the different kinds of editing commands for the QBasic editor and their keystrokes.

Table 2.3. The editing commands for the QBasic editor.

Cursor Move

Keystroke	The cursor is moved...
Left arrow	one character to the left
Right arrow	one character to the right
Ctrl+Left arrow	one word to the left
Ctrl+Right arrow	one word to the right
Up arrow	one line up
Down arrow	one line down
Home	to the beginning of the current line
End	to the end of the current line
F6	to the next window

Text Scrolling

Keystroke	The text scrolls...
Ctrl+Up arrow	one line up
Ctrl+Down arrow	one line down
PgUp	one page up
PgDn	one page down

Text Selection

Keystroke	Selects...
Shift+Left arrow	the left character
Shift+Right arrow	the right character
Shift+Ctrl+Left arrow	the left word
Shift+Ctrl+Right arrow	the right word
Shift+Down arrow	the current line
Shift+Up arrow	the line above the current line

continues

2

Table 2.3. continued

Text Selection

Keystroke	Selects...
Shift+PgUp	the screen up
Shift+PgDn	the screen down
Shift+Ctrl+Home	all text to the beginning of the line
Shift+Ctrl+End	all text to the end of the line

Cut, Copy, and Delete

Keystroke	Operation
Ctrl+Ins	Copy text from clipboard
Shift+Del	Delete selected text to clipboard
Ctrl+Y	Delete the current line and copy it to the clipboard
Ctrl+Q, Y	Delete the characters to the end of the line and copy them to the clipboard
Shift+Ins	Insert contents of clipboard
Home, Ctrl+N	Insert a blank line above the cursor position
Ctrl+P, Ctrl+key	Insert a special character
Backspace	Delete the character to the left of the cursor
Del	Delete the character at the cursor
Del	Delete selected text
Shift+Tab	Delete the leading spaces from the current line
Ins	Toggle between insert and overwrite modes

Bookmarks

Keystroke	Operation
Ctrl+K, 0 to 3	Set bookmarks 0 to 3
Ctrl+Q, 0 to 3	Move to bookmark 0 to 3

Window Commands

Keystroke	Operation
Alt+Plus	Increase the size of the active window
Alt+Minus	Decrease the size of the active window
Ctrl+F10	Zoom in and out of the active window
Ctrl+PgUp	Move left one window
Ctrl+PgDn	Move right one window

2

Summary

This chapter introduced you to various aspects of the QBasic environment. You learned about the following topics:

- QBasic offers options that you can invoke from the DOS prompt while loading QBasic. These options permit you to fine-tune certain aspects of displaying text and operating the QBasic environment.

- QBasic offers three ways to choose menu selections, including using the mouse, shortcut keys, and the up and down arrows.

- The **File** option enables you to open a new window for editing, load an existing QBasic program, save QBasic programs, print a file, and exit QBasic.

- The **Edit** option offers selections that support text-editing operations, such as cut, copy, paste, and delete.

- The **View** option provides selections to split the screen, view the subprograms in a QBasic programs, and examine the output screen.

☐ The **S**earch option, using versatile dialog boxes, provides selections to find and change text.

☐ The **R**un option manages running, restarting, and resuming QBasic programs.

☐ The **D**ebug option offers selections that enable you to execute a program in single steps.

☐ The **O**ptions option provides selections to customize the colors of the QBasic environment, specify the directory that contains the QBasic help file, and toggle the syntax checking feature.

☐ The **H**elp option supplies you with selections that support context-sensitive online help. The QBasic help system uses hypertext links to enable you to jump between various locations in the help system.

☐ QBasic offers a family of menu shortcut keys to accelerate invoking certain menu options and selections.

☐ QBasic supports editing keys for moving the cursor, managing bookmarks, manipulating the Program editing and Immediate windows, and scrolling, selecting, inserting, deleting, and copying text.

Q&A

Q. Can I use QBasic to edit my AUTOEXEC.BAT and CONFIG.SYS files?

A. Yes, as long as you invoke the /EDITOR or /ED options. Here is what you need to type at the DOS prompt to edit these files:

```
> QBASIC \AUTOEXEC.BAT /ED
```

and

```
> QBASIC \CONFIG.SYS /ED
```

Q. If I want to share my QBasic programs with my friends, do I have to do anything special?

A. No. Your friends must have QBasic on their machine, however. This requirement is easy to meet if your friends use DOS 5.0.

Q. Does QBasic create a backup file when I use the Save selection in the File menu option?

A. No. QBasic overwrites the contents of the program file.

WorkShop

The Workshop provides quiz questions to help you solidify your understanding of the material covered and exercises to provide you with experience in using what you've learned. Try to understand the quiz and exercise answers before continuing on to the next chapter. Answers are provided in Appendix B, "Answers."

2

Quiz

1. True or false: The shortcut key for exiting QBasic is Alt+X.

2. True or false: The F5 function key starts running QBasic programs.

3. True or false: The Del key clears a block of selected text.

4. True or false: The keystrokes Alt+F and S save the currently edited program in the same file.

5. True or false: QBasic creates a backup file when you use the **S**ave selection in the **F**ile menu option.

DAY
3

Data Types, Variables, and Constants

This chapter covers manipulating data (such as data types, variables, and constants) in a QBasic program. Today, you will learn about the following topics:

- [ ] The predefined data types in QBasic
- [ ] Naming items in QBasic
- [ ] What is a variable?
- [ ] Creating and using variables
- [ ] The INPUT statement
- [ ] Explicit data typing of variables
- [ ] Implicit data typing of variables
- [ ] What is a constant?
- [ ] Creating and using constants

Predefined QBasic Data Types

Computers are good at learning instructions and executing them obediently. Contrary to what you might believe, computers are very stupid. For example, computer math revolves around two numbers—0 and 1! So why are computers so popular, powerful, and revered? The answer lies in what programmers have done with computers. A computer's ability is a true testament to the human genius.

From Bits To Bytes

Computers do binary math—they only can count from zero to one. Computer scientists, hardware manufacturers, and programmers have devised smart schemes that employ the binary math of computers. By looking at groups of bits (a *bit* is a binary digit, taking a value of 0 or 1), you can create numbers to use in calculations. Groups of bits are called *bytes, words,* and *long words.* A byte is made up of 8 bits. A word contains 16 bits. A long word contains 32 bits. Figure 3.1 shows a schema depicting the 8 bits in a byte. The bits are numbered 0 to

7 from right to left. Bit number 0 is the least significant bit, whereas bit number 7 is the most significant bit. The 8 bits in a byte enable you to create 256 different combinations of zeroes and ones. Consequently, you can use a byte to count from 0–255. In Figure 3.1 the bits of the top byte are all ones. This bit combination represents the integer 255. The middle byte in the same figure has all of its bits set to zero. This combination of bits represents the integer 0. The bottom byte in the figure has ones in all of the first seven bits and zero in the most significant bit. This combination of bits represents the integer 127.

7	6	5	4	3	2	1	0	← bit number
1	1	1	1	1	1	1	1	= 255 (or -128)

7	6	5	4	3	2	1	0	← bit number
0	0	0	0	0	0	0	0	= 0

7	6	5	4	3	2	1	0	← bit number
0	1	1	1	1	1	1	1	= 127

Figure 3.1. The 8 bits of a byte.

3

If you want to count positive and negative numbers, you can use bit number 7 as a sign bit. Under this scheme, a byte represents values that range from –128 to 127. The top byte in Figure 3.1 represents the number –128 when you employ the most significant bit as a sign bit. The second byte in Figure 3.1 is zero. The third byte in the same figure is positive because bit number 8 is 0.

Words and Long Words

A word stores 16 bits. Applying the bit-counting schemes I just presented, you can use a word to represent **unsigned integers** (that is, non-negative integers) in the range of 0–65535. If you want to represent signed integers, using the most significant bit as a sign bit, you can use a word to represent integers from –32768 to 32767. Figure 3.2 shows the schema for the 16-bit word. When you compare the range of numbers represented by a byte (256) and the range of numbers represented by a word (65,536), you might notice that doubling the number of bits from 8 to 16 squares the range of available values (256 squared equals 65536).

In the case of a long word (also shown in Figure 3.2), you are able to cover an even wider range of numbers. Just counting positive numbers, you can represent 0 to 4,294,967,295. When you want to cover positive and negative numbers, you can represent –2,147,483,648 to 2,147,483,647. This huge range of integers is usually enough for most applications.

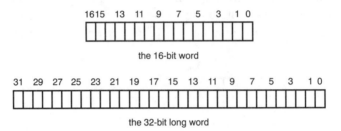

the 16-bit word

the 32-bit long word

Figure 3.2. A word and a long word.

Floating-Point Numbers

Computer scientists also use groups of bits to represent floating-point numbers, but the topic is beyond the scope of this book. However, the basic approach still revolves around manipulating various groups of bits. There are basically three kinds of bits used to represent a floating-point number in scientific format. First, there is the sign bit. Second, there are the bits that store the mantissa of a number (its digits). Third, there are the bits that store the exponent.

Character Representation

Now that you know about numbers, your next question might be how does a computer store text? The building blocks for text are characters—letters and symbols (such as punctuation marks). Computer scientists have devised a method in which each character is represented by a unique integer value. These integers are known as the ASCII (American Standard for Code Information Interchange) codes. These codes serve as an ID or social security number, if you like, for the individual characters. Because computers manipulate numbers (especially integers) very well, associating characters with integers (that is, their ASCII codes) is the adopted method for storing and manipulating characters in

the computer. Therefore, computers store text as sequences of ASCII codes, and your hardware and operating system translate these codes to the characters that appear on your screen or printer.

QBasic Data Types

In the previous subsections I talked in general terms about the schemes that enable computers to manipulate integers, floating-point numbers, and characters. What about QBasic in particular? What kind of data types does it offer? QBasic supports two main data types: numbers and strings of characters. There are two kinds of numbers supported by QBasic: integers and floating-point numbers. Table 3.1 lists the predefined data types in QBasic.

Table 3.1. Shows the predefined data types in QBasic.

Data Type (byte size)	Minimum Value	Maximum Value
String length (varies)	0 characters	32,767 characters
Integers (2 bytes)	−32,768	32,767
Long integers (4 bytes)	−2,147,483,648	2,147,483,647
Single-precision numbers: (4 bytes)		
Positive	2.802597E−45	3.402823E+38
Negative	−3.402823E+38	−2.802597E−45
Double-precision numbers: (8 bytes)		
Positive	4.940656458412465D−324	1.79769313486231D+308
Negative	−1.79769313486231D+308	−4.940656458412465D−324

3

Let's look at examples of different values for the various predefined data types.

Strings contain a series of characters enclosed in a pair of quotation marks. Here are some examples of strings:

```
"This is a typical string"
"Hello World!"
"Can't touch that!"
"c"
" "
```

The first two examples are typical strings. The third string contains a single quotation mark. This character does not affect the string. The fourth example is a single-character string. The last example shows an empty (also called **null**) string.

☐ **New Term** A string of characters enclosed in a pair of double quotes is called a *string literal.* The five string examples just covered are string literals.

Integers have values that range from –32768 to 32767. Here are some examples of valid integers:

```
123
-10000
31000
-1
0
```

Long integers have a much wider range. Here are some examples of valid long integers:

```
65000
-70000
1000000
1233333
```

Single-precision floating-point numbers cover a range of numbers that is useful when your application needs a more exact number. Here are examples of single-precision floating-point numbers:

```
3.1417
-24.98
```

```
65000.12
1.2E+12
4.565E-05
-6.87E-09
```

Notice that the last three examples represent numbers using the scientific notation using the letter E. The number to the left of the E is the mantissa and the number to the right of the E is the power of ten. Thus, 1.2E+12 is the same as:

```
1.2 * 10
```
$1.2 * 10^{12}$

Double-precision, floating-point numbers cover a wide range of numbers and are more exact than single-precision numbers. Here are examples of double-precision floating-point numbers:

```
3.1417D+100
-6.87D-129
2.3#
```

The # character specifies that the number 2.3 is a double-precision floating-point number. The first two examples use the letter D to indicate the exponent of a double-precision number. Therefore, you can distinguish between single-precision and double-precision numbers in scientific notation by the letters E and D.

Naming Items in QBasic

All programming languages, including QBasic, permit you to create data items and program components. To use and manage these objects, you first must name them. QBasic requires that you follow a simple set of rules when naming objects. These rules are:

1. The first character in a name must be a letter. It can be uppercase or lowercase.

2. The subsequent characters, if used, can be letters, digits, or the dot.

3. The name you define cannot match a QBasic keyword. However, it can include a QBasic keyword.

4. Names can be as many as 40 characters long.

5. QBasic names are not case-sensitive.

Here are some examples of valid names:

```
LastName
LASTNAME
interestrate
interestRate
Last.Name
Day1.Hour1
Day1.Hour2
Day1
Minute34Reading
Day1Hour2
PRINTIT
X
i
```

Notice that the first two examples (LastName and LASTNAME) refer to the same name because QBasic names are not case-sensitive. The same is true for the third and fourth examples (interestrate and interestRate). QBasic does not force on you any style for choosing names. A naming style that has become popular in recent years is demonstrated in the first and third names. Notice that the uppercase letters are used on the first letter of each word in a name that contains multiple words. This style enables you to easily read such names. The last two are examples of single-letter names.

Here are some examples of invalid names:

```
1stDay
first index
long_integer
print
```

The first name starts with a digit, which violates the first naming rule. The second example contains a space in the middle. This example actually shows two distinct and valid names. The third example uses the underscore character. Some languages such as Pascal and C allow the underscore. QBasic does not. The last example uses a QBasic keyword in lowercase.

What is a Variable?

The computer's memory contains programs and data. When you start to run a program, QBasic designates a memory block to allow your program to store and recall information. The input part of a program moves data into the memory. The processing part of a program recalls the data in memory, possibly alters the data, and stores the updated information back in memory. The output part of a program recalls the data in memory and sends it to the screen or to the printer.

You might ask yourself, what part of the memory contains my data? How do I get to that data in the machine's memory? There are two ways to access data in the computer's memory: the hard way and the easy way. The hard way requires you to know the actual numeric address of the memory location, such as 0345:0012, that contains your data—in fact, each piece of data has its own address and number of bytes it occupies.

If this were the only way to access data in a program, only a handful of people would be programming computers today. The good news is that programming languages such as QBasic provide a much easier alternative. Instead of remembering abstract numbers that represent memory locations (and going insane in a matter of hours), QBasic enables you to name these memory locations—you can have a name for each distinct data item. The beauty of this scheme is that the names you use absolve you from knowing (or even caring about knowing) the exact memory location of your data. The name of each data item becomes a handle that you use to control storing and recalling data to that memory location. To share even more good news, QBasic (and all high-level programming languages) manages the memory resources in a highly automatic fashion.

So, what is a variable? A *variable* is the name of a memory location that contains data item. Why use the name **variable**? Why not call the memory locations, for example, **memory tags**, **data labels**, or **data boxes**? The answer probably has something to do with FORTRAN (one of the earliest programming languages). FORTRAN (which stands for FORmula TRANslation) is a language geared to mathematicians and scientists. FORTRAN programmers deal with algebraic equations involving variables. In addition, the name variable is a good reminder that you can alter the data in the memory.

3

Using a variable, you can store and recall data in a memory location. Figure 3.3 shows the scheme for accessing memory locations using variables. The figure shows an internal table used (and completely maintained) by QBasic programs. This table enables a program to perform the following tasks:

1. Determine when to allocate a new memory address and associate it with a new variable.

2. Store new data in the memory address associated with a new or an existing variable.

3. Recall data from the memory address associated with a specified variable.

Figure 3.3 illustrates a QBasic program in the process of accessing the data associated with a variable named index. The internal table provides the QBasic program with the sought memory address, which contains the data associated with the variable index.

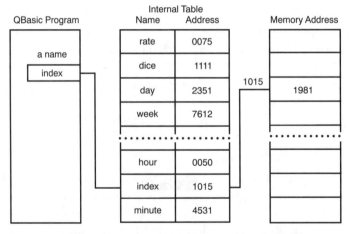

Figure 3.3. The scheme for accessing memory using variables.

Creating and Using Variables

QBasic is very flexible and forgiving about declaring variables. Other programming languages, such as C and Pascal, are not so tolerant. In QBasic you declare a variable either explicitly or implicitly. When you use a new variable, QBasic

creates it for you. By use I mean assign a value to it. I can better illustrate this point with an example that uses a variable. Listing 3.1 shows a dice-throwing program, DICE3.BAS, that uses a simple variable.

Listing 3.1. A dice-throwing program, DICE3.BAS, that uses a simple variable.

```
 1: REM Program that throws a dice
 2: REM Version 1.0
 3: REM Created 12/17/1992    Last Update 12/18/1992
 4: REM
 5: CLS ' clear the screen
 6: RANDOMIZE ' get a new seed
 7: ' assign a value to the variable Dice
 8: Dice = INT(RND(1) * 6) + 1
 9: ' output number between 1 and 6
10: PRINT "Dice throw is"; Dice
11: END
```

Here is a sample output for the program in Listing 3.1:

```
Random-number seed (-32768 to 32767)? 555
Dice throw is 1
```

The program in Listing 3.1 uses a single variable named Dice. Line 8 assigns a value to Dice. The value is supplied by the predefined QBasic functions RND and INT. Because this is the first program line that mentions Dice, the program also creates the variable Dice. From that point the program is aware of Dice. On Line 10, the PRINT statement outputs the value of the dice throw, stored in Dice. Notice that PRINT displays a string literal and the numeric value of a single-precision, floating-point number. The two data items are separated by a semicolon. The PRINT statement is versatile enough to display any number of data items and any combination of data types predefined by QBasic.

You might wonder about the data type of the variable Dice. By default, QBasic variables have the single-precision, floating-point type. This means that Dice also can store fractions.

3

To give you a better idea of how the program handles `Dice` (and variables in general), think of a variable as a labeled box containing data. On line 8, the program calculates the value of the dice throw and then assigns it to the variable `Dice`. The program at this point looks for a data box labeled `Dice`. The program quickly concludes that there is no such box. Therefore, it creates a new data box, labels it `Dice`, and inserts the numeric value in that box. As soon as the program completes this task, it moves on, executing the next program line. When the program reaches the `PRINT` statement, it displays the quoted text and then comes across the variable `Dice`. Once again, the program looks for a data box labeled `Dice`. This time it finds such a box and passes a copy of the information in that box to the `PRINT` statement, which then displays the copied value. Notice that I said *passes a copy of the information* and not moves the information, because accessing data stored in a variable **does not remove** that data from the variable.

Let's modify the program in Listing 3.1 to make it throw two dice. Listing 3.2 shows the new version of the dice-throwing program, DICE4.BAS, which uses two variables.

Listing 3.2. A dice-throwing program, DICE4.BAS, that uses two variables.

```
1: REM Program that throws two dices
2: REM Version 1.0
3: REM Created 12/17/1992   Last Update 12/18/1992
4: REM
5: CLS ' clear the screen
6: RANDOMIZE ' get a new seed
7: ' assign a value to the variable Dice1
8: Dice1 = INT(RND(1) * 6) + 1
9: ' assign a value to the variable Dice2
10: Dice2 = INT(RND(1) * 6) + 1
11: ' output numbers between 1 and 6
12: PRINT "Dice throws are "; Dice1; " and "; Dice2
13: END
```

Here is a sample output for the program in Listing 3.2:

```
Random-number seed (-32768 to 32767)? 456
Dice throws are  6  and  5
```

The program in Listing 3.2 uses two variables, Dice1 and Dice2. On line 8 the program creates the first variable, Dice1, and assigns it an integer. On line 10 the program creates the second variable, Dice2, and assigns it an integer. The PRINT statement on line 12 displays the values of the two dice throws, which are stored in Dice1 and Dice2.

When I first learned to program, I was unaware that you could reassign new values to the same variable. Consequently, I created a new variable every time I wanted to store a new number or value. I soon learned that this approach wastes a lot of memory. To demonstrate how to assign a new value to the same variable, I present Listing 3.3, a modified version of Listing 3.2. The new version uses one variable, Dice, to store the values for the two dice throws.

Listing 3.3. A dice-throwing program, DICE5.BAS, that uses a single variable.

```
 1: REM Program that throws two dices
 2: REM Version 1.0
 3: REM Created 12/17/1992   Last Update 12/18/1992
 4: REM
 5: CLS ' clear the screen
 6: RANDOMIZE ' get a new seed
 7: ' assign a value to the variable Dice
 8: Dice = INT(RND(1) * 6) + 1
 9: ' output the first dice throw
10: PRINT "Dice throws are "; Dice;
11: ' assign another value to the variable Dice
12: Dice = INT(RND(1) * 6) + 1
13: ' output the second dice throw
14: PRINT " and "; Dice
15: END
```

Here is a sample output for the program in Listing 3.3:

```
Random-number seed (-32768 to 32767)? 625
Dice throws are  1  and  3
```

In Listing 3.3, the program creates the variable Dice and assigns its first value on line 8. The value stored in Dice represents the first dice throw. On line 10 the PRINT statement displays the leading text and the value of the first dice throw (stored in Dice). On line 12, the program assigns a second value to Dice. The program (using the data box analogy) calculates the value on the right side of the equal sign and assigns it to Dice. As before, the program searches for and finds a data box labeled Dice. The program overwrites the old contents of the data box with the new value. On line 14, the second PRINT statement displays the string " and " and the new value stored in Dice.

The *INPUT* Statement

The only input you have done so far has been entering a number to seed the random-number generator. QBasic offers other input commands. On Day 8, "Keyboard and Program Input," I discuss the various QBasic input mechanisms. I'd like to present more interactive programs before then, so I'll define the INPUT statement.

The general syntax of QBasic commands and structures includes special characters to indicate optional and alternate components. Components enclosed in square brackets are optional. Alternate components are enclosed in a pair of braces and contain the bar character, ¦.

Syntax

The INPUT Statement

The general syntax for the INPUT statement is:

```
INPUT [;] ["prompt"{; ¦ ,}] variablelist
```

The *prompt* is an optional string literal that appears before the user types in the data. A semicolon after *prompt* appends a question mark to the prompt string. The *variablelist* represents one or more variables, separated by commas, that store the data you enter from the keyboard. If the *variableList* contains two or more variables, you must separate the variables with commas. Otherwise, the INPUT statement displays an error message. When you finish entering data for the INPUT statement, you must press the Return key.

Examples:

```
' use prompt to enter a single value
INPUT "Enter your age ";Age

' Use PRINT to prompt
PRINT "Enter your age ";
INPUT Age

' Prompt for two data items
INPUT "Enter name and age : ",YourName$, YourAge

' Prompt for three data items
INPUT "Enter three integers "; int1, int2, int3
```

Let's look at a few examples of using the INPUT statement. Listing 3.4 shows the program HELLO2.BAS. The program prompts you to enter your name and then displays a greeting that includes your name.

3

Listing 3.4. **The program HELLO2.BAS.**

```
 1: REM Program to prompt you for your name
 2: REM and greet you
 3: REM
 4: CLS ' clear the screen
 5: ' prompt you to enter your name
 6: INPUT "Enter your name "; You$
 7: PRINT ' display a blank line
 8: ' display a greeting message
 9: PRINT "Hello "; You$; ", how are you?"
10: END
```

Here is a sample session with the program in Listing 3.4:

```
Enter your name ? Namir Shammas

Hello Namir Shammas, how are you?
```

On line 6 the program uses the INPUT statement to prompt you for your name. The literal string "Enter your name" tells you what to enter. The semicolon after the string adds a question mark to the end of the string. The program displays the string and waits for you to type in your input. When you finish, press Return to tell the INPUT statement you have finished typing. The INPUT statement places what you have typed in the variable You$. The $ indicates that the variable stores a string of characters. It is worth mentioning that the program creates You$ when it executes line 6. Line 9 has a PRINT statement that displays your input as part of a greeting. Notice that the PRINT statement uses semicolons between the different items to concatenate (join together) the output.

Take a look at another program that uses the INPUT statement, this time with two variables in the variable list. Listing 3.5 shows the program HELLO3.BAS, which prompts you to enter your first and last names. The program displays a greeting and a question about a family member.

Listing 3.5. The program HELLO3.BAS, which uses an INPUT statement with multiple data input.

```
 1: REM Program to prompt you for your name
 2: REM and greet you
 3: REM
 4: CLS ' clear the screen
 5: ' prompt you to enter your first and last names
 6: PRINT "Please separate multiple input by commas"
 7: INPUT "Enter your first and last names : ", First$, Last$
 8: PRINT ' display a blank line
 9: ' display a greeting message
10: PRINT "Hello "; First$; " "; Last$; ", how are you?"
11: PRINT "Are you related to Silverster "; Last$; "?"
12: END
```

Here is a sample session with the program in Listing 3.5:

```
Please separate multiple input by commas
Enter your first and last names : Namir,Shammas

Hello Namir Shammas, how are you?
Are you related to Silverster Shammas?
```

 In Listing 3.5 line 6 uses a PRINT statement to display a reminder about separating your input with a comma. This statement is an example of making your programs display messages that guide the user's input. Line 7 contains an INPUT statement that uses a prompt string and stores your input in the variables First$ and Last$. Line 10 contains a PRINT statement that displays the strings in First$ and Last$ as part of the greeting. Line 11 has another PRINT statement that uses Last$ to inquire about your relation with a possible family member.

 DO add messages that guide the user in entering data. This information makes your programs more user-friendly.

DON'T assume that people who use your QBasic programs are mind readers and know what is expected of them.

The program in Listing 3.5 prompts you to enter more than one data item using a single INPUT statement. Good programming practices encourage you to use a separate INPUT statement for each data item you input. Listing 3.6 shows the modified version of Listing 3.5, employing an INPUT statement for each data item.

 Listing 3.6. The program HELLO4.BAS.

```
 1: REM Program to prompt you for your name
 2: REM and greet you
 3: REM
 4: CLS ' clear the screen
 5: ' prompt you to enter your first name
 6: INPUT "Enter your first name : ", First$
 7: ' prompt you to enter your last name
 8: INPUT "Enter your last name : ", Last$
 9: PRINT ' display a blank line
10: ' display a greeting message
11: PRINT "Hello "; First$; " "; Last$; ", how are you?"
12: PRINT "Are you related to Silverster "; Last$; "?"
13: END
```

Here is a sample session with the program in Listing 3.6:

```
Enter your first name : Namir
Enter your last name : Shammas

Hello Namir Shammas, how are you?
Are you related to Silverster Shammas?
```

 Notice that the new program version does not have a PRINT statement before the INPUT statement on line 6. You don't need to inform the user about separating multiple input with a comma because there is no multiple input. Lines 6 and 7 use INPUT statements to prompt you for your first and last names, storing your input in the variables First$ and Last$, respectively. The remaining program lines are the same as those in Listing 3.5.

Explicit Data Typing of Variables

Every variable in QBasic is associated with a data type. The default data type is a single-precision, floating-point number. QBasic offers two methods for explicitly declaring the data type associated with a variable—data-type suffixes and the DIM statement.

Using Data-Type Suffixes

In QBasic you can append special data-type suffixes to declare explicitly the types of variables. Table 3.2 lists the data type suffixes. QBasic has inherited these suffixes from GW-BASIC.

Table 3.2. The data type suffixes.

Suffix	Data Type
$	String
%	Integer
&	Long integer

Suffix	Data Type
!	Single-precision, floating-point number
#	Double-precision, floating-point number

Here are some examples of explicitly typed variables:

```
MyName$               ' string
InterestRate!         ' single-precision float
MachineTolerance#     ' double-precision float
DayNumber%            ' integer
index%                ' integer
fileSize&             ' long integer
```

Let's look at a program that uses data-type suffixes. Listing 3.7 contains the program VOLUME1.BAS, which prompts you to enter the radius and height of a cylinder. The program calculates the base area and volume of the cylinder, displaying the volume.

3

 Listing 3.7. The program VOLUME1.BAS, which uses data-type suffixes.

```
 1: REM Program that calculates the volume of a cylinder
 2: REM
 3: CLS
 4: INPUT "Enter the cylinder radius (ft.) "; Radius!
 5: INPUT "Enter the cylinder height (ft.) "; Height!
 6: PRINT
 7: Pi# = 4 * ATN(1) ' calculate pi
 8: ' calculate the base area of the cylinder
 9: Area# = Pi# * Radius! * Radius!
10: ' calculate the cylinder volume
11: Volume# = Area# * Height!
12: PRINT "Volume of cylinder = "; Volume#; " cuft"
13: END
```

Here is a sample output for the program in Listing 3.7:

```
Enter the cylinder radius (ft.) ? 1
Enter the cylinder height (ft.) ? 10

Volume of cylinder =  31.41592653589793  cuft
```

The program uses the variables Radius!, Height!, Pi#, Area#, and Volume#. The variables are explicitly typed using the type suffixes. The first two variables are single-precision floats (that's short for floating-point numbers), whereas the other three variables are double-precision floats. The program uses the variables Pi# and Area# to store intermediate results. The program uses the ATN function to return the arctangent value. Because QBasic does not supply a predefined constant for Pi, you need to provide your programs with a good approximation of Pi. The expression 4 * ATN(1) produces a very good approximation of Pi.

Potential Problems with Data-Type Suffixes

There is one potential problem with using data-type suffixes. QBasic considers the data-type suffix as part of the variable name. Consequently, you can have as many as five variables in a program that have the same name but different type suffixes. For example, a program can use the variables X$, X#, X!, X&, and X% to store five different pieces of information. Many programmers (rightfully) consider this misuse of data-type suffixes heresy because it reduces the clarity of a program, making it easy to mix up variables. The advice given by professional programmers is to use distinct names for your variables.

DO use distinct variable names.

DON'T use the same variable name with more than one data type suffix.

To illustrate this problem, consider the program in Listing 3.8. I created this program by modifying Listing 3.7. Examine the listing, type it in, and then run the program.

Listing 3.8. The program VOLUME2.BAS with a type suffix problem.

```
 1: REM Program that calculates the volume of a cylinder
 2: REM
 3: REM ************************************************
 4: REM
 5: REM NOTE: The program has an error due to use of
 6: REM variable Height# in addition to variable Height!
 7: REM
 8: REM ************************************************
 9: REM
10: CLS
11: INPUT "Enter the cylinder radius (ft.) "; Radius!
12: INPUT "Enter the cylinder height (ft.) "; Height!
13: PRINT
14: Pi# = 4 * ATN(1) ' calculate pi
15: ' calculate base area of cylinder
16: Area# = Pi# * Radius! * Radius!
17: ' calculate the cylinder volume
18: Volume# = Area# * Height#
19: PRINT "Volume of cylinder = "; Volume#; " cuft"
20: END
```

3

Here is a sample output for the program in Listing 3.8:

```
Enter the cylinder radius (ft.) ? 1
Enter the cylinder height (ft.) ? 10

Volume of cylinder =  0  cuft
```

Notice that the program displays the cylinder volume as 0. You get the volume no matter what numbers you type in for the radius and height. Why? Examine lines 12 and 18. On line 12, the INPUT statement stores your cylinder height in the variable Height!. On line 18 the program calculates the cylinder volume by multiplying the values stored in the variables Area# and Height#. You might ask, "wait a minute, should the variable Height# be Height!?" Indeed, on line 18, the program creates a new variable called Height#. Because Height# is new, the program creates it and assigns the default value of 0. Multiplication by zero always yields zero, which is stored in the variable Volume#.

Using the *DIM* Statement

QBasic allows you to associate a variable with a data type using the DIM statement. The DIM statement also enables you to create variables because the variables in the DIM statement must not appear in previous lines.

The DIM Statement

The general syntax for the DIM statement is:

```
DIM variableName AS dataType
```

The *variableName* is the name of a variable you want to associate with the data type *dataType*. The names of the predefined QBasic data types are INTEGER, LONG (long integer), SINGLE (single-precision float), DOUBLE (double-precision float), and STRING.

Examples:

```
DIM MyName AS STRING
DIM InterestRate AS SINGLE
DIM MachineTolerance AS DOUBLE
DIM DayNumber AS INTEGER
DIM index AS INTEGER
DIM fileSize AS LONG
```

DO develop the habit of declaring your program's variables using the DIM statement. This habit pays off now and in the long run. Declaring variables with the DIM statement enables you to avoid using the error-prone data type suffixes. In the long run, if you move to another programming language, such as Pascal or C, you will find that this habit has prepared you adequately for these languages, which require the declaration of all variables.

Let's look at a program that uses the DIM statement to explicitly declare the data type of its variables. Listing 3.9 is another version of Listing 3.7 and uses the DIM statement.

Listing 3.9. The VOLUME3.BAS program, which uses the DIM statement to explicitly declare the data types of its variables.

```
 1: REM Program that calculates the volume of a cylinder
 2: REM
 3: ' declare the variables
 4: DIM Radius AS SINGLE
 5: DIM Height AS SINGLE
 6: DIM Pi AS DOUBLE
 7: DIM Area AS DOUBLE
 8: DIM Volume AS DOUBLE
 9: '
10: CLS
11: INPUT "Enter the cylinder radius (ft.) "; Radius
12: INPUT "Enter the cylinder height (ft.) "; Height
13: PRINT
14: Pi = 4 * ATN(1) ' calculate pi
15: ' calculate the base area of the cylinder
16: Area = Pi * Radius * Radius
17: ' calculate the cylinder volume
18: Volume = Area * Height
19: PRINT "Volume of cylinder = "; Volume; " cuft"
20: END
```

Here is a sample output for the program in Listing 3.9:

```
Enter the cylinder radius (ft.) ? 1
Enter the cylinder height (ft.) ? 10

Volume of cylinder =  31.41592653589793  cuft
```

The program in Listing 3.9 uses a series of DIM statements to declare the data types for all of its variables. This approach frees the program from having to specify the data-type prefix for its variables. Consequently, you save keystrokes when typing the names of variables. More importantly, using DIM statements eliminates the possibility of keying in the wrong data-type suffix with the names of variables.

Implicit Data Typing of Variables

The default data type of a variable is single-precision float. QBasic enables you to alter the default data type by using a family of DEF*type* statements.

The DEF*type* Statements

The general syntax for the DEF*type* statements is:

```
DEFINT letterrange [,letterrange]...
DEFLNG letterrange [,letterrange]...
DEFSNG letterrange [,letterrange]...
DEFDBL letterrange [,letterrange]...
DEFSTR letterrange [,letterrange]...
```

The *letterrange* is a letter (such as A or X) or range of letters (such as C–P). QBasic sets the default data type for variables whose names begin with the specified letter or letters, as follows:

Statement	Default Data Type
DEFINT	Integer
DEFLNG	Long integer
DEFSNG	Single precision
DEFDBL	Double precision
DEFSTR	String

The following rules apply:

1. The single-precision is the default data type if you do not specify a DEF*type* statement.

2. A data-type suffix (%, &, !, #, or $) always takes precedence over a DEF*type* statement.

3. A DEF*type* statement can override the DEF*type* statements that appear before it.

Examples:

```
' declare all variables to be integers
DEFINT A-Z
```

```
' declare all variables to be double-precision floats,
' except the ones that start with I to O
DEFDBL A-Z
DEFINT I-O ' override the above DEFtype in the range I to O


declare all variables that begin with S and Z as strings
DEFSTR S, Z


' declare all variables that starts with A to C, I to O,
' and Z as integers
DEFINT A-C, I-O, Z
```

Let's look at a simple example that uses the DEF*type* statement. Listing 3.10, HELLO5.BAS, uses DEFSTR to declare strings the default type for all variables. The program performs the same tasks as HELLO4.BAS, found in Listing 3.6.

Listing 3.10. The program HELLO5.BAS, which uses DEFSTR to set the default types of all program variables as strings.

3

```
 1: REM Program to prompt you for your name
 2: REM and greet you
 3: REM
 4: ' declare all of the variables to have a default string type
 5: DEFSTR A-Z
 6: CLS ' clear the screen
 7: ' prompt you to enter your first name
 8: INPUT "Enter your first name : ", First
 9: ' prompt you to enter your last name
10: INPUT "Enter your last name : ", Last
11: PRINT ' display a blank line
12: ' display a greeting message
13: PRINT "Hello "; First; " "; Last; ", how are you?"
14: PRINT "Are you related to Silverster "; Last; "?"
15: END
```

Here is a sample session with the program in Listing 3.10:

```
Enter your first name : John
Enter your last name : Roche

Hello John Roche, how are you?
Are you related to Silverster Roche?
```

On line 5 of Listing 3.10, the program declares the string type as the default data type for all variables. The program uses two variables, First and Last. Because the names of the variables have no type suffixes and there are no DIM statements, the program associates the default string type with the two variables. As such, the INPUT statements on lines 8 and 10 store strings in these variables. Similarly, the PRINT statement on lines 13 and 14 displays the strings stored in these variables.

Here is another example of using the DEF*type* statement. Listing 3.11 shows the program VOLUME4.BAS (a version of program VOLUME3.BAS). VOLUME4.BAS uses the DEFDBL statement and then overrides it with data-type suffixes.

Listing 3.11. The program VOLUME4.BAS, which uses the DEFDBL statement and overrides it with data type suffixes.

```
 1: REM Program that calculates the volume of a cylinder
 2: REM
 3: ' declare that all of the variables are double-precision
 4: ' floats by default
 5: DEFDBL A-Z
 6: '
 7: CLS
 8: INPUT "Enter the cylinder radius (ft.) "; Radius!
 9: INPUT "Enter the cylinder height (ft.) "; Height!
10: PRINT
11: Pi = 4 * ATN(1) ' calculate pi
12: ' calculate the base area of the cylinder
13: Area = Pi * Radius! * Radius!
14: ' calculate the cylinder volume
15: Volume = Area * Height!
16: PRINT "Volume of cylinder = "; Volume; " cuft"
17: END
```

Here is a sample session with the program in Listing 3.11:

```
Enter the cylinder radius (ft.) ? 1
Enter the cylinder height (ft.) ? 10

Volume of cylinder =  31.41592653589793  cuft
```

Line 5 in Listing 3.11 declares that the default data type for all program variables is double-precision float. This is a sound choice for a default; most of the variables have the double-precision float type. The variables Radius! and Height! are the exceptions because they have data-type suffixes explicitly declaring them as single-precision floats.

What is a Constant?

When I introduced you to variables, I also mentioned the ability to alter the data associated with variables. What if you want to assign a fixed value to a name? In other words, what if you want a special kind of variable that takes on a fixed value that it retains throughout a QBasic program? Programming languages, including QBasic, appropriately call these special variables *constants*.

Constants are names that have a fixed value associated with them. Using constants has several advantages:

- ☐ Constants make your programs more readable because you replace abstract numbers with more descriptive names.

- ☐ Constants resolve the possible confusion created when the same number has two or more meanings in the program.

- ☐ Constants enable you to centralize changing a value throughout a program. Instead of performing a text change operation throughout the text (which can erroneously alter the same number used in a different context), you alter only the value assigned to the constant.

DO use constants to write programs that are easier to read and easier to maintain.

Declaring and Using Constants

QBasic enables you to declare constants using the CONST statement. You must declare a constant before you use it in a program statement.

Syntax

The CONST statement

The general syntax for declaring a constant is:

```
CONST constantName = value,...
```

The `constantName` represents the name of the constant and `value` represents the value assigned to the constant. When you name constants, follow the same rules as naming variables. You can include a data-type suffix with the constant's name to associate the constants with a specific data type. If you omit the type prefix, QBasic uses the type of assigned value as the data type associated with the constant.

Examples:

```
CONST WEEKDAYS% = 7
CONST HOURSPERDAY! = 24
CONST SecondPerMinute% = 60, MinutePerHour% = 60
CONST FirstWorkDay$ = "Monday"
CONST MinimumFileSize& = 60000
CONST Version = "1.12"
CONST Me$ = "Namir Shammas"
```

Using constants is similar to using variables, except you cannot place a constant on the left side of an equal sign in an assignment statement. If you use a data-type suffix in the declaration of the constant, you don't need to include the suffix with the constant name anywhere else in the program.

Let's look at a program that uses constants. Listing 3.12, TEMP1.BAS, uses constants to convert temperatures from Fahrenheit to Celsius. The program prompts you to enter a temperature in Fahrenheit. The program then calculates the equivalent Celsius temperature. Finally, the program displays the temperature in both temperature scales.

Listing 3.12. TEMP1.BAS, which uses constants to convert temperatures.

```
 1: REM Program that converts Fahrenheit Temperatures to Celsius
 2: REM
 3: ' declare the constants SHIFT# and SCALE#
 4: CONST SHIFT# = 32#   ' explicit type association
 5: CONST SCALE = 1.8#   ' implicit type association
 6: CONST TFChar = "F "  ' implicit type association
 7: CONST TCchar = "C "  ' implicit type association
 8: ' declare the program variables as double-precision floats
 9: DIM TF AS DOUBLE
10: DIM TC AS DOUBLE
11: CLS
12: ' obtain input temperature
13: INPUT "Enter a Fahrenheit temperature "; TF
14: ' convert the temperature to Celsius
15: TC = (TF - SHIFT) / SCALE
16: ' display the result
17: PRINT TF; TFChar; "="; TC; TCchar
18: END
```

3

Here is a sample session with the program in Listing 3.12:

```
Enter a Fahrenheit temperature ? 50
 50 F = 10 C
```

The program in Listing 3.12 declares four constants on lines 4–7. Line 4 contains the declaration of the constant SHIFT. The declaration uses the # data type suffix for an explicit type association—a double-precision floating-point number. Line 5 declares the constant SCALE and assigns it the value 1.8# (a double-precision number). Consequently, the data type associated with SCALE is also a double-precision float. Lines 6 and 7 declare the constants TFchar and TCchar and assign them two-character strings. Consequently, the data type associated with these constants is the string type.

The program uses DIM statements on lines 9 and 10 to declare the variables TC and TF as double-precision floats. Line 15 calculates the Celsius temperature. The statement uses the variables TC and TF, as well as the numeric constants SHIFT and SCALE. Notice that SHIFT does not have the # data type suffix. Line 17 contains a PRINT statement that displays both temperatures. This statement displays the values in TC and TF, as well as the contents of TCchar and TFchar.

Summary

This chapter covered manipulating data in programs. You learned about the following topics:

- [ ] The predefined data types in QBasic are integer, long integer, single-precision, floating-point numbers, double-precision, floating-point numbers, and strings.

- [ ] Naming items in QBasic follows a few simple rules. Names can be as many as 40 characters long, must begin with a letter, and can be followed by letters, digits, or the dot character.

- [ ] A variable is a label for a memory location that stores and recalls data.

- [ ] QBasic permits you to create variables either explicitly or implicitly. To create a variable explicitly, use the DIM statement. To create a variable implicitly, assign it a value the first time you use it.

- [ ] Explicit data typing of variables uses either the data type suffixes or the DIM statement. The data-type suffixes include %, &, !, #, and $ for the integer, long, single, double, and string types, respectively. The DIM statement sets the default data type of variables by specifying the INTEGER, LONG, SINGLE, DOUBLE, and STRING types.

- [ ] For another way to type data implicitly, you can use the DEF*type* statements. The DEF*type* statements set the default data type of variables by specifying the first letters in the names of variables.

- [ ] Constants are names associated with fixed values. Using constants makes your programs more clear and easier to update.

- [ ] QBasic allows you to declare constants using the CONST statements. You can create constants with any predefined data type. If you do not specify the data type associated with a constant (by using the type suffix), QBasic deduces the data type from the type of the assigned value.

Q&A

Q. What happens if I use a variable without assigning it a value?

A. When QBasic creates a variable, the variable is assigned the proper default value. Thus, QBasic assigns empty strings to string variables and zeros to numeric variables. To illustrate this feature, consider the following one-line program:

```
PRINT "The contents of the uninitialized variable X$ is
   '";X$;"'"
```

The program displays the following output to indicate that the uninitialized variable X$ has the default value of an empty string:

```
The contents of the uninitialized variable X$ is ''
```

Q. How can I avoid accidently using QBasic keywords as variable and constant names in a program?

A. The QBasic editor scans your program lines as you enter them. The editor will display a syntax error message box when you use a QBasic keyword as a variable or a constant.

Q. What happens if I type in a string instead of a number in an INPUT statement that expects a number?

A. The INPUT statement issues a **Redo from start** error message and prompts you again for the correct input.

Q. What happens if I type in a floating-point number in an INPUT statement that expects an integer value?

A. The INPUT statement ignores the fractional part of your input.

Q. How can I make the prompt in the INPUT statement more flexible?

A. You can place a PRINT statement right before the INPUT statement. The PRINT statement then can use a variable or a constant to display the prompt message. Here is an example:

```
1: CONST Message = "Enter a number "
2: PRINT Message;
3: INPUT N%
4: PRINT "You entered ";N%
5: END
```

Workshop

The Workshop provides quiz questions to help you solidify your understanding of the material covered and exercises to provide you with experience in using what you've learned. Try to understand the quiz and exercise answers before continuing on to the next chapter. Answers are provided in Appendix B, "Answers."

Quiz

1. True or false: the variables `Index` and `INDEX` are different.

2. True or false: the variables `Index%` and `INDEX!` are different.

3. True or false: the variable `Input` is valid.

4. True or false: the following statement erases the content of the variable `index`:

   ```
   index = index
   ```

5. What is the output of the following program?

   ```
   1: INPUT "Enter a number ";N
   2: N = 12
   3: PRINT "Number is ";N
   ```

6. What is wrong with the following statement?

   ```
   index% = 33000
   ```

7. How can you fix the statement in question 6?

8. What is the output of the following program?

```
1: DIM N AS DOUBLE
2: N = 10
3: PRINT "N = ";N#
```

Exercises

1. Write a program that calculates the volume of a sphere for a given sphere radius. Make the program prompt for the radius and display the calculated volume. To obtain the value of pi, use the value 4 * ATN(1). The equation for calculating the volume of a sphere is

```
volume = (pi/3) * radius3
```

2. Write a program that compares the following approximation of pi:

```
pi = 355 / 113
```

with the value obtained using 4 * ATN(1). Calculate the error of the above approximation using the equation:

```
error (per billion) = (piApproximate - piAccurate) /
piAccurate * 1000000000
```

```
represent the piAccurate using 4 * ATN(1) and piApproximate
using 355 / 113.
```

3. Modify the program TEMP1.BAS, shown in Listing 3.12, to use a constant (call it Message) for a prompt string. There's a hint for the program modification in the Q&A section.

3

DAY

4

Operators and Expressions

This chapter covers data manipulation in QBasic. You will learn about the following topics:

- [ ] An overview of operators and expressions

- [ ] The assignment operator

- [ ] Numeric data conversion

- [ ] Math operators

- [ ] The Boolean truth table

- [ ] Relational operators

- [ ] Logical operators

- [ ] String operators

- [ ] Math expressions

Overview of Operators and Expressions

Let me start by giving you a brief and general introduction to operators and expressions. In the later sections of this chapter, I discuss the QBasic operators and expressions in detail.

What is an operator? Let me answer this question by giving simple examples. Consider the mathematical term 1 + 2. The + symbol is the addition operator, indicating the addition of the numbers 1 and 2 (which are called *operands*). Similarly, the mathematical term 4 − 5 contains the − symbol, the subtraction operator. As the name suggests, an *operator* is a special character, symbol, or name that operates on data in a specific way. QBasic supports a variety of operators. They include assignment, math, relational, logical, and string operators.

What is an expression? An *expression* is a series of operators and operands that yields a result when evaluated. Here are some examples of simple expressions (the expressions are on the right side of the equal signs):

```
y = 2 * (index% + 5) / 3
x# = 25 / (7 * (X# - 2) / 2)
```

```
Sum% = 1 + day1% + day2% + day3%
pi# * radius! * radius!
i% = index%
J% = 3
```

The above examples show you that even a numeric constant or a variable constitutes an expression, albeit a simple one. QBasic supports a variety of expressions, including math, logical, and string expressions.

The Assignment Operator

The assignment operator has special meaning in programming languages. QBasic and most programming languages use the = character for the assignment operator.

Syntax

The Assignment Operator (=)

The general syntax for using the assignment operator is

variableName = expression

The *expression* can be a constant, variable, or series of one or more operators and operands. The *variableName* is the name of the variable that receives the value of the *expression*. If the *expression* is a string, the *variableName* must be a string-typed variable. In the case of numeric expressions, QBasic allows you to mix the different data types. However, the *expression* value must not overflow the *variableName*. More about this in the next section.

4

Example:

```
index% = 1 ' assign constant value
Me$ = "Namir" ' assign string literal
charPosition% = index% ' assign variable
Pi = 355 / 113 ' assign an expression with operators
                  and operands
```

In QBasic the variable that appears on the left side of the = operator also can appear in the expression on the right side of the operator. This programming feature is found in just about all programming languages. What is the effect of using a variable on both sides of the assignment operator? Let me answer the question with an example. Consider the following program:

```
I% = 1
I% = I% + 3
PRINT "I% = ";I%
```

The first statement assigns 1 to the variable I% using the assignment operator. In the second statement the variable I% appears on both sides of the assignment operator. Here is how the QBasic program executes the second statement:

1. The program determines that the first operand is a variable named I%. Because the variable exists (thanks to the first statement), the program recalls 1, the value *currently* stored in I%.

2. Next, the program determines that the operator is the addition operator.

3. The program then determines that the second operand is the constant 3.

4. The program adds the numbers 1 and 3 to obtain 4, the value of the expression on the right side of the assignment operator. The program saves this value internally.

5. Finally, the program determines that the variable receiving the value of the expression is I%. Because this variable exists, the program overwrites the previous contents of I% with 4, the result of the expression.

Numeric Data Conversion

QBasic supports four numeric data types, two integer types and two floating-point types. As I showed you on Day 3, "Data Types, Constants, and Variables," each numeric data type has a specific range of values. Does QBasic allow you to assign a value of a particular numeric type to a variable associated with another numeric type? The answer is yes, provided that you observe the guidelines listed in Table 4.1. This table indicates the rules and limitations for assigning one type of numeric data to another one.

Table 4.1. Numeric conversion guidelines.

From	To	Remarks
Integer	Long	all values
	Single	all values
	Double	all values
Long	Integer	number must be in the range of the type integer
	Single	all values
	Double	all values
Single	Integer	number must be in the range of the type Integer. In addition, the number loses its fractional part.
	Long	number must be in the range of the type Long. In addition, the number loses its fractional part.
	Double	all values
Double	Integer	number must be in the range of the type Integer. In addition, the number loses its fractional part.
	Long	number must be in the range of the type Long. In addition, the number loses its fractional part.
	Single	number must be in the range of the type Single.

Implicit Numeric Conversion

Under the guidelines for numeric conversion shown in Table 4.1, QBasic performs implicit (or automatic, if you prefer) numeric conversion. Let me present two programs that demonstrate the numeric conversion of integer and single-precision floats.

Listing 4.1, ASSIGN1.BAS, assigns an integer value to variables of the other numeric data types. The program requires no input. It simply displays numbers of different numeric types and precisions.

Listing 4.1. **ASSIGN1.BAS, which assigns an integer value to variables of other numeric data types.**

```
 1: REM Program demonstrates assigning an integer to
 2: REM the other numeric data types
 3: REM
 4: ' declare the program variables
 5: DIM IntVar AS INTEGER
 6: DIM LongVar AS LONG
 7: DIM SingleVar AS SINGLE
 8: DIM DoubleVar AS DOUBLE
 9: '
10: CLS
11: ' Assign values to the integer variable
12: IntVar = 45
13: PRINT "IntVar = "; IntVar
14: ' copy integer value to long variable
15: LongVar = IntVar
16: PRINT "LongVar = "; LongVar
17: ' copy integer value to single variable
18: SingleVar = IntVar
19: PRINT "SingleVar = "; SingleVar
20: ' copy integer value to double variable
21: DoubleVar = IntVar
22: PRINT "DoubleVar = "; DoubleVar
23: END
```

Here is a sample output for the program in Listing 4.1:

```
IntVar =   45
LongVar =   45
SingleVar =   45
DoubleVar =   45
```

In Listing 4.1 lines 5–8 declare four program variables: IntVar, LongVar, SingleVar, and DoubleVar. The name of each variable is derived from the numeric data type associated it. On line 12 the program assigns the value of 45 to IntVar. The program then assigns the contents of IntVar to the other

variables on lines 15, 18, and 21. The program uses PRINT statements on lines 13, 16, 19, and 22 to display the contents of the four variables. The program output indicates that the program successfully stores the number 45 in all four variables. Each variable stores 45 in its own numeric type and precision.

Listing 4.1 illustrates the successful conversion between the integer data type and the other numeric types. This is true because the integer type has the narrowest range of values. Consequently, converting from an integer to another numeric type is safe and proceeds without any overflow error. An overflow error occurs if you attempt, for example, to convert a long integer value of 65535 to an integer.

Let's look at Listing 4.2, a program that illustrates the effect of converting a single-precision float to the other numeric types. Again, the program requires no input. It displays the numbers it converted from single-precision to the other numeric types.

Listing 4.2. ASSIGN2.BAS, which assigns a single-precision float value to variables of the other numeric data types.

```
 1: REM Program demonstrates assigning a single to
 2: REM the other numeric data types
 3: REM
 4: ' declare the program variables
 5: DIM IntVar AS INTEGER
 6: DIM LongVar AS LONG
 7: DIM SingleVar AS SINGLE
 8: DIM DoubleVar AS DOUBLE
 9: '
10: CLS
11: ' assign value to the single variable
12: SingleVar = 1000.4
13: PRINT "SingleVar = "; SingleVar
14: IntVar = SingleVar
15: PRINT "IntVar = "; IntVar
16: ' copy single value to long variable
17: LongVar = SingleVar
18: PRINT "LongVar = "; LongVar
19: ' copy single value to double variable
20: DoubleVar = SingleVar
21: PRINT "DoubleVar = "; DoubleVar
22: END
```

Here is a sample output for the program in Listing 4.2:

```
SingleVar =  1000.4
IntVar =  1000
LongVar =  1000
DoubleVar =  1000.400024414062
```

In Listing 4.2 lines 5–8 declare four program variables: IntVar, LongVar, SingleVar, and DoubleVar. On Line 12 the program assigns the value 1000.4 to SingleVar. The program then assigns the contents of SingleVar to the other variables on lines 14, 17, and 20. The program uses PRINT statements on lines 13, 15, 18, and 21 to display the contents of the four variables. The program output indicates that the conversion from single-precision to integer and long integer causes the loss of the fractional part.

Explicit Numeric Conversion

QBasic enables you to perform explicit numeric conversions using the family of Ctype functions. These functions convert from one numeric data type to another and follow the conversion guidelines shown in Table 4.1.

The Ctype functions

The general syntax for the Ctype numeric conversion functions is

```
CINT(numericExpression)
CLNG(numericExpression)
CSNG(numericExpression)
CDBL(numericExpression)
```

The *numericExpression* is a numeric constant, variable, or expression. The first three functions generate an overflow error at runtime if the *numericExpression* value is out of range.

Examples:

```
PRINT CINT(23.4 / 12.3)
PRINT CLNG(123.8 * 8.3)
PRINT CSNG(4 + 2)
PRINT CDBL(3 / 4)
```

Let's look at a program that uses the CINT, CLNG, CSNG, and CDBL conversion functions. Listing 4.3 tests the conversion functions using integers and single-precision numbers. The program requires no input; it assigns data internally.

Listing 4.3. **ASSIGN3.BAS, which uses the Ctype numeric conversion functions.**

```
1: REM Program demonstrates using the CINT,
2: REM CLNG, CSNG, and CDBL numeric conversion functions
3: REM
4: ' declare the program variables
5: DIM IntVar1 AS INTEGER
6: DIM IntVar2 AS INTEGER
7: DIM SngVar1 AS SINGLE
8: DIM SngVar2 AS SINGLE
9: '
10: CLS
11: ' assign values to the variables
12: IntVar1 = 355
13: IntVar2 = 113
14: SngVar1 = 122.5
15: SngVar2 = 56.32
16:
17: ' Test the CINT, CLNG, CSNG and CDBL functions with
18: ' the integer variables
19: PRINT "IntVar1 = "; IntVar1
20: PRINT "IntVar2 = "; IntVar2
21: PRINT "IntVar1 / IntVar2 = "; CINT(IntVar1 / IntVar2)
22: PRINT "CLNG(IntVar1 / IntVar2) = "; CLNG(IntVar1 / IntVar2)
23: PRINT "CSNG(IntVar1 / IntVar2) = "; CSNG(IntVar1 / IntVar2)
24: PRINT "CDBL(IntVar1 / IntVar2) = "; CDBL(IntVar1 / IntVar2)
25: PRINT
26:
27: ' Test the CINT, CLNG, and CDBL functions with
28: ' the single-precision variables
29: PRINT "SngVar1 = "; SngVar1
30: PRINT "SngVar2 = "; SngVar2
31: PRINT "SngVar1 / SngVar2 = "; SngVar1 / SngVar2
32: PRINT "CINT(SngVar1 / SngVar2) = "; CINT(SngVar1 / SngVar2)
33: PRINT "CLNG(SngVar1 / SngVar2) = "; CLNG(SngVar1 / SngVar2)
```

4

Listing 4.3. continued

```
34: PRINT "CDBL(SngVar1 / SngVar2) = "; CDBL(SngVar1 / SngVar2)
35:
36: END
```

Here is a sample output for the program in Listing 4.3:

```
IntVar1 =   355
IntVar2 =   113
IntVar1 / IntVar2 =   3
CLNG(IntVar1 / IntVar2) =   3
CSNG(IntVar1 / IntVar2) =   3.141593
CDBL(IntVar1 / IntVar2) =   3.141592920353983

SngVar1 =   122.5
SngVar2 =   56.32
SngVar1 / SngVar2 =   2.175071
CINT(SngVar1 / SngVar2) =   2
CLNG(SngVar1 / SngVar2) =   2
CDBL(SngVar1 / SngVar2) =   2.175071034513122
```

Analysis

In Listing 4.3 lines 5–8 declare two integer variables, IntVar1 and IntVar2, and two single-precision variables, SngVar1 and SngVar2. Lines 12–15 contain statements that assign values to the four variables. On lines 19 and 20, the program uses PRINT statements to display the values in IntVar1 and IntVar2. Line 21 displays the integer ratio of IntVar1 and IntVar2. Notice that the PRINT statement uses the CINT function to obtain the integer result. Why? The / operator performs floating-point divisions, even on integers. So the program must use CINT to convert the answer to an integer. In the next section I present the math operators and show you the operator for integer division. For now, using the / operator is fine. Line 22 uses the CLNG function with the ratio of the integer variables. Lines 23 and 24 use the CSNG and CDBL functions to display the ratios as single-precision and double-precision numbers, respectively.

Lines 29 and 30 display the values in the single-precision variables SngVar1 and SngVar2, respectively. The PRINT statement on line 31 displays the ratio of these two variables. The output is a single-precision number. On line 32 CINT converts the ratio of the variables (a single-precision number) to an integer. This conversion chops off the fractional part of the ratio. Line 33 performs a similar task when function CLNG converts the single-precision ratio to a long integer.

Math Operators

QBasic supports math operators to perform the four basic operations (addition, subtraction, multiplication, and division) as well as integer division, integer division remainder (also called modulo), and exponentiation (raising a value to a power). Table 4.2 lists the QBasic math operators and offers simple examples.

Table 4.2. **The QBasic math operators.**

Operator	Meaning	Examples
+	+ unary	`i% = +3`
-	- unary	`i% = -123`
+	addition	`i% = 23 + 34 ' = 57`
-	subtraction	`index% = 78 - i% ' = 21`
*	multiplication	`L& = i% * index% ' = 78`
/	division	`X# = i% / 12.3 ' = 4.63415`
\	integer division	`i% = index% \ 12 ' = 1`
^	raising to power	`X# = 2.1^8.3 ' = 472.51995`
		`Y# = 3^7 ' = 2187`
MOD	division remainder	`J% = 12 MOD 2 ' = 0`

Note: The **MOD** operator converts its operands to integers.

Warning: The /, \, and MOD operators generate a division-by-zero runtime error if the second operand is 0.

Let's look at a simple program that tests the QBasic math operators. Listing 4.4, MATHOP1.BAS, uses the various math operators. The program prompts you to enter two operands, one at a time. The top of the screen displays a notice requesting that you enter small positive numbers to avoid possible runtime errors. The program then displays the product of the various math operations using the two numbers you entered.

Listing 4.4. MATHOP1.BAS, which tests the QBasic math operators.

```
 1: REM Program that demonstrates the QBasic math operators
 2: REM
 3: ' declare the program variables
 4: DIM Operand1 AS SINGLE
 5: DIM Operand2 AS SINGLE
 6:
 7: CLS
 8: PRINT "Notice: Enter small positive numbers"
 9: INPUT "Enter the first operand : ", Operand1
10: INPUT "Enter the second operand : ", Operand2
11:
12: PRINT Operand1; " + "; Operand2; " = "; Operand1 + Operand2
13: PRINT Operand1; " - "; Operand2; " = "; Operand1 - Operand2
14: PRINT Operand1; " * "; Operand2; " = "; Operand1 * Operand2
15: PRINT Operand1; " / "; Operand2; " = "; Operand1 / Operand2
16: PRINT Operand1; " ^ "; Operand2; " = "; Operand1 ^ Operand2
17: PRINT Operand1; " \ "; Operand2; " = "; Operand1 \ Operand2
18: PRINT Operand1; " MOD "; Operand2; " = "; Operand1 MOD Operand2
19: END
```

Here is a sample output for the program in Listing 4.4:

```
Notice: Enter small positive numbers
Enter the first operand : 3.5
Enter the second operand : 2
  3.5  +  2  =  5.5
  3.5  -  2  =  1.5
  3.5  *  2  =  7
  3.5  /  2  =  1.75
  3.5  ^  2  =  12.25
  3.5  \  2  =  2
  3.5  MOD  2  =  0
```

Lines 4 and 5 in Listing 4.4 declare two single-precision variables Operand1 and Operand2. This declaration is optional because QBasic variables are single-precision by default. I included these statements to be consistent with my recommendation of using DIM statements to declare variables. Line 8 contains a PRINT statement that displays the notice about entering small

numbers. Lines 9 and 10 contain INPUT statements that prompt you to enter the two operands, storing these values in the variables Operand1 and Operand2. Lines 12–18 contain a series of PRINT statements. Each statement displays the first operand, the math operator (as a string), the second operand, and the result of the operation.

The Boolean Truth Table

A computer's versatility depends on how it can view binary digits as well as integers. In addition, the power of a computer comes from its ability to make quick and accurate decisions. Consequently, computer programs must be able to examine data and determine whether certain conditions are true or false. There's a similarity between the binary values (0 and 1) and the two logical states of a condition: true and false. Computer scientists quickly drew the relationship between binary digits (and integer values) and logical values. 19th-century English mathematician George Boole, who lived before computers were invented, studied logic and logical values (true and false). Boole devised a set of operations for the logical values. Boole's work has had such an influence that among programmers the word *Boolean* has become synonymous with the word logical.

Boole invented the truth table, the logical equivalent of the multiplication table in arithmetic. Table 4.3 lists the Boolean truth table. The table contains most of the Boolean operations. (The ones not shown are not implemented in QBasic.)

4

Table 4.3. **The Boolean Truth Table.**

Boolean Operand 1	Boolean Operand 2	Boolean Operation	Result
True	True	Conjunction	True
True	False	(AND)	False
False	True		False
False	False		False
True	True	Disjunction	True

continues

85

Table 4.3. continued

Boolean Operand 1	Boolean Operand 2	Boolean Operation	Result
True	False	(OR)	True
False	True		True
False	False		False
True	True	Exclusive OR	False
True	False	(XOR)	True
False	True		True
False	False		False
True	True	Equivalence	True
True	False		False
False	True		False
False	False		True
True	True	Implication	True
True	False		False
False	True		True
False	False		True
True		Complement	False
False		(NOT)	True

How does QBasic manage Boolean values, you might ask? QBasic considers the integer 0 false and the integer -1 true. In the next sections I discuss how QBasic statements translate expressions into Boolean values.

Relational Operators

The relational operators enable a program statement to examine a condition by comparing compatible values and producing a Boolean result. Table 4.4 lists the QBasic relational operators. A relational operator yields -1 (true) if the examined condition is true. Otherwise, the operator produces 0 (false). For example, if I%=1, the following condition is true:

```
OK% = I% <> 0
```

The <> operator yields -1, and the statement assigns -1 to the variable OK%.

Table 4.4. The QBasic relational operators.

Operator	Meaning	Example
<	less than	12 < 4
<=	less than or equal to	i% <= 0
>	greater than	X > Y
>=	greater than or equal to	X >= 1
<>	not equal to	Z& <> 0
=	equal to	I% = 0

Let's look at a program that uses the various relational operators. Listing 4.5, RELOP1.BAS, prompts you to enter two integers. The program displays the Boolean values of 0 or -1, based on applying the various relational operators to your input.

Listing 4.5. RELOP1.BAS, which tests the QBasic relational operators.

```
1: REM Program illustrates the relational operators in QBasic
2: REM
3: ' declare the variables
4: DIM Operand1 AS INTEGER
5: DIM Operand2 AS INTEGER
6:
```

Listing 4.5. **continued**

```
 7: CLS
 8: INPUT "Enter an integer : ", Operand1
 9: INPUT "Enter another integer : ", Operand2
10: ' test the various relational operators using the input values
11: PRINT "Condition: "; Operand1; " = "; Operand2; "  is ";
12: PRINT Operand1 = Operand2
13: PRINT "Condition: "; Operand1; " <> "; Operand2; " is ";
14: PRINT Operand1 <> Operand2
15: PRINT "Condition: "; Operand1; " > "; Operand2; "  is ";
16: PRINT Operand1 > Operand2
17: PRINT "Condition: "; Operand1; " >= "; Operand2; " is ";
18: PRINT Operand1 >= Operand2
19: PRINT "Condition: "; Operand1; " < "; Operand2; "  is ";
20: PRINT Operand1 < Operand2
21: PRINT "Condition: "; Operand1; " <= "; Operand2; " is ";
22: PRINT Operand1 <= Operand2
23: END
```

Here is a sample output for the program in Listing 4.5:

```
Notice: Enter small positive numbers
Enter an integer : -5
Enter another integer : 3
Condition: -5  =  3   is  0
Condition: -5  <>  3   is -1
Condition: -5  >  3   is  0
Condition: -5  >=  3   is  0
Condition: -5  <  3   is -1
Condition: -5  <=  3   is -1
```

The program in Listing 4.5 uses the integer variables declared in lines 4 and 5, Operand1 and Operand2. Lines 8 and 9 contain INPUT statements that prompt you for the two integers. Lines 11–22 contain a set of PRINT statement pairs. Each pair displays the first number, the relational operator (as a string), the second number, and the Boolean value produced by applying that relational operator to the two values.

Logical Operators

The relational operators produce Boolean values (represented by 0 and -1) by comparing pairs of compatible data items. QBasic provides you with logical (or Boolean, if you prefer) operators than can take these Boolean values and manipulate them in accordance with the Boolean truth table. In addition, the Boolean operators supplement relational operators and thus enable you to test more sophisticated conditions. Table 4.5 lists the QBasic logical operators and offers simple examples. The most commonly used logical operators are AND, OR, XOR, and NOT. I have yet to come across an application that uses the EQV or IMP operators.

Table 4.5. The QBasic logical operators.

Logical Operator	Meaning	Example
NOT	Bit-wise complement	ok = NOT (i% > 0)
AND	Conjunction	ok = (i>0) AND (i<9)
OR	Disjunction (inclusive "or")	ok = (i=0) OR (i=1)
XOR	Exclusive "or"	er = (i=1) XOR (i=2)
EQV	Equivalence	er = (j=9) EQV (k=1)
IMP	Implication	er = (j=9) IMP (k=1)

New Term The term *condition* refers to a statement that uses at least a one relational operator. A condition also might include one or more Boolean operators. Here are some examples of conditions:

```
isPositive% = I% > 0
inRange1To9% = J% >= 1 AND J% <= 9
isOdd% = I%=1 OR I%=3 OR I%=5 OR I%=7 OR I%=9
```

Take a look at Listing 4.6, a program that uses the logical operators AND, OR, XOR, and NOT. I created this program by editing the RELOP1.BAS program in Listing 4.5. I added PRINT statements that display the value produced by both the logical and relational operators.

Listing 4.6. **RELOP2.BAS, which tests the QBasic logical operators.**

```
1: REM Program illustrates the logical operators in QBasic
2: REM
3: ' declare the variables
4: DIM Operand1 AS INTEGER
5: DIM Operand2 AS INTEGER
6:
7: CLS
8: INPUT "Enter an integer : ", Operand1
9: INPUT "Enter another integer : ", Operand2
10: PRINT
11: ' use the various relational operators using the input values
12: PRINT "Condition: "; Operand1; " = "; Operand2; "  is ";
13: PRINT Operand1 = Operand2
14: PRINT "Condition: "; Operand1; " <> "; Operand2; " is ";
15: PRINT Operand1 <> Operand2
16: PRINT "Condition: "; Operand1; " > "; Operand2; "  is ";
17: PRINT Operand1 > Operand2
18: PRINT "Condition: "; Operand1; " >= "; Operand2; " is ";
19: PRINT Operand1 >= Operand2
20: PRINT "Condition: "; Operand1; " < "; Operand2; "  is ";
21: PRINT Operand1 < Operand2
22: PRINT "Condition: "; Operand1; " <= "; Operand2; " is ";
23: PRINT Operand1 <= Operand2
24: PRINT
25: ' now apply the logical operators
26: ' test AND
27: PRINT "Condition: "; Operand1; " >  "; Operand2; " AND ";
28: PRINT Operand1; " >   0 is ";
29: PRINT Operand1 > Operand2 AND Operand1 > 0
30: ' test OR
31: PRINT "Condition: "; Operand1; " <> "; Operand2; " OR   ";
32: PRINT Operand1; " <   0 is ";
33: PRINT Operand1 <> Operand2 OR Operand1 < 0
34: ' test XOR
35: PRINT "Condition: "; Operand1; " <> "; Operand2; " XOR ";
36: PRINT Operand1; " <=  0 is ";
37: PRINT Operand1 <> Operand2 XOR Operand1 <= 0
38: ' test NOT
39: PRINT "Condition: NOT "; Operand1; " <> "; Operand2; " is ";
40: PRINT NOT Operand1 <> Operand2
41: END
```

Here is a sample output for the program in Listing 4.6:

```
Enter an integer : 6
Enter another integer : 3

Condition:  6  =  3   is  0
Condition:  6  <> 3   is -1
Condition:  6  >  3   is -1
Condition:  6  >= 3   is -1
Condition:  6  <  3   is  0
Condition:  6  <= 3   is  0

Condition:  6  >  3  AND  6  >  0 is -1
Condition:  6  <> 3  OR   6  <  0 is -1
Condition:  6  <> 3  XOR  6  <= 0 is -1
Condition: NOT 6  <> 3   is  0
```

The statements on the first 23 lines of Listing 4.6 match the beginning of Listing 4.5. These lines contain PRINT statements that display the Boolean values produced by applying relational operators to your input. The statements on line 27 to the end of the program contain PRINT statements that apply the AND, OR, XOR, and NOT operators to your input. You can use the output of the statements in lines 12–23 to double-check the outcome of the Boolean operators.

String Operators

QBasic supports only one operator for string manipulation. The + operator enables you to **concatenate** (append) string literals, string constants, and string variables. QBasic strings rely on built-in functions to manipulate strings. On Day 5, "String Manipulation," I discuss the string-manipulating functions.

Let's look at a program that uses the + operator with strings. Listing 4.7, STRING1.BAS, concatenates string literals, string constants, and string variables. The program prompts you to enter your first and last names and then displays a message that includes other text. In fact, the program displays the message twice. I'll explain this duplicate output when I discuss the program listing.

Listing 4.7. STRING1.BAS, which illustrates using the + operator to concatenate string literals, string constants, and string variables.

```
 1: REM Program demonstrates the + operator to
 2: REM concatenate strings
 3: REM
 4: ' declare string constants
 5: CONST FIRST = "John"
 6: CONST LAST = "Lennon"
 7: ' declare program variables
 8: DIM MyFirst AS STRING
 9: DIM MyLast AS STRING
10: DIM Message AS STRING
11: CLS
12: INPUT "Enter your first name : ", MyFirst
13: INPUT "Enter your last name : ", MyLast
14: PRINT
15:
16: ' concatenate string in preparation for output
17: Message = MyFirst + " " + MyLast
18: Message = Message + " is a fan of " + FIRST + " " + LAST
19: ' now output the string to the screen
20: PRINT Message
21:
22: ' display the same text by using semicolons between the
23: ' various data items
24: PRINT MyFirst; " "; MyLast; " is a fan of "; FIRST; " "; LAST
25: END
```

Here is a sample output for the program in Listing 4.7:

```
Enter your first name : Namir
Enter your last name : Shammas


Namir Shammas is a fan of John Lennon
Namir Shammas is a fan of John Lennon
```

The program in Listing 4.7 declares two string constants, FIRST and LAST, on lines 5 and 6. On lines 8–10, the program declares three string variables: MyFirst, MyLast, and Message. Lines 12 and 13 contain INPUT statements that prompt you for your first and last names. The program stores your input

in `MyFirst` and `MyLast`. On line 17 the program uses the + operator to concatenate the contents of `MyFirst` with a single-space string and the contents of variable `MyLast`. The statement assigns the resulting string value to the variable `Message`. On line 18 the program concatenates the contents of variable `Message` with other string literals and the string constants `FIRST` and `LAST`. The statement assigns the resulting string value back to `Message`. The statements on lines 17 and 18 illustrate a simple method that you can use to build a long string made from either many string items or long string literals. Line 20 displays the contents of `Message` using a `PRINT` statement. Line 24 uses another `PRINT` statement to display the same text displayed by line 20. This time, the `PRINT` statement displays the string items by concatenating them with semicolons. The program shows how you can output a concatenated string in two ways: by building the output in a string variable and then displaying that variable, or by concatenating the output in a `PRINT` statement.

Math Expressions

So far I've presented programs that contain simple mathematical expressions. Each expression uses one mathematical operator. In this section I discuss mathematical expressions that involve multiple operators. The main issue raised by such expressions is how QBasic evaluates them. In the case of single-operator expressions, such as 2 * 4 or 56 - 34, things are simple. You take the two operands and perform the operation specified by the operator. In the next subsections I discuss exactly how QBasic deals with multiple-operator expressions.

Operator Precedence

Pop quiz! What is the value assigned to the variable `I%` in the following statement?

```
I% = 3 + 6 * 2 + 1
```

If the operators are systematically applied from left to right the answer is 19. If the operators are applied in the reverse direction, the answer is 21. In reality, QBasic does not utilize such directional schemes for applying operators. Instead, QBasic (and many programming languages) considers the mathematical operators to have different precedence. According to the precedence in Table 4.6, the above QBasic statement evaluates to 16—first the multiplication is performed and then the addition operations. In the next subsection I take a closer look at how such an expression is evaluated.

Table 4.6. The precedence of QBasic mathematical operators.

(Top level is the highest, and each line is the next level down.)

exponentiation (^)

unary addition and subtraction

multiplication (*), division (/)

integer division (\), integer remainder (MOD)

addition (+) and subtraction (-)

Evaluating Math Expressions

Let me use an example to explain how QBasic evaluates a math expression. Figure 4.1 shows the steps involved in evaluating a sample math expression with multiple operators that have different precedence. Notice that the mathematical expression in Figure 4.1 has no parentheses. In the next subsection, I discuss using parentheses in mathematical expressions and how they alter the evaluation of these expressions.

The rules for evaluating a math expression (without parentheses) are:

1. The higher precedence operators are applied before the ones with lower precedence.

2. When there are multiple operators that have the same precedence, the evaluation applies the operators from left to right.

The steps for evaluating a mathematical expression in Figure 4.1 also reflect the above rules.

Using Parentheses

Using parentheses enables you to alter the precedence of operators. QBasic applies the following rules when you use parentheses in mathematical expressions:

1. The higher precedence operators are applied before the ones with lower precedence.

2. When there are multiple operators that have the same precedence, the evaluation applies the operators from left to right.

3. The operators in parentheses are evaluated first.

4. Nested parentheses have a higher evaluation precedence that the ones that contain them.

5. The evaluation of an expression starts with the most nested parentheses and gradually proceeds to the operators that are outside any parentheses.

6. Within a set of parentheses, the operators are applied using rules 1 and 2.

Figure 4.2 shows the steps involved in evaluating a sample math expression with multiple operators and a single-level parentheses. Figure 4.3 shows the steps involved in evaluating a sample math expression with multiple operators and multilevel parentheses.

4

```
              1 + 5 * 4 – 16 / 2 ^ 3           initial expression
   step 1:  raise the number 2 to power 3
              1 + 5 * 4 – 16 / 2 ^ 3           yields
                              |___|
              1 + 5 * 4 – 16 /    8
   step 2:  multiply the numbers 5 and 4
              1 + 5 * 4 – 16 /    8            yields
                  |___|
              1 +   20  – 16 /    8
   step 3:  divide the numbers 16 and 8
              1 +  20  – 16 /    8             yields
                          |____|
              1 +  20  –     2
   step 4:  add the numbers 1 and 20
              1 +  20  –     2                 yields
              |____|
               21    –     2
   step 5:  subtract 2 from 21
               21    –    2
               |_____|
                    19                         the expression value
```

Figure 4.1. Evaluating a math expression with multiple operators that have different precedence.

```
( 1 + 5 ) * ( 14 − 6 ) / 2 ^ 3        initial expression
step 1:  add the numbers 1 and 5 in the first parentheses
( 1 + 5 ) * ( 14 − 6 ) / 2 ^ 3        yields
    6     * ( 14 − 6 ) / 2 ^ 3
step 2:  subtract the number 6 from the number 14
    6     * ( 14 − 6 ) / 2 ^ 3        yields
    6     *     8     / 2 ^ 3
step 3:  raise the number 2 to power 3
    6     *     8     / 2 ^ 3         yields
    6     *     8     /   8
step 4:  multiply 6 and 8
    6     *     8     /   8          yields
        48            /   8
step 5:  divide 48 by 8
        48                /   8
                6                    the expression value
```

Figure 4.2. Evaluating a math expression with multiple operators and single-level parentheses.

```
( 12 * ( 1 + 5 ) + ( 14 − 6 ) ) / 2 ^ 3        initial expression
step 1:  add the numbers 1 and 5 in the first parentheses
( 12 * ( 1 + 5 ) + ( 14 − 6 ) ) / 2 ^ 3        yields
( 12 *    6     + ( 14 − 6 ) ) / 2 ^ 3
step 2:  subtract 6 from 14
( 12 *    6     + ( 14 − 6 ) ) / 2 ^ 3         yields
( 12 *    6     +     8     ) / 2 ^ 3
step 3:  multiply 12 and 6
( 12 *    6     +     8     ) / 2 ^ 3           yields
(     72        +     8     ) / 2 ^ 3
step 4:  add the numbers 72 and 8
(     72        +     8     ) / 2 ^ 3           yields
            80              / 2 ^ 3
step 5:  raise the number 2 to power 3
            80              / 2 ^ 3             yields
            80              /   8
step 6:  divide 80 by 8
            80                /   8             the expression value
                    10
```

Figure 4.3. Evaluating a math expression with multiple operators and multi-level parentheses.

Let's look at a QBasic program that evaluates mathematical expressions and displays their results. Listing 4.8, MATHOP2.BAS, evaluates a selection of mathematical expressions. The program requires no input. It merely displays text image of the expressions along with their results.

Listing 4.8. MATHOP2.BAS, which evaluates a selection of mathematical expressions.

```
 1: REM Program tests various math expressions
 2: REM
 3: CLS
 4: PRINT "Sample mathematical expressions"
 5: PRINT
 6: PRINT "2 + 5 * 3 + 6 = "; 2 + 5 * 3 + 6
 7: PRINT "2 + 3 * 4 - 16 / 8 = "; 2 + 3 * 4 - 16 / 8
 8: PRINT "(2 + 5) * (3 + 6) = "; (2 + 5) * (3 + 6)
 9: PRINT "((2 + 3) * 4 - 16) / 2 = "; ((2 + 3) * 4 - 16) / 2
10: PRINT "((12 + 4) * 2) / ((2 + 3) * 4 - 16) = ";
11: PRINT ((12 + 4) * 2) / ((2 + 3) * 4 - 16)
12: END
```

Here is a sample output for the program in Listing 4.8:

```
Sample mathematical expressions

2 + 5 * 3 + 6 =  23
2 + 3 * 4 - 16 / 8 =  12
(2 + 5) * (3 + 6) =  63
((2 + 3) * 4 - 16) / 2 =  2
((12 + 4) * 2) / ((2 + 3) * 4 - 16) =  8
```

The program in Listing 4.8 uses no variables. The core of the program consists of the PRINT statements that display the text image of the various mathematical expressions along with their values.

4

DO remember operator precedence when adding math expressions to your program.

DON'T use needless parentheses; they slow down the evaluation of an expression. Here is an example of what to avoid:

```
I% = ((((2) + 6)) / (4 + 89)) + 1
```

A simpler version of the statement is:

```
I% = (2 + 6) / (4 + 89) + 1
```

Summary

The chapter covered QBasic data manipulation. You learned about the following topics:

☐ An overview of operators and expressions. Operators are special symbols or names that manipulate data, called the operands. Expressions contain multiple operators and operands.

☐ The assignment operator (the = character) enables you to assign a constant, variable, or expression to a variable. The assigned value must be compatible with the variable receiving the value.

☐ QBasic performs automatic numeric conversion. This conversion accommodates assigning a numeric value (of a certain type) to a variable associated with a different numeric data type.

☐ Math operators in QBasic include the +, -, /, \(integer division), *, ^ (raising to power), and MOD (division remainder).

☐ The Boolean truth table shows how the logical operators manipulate the logical values true and false. QBasic regards -1 as true and 0 as false when dealing with Boolean (logical) values.

- Relational operators in QBasic are <, <=, >, >=, <>, and =. These operators compare compatible data items (constants, variables, and expression) and yield -1 (if the comparison is true) or 0 (if the comparison is false).

- Logical operators in QBasic are AND, OR, XOR, NOT, EQV, and IMP. These operators manipulate -1 (true) and 0 (false) values and yield a -1 (true) or 0 (false) in accordance with the Boolean truth table.

- The only string operator in QBasic is the + operator, which concatenates string literals, string constants, and string variables.

- Math expressions are evaluated by using operator precedence rules. These precedence rules are fairly standard among programming languages. Using parentheses enables you to alter the precedence of applying an operator.

Q&A

Q.   What's the best way for me to check whether the value of a variable lies within a range of values?

A.   The general expression to verify that a value is within a range is:

```
aVar >= lowerLimitValue AND aVar <= upperLimitValue
```

To check for a value that is strictly **inside** a given range (that is, not equal to either boundary) use the following general form:

```
aVar > lowerLimitValue AND aVar < upperLimitValue
```

Q.   How can I check whether the value of a variable lies outside a range of values?

A.   The general expression for checking that a value is outside a range of value is:

```
aVar >= lowerLimitValue XOR aVar <= upperLimitValue
```

You also can use the following general expression:

```
aVar < lowerLimitValue OR aVar > upperLimitValue
```

4

Q. Can I assign the same value to several variables in a single statement, such as:

```
A = B = C = D = 10
```

A. No. QBasic only considers the leftmost = operator as an assignment operator. The other = operators are treated as relational operators that test equality of values.

Q. Can I write Boolean expressions that use relational operators, each with different data types, such as:

```
(X# > 0 AND I% < 10) OR (Me$ <> "Namir)
```

A. Yes. Each relational subexpression yields a Boolean true (-1) or false (0). The Boolean operators then work with -1 or 0.

Workshop

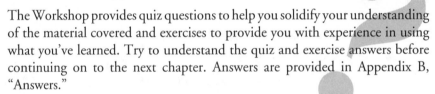

The Workshop provides quiz questions to help you solidify your understanding of the material covered and exercises to provide you with experience in using what you've learned. Try to understand the quiz and exercise answers before continuing on to the next chapter. Answers are provided in Appendix B, "Answers."

Quiz

1. What is the value stored in variable I% in the following statements:

```
J% = 10
I% = J% = 10
```

2. What are the values produced by the following mathematical expressions?

```
a. 2 ^ 3 ^ 2
b. 2 ^ (3 ^ 2)
c. 2 * 3 / 12 + 1
d. (20 + 5) / (2 + 3)
```

3. True or false: the following statements execute without a runtime error:

```
N& = 32768
I% = N%
```

4. What is wrong with the following statement?

```
PRINT "Area = " + Area# + " square feet"
```

5. What is wrong with the second statement in the following set of statements?

```
INPUT "Enter a number ";J%
I% = J% > 0 OR J% < 10    and
PRINT "Condition : "; J%; " is in range of 1 to 9 is "; I%
```

6. What is wrong with the second statement in the following set of statements?

```
INPUT "Enter a number ";J%
I% = J% = 0 AND J% = 10    or
PRINT "Condition : "; J%; " = 0 or 10 is "; I%
```

7. In question 6, can you correct the second statement by writing the following?

```
I% = J% = 0 XOR J% = 10
```

8. Simplify the following mathematical expressions:

```
a. I% = (((((((((1)))))))))    1
b. J% = (2 * 3) + 1    2x3+1
c. K% = (4 * 5) + (6 * 7) + 1    4x5+6x7 +1
d. M! = ((1 + 4) / (5 + 9))    (1+4)/(5+9)
```

9. What is wrong with the following expression?

```
D# = (2 + 3) * (47 - 12    missing
                          Parenthesis
```

Exercises

1. Write a QBasic statement that toggles the Boolean value stored in a variable named Flag%.

4

2. Write an expression that determines whether the contents of an integer variable (call it N%) is an odd or even number. Use the MOD operator in the expression that returns -1 (True) if N% stores an even number, and 0 (False) otherwise.

3. Write a program that uses both relational and logical operators to guard against converting out-of-range single-precision numbers into integers. Your program should prompt for input and store it in a single-precision, float variable. Save the program in a file named ASSIGN4.BAS.

4. Simplify the following Boolean expressions:

   a. NOT (NOT A > 10)
   b. NOT (X > 0 AND X < 10)
   c. X = 0 OR X = 1 OR X = 2 OR X = 3 OR X = 4

5. Modify ASSIGN1.BAS in Listing 4.1 to assign the long integer variable, LongVar, to the other variables. Save the modified program under the filename ASSIGN5.BAS.

6. Modify ASSIGN2.BAS in Listing 4.2 to assign the double-precision float variable, DoubleVar, to the other variables. Save the modified program under the filename ASSIGN6.BAS.

DAY
5

String
Manipulation

Many programs involve managing strings such as names, addresses, ZIP codes, and so on. QBasic provides a rich set of functions that manipulates strings. In this chapter you learn about the following topics:

☐ Obtaining the number of characters in a string using the LEN function

☐ Converting a character into its integer ASCII code using the ASC function

☐ Converting an ASCII code number into a character using the CHR$ function

☐ Converting strings to numbers and vice versa using the STR$ and VAL functions

☐ Extracting substrings using the LEFT$, RIGHT$, and MID$ functions

☐ Overwriting part of a string with the MID$ statement

☐ Locating substrings using the INSTR function

☐ Converting the character case of a string using the LCASE$ and UCASE$ functions

There are other, more advanced, string functions, and they are covered in Chapter 17, "Advanced String Manipulation."

Before I discuss the various string functions in QBasic, here is a list of terms you should become familiar with.

■**New Term**   The term *substring* refers to any portion of a string.

■**New Term**   A QBasic *function* is program component that takes a number of values, called *arguments*, and returns a single value. Functions in programming languages are similar to mathematical functions. QBasic provides a rich number of predefined functions. This chapter deals with the QBasic functions that manipulate strings. Although some of these functions take single arguments, others take two or three arguments.

■**New Term**   The *parameter* of a function is the formal name of an argument. When I present a function, I discuss the role of its various parameters.

■**New Term**   The term *function call* refers to using (or calling, which is where the term comes from) a function with a set of values. For example, CINT(12.3) is a function call that invokes the CINT function and supplies it with the value 12.3.

■**New Term** The terms *case-sensitive* and *case-insensitive* are often involved when searching for characters in a string. Case-sensitive indicates that the character comparison (or search) distinguishes between uppercase and lowercase letters. By contrast, case-insensitive indicates that the character comparison (or search) does not distinguishes between uppercase and lowercase letters.

Getting the Length of a String

The manipulation of a string often involves knowing the number of characters it contains (its lengths.) QBasic offers the built-in LEN function to obtain the number of characters in a string.

Syntax

The LEN Function

The general syntax for the LEN function is

```
LEN(stringExpression)
```

The *stringExpression* parameter is either a string literal, string constant, string variable, string function, or an expression that contains these different components. The LEN function returns the number of characters in the parameter *stringExpression*. If *stringExpression* is an empty string, LEN returns 0.

Figure 5.1 depicts the function LEN("Hello"), which returns 5, the number of characters in the string literal "Hello".

Examples:

```
' apply LEN to a string literal
L% = LEN("This is a string literal")


' apply LEN to a string constant
CONST VERSION = "Version 1.0"
L% = LEN(VERSION)


' apply LEN to a string variable
DIM aString AS STRING
```

5

```
aString = "Hello"
PRINT aString; " has "; LEN(aString); " characters"

' apply LEN to a string expression
DIM aString AS STRING
DIM L AS INTEGER
aString = "Namir Shammas"
L = LEN("My name is " + aString)
```

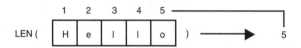

Figure 5.1. The function LEN("Hello") returns the integer 5.

Let's look at an example that uses the LEN function. Listing 5.1, STRING2.BAS, utilizes the LEN function to determine the length of two input strings. The program prompts you to input two strings. The program then displays the following information:

☐ A character ruler.

☐ The strings you entered. Each string appears on a separate line.

☐ The length of each string.

☐ The set of Boolean values (-1 or 0) that determines whether the first string is longer, shorter, or equal to the second string.

 Listing 5.1. STRING2.BAS, which illustrates the LEN function.

```
1: REM Program that tests the LEN function
2: REM
3: ' declare the program variables
4: DIM Len1 AS INTEGER
5: DIM Len2 AS INTEGER
6: DIM S1 AS STRING
7: DIM S2 AS STRING
8:
9: CLS
```

```
10: PRINT "Enter a first string (with no commas)"
11: INPUT S1
12: PRINT "Enter a second string (with no commas)"
13: INPUT S2
14: PRINT
15: ' store the length of the string S1 in Len1
16: Len1 = LEN(S1)
17: ' store the length of the string S2 in Len2
18: Len2 = LEN(S2)
19: PRINT "          1         2         3         4         5"
20: PRINT "12345678901234567890123456789012345678901234567890"
21: PRINT
22: PRINT S1
23: PRINT S2
24: PRINT
25: PRINT "String 1 has "; Len1; " characters"
26: PRINT "String 2 has "; Len2; " characters"
27: PRINT "Condition: 'String 1 is longer than String 2' is ";
28: PRINT Len1 > Len2
29: PRINT "Condition: 'String 1 is shorter than String 2' is ";
30: PRINT Len1 < Len2
31: PRINT "Condition: 'Both strings have the same length' is ";
32: PRINT Len1 = Len2
33: END
```

Here is a sample output for the program in Listing 5.1:

```
Enter a first string (with no commas)
? California
Enter a second string (with no commas)
? Virginia

          1         2         3         4         5
12345678901234567890123456789012345678901234567890

California
Virginia

String 1 has  10  characters
String 2 has  8  characters
```

5

```
Condition: 'String 1 is longer than String 2' is -1
Condition: 'String 1 is shorter than String 2' is  0
Condition: 'Both strings have the same length' is  0
```

The program in Listing 5.1 declares its variables on lines 4–7. The program declares the integer variables Len1 and Len2 to store the length of the two strings you enter. The string variables S1 and S2 store the keyboard input. Using a PRINT statement, line 10 displays the message that prompts you for the first string. Line 11 uses an INPUT statement, with no prompt string, to obtain the first string. Lines 12 and 13, which perform tasks similar to lines 10 and 11, obtain the second string. Lines 16 and 18 apply the LEN function to strings S1 and S2, respectively, and assign the string lengths to Len1 and Len2, respectively. Lines 19 and 20 contain PRINT statements that display the character ruler. Lines 22 and 23 display the strings you entered. Lines 25 and 26 display the number of characters in each string. Lines 27 and 28 display whether the first string is longer than the second string. The program calculates the Boolean result using the expression Len1 > Len2. Lines 29 and 30 perform a similar task to determine whether the first string is shorter than the second string. Lines 31 and 32 determine whether the two strings are of equal lengths.

Converting a Character into an ASCII Code

On Day 3, "Data Types, Constants, and Variables," I mentioned that computers represent characters using unique integer values (or integer codes, if you prefer). I also mentioned that these codes are known as the ASCII codes. QBasic offers a built-in function that returns the ASCII code of the first character in a string. The QBasic help system has an online ASCII table. Using this table, you can look up the ASCII code for a specific character. The first 128 characters are standard for all computers and operating systems that use ASCII code. The second 128 characters are called extended ASCII characters. The IBM corporation established these characters and their codes for the IBM PC. These values are valid for QBasic and for other programming languages running under DOS.

The ASC Function

The general syntax for ASC function is:

```
ASC(stringExpression)
```

The *stringExpression* parameter is either a string literal, string constant, string variable, string function, or an expression that contains these different components. The ASC function returns the ASCII code for only the first character in *stringExpression*. The function ignores any other characters in *stringExpression*.

Figure 5.2 shows how the ASC function works only on the first character of a string.

Examples:

```
' apply ASC to a string literal
L% = ASC("T")


' apply ASC to a string constant
CONST DRIVE = "A:"
L% = ASC(DRIVE)


' apply ASC to a string variable
DIM aString AS STRING
aString = "H"
PRINT "The ASCII code for "; aString; " is "; ASC(aString)


' apply ASC to a string expression
DIM DriveLetter AS STRING
DIM L AS INTEGER
DriveLetter = "A"
L = ASC(DriveLetter + ":\")
```

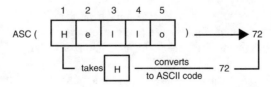

Figure 5.2. The ASC function works only on the first character of a string.

Let's look at a simple program that uses the ASC function. Listing 5.2, STRING3.BAS, uses the ASC functions to display the ASCII codes for the four strings that you enter.

Listing 5.2. STRING3.BAS, which illustrates the ASC function.

```
 1: REM Program that tests the ASC function
 2: REM
 3: ' declare the program variables
 4: DIM Char1 AS STRING
 5: DIM Char2 AS STRING
 6: DIM Char3 AS STRING
 7: DIM Char4 AS STRING
 8:
 9: CLS
10: INPUT "Enter first character (except a comma) "; Char1
11: INPUT "Enter second character (except a comma) "; Char2
12: INPUT "Enter third character (except a comma) "; Char3
13: INPUT "Enter fourth character (except a comma) "; Char4
14: PRINT
15: PRINT "The ASCII code for character "; Char1; " is ";
   ➥ASC(Char1)
16: PRINT "The ASCII code for character "; Char2; " is ";
   ➥ASC(Char2)
17: PRINT "The ASCII code for character "; Char3; " is ";
   ➥ASC(Char3)
18: PRINT "The ASCII code for character "; Char4; " is ";
   ➥ASC(Char4)
19: END
```

Here is a sample output for the program in Listing 5.2:

```
Enter first character (except a comma) ? A
Enter second character (except a comma) ? a
Enter third character (except a comma) ? 1
Enter fourth character (except a comma) ? !

The ASCII code for character A is  65
The ASCII code for character a is  97
```

```
The ASCII code for character 1 is  49
The ASCII code for character ! is  33
```

Analysis

The program in Listing 5.2 declares its variables on lines 4–7. The variables Char1, Char2, Char3, and Char4 have the string data type. Lines 10–13 use INPUT statements to prompt you to enter a single character (except the comma, which is used by the INPUT statement to separate multiple data input). You can enter a multicharacter string, but only the first character is significant. Lines 15–18 displays the characters you enter and their accompanying ASCII codes. The PRINT statements in these lines use the ASC function to display the ASCII codes.

Converting an ASCII Code into a Character

The ASC function offers a way to convert a character into an ASCII code. QBasic compliments the ASC function with the predefined CHR$ function to convert an ASCII code into a character.

Syntax

The CHR$ Function

The general syntax for CHR$ function is

```
CHR$(numericExpression)
```

The *numericExpression* parameter is either a numeric constant, named numeric constant, numeric variable, numeric function, or an expression that contains these different components. *numericExpression* must be in the range of 0–255. CHR$ returns the character that corresponds to the ASCII code represented by numericExpression. If *numericExpression* is a floating-point number, CHR$ uses the integer part only.

Examples:

```
' apply CHR$ to numeric constants
C$ = CHR$(65)
D$ = CHR$(65.1)
```

5

```
' apply CHR$ to a named numeric constant
CONST ASCII.CODE = 65
C$ = CHR$(ASCII.CODE)

' apply CHR$ to a numeric variable
DIM IntVar AS INTEGER
DIM C AS STRING
IntVar = 68
C = CHR$(IntVar)

' apply CHR$ to a numeric expression
DIM DriveLetter AS STRING
DIM NumberOfDrives AS INTEGER
INPUT "Enter number of drives "; NumberOfDrives
DriveLetter = CHR$(ASC("A") + NumberOfDrives)
PRINT "Last drive is "; DriveLetter
```

Note: Using the CHR$ function enables you to display the double-quotation mark character and incorporate it in string expressions. Because the ASCII code for the double-quotation mark character is 34, the function call CHR$(34) produces the double-quotation mark character.

Let me present a program that uses the CHR$ function. Listing 5.3, STRING4.BAS, uses the CHR$ function to determine the previous and next characters of an input character. The program prompts you to enter a single letter (except the comma). The program then displays the ASCII code for the character you enter. In addition, the program displays the characters that are before and after the input character. The displayed sequence of characters is based on the ASCII code table.

Listing 5.3. STRING4.BAS, which uses the CHR$ function to determine the previous and next characters of an input character.

```
1: REM Program that tests the CHR$ function
2: REM
3: ' declare the program variables
4: DIM aChar AS STRING
5: DIM NextChar AS STRING
6: DIM PrevChar AS STRING
7: DIM Ascii AS INTEGER
8:
9: CLS
10: INPUT "Enter a character (except a comma) "; aChar
11: Ascii = ASC(aChar)
12: NextChar = CHR$(Ascii + 1)
13: PrevChar = CHR$(Ascii - 1)
14: PRINT
15: PRINT "The ASCII code for "; aChar; " is "; Ascii
16: PRINT "Character "; PrevChar; " comes before "; aChar
17: PRINT "Character "; NextChar; " comes after "; aChar
18: END
```

Here is a sample output for the program in Listing 5.3:

```
Enter a character (except a comma) ? H

The ASCII code for H is  72
Character G comes before H
Character I comes after H
```

The program in Listing 5.3 declares its variables on lines 4–7. Line 10 uses an INPUT statement to prompt you for a single character and stores your input in the variable aChar. Line 11 uses the ASC function to save the ASCII code of the input character in the variable Ascii. Line 12 contains an assignment statement that obtains the next character and saves it in NextChar. The assignment statement uses the numeric expression Ascii + 1 to calculate the ASCII code for the next character. Then the statement applies the CHR$ function to assign the next character itself to the variable NextChar. Line 13 performs a similar task to calculate and to assign the previous character in the variable

PrevChar. Line 15 contains a PRINT statement that displays the ASCII code of the input character. Lines 16 and 17 contain PRINT statements that show the characters that come before and after the input character in the ASCII code table.

Converting Between Strings and Numbers

On Day 3 I presented the CINT, CLNG, CSNG, and CLNG functions, which convert between various numeric data types. QBasic offers predefined functions VAL and STR$ to convert between strings and the numeric data types.

The *VAL* Function

The predefined function VAL converts a string into a number.

The VAL Function

The general syntax for VAL function is:

```
VAL(stringExpression)
```

The *stringExpression* parameter is either a string literal, string constant, string variable, string function, or an expression that contains these different components. VAL attempts to convert the characters in *stringExpression* from left to right. The conversion stops when VAL comes across a character that is not part of the string image of a number. The function ignores leading and intermediate spaces. The VAL function returns the value of the characters it is able to convert. If the first character is not a digit, a plus sign, a minus sign, or a decimal point, the VAL function returns 0.

Figure 5.3 shows the VAL function converting a string with leading digits.

Examples:

```
' apply VAL to a string literal
L% = VAL("12.3")
M% = VAL("25.4 Tons")

' apply VAL to a string constant
CONST MEMORY = "2Kb"
RAM% = VAL(MEMORY)

' apply VAL to a string variable
DIM aString AS STRING
DIM X AS SINGLE
aString = "-1.23E+09"
X = VAL(aString)

' apply VAL to a string expression
DIM numberImage AS STRING
DIM L AS INTEGER
numberImage = "123"
L = VAL("21" + aString)
```

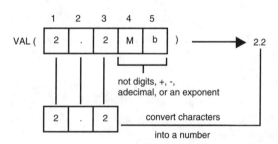

Figure 5.3. The VAL function converting a string with leading digits.

Let's look at a program that uses the VAL functions with the various kinds of string expressions. Listing 5.4, STRING5.BAS, displays the strings being converted and the conversion results.

5

DAY 5

Type Listing 5.4. STRING5.BAS, which uses the VAL function with various types of strings.

```
 1: REM Program that tests the VAL function
 2: REM
 3: ' declare the program variables
 4: DIM Astring AS STRING
 5: DIM X AS DOUBLE
 6: DIM Q AS STRING
 7:
 8: CLS
 9: ' assign the double-quote character to variable Q
10: Q = CHR$(34)
11: ' string contains the image of an integer
12: Astring = "245"
13: X = VAL(Astring)
14: PRINT "VAL("; Q + Astring + Q; ")= "; X
15: ' string contains the image of a single-precision float
16: Astring = "-12.345"
17: X = VAL(Astring)
18: PRINT "VAL("; Q + Astring + Q; ")= "; X
19: ' string contains the image of a double-precision float
20: Astring = "-1.2345D-03"
21: X = VAL(Astring)
22: PRINT "VAL("; Q + Astring + Q; ")= "; X
23: ' string contains the image of an integer with extra text
24: Astring = "16MB of RAM"
25: X = VAL(Astring)
26: PRINT "VAL("; Q + Astring + Q; ")= "; X
27: ' string contains the image of a single-precision
28: ' float with a intermediate spaces
29: Astring = "   16.45 12 15"
30: X = VAL(Astring)
31: PRINT "VAL("; Q + Astring + Q; ")= "; X
32: ' string contains the image of a single-precision
33: ' float that comes AFTER some text
34: Astring = "Temperature = 16.45 Celsius"
35: X = VAL(Astring)
36: PRINT "VAL("; Q + Astring + Q; ")= "; X
37: END
```

Here is a sample output for the program in Listing 5.4:

```
VAL("245")=  245
VAL("-12.345")= -12.345
VAL("-1.2345D-03")= -.0012345
VAL("16MB of RAM")=  16
VAL("   16.45 12 15")=  16.451215
VAL("Temperature = 16.45 Celsius")=  0
```

The program in Listing 5.4 declares its three variables on lines 4–6. The program uses the variable Astring to store the strings to be converted. The program uses the variable X to store the numbers converted by applying VAL to the Astring. The variable Q stores the double-quotation mark character, used by the program in the various PRINT statements.

On line 12 the program assigns the string image of an integer to Astring. Line 13 contains the assignment statement that applies the VAL function to Astring and stores the result in variable X. Line 14 contains a PRINT statement that displays the string image and the converted number. The output indicates that the VAL function converts the string "245" to the number 245. The conversion is correct and uses all of the characters in Astring. On line 16 the program assigns the string image of a single-precision number to Astring. Lines 17 and 18 perform the numeric conversion and display the data. The output indicates the VAL function converts the string "-12.345" into the number –12.345. The conversion is again correct and utilizes all of the characters in Astring. Lines 20–22 perform a similar set of tasks, this time using the string image of a double-precision number.

On line 24, the program assigns the string "16MB of RAM" to Astring. Notice that only the first two characters in the string make up the image of the number 16. Consequently, the call to VAL on line 25 yields the value 16, which is assigned to X. The output, produced by the PRINT statement on line 26, confirms that X stores the number 16. On line 29 the program assigns the string "   16.45 12 15" to Astring. This case shows a string with leading and intermediate spaces. VAL converts the string to the number 16.451215. The program output confirms the result of this conversion.

On line 34 the program assigns the string "Temperature = 16.45 Celsius" to Astring. In this example the VAL function fails to convert the number that appears somewhere in the middle of the string. Because the first string character is T, the call to VAL on line 35 gives up and returns 0. The PRINT statement on line 36 displays 0, confirming the failed string conversion.

5

The *STR$* Function

The counterpart of VAL is the built-in function STR$. This function converts a numeric expression into a string.

The STR$ Function

The general syntax for the STR$ function is

```
STR$(numericExpression)
```

The *numericExpression* parameter is either a numeric constant, named numeric constant, numeric variable, numeric function, or an expression that contains these different components. STR$ returns the string image of the number represented by *numericExpression*. If the converted number is positive, the STR$ function returns a string that begins with a space. If the converted number is negative, the STR$ function returns a string that begins with the minus sign.

Examples:

```
' apply STR$ to numeric constants
C$ = STR$(65)
D$ = STR$(65.1)

' apply STR$ to a named numeric constant
CONST ASCII.CODE = 65
C$ = STR$(ASCII.CODE)

' apply STR$ to a numeric variable
DIM IntVar AS INTEGER
DIM C AS STRING
IntVar = 68
C = STR$(IntVar)
```

Here is a program that illustrates the STR$ function. Listing 5.5, STRING6.BAS, uses the STR$ function to convert numbers into their string images. The program requires no input. Instead, it internally assigns values to variables of different numerical types, converts the stored numeric values into strings, and displays the strings.

Listing 5.5. **STRING6.BAS, which uses the STR$ function to convert numbers into their string images.**

```
 1: REM Program that tests the STR$ function
 2: REM
 3: ' declare the program variables
 4: DIM IntVar AS INTEGER
 5: DIM LngVar AS LONG
 6: DIM SngVar AS SINGLE
 7: DIM DblVar AS DOUBLE
 8: DIM Q AS STRING
 9:
10: CLS
11: ' assign the double-quote character to variable Q
12: Q = CHR$(34)
13: IntVar = 41
14: LngVar = 65535
15: SngVar = 2.34
16: DblVar = -.34#
17: PRINT "STR$("; IntVar; ") = "; Q + STR$(IntVar) + Q
18: PRINT "STR$("; LngVar; ") = "; Q + STR$(LngVar) + Q
19: PRINT "STR$("; SngVar; ") = "; Q + STR$(SngVar) + Q
20: PRINT "STR$("; DblVar; ") = "; Q + STR$(DblVar) + Q
21: END
```

Here is a sample output for the program in Listing 5.5:

```
STR$( 41 ) = " 41"
STR$( 65535 ) = " 65535"
STR$( 2.34 ) = " 2.34"
STR$(-.34 ) = "-.34"
```

The program in Listing 5.5 declares its variables on lines 4–8. The program uses the variables IntVar, LngVar, SngVar, and DblVar to store an integer, a long integer, a single-precision float, and a double-precision float, respectively. On lines 13–16 the program assigns values to the various numerical variables. On lines 17–20 the program uses a series of PRINT statements to display the numeric value stored in each numeric variable and the corresponding string image produced by function STR$.

5

Extracting Substrings

The manipulation of a string often includes the ability to extract part of the string. QBasic offers built-in functions that enable you to extract the leading (the leftmost) characters, the trailing (the rightmost) characters, and the internal characters in a string. The QBasic functions that perform these tasks are LEFT$, RIGHT$, and MID$, respectively. The next subsections discuss these functions.

The *LEFT$* Function

The LEFT$ function extracts the leading characters of a string.

The LEFT$ Function

The general syntax for LEFT$ function is

```
LEFT$(stringExpression, count)
```

The *stringExpression* parameter is either a string literal, string constant, string variable, string function, or an expression that contains these different components. The count parameter is the number of leading characters to extract. If the value of *count* is 0, the LEFT$ function returns an empty string. If the value of count is greater than the number of characters in *stringExpression*, LEFT$ returns the *stringExpression* without padding it with extra characters.

Figure 5.4 shows the LEFT$ function extracting the first three characters of the string literal "There".

Examples:

```
' apply LEFT$ to a string literal
L$ = LEFT$("12.3", 2) ' L$ stores "12"

' apply LEFT$ to a string constant
CONST MEMORY = "2Kb Memory"
RAM$ = LEFT$(MEMORY, 3) ' RAM$ contains "2Kb"

' apply LEFT$ to a string variable
DIM Str1 AS STRING
DIM Str2 AS STRING
```

```
Str1 = "Hello"
Str2 = LEFT$(Str1, 2) ' Str2 stores "He"

' apply LEFT$ to a string expression
DIM Str1 AS STRING
DIM Str2 AS STRING
Str1 = "Me"
Str2 = LEFT$(Str1 + "re mortal", 4) ' Str2 stores "Mere"
```

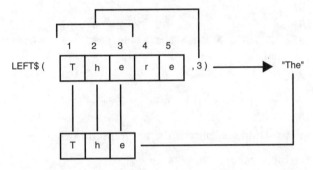

Figure 5.4. The LEFT$ function extracting the first three characters of the string literal "There".

Let's look at a simple program that uses the LEFT$ function. Listing 5.6, STRING7.BAS, uses the LEFT$ function to extract the leading characters of a string. The program prompts to enter a string and the number of leading characters to extract. Then the program displays a character rule, your input, and the extracted string.

Listing 5.6. STRING7.BAS, which uses the LEFT$ function to extract the leading characters of a string.

```
1: REM Program that tests the LEFT$ function
2: REM
3: ' declare the program variables
4: DIM InString AS STRING
5: DIM OutString AS STRING
6: DIM Count AS INTEGER
7: DIM Q AS STRING
```

continues

Listing 5.6. continued

```
 8:
 9: CLS
10: ' assign the double-quote character to variable Q
11: Q = CHR$(34)
12: INPUT "Enter a string : ", InString
13: INPUT "Enter number of leading characters to extract"; Count
14: OutString = LEFT$(InString, Count)
15: PRINT
16: PRINT "        1         2         3         4         5"
17: PRINT "12345678901234567890123456789012345678901234567890"
18: PRINT InString
19: PRINT "Extracted string is " Q + OutString + Q
20: END
```

Here is a sample output for the program in Listing 5.6:

```
Enter a string : QuickBasic
Enter number of leading characters to extract? 5

        1         2         3         4         5
12345678901234567890123456789012345678901234567890
QuickBasic
Extracted string is "Quick"
```

 The program in Listing 5.6 declares its variables on lines 4–7. Lines 12 and 13 contain INPUT statements that prompt you to enter a string and the number of leading characters to extract from the string. The statement on line 12 stores the string you type in the variable InString. The statement on line 13 saves the number you enter in the variable Count. Line 14 contains an assignment statement that uses the LEFT$ function to extract Count characters from InString. Lines 16–19 display the character ruler, the input string, and the extracted strings.

The *RIGHT$* Function

QBasic offers the built-in function RIGHT$ to extract the trailing character of a string.

The RIGHT$ Function

The general syntax for the RIGHT$ function is:

```
RIGHT$(stringExpression, count)
```

The *stringExpression* parameter is either a string literal, string constant, string variable, string function, or an expression that contains these different components. The *count* parameter is the number of trailing characters to extract. If the value of *count* is 0, RIGHT$ returns an empty string. If the value of *count* is greater than the number of characters in *stringExpression*, RIGHT$ returns *stringExpression* without padding it with extra characters.

Figure 5.5 shows the RIGHT$ function extracting the last three characters of the string literal "Flair".

Examples:

```
' apply RIGHT$ to a string literal
L$ = RIGHT$("12.3", 2) ' L$ stores "2.3"


' apply RIGHT$ to a string constant
CONST MEMORY = "2Kb Memory"
RAM$ = RIGHT$(MEMORY, 6) ' RAM$ contains "Memory"


' apply RIGHT$ to a string variable
DIM Str1 AS STRING
DIM Str2 AS STRING
Str1 = "Hello"
Str2 = RIGHT$(Str1, 2) ' Str2 stores "lo"


' apply RIGHT$ to a string expression
DIM Str1 AS STRING
DIM Str2 AS STRING
Str1 = "Me"
Str2 = RIGHT$(Str1 + "re mortal", 5) ' Str2 stores "mortal"
```

5

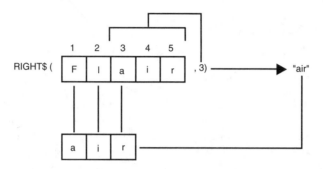

Figure 5.5. The RIGHT$ function extracting the last three characters of the string literal "Flair".

Let's look at a simple program that uses the RIGHT$ function. Listing 5.7, STRING8.BAS, uses RIGHT$ to extract the trailing characters of a string. The program prompts to enter a string and the number of trailing characters to extract. The program displays a character rule, your input, and the extracted string.

 Listing 5.7. STRING8.BAS

```
1: REM Program that tests the RIGHT$ function
2: REM
3: ' declare the program variables
4: DIM InString AS STRING
5: DIM OutString AS STRING
6: DIM Count AS INTEGER
7: DIM Q AS STRING
8:
9: CLS
10: ' assign the double-quote character to variable Q
11: Q = CHR$(34)
12: INPUT "Enter a string : ", InString
13: INPUT "Enter number of trailing characters to extract"; Count
14: OutString = RIGHT$(InString, Count)
15: PRINT
16: PRINT "          1         2         3         4         5"
17: PRINT "12345678901234567890123456789012345678901234567890"
```

```
18: PRINT InString
19: PRINT "The extracted string is "; Q + OutString + Q
20: END
```

Here is a sample output for the program in Listing 5.7:

```
Enter a string : QuickBasic
Enter number of trailing characters to extract? 5

          1         2         3         4         5
12345678901234567890123456789012345678901234567890
QuickBasic
The extracted string is "Basic"
```

The program in Listing 5.7 declares its variables on lines 4–7. Lines 12 and 13 contain INPUT statements that prompt you to enter a string and the number of trailing characters to extract from the input string. The statement on line 12 stores the string you type in the variable InString. The statement on line 13 saves the number you enter in the variable Count. Line 14 contains an assignment statement that uses the RIGHT$ function to extract Count characters from InString. Lines 16–19 display the character ruler, the input string, and the extracted strings.

The MID$ Function

In addition to the LEFT$ and RIGHT$ functions, QBasic offers the versatile function MID$ that enables you to extract characters from any part of a string.

5

The MID$ Function

The general syntax for MID$ function is:

```
MID$(stringExpression, start[, count])
```

The *stringExpression* parameter is either a string literal, string constant, string variable, string function, or an expression that contains these different components. The start parameter specifies the index of the first character to extract. The optional *count* parameter is the number of characters to extract. When omitted, MID$ extracts the characters to the end of the *stringExpression*. When assigning values to the parameters *start* and *count*, follow these rules:

1. The value of *start* must be in the range of 1–32767.

2. If the value of *start* is greater than the size of *stringExpression*, MID$ returns an empty string.

3. If the value of *count* is 0, MID$ returns an empty string.

4. If the value of *start* + *count* exceeds the size of the *stringExpression*, MID$ ignores the excess value of *start* + *count*.

Figure 5.6 shows the MID$ function extracting the three characters in the string literal "Drowns."

Examples:

```
' apply MID$ to a string literal
L$ = MID$("12.3", 2, 2) ' L$ stores "2."

' apply MID$ to a string constant
CONST MEMORY = "2Kb Memory"
RAM$ = MID$(MEMORY, 2, 2) ' RAM$ contains "Kb"

' apply MID$ to a string variable
DIM Str1 AS STRING
DIM Str2 AS STRING
Str1 = "Hello World"
Str2 = MID$(Str1, 4) ' Str2 stores "lo World"

' apply MID$ to a string expression
DIM Str1 AS STRING
DIM Str2 AS STRING
Str1 = "Me"
Str2 = MID$(Str1 + "re mortal", 2, 3) ' Str2 stores "ere"
```

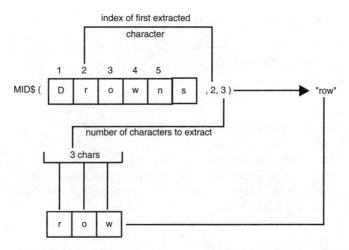

Figure 5.6. The MID$ function extracting the three characters in the string literal "Drowns".

Let's look at a simple program that uses the MID$ function. Listing 5.8, STRING9.BAS, uses MID$ to extract characters from a string. The program prompts to enter a string, the index of the first extracted character, and the number of characters to extract. The program then displays the following:

☐ A character rule

☐ Your input string

☐ The extracted string

☐ The first, second, third, and last characters in the string you entered

 Listing 5.8. STRING9.BAS

```
1: REM Program that tests the MID$ function
2: REM
3: ' declare the program variables
4: DIM InString AS STRING
5: DIM OutString AS STRING
6: DIM Start AS INTEGER
7: DIM Count AS INTEGER
```

continues

Listing 5.8. continued

```
 8: DIM StrLen AS INTEGER
 9: DIM Q AS STRING
10:
11: CLS
12: ' assign the double-quote character to variable Q
13: Q = CHR$(34)
14: INPUT "Enter a string : ", InString
15: INPUT "Enter index of first character to extract"; Start
16: INPUT "Enter number of characters to extract"; Count
17: StrLen = LEN(InString)
18: OutString = MID$(InString, Start, Count)
19: PRINT
20: PRINT "          1         2         3         4         5"
21: PRINT "12345678901234567890123456789012345678901234567890"
22: PRINT InString
23: PRINT "The extracted string is "; Q + OutString + Q
24: ' display the first three and the last characters
25: PRINT "First input character is "; MID$(InString, 1, 1)
26: PRINT "Second input character is "; MID$(InString, 2, 1)
27: PRINT "Third input character is "; MID$(InString, 3, 1)
28: PRINT "Last input character is "; MID$(InString, StrLen, 1)
29: END
```

Here is a sample output for the program in Listing 5.8:

```
Enter a string : 123456789
Enter index of first character to extract? 3
Enter number of characters to extract? 2


          1         2         3         4         5
12345678901234567890123456789012345678901234567890
123456789
The extracted string is "34"
First input character is 1
Second input character is 2
Third input character is 3
Last input character is 9
```

Analysis The program in Listing 5.8. declares its variable on lines 4–9. Lines 14–16 contain INPUT statements that prompt you to enter a string, the index of the first extracted character, and the number of characters to extract. The INPUT statement on line 14 stores the string input in the variable InString. The INPUT statement on line 15 saves the input for the starting index in the variable Start. The INPUT statement on line 16 stores the input for the number of extracted characters in the variable Count. On line 17 the program uses an assignment statement to store the size of the string you entered in the integer variable StrLen. On line 18 MID$ extracts the characters from InString and saves them in the variable OutString. Lines 20 and 21 use PRINT statements to display the character ruler. The PRINT statement on line 22 displays your input string. The PRINT statement on the next line displays the extracted string, stored in OutString. The PRINT statements in lines 25–28 display the first, second, third, and last characters of the input string using the MID$ function. Notice that in each statement, the value for *count* is 1, the size of a single-character string. In addition, notice the values for the *start* parameter are 1, 2, 3, and StrLen. These values represent the indices for the extracted characters. In the case of line 28, I do not need to supply MID$ with a value for *count*. Instead, I can use the function call MID$(InString, StrLen) to obtain the same result. Why? The value of StrLen sets the first extracted character at the last character in InString. When you omit the value for *count*, you extract the rest of the string, which is only 1 character long.

Overwriting Substrings with the *MID$* Statement

In addition to enabling you to extract any portion of a string with the MID$ function, QBasic offers the MID$ statement (that does not return a value) which enables you to overwrite parts or all of a string.

5

The MID$ Statement

The general syntax for `MID$` statement is

```
MID$(stringVariable, start[, count]) = stringExpression
```

The *stringVariable* parameter is a string variable. The *start* parameter specifies the index of the first character in *stringVariable* to overwrite. The optional *count* parameter is the number of characters to overwrite. When you omit the value of *count*, the `MID$` statements overwrite the rest of the string in *stringVariable*. The *stringExpression* parameter is either a string literal, string constant, string variable, string function, or an expression that contains these different components. The rules for assigning values to *stringVariable*, *start* and *count* are the following:

1. The value for *start* must be between 1 and the length of the string in *stringVariable*.

2. If the value for *start* is greater than the size of the value for *stringExpression*, `MID$` does not alter the *stringVariable*.

3. If the value of *count* is 0, `MID$` does not alter the *stringVariable*.

4. If the value of *start* + *count* is smaller than the size of *stringExpression*, `MID$` ignores the excess characters in *stringExpression*. In other words, `MID$` does not expand the *stringVariable* to accommodate a larger *stringExpression*.

5. The *stringVariable* in the `MID$` statement cannot be an empty string. This condition generates a runtime error.

Figure 5.7 shows the `MID$` statement overwriting a part of string variable with parts of a string.

Example:

```
L$ = "00000"
MID$(L$, 2, 2) = "123" ' L$ stores "01200"
```

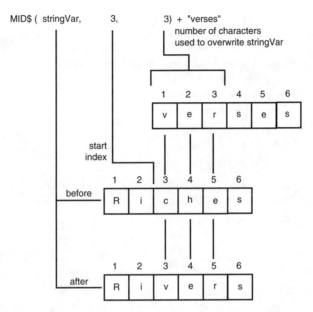

Figure 5.7. Overwriting part of a string variable with parts of a string using the MID$ statement.

Let's look at a program that overwrites parts of a string using the MID$ statement. Listing 5.9, STRING10.BAS, prompts you to enter the following data:

☐ The main string

☐ The overwriting string

☐ The index of first character to overwrite

☐ The number of characters to overwrite

The program displays a character ruler and various cases of overwriting the main string.

5

Listing 5.9. STRING10.BAS, which uses the MID$ statement to overwrite a portion of a string.

```
 1: REM Program that tests the MID$ statement
 2: REM
 3: ' declare the program variables
 4: DIM MainString AS STRING
 5: DIM CopyMainString AS STRING
 6: DIM SecString AS STRING
 7: DIM Start AS INTEGER
 8: DIM Count AS INTEGER
 9:
10: CLS
11: INPUT "Enter the main string : ", MainString
12: INPUT "Enter the overwriting string : ", SecString
13: INPUT "Enter index of first character to overwrite"; Start
14: INPUT "Enter number of characters to overwrite"; Count
15: PRINT
16: PRINT "          1         2         3         4         5"
17: PRINT "12345678901234567890123456789012345678901234567890"
18: PRINT "The original input string is:"
19: PRINT MainString
20: CopyMainString = MainString
21: MID$(MainString, Start, Count) = MID$(SecString, 1, Count - )
22: PRINT "The first modification gives:"
23: PRINT MainString
24: MainString = CopyMainString
25: MID$(MainString, Start, Count) = SecString
26: PRINT "The second modification gives:"
27: PRINT MainString
28: MainString = CopyMainString
29: MID$(MainString, Start) = SecString
30: PRINT "The third modification gives:"
31: PRINT MainString
32: END
```

Here is a sample output for the program in Listing 5.9:

```
Enter the main string : Namir Shammas
Enter the overwriting string : Keith Richards
```

```
Enter index of first character to overwrite? 1
Enter number of characters to overwrite? 5


             1         2         3         4         5
12345678901234567890123456789012345678901234567890
The original input string is:
Namir Shammas
The first modification gives:
Keitr Shammas
The second modification gives:
Keith Shammas
The third modification gives:
Keith Richard
```

The program in Listing 5.9 declares its variables on lines 4–8. The INPUT statement on line 11 prompts you to enter the main string and saves your input to the variable MainString. The INPUT statement on line 12 prompts you to enter the overwriting string and stores your input to the variable SecString. The INPUT statement on line 13 prompts you to enter the index of the first overwritten character and saves your input to the variable Start. The INPUT statement on line 14 prompts you to enter the number of characters to overwrite and saves your input to the variable Count.

Lines 16 and 17 contain PRINT statements that display the character ruler. The next two lines use PRINT statements to display the original input. On line 20 the program assigns the contents of MainString to CopyMainString. The program maintains the original input in CopyMainString while manipulating the characters in MainString.

The statement on line 21 overwrites the main string with the first Count-1 characters in SecString. The MID$ statement specifies Count characters to overwrite, but the size of the overwriting string is Count - 1. Consequently, the smaller value prevails and only Count - 1 characters in MainString are overwritten. The PRINT statements on lines 22 and 23 display the modified string MainString.

The statement on line 24 assigns the original input to MainString. On line 25 the characters in SecString overwrite Count characters in MainString. The number of overwritten characters is the smaller value of Count and the number of characters in SecString. The PRINT statements on lines 26 and 27 display the modified string MainString.

5

The statement on line 28 assigns the original input to MainString. On line 29, all the characters in SecString overwrite the characters in MainString, beginning with character number Start. The number of overwritten characters is equal to the number of characters in SecString. The PRINT statements on lines 30 and 31 display the modified string MainString.

Locating Substrings

QBasic offers the predefined function INSTR to search for a string in another string. This function performs a case-sensitive search and enables you to specify the first searched character in the searched (which I'll call scanned) string.

Syntax

The INSTR Function

The general syntax for the INSTR function is

```
INSTR([start,] stringExpress1, stringExpress2)
```

The optional *start* parameter specifies the index of the first scanned character in *stringExpress1*. The *stringExpress1* parameter is the scanned string and can be a string literal, string constant, string variable, string function, or an expression that contains these different components. The *stringExpress2* parameter is the search string and can be a string literal, string constant, string variable, string function, or an expression that contains these different components. INSTR returns the index of the first character where *stringExpress2* occurs in *stringExpress1*. If there is no match, the function returns 0.

Figure 5.8 shows the INSTR("Here", "re") function call, which returns the index of the first matching character of "re" in "Here".

Examples:

```
' apply INSTR to a string literal
L% = INSTR("This is a string literal", "his") ' L% is 2

' apply INSTR to a string constant
CONST VERSION = "Version 1.0"
L% = INSTR(VERSION, ".0") ' L% is 10
```

```
' apply INSTR to a string variable
DIM aString AS STRING
aString = "Hello Heidy"
PRINT "Match at "; INSTR(3, aString, "He")

' apply INSTR to a string expression
DIM aString AS STRING
DIM L AS INTEGER
aString = "Namir Shammas"
L = INSTR("My name is " + aString, RIGHT$(aString, 5))
```

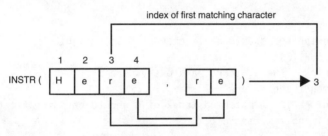

Figure 5.8. The INSTR("Here", "re") function, which returns the index of the first matching character of "re" in "Here."

Let's look at an example that searches for a string in another string. Listing 5.10, STRING11.BAS, searches for the string `"ere"` in the string `"Here, there, and everywhere"`. The program requires no keyboard input. Instead, it internally supplies data to the scanned and search strings. The program displays the three character indices in `"Here, there, and everywhere"` where `"ere"` appears. I made this program more controlled to ensure that I can display the results I want to show you. A typical use of the `INSTR` in QBasic programs also involves the `IF` statement to test the outcome of the string search. I don't discuss the `IF` statement until Day 6, "Decision Making," so I don't use it in this program.

5

Listing 5.10. STRING11.BAS, which searches for the string "ere" in the string "Here, there, and everywhere."

```
 1: REM Program that tests the INSTR function
 2: REM
 3: ' declare the program variables
 4: DIM AString AS STRING
 5: DIM SearchString AS STRING
 6: DIM Start AS INTEGER
 7: DIM I AS INTEGER
 8: DIM Q AS STRING
 9:
10: CLS
11: ' assign the double-quote character to variable Q
12: Q = CHR$(34)
13: AString = "Here, there, and everywhere"
14: SearchString = "ere"
15: PRINT "NOTE: A matching index of 0 should be interpreted"
16: PRINT "as a mismatch"
17: PRINT
18: PRINT "         1         2         3         4         5"
19: PRINT "12345678901234567890123456789012345678901234567890"
20: ' search from the beginning of string AString
21: I = INSTR(AString, SearchString)
22: PRINT AString; " <-- Main string"
23: PRINT Q; SearchString; Q; " <--- Search string"
24: PRINT
25: PRINT "Found match at index"; I;
26: PRINT "when search start at character 1"
27: ' search starts at character 3 of string AString
28: Start = 3
29: I = INSTR(Start, AString, SearchString)
30: PRINT "Found match at index"; I;
31: PRINT "when search start at character"; Start
32: ' search starts at character 10 of string AString
33: Start = 10
34: I = INSTR(Start, AString, SearchString)
35: PRINT "Found match at index"; I;
36: PRINT "when search start at character"; Start
37: ' search starts at character 26 of string AString
38: Start = 26
```

```
39: I = INSTR(Start, AString, SearchString)
40: PRINT "Found match at index"; I;
41: PRINT "when search start at character"; Start
42: END
```

Here is a sample output for the program in Listing 5.10:

```
NOTE: A matching index of 0 should be interpreted
as a mismatch


         1         2         3         4         5
12345678901234567890123456789012345678901234567890
Here, there, and everywhere <-- Main string
"ere" <--- Search string

Found match at index 2 when search start at character 1
Found match at index 9 when search start at character 3
Found match at index 25 when search start at character 10
Found match at index 0 when search start at character 26
```

The program in Listing 5.10 declares its variables on lines 4–8. On line 13 the program assigns the string literal `"Here, there, and everywhere"` to the variable `AString`. On line 14 the program assigns the string literal `"ere"` to the variable `SearchString`. Lines 15 and 16 contain `PRINT` statements that display a comment about interpreting the values of the matching indices. Lines 18 and 19 contain `PRINT` statements that display the character ruler.

The string search begins after line 20. The statement on line 21 invokes `INSTR`, passing `AString` and `SearchString`. Consequently, this call to `INSTR` begins searching for `SearchString` at the first character of `AString`. The statement assigns the result of the search to the variable `I`. Lines 22 and 23 display the contents of `AString` and `SearchString`. On Line 25 the program displays the value of `I`, which is 2. The `PRINT` statement on line 26 displays text that reports the result of the first search.

On line 28 the program assigns the value 3 (which is greater than 2, the current value of `I`) to `Start`. The statement on line 29 calls `INSTR` and passes the values in `Start`, `AString`, and `SearchString`. This function call causes the search to begin at the third character in `AString`. The function `INSTR` returns 9, the index of the second occurrence of `SearchString` in `AString`. The `PRINT` statements display the results of the second search.

5

The rest of the program lines repeats the steps in lines 28–31 two more times. On line 33 the program assigns 10 (one value higher than the result returned by the last call to INSTR) to Start. This time, INSTR returns 25. On line 38, the program assigns 26 (once again, one value higher than the result returned by the last call to INSTR) to Start. However, this time INSTR fails to find a match for SearchString and consequently returns 0.

Converting the Character Case of a String

QBasic offers the UCASE$ and LCASE$ functions to convert the characters of a string into uppercase and lowercase, respectively. These functions are valuable in eliminating the different character cases in a string. Used with the INSTR, either function enables you to perform a case-insensitive search.

The *UCASE$* Function

The UCASE$ function converts the characters of a string to uppercase. The function only affects lowercase characters. All other characters remain intact.

Syntax

The UCASE$ Function
The general syntax for UCASE$ function is

```
UCASE$(stringExpression)
```

The *stringExpression* parameter is either a string literal, string constant, string variable, string function, or an expression that contains these different components. Figure 5.12 shows the UCASE$ function changing the string "Hello" to "HELLO".

Examples:

```
' apply UCASE$ to a string literal
L$ = UCASE$("Hello") ' L$ stores "HELLO"

' apply UCASE$ to a string constant
CONST MEMORY = "2Kb Memory"
RAM$ = UCASE$(MEMORY, 3) ' RAM$ contains "2KB MEMORY"
```

```
' apply UCASE$ to a string variable
DIM Str1 AS STRING
DIM Str2 AS STRING
Str1 = "Hello"
Str2 = UCASE$(Str1, 2) ' Str2 stores "HELLO"

' apply UCASE$ to a string expression
DIM Str1 AS STRING
DIM Str2 AS STRING
Str1 = "Me"
Str2 = UCASE$(Str1 + "re mortal", 4) ' Stores "MERE MORTAL"
```

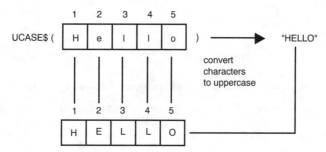

Figure 5.9. The UCASE$ function converting the string "Hello" to "HELLO".

Listing 5.11, STRING14.BAS, uses the UCASE$ function to convert the characters of a string to uppercase. The program prompts you for a string. The program displays the character ruler along with the original input and the uppercase character version of the input.

Listing 5.11. STRING14.BAS, which uses the UCASE$ function to convert the characters of a string to uppercase.

```
1: REM Program that tests the UCASE$ function
2: REM
3: ' declare the program variables
4: DIM InString AS STRING
5: DIM OutString AS STRING
```

continues

139

Listing 5.11. continued

```
 6: DIM Q AS STRING
 7:
 8: CLS
 9: ' assign the double-quote character to variable Q
10: Q = CHR$(34)
11: INPUT "Enter a string : ", InString
12: OutString = UCASE$(InString)
13: PRINT
14: PRINT "          1         2         3         4         5"
15: PRINT " 12345678901234567890123456789012345678901234567890"
16: PRINT Q; InString; Q
17: PRINT Q; OutString; Q
18: END
```

Here is a sample output for the program in Listing 5.11:

```
Enter a string : The filename is MATH.BAS

          1         2         3         4         5
 12345678901234567890123456789012345678901234567890
"The filename is MATH.BAS"
"THE FILENAME IS MATH.BAS"
```

The program in Listing 5.11 declares its variables on lines 4–6. The INPUT statement on line 11 prompts you to enter a string and stores your input in the variable InString. On line 12 the program uses an assignment statement that calls UCASE$. This function call converts the characters in InString to uppercase. The statement assigns the resulting string to the variable OutString. On lines 14 and 15 the program uses PRINT statements to display the character ruler. The PRINT statements on lines 16 and 17 display the original input and its uppercase version.

The *LCASE$* Function

The LCASE$ function converts the characters of a string into lowercase. The function only affects uppercase characters. All other characters remain intact.

Syntax

The LCASE$ Function

The general syntax for the LCASE$ function is

LCASE$(*stringExpression*)

The *stringExpression* parameter is either a string literal, string constant, string variable, string function, or an expression that contains these different components. Figure 5.13 illustrates the LCASE$ function converting the characters of the string "BASIC" to lowercase.

Examples:

```
' apply LCASE$ to a string literal
L$ = LCASE$("BASIC") ' L$ stores "basic"


' apply LCASE$ to a string constant
CONST MEMORY = "2Kb Memory"
RAM$ = LCASE$(MEMORY, 3) ' RAM$ contains "2kb memory"


' apply LCASE$ to a string variable
DIM Str1 AS STRING
DIM Str2 AS STRING
Str1 = "Hello"
Str2 = LCASE$(Str1, 2) ' Str2 stores "hello"


' apply LCASE$ to a string expression
DIM Str1 AS STRING
DIM Str2 AS STRING
Str1 = "Me"
Str2 = LCASE$(Str1 + "re mortal", 4) ' Stores "mere mortal"
```

5

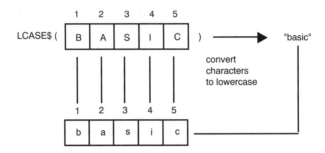

Figure 5.10. The LCASE$ function converting the characters of "BASIC" to lowercase.

Listing 5.12, STRING15.BAS, uses the LCASE$ function to convert the characters of a string to lowercase. The program prompts you for a string. The program displays the character ruler along with the original input and the lowercase character version of the input.

Listing 5.12. STRING15.BAS, that uses the LCASE$ function to convert the characters of a string to lowercase.

```
1: REM Program that tests the LCASE$ function
2: REM
3: ' declare the program variables
4: DIM InString AS STRING
5: DIM OutString AS STRING
6: DIM Q AS STRING
7:
8: CLS
9: ' assign the double-quote character to variable Q
10: Q = CHR$(34)
11: INPUT "Enter a string : ", InString
12: OutString = LCASE$(InString)
13: PRINT
14: PRINT "          1         2         3         4         5"
15: PRINT " 12345678901234567890123456789012345678901234567890"
16: PRINT Q; InString; Q
17: PRINT Q; OutString; Q
18: END
```

Here is a sample output for the program in Listing 5.12:

```
Enter a string : The filename is MATH.BAS


          1         2         3         4         5
12345678901234567890123456789012345678901234567890
"The filename is MATH.BAS"
"the filename is math.bas"
```

The program in Listing 5.12 declares its variables on lines 4–6. The INPUT statement on line 11 prompts you to enter a string and stores your input in the variable InString. On line 12 the program uses an assignment statement that calls LCASE$. This function call converts the characters in InString to lowercase. The statement assigns the resulting string to the variable OutString. On lines 14 and 15 the program uses PRINT statements to display the character ruler. The PRINT statements on lines 16 and 17 display the original input and its lowercase version.

Summary

This chapter presented some of the various QBasic functions that manipulate strings. You learned about the following:

☐ Obtaining the number of characters in a string by using the LEN function. This function takes string literals, string constants, string variables, string functions, and string expressions.

☐ Converting a character into its integer ASCII code using the ASC function. This function converts only the first character in a string value.

☐ Converting an ASCII code into a character using the CHR$ function. The function converts an integer (in the range of 0–255) that represents an ASCII code value to its corresponding single-character string.

☐ Converting strings to numbers and vice versa involves using the VAL and STR$ functions. VAL converts its string argument into a number. The leading characters of the string must contain a string image of a number. The conversion proceeds until either the entire string is converted or until a character that is not part of the string image of a number is reached. The VAL function ignores the space character during the conversion. The STR$ function converts a numeric expression into its string image.

☐ Extracting substrings using the LEFT$, RIGHT$, and MID$ functions. The LEFT$ function extracts a specified number of the leftmost (or leading) characters in a string. The RIGHT$ function extracts a specified number of the rightmost (or trailing) characters in a string. The MID$ function extracts a specified number of characters from anywhere in a string.

☐ Overwriting part of a string with the MID$ statement. The MID$ statement does not expand the string if the assigned string expression is larger than the overwritten string variable.

☐ Locating substrings using the INSTR function. The function returns the index of the first character in the scanned string where the search string occurs. The function has an optional parameter that specifies the number of characters to skip when conducting the search.

☐ Converting the character case of a string with the UCASE$ and LCASE$ functions. The UCASE$ function converts the lowercase characters of a string expression into uppercase. The LCASE$ function performs the reverse action.

Q&A

Q.   Other than telling me the length of a string, can LEN do anything else?

A.   Yes. Recently Microsoft extended the use of LEN in its various implementations of BASIC. LEN now can produce the byte size of a variable. Therefore, the following short program displays the byte size of integers:

```
DIM I AS INTEGER
PRINT "Byte size of integers = "; LEN(I)
```

Q.   What if I try to use an out-of-range index with a string?

A.   The valid character indices for the various QBasic string func-
     tions is 1 to the length of the string or 32767 (whichever is
     smaller). Values less than 1 produce runtime errors. By contrast,
     values that exceed the length of the string are adjusted automati-
     cally to equal the length of the string.

Q.   Can I display graphics characters (the ones that are part of the
     extended ASCII characters)?

A.   Yes. Use the CHR$ or STRING$ functions and supply these func-
     tions the ASCII code for the graphic characters you want to
     display.

Q.   If VAL returns a 0, how can I tell whether the string was equal to
     zero or the function is signaling its total failure in converting a
     string into a number?

A.   You can't. To avoid some confusion, you might want to use the
     following trick to convert the bad result into a large negative
     number (assuming that your applications do not regard such a
     number as valid):

```
1: CONST BAD.NUMBER = -32767
2: DIM Number AS INTEGER
3: DIM S AS STRING
4: S = "Hello"
5: Number = VAL(S)
6: Number = Number - BAD.NUMBER * (LEFT$(S, 1) <> "0")
```

In these lines VAL converts the contents of S to the numeric value
assigned to Number. The assignment statement on line 5 stores the value
of 0 in the variable Number. Line 6 uses the LEFT$ function to examine
the first character in S. If that character is not zero, there is a conversion error and the variable Number gets assigned –32767.

5

Workshop

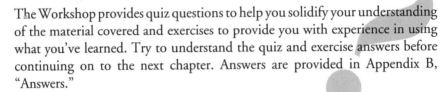

The Workshop provides quiz questions to help you solidify your understanding of the material covered and exercises to provide you with experience in using what you've learned. Try to understand the quiz and exercise answers before continuing on to the next chapter. Answers are provided in Appendix B, "Answers."

Quiz

1. In Listing 5.6, what is the extracted string if you enter the following values for the numeric prompt?

   a. 0
   b. 40

2. True or false: The LEFT$ function pads the string it manipulates if you request to extract more characters than there are in the string.

3. True or false: The following statements result in assigning the value −1 (true) to the variable areEqual:

```
DIM S AS STRING
DIM L AS INTEGER
DIM areEqual AS INTEGER
S = "Hello"
L = LEN(S)
areEqual = (MID$(S, 2) = MID$(S, 2, L - 1)
```

4. True or false: in question 3 areEqual is assigned −1 if the last statement is

```
areEqual = (MID$(S, 2) = MID$(S, 2, L)
```

5. True or false: The following statements assign −1 (true) to the variable areEqual:

```
DIM S AS STRING
DIM L AS INTEGER
DIM areEqual AS INTEGER
S = "Hello"
L = LEN(S)
areEqual = (RIGHT$(S, L) = LEFT$(S, L))
```

6. Simplify the following function calls by (possibly) using a different function that requires fewer values (Assume that the variable AString stores a string that is 40 character long):

    a. `MID$(AString, 2, LEN(AString))`
    b. `MID$(AString, 1, LEN(AString))`
    c. `MID$(AString, 1, LEN(AString) / 2)`
    d. `MID$(AString, LEN(AString), 1)`

Exercises

1. Write a set of QBasic statements that uses the MID$ function to emulate the LEFT$ function shown in the statements that follow:

```
DIM Str1 AS STRING
DIM Str2 AS STRING
DIM N AS INTEGER
N = 5
Str1 = "QuickBasic"
Str2 = LEFT$(Str1, N)
```

2. Write a set of QBasic statements that uses the MID$ function to emulate the RIGHT$ function shown in the following statements:

```
DIM Str1 AS STRING
DIM Str2 AS STRING
DIM N AS INTEGER
N = 5
Str1 = "QuickBasic"
Str2 = RIGHT$(Str1, N)
```

3. In the following statements, the function INSTR performs a case-sensitive search. Modify the INSTR statement to make the search case-insensitive (this alters the displayed result):

```
DIM MainString AS STRING
DIM SearchStr AS STRING
DIM I AS INTEGER
MainString = "I still use Dos"
SearchStr = "DOS"
I = INSTR(MainString, SearchStr)
PRINT "Matching "; SearchStr; " @ "; I
```

4. Write a short program that performs the following tasks:

☐ Prompts you to enter your first and last names, using two separate INPUT statements.

☐ Uses string manipulation functions to ensure that your first and last names appear in the proper letter cases (the first letter is capitalized and the rest of the characters are in lowercase).

☐ Displays a greeting message that includes your first and last names.

DAY
6

Decision Making

Computers excel in processing large amounts of data quickly and efficiently. Processing data includes making various decisions related to reading, manipulating, and updating information. Depriving programming languages the ability to make decisions renders computers practically useless. So far, the programs I have presented make no decisions. These programs execute every statement from start to finish in a sequential manner. The decision-making features of a language permit programs to execute certain statements when tested conditions are true or false. This chapter presents the various decision-making statements in QBasic. You learn about the following topics:

- Program pseudocode
- The single-alternative IF-THEN statement
- Single-stepping through a program
- The dual-alternative IF-THEN-ELSE statement
- The multiple-alternative IF-THEN-ELSEIF statement
- The multiple-alternative SELECT-CASE statement
- Nested IF statements
- Nested IF and SELECT-CASE statements

Program PseudoCode

If you want to develop non-trivial programs, you need to give such programs more forethought and planning. To do this, you have two general options: flowcharts and pseudocode.

Using flowcharts, as the name might suggest, involves drawing a schema for the various program components and how they connect with each other. Each component represents a task that is carried out by one or more program statements.

Using pseudocode involves an outline that specifies the sequence of tasks your program needs to perform, stated in plain English. Don't concern yourself about the actual function calls or the exact form of a statement when you write the pseudocode of a program. All you need to do is to plan the program.

Because pseudocode involves typing text (and not drawing shapes, as is the case with flowcharts) I use this method to show you how to plan your programs. Let's look at an example. On Day 5, "String Manipulation," I presented the program STRING10.BAS, which searches for the string "ere" in the string "Here, there, and everywhere". Here is the pseudocode for that program:

1. Clear the screen.

2. Assign the string literal "Here, there, and everywhere" to the scanned variable.

3. Assign the string literal to the search variable.

4. Display instructions about interpreting the value of the matching index.

5. Display the character ruler.

6. Locate the first occurrence of the search string in the scanned string. Store the search index in the index variable.

7. Display the scanned string.

8. Display the search string.

9. Display the value in the index variable.

10. Assign 3 to the offset variable.

11. Locate the next occurrence of the search string in the scanned string. Store the result in the index variable

12. Display the value in the index variable.

13. Repeat steps 10 to 13 by assigning 13 and 26 to the offset variable.

This pseudocode gives a general description for the program tasks. This description is independent of the language. You can refine the above pseudocode to describe language related tasks, such as declaring the program's variables. Listing 6.1 shows the program STRING11.BAS.

Listing 6.1. STRING11.BAS, which searches for the string "ere" in the string "Here, there, and everywhere."

```
 1: REM Program that tests the INSTR function
 2: REM
 3: ' declare the program variables
 4: DIM AString AS STRING
 5: DIM SearchString AS STRING
 6: DIM Start AS INTEGER
 7: DIM I AS INTEGER
 8: DIM Q AS STRING
 9:
10: CLS
11: ' assign the double-quote character to variable Q
12: Q = CHR$(34)
13: AString = "Here, there, and everywhere"
14: SearchString = "ere"
15: PRINT "NOTE: A matching index of 0 should be interpreted"
16: PRINT "as a mismatch"
17: PRINT
18: PRINT "           1         2         3         4         5"
19: PRINT "12345678901234567890123456789012345678901234567890"
20: ' search from the beginning of string AString
21: I = INSTR(AString, SearchString)
22: PRINT AString; " <-- Main string"
23: PRINT Q; SearchString; Q; " <--- Search string"
24: PRINT
25: PRINT "Found match at index"; I;
26: PRINT "when search start at character 1"
27: ' search starts at character 3 of string AString
28: Start = 3
29: I = INSTR(Start, AString, SearchString)
30: PRINT "Found match at index"; I;
31: PRINT "when search start at character"; Start
32: ' search starts at character 10 of string AString
33: Start = 10
34: I = INSTR(Start, AString, SearchString)
35: PRINT "Found match at index"; I;
36: PRINT "when search start at character"; Start
37: ' search starts at character 26 of string AString
38: Start = 26
```

```
39: I = INSTR(Start, AString, SearchString)
40: PRINT "Found match at index"; I;
41: PRINT "when search start at character"; Start
42: END
```

The *IF-THEN* Statement

The IF-THEN statement examines a condition and executes a set of statements if the condition is true.

The IF-THEN Statement

The general syntax for the single-alternative IF-THEN statement is

```
IF condition THEN
     sequence of statements
END IF
```

The general syntax for the short form of the IF-THEN statement is

```
IF condition THEN statement
```

The condition represents a Boolean expression that yields a true (−1) or false (0) value. When the tested condition is true, the program executes the statement(s) in the THEN clause. Otherwise, the program proceeds to the statement that comes after the IF-THEN statement.

Figure 6.1 shows the program flow in the single-alternative IF-THEN statement.

Example:

```
DIM I AS INTEGER
INPUT "Enter a positive integer "; I
' adjust non-positive values to 1
IF I <= 0 THEN I = 1

DIM First AS INTEGER
DIM Second AS INTEGER
DIM Temp AS INTEGER
INPUT "Enter a first integer "; First
```

```
INPUT "Enter a second integer "; Second
IF Second > First THEN
    ' swap the values in the variables
    Temp = First
    First = Second
    Second = Temp
END IF
PRINT First; " is greater than or equal to "; Second
```

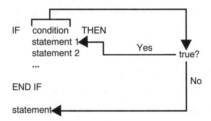

Figure 6.1. The single-alternative IF-THEN statement.

Listing 6.2, IF1.BAS, uses the IF-THEN statement to search for a string in another string. The program prompts you to enter the scanned string, the search string, and a Yes/No answer to indicate whether to conduct a case-sensitive search. The program displays the function ruler, the scanned string, the search string, and the search outcome. If the program finds a match in the scanned string, it displays the index of the first matching character. Otherwise, the program displays a message stating that there is no match for the search string.

Here is the pseudocode for the program:

1. Input the scanned string and store it in MainStr.

2. Input the search string and store it in FindStr.

3. Prompt for a Yes/No answer to ask whether the user wants to conduct a case-sensitive search. Store the input in Answer.

4. Store the contents of MainStr and FindStr in MainStrCopy and FindStrCopy.

5. Assign the first character of Answer back to variable Answer.

6. If Answer does not contain the letter Y, then perform the following steps:

6.1. Store the uppercase characters of MainStr in MainStr.

6.2. Store the uppercase characters of FindStr in FindStr.

7. Locate the occurrence of the search string in the scanned string. Assign the index value to the variable Index.

8. Display the character ruler.

9. Display the contents of MainStrCopy (which contains the original scanned string).

10. If Index stores a positive value, display the search string and the value of Index.

11. If Index is 0, display a message to inform you that no match was found for the search string.

Listing 6.2. IF1.BAS, which uses the IF-THEN statement to search for a string in another string.

```
 1: REM Program tests the IF-THEN statement
 2: REM
 3: ' declare the program variables
 4: DIM MainStr AS STRING
 5: DIM MainStrCopy AS STRING
 6: DIM FindStr AS STRING
 7: DIM FindStrCopy AS STRING
 8: DIM Answer AS STRING
 9: DIM Index AS INTEGER
10: DIM Q AS STRING
11: CLS
12: Q = CHR$(34)
13: INPUT "Enter the main string : ", MainStr
14: INPUT "Enter the search string : ", FindStr
15: INPUT "Is search case-sensitive? (Y/N) ", Answer
16: ' store copies of the main and search strings
17: MainStrCopy = MainStr
18: FindStrCopy = FindStr
19: ' extract the uppercase of the first character
20: ' in variable Answer
21: Answer = UCASE$(LEFT$(Answer, 1))
22: ' convert MainStr and FindStr to uppercase if the search
```

continues

Listing 6.2. continued

```
23: ' is NOT case-sensitive
24: IF Answer <> "Y" THEN
25:   MainStr = UCASE$(MainStr)
26:   FindStr = UCASE$(FindStr)
27: END IF
28: ' find the index of the first matching character in MainStr
29: Index = INSTR(MainStr, FindStr)
30: ' display character ruler
31: PRINT
32: PRINT "         1         2         3         4"
33: PRINT " 12345678980123456789801234567898012345678980"
34: PRINT Q; MainStrCopy; Q
35: ' display message if found match
36: IF Index > 0 THEN
37:   PRINT "Found a match for "; Q; FindStrCopy; Q;
38:   PRINT " @ index "; Index
39: END IF
40: ' display message if not match was found
41: IF Index = 0 THEN
42:   PRINT "Cannot find a match for search string ";
43:   PRINT Q; FindStrCopy; Q
44: END IF
45: END
```

Here is a sample output for the program in Listing 6.2:

```
Enter the main string : Hello World!
Enter the search string : llo
Is search case-sensitive? (Y/N) y

          1         2         3         4
 12345678980123456789801234567898012345678980
"Hello World!"
Found a match for "llo" @ index  3
```

The program in Listing 6.2 declares its variables on lines 4–10. The INPUT statement on line 13 prompts you to enter the scanned string and stores it in the variable MainStr. The INPUT statement on line 14 prompts you to

enter the search string and saves it in the variable FindStr. The INPUT statement on line 15 asks you whether you want to conduct a case-sensitive search. The statement stores your input in the variable Answer. The statements on lines 17 and 18 save copies of MainStr and FindStr in the variable MainStrCopy and FindStrCopy. The statement on line 21 assigns the uppercase version of the first character in Answer back to the same variable.

The IF-THEN statement (the first of three such statements) on line 24 examines the condition where the contents of Answer are not equal to the literal string "Y". If this condition is true, the program executes the THEN clause statements found on lines 25 and 26. These statements replace characters of MainStr and FindStr with their uppercase versions. On line 29 the program uses the INSTR function to search for FindStr in MainStr. The statement assigns the value returned by INSTR to the variable Index. The PRINT statements on lines 32 and 33 display the character ruler. The PRINT statement on line 34 displays the scanned string, enclosed in double quotation marks.

The IF-THEN statement on line 36 examines the condition of Index storing a positive number (that is, whether the search string was found in the scanned string). If this condition is true, the program executes the THEN clause statements on lines 37 and 38. These lines contain PRINT statements that display the search string and the index of the first matching character.

The IF-THEN statement on line 41 examines the condition of Index storing a zero (that is, whether the search string was not found in the scanned string). If this condition is true, the program executes the THEN clause statements on lines 42 and 43. These lines contain PRINT statements that inform you that the INSTR function did not find a match for the search string.

Single-Stepping Through a Program

QBasic enables you to execute your program one statement at a time. This slow-motion mode permits you to follow the execution of each statement. This feature is handy in tracing the execution of IF statements. The QBasic environment responds to the F8 function key by single-stepping in your program.

Let's look at a session that single-steps through the program in Listing 6.2. Load the program IF1.BAS and press the F8 function key to start single-stepping through the program. The program stops at line 4. Now every time you press the F8 key, the program executes the next statement. When the program reaches the INPUT statements, QBasic displays the output screen and prompts you for input. Type in the same data you see in the session of program IF1.BAS. When you press Return, QBasic switches back to the program listing. The program single-steps through every statement until it reaches line 24. Because Answer stores "Y", the condition Answer <> "Y" is false. Consequently, the next time you press F8, the program jumps to line 29, bypassing the statements in the THEN clause. The program executes the statements on lines 29–34.

On line 36 the program evaluates the condition Index > 0. Because Index stores 3, the condition is true. Consequently, the program executes the statements on lines 37 and 38 when you repeatedly press the F8 key. On line 41 the program evaluates the condition Index = 0. Because this condition is false, the program execution jumps to the END statement.

The *IF-THEN-ELSE* Statement

The IF-THEN-ELSE statement examines a condition and offers two alternate courses of action. Each course of action is implemented using one or more statements.

The IF-THEN-ELSE Statement

The general syntax for the dual-alternative IF-THEN-ELSE statement is

```
IF condition THEN
    first sequence of statements
ELSE
    second sequence of statements
END IF
```

The general syntax for the short form of the IF-THEN-ELSE statement is

```
IF condition THEN statement1 ELSE statement2
```

The *condition* represents a Boolean expression that yields a true (−1) or false (0) value. When the tested *condition* is true, the program executes the set of statements in the THEN clause. Otherwise, the program executes the sequence of statements in the ELSE clause.

Figure 6.2 shows the program flow in the dual-alternative IF-THEN-ELSE statement.

Examples:

```
IF Answer <> "" THEN
     Answer = UCASE$(LEFT$(Answer, 1))
ELSE
     Answer = "N"
END IF


IF CaseSenseSearch = "Y" THEN
     Index = INSTR(MainString, FindString)
ELSE
     Index = INSTR(UCASE$(MainString), UCASE$(FindString))
END IF
```

6

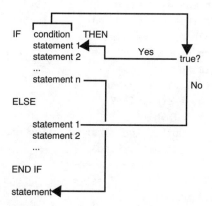

Figure 6.2. The dual-alternative IF-THEN-ELSE statement.

String Search Example

In Listing 6.2 the program uses two separate IF-THEN statements to examine the value stored in the variable Index. The first IF-THEN statement uses the Boolean expression Index > 0, whereas the second statement uses the Boolean expression Index = 0. Because these conditions are essentially the reverse of each other, I can replace the two IF-THEN statements with a single IF-THEN-ELSE statement. Listing 6.3 shows the resulting program, IF2.BAS.

Listing 6.3. IF2.BAS, a version of IF1.BAS that uses the IF-THEN-ELSE statement.

```
1: REM Program tests the IF-THEN-ELSE statement
2: REM
3: ' declare the program variables
4: DIM MainStr AS STRING
5: DIM FindStr AS STRING
6: DIM Answer AS STRING
7: DIM Index AS INTEGER
8: DIM Q AS STRING
9: CLS
10: Q = CHR$(34)
11: INPUT "Enter the main string : ", MainStr
12: INPUT "Enter the search string : ", FindStr
13: INPUT "Is search case-sensitive? (Y/N) ", Answer
14: ' extract the uppercase of the first character
15: ' in variable Answer
16: Answer = UCASE$(LEFT$(Answer, 1))
17: ' is search case-sensitive?
18: IF Answer = "Y" THEN
19:    ' find the index of the first matching character in MainStr
20:    Index = INSTR(MainStr, FindStr)
21: ELSE
22:    ' find the index of the first matching character
23:    ' in UCASE$(MainStr)
24:    Index = INSTR(UCASE$(MainStr), UCASE$(FindStr))
25: END IF
26: ' display character ruler
27: PRINT
28: PRINT "             1         2         3         4"
29: PRINT " 12345678980123456789801234567898012345678980"
```

```
30: PRINT Q; MainStr; Q
31: ' was match found?
32: IF Index > 0 THEN
33:   PRINT "Found a match for "; Q; FindStr; Q;
34:   PRINT " @ index "; Index
35: ELSE
36:   PRINT "Cannot find a match for search string "; Q; FindStr; Q
37: END IF
38: END
```

6

Here is a sample output for the program in Listing 6.3:

```
Enter the main string : Hello World!
Enter the search string : llo
Is search case-sensitive? (Y/N) y


            1         2         3         4
   12345678980123456789801234567898012345678980
   "Hello World!"
   Found a match for "llo" @ index  3
```

Because IF2.BAS is a modified version of IF1.BAS, let me focus on the different lines of IF2.BAS. On line 32 the IF-THEN-ELSE statement examines the condition Index > 0. If this condition is true, the program executes the THEN clause statements on lines 33 and 34. Otherwise, the program executes the ELSE clause statement on line 36.

Quadratic Equation Example

Let me present another example that uses the IF-THEN-ELSE statement. IF3.BAS, shown in Listing 6.4, solves for the roots of the quadratic equation:

$$A X^2 + B X + C = 0$$

The roots of the equation are the values of X that make the equation equal 0 for given values of A, B, and C. The program in Listing 6.4 prompts you to enter the values for these coefficients and displays the roots of the quadratic equation. The roots of the equation are either real or imaginary, depending on the value of the expression $B^2 - 4AC$, which is called the **discriminant**. If the discriminant is negative, the roots are imaginary. Otherwise, the roots are real.

> **Listing 6.4. IF3.BAS, which solves for the roots of a quadratic equation using the IF-THEN-ELSE statement.**

> Type

```
 1: REM Program tests the IF-THEN-ELSE statement
 2: REM
 3: ' declare the program variables
 4: DIM A AS DOUBLE
 5: DIM B AS DOUBLE
 6: DIM C AS DOUBLE
 7: DIM Discrim AS DOUBLE
 8: DIM D AS DOUBLE
 9: DIM TwoA AS DOUBLE
10: DIM Root1 AS DOUBLE
11: DIM Root2 AS DOUBLE
12:
13: CLS
14: PRINT "For the quadratic equation:"
15: PRINT
16: PRINT "      A X^2 + BX + C = 0"
17: PRINT
18: INPUT "Enter non-zero value for A "; A
19: ' handle the case when A is zero
20: IF A = 0 THEN
21:    PRINT
22:    PRINT "Error: Value for A must not be zero!"
23:    PRINT
24:    END
25: END IF
26: INPUT "Enter value for B "; B
27: INPUT "Enter value for C "; C
28: PRINT
29: Discrim = B * B - 4 * A * C
30: TwoA = A + A
31: IF Discrim >= 0 THEN
32:    Root1 = (-B + SQR(Discrim)) / TwoA
33:    Root2 = (-B - SQR(Discrim)) / TwoA
34:    PRINT "Root #1 = "; Root1
35:    PRINT "Root #2 = "; Root2
36: ELSE
37:    Discrim = -Discrim
38:    PRINT "Root #1 = "; (-B / TwoA);
```

```
39:    PRINT "+i("; SQR(Discrim) / TwoA; ")"
40:    PRINT "Root #2 = "; (-B / TwoA);
41:    PRINT "-i("; SQR(Discrim) / TwoA; ")"
42: END IF
43: END
```

Here is a sample output for the program in Listing 6.4:

```
For the quadratic equation:
A X^2 + BX + C = 0

Enter non-zero value for A ? 2
Enter value for B ? -6
Enter value for C ? 3

Root #1 =  2.366025403784439
Root #2 =  .6339745962155614
```

Here is a second sample output for the program in Listing 6.4. This one shows complex roots:

```
For the quadratic equation:
A X^2 + BX + C = 0

Enter non-zero value for A ? 1
Enter value for B ? 1
Enter value for C ? 1

Root #1 = -.5 +i( .8660254037844386 )
Root #2 = -.5 -i( .8660254037844386 )
```

The program in Listing 6.4 declares its variables on lines 4–11. All variables have the DOUBLE data type. Lines 14–16 contain PRINT statements that define a quadratic equation and specify the names of the coefficients A, B, and C. The INPUT statement on line 18 prompts you to enter the value for coefficient A and stores this value in the variable A. The program uses an IF-THEN statement on line 20 to detect assigning 0 to A. If this condition is true, the program executes the THEN clause statements on lines 21–24. These statements display a warning message and end the program. This drastic action prevents a division-by-zero error.

The INPUT statements on lines 26 and 27 prompt you to enter the values for coefficients B and C and store these values in the variables B and C. On line 29 the program calculates the discriminant and stores it in the variable Discrim. In the next line, the program assigns the value of 2A (evaluated using the addition expression A + A) to the variable TwoA.

The program uses an IF-THEN-ELSE statement on line 31 to test whether the value in Discrim is non-negative. If this condition is true, the program executes the THEN clause statements on lines 32–35. Otherwise, the program executes the ELSE clause statements on lines 37–41.

The statements in the THEN clause calculate the two real roots and store them in the variables Root1 and Root2. SQR is the QBasic square root function. The PRINT statements on lines 34 and 35 display the values of the roots.

The statements in the ELSE clause calculate and display the real and imaginary components of the two complex roots.

The *IF-THEN-ELSEIF* Statement

QBasic extends the number of alternatives by offering the versatile IF-THEN-ELSEIF statement. This kind of IF statement enables you to set multiple alternatives, needed when your program has to handle more than two related conditions.

The IF-THEN-ELSEIF Statement

The general syntax for the multiple-alternative IF-THEN-ELSEIF statement is

```
IF condition1 THEN
    statement sequence #1
ELSEIF condition2 THEN
    statement sequence #2
ELSEIF condition3 THEN
    statement sequence #3
```

```
....
ELSE
     statement sequence #n
END IF
```

The IF-THEN-ELSEIF statement contains a set of conditions. The first condition tested is *condition1*. If this condition is true, the program executes *statement sequence #1* and then jumps to after the END IF clause. By contrast, if *condition1* is false, the program evaluates *condition2*. If this condition is true, the program executes *statement sequence #2* and then jumps to after the END IF clause. If *condition2* is also false, the program evaluates the next condition, and so on. If all the conditions in the IF-THEN-ELSEIF statement fail, the program executes the statements in the catch-all ELSE clause (if one is included).

Figure 6.3 shows the program flow in the multiple-alternative IF-THEN-ELSEIF statement.

Example:

```
DIM DayNumber AS INTEGER
INPUT "Enter a week day number "; DayNumber
IF DayNumber = 1 THEN
     PRINT "Sunday"
ELSEIF DayNumber = 2 THEN
     PRINT "Monday"
ELSEIF DayNumber = 3 THEN
     PRINT "Tuesday"
ELSEIF DayNumber = 4 THEN
     PRINT "Wednesday"
ELSEIF DayNumber = 5 THEN
     PRINT "Thursday"
ELSEIF DayNumber = 6 THEN
     PRINT "Friday"
ELSEIF DayNumber = 7 THEN
     PRINT "Saturday"
ELSE
     PRINT "Invalid weekday number"
END IF
```

6

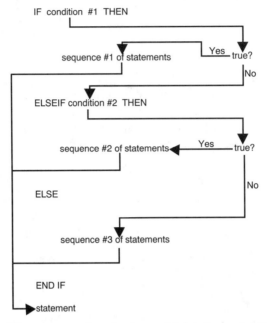

IF condition #1 THEN

sequence #1 of statements

Yes ___ true?

No

ELSEIF condition #2 THEN

sequence #2 of statements

Yes ___ true?

No

ELSE

sequence #3 of statements

END IF

statement

Figure 6.3. The program flow in the multiple-alternative IF-THEN-ELSEIF statement.

DO make the IF-THEN-ELSEIF statement operate more efficiently by placing the conditions in a descending order of their likelihood of being true. Such an order should reduce the average number of tested conditions.

DON'T forget to use the catch-all ELSE clause in an IF-THEN-ELSEIF statement. The ELSE clause ensures that the IF statement deals with all conditions.

Take a look at an example. Listing 6.5, IF4.BAS, classifies an input character using an IF-THEN-ELSEIF statement. The program prompts you to enter a character and then displays the type of character you entered. The program even can detect when you only press the Return key and provide no input.

Listing 6.5. IF4.BAS, which classifies an input character using the IF-THEN-ELSEIF statement.

```
 1: REM Program tests the multiple-alternative
 2: REM IF-THEN-ELSE statement
 3: REM
 4: ' declare set of punctuation characters
 5: CONST PUNCT.CHARS = "!@#$%^&*()_-+={[}]:;'`~?/>.<,"
 6: ' declare the program variables
 7: DIM Char AS STRING
 8: DIM Q AS STRING
 9: CLS
10:
11: Q = CHR$(34)
12: INPUT "Enter a character : ", Char
13: PRINT
14: ' extract the first character from Char
15: Char = LEFT$(Char, 1)
16: IF Char = "" THEN
17:    PRINT "You did not enter a character!"
18: ' is the character an uppercase letter?
19: ELSEIF Char >= "A" AND Char <= "Z" THEN
20:    PRINT Char; " is an uppercase character"
21: ' is the character a lowercase letter?
22: ELSEIF Char >= "a" AND Char <= "z" THEN
23:    PRINT Char; " is a lowercase character"
24: ' is the character digit?
25: ELSEIF Char >= "0" AND Char <= "9" THEN
26:    PRINT Char; " is digit"
27: ' is the character a space?
28: ELSEIF Char = " " THEN
29:    PRINT "You entered the space character"
30: ' is the character a punctuation character?
31: ELSEIF INSTR(PUNCT.CHARS + Q, Char) > 0 THEN
32:    PRINT Char; " is a punctuation character"
33: ' is the character a control character?
34: ELSEIF ASC(Char) <= 31 THEN
35:    PRINT Char; " is a control character"
36: ' is the character an extended ASCII character?
37: ELSEIF ASC(Char) > 127 THEN
38:    PRINT Char; " is an extended ASCII character"
```

continues

Listing 6.5. continued

```
39: ' this is the catch-all clause
40: ELSE
41:   PRINT "Sorry! I cannot identify the character "; Char
42: END IF
43: END
```

Here is a sample output for the program in Listing 6.5:

```
Enter a character : B

B is an uppercase character
```

Run the program again and enter lowercase characters, digits, and punctuation characters. Each time the output echoes the type of character you enter.

The program in Listing 6.5 declares the constant PUNCT.CHARS on line 5. This constant contains the punctuation characters. The program also declares its two variables, Char and Q, on lines 7 and 8. The INPUT statement on line 12 prompts you to enter a character and stores it in the variable Char. Line 15 contains an assignment statement that extracts the first character in Char and assigns it back to the same variable.

Line 16 contains the beginning of the IF-THEN-ELSEIF statement. Table 6.1 lists the conditions tested in the different lines. Line 40 contains the catch-all ELSE clause. Notice the condition tests vary in form. On line 31 the condition test involves the INSTR function. On lines 34 and 37 the condition tests use the ASC function.

Table 6.1. The conditions tested at the various lines of Listing 6.5.

Line Number	Condition/Purpose
16	Char = "" Char is an empty string (no input)
19	Char >= "A" AND Char <= "Z" input is an uppercase character
22	Char >= "a" AND Char <= "z" input is a lowercase character

Line Number	Condition/Purpose
25	`Char >= "0" AND Char <= "9"` input is a digit
28	`Char = " "` input is a space
31	`INSTR(PUNCT.CHARS + Q, Char) > 0` input is a punctuation character
34	`ASC(Char) <= 31` input is a control character (generated by pressing a letter key while holding down the Ctrl key)
37	`ASC(Char) > 127` input is an extended ASCII character (generated by pressing the Alt key and typing in the three-digit ASCII code)

6

The *SELECT-CASE* Statement

QBasic offers the multiple-alternative SELECT-CASE statement as a short form for the IF-THEN-ELSEIF statement.

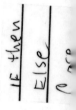

Syntax

The SELECT-CASE Statement

The general syntax for the multiple-alternative SELECT-CASE statement is

```
SELECT CASE testExpression
    CASE matchExpression1
        statement sequence #1
    CASE matchExpression2
        statement sequence #2
    CASE matchExpression3
        statement sequence #3
    ....
    CASE ELSE
    statement sequence #n
END SELECT
```

The *testExpression* is a string, numeric variable, function call, or expression. The SELECT-CASE statement evaluates the *testExpression* and then searches for a matching expression in the various CASE clauses. The basic types of matching expressions are

1. A list of values with the following general format:

   expression1, expression2, ...

2. A range of values with the following general format:

   lowerLimitExpression TO *upperLimitExpression*

The range of values is defined by the expressions *lowerLimitExpression* and *upperLimitExpression*. For example, the statement CASE 3 To 7 will trap all values between these two numbers.

3. Partial relational expression with the following general format:

   IS *relationalOperator expression*

The *relationalOperator* is =, <>, <, <=, >, and >=. For example, the statement IS > 0 will trap all positive numbers.

A CASE clause can include a combination of these basic matching expressions.

Figure 6.4 shows the program flow in the multiple-alternative SELECT-CASE statement.

Example:

```
DIM DayNumber AS INTEGER
INPUT "Enter a week day number "; DayNumber
SELECT CASE DayNumber
    CASE 1, 7
        PRINT "The WeekEnd!"
    CASE 6
        PRINT "It's Friday!"
    CASE IS > 1, IS < 6
        PRINT "Just an ordinary weekday"
    CASE ELSE
        PRINT "Invalid weekday number"
END SELECT
```

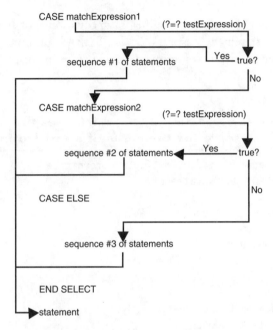

Figure 6.4. The program flow in the multiple-alternative SELECT-CASE statement.

DO make the SELECT-CASE statement operate more efficiently by placing the matching expressions in the descending order of their likelihood to match the tested expression. Such an order should reduce the average number of tested conditions.

DON'T forget to use the catch-all CASE ELSE clause in an SELECT-CASE statement. The CASE ELSE clause ensures that the SELECT-CASE statement deals with all conditions.

Quadratic Equation Example

Let me present a version of the quadratic equation root solver that uses the SELECT-CASE statement. Listing 6.6, CASE1.BAS, prompts you to enter the values for the coefficients of the quadratic equation and displays the roots of the equation.

Listing 6.6. CASE1.BAS, which uses the SELECT-CASE to solve for the roots of a quadratic equation.

```
 1: REM Program tests the multiple-alternative
 2: REM SELECT-CASE statement
 3: REM
 4: ' declare the program variables
 5: DIM A AS DOUBLE
 6: DIM B AS DOUBLE
 7: DIM C AS DOUBLE
 8: DIM Discrim AS DOUBLE
 9: DIM D AS DOUBLE
10: DIM TwoA AS DOUBLE
11: DIM Root1 AS DOUBLE
12: DIM Root2 AS DOUBLE
13:
14: CLS
15: PRINT "For the quadratic equation:"
16: PRINT
17: PRINT "      A X^2 + BX + C = 0"
18: PRINT
19: INPUT "Enter non-zero value for A "; A
20: ' handle the case when A is zero
21: IF A = 0 THEN
22:    PRINT
23:    PRINT "Error: Value for A must not be zero!"
24:    PRINT
25:    END
26: END IF
27: INPUT "Enter value for B "; B
28: INPUT "Enter value for C "; C
29: PRINT
30: Discrim = B * B - 4 * A * C
31: TwoA = A + A
```

```
32: SELECT CASE Discrim
33:  CASE IS > 0
34:   Root1 = (-B + SQR(Discrim)) / TwoA
35:   Root2 = (-B - SQR(Discrim)) / TwoA
36:   PRINT "Root #1 = "; Root1
37:   PRINT "Root #2 = "; Root2
38:
39:  CASE IS < 0
40:   Discrim = -Discrim
41:   PRINT "Root #1 = "; (-B / TwoA); "+i(";
42:   PRINT SQR(Discrim) / TwoA; ")"
43:   PRINT "Root #2 = "; (-B / TwoA); "-i(";
44:   PRINT SQR(Discrim) / TwoA; ")"
45:
46:  CASE ELSE
47:   Root1 = -B / TwoA
48:   Root2 = Root1
49:   PRINT "Root #1 = "; Root1
50:   PRINT "Root #2 = "; Root2
51: END SELECT
52: END
```

Here is a sample output for the program in Listing 6.6:

```
For the quadratic equation:
A X^2 + BX + C = 0

Enter non-zero value for A ? 1
Enter value for B ? -4
Enter value for C ? 4

Root #1 =  2
Root #2 =  2
```

The program in Listing 6.6 declares its variables on lines 5–12. All the variables have the DOUBLE data type. The statements on lines 15–17 contain PRINT statements that define a quadratic equation and specify the names of the coefficients A, B, and C. The INPUT statement on line 19 prompts you to enter the value for coefficient A and stores the value in the variable A. The program uses an IF-THEN statement on line 21 to detect whether A is equal to zero. If this condition is true, the program executes the THEN clause statements on lines 22–25. These statements display a warning message and end the program to avoid division by 0.

The INPUT statements on lines 27 and 28 prompt you to enter the values for coefficients B and C and store these values in the variables B and C. On line 30 the program calculates the discriminant and stores it in the variable Discrim. On the next line the program assigns the value of A+A to the variable TwoA.

The program uses the SELECT-CASE statement on line 32 to determine the three possible solutions. The SELECT-CASE statement uses the variable Discrim as the test expression. The matching expressions are:

1. The IS > 0 matching expression tests whether Discrim stores a positive value. In this case the roots are real and distinct. The sequence of statements on lines 34–37 calculates and displays the roots.

2. The IS < 0 matching expression tests whether Discrim stores a negative value. In this case the roots are complex. The sequence of statements on lines 40–44 calculates and displays the roots.

3. The ELSE clause handles the remaining case—Discrim stores zero. In this case the roots are real and have the same value. The sequence of statements on lines 47–50 calculates and displays the roots.

Character Classification Example

Let's look at the character-classification program. The IF5.BAS program in Listing 6.4 uses the IF-THEN-ELSEIF statement to classify a character that you enter. Listing 6.7, CASE2.BAS, uses the SELECT-CASE statement instead. CASE2.BAS prompts you for a character and displays its category.

Listing 6.7. CASE2.BAS, which classifies an input character using the SELECT-CASE statement.

```
1: REM Program tests the multiple-alternative
2: REM SELECT-CASE statement
3: REM
4: ' declare the program variables
5: DIM Char AS STRING
6: DIM Q AS STRING
```

```
 7: CLS
 8:
 9: Q = CHR$(34)
10: INPUT "Enter a character : ", Char
11: PRINT
12: ' extract the first character from Char
13: Char = LEFT$(Char, 1)
14:
15: SELECT CASE Char
16:   CASE IS = ""
17:     PRINT "You did not enter a character!"
18:
19:   ' is the character an uppercase letter?
20:   CASE "A" TO "Z"
21:     PRINT Char; " is an uppercase character"
22:
23:   ' is the character a lowercase letter?
24:   CASE "a" TO "z"
25:     PRINT Char; " is a lowercase character"
26:
27:   ' is the character digit?
28:   CASE "0" TO "9"
29:     PRINT Char; " is a digit"
30:
31:   ' is the character a space?
32:   CASE IS = " "
33:     PRINT "You entered the space character"
34:
35:   ' is the character a punctuation character?
36:   CASE "!" TO "/", ":" TO "@", "[" TO "`", "{" TO "~"
37:     PRINT Char; " is a punctuation character"
38:
39:   ' is the character a control character?
40:   CASE IS <= CHR$(31)
41:     PRINT Char; " is a control character"
42:
43:   ' is the character an extended ASCII character?
44:   CASE IS > CHR$(127)
45:     PRINT Char; " is an extended ASCII character"
46:
47:   ' this is the catch-all clause
```

continues

6

Listing 6.7. continued

```
48:    CASE ELSE
49:       PRINT "Sorry! I cannot identify the character "; Char
50: END SELECT
51: END
```

Here is a sample output for the program in Listing 6.7:

```
Enter a character : 1

1 is a digit
```

 The main difference between IF4.BAS and CASE2.BAS is that the latter uses the SELECT-CASE statement instead of the IF-THEN-ELSEIF statement. Table 6.3 lists the matching expressions at the various lines of Listing 6.7. The range and simple relational matching expressions are the most common. The matching expression on line 36 is the most advanced. It contains a series of value ranges to cover the punctuation characters. Notice that all the ranges in the SELECT-CASE are based on the character order in the ASCII table.

Table 6.3. The matching expression at the various lines of Listing 6.7.

Line Number	Matching Expression/Purpose
16	IS = "" Char is an empty string (no input)
20	"A" TO "Z" input is an uppercase character
24	"a" TO "z" input is a lowercase character
28	"0" TO "9" input is a digit
32	IS = " " input is a space
36	"!" TO "/", ":" TO "@", "[" TO "`", "{" TO "~" input is a punctuation character
40	IS <= CHR$(31) input is a control character (generated by pressing a letter key while holding down the Ctrl key)

176

Line Number	Matching Expression/Purpose
44	IS > CHR$(127) input is an extended ASCII character (generated by pressing the Alt key and then typing in the three digit ASCII code)

Nested *IF* Statements

6

You can nest various types of IF statements in a program to implement more sophisticated decisions. You cannot overlap the THEN or ELSE clauses of the various IF statements, however. The inner IF statements must be completely contained in the outer ones.

Take a look at a simple example. Listing 6.8, IF5.BAS, uses nested IF statements. The program prompts you to enter a string. If you just press the Return key, the program ends. By contrast, if you type in a set of characters, the program prompts you whether you want to see your input echoed in uppercase or lowercase. The typical input is either U (for uppercase) or L (for lowercase)—you can type in your input in either uppercase or lowercase. If you just press the Return key, the program interprets your action as a request to display the first input in uppercase characters.

Listing 6.8. IF5.BAS, which uses nested IF statements.

```
 1: REM Program tests the nested
 2: REM IF-THEN-ELSE statements
 3: REM
 4: ' declare the program variables
 5: DIM InString AS STRING
 6: DIM OutString AS STRING
 7: DIM ToCase AS STRING
 8:
 9: CLS
10: INPUT "Enter a string : ", InString
11: IF InString <> "" THEN
12:    INPUT "Convert to Uppercase or Lowercase? (U/L) ", ToCase
```

continues

Listing 6.8. continued

```
13:   ' process choice
14:   IF ToCase <> "" THEN
15:     ToCase = UCASE$(LEFT$(ToCase, 1))
16:   ELSE
17:     ToCase = "U"
18:   END IF
19:
20:   ' convert input according to choice
21:   IF ToCase = "U" THEN
22:     OutString = UCASE$(InString)
23:   ELSE
24:     OutString = LCASE$(InString)
25:   END IF
26:
27:   PRINT "Input string is: "; InString
28:   PRINT "Output string is: "; OutString
29: END IF
30:
31: PRINT
32: PRINT "End of program"
33: END
```

Here is a sample output for the program in Listing 6.8:

```
Enter a string : QBasic
Convert to Uppercase or Lowercase? (U/L) u

Input string is: QBasic
Output string is: QBASIC

End of program
```

The program in Listing 6.8 declares its three string variables on lines 5–7. The INPUT statement on line 10 prompts you to enter a string and stores it in the variable InString. Line 11 contains the outer IF statement. The IF statement executes the THEN clause statements only when InString is not an empty string. Otherwise, the program resumes at the PRINT statement on line 31.

Inside the THEN clause of the outer IF statement are two inner IF-THEN-ELSE statements, located on lines 14 and 21. The INPUT statement on line 12 prompts you to choose the character-case conversion mode. The statement stores your input in ToCase. The IF-THEN-ELSE statement on line 14 processes the contents of ToCase. If the variable stores a non-empty string, the program executes the THEN clause statement on line 15. This statement replaces the contents of ToCase with the uppercase of its first character. If the tested condition is false (ToCase stores an empty string) the program executes the ELSE statement on line 17. This statement assigns the string literal "U" to ToCase.

The second nested IF statement processes the contents of InString. The IF statement compares the contents of ToCase with the string literal "U". If this condition is true, the program executes the THEN clause statement on line 22. This statement stores the uppercase characters of InString in the variable OutString. By contrast, when the tested condition is false, the program executes the ELSE clause statement on line 24. This statement saves the lowercase characters of InString in OutString.

Line 32 contains a PRINT statement that displays a message indicating that the program has ended. This message is displayed when you do not enter any characters for the first prompt.

Nested *IF* and *SELECT-CASE* Statements

QBasic also enables you to nest IF and SELECT-CASE statements. Either type of decision-making statement can be the outer statement. The choice depends on the actual program. Again, the rule to watch is not to overlap clauses from the IF and SELECT-CASE statements.

Let's look at an example. Listing 6.9, CASE3.BAS, implements a four-function calculator. The program prompts you to enter the first operand, the mathematical operator (+, -, /, and *), and the second operand. The program displays the operands, the operator, and the result when there are no errors. Such errors occur when you attempt to divide by zero, or when you enter an invalid operator.

Listing 6.9. CASE3.BAS, which implements a
four-function calculator.

```
1: REM Program shows an IF statement nested
2: REM inside a SELECT-CASE statement
3: CONST TRUE% = -1
4: CONST FALSE% = 0
5: ' declare the program variables
6: DIM X AS DOUBLE
7: DIM Y AS DOUBLE
8: DIM Z AS DOUBLE
9: DIM OpChar AS STRING
10: DIM MathError AS INTEGER
11:
12: CLS
13: ' input operands and operators
14: INPUT "Enter the first operand"; X
15: INPUT "Enter the operator [in '+-*/']: ", OpChar
16: INPUT "Enter the second operand"; Y
17:
18: ' clear math error by default
19: MathError = FALSE
20:
21: SELECT CASE LEFT$(OpChar, 1)
22:
23:    CASE "+"
24:       Z = X + Y
25:
26:    CASE "-"
27:       Z = X - Y
28:
29:    CASE "*"
30:       Z = X * Y
31:
32:    CASE "/"
33:       ' dividing by a number other than zero?
34:       IF Y <> 0 THEN
35:          Z = X / Y
36:       ELSE
37:          ' division-by-zero error!
38:          MathError = TRUE
39:       END IF
```

```
40:
41:    CASE ELSE
42:       ' bad operator error
43:       MathError = TRUE
44: END SELECT
45:
46: PRINT
47: IF MathError = FALSE THEN
48:    PRINT X; OpChar; Y; "= "; Z
49: ELSE
50:    PRINT "Bad operator or division-by-zero error"
51: END IF
52: END
```

6

Here is a sample output for the program in Listing 6.9:

```
Enter the first operand? 355
Enter the operator [in '+-*/']: /
Enter the second operand? 113


   355 / 113 =   3.141592920353983
```

The program in Listing 6.9 declares the constants TRUE% and FALSE% on lines 3 and 4. The program uses these constants to manage the error status.

On lines 6–10 the program declares its variables. The INPUT statements on lines 14–16 prompt you to enter the first operand, the operator, and the second operand. The statements save your input in the variables X, OpChar, and Y. On line 19 the program assigns the constant FALSE to the variable MathError, which acts as a logical flag or switch that maintains the error status.

The SELECT-CASE statement on line 21 tests the expression LEFT$(OpChar, 1) with the CASE clauses on lines 23, 26, 29, and 32. Each CASE clause contains a string literal that represents a mathematical operator. The statements in the first three CASE clauses add, subtract, and multiply the operands in a straightforward fashion. By contrast, the CASE clause on line 32 uses a nested IF-THEN-ELSE statement to guard against an attempt to divide by zero. The IF statement examines the condition Y is not equal to zero. If this condition is true, the program performs the division on line 35. Otherwise, the program executes the ELSE clause statement on line 38. This statement assigns the constant TRUE to the variable MathError, signaling an error.

The catch-all ELSE clause of the SELECT-CASE statement also assigns TRUE to MathError when the tested expression does not match any CASE clause (because the operator is not valid).

The IF-THEN-ELSE statement on line 47 examines the error status, stored in MathError. If there are no errors, the program displays the operands, operator, and result using the PRINT statement in line 48. Otherwise, the program displays an error message using the PRINT statement on line 50.

Summary

This chapter covered the QBasic decision-making statements. These statements allow your programs to examine conditions and take action accordingly. You learned about the following topics:

☐ Program pseudocode is essentially an outline, in plain English, that lists the sequence of program tasks.

☐ The single-alternative IF-THEN statement executes a sequence of statements in the THEN clause when the tested condition is true. Otherwise, the program execution resumes after the IF statement.

☐ Single-stepping through a program enables you to execute the program statements one at a time. This slow-motion mode enables you to determine exactly which statements are being executed in an IF or SELECT-CASE statement.

☐ The dual-alternative IF-THEN-ELSE statement examines a condition and executes the statements in the THEN clause if the condition is true. Otherwise, the statements in the ELSE clause are executed.

☐ The multiple-alternative IF-THEN-ELSEIF statement examines a series of conditions and executes the statements that correspond to the first condition that is true. If none of the tested conditions are true, the statements in the catch-all ELSE clause (if present) are executed.

☐ The multiple-alternative SELECT-CASE statement is a short form of the IF-THEN-ELSEIF statement. The SELECT-CASE statement compares a tested expression with different matching expressions. Each matching expression is placed in a CASE clause. The building blocks for matching expressions are lists of values, range of values, and partial relational expressions.

☐ Nested IF statements are allowed by QBasic. You can nest any kinds of IF statements as long as their THEN and ELSE clauses do not overlap.

☐ Nested IF and SELECT-CASE statements are permitted by QBasic. You can nest IF and SELECT-CASE statements as long as their clauses do not overlap.

Q&A

6

Q. Does QBasic impose any rules for indenting statements in the THEN and ELSE clauses of IF statements?

A. No. The indentation is purely up to you. Typical indentations range from 2 to 4 spaces. Using indentations makes your listings much more readable. Here is the case of an IF statement with unindented THEN and ELSE clause statements:

```
IF I > 0 THEN
J = I * I
ELSE
J = 10 - I
END IF
```

Compare the readability of the unindented listing with the indented version that follows:

```
IF I > 0 THEN
  J = I * I
ELSE
  J = 10 - I
END IF
```

The indented version is much easier to read.

Q. What are the rules for writing the condition of an IF-THEN-ELSE statement?

A. There are two schools of thought. The first one recommends that you write the condition such that it is true more often than false. The second school recommends avoiding negative expressions (those that use the relational operator <> and the Boolean operator NOT). Programmers in this camp would translate the following IF statement:

```
IF I <> 0 THEN
    J = 100 \ I
ELSE
    J = 1
END IF
```

into the following equivalent form:

```
IF I = 0 THEN
    J = 1
ELSE
    J = 100 \ I
END IF
```

even though the likelihood of I storing 0 might be very low!

Q. How can I avoid the possibility of division by zero, such as in the following code snippet:

```
IF I <> 0 AND 1/I > 1 THEN
    J = I * I
END IF
```

A. Because QBasic evaluates the entire condition, the above example generates a runtime error when I contains 0. To solve the problem, use nested IF statements:

```
IF I <> 0 THEN
    IF 1/I > 1 THEN
        J = I * I
    END IF
END IF
```

The condition in the outer IF statement protects the condition in the inner IF statement from dividing by zero.

Q. Do I have to include an ELSE clause in IF-THEN-ELSEIF and SELECT-CASE statements?

A. Programmers **highly recommend** that you include these catch-all clauses to ensure that multiple-alternative statements handle all conditions.

Workshop

The Workshop provides quiz questions to help you solidify your understanding of the material covered and exercises to provide you with experience in using what you've learned. Try to understand the quiz and exercise answers before continuing on to the next chapter. Answers are provided in Appendix B, "Answers."

6

Quiz

1. Simplify the following nested IF statements by replacing them with a single IF statement:

   IF I>0 and I<10 then

   ```
   IF I > 0 THEN
       IF I < 10 THEN
           PRINT "I = "; I
       END IF
   END IF
   ```

2. Simplify the following IF statements by replacing them with a single IF statement:

   ```
   IF I > 0 THEN
       J = I * I
       PRINT "J = "; J
   END IF
   IF I < 0 THEN
       J = 4 * I
       PRINT "J = "; J
   END IF
   IF I = 0 THEN
       J = 10 + I
       PRINT "J = "; J
   END IF
   ```

3. True or false: The following IF-THEN statements perform the same tasks as the IF-THEN-ELSE statement:

   ```
   IF I < 0 THEN
       I = 10 + I
   ```

```
            J = I * I
            PRINT "I = "; I
            PRINT "J = "; J
        END IF
        IF I >= 0 THEN
            K = 4 * I + 1
            PRINT "K = "; K
        END IF

        IF I < 0 THEN
            I = 10 - I
            J = I * I
            PRINT "I = "; I
            PRINT "J = "; J
        ELSE
            K = 4 * I + 1
            PRINT "K = "; K
        END IF
```

4. Simplify the following IF-THEN-ELSE statement:

```
    IF I > 0 AND I < 100 THEN
        J = I * I
    ELSEIF I > 10 AND I < 50 THEN
        J = 10 + I
    ELSEIF I >= 100 THEN
        J = I
    ELSE
        J = 1
    END IF
```

5. What is wrong with the following IF statement?

```
    IF I > (1 + I * I) THEN
        J = I * I
        PRINT "I = "; I; " and J = "; J
    END IF
```

Exercises

1. Modify the program IF2.BAS to use the `IF-THEN-ELSEIF` statement. Make the new program, IF6.BAS, test the condition `Discrim > 0` and `Discrim < 0`. Use the catch-all `ELSE` clause for the case when `Discrim` is 0.

2. Write the pseudocode for CASE3.BAS.

3. Single-step though the programs CASE2.BAS and CASE3.BAS using the F8 function key.

6

187

DAY 7

Looping

Computers are very good at tirelessly and accurately repeating tasks. Add the speed of processing and you get efficient and accurate computing machines. The feature of repeating a task is called *looping*. In this chapter you will learn about the basics of looping and the various QBasic loop statements. The topics covered in this chapter include:

- The GOTO statement
- An overview of loops
- Creating loops with the GOTO statement
- The FOR-NEXT loop
- Nested loops
- The conditional DO-WHILE loop
- The conditional DO-UNTIL loop
- Exiting loops
- The open DO-LOOP

New Term The term **iteration** refers to executing the statements inside a loop.

The *GOTO* Statement

The GOTO statement enables you to jump from one location in a program to another. The most controversial statement in programming languages, especially BASIC, is GOTO. Many programmers and teachers believe that the GOTO statement encourages novice programmers to write programs with zig-zagging flow, known as *spaghetti code*. Such programs are hard to read, understand, and update. Fortunately, QBasic is a more structured implementation of BASIC and enables you to minimize or eliminate the use of GOTO statements.

Syntax

The GOTO Statement

The general syntax for the GOTO statement is

```
GOTO label
```

The `label` is a program location that is either a unique name or number, followed by a colon. Labels must appear on separate lines.

Example:

```
IF I = 0 THEN GOTO nextStatement
I = 1
J = I * I
nextStatement:
```

In the previous example the program jumps to the label `nextStatement` when the variable `I` contains zero. Otherwise, the program executes the two assignment statements and then reaches the label `nextStatement`.

7

The `GOTO` statement is useful (when used sparingly) in special cases, such as when you need to exit a program after executing a set of statements that wind down the program.

Let's look at an example. Listing 7.1, GOTO1.BAS, uses the `GOTO` statement to exit the string searching program due to the lack of input. The program prompts you to enter the scanned string and the search string. If you only press the Return key for either prompt, the program displays a message and ends. The message states that you need to enter at least one character. Of course, you need to run the program again and supply it with the correct input.

Listing 7.1. GOTO1.BAS, which uses the GOTO statement to exit the string searching program due to the lack of input.

```
 1: REM Program tests the GOTO statement
 2: REM
 3: ' declare the program variables
 4: DIM MainString AS STRING
 5: DIM FindString AS STRING
 6: DIM I AS INTEGER
 7:
 8: CLS
 9: INPUT "Enter the main string : ", MainString
10: IF MainString = "" THEN GOTO BAD.INPUT
11: INPUT "Enter the search string : ", FindString
12: IF FindString = "" THEN GOTO BAD.INPUT
13: I = INSTR(MainString, FindString)
```

continues

Listing 7.1. continued

```
14: PRINT
15: IF I > 0 THEN
16:   PRINT "Found search string at character "; I
17: ELSE
18:   PRINT "No match for search string"
19: END IF
20:
21: END
22:
23: BAD.INPUT:
24: PRINT
25: PRINT "You must enter at least one character!"
26: PRINT
27: PRINT "End of program"
28: PRINT
29: END
```

Here is a sample output for the program in Listing 7.1:

```
Enter the main string : QuickBasic
Enter the search string :

You must enter at least one character!

End of program
```

The program in Listing 7.1 declares its variables on lines 4–6. The INPUT statement on line 9 prompts you to enter the scanned string and stores it in the variable MainString. The IF statement on line 10 determines whether MainString contains an empty string (as a result of you only pressing the Return key). If this condition is true, the program executes the GOTO statement in the THEN clause. The GOTO statement causes the program execution to jump to the label BAD.INPUT, located at line 23.

The INPUT statement on line 11 prompts you to enter the search string and saves it in the variable FindString. The IF statement on line 12 determines whether FindString contains an empty string. If this condition is true, the

program executes the GOTO statement in the THEN clause. The GOTO statement causes the program execution to jump to the label BAD.INPUT.

The assignment statement on line 13 calls the function INSTR and returns the first character index where the variable FindString occurs in MainString. The statement assigns the result of INSTR to the variable I. The IF-THEN-ELSE statement on line 15 determines whether I is positive. If the condition is true, the program displays the value in I using the PRINT statement on line 16. Otherwise, the program executes the ELSE clause statement on line 18. The line contains a PRINT statement that displays a message indicating the failure of the string search. The program then ends when it executes the END statement at line 21.

The BAD.INPUT label on line 23 is followed by a set of PRINT statements (on lines 24–28) that display the program's complaint for the lack of input. The program ends when it executes the END statement on line 29.

Looping—An Overview

A program loop, in general, is a sequence of statements that typically is executed many times. Loops implement repetitive tasks of one or more program statements.

There are three general types of loops: fixed, conditional, and open. The fixed loops repeat their statements for a predetermined number of times. Conditional loops repeat their statements while or until a tested condition is true. Open loops, basically, repeat their statements indefinitely. Although there are a few applications that loop indefinitely (the best example is MS-DOS), most open loops have an escape mechanism to stop iterating.

Looping with *GOTO*s

Before I introduce you to the different QBasic loops, let me show you how to build a simple loop using the IF-THEN and GOTO statements. I present this discussion not to teach you a programming technique, but rather to give you insight about how loops work.

The general forms for creating loops with the IF-THEN and GOTO statements are as follows:

```
StartOfLoop:
    sequence of statements
IF condition THEN GOTO StartOfLoop
```

```
StartOfLoop:
IF condition THEN GOTO EndOfLoop
    sequence of statements
GOTO StartOfLoop
EndOfLoop:
```

The first form executes a sequence of statements and then tests a Boolean condition. If that condition is true, the GOTO statement sends the program flow back to the label StartOfLoop to perform another iteration.

The second form uses two labels. This kind of loop tests a condition first. If it is true, the GOTO statement jumps to label EndOfLoop, the end of the loop. Otherwise, the loop executes a sequence of statements and then executes the GOTO StartOfLoop statement. This statement causes the program execution to jump to the beginning of the loop, to label StartOfLoop.

Let's look at a simple program that applies the first form of a simple loop. Listing 7.2, GOTO2.BAS, implements a simple counting loop using the IF-THEN and GOTO statements. The program requires no keyboard input and executes the simple loop that displays integers that range from 1–15. Each value appears on a separate line.

Listing 7.2. GOTO2.BAS, which implements a simple counting loop using the IF-THEN and GOTO statements.

```
1: REM Program uses the GOTO statement
2: REM to create a simple loop
3: REM
4: ' declare the program variables
5: DIM I AS INTEGER
6: CLS
7: ' initialize variable for the loop
8: I = 0
9: ' loop starts next
```

```
10: Top:
11:   I = I + 1
12:   PRINT "Variable I now stores "; I
13:   IF I < 15 THEN GOTO Top
14: ' end of loop
15: PRINT
16: PRINT "End of loop"
17: END
```

Here is a sample output for the program in Listing 7.2:

```
Variable I now stores  1
Variable I now stores  2
Variable I now stores  3
Variable I now stores  4
Variable I now stores  5
Variable I now stores  6
Variable I now stores  7
Variable I now stores  8
Variable I now stores  9
Variable I now stores  10
Variable I now stores  11
Variable I now stores  12
Variable I now stores  13
Variable I now stores  14
Variable I now stores  15

End of loop
```

The program in Listing 7.2 declares the variable I on line 5. On line 8 the program assigns 0 to I as part of setting up the loop. The program uses I to control how many times the loop iterates. The loop itself begins at the label Top, on line 10, and ends at line 13.

On line 11 the program increments I by 1. The PRINT statement on line 12 displays text and the value in I. This statement provides the output of each loop iteration. The IF statement on line 13 determines whether I contains a number smaller than 15. If this condition is true, the program executes the GOTO statement in the THEN clause. The GOTO statement makes the program flow resume at the top of the loop.

The PRINT statement on line 16 displays a message indicating the end of the looping.

The *FOR-NEXT* Loop

The *FOR-NEXT* loop is the fixed loop in QBasic. This loop iterates for a predefined number of times. There are two types of *FOR-NEXT* loops: the upward-counting and the downward-counting loops.

Syntax

The Upward-Counting **FOR-NEXT** Loop

The general syntax for the upward-counting FOR-NEXT loop is

```
FOR loopControlVariable = lowVal TO highVal [STEP increment]
    sequence of statements
NEXT [loopControlVariable]
```

The *loopControlVariable* is the variable used to control the number of iterations in the FOR-NEXT loop. When the loop starts iterating, it assigns the numeric value *lowVal* to *loopControlVariable*. At the end of each iteration, the program adds the *increment* value (or 1 if the STEP clause is not present) to the *loopControlVariable*. The FOR-NEXT loop resumes iterating as long as the value in the *loopControlVariable* is less than or equal to the numeric value *HighVal*. The loop does not iterate if the value of *lowVal* is greater than the value of *HighVal*. The number of loop iterations is:

```
number of iterations = (highVal - lowVal + 1) / increment
```

Figure 7.1 shows a sample upward-counting FOR-NEXT loop with the STEP clause.

Examples:

```
FOR I = 1 TO 10
    PRINT I
NEXT I


FOR Year = 1981 TO 1990
    PRINT "In "; Year; " income is "; INT(RND * 50000)
NEXT


FOR I = 104 TO 345 STEP 3
    PRINT I * I
NEXT I
```

SAMS PUBLISHING

The Downward-Counting FOR-NEXT Loop

The general syntax for the downward-counting FOR-NEXT loop is

```
FOR loopControlVariable = highVal TO lowVal [STEP decrement]
    sequence of statements
NEXT [loopControlVariable]
```

The *loopControlVariable* is the variable used to control the number of iterations in the FOR-NEXT loop. When the loop starts iterating, it assigns the numeric value *highVal* to the *loopControlVariable*. At the end of each iteration, the program adds the value of *decrement* (*decrement* must be negative) to the *loopControlVariable*. The FOR-NEXT loop resumes iterating as long as the value in the *loopControlVariable* is greater than or equal to the numeric value *lowVal*. The loop does not iterate if the value of *highVal* is less than the value of *lowVal*. The number of loop iterations is (the minus sign is used because the decrement value is negative):

```
number of iterations = -(highVal - lowVal + 1) / decrement
```

Figure 7.2 shows a sample downward-counting FOR-NEXT loop with the STEP clause.

Example:

```
FOR I = 10 TO 1 STEP -1
    PRINT I
NEXT I


FOR Year = 1990 TO 1981 STEP -1
    PRINT "In "; Year; " income is "; INT(RND * 50000)
NEXT


FOR I = 345 TO 104 STEP -3
    PRINT I * I
NEXT I
```

7

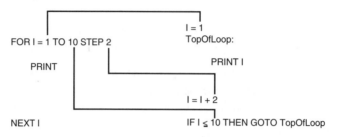

Figure 7.1. A sample upward-counting FOR-NEXT loop with the STEP clause.

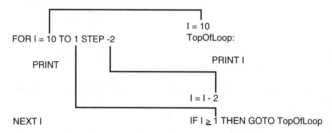

Figure 7.2. A sample downward-counting FOR-NEXT loop with the STEP clause.

DO use STEP values that are consistent with the data type of the loop-control variable.

DON'T use 0 in the STEP clause of a FOR-NEXT loop. It will cause the loop to iterate indefinitely.

The QBasic FOR-NEXT loop allows you to use any numeric data type for the loop-control variable and the loop's limits. You cannot use string variables as the loop-control variable and string expressions for the loop's limits.

In the next subsections I present a number of programs that illustrate different basic ways of using the FOR-NEXT loop.

Iteration Counting

One way to use the FOR-NEXT loop is to repeat a set of statements a fixed number of times. The loop-control variable does not appear in the repeated statements. Instead, it merely serves to monitor the number of iterations.

Listing 7.3, FOR1.BAS, uses the FOR-NEXT loop to replicate string patterns. The program prompts you to enter a string pattern (your input should be a small string) and the number of times to replicate the pattern (the number also should be small). The program displays the string produced by replicating the pattern for the specified number of times.

 Listing 7.3. FOR1.BAS, which uses the FOR-NEXT loop to replicate string patterns.

```
 1: REM Program that uses the FOR loop
 2: REM to replicate a multi-character pattern
 3: ' declare the variables
 4: DIM MainString AS STRING
 5: DIM StrPattern AS STRING
 6: DIM Q AS STRING
 7: DIM N AS INTEGER
 8: DIM I AS INTEGER
 9:
10: Q = CHR$(34)
11: CLS
12: INPUT "Enter string pattern : ", StrPattern
13: INPUT "Enter number of times to replicate pattern "; N
14: ' initialize string
15: MainString = ""
16: ' loop to build the replicated pattern
17: FOR I = 1 TO N
18:    MainString = MainString + StrPattern
19: NEXT I
20: PRINT "Replicated string is "; Q; MainString; Q
21: END
```

Here is a sample output for the program in Listing 7.3:

```
Enter string pattern : -+
Enter number of times to replicate pattern ? 10
Replicated string is "-+-+-+-+-+-+-+-+-+-+"
```

The program in Listing 7.3 declares its variables on lines 4–8. The INPUT statement on line 12 prompts you to enter the string pattern and saves it in the variable StrPattern. The INPUT statement on line 13 prompts you to enter the number of times to replicate the pattern. The statement stores your input in the variable N. On line 15 the program initializes the string variable MainString, which is used to store the replicated pattern. Line 17 contains the start of the FOR-NEXT loop. The loop uses the variable I as the loop-control variable and iterates in the range of 1 to N (the times of times to replicate the pattern). The FOR-NEXT loop encompasses the single assignment statement on line 18. This statement concatenates the previous contents of MainString with the pattern stored in StrPattern. Each iteration assigns the resulting string back to MainString. The NEXT clause on line 19 specifies the end of the loop. The PRINT statement on line 20 displays the replicated pattern.

Using the Value of the Loop-Control Variable

In Listing 7.3 notice the loop statement on line 18 does not utilize the loop-control variable I. There are many tasks that do use the variable to provide values for expressions in the loop statements.

Let's look at a simple example. Listing 7.4, FOR2.BAS, uses a FOR-NEXT loop to sum up integers. The program prompts you to enter the number of integers to sum (from 1 to the number you specify). The program calculates the sum of integers using a FOR-NEXT loop and using the Gauss equation. The Gauss equation, which calculates the sum of integers, follows:

```
sum of integers from 1 to N = N (N + 1) / 2
```

The output includes both values, which should match.

 Listing 7.4. FOR2.BAS, which uses the FOR-NEXT loop to sum up integers.

```
1: REM Program that uses the FOR loop
2: REM calculate the sum of integers
3: ' declare the variables
4: DIM N AS INTEGER
5: DIM I AS INTEGER
6: DIM Sum AS DOUBLE
7: DIM Ndbl AS DOUBLE
8:
9: CLS
10: INPUT "Enter number integers to sum "; N
11: Ndbl = N ' store a DOUBLE-typed version of N in Ndbl
12: PRINT
13: PRINT "Wait please..."
14: PRINT
15: ' initialize sum
16: Sum = 0
17: ' loop to accumulate the sum of integers
18: FOR I = 1 TO N
19:    Sum = Sum + I
20: NEXT I
21:
22: PRINT "Sum of "; N; " integers = "; Sum; " using loop"
23: PRINT "Sum of "; N; " integers = "; Ndbl * (Ndbl + 1) / 2;
24: PRINT " using the Gauss equation"
25: END
```

7

Here is a sample output for the program in Listing 7.4:

```
Enter number integers to sum ? 30000

Wait please...

Sum of  30000  integers =  450015000  using loop
Sum of  30000  integers =  450015000  using the Gauss equation
```

The program in Listing 7.4 declares its variables on lines 4–7. The INPUT statement on line 10 prompts you to enter the number of integers to sum. The statement stores your input in the integer variable N. On line 11 the program stores the value of N in the double-typed variable Ndbl. The PRINT statement on line 13 displays a "Wait please..." message.

Because the loop takes the sum of numbers, the program needs a statement to properly initialize the variable that stores the sum—in this case the variable is called Sum. Line 16 assigns 0 to Sum before it starts executing the FOR-NEXT loop on line 18. The loop uses the variable I as the loop-control variable and iterates in the range of 1 to N. The loop uses only one statement, located on line 19, to accumulate the sum of integers in Sum. Notice that the statement on line 19 uses I to provide the integer values to be accumulated in Sum. Line 20 contains the NEXT clause, which declares the end of the FOR-NEXT loop.

The PRINT statements on lines 22–24 display the sum of integers using the loop and using the Gauss equation.

Indexing with the Loop-Control Variable

You also can use the loop-control variable of a FOR-NEXT loop as an index to the various characters of a string. For example, if S is a string variable, and I is a loop-control variable, the function call MID$(S, I, 1) retrieves character number I from string S. Similarly, you can use the statement MID$(S, I, 1) to overwrite a character number I in string S.

Here's an example. Listing 7.5, FOR3.BAS, uses a FOR-NEXT loop to access the individual characters of a string. The program prompts you to enter a string and then displays your input along with its reversed characters.

Listing 7.5. FOR3.BAS, which uses a FOR-NEXT loop to access the individual characters of a string.

```
 1: REM Program that uses the FOR loop
 2: REM to access the characters of a string
 3: ' declare the variables
 4: DIM AString AS STRING
 5: DIM RevString AS STRING
 6: DIM Q AS STRING
 7: DIM L AS INTEGER
 8: DIM I AS INTEGER
 9:
10: CLS
11: Q = CHR$(34)
12: INPUT "Enter a string : ", AString
13: L = LEN(AString)
14: RevString = ""
15: FOR I = L TO 1 STEP -1
16:    RevString = RevString + MID$(AString, I, 1)
17: NEXT I
18: PRINT
19: PRINT "Input string is : "; Q; AString; Q
20: PRINT "Reversed string is : "; Q; RevString; Q
21: END
```

Here is a sample output for the program in Listing 7.5:

```
Enter a string : QBasic

Input string is : "QBasic"
Reversed string is : "cisaBQ"
```

The program in Listing 7.5 declares its variables on lines 4–8. The INPUT statement on line 12 prompts you to enter a string and stores it in the variable AString. The statement on line 13 calls the function LEN to assign the length of the string in AString to the variable L. Line 14 assigns an empty string to the variable RevString. The program uses this variable to store the characters of AString in a reverse order. This statement provides the required initialization for the program's loop. Line 15 contains the beginning of the downward-counting FOR-NEXT loop. The loop uses the control variable I and iterates from L to 1 in steps of −1. Using the downward-counting loop provides a more intuitive way of recalling the characters in AString in the reverse order (from right to left.) The loop statement on line 16 concatenates the contents of RevString with character number I in AString. The statement assigns the resulting string back to RevString. Line 17 contains the NEXT clause, defining the end of the loop. The PRINT statements on lines 19 and 20 display the input and reversed strings.

Floating-Point Loop-Control Variables

The FOR-NEXT loops that I presented so far use integer-typed loop-control variables. QBasic also enables you to use control variables that are floating-point data types. Such loop-control variables are useful in supplying floating-point numbers to the statements inside the loop. Typical applications that use floating-point loop-control variables include mathematical, scientific, and graphics applications.

Let me present an example for this kind of loop-control variable. Listing 7.6, FOR4.BAS, uses a double-typed loop-control variable to find the approximate roots of a quadratic equation. The program requires no input because the coefficients of the equation are defined in the program. Instead, the program calculates and displays the approximate roots and the value of the function at these roots.

The program applies a simple method (although it requires a lot of computations) that uses a FOR-NEXT loop to examine the value of the following function Y:

$$Y = A X^2 + B X + C$$

The program examines the values of Y in a specified range of X values, calculating values of Y at small increments of X—small enough to detect when the values of Y change sign. When the values change sign, the program concludes that the current value of X is near a root (the value of X where function Y is 0).

Listing 7.6. FOR4.BAS, which uses a double-typed loop-control variable to find the approximate roots of a quadratic equation.

```
 1: REM Program that uses the FOR loop
 2: REM to get the approximate roots of
 3: REM a quadratic equation
 4: CONST FIRST# = 10
 5: CONST LAST# = -10
 6: CONST INCREM# = -.005
 7: CONST A# = -2
 8: CONST B# = 1
 9: CONST C# = 10
10: ' declare the variables
11: DIM X AS DOUBLE
12: DIM Y1 AS DOUBLE
13: DIM Y2 AS DOUBLE
14: DIM Xroot AS DOUBLE
15: DIM Yroot AS DOUBLE
16: CLS
17: PRINT "Wait please..."
18: PRINT
19: X = FIRST
20: Y1 = A * X * X + B * X + C
21: FOR X = FIRST + INCREM TO LAST STEP INCREM
22:    Y2 = A * X * X + B * X + C
23:    IF Y2 * Y1 < 0 THEN
24:      Xroot = X - INCREM / 2
25:      Yroot = A * Xroot * Xroot + B * Xroot + C
26:      PRINT "Root near X = "; Xroot;
27:      PRINT " F(X) = "; Yroot
28:    END IF
29:    Y1 = Y2
30: NEXT X
31: PRINT
32: PRINT "End of program"
33: END
```

Here is a sample output for the program in Listing 7.6:

```
Wait please...

Root near X =  2.497500167693943  F(X) =
2.248599243139812D-02
Root near X = -2.002499731723219  F(X) =
-2.251008282634854D-02

End of program
```

The program in Listing 7.6 declares a set of constants on lines 4–9. The constants FIRST# and LAST# define the range of root values for X. The constant INCREM# defines how much X is incremented when searching for the root. The constants A#, B#, and C# are the coefficients of the quadratic equation. You can experiment with changing the values of these constants. The program declares its variables on lines 11–15. The PRINT statement on line 17 displays a "Wait please..." message. On line 19 the program assigns the value of FIRST to the variable X. On line 20 the program calculates the value of Y at X = FIRST and assigns the value to variable Y1. The statements on lines 19 and 20 prepare for the work of the FOR-NEXT loop.

The search for the root starts at line 21, which contains the beginning of the FOR-NEXT loop. The loop uses the control variable X and iterates from the value FIRST + INCREM to LAST in steps of INCREM. Unlike the FOR-NEXT loops in the previous programs, this loop contains multiple statements and even an IF statement. The first statement on line 22 calculates the value of Y at the current value of X and stores it in Y2. The IF statement on line 23 detects a change of sign between the last two values of Y (stored in Y1 and Y2). The IF statement tests the condition Y1 * Y2 < 0. If this condition is true, the last two values of Y have changed sign around a root value. Consequently, the program executes the THEN clause statements. The first statement on line 24 calculates an average value of X in the current interval (defined by the values X - INCREM and X) and saves it in the variable Xroot. Line 25 calculates the value of Y at Xroot and stores it in Yroot. The PRINT statements on lines 26 and 27 display the values of Xroot and Yroot. The last statement inside the FOR-NEXT loop assigns the contents of Y2 to Y1. This shift in value prepares the loop for the next iteration. Line 30 contains the NEXT clause that defines the end of the loop. The PRINT statement on line 32 displays a message informing you that the program has ended.

Nested Loops

There are many program tasks that require more than one FOR-NEXT loops, nested inside each other. Each iteration of the outer FOR-NEXT loops requires the complete execution of the inner FOR-NEXT loops. These nested loops work like the short and long hands of a typical clock, which turn at different speeds.

Nesting FOR-NEXT Loops

The general syntax for nesting FOR-NEXT loops is:

```
FOR var1 = low1 TO high1 [STEP increment1]
    [sequence of statements]
    FOR var2 = low2 TO high2 [STEP increment2]
        [sequence of statements]
        ....
        FOR varn = lown TO highn [STEP incrementn]
            sequence of statements
        NEXT [varn]
        [sequence of statements]
    NEXT [var2]
[sequence of statements]
NEXT [var1]
```

QBasic allows you to consolidate the NEXT clauses of the nested FOR-NEXT loops if there are statements between them:

```
FOR var1 = low1 TO high1 [STEP increment1]
    [sequence of statements]
    FOR var2 = low2 TO high2 [STEP increment2]
        [sequence of statements]
        ...
        FOR varn = lown TO highn [STEP incrementn]
            sequence of statements
NEXT varn, ..., var2, var1
```

The iteration of the outer FOR-NEXT loops requires the complete execution of the inner FOR-NEXT loops. The total number of times to execute the statements in the innermost loop is:

```
total = (high1 - low1 + 1)(high2 - low2 + 1)...(highn - lown + 1)
```

As you can see from the equation, the number dramatically increases with the number of nested loops and the iteration range of each loop.

Examples:

```
FOR I = 1 TO 10 STEP 3
    FOR J = 1 TO 3
        PRINT I * J
    NEXT J
NEXT I


FOR I = 10 TO 4 STEP -2
    FOR J = 1 TO 3
        PRINT I * J
NEXT J, I
```

DO make sure that inner FOR-NEXT loops are completely contained in the outer nested loops.

DON'T overlap the NEXT clauses of nested FOR loops.

Let's look at an example. Listing 7.7, FOR5.BAS, uses a nested FOR-NEXT loop to time character concatenation in QBasic. The program uses the outer FOR-NEXT loop to repeat the concatenation process (which itself uses the inner FOR-NEXT loop) enough times to measure the duration of the process. The program requires no keyboard input. Instead, it displays a message asking you to wait and then displays the time required to repeat the process a set number of times. The program also presents the time per concatenated character. The small value of the latter result indicates how fast a single character can be concatenated to a string.

Listing 7.7. FOR5.BAS, which uses a nested FOR-NEXT loop to time character concatenation in QBasic.

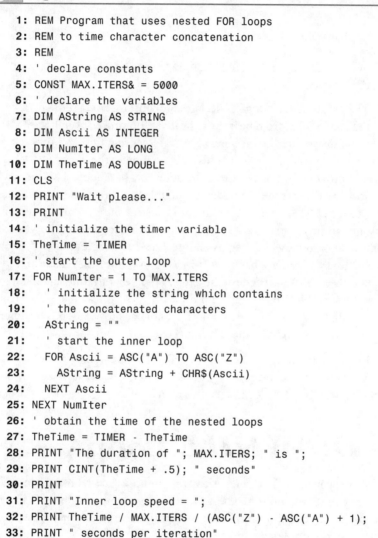

```
1: REM Program that uses nested FOR loops
2: REM to time character concatenation
3: REM
4: ' declare constants
5: CONST MAX.ITERS& = 5000
6: ' declare the variables
7: DIM AString AS STRING
8: DIM Ascii AS INTEGER
9: DIM NumIter AS LONG
10: DIM TheTime AS DOUBLE
11: CLS
12: PRINT "Wait please..."
13: PRINT
14: ' initialize the timer variable
15: TheTime = TIMER
16: ' start the outer loop
17: FOR NumIter = 1 TO MAX.ITERS
18:    ' initialize the string which contains
19:    ' the concatenated characters
20:    AString = ""
21:    ' start the inner loop
22:    FOR Ascii = ASC("A") TO ASC("Z")
23:       AString = AString + CHR$(Ascii)
24:    NEXT Ascii
25: NEXT NumIter
26: ' obtain the time of the nested loops
27: TheTime = TIMER - TheTime
28: PRINT "The duration of "; MAX.ITERS; " is ";
29: PRINT CINT(TheTime + .5); " seconds"
30: PRINT
31: PRINT "Inner loop speed = ";
32: PRINT TheTime / MAX.ITERS / (ASC("Z") - ASC("A") + 1);
33: PRINT " seconds per iteration"
34: END
```

7

Here is a sample output for the program in Listing 7.7 (the results you get depend on your computer setup):

```
Wait please...

The duration of  5000  is  27  seconds

Inner loop speed =  2.028545673076923D-04  seconds per
iteration
```

The program in Listing 7.7 declares the constant MAX.ITERS& to define the number of times to repeat the concatenation process. On lines 7–10, the program declares its variables. The statement on line 15 stores the result of TIMER in the variable TheTime. This statement takes the initial TIMER reading before the program begins executing the outer FOR-NEXT loop. This loop, which begins on line 17, uses the loop-control variable NumIter with values that range from 1 to MAX.ITERS. The first statement inside the outer loop, located on line 20, assigns an empty string to AString. This statement prepares the work of the inner FOR-NEXT loop, which begins on line 22. The latter loop uses the control variable Ascii with values that range from ASC("A"), the ASCII code of the letter A, to ASC("Z"), the ASCII code of the letter Z. There is only one statement inside the inner loop. This statement, found on line 23, concatenates the string in AString with CHR$(Ascii) and assigns the result back to AString. The inner and outer loops end at lines 24 and 25, respectively.

On line 27 the program assigns the elapsed time to the variable TheTime by calling the TIMER a second time. The PRINT statements on lines 28–33 display the timing results for the character concatenation.

The *DO-WHILE* Loop

Sometimes, you might have a repetitive programming task, but you don't know how many times you need to repeat the steps. Instead, the number of iterations depends on a tested condition. While (or until) such a condition is true, the loop iterates. QBasic implements two conditional loops: the DO-WHILE and the DO-UNTIL loops. In this section I discuss the DO-WHILE conditional loop.

Syntax

The DO-WHILE Loop

There are two forms of the DO-WHILE loop:

```
DO WHILE condition
    sequence of statements
LOOP
```

```
DO
    sequence of statements
LOOP WHILE condition
```

The first form of the DO-WHILE loop executes its statements as long as the tested *condition* is true. Because the loop condition is tested before executing the loop statements, it's possible that the loop never executes its statements (when the tested condition is initially false). Figure 7.3 shows a sample DO-WHILE loop and an equivalent loop made up of IF and GOTO statements.

The second form of the DO-WHILE loop executes the loop statements first and then tests the condition. The loop iterates while the condition is true. Because the condition appears after the loop statements, this form of the DO-WHILE loop executes its statements at least once.

QBasic also supports another form of the DO-WHILE loop:

```
WHILE condition
    sequence of statements
WEND
```

This second form is inherited from the BASICA and GW-BASIC implementations. The two forms differ in keywords only. Otherwise, both work identically.

Examples:

```
I = 1
DO WHILE I <= 10
    PRINT I
    I = I + 2
LOOP
```

7

```
I = 1
WHILE I <= 10
     PRINT I
     I = I + 2
WEND


I = 1
DO
     PRINT I
     I = I + 2
LOOP WHILE I <= 10
```

```
I = 1                          I = 1
DO WHILE I ≤ 10                IF I > 10 THEN GOTO EndOfLoop
                               Top:



     PRINT I                       PRINT I
     I = I + 1                     I = I + 1


     LOOP                         GOTO Top
                                  EndOfLoop:
```

Figure 7.3. A sample DO-WHILE loop and an equivalent loop made up of IF and GOTO statements.

DO include statements inside the DO-WHILE to update the tested condition of the loop. Otherwise, the loop iterates indefinitely and your program is stuck in the loop!

DON'T forget to place statements before the DO-WHILE loop that assist in setting up the loop. You might need to use one or more statements after the loop to process any pending values.

Let's look at an example that employs the DO-WHILE loop. Listing 7.8, WHILE1.BAS, uses a DO-WHILE loop to search for multiple occurrences of a search string in a scanned string. The program prompts you to enter the scanned string and the search string. The program displays a character ruler, the input strings, and the indices of the characters where the search string occurs. If the program is unable to find any match, it displays a message to that effect.

Listing 7.8. WHILE1.BAS, which uses a DO-WHILE loop to search for the multiple occurrences of a search string in a scanned string.

```
1: REM Program that tests the DO-WHILE loop
2: REM
3: ' declare the program variables
4: DIM AString AS STRING
5: DIM SearchString AS STRING
6: DIM Count AS INTEGER
7: DIM I AS INTEGER
8: DIM Q AS STRING
9:
10: CLS
11: ' assign the double-quote character to variable Q
12: Q = CHR$(34)
13: ' prompt for a non-empty scanned string
14: AString = ""
15: DO WHILE AString = ""
16:   INPUT "Enter the string to scan : ", AString
17: LOOP
18: ' prompt for a non-empty search string
19: SearchString = ""
20: DO WHILE SearchString = ""
21:   INPUT "Enter the search string : ", SearchString
22: LOOP
23: PRINT
24: PRINT "          1         2         3         4         5"
25: PRINT "12345678901234567890123456789012345678901234567890"
26: ' search from the beginning of string AString
27: I = INSTR(AString, SearchString)
28: ' initialize the number of matches
29: Count = 0
```

continues

Listing 7.8. continued

```
30: PRINT AString; " <-- scanned string"
31: PRINT Q; SearchString; Q; " <--- search string"
32: PRINT
33: DO WHILE I > 0
34:   Count = Count + 1
35:   PRINT "Found match at index"; I
36:   I = INSTR(I + 1, AString, SearchString)
37: LOOP
38: ' no matches found?
39: IF Count = 0 THEN PRINT "No matching search string was found"
40: END
```

Here is a sample output for the program in Listing 7.8:

```
Enter the string to scan : Hello mellow yellow!
Enter the search string : llo

         1         2         3         4         5
12345678901234567890123456789012345678901234567890
Hello mellow yellow! <-- scanned string
"llo" <--- search string

Found match at index 3
Found match at index 9
Found match at index 16
```

The program in Listing 7.8 declares its variables on lines 4–8. The program uses two DO-WHILE loops to ensure that you do not enter empty strings. Line 14 assigns an empty string to AString to prepare for the DO-WHILE loop that begins on line 15. This loop iterates as long as AString contains an empty string. The INPUT statement inside the DO-WHILE loop prompts you to enter the scanned string and saves it in AString. The program performs a similar set of tasks to obtain the search string on lines 19–22.

The PRINT statements on lines 24 and 25 display the character ruler. On line 27 the program searches for the first occurrence of FindString in AString. The statement calls INSTR and assigns the function result to I. On line 29 the

program initializes the number of occurrences of the search string to 0. The program uses the variable Count to keep track of this information. The PRINT statements on lines 30 and 31 display the scanned and search strings.

 The DO-WHILE loop that begins on line 33 iterates as long as I stores a positive number. Such a number indicates that the last call to INSTR found a match to the search string in the scanned string. If the scanned string does not contain the search string, the condition of the DO-WHILE loop is initially false. Consequently, the program does not execute the statements inside the loop.

The first statement in the DO-WHILE loop increments the contents of Count. The second statement, on line 35, displays the variable of I. The last statement in the loop calls INSTR to search for the next occurrence of FindString in AString. Notice that this function call uses the offset character of I + 1, to ensure that the function does not return the index of the last match (which causes the loop to iterate indefinitely!).

The IF statement on line 39 displays a no-match message if the Count stores 0.

The *DO-UNTIL* Loop

The DO-UNTIL loop is the other conditional loop in QBasic. This loop iterates until a condition is true.

The DO-UNTIL Loop

The DO-UNTIL loop has two general forms:

```
DO
     sequence of statements
LOOP UNTIL condition


DO UNTIL condition
     sequence of statements
LOOP
```

The first form of the DO-UNTIL loop executes the sequence of statements and then examines the loop condition. If the condition is false, the loop iterates again. Because the loop condition appears after the sequence of statements, the DO-UNTIL loop executes its statements at least once. Figure 7.4 shows a sample DO-UNTIL loop and an equivalent loop made up of IF and GOTO statements.

The second form of the DO-UNTIL loop tests the condition before executing the statements inside the loop. Consequently, the loop might not execute its statements at all if the tested condition is initially true.

Examples:

```
I = 1
DO
    PRINT I * I
    I = I + 2
LOOP UNTIL I > 12


DO
    INPUT "More calculations? (Y/N) ", Answer
    Answer = UCASE$(LEFT$(Answer, 1))
LOOP UNTIL Answer = "Y" OR Answer = "N"


I = 1
DO LOOP UNTIL I > 12
    PRINT I * I
    I = I + 2
LOOP
```

DO include statements inside the DO-UNTIL to update the tested condition of the loop. Otherwise, the loop iterates indefinitely!

DON'T forget to place statements before the DO-UNTIL loop that assist in setting up the loop. You might need to use one or more statements after the loop to process any pending values.

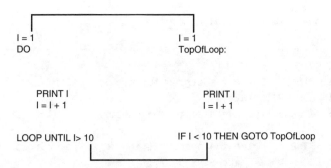

```
I = 1                           I = 1
DO                              TopOfLoop:


    PRINT I                         PRINT I
    I = I + 1                       I = I + 1


LOOP UNTIL I> 10            IF I < 10 THEN GOTO TopOfLoop
```

Figure 7.4. A sample DO-UNTIL loop and an equivalent loop made up of IF and GOTO statements.

Take a look at an example. Listing 7.9, UNTIL1.BAS, uses a `DO-UNTIL` loop to search for multiple occurrences of a search string in a scanned string. I created this program by modifying the WHILE1.BAS (in Listing 7.8) and replacing the `DO-WHILE` loops with `DO-UNTIL` loops. The program prompts you to enter the scanned string and the search string. The program displays a character ruler, the input strings, and the indices of the characters where the search string occurs. If the program is unable to find any match, it displays a message to that effect.

Listing 7.9. UNTIL1.BAS, which uses a DO-UNTIL loop to search for the multiple occurrences of a search string in a scanned string.

```
 1: REM Program that tests the DO-UNTIL loop
 2: REM
 3: ' declare the program variables
 4: DIM AString AS STRING
 5: DIM SearchString AS STRING
 6: DIM Count AS INTEGER
 7: DIM I AS INTEGER
 8: DIM Q AS STRING
 9:
10: CLS
11: ' assign the double-quote character to variable Q
12: Q = CHR$(34)
13: ' prompt for a non-empty scanned string
```

continues

Listing 7.9. continued

```
14: DO
15:   INPUT "Enter the string to scan : ", AString
16: LOOP UNTIL AString <> ""
17: ' prompt for a non-empty search string
18: DO
19:   INPUT "Enter the search string : ", SearchString
20: LOOP UNTIL SearchString <> ""
21: PRINT
22: PRINT "            1         2         3         4         5"
23: PRINT "12345678901234567890123456789012345678901234567890"
24: ' initialize the number of matches
25: Count = 0
26: PRINT AString; " <-- scanned string"
27: PRINT Q; SearchString; Q; " <--- search string"
28: PRINT
29: ' search from the beginning of string AString
30: I = 0
31: DO
32:   I = INSTR(I + 1, AString, SearchString)
33:   IF I > 0 THEN
34:     Count = Count + 1
35:     PRINT "Found match at index"; I
36:   END IF
37: LOOP UNTIL I = 0
38: ' no matches found?
39: IF Count = 0 THEN PRINT "No matching search string was found"
40: END
```

Here is a sample output for the program in Listing 7.9:

```
Enter the string to scan : Hello mellow yellow!
Enter the search string : llo

            1         2         3         4         5
12345678901234567890123456789012345678901234567890
Hello mellow yellow! <-- scanned string
"llo" <--- search string
```

```
Found match at index 3
Found match at index 9
Found match at index 16
```

Because the program in Listing 7.9 is similar to the program in Listing 7.8, let me focus on the main differences between the two listings, the DO-UNTIL loops. Line 14 contains the beginning of the DO-UNTIL loop used to prompt you for a nonempty scanned string. Notice there is no statement before the loop to assign an empty string to AString. Using a DO-UNTIL loop proves to be better than the DO-WHILE loop in this respect. The same comments are true for the second DO-UNTIL loop that starts on line 18.

The program uses a third DO-UNTIL loop to locate the occurrences of the search string in the scanned string. Line 30 prepares for the DO-UNTIL loop by assigning 0 to I (which is used in the loop to store the result of INSTR.) The DO-UNTIL loop starts on line 31. The first statement inside the loop calls INSTR and supplies it three arguments, the first being the value I + 1. The first time the loop iterates, the value of I + 1 is 1, the index of the first character in AString. In the other iterations the value of I + 1 gives a character offset that enables INSTR to skip over the previous occurrences it found. Line 33 contains an IF statement that detects a positive value in I. If this condition is true, the THEN clause statement increments Count and displays the value in I. The DO-UNTIL loop ends on line 37 where the loop examines the condition I = 0. When this condition is true, the loop stops iterating.

Exiting Loops

QBasic offers statements that enable you to exit from the FOR-NEXT, DO-WHILE, DO-UNTIL, and DO-LOOP (which I present in the next section) loops. The EXIT FOR statement enables you to exit the current FOR-NEXT loop. The EXIT DO statement enables you to exit DO-WHILE, DO-UNTIL, and DO-LOOP loops.

Let me present an example that uses the EXIT FOR statement. Listing 7.10, FOR6.BAS, uses the EXIT FOR statement to end the search for the roots of a quadratic equation. I created FOR6.BAS from FOR4.BAS. When you ran the latter program, you might recall that there was a little waiting period between displaying the second (and last) root and the end of the program. This period represents wasted computing efforts because the program has already located the approximate values for the two roots. FOR6.BAS employs a smarter scheme. It counts the number of roots discovered. When the number reaches 2, it exits the root-seeking FOR-NEXT loop.

Listing 7.10. FOR6.BAS, which uses the EXIT FOR statement to end the search for the roots of a quadratic equation.

```
 1: REM Program that uses the FOR loop and EXIT FOR
 2: REM to get the approximate roots of
 3: REM a quadratic equation
 4: CONST FIRST# = 10
 5: CONST LAST# = -10
 6: CONST INCREM# = -.005
 7: CONST A# = -2
 8: CONST B# = 1
 9: CONST C# = 10
10: ' declare the variables
11: DIM X AS DOUBLE
12: DIM Y1 AS DOUBLE
13: DIM Y2 AS DOUBLE
14: DIM Xroot AS DOUBLE
15: DIM Yroot AS DOUBLE
16: DIM RootCount AS INTEGER
17: CLS
18: PRINT "Wait please..."
19: PRINT
20: ' initialize the number of roots found
21: RootCount = 0
22: X = FIRST
23: Y1 = A * X * X + B * X + C
24: FOR X = FIRST + INCREM TO LAST STEP INCREM
25:    Y2 = A * X * X + B * X + C
26:    IF Y2 * Y1 < 0 THEN
27:      Xroot = X - INCREM / 2
28:      Yroot = A * Xroot * Xroot + B * Xroot + C
29:      PRINT "Root near X = "; Xroot;
30:      PRINT " F(X) = "; Yroot
31:      RootCount = RootCount + 1
32:      IF RootCount >= 2 THEN EXIT FOR
33:    END IF
```

```
34:    ' can also place the EXIT FOR here
35:    ' IF RootCount >= 2 THEN EXIT FOR
36:    Y1 = Y2
37: NEXT X
38: PRINT
39: PRINT "End of program"
40: END
```

Here is a sample output for the program in Listing 7.10:

```
Wait please...

Root near X =  2.497500167693943  F(X) =  2.248599243139812D-02
Root near X = -2.002499731723219  F(X) = -2.251008282634854D-02

End of program
```

Because FOR6.BAS is very similar to FOR4.BAS, let me focus on the differences. FOR6.BAS uses the variable RootCount to count the number of roots found. Line 21 initializes RootCount. Line 32, located inside the IF statement, increments RootCount. The next statement contains an IF statement that executes the EXIT FOR statement when the value in RootCount is 2 or more. As the program listing shows, I also can place the loop-exiting IF statement after line 33.

The Open *DO-LOOP*

In principle, the open DO-LOOP iterates indefinitely. This kind of iteration finds few uses in real applications. Therefore, open loops in various programming languages, including QBasic, provide an escape mechanism. QBasic uses the EXIT DO statement to implement this escape mechanism.

The DO-LOOP Loop

The general syntax for the DO-LOOP with an EXIT DO statement is

```
DO
        [sequence #1 of statements]
        IF condition THEN
                [sequence #2 of statements]
```

221

```
            EXIT DO
        END IF
        [sequence #3 of statements]
    LOOP
```

The open loop executes the first sequence of statements and then the IF statement. When the tested condition is true, the IF statement executes the statements in the THEN clause. This clause might contain statements that perform clean-up operations (such as updating variables) before executing the EXIT DO statement. If the tested condition in the IF statement is false, the open loop executes another set of statements to end the iteration. The host program then starts another iteration, and so on. Figure 7.5 shows a sample DO-LOOP and an equivalent loop constructed with GOTO statements.

Example:

```
I = 1
DO
    PRINT I
    IF I > 10 THEN EXIT DO
    I = I + 1
LOOP
```

```
    I = 1                           I = 1

    DO                              TopOfLoop:


        PRINT I                     PRINT I
        IF I > 10 THEN EXIT DO      IF I > 10 THEN GOTO EndDo
        I = I + 1                   I = I + 1


    LOOP                            GOTO TopOfLoop
                                    EndDo:
```

Figure 7.5. A sample DO-LOOP.

DO use an `IF` statement with an `EXIT DO` statement to stop the iteration of an open loop.

DON'T forget to include statements that update the condition tested by the loop-escaping `IF` statement.

Here's an example of an open loop I hope you find interesting. Listing 7.11, SHELL.BAS, implements a simple, yet versatile, QBasic DOS shell. The program prompts you to enter a DOS command. You can type in internal DOS commands, such as DIR, or external DOS commands, such as XCOPY. You even can run other programs, such as invoking another copy of QBasic (memory permitting). To exit the program, type in EXIT (in either uppercase or lowercase).

 Listing 7.11. SHELL.BAS, which implements a simple, yet functional, QBasic DOS shell.

```
 1: REM Program that uses an open DO-LOOP
 2: REM
 3: ' declare program variables
 4: DIM DOScommand AS STRING
 5: CLS
 6: DO
 7:  PRINT "Type EXIT to exit the shell"
 8:  LINE INPUT "QBasic> "; DOScommand
 9:  IF UCASE$(DOScommand) = "EXIT" THEN EXIT DO
10:  ' invoke the DOS shell
11:  IF DOScommand <> "" THEN
12:    SHELL (DOScommand)
13:  ELSE
14:    CLS
15:  END IF
16: LOOP
17:
18: PRINT "Out of QBasic DOS shell"
19: END
```

Here is a sample output for the program in Listing 7.11:

```
Type EXIT to exit the shell
QBasic> dir goto?.bas

 Volume in drive C is HD 100Meg
 Volume Serial Number is 16C8-84EC
 Directory of C:\BASIC

GOTO1     BAS         605 12-30-92    1:32p
GOTO2     BAS         323 12-26-92    1:27a
GOTO3     BAS         631 12-30-92    2:01p
          3 file(s)         1559 bytes
                        24424448 bytes free
Type EXIT to exit the shell
QBasic> exit
Out of QBasic DOS shell
```

The program in Listing 7.11 declares the variable DOScommand on line 4. The open loop starts on line 6. The first statement inside the loop, located on line 7, is a PRINT statement that reminds you to type in EXIT to exit from the shell. Line 8 contains a special input statement, LINE INPUT, that enables you to enter a line of characters, including leading spaces and commas (more about LINE INPUT on Day 8, "Keyboard and Program Input"). The LINE INPUT statement stores your input in DOScommand. Line 9 contains an IF statement that determines whether an uppercase version of your input is EXIT. If this condition is true, the IF statement executes the EXIT DO statement in the THEN clause. If the tested condition is false, the program executes the IF statement (on line 11) that determines whether the DOS command does not contain an empty string. If this condition is true, the program executes the command in SHELL statement in the THEN clause. The SHELL command invokes a copy of DOS and passes the DOS command stored in DOScommand. If the condition on line 11 is false, the program executes the CLS statement in the ELSE clause. As soon as you exit the open loop, the program displays a message using the PRINT statement on line 18. The message confirms that you are out of the QBasic shell.

Summary

This chapter presented the various types of QBasic loops, including fixed, conditional, and open loops. You learned about the following topics:

- ☐ The GOTO statement enables program execution to jump from one location to another. The targeted location is marked by program labels. Use the GOTO statement sparingly, if at all.

- ☐ Creating loops with the GOTO statement also includes using labels and IF statements. These three components enable you to simulate any type of loop.

- ☐ The FOR-NEXT loop is the QBasic fixed iteration loop. The loop uses a control variable and assigns it a range of values and an optional increment (the default is 1) value. FOR-NEXT loops can be either upward-counting or downward-counting. An upward-counting loop increases the value of its control variable in each iteration. By contrast, a downward-counting loop decreases the value of its control variable in each iteration. QBasic restricts the loop-control variables to numeric types. You cannot use strings.

- ☐ Not only does QBasic enable you to use nested FOR-NEXT loops, you can use a special syntax to consolidate the loop-control variables in a single NEXT clause. The nested loops must not overlap.

- ☐ The conditional DO-WHILE loop iterates as long as a tested condition is true. The tested condition appears before the statements inside the loop. Consequently, if the tested condition is initially false, the DO-WHILE loop never executes its statements.

- ☐ The conditional DO-UNTIL loop iterates until a condition is true. The tested condition appears after the statements inside the loop. Consequently, the DO-UNTIL loop executes its statements at least once.

- ☐ If you need to exit a loop, you can use the EXIT FOR statement to exit a FOR-NEXT loop and the EXIT-DO statement to exit the other types of loops. The EXIT statements exit the current loop.

- ☐ The open DO-LOOP is essentially an endless loop. However, practical applications employ IF statements with EXIT DO statements to exit the open loop.

7

Q&A

Q. Can I use a DO-WHILE loop to do the same thing as a FOR-NEXT loop?

A. Yes. Here is a simple example that explains how a DO-WHILE loop can simulate a FOR-NEXT loop:

```
                              I = 1
FOR I = 1 TO 10 STEP 2        DO WHILE I <= 10
    PRINT I                       PRINT I
                                  I = I + 2
NEXT I                        LOOP
```

The DO-WHILE loop needs a leading statement that initializes the loop-control variable. Also, notice the DO-WHILE loop uses a statement inside it to alter the value of the loop-control variable.

Q. Can I use a DO-WHILE loop to do the same thing as a DO-UNTIL loop?

A. Here is a simple example that explains how a DO-WHILE loop can simulate a DO-UNTIL loop:

```
I = 1                         I = 1
DO                            DO WHILE I <= 10
    PRINT I                       PRINT I
    I = I + 2                     I = I + 2
LOOP UNTIL I > 10             LOOP
```

The DO-WHILE loop uses a condition that is the reverse of the condition in the DO-UNTIL loop.

Q. Can the DO-LOOP emulate the other QBasic loops?

A. The DO-LOOP is able to emulate the other QBasic loops by placing the loop-escaping IF statement near the DO or LOOP clause. Here is how the DO-LOOP emulates a sample FOR-NEXT loop:

```
                              I = 1
FOR I = 1 TO 10 STEP 2        DO
                                  IF I > 10 THEN EXIT DO
    PRINT I                       PRINT I
                                  I = I + 2
NEXT I                        LOOP
```

The loop-escaping IF statement appears after the DO clause and tests whether the loop-control variable, I, is greater than the upper limit of the FOR-NEXT loop. Also notice that the DO-LOOP uses a leading statement that initializes the loop-control variable.

Here is a simple example of how the DO-LOOP can emulate a DO-WHILE loop:

```
I = 1                           I = 1
DO WHILE I <= 10                DO
                                    IF I > 10 THEN EXIT DO
    PRINT I                         PRINT I
    I = I + 2                       I = I + 2
LOOP                            LOOP
```

Notice the DO-LOOP uses a loop-escaping IF statement right after the DO clause. The condition tested by the IF statement is the logical reverse of the DO-WHILE loop condition.

Here is a simple example of how the DO-LOOP can emulate a DO-UNTIL loop:

```
I = 1                           I = 1
DO                              DO
    PRINT I                         PRINT I
    I = I + 2                       I = I + 2
                                    IF I > 10 THEN EXIT DO
LOOP UNTIL I > 10               LOOP
```

The DO-LOOP uses a loop-escaping IF statement right before the LOOP clause. The IF statement tests the same condition as the DO-UNTIL loop.

Q. In nested FOR-NEXT loops, can I use the loop-control variable of the outer loop as part of the range of values for the inner loop?

A. Yes. QBasic does not object to such use. Here is a simple example:

```
FOR I = 1 TO 100 STEP 5
    FOR J = I TO 100
        PRINT I * J
    NEXT J
NEXT I
```

Q. Can I nest any combination of loops?

A. Yes. You can nest any combination of loops in a QBasic program.

Q. How can I translate a DO-WHILE loop into a DO-UNTIL loop (where both loops test the looping condition before executing their statements)?

A. To translate the DO-WHILE loop into the DO-UNTIL loop, use the Boolean operator NOT to reverse the condition of the DO-WHILE loop, as shown in the following general form:

```
DO WHILE condition                 DO UNTIL NOT condition
    sequence of statements             sequence of statements
LOOP                               LOOP
```

Q. How can I translate a DO-WHILE loop into a DO-UNTIL loop (where both loops test the looping condition after executing their statements)?

A. To translate the DO-WHILE loop into the DO-UNTIL loop, use the Boolean operator NOT to reverse the condition of the DO-WHILE loop, as shown in the general following form:

```
DO                                 DO
    sequence of statements             sequence of statements
LOOP WHILE condition               LOOP UNTIL NOT condition
```

Workshop

The Workshop provides quiz questions to help you solidify your understanding of the material covered and exercises to provide you with experience in using what you've learned. Try to understand the quiz and exercise answers before continuing on to the next chapter. Answers are provided in Appendix B, "Answers."

Quiz

1. What is wrong with the following loop?

```
I = 1
DO WHILE I < 10
    J = I * I - 1
    K = 2 * J - I
    PRINT "I = "; I
    PRINT "J = "; J
    PRINT "K = "; K
LOOP
```

2. What is the output of the following simple program?

```
DIM I AS INTEGER
FOR I = 5 TO 9 STEP 2
    PRINT I - 2
NEXT I
END
```

3. What is the output of the following simple program?

```
DIM I AS INTEGER
FOR I = 5 TO 9 STEP 0
    PRINT I - 2
NEXT I
END
```

4. What is wrong with the following program?

```
FOR I = 1 TO 10
    FOR I = 8 TO 12
        PRINT I
    NEXT I
NEXT I
```

5. Where is the error in the following program?

```
FOR I = 1 TO 10
    FOR J = I TO 12
        PRINT I * J
    NEXT I
NEXT J
```

6. What is wrong with the following program?

```
FOR I = 1 TO 10
    FOR J = I TO 12
        PRINT I * J
NEXT
```

7. Where is the error in the following program?

```
I = 1
DO WHILE 1 > 0
    PRINT I
    I = I + 1
LOOP
```

8. What is wrong with the following program?

```
I = INSTR(MainString, FindString)
DO WHILE I > 0
    PRINT "Found match at character "; I
    I = INSTR(MainString, FindString)
LOOP
```

9. The factorial of a number is the product of the sequence of integers from 1 to that number. The following general equation defines the factorial (which uses the symbol !):

```
n! = 1 * 2 * 3 * ... * n
```

Here is a QBasic program that calculates the factorial of a number. The problem is that for whatever positive value you enter, the program displays 0 for the factorial. Where is the error in the program?

```
DIM I AS INTEGER
DIM N AS INTEGER
DIM Factorial AS DOUBLE
CLS
INPUT "Enter positive integer "; N
FOR I = 1 TO N
    Factorial = Factorial * I
NEXT I
PRINT N; "! = "; Factorial
END
```

Exercises

1. Alter GOTO1.BAS in Listing 7.1 such that you replace the first END statement with a GOTO statement that jumps to the second END statement on line 29. Call the new program GOTO3.BAS.

2. Write a program (call it FOR7.BAS) that uses a FOR-NEXT loop to obtain and display the sum of odd integers in the range of 11 to 121.

3. Write a program (call it WHILE2.BAS) that uses a DO-WHILE loop to obtain and display the sum of the squared odd integers in the range of 11 to 121.

4. Write a program (call it UNTIL2.BAS) that uses a DO-UNTIL loop to obtain and display the sum of the squared odd integers in the range of 11 to 121.

7

Week 1 in Review

This special section presents a program that uses what you have learned so far. The program manages a to-do list and supports the following operations:

1. Add a new task

2. Delete the last task

3. Quit

To print the to-do list, you need to turn on your printer and press the PrtScr key (Print Screen key on some keyboards).

This list of features should indicate that this first version is rather primitive and contains a lot of rough edges. In the reviews of the second and third weeks, I present more polished versions of this program. Each version adds a few more features and also improves on the programming.

> **Type**
>
> Listing 1. **TODO1.BAS, a simple version of a program that manages a to-do list.**

```
1: REM Program which manages a To-Do list
2: REM
3: REM  Version 1.0           1/20/93
4: REM
5: ' declare constants
6: CONST MARK = "◊ "
7: CONST MENU = "A)dd to do, D)elete last to do, Q)uit"
8: CONST MSG = "Print screen by pressing the PrtScr key"
9: CONST MAX.TODO = 15
```

continues

Listing 1. continued

```
10: CONST MAX.SPACES = MAX.TODO * 80
11: ' declare variables
12: DIM Choice AS STRING
13: DIM DateStr AS STRING
14: DIM ToDo AS STRING
15: DIM NL AS STRING
16: DIM S AS STRING
17: DIM I AS INTEGER
18: DIM ToDoCount AS INTEGER
19:
20: S = ""
21: ToDoCount = 0
22: ' new line
23: NL = CHR$(10)
24: DO
25:   CLS
26:   PRINT S; SPACE$(MAX.SPACES - LEN(S))
27:   PRINT MENU
28:   PRINT MSG
29:   INPUT ">", Choice
30:   Choice = UCASE$(LEFT$(Choice, 1))
31:   SELECT CASE Choice
32:     CASE "A"
33:       IF ToDoCount < MAX.TODO THEN
34:         PRINT
35:         DO
36:           INPUT "Enter date : ", DateStr
37:         LOOP UNTIL DateStr <> ""
38:         DO
39:           INPUT "Enter task : ", ToDo
40:         LOOP UNTIL ToDo <> ""
41:         S = S + MARK + DateStr
42:         S = S + SPACE$(12 - LEN(DateStr)) + ToDo + NL
43:         ToDoCount = ToDoCount + 1
44:       END IF
45:
46:     CASE "D" ' delete the last entry
47:       IF ToDoCount > 0 THEN
48:         ' find the last task marker
```

```
49:          I = LEN(S) - 1
50:          DO WHILE I > 0 AND MID$(S, I, 2) <> MARK
51:            I = I - 1
52:          LOOP
53:          ' extract the other tasks
54:          S = LEFT$(S, I - 1)
55:          ToDoCount = ToDoCount - 1
56:        END IF
57:      END SELECT
58: LOOP UNTIL Choice = "Q"
59: END
```

Here is some sample output for the program in Listing 1:

```
◊ 01/18/93      Deadline for QBasic book
◊ 02/02/93      Meeting with D. Jenkins in NY City
◊ 03/04/93      Nancy's birthday
◊ 05/03/93      QBasic conference in London
◊ 06/15/93      Regional sales meeting in Chicago
◊ 11/15/93      Comdex Fall 93 in Las Vegas
◊ 12/01/93      QBasic conference in Tokyo
```

```
A)dd to do, D)elete last to do, Q)uit
Print screen by pressing the PrtScr key
>q
```

The program in Listing 1 declares its constants on lines 6–10. The program declares its variable on lines 12–18. The program stores the tasks on separate lines using the string variable S. The statement on line 20 initializes S to an empty string. The statement on line 21 initializes the task counter, ToDoCount. The statement on line 23 assigns the newline character to the variable NL.

The program uses the DO-UNTIL loop on lines 24–58 to perform the tasks offered by the online menu. The program systematically clears the screen using the CLS statement on line 25. The PRINT statement on line 26 displays the string S, with its current tasks. To ensure that the menu appears at the same location in every loop iteration, the PRINT statement calls function SPACE$ to append MAX.SPACES - LEN(S) spaces. These spaces move the cursor to the sought screen row. The PRINT statements on lines 27 and 28 display the one-line menu and the instruction to print, respectively. The INPUT statement on line 29 displays a DOS-like prompt and awaits your input. The statement stores your input in the variable Choice. The statement on line 30 extracts the uppercase of the first character in Choice.

To execute the specific command you requested, the program uses the SELECT-CASE statement on lines 31–57. There are two CASE clauses in the SELECT-CASE statement. These clauses handle the first two menu options.

The first CASE clause on line 32 handles adding a new task. The program ensures that you have not exceeded the maximum number of tasks allowed. If this condition is true, the program uses the INPUT statements on lines 36 and 39 to prompt you for the date and task. The program stores the date and task in the variables DateStr and ToDo. Notice that both INPUT statements are inside DO-UNTIL loops. These loops ensure that you do not enter empty strings. The statements on lines 41 and 42 append the constant MARK, the variable DateStr, a few spaces, the variable ToDo, and the variable NL to the current string in S. The variable NL enables the string to display line breaks. The statement on line 43 increments the value in the variable ToDoCount.

The second CASE clause (on line 46) handles deleting the last task. The program determines whether there are any tasks. If this condition is true, the program locates the last occurrence of the constant MARK. This location marks the beginning of the last task. Once located, using the variable I, the program extracts the first I - 1 characters in S. The statement on line 55 decrements the number of tasks stored in ToDoCount.

The UNTIL clause of the loop exits the loop when the variable Choice stores the letter Q.

In the next week in review I present a new version that uses the QBasic statements I present on Days 8–14.

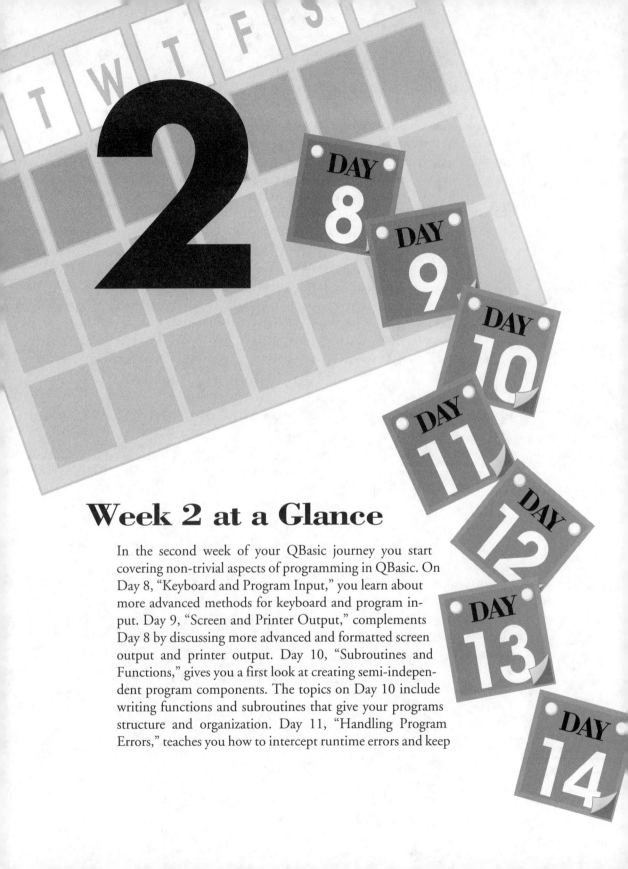

Week 2 at a Glance

In the second week of your QBasic journey you start covering non-trivial aspects of programming in QBasic. On Day 8, "Keyboard and Program Input," you learn about more advanced methods for keyboard and program input. Day 9, "Screen and Printer Output," complements Day 8 by discussing more advanced and formatted screen output and printer output. Day 10, "Subroutines and Functions," gives you a first look at creating semi-independent program components. The topics on Day 10 include writing functions and subroutines that give your programs structure and organization. Day 11, "Handling Program Errors," teaches you how to intercept runtime errors and keep your programs running. Days 12, "Simple Arrays," and 13, "Multidimensional Arrays," present the different types of arrays, which are special variables that store multiple values, adding flexibility to managing data. For the mathematically inclined readers, Day 14, "Math Functions," presents the math functions supported by QBasic. These functions include common, logarithmic, and trigonometric functions.

DAY

8

Keyboard and Program Input

QBasic supports four sources of input. They are the keyboard, data files, serial communication ports, and program-coded data. This chapter looks at the first and last methods of input. On Days 18, "Text File Input/Output," and 19, "Random-Access and Binary File Input/Output," I discuss data input from files. The subject of input from communication ports is beyond the scope of this book. Today you will learn about the following topics:

- ☐ Reading a string with the LINE INPUT statement

- ☐ Reading characters with the INPUT$ function

- ☐ Implementing simple menu systems with the INPUT$ function

- ☐ Reading characters with the INKEY$ function

- ☐ Reading special keys with the INKEY$ function

- ☐ Reading internal program data using the READ statement

The *LINE INPUT* Statement

On Day 2, "The QBasic Environment," I introduced you to the INPUT statement, which enables you to type in strings and numbers. With the INPUT statement, you can enter multiple data items. You must separate these items with commas. What happens if a comma is part of the text you want to enter, such as Ann Arbor, MI 48104? Because the INPUT statement is not a mind reader, it assumes that you entered two separate strings, "Ann Arbor" and " MI 48104". There are two solutions for this problem. The first solution requires you to enclose the string in a pair of double-quotes. The second solution for this problem is the LINE INPUT statement.

The LINE INPUT Statement

The general syntax for the LINE INPUT statement is

```
LINE INPUT [;] ["prompt";] stringVariable
```

The *prompt* string is the input prompt. The LINE INPUT stores the input in the string variable *stringVariable*. Figure 8.1 shows the LINE INPUT statement.

Examples:

```
LINE INPUT "Enter city, state, and zip code "; CSZ$
LINE INPUT "Enter a string : "; S$
LINE INPUT ; A$
```

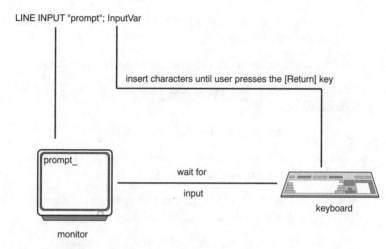

Figure 8.1. The LINE INPUT statement.

Take a look at a program that illustrates using the LINE INPUT statement and extracting space-delimited words from a string. Listing 8.1, LINEINP1.BAS, performs these tasks. The program prompts you to enter a string. Then the program processes your input to extract and display the individual words.

The basic method for extracting space-delimited words is to use the spaces right before and right after a word as markers. Using these two markers, a program easily can extract an enclosed word using the MID$ function. A programming trick that makes the implementation of this method easier ensures that the first and last characters of the scanned string are spaces. This trick enables the first and last words in the scanned string to be treated just like any other internal words. Consequently, you only have to deal with one kind of word (each word is enclosed in spaces) instead of three kinds of words (the leading, internal, and trailing words).

8

Here is the pseudocode for this program:

1. Clear the screen.

2. Input a string and save it in S.

3. Remove the leading and trailing spaces in S.

4. Add a single leading and trailing space (to make scanning the characters in the string easier.)

5. Initialize the counter for the extracted words, Count, to 0.

6. Assign the index of the first space character, 1, to the first indexing variable, I1.

7. Copy the value of I1 into the second indexing variable, I2.

8. Repeat the following steps as long as I2 is greater than 0 and less than the length of the string in variable S.

   8.1.   Find the index of the space character that comes *immediately after* a word. Save that index in variable I2.

   8.2.   Increment the words counter variable Count.

   8.3.   Display partial output to include the value of the variable Count.

   8.4.   Display the substring that starts at character index I1 + 1 and is I2 - I1 - 1 characters long.

   8.5.   Increment the value in variable I2 as long as the character at index I2 is a space. When this repetitive task is done, the variable I2 stores the index of the first nonspace character beyond the possible sequence of spaces.

   8.6.   Assign I2 - 1 to variable I1. The variable I1 now contains the index of the space character that comes *immediately before* the next word.

9. End the program.

Listing 8.1. LINEINP1.BAS, which uses the LINE INPUT statement and extracts the space-delimited words in a string.

```
1: REM Program tests the LINE INPUT statement
2: REM
3: ' declare the variables
4: DIM S AS STRING
5: DIM aWord AS STRING
6: DIM I1 AS INTEGER
7: DIM I2 AS INTEGER
8: DIM Count AS INTEGER
9:
10: CLS
11: LINE INPUT "Enter a string : "; S
12: PRINT
13: ' remove leading and trailing spaces
14: S = RTRIM$(LTRIM$(S))
15: ' add a single space before and after the string S
16: S = " " + S + " "
17: Count = 0
18: ' assign the index of the first space character to variable I1
19: I1 = 1
20: I2 = 1
21: DO WHILE I2 > 0 AND I2 < LEN(S)
22:     ' find the next space
23:     I2 = INSTR(I1 + 1, S, " ")
24:     ' increment words counter
25:     Count = Count + 1
26:     ' display the currently extracted word
27:     PRINT "Word # "; Count; " is ";
28:     PRINT MID$(S, I1 + 1, I2 - I1 - 1)
29:     ' move over any consecutive multiple spaces
30:     DO WHILE MID$(S, I2, 1) = " "
31:         I2 = I2 + 1
32:     LOOP
33:     ' set I1 as the index of the space right before a word
34:     I1 = I2 - 1
35: LOOP
36: END
```

Here is some sample output for the program in Listing 8.1:

```
Enter a string :   One   Two      Three    Four

Word #  1   is One
Word #  2   is Two
Word #  3   is Three
Word #  4   is Four
```

The program in Listing 8.1 declares its variables on lines 4–8. The LINE INPUT statement on line 11 prompts you to enter a string and stores it in the variable S. The statement on line 14 uses the RTRIM$ and LTRIM$ functions to remove all leading and trailing spaces. The assignment statement on line 16 inserts a space before and after the current contents of S. The statement stores the resulting string back in S. Now S contains a string that begins and ends with space characters. On line 17, the program initializes the words counter variable Count. The assignment statements on lines 19 and 20 assign 1, the index of the first space in S, to the character-indexing variables I1 and I2.

The word-extracting DO-WHILE loop starts on line 21. The condition tested iterates the loop as long as the variable I2 contains a positive value that is less than the number of characters in S. Line 23, which contains the first statement inside the loop, searches for the first space character after character I1. The statement assigns the result of the INSTR function call to variable I2. Notice that the program does not check whether or not variable I2 stores 0. Why? By inserting spaces at the first and last characters of the scanned string, the program ensures that variable I2 is never assigned 0.

Line 25 increments the words counter variable Count. The PRINT statements on lines 27 and 28 display the extracted word. The statements display this word by calling the MID$ function. The extracted word is located at index I1 + 1 of S, and is I2 - I1 - 1 characters long.

The current value in I2 points to the space immediately after the currently extracted words. What if there are multiple spaces between the currently extracted word and the next one? The program handles this possible case by using another DO-WHILE loop. This loop iterates as long as the character at index I2 is a space. The single statement in this loop increments the value in I2. This statement enables the program to increase the value in I2 until it points to the first character of the next word. If the value in I2 exceeds the length of the scanned string, the MID$ function returns an empty string. This function value also stops the iteration, even though the value in variable I2 does not point to the first character in the next word.

The assignment statement on line 34 assigns the value of I2 - 1 to variable I1. This value either points to the first character in the next word or the trailing space in the scanned string. The outer DO-WHILE loop ends on line 35.

The *INPUT$* Function

The INPUT$ function reads one or more characters from the keyboard. This function is suitable for the quick input of a few characters. You don't need to press the Return key because the function instantly accepts every character you type. Therefore, use the INPUT$ function carefully.

Syntax

The INPUT$ Function

The general syntax for the INPUT$ function is

```
INPUT$(count)
```

The parameter *count* specifies the number of characters to read from the keyboard. The typical value for this parameter is 1. You don't need to press the Return key to end your input. The INPUT$ function does not automatically display your input—you need to use PRINT statements to echo the input on the screen. Figure 8.2 shows how the INPUT$(1) function call works.

Example:

```
DO
      PRINT "More calculations? (Y/N) ";
      aChar = INPUT$(1)
      PRINT aChar
      aChar = UCASE$(aChar)
LOOP UNTIL aChar = "Y" OR aChar = "N"
```

8

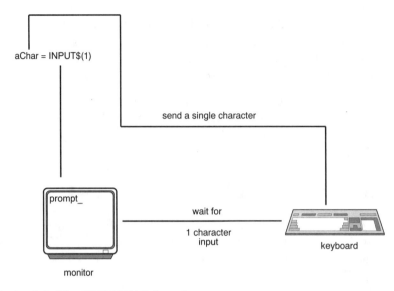

Figure 8.2. The INPUT$(1) function.

Here is an example that shows the typical use of the INPUT$ function. Listing 8.2, INPUT$1.BAS, uses the INPUT$ function for a quick Yes/No answer. The program prompts you for a string. Then the program displays your input and its uppercase version. Next, the program prompts you for a Y/N answer (the single-character response for a Yes/No answer) regarding whether you want to enter another string. The highlight of the program is the Yes/No prompt, which uses the INPUT$ function.

 Listing 8.2. INPUT$1.BAS, which uses the INPUT$ function for a quick Yes/No answer.

```
 1: REM Program that tests the INPUT$ function
 2: REM
 3: ' declare variables
 4: DIM AString AS STRING
 5: DIM K AS STRING
 6: DIM Q AS STRING
 7:
 8: CLS
 9: Q = CHR$(34)
10: DO
```

```
11:   LINE INPUT "Enter a string : "; AString
12:   PRINT
13:   PRINT "The uppercase of string "; Q; AString; Q;
14:   PRINT " is "; Q; UCASE$(AString); Q
15:   ' prompt for another input
16:   DO
17:     PRINT
18:     PRINT "Input another string? (Y/N) ";
19:     ' wait for keyboard input
20:     K = INPUT$(1)
21:     PRINT K
22:     K = UCASE$(K)
23:     PRINT
24:   LOOP UNTIL K = "Y" OR K = "N"
25: LOOP UNTIL K = "N"
26: END
```

Here is some sample output for the program in Listing 8.2:

```
Enter a string : QBasic

The uppercase of string "QBasic" is "QBASIC"

Input another string? (Y/N) j


Input another string? (Y/N) y

Enter a string : QuickBasic

The uppercase of string "QuickBasic" is "QUICKBASIC"

Input another string? (Y/N) n
```

The program in Listing 8.2 declares its variables on lines 4–6. The program uses an outer DO-UNTIL loop that starts on line 10 and ends on line 25. The first statement in the outer loop, on line 11, uses a LINE INPUT statement to prompt you for a string. The statement stores your input in the variable AString. The PRINT statements on lines 13 and 14 display your input and its uppercase version.

On lines 16–24 the program uses an inner DO-UNTIL loop to obtain either the character Y or N. The PRINT statement on line 18 displays the prompting message. Line 20 contains the assignment statement, which calls the INPUT$ function to read one character and stores the input in variable K. The PRINT statement on line 21 echoes the input to the screen. The assignment statement on line 22 converts the character in K to uppercase. The LOOP UNTIL clause on line 25 shows that the inner DO-UNTIL loop iterates until the character in variable K is either Y or N.

The LOOP UNTIL clause on line 24 shows that the outer DO-UNTIL loop iterates until the character in variable K is N.

Simple Menus Using *INPUT$*

Using INPUT$, you can create nested menus that support quick single-character selections. The INPUT$ function supports this quick input feature because you don't need to press the Return key to confirm your input. The biggest disadvantage with using INPUT$ is the inability to correct erroneous input. The remedy for this problem in nested menus is to provide an exit option or selection at every menu level.

The general pseudocode for creating a set of menu options and selections is to repeat the following steps until the exit choice is selected:

1. Display the menu title (usually centered).

2. Display the main choices.

3. Prompt the user to make a choice.

4. Use a SELECT-CASE statement to examine the menu choice.

Figure 8.3 shows a sample nested-menu structure. Listing 8.3, INPUT$2.BAS, uses the INPUT$ function to implement a simple nested-menu structure. The menu selections are dummies to make the program short. You may choose a menu option/selection either by number or by shortcut key (the uppercase character in the menu option/selection indicates the shortcut key). When you choose a menu selection, the program displays a message that says the feature you invoked is not yet implemented. You can press either the 4 or X keys and then press Enter, or press the Escape key to exit from menu selections or menu options.

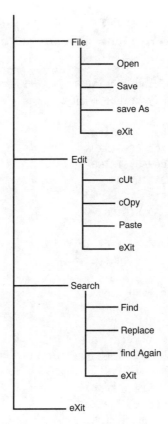

File
   Open
   Save
   save As
   eXit

Edit
   cUt
   cOpy
   Paste
   eXit

Search
   Find
   Replace
   find Again
   eXit

eXit

Figure 8.3. The sample nested menu structure.

8

DO provide a choice to exit the current option or selection in a menu system.

DON'T implement critical tasks without asking for confirmation from the enduser.

Listing 8.3. **INPUT$2.BAS, which uses the INPUT$ function to implement a simple nested menu structure.**

```
 1: REM Program uses the INPUT$ function
 2: REM to quickly select menu options
 3: REM
 4: ' declare the variables
 5: DIM MainChoice AS STRING
 6: DIM SecChoice AS STRING
 7: DIM Title AS STRING
 8: DIM C AS STRING
 9: DIM ExitStr AS STRING
10:
11: ' setup the characters in the exit string
12: ExitStr = "4X" + CHR$(27)
13:
14: ' start main menu loop
15: DO
16:    CLS
17:    Title = "M A I N    M E N U"
18:    PRINT SPACE$(40 - LEN(Title) \ 2); Title
19:    PRINT
20:    PRINT "1. File": PRINT
21:    PRINT "2. Edit ": PRINT
22:    PRINT "3. Search": PRINT
23:    PRINT "4. eXit": PRINT
24:    PRINT "Select option by number or shortcut key: ";
25:    MainChoice = INPUT$(1)
26:    IF MainChoice <> CHR$(27) THEN
27:      PRINT MainChoice
28:      MainChoice = UCASE$(MainChoice)
29:    END IF
30:
31:    SELECT CASE MainChoice
32:      ' display the selections in the File option
33:      CASE "1", "F"
34:        DO
35:          CLS
36:          Title = "F I L E    O P T I O N"
37:          PRINT SPACE$(40 - LEN(Title) \ 2); Title
38:          PRINT
```

```
39:          PRINT "1. Open": PRINT
40:          PRINT "2. Save": PRINT
41:          PRINT "3. save As": PRINT
42:          PRINT "4. eXit": PRINT
43:          PRINT
44:          PRINT "Select option by number or shortcut key: ";
45:          SecChoice = INPUT$(1)
46:          IF SecChoice <> CHR$(27) THEN
47:            PRINT SecChoice
48:            SecChoice = UCASE$(SecChoice)
49:          END IF
50:          IF INSTR("123OSA", SecChoice) > 0 THEN
51:            PRINT : PRINT : PRINT : PRINT
52:            PRINT "Feature not yet implemented!"
53:            PRINT
54:            PRINT "Press any key to continue..."
55:            C = INPUT$(1)
56:          END IF
57:        LOOP UNTIL INSTR(ExitStr, SecChoice) > 0
58:
59:        ' display the selections in the Edit option
60:        CASE "2", "E"
61:          DO
62:            CLS
63:            Title = "E D I T   O P T I O N"
64:            PRINT SPACE$(40 - LEN(Title) \ 2); Title
65:            PRINT
66:            PRINT "1. cUt": PRINT
67:            PRINT "2. cOpy": PRINT
68:            PRINT "3. Paste": PRINT
69:            PRINT "4. eXit": PRINT
70:            PRINT
71:            PRINT "Select option by number or shortcut key: ";
72:            SecChoice = INPUT$(1)
73:            IF SecChoice <> CHR$(27) THEN
74:              PRINT SecChoice
75:              SecChoice = UCASE$(SecChoice)
76:            END IF
77:            SecChoice = UCASE$(SecChoice)
78:            IF INSTR("123UOP", SecChoice) > 0 THEN
79:              PRINT : PRINT : PRINT : PRINT
```

continues

Listing 8.3. continued

```
 80:            PRINT "Feature not yet implemented!"
 81:            PRINT
 82:            PRINT "Press any key to continue..."
 83:            C = INPUT$(1)
 84:          END IF
 85:      LOOP UNTIL INSTR(ExitStr, SecChoice) > 0
 86:
 87:      ' display the selections in the Search options
 88:      CASE "3", "S"
 89:        DO
 90:          CLS
 91:          Title = "S E A R C H    O P T I O N"
 92:          PRINT SPACE$(40 - LEN(Title) \ 2); Title
 93:          PRINT
 94:          PRINT "1. Find": PRINT
 95:          PRINT "2. Replace": PRINT
 96:          PRINT "3. find Again": PRINT
 97:          PRINT "4. eXit": PRINT
 98:          PRINT
 99:          PRINT "Select option by number or shortcut key: ";
100:          SecChoice = INPUT$(1)
101:          IF SecChoice <> CHR$(27) THEN
102:            PRINT SecChoice
103:            SecChoice = UCASE$(SecChoice)
104:          END IF
105:          SecChoice = UCASE$(SecChoice)
106:          IF INSTR("123FRA", SecChoice) > 0 THEN
107:            PRINT : PRINT : PRINT : PRINT
108:            PRINT "Feature not yet implemented!"
109:            PRINT
110:            PRINT "Press any key to continue..."
111:            C = INPUT$(1)
112:          END IF
113:      LOOP UNTIL INSTR(ExitStr, SecChoice) > 0
114:
115:      CASE ELSE
116:        IF INSTR(ExitStr, MainChoice) = 0 THEN
```

```
117:          PRINT : PRINT : PRINT : PRINT
118:          PRINT "Invalid choice"
119:          PRINT
120:          PRINT "Press any key to continue..."
121:          C = INPUT$(1)
122:        END IF
123:
124:   END SELECT
125:
126: LOOP UNTIL INSTR(ExitStr, MainChoice) > 0
```

Here is some sample output for the program in Listing 8.3 (note that the screen clears after you choose a menu option/selection or press a key when prompted to do so):

```
          M A I N    M E N U

1. File

2. Edit

3. Search

4. eXit

Select option by number or shortcut key: s




          S E A R C H    O P T I O N

1. Find

2. Replace

3. find Again

4. eXit
```

8

```
Select option by number or shortcut key: f



Feature not yet implemented!

Press any key to continue...


              S E A R C H   O P T I O N

1. Find

2. Replace

3. find Again

4. eXit


Select option by number or shortcut key: x


              M A I N    M E N U

1. File

2. Edit

3. Search

4. eXit

Select option by number or shortcut key: x
```

The program in Listing 8.3 declares its variables on lines 5–9. The statement on line 12 assigns the 4, X, and escape characters to the string variable ExitStr.

The program implements the main menu using the DO-UNTIL loop that starts on line 15 and ends on line 126. The outer loop assigns the title of the main menu to the variable Title. The PRINT statement on line 18 displays the title

centered on the first line of the screen. The PRINT statements in lines 20–24 display the menu options and prompt you for input. The statement on line 25 uses the INPUT$ statement to read the single-character choice and to store it in the variable MainChoice. The IF-THEN statement on line 26 determines whether the character in variable MainChoice is the escape character. If this condition is true (the character is not the escape character), the program executes the statements in the THEN clause. These statements display the input character and then convert it into uppercase.

The SELECT-CASE statement, which starts on line 31 and ends on line 124, contains the CASE clauses to handle the various menu options. Each option contains its own DO-UNTIL loop and SELECT-CASE statement to display its menu selections and process your selection. The LOOP UNTIL clauses examine the condition INSTR(ExitStr, SecChoice) > 0 to determine when to exit back to the main menu. The tested condition is true when you enter 4, X, x, or when you press the Escape key. The LOOP UNTIL clause for the outer loop examines the condition INSTR(ExitStr, MainChoice) > 0 to determine whether to stop the program.

The *INKEY$* Function

QBasic supports the versatile INKEY$ keyboard input function. Unlike the INPUT, LINE INPUT, and INPUT$ statements, the INKEY$ function reads the keyboard at the instant you call it. The function does not wait for you to input data!

The INKEY$ Function

The general syntax for the INKEY$ function is

```
INKEY$
```

The INKEY$ function instantly reads the key pressed and does not echo the input to the screen. The function returns the following results:

1. An empty string when there is no keyboard input.

2. A single-character string when you press the keys for letters, digits, or punctuation characters.

3. A two-character string when you press a function key, cursor control key, and other alternate keys. The first character in the value returned by the function is an ASCII 0. The second character has an ASCII code value that depends on the special key you press (see Table 8.1). Figure 8.4 shows how the INKEY$ function works.

Example:

```
DO
     InChar = INKEY$
LOOP UNTIL InChar <> " "
IF LEN(InChar) = 1 THEN
     PRINT "You pressed "; InChar
ELSE
PRINT "You pressed a function key or cursor ";
     PRINT "control character"
END IF
```

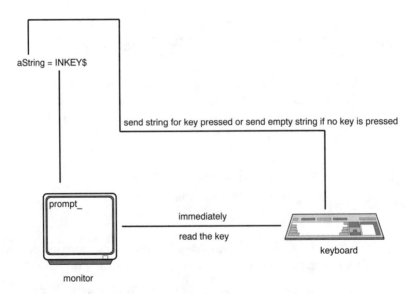

Figure 8.4. The INKEY$ function at work.

DO place the call to the INKEY$ function in a DO-UNTIL or DO-WHILE loop.

DON'T assume that there is always a keystroke available when a program calls the INKEY$ function.

Here is an example that uses the INKEY$ function in a manner similar to the INPUT$ function. Listing 8.4, INKEY1.BAS, uses the INKEY$ function to obtain a Yes/No answer. I created this program by modifying INPUT$1.BAS from Listing 8.2. The program prompts you for a string. Then the program displays your input and its uppercase version. Next, the program prompts you for a Y/N answer (which is the single-character response for a Yes/No answer) regarding whether you want to enter another string.

 Listing 8.4. INKEY1.BAS, which uses the INKEY$ function to obtain a Yes/No answer.

```
 1: REM Program that tests the INKEY$ function
 2: REM
 3: ' declare variables
 4: DIM AString AS STRING
 5: DIM K AS STRING
 6: DIM Q AS STRING
 7:
 8: CLS
 9: Q = CHR$(34)
10: DO
11:   LINE INPUT "Enter a string : "; AString
12:   PRINT
13:   PRINT "The uppercase of string "; Q; AString; Q;
14:   PRINT " is "; Q; UCASE$(AString); Q
15:   ' prompt for another input
16:   DO
17:     PRINT
18:     PRINT "Input another string? (Y/N) ";
19:     ' wait for keyboard input
20:     DO
```

continues

Listing 8.4. continued

```
21:       K = INKEY$
22:     LOOP UNTIL K <> ""
23:     PRINT K
24:     K = UCASE$(K)
25:     PRINT
26:   LOOP UNTIL K = "Y" OR K = "N"
27: LOOP UNTIL K = "N"
28: END
```

Here is some sample output for the program in Listing 8.4:

```
Enter a string : QBasic

The uppercase of string "QBasic" is "QBASIC"

Input another string? (Y/N) j


Input another string? (Y/N) y

Enter a string : QuickBasic

The uppercase of string "QuickBasic" is "QUICKBASIC"

Input another string? (Y/N) n
```

Because the program in Listing 8.4 is very similar to the one in Listing 8.2, I focus only on the different programs lines. These lines are located in the inner DO-UNTIL loop, which starts on line 16 and ends on line 26. The PRINT statement on line 18 displays the prompting message. Lines 20–22 contain yet another nested DO-UNTIL loop. This loop contains the statement that calls the INKEY$ function and assigns the result to the variable K. The loop iterates until the variable does not contain an empty string. The PRINT statement on line 23 echoes the input on the screen. The assignment statement on line 24 converts the character in K to uppercase. The LOOP UNTIL clause on line 26 shows that the inner DO-UNTIL loop iterates until the character in K is either Y or N.

Reading Special Keys

The INKEY$ function allows your programs to read the function keys and the cursor control keys. Table 8.1 contains a selection of scan code values for special keys. The integers in the table represent the ASCII code for the second character in the string that INKEY$ returns when you press a function key or a cursor control key.

Table 8.1. A selection of scan code values for special keys.

Key	Scan Code	Key	Scan Code
F1	59	Home	71
F2	60	End	79
F3	61	Num Lock	69
F4	62	Scroll Lock	70
F5	63	Caps Lock	58
F6	64	Up arrow	72
F7	65	Down arrow	80
F8	66	Left arrow	75
F9	67	Right arrow	77
F10	68	Page Up	73
F11	133	Page Down	81
F12	134	Insert	82
		Delete	83

Listing 8.5, INKEY2.BAS, illustrates the use of the INKEY$ function to read special keys. The program displays a message reminding you that to end the program you need to press the Escape key. Then the program monitors the keys you press and displays a message that identifies or classifies the key you just pressed.

Listing 8.5. INKEY2.BAS, which illustrates the use of function INKEY\$ to read special keys.

```
 1: REM Program that tests the INKEY$ function
 2: REM
 3: ' declare variables
 4: DIM K AS STRING
 5: DIM S AS STRING
 6: DIM ScanCode AS INTEGER
 7:
 8: CLS
 9: PRINT "Press the Esc key to exit"
10: DO
11:    DO
12:       K = INKEY$
13:    LOOP UNTIL K <> ""
14:    IF LEN(K) = 1 THEN
15:      IF K <> CHR$(27) THEN
16:         PRINT "You entered "; K
17:      END IF
18:    ELSE
19:      ScanCode = ASC(MID$(K, 2, 1))
20:      SELECT CASE ScanCode
21:        CASE 59 TO 68
22:           S = MID$(STR$(ScanCode - 58), 2)
23:           PRINT "You pressed the F"; S; " function key"
24:        CASE 133 TO 134
25:           S = MID$(STR$(ScanCode - 122), 2)
26:           PRINT "You pressed the F"; S; " function key"
27:        CASE 72
28:           PRINT "You pressed the up arrow key"
29:        CASE 80
30:           PRINT "You pressed the down arrow key"
31:        CASE 75
32:           PRINT "You pressed the left arrow key"
33:        CASE 77
34:           PRINT "You pressed the right arrow key"
35:        CASE 73
36:           PRINT "You pressed the page up key"
37:        CASE 81
38:           PRINT "You pressed the page down key"
39:        CASE ELSE
```

```
40:          PRINT "You pressed a function/cursor key"
41:     END SELECT
42:   END IF
43: LOOP UNTIL K = CHR$(27)
44: END
```

Here is some sample output for the program in Listing 8.5:

```
Press the Esc key to exit
You pressed the up arrow key
You pressed the left arrow key
You pressed the down arrow key
You pressed the right arrow key
You pressed the page up key
You pressed the page down key
You pressed the F1 function key
You pressed the F2 function key
You pressed the F3 function key
You pressed the F4 function key
You pressed the F5 function key
You pressed the F6 function key
You pressed the F7 function key
You pressed the F8 function key
You pressed the F7 function key
You pressed the F8 function key
You pressed the F9 function key
You pressed the F10 function key
You pressed the F11 function key
You pressed the F12 function key
You pressed a function/cursor key
```

The program in Listing 8.5 declares its variables on lines 4–6. The PRINT statement on line 9 displays a message reminding you that you need to press the Escape key to exit from the program. The outer DO-UNTIL loop starts on line 10 and ends on line 43. The first statement inside the outer loop is the start of the inner DO-UNTIL loop. This loop contains a single statement that calls the INKEY$ function and assigns its result to the string variable K. The LOOP UNTIL clause of the inner loop is on line 13. The tested condition iterates the loop until K contains a nonempty string.

On lines 14–42, the program contains an IF-THEN-ELSE that examines the string in K. The condition of the IF statement compares the length of K with 1. If this condition is true, you pressed an ordinary key. The program executes the THEN clause statement on line 16. This statement displays the character you entered. If the tested condition is false, the program executes the statement in the ELSE clause. The first statement, found on line 19, obtains the ASCII code for the second function in the variable K and stores it in the variable ScanCode. The SELECT-CASE statement on line 20 examines the value in ScanCode.

The first CASE clause, on line 21, detects the function keys F1–F9. The CASE clause specifies the range of values that belong to these function keys (see Table 8.1). The statement on line 22 obtains the string image of the function key number. The PRINT statement on line 23 displays a string that identifies the exact function key.

The second CASE clause, on line 24, detects the function keys F11 and F12. The CASE clause specifies the range of values that belong to these function keys (see Table 8.1). The statement on line 25 obtains the string image of the function key number. The PRINT statement on line 26 displays a string that identifies the exact function key.

The CASE clauses on lines 27–37 detect pressing the Up arrow, Down arrow, Left arrow, Right arrow, Page Up, and Page Down keys. The CASE ELSE clause on line 39 is the catch-all clause that displays a message for all other special keys.

Line 43 contains the LOOP UNTIL clause for the outer loop. The clause examines the condition K = CHR$(27). This condition causes the loop to iterate until you press the Escape key.

The *READ* Statement

In the previous sections of this chapter I presented various statements and functions that support keyboard input. In this section I present a set of statements that enable you to obtain data imbedded in a QBasic program. There are two general reasons why you would want to include data in a program's .BAS file:

☐ The imbedded information represents predefined parameters. Consequently, it is easier to obtain them from the program itself than it is to enter them from the keyboard every time you run the program.

☐ The scheme enables you to incorporate your own data with the program. You can change the imbedded data and save the program to update the imbedded information.

QBasic offers the READ statement that enables you to read strings and numbers from DATA statements.

The DATA Statement

The general syntax for the DATA statement is

```
DATA value1 [, value2, value3, ...]
```

The DATA statement must contain at least one value. You must separate multiple values with commas. The values in a DATA statement can either be strings or valid numbers. You only have to enclose strings in double quotes if the strings contain commas. Otherwise, the double quotes are optional. You can place any combination of valid data types in a single DATA statement.

Examples:

```
DATA QBasic, QuickBasic          ' two items
DATA "QBasic", "QuickBasic"      ' two items
DATA "QBasic, QuickBasic"        ' one item
DATA London, 1, 2, 3
DATA 3.45, California
DATA -9.8E+03, 1.2D+11, -1
```

The READ Statement

The general syntax for the READ statement is

```
READ variable1 [,variable2, variable3, ...]
```

The READ statement must contain at least one variable. You must separate multiple variables with commas. The variables can be any predefined type in QBasic. Figure 8.5 depicts the READ and DATA statements at work.

8

Examples:

```
READ MyName$
READ Age, Weight
PRINT MyName; " is "; Age; " years old and weighs ";
PRINT Weight; " pounds"
DATA "John Stewart", 39, 190
```

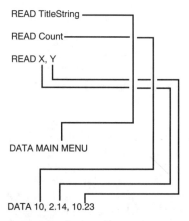

Figure 8.5. The READ and DATA statements at work.

How do the READ and DATA statements work? Here is a likely scenario. When a QBasic program executes the first READ statement, it searches for the first DATA statement in the program. If the program does not contain any DATA statements, the program stops and displays an error. If the program does contain a DATA statement, the program performs the following steps:

1. It sets up an internal pointer to remember the location of the first value in the DATA statement.

2. It reads the first value in the DATA statement. If that value has a data type incompatible with the input variable in the READ statement, the program raises an error. Otherwise, the program execution resumes.

For subsequent DATA input (this occurs when the first READ statement has multiple variables, or when the program executes the next READ statement), the program performs the following steps:

1. It uses the internal DATA value pointer to find the next value to read. This value may be in the same DATA statement or in a subsequent one—it makes no difference for the program. If the program does not find the next value, it raises an error.

2. It reads the next value in a DATA statement. If that value has a data type that is incompatible with the input variable in the READ statement, the program raises an error. Otherwise, the program execution resumes.

The previous scenario indicates that QBasic places no restrictions on relating the number of variables in a READ statement with the number of values in a DATA statement. As long as there is a value for each variable in a READ statement, everything is fine. In fact, you can have more values in DATA statements than variables in the READ statements. The extra values are simply never read.

DO make the total number of values in a DATA statement equal to or even greater than the total number of variables in the READ statement.

DON'T forget to enclose a string value within a pair of double quotes if that string includes one or more commas.

Take a look at an example. Listing 8.6, DATA1.BAS, uses the READ statement to obtain information in DATA statements. The program reads the title, date, and data from a set of DATA statements. The data contain steel thickness observations taken from various steel bar samples. The program then calculates the average value and standard deviation for the observations. Finally, the program displays the number of observations and their statistics.

Listing 8.6. DATA1.BAS, which uses the READ statement to obtain information in DATA statements.

```
1: REM Program uses the READ and DATA statements
2: REM
3: ' declare variables
4: DIM Title AS STRING
```

continues

```
 5: DIM DateStr AS STRING
 6: DIM X AS DOUBLE
 7: DIM Sum AS DOUBLE
 8: DIM SumX AS DOUBLE
 9: DIM SumXX AS DOUBLE
10: DIM Mean AS DOUBLE
11: DIM Sdev AS DOUBLE
12: DIM N AS INTEGER
13: DIM I AS INTEGER
14:
15: CLS
16: READ Title
17: READ DateStr
18: PRINT SPACE$(40 - LEN(Title) \ 2); Title
19: PRINT
20: PRINT "Date collected " + DateStr
21:
22: PRINT
23: ' initialize the summations variables
24: SumX = 0
25: SumXX = 0
26: ' read the number of observations
27: READ N
28: Sum = N
29: FOR I = 1 TO N
30:    ' read the next observation
31:    READ X
32:    SumX = SumX + X
33:    SumXX = SumXX + X * X
34: NEXT I
35:
36: Mean = SumX / Sum
37: Sdev = SQR((SumXX - SumX * SumX / Sum) / (Sum - 1))
38: PRINT "Number of observations = "; N
39: PRINT "Mean value = "; Mean
40: PRINT "Standard deviation = "; CINT(Sdev * 100) / 100
41:
42: DATA Sample Steel Bar Thickness Data
43: DATA 1/23/93
```

```
44: DATA 10
45: DATA 3.4, 5.6, 9.8, 1.2, 6.5, 3.4
46: DATA 5.6, 8.1, 2.3, 4.5
```

Here is some sample output for the program in Listing 8.6:

```
Sample Steel Bar Thickness Data

Date collected 1/23/93

Number of observations =  10
Mean value =  5.04
Standard deviation =  2.64
```

The program in Listing 8.6 declares its variables on lines 4–13. The READ statement on line 16 reads the first value in the set of DATA statements, located on line 42. The statement saves the string in the variable Title. The READ statement on line 17 reads the second value in the set of DATA statements, located on line 43. The statement stores the second value in the variable DateStr. The PRINT statements on lines 18 and 20 display the centered title and the date, respectively.

The statements on lines 24 and 25 initialize the statistical summation variables SumX and SumXX. The READ statement on line 27 reads the third value in the set of DATA statements, located on line 44. The statement stores this value in the variable N. The statement on line 28 assigns the value of N to the variable Sum, which represents the sum of observations. The program uses a FOR-NEXT loop, which starts on line 29 and ends on line 34. The loop has the control variable I and iterates from 1 to N. Line 31 contains a READ statement that reads a floating-point number from the DATA statements and stores it in X. The statements on lines 32 and 33 update the summation variables SumX and SumXX with the value of X and its square, respectively. The statements on lines 36 and 37 calculate the mean and standard deviation values for the observations found in the DATA statements.

The PRINT statements on lines 38–40 display the number of observations, the mean value, and the standard deviation. Lines 42–46 contain the DATA statements.

The *RESTORE* Statement

The READ statement sequentially accesses the values in DATA statements. There are many cases where you need to reread some of the values in DATA statements. QBasic offers the RESTORE statement to support such an operation.

The RESTORE Statement

The general syntax for the RESTORE statement is

```
RESTORE label
```

label is the name of an existing program label. The next READ statement obtains its input from the first value in the first DATA statement after the specified label. If there are no DATA statements after the label, the program raises a runtime error.

Example:

```
READ N
FOR I = 1 TO N
    Sum = 0
    FOR J = 1 TO I
        READ X
        Sum = Sum + X
    NEXT J
    RESTORE dataLBL
    PRINT "Moving average = "; Sum / I
    PRINT
NEXT I

dataLBL:

DATA 10
DATA 2.3, 4.5, 4.5, 3.4, 9.2
DATA 1.4, 7.3, 8.1, 2.2, 1.1
```

> **DO** place only the values to reread in a DATA statement *after* the label mentioned in a RESTORE statement.
>
> **DON'T** use a label name in a RESTORE statement if the label itself is not followed by a DATA statement.

Take a look at an example. Listing 8.7, DATA2.BAS, uses the RESTORE statement to reread values from DATA statements. The DATA statements contain a miniature database with the first name, last name, and phone number for a few people. The program prompts you to enter the last name of a contact. The program rereads the contact list in the DATA statement looking for a last name that matches your input. To make the program flexible, I offer the following features:

The search for the matching last name is non-case-sensitive.

The input needs to match any part of a last name in a DATA statement.

If the program finds a matching last name, it displays the full name and phone number of the contact. Otherwise, the program displays a message telling you that the name you entered is not in the database.

Finally, the program prompts you for a Y/N answer to search for more names.

 Listing 8.7. DATA2.BAS, which uses the RESTORE statement to reread values from DATA statements.

```
 1: REM Program uses the READ, DATA and
 2: REM RESTORE statements
 3: ' declare constants
 4: CONST TRUE% = -1
 5: CONST FALSE% = 0
 6: ' declare variables
 7: DIM aName AS STRING
 8: DIM FirstName AS STRING
 9: DIM LastName AS STRING
10: DIM Phone AS STRING
11: DIM C AS STRING
```

continues

```
12: DIM N AS INTEGER
13: DIM I AS INTEGER
14: DIM Found AS INTEGER
15:
16: READ N
17: CLS
18: DO
19:    ' input search name
20:    LINE INPUT "Enter name : "; aName
21:    PRINT
22:    ' set search flag to false
23:    Found = FALSE
24:    ' use loop to search
25:    FOR I = 1 TO N
26:       ' read the next data set
27:       READ FirstName, LastName, Phone
28:       ' find a match?
29:       IF INSTR(UCASE$(LastName), UCASE$(aName)) > 0 THEN
30:          Found = TRUE
31:          EXIT FOR
32:       END IF
33:    NEXT I
34:
35:    ' reset DATA statement pointer
36:    RESTORE DataList
37:
38:    ' was a match found?
39:    IF Found = TRUE THEN
40:       PRINT "The phone number of "; FirstName; " "; LastName;
41:       PRINT " is "; Phone
42:    ELSE
43:       PRINT aName; " is not in the database"
44:    END IF
45:
46:    ' prompt user for more search
47:    DO
48:       PRINT
49:       PRINT "Search for another name? (Y/N) ";
50:       C = INPUT$(1)
```

```
51:    PRINT C
52:    C = UCASE$(C)
53:    PRINT
54:  LOOP UNTIL C = "Y" OR C = "N"
55:
56: LOOP UNTIL C <> "Y"
57:
58: '****************** DATA Statements Section *********
59:
60: DATA 7
61: DataList:
62: DATA "Paul", "Hammer", "555-3232"
63: DATA "Jim", "Chataway", "555-9987"
64: DATA "Richard", "Lynch", "555-5432"
65: DATA "Kim", "Chin", "555-8765"
66: DATA "Darryl", "Lanz", "555-9263"
67: DATA "Jean", "Jarre", "555-2222"
68: DATA "Paul", "Jarvis", "555-9283"
69:
70: END
```

8

Here is some sample output for the program in Listing 8.7:

```
Enter name : lanz

The phone number of Darryl Lanz is 555-9263

Search for another name? (Y/N) y

Enter name : Jar

The phone number of Jean Jarre is 555-2222

Search for another name? (Y/N) y

Enter name : Shammas

Shammas is not in the database

Search for another name? (Y/N) n
```

The program in Listing 8.7 declares the constants `TRUE%` and `FALSE%` on lines 4 and 5, respectively. Lines 7–14 contain the declarations of the variables. The `READ` statement on line 16 obtains the number of contact records in the `DATA` statements. The program reads this information only once.

Lines 18–56 contain the outer `DO-UNTIL` loop. This loop prompts you for input, searches for data, displays the search result, and prompts you to search for more data. The `LINE INPUT` statement on line 20 prompts you to enter a name and stores it in the variable `aName`. The statement on line 23 assigns the constant `FALSE` to the variable `Found`. This statement initializes the search flag, `Found`, with a pessimistic value. The `FOR-NEXT` loop on lines 25–33 performs the search for a matching last name. The loop uses the control variable `I` and iterates from 1 to `N`. Line 27 contains a `READ` statement that obtains values for the variables `FirstName`, `LastName`, and `Phone`. The `IF-THEN` statement on line 29 uses the `INSTR` and `UCASE$` functions to perform a case-insensitive search. If the `INSTR` function yields a positive value, the program executes the `THEN` clause statements. The first statement assigns the constant `TRUE` to the variable `Found`. The second statement executes an `EXIT FOR` statement to exit from the loop, now that the program has found a match.

Line 36 contains the `RESTORE` statement, which resets the internal `DATA` statement pointer to the first value in the first `DATA` statement after the label `DataList`. The `IF-THEN-ELSE` statement on line 39 displays the result of the search if variable `Found` contains `TRUE`. Otherwise, the statements in the `ELSE` clause display a failed-search message.

The program uses the `DO-UNTIL` loop on lines 47–54 to prompt you for another search. Line 56 contains the `LOOP UNTIL` clause for the outer loop. This clause examines the condition where the variable `C` does not contain the string `"Y"`. If this condition is true, the outer `DO-UNTIL` loop stops iterating.

Lines 60–68 contain the `DATA` statement and the special label `DataList`. If you add more `DATA` statements, make sure that you increase the value in line 60 accordingly.

Summary

This chapter looks at the keyboard and internal methods of input. Today you learned about the following topics:

□ The LINE INPUT statement enables you to enter a line of text that contains any character, including commas, leading spaces, and trailing spaces. The variable that receives the input from the LINE INPUT statement must have the string data type.

□ The INPUT$ function enables you to read one or more characters from the keyboard without pressing the Return key to end the input. The INPUT$ function is suitable for fast input that requires a few characters.

□ The INKEY$ function enables you to read both ordinary characters and special keystrokes. These keystrokes include the function keys and the cursor keys. Like the INPUT$ function, the INKEY$ function does not require you to press the Return key to end the input. The INKEY$ function is also suitable for fast input that requires a few characters.

□ The READ statement enables you to obtain input from DATA statements that contain values imbedded in the program. The READ statement accepts one or more variables. The DATA statement accepts one or more values. You don't need to enclose the strings in DATA statements in double quotation marks unless they contain a comma as part of the text. To avoid a runtime error, a QBasic program must have enough values in DATA statements to accommodate the number of variables in the READ statements. In addition, the data types of the variables in the READ statements must be compatible with the values in the DATA statements.

□ The RESTORE statement enables you to reset the internal DATA statement pointer. Consequently, you can reread data from DATA statements without raising a runtime error.

Q&A

Q. Where in a program should I place the DATA statements?

A. QBasic enables you to place the DATA statements any where in a program. However, it is a good programming practice to place them at the end. In addition, commenting the DATA statements adds clarity to what the values are all about.

Q. Can a program execute a RESTORE statement before a READ statement?

A. Yes. You can use the RESTORE statement to select the DATA statements that will supply the input for the READ statements. This feature enables you to select alternate sets of DATA statements for input.

Workshop

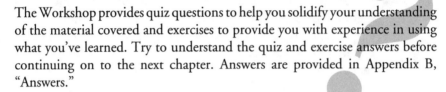

The Workshop provides quiz questions to help you solidify your understanding of the material covered and exercises to provide you with experience in using what you've learned. Try to understand the quiz and exercise answers before continuing on to the next chapter. Answers are provided in Appendix B, "Answers."

Quiz

1. What is the output of the following program?

```
DIM AString AS STRING
READ AString
PRINT AString
PRINT LEN(AString)
DATA 1.23E+08
```

2. Where is the error in the following set of statements?

```
DIM X AS DOUBLE
DIM N AS INTEGER
DIM S AS STRING

READ S
READ N
READ X
PRINT "S = "; S
PRINT "N = "; N
PRINT "X = "; X

DATA "Version 1.0", 3
```

3. Where is the error in the following set of statements?

```
DIM X AS DOUBLE
DIM N AS INTEGER
DIM S AS STRING

READ S
READ N
READ X
PRINT "S = "; S
PRINT "N = "; N
PRINT "X = "; X

DATA 3, "Version 1.0", 2.3
```

4. What is wrong with the following program?

```
DIM X AS DOUBLE
CLS
LINE INPUT "Enter a number "; X
PRINT "You entered "; X
END
```

5. Where is the error in the following set of statements?

```
DIM X AS DOUBLE
DIM N AS INTEGER
DIM S AS STRING

READ S
READ N
READ X
PRINT "S = "; S
PRINT "N = "; N
PRINT "X = "; X
RESTORE MoreData:
READ S
READ N
READ X
```

```
PRINT "S = "; S
PRINT "N = "; N
PRINT "X = "; X

DATA "Version 1.0", 2.3, 3
MoreData:
END
```

Exercises

1. Write the program DATA3.BAS, using the READ, DATA, and RESTORE statements, to enable you to select between the following data sets:

```
DATA Sample Steel Bar Thickness Data
DATA 1/23/93
DATA 10
DATA 3.4, 5.6, 9.8, 1.2, 6.5, 3.4
DATA 5.6, 8.1, 2.3, 4.5

DATA Sample Steel Bar Thickness Data
DATA 2/13/93
DATA 10
DATA 2.4, 7.6, 8.8, 2.2, 3.5, 8.4
DATA 3.6, 7.9, 2.8, 3.9

DATA Sample Steel Bar Thickness Data
DATA 3/3/93
DATA 10
DATA 4.1, 6.1, 9.1, 1.1, 5.9, 4.5
DATA 3.5, 9.1, 3.7, 3.2
```

2. Write a version of DATA2.BAS—call it DATA4.BAS—that can automatically detect the last DATA statement. To implement this method, use a special set of strings—say "!"—for the last name, first name, and phone numbers. Assign the special string (the "!") to the constant EOD (short for End Of DATA).

Hint: Replace the FOR-NEXT loop with a DO-UNTIL loop that searches for a matching last name. You also can take advantage of the DO-UNTIL loop to simplify the IF-THEN statement inside the loop.

3. Modify INKEY1.BAS to create a special version—call it INKEY3.BAS. In the new version, use the TIMER function to exit from the DO-UNTIL loop (which contains the call to the function INKEY$) after a few seconds—say three seconds. Write the program so that if the loop ends on a time out, the program assigns the string literal "N" to variable K.

8

DAY
9

Screen and Printer Output

The programs presented so far do not explore the versatile output statements and functions in QBasic. In this chapter I present the means to format your output. In addition, I present the statements that enable you to send output to your printer. Finally, the chapter looks at statements and functions that support manipulating the screen cursor. Today you will learn about the following topics:

- [ ] Tabbing output with the `PRINT` statement
- [ ] Tabbing output with the `TAB` function
- [ ] Spacing output with the `SPC` function
- [ ] Formatting output with the `PRINT USING` statement
- [ ] Printing output using the `LPRINT` and `LPRINT USING` statements
- [ ] Locating the screen cursor with the `CSRLIN` and `POS` functions
- [ ] Moving the screen cursor with the `LOCATE` statement

Tabbing with *PRINT*

The `PRINT` statement is a versatile command. You can use it without any value to print a blank line, or you can display one or more values in a `PRINT` statement. When you provide the `PRINT` statement with multiple values, you must separate these values with either semicolons or commas. The programs that I have presented so far use the semicolon to separate multiple values in a `PRINT` statement. The semicolon tells the `PRINT` statement to chain the output. The comma tells the `PRINT` statement to display the next item in a predefined printing zone.

Here are the rules that specify how the comma affects the output in a `PRINT` statement:

- [ ] The commas specify the next printing zone. Each zone is 14 characters wide. Thus, the following statement displays the characters A, B, and C in columns 1, 15, and 29, respectively:

    ```
    PRINT "A", "B", "C"
    ```

- [ ] A `PRINT` statement may contain a comma before and/or after any displayed values. Here are some examples:

```
PRINT , "A", "B",;
PRINT "C"
```

These statements display the letters A, B, and C at columns 15, 29, and 43, respectively.

☐ If the PRINT statement writes a value (such as a string) that is longer than 14 characters, the subsequent value appears in the next printing zone. (Remember, each zone is 14 characters long.)

Take a look at a simple program that compares the semicolons with the commas in a list of values displayed by a PRINT statement. Listing 9.1 shows the program PRINT1.BAS, which performs the comparison. The program prompts you to enter a string, a positive number, a negative number, and a number (which can be positive, zero, or negative). Then the program displays the following:

1. The character ruler displays.

2. Carat characters appear immediately below the character ruler, indicating where each printing zone begins.

3. The data you entered appears chained if you used a PRINT statement with semicolons.

4. The data you entered appears more spaced out if you used a PRINT statement with commas.

9

Listing 9.1. PRINT1.BAS, which displays a list of items using the semicolon and comma delimiters in PRINT statements.

```
 1: REM Program that shows how to print
 2: REM multiple items with the PRINT statement
 3: REM using the comma and semicolon
 4: REM
 5: ' declare the variables
 6: DIM X AS DOUBLE
 7: DIM Y AS DOUBLE
 8: DIM Z AS DOUBLE
 9: DIM S AS STRING
10:
```

continues

Listing 9.1. continued

```
11: CLS
12: DO
13:   PRINT "Enter a string that has less than 14 characters:"
14:   PRINT "          1"
15:   PRINT "12345678901234"
16:   LINE INPUT ; S
17:   PRINT
18: LOOP UNTIL S <> "" AND LEN(S) < 14
19:
20: DO
21:   INPUT "Enter positive number"; X
22: LOOP UNTIL X > 0
23:
24: DO
25:   INPUT "Enter the negative number"; Y
26: LOOP UNTIL Y < 0
27:
28: INPUT "Enter a number"; Z
29: PRINT : PRINT
30: PRINT "          1         2         3         4         5"
31: PRINT "12345678901234567890123456789012345678901234567890"
32: PRINT "^", "^", "^", "^"
33:
34: PRINT "Using semicolons the output is"
35: PRINT S; X; Y; Z
36:
37: PRINT "Using commas the output is"
38: PRINT S, X, Y, Z
39:
40: END
```

Here is some sample output for the program in Listing 9.1:

```
Enter a string that has less than 14 characters:
          1
12345678901234
QuickBasic
Enter positive number? 10.25
```

```
Enter the negative number? -8.5
Enter a number? 144000


          1         2         3         4         5
12345678901234567890123456789012345678901234567890
^         ^         ^         ^

Using semicolons the output is
QuickBasic 10.25 -8.5  144000
Using commas the output is
QuickBasic    10.25        -8.5           144000
```

Analysis The program in Listing 9.1 declares its variables on lines 6–9. Lines 12–18 contain a DO-UNTIL loop that obtains a non-empty string containing less than 14 characters. The PRINT statements on lines 13–15 display the prompting message and the character ruler. The LINE INPUT statement on line 16 prompts you to enter a string. The LOOP UNTIL clause on line 18 ensures that the loop iterates until the string in S is not empty and stores fewer than 14 characters.

The DO-UNTIL loop on lines 20–22 obtains a positive number. The INPUT statement on line 21 prompts you to enter a positive number and stores it in the variable X. The LOOP UNTIL clause on line 22 causes the loop to iterate until X contains a positive number.

The DO-UNTIL loop on lines 24–26 obtains a positive number. The INPUT statement on line 25 prompts you to enter a negative number and stores it in variable Y. The LOOP UNTIL clause on line 26 causes the loop to iterate until the variable Y contains a negative number.

The INPUT statement on line 28 prompts you to enter a number. The statement stores your input in Z. The PRINT statements on lines 30 and 31 display the character ruler. The PRINT statement on line 32 displays four single-carat characters, separated by commas. This statement shows the start of the first four printing zones. The PRINT statement on line 35 displays the contents of S, X, Y, and Z using semicolons. The sample program output shows that the PRINT statement automatically places a space between each neighboring value. The PRINT statement on line 38 displays the contents of S, X, Y, and Z using commas. The sample program output shows these values appearing at the start of the printing zones.

9

Tabulated Output

Now take a look at a simple example that displays a table of numeric values using commas in a PRINT statement. Listing 9.2, PRINT2.BAS, displays tables of squares and cubes for integers ranging from 10 through 20.

 Listing 9.2. **PRINT2.BAS, which displays a table using a PRINT statement with commas.**

```
 1: REM Program that displays a table using
 2: REM the PRINT statement
 3: REM
 4: CONST TITLE1 = "Sample Table of Squares and Cubes"
 5: CONST TITLE2 = "(using the PRINT statement and commas)"
 6: CONST FIRST = 10
 7: CONST LAST = 20
 8: ' declare the variables
 9: DIM N AS INTEGER
10:
11: CLS
12: PRINT
13: PRINT SPACE$(40 - LEN(TITLE1) \ 2); TITLE1
14: PRINT SPACE$(40 - LEN(TITLE2) \ 2); TITLE2
15: PRINT
16: PRINT
17:
18: PRINT , "  N", "N ^ 2", " N ^ 3"
19: PRINT , STRING$(35, "-")
20: FOR N = FIRST TO LAST
21:   PRINT , N, N * N, N * N * N
22: NEXT N
23:
24: END
```

Here is some sample output for the program in Listing 9.2:

Sample Table of Squares and Cubes
      (using the PRINT statement and commas)

```
   N           N ^ 2          N ^ 3
- - - - - - - - - - - - - - - - - - - - - - - - - - - - - - -
   10          100            1000
   11          121            1331
   12          144            1728
   13          169            2197
   14          196            2744
   15          225            3375
   16          256            4096
   17          289            4913
   18          324            5832
   19          361            6859
   20          400            8000
```

The program in Listing 9.2 declares four constants on lines 4–7. The first two constants define the title of the table. The last two constants define the range of integer values displayed in the table. The PRINT statements on lines 13 and 14 display the centered title of the table. The statements use the SPACE$ function to insert the leading spaces that center the text of the titles. The PRINT statements on lines 18 and 19 display the table heading. The FOR-NEXT loop on lines 20–22 display the tabulated values. The loop uses the control variable N and iterates from FIRST to LAST. The PRINT statement inside the loop displays the values of N, N squared, and N cubed. Notice that the PRINT statements on lines 18, 19, and 21 contain a comma before the displayed values. This comma ensures that the table is indented to the right and does not appear at the first column of the screen.

Tabbing with the *TAB* Function

The commas in the PRINT statement do not enable you to specify the exact column position. QBasic offers the TAB function to cure this shortcoming. The TAB function moves the cursor to the column position you specify.

The TAB Function

The general syntax for the TAB function is:

```
TAB(columnPosition)
```

The parameter `columnPosition` specifies the position where the next item of a PRINT statement appears. The parameter can be a numeric constant, named numeric constant, variable, numeric function, or numeric expression. The TAB function rounds up `columnPosition`. If the current output position is beyond the column position specified by the TAB function, the function displays the next item on the next line (at the specified column position).

Examples:

```
PRINT TAB(10); "at 10"


FOR I = 5 TO 40 STEP 5
    PRINT TAB(I); I
NEXT I
```

Now, take a look at an example. Listing 9.3, TAB1.BAS, displays a table using a TAB function. I created this program by editing the PRINT2.BAS program in Listing 9.2. The program displays tables of squares and cubes for integers ranging from 10 to 20.

Listing 9.3. TAB1.BAS, which displays a table using a TAB function.

```
 1: REM Program that uses the TAB function
 2: REM
 3: ' declare the constants
 4: CONST TAB1 = 25
 5: CONST TAB2 = 35
 6: CONST TAB3 = 45
 7: CONST TITLE1 = "Sample Table of Squares and Cubes"
 8: CONST TITLE2 = "(using the TAB function)"
 9: CONST FIRST = 10
10: CONST LAST = 20
11: ' declare the variables
```

```
12: DIM N AS INTEGER
13:
14: CLS
15: PRINT
16: PRINT TAB(40 - LEN(TITLE1) \ 2); TITLE1
17: PRINT TAB(40 - LEN(TITLE2) \ 2); TITLE2
18: PRINT
19: PRINT
20:
21: PRINT TAB(TAB1); " N"; TAB(TAB2); "N ^ 2"; TAB(TAB3); " N ^ 3"
22: PRINT TAB(TAB1 - 3); STRING$(60 - TAB1, "-")
23: FOR N = FIRST TO LAST
24:    PRINT TAB(TAB1); N; TAB(TAB2); N * N; TAB(TAB3); N * N * N
25: NEXT N
26: END
```

Here is some sample output for the program in Listing 9.3:

```
      Sample Table of Squares and Cubes
             (using the TAB function)



         N         N ^ 2      N ^ 3
      ------------------------------------
        10         100        1000
        11         121        1331
        12         144        1728
        13         169        2197
        14         196        2744
        15         225        3375
        16         256        4096
        17         289        4913
        18         324        5832
        19         361        6859
        20         400        8000
```

Analysis The program in Listing 9.3 declares a set of constants on lines 4–10. The constants on lines 4–6 define the tab positions for the columns in the table. The constants on lines 7 and 8 define the titles of the table. The constants on lines 9 and 10 define the range of integers used to display the squares and cubes.

The PRINT statements on lines 16 and 17 display the centered title. Notice that these statements use the TAB function instead of the SPACE$ function to display the centered text.

The PRINT statements on lines 21 and 22 display the table heading. These statements use the TAB function to display the components of the table heading at their proper locations. The program uses the FOR-NEXT loop on lines 23–25 to display the tabulated numeric values. The loop uses the control variable N and iterates from FIRST to LAST. The PRINT statement inside the loop displays the values of N, N squared, and N cubed. Each item is preceded by a call to TAB to specify its column position.

Spacing Output with the *SPC* Function

QBasic offers the SPC function to complement the TAB function. SPC moves the next output position by a specified number of spaces.

The SPC Function

The general syntax for the SPC function is

```
SPC(spacingValue)
```

The parameter *spacingValue* defines the number of spaces between the last and next displayed items. The parameter can be a numeric constant, named numeric constant, variable, numeric function, or numeric expression. The SPC function rounds up the argument *spacingValue*.

The arguments for the TAB function are absolute column positions. The arguments for the SPC function are differences in column positions.

Example:

```
PRINT SPC(10); "at 10"


FOR I = 5 TO 40 STEP 5
    PRINT SPC(5); I
NEXT I
```

Take a look at another example. Listing 9.4, SPC1.BAS, displays a table using a SPC function. I created this program by editing the TAB1.BAS program in Listing 9.3. The program displays tables of squares and cubes for integers ranging from 10 to 20.

 Listing 9.4. SPC1.BAS, which displays a table using a SPC function.

```
1: REM Program that uses the SPC function
2: REM
3: ' declare the constant
4: CONST MARGIN = 25
5: CONST SV = 10
6: CONST TITLE1 = "Sample Table of Squares and Cubes"
7: CONST TITLE2 = "(using the SPC function)"
8: CONST FIRST = 10
9: CONST LAST = 20
10: ' declare the variables
11: DIM N AS INTEGER
12:
13: CLS
14: PRINT
15: PRINT SPC(40 - LEN(TITLE1) \ 2); TITLE1
16: PRINT SPC(40 - LEN(TITLE2) \ 2); TITLE2
17: PRINT
18: PRINT
19:
20: PRINT SPC(MARGIN); " N"; SPC(SV);
21: PRINT "  N ^ 2"; SPC(SV); " N ^ 3"
22: PRINT SPC(MARGIN - 3); STRING$(60 - MARGIN + 3, "-")
23: FOR N = FIRST TO LAST
24:    PRINT SPC(MARGIN); N; SPC(SV); N * N; SPC(SV); N * N * N
25: NEXT N
26: END
```

9

Here is some sample output for the program in Listing 9.4:

```
Sample Table of Squares and Cubes
      (using the SPC function)


    N              N ^ 2            N ^ 3
-------------------------------------------
    10              100             1000
    11              121             1331
    12              144             1728
    13              169             2197
    14              196             2744
    15              225             3375
    16              256             4096
    17              289             4913
    18              324             5832
    19              361         ,   6859
    20              400             8000
```

The program in Listing 9.4 declares a set of constants on lines 4–9. The constants on lines 4 and 5 define the left margin and column spacing. The constants on lines 6 and 7 define the titles of the table. The constants on lines 8 and 9 define the range of integers used to display the squares and cubes.

The PRINT statements on lines 15 and 16 display the centered title. Notice that these statements use the SPC function instead of the SPACE$ or TAB functions to display the centered text. These statements illustrate a third method for displaying centered text.

The PRINT statements on lines 20–22 display the table heading. These statements use the SPC function to display the components of the table heading at their proper locations. The program uses the FOR-NEXT loop on lines 23–25 to display the tabulated numeric values. The loop uses the control variable N and iterates from FIRST to LAST. The PRINT statement inside the loop displays the values of N, N squared, and N cubed. Each item is preceded by a call to the function SPC to specify intercolumn spacing. The first calls to the SPC function on lines 20, 22, and 24 use the argument MARGIN to specify the left margin. The other calls to the SPC function in these statements use the argument SV to specify the spacing between the columns of the table.

Formatting Output with the *PRINT USING* Statement

The comma, TAB function, and SPC function offer you control over the location of the output. However, they do not affect the appearance of the output. Displaying numbers with a lot of decimal places does not really look neat on a report. The numerous digits are too much for the eyes and might even be insignificant. Fortunately, QBasic offers a mechanism to tame the output. The champion of this mechanism is the USING clause, which can appear in the PRINT statement. Thus, the PRINT USING statement enables you to display formatted output.

The PRINT USING Statement

The general syntax for the PRINT USING statement is

```
PRINT USING formatStr; value1[, value2, ...] [{; ¦ ,}]
```

The *formatStr* parameter is a string expression. The arguments for this parameter may be a string literal, a string constant, a string variable, a string function, or any combination of these basic components.

Because QBasic supports a rich set of control codes for strings and numeric data, I present these codes in the next subsections.

Example:

```
DIM A AS SINGLE
A = 2.3
PRINT USING "#.####"; A

DIM X AS DOUBLE
X = 355 / 113
PRINT USING "+#.###^^^^^";  X
```

9

Formatting String Output

Table 9.1 shows the string control codes for the PRINT USING statement. Table 9.2 shows the string formats to display portions of a string.

Table 9.1. The string control codes for the PRINT USING statement.

Control Code	Purpose
!	Displays only the first character of a string. Here is a simple example: `PRINT USING "'!'"; "QBasic" ' displays 'Q'`

\\	Displays a minimum of two characters of a string (one for each backslash character). You can insert spaces between the backslash characters. The PRINT USING statement displays an additional character for each space between the backslash characters. Here are a few simple examples:
	
	`PRINT USING "'\\'"; "QBasic" ' displays 'QB'`
	
	`PRINT USING "'\ \'"; "QBasic" ' displays 'QBa'`
	
	`PRINT USING "'\  \'"; "QBasic" ' displays 'QBas'`

&	Displays the entire string. Here is a simple example: `PRINT USING "'&'"; "QBasic" ' displays 'QBasic'`
_	Displays verbatim the character that comes after the underscore. By using the __, _!, _\, and _& combinations, you can display the _, !, \, and & characters, respectively, in a PRINT USING statement. Here is a simple example: `PRINT USING "'!_!'"; "QBasic" ' displays 'Q!'`

Table 9.2. **The string formats to display portions of a string.**

Format	Number of Displayed Characters
!	1
\\	2
\ \	3
\ \	4
\ \	5
\ <n spaces> \	n+2
&	LEN(string)

Listing 9.5, USING1.BAS, displays formatted strings. The program prompts you to enter a string that has between 5 and 20 characters. The program then displays a table that shows part and all of the string using the various string control codes in Table 9.1.

 Listing 9.5. **USING1.BAS, which displays formatted strings.**

```
1: REM Program demonstrates the PRINT USING
2: REM statement with strings
3: REM
4: ' declare the variables
5: DIM AString AS STRING
6: DIM FrmtStr AS STRING
7: DIM Q AS STRING
8: DIM L AS INTEGER
9: DIM I AS INTEGER
10:
11: CLS
12: Q = CHR$(34)
13: DO
14:    PRINT "Enter a string that is between 5 and 20 ";
15:    PRINT "characters long:"
16:    PRINT "          1         2"
17:    PRINT "12345678901234567890"
```

continues

9

Listing 9.5. continued

```
18:    LINE INPUT ; AString
19:    PRINT
20:    L = LEN(AString)
21: LOOP UNTIL L >= 5 AND L <= 20
22:
23: PRINT
24: ' display table heading
25: PRINT TAB(10); "Format"; TAB(40); "Output"
26: PRINT STRING$(60, "-")
27: ' display first table entry
28: PRINT TAB(10); "!";
29: PRINT TAB(40); Q;
30: PRINT USING "!"; AString;
31: PRINT Q
32: ' display varying length output
33: FOR I = 2 TO L STEP 2
34:    ' build the format string
35:    FrmtStr = "\" + SPACE$(I - 2) + "\"
36:    PRINT TAB(10);
37:    ' display the format string itself
38:    'PRINT USING "The format string &&& yields "; Q; FrmtStr; Q;
39:    PRINT FrmtStr;
40:    ' display the string
41:    PRINT TAB(40);
42:    PRINT USING "!"; Q;
43:    PRINT USING FrmtStr; AString;
44:    PRINT USING "!"; Q
45: NEXT I
46: ' display the entire string using the & format
47: PRINT TAB(10); "&";
48: PRINT TAB(40); Q;
49: PRINT USING "&"; AString;
50: PRINT Q
51: END
```

Here is some sample output for the program in Listing 9.5:

```
Enter a string that is between 5 and 20 characters long:
         1         2
12345678901234567890
I use QBasic

         Format                              Output
-------------------------------------------------------------
           !                                "I"
           \ \                              "I "
           \   \                            "I us"
           \     \                          "I use "
           \       \                        "I use QB"
           \         \                      "I use QBas"
           \           \                    "I use QBasic"
           &                                "I use QBasic"
```

The program in Listing 9.5 declares its variables on lines 5–9. The program uses the DO-UNTIL loop on lines 13–21 to obtain a string that is from 5 to 20 characters long. The PRINT statements on lines 14–17 display the prompt and the character ruler. The LINE INPUT statement on line 18 prompts you for a string and saves your input in the variable AString. The statement on line 21 assigns the length of the string in AString to the variable L. The LOOP UNTIL clauses examine the condition where L contains a value from 5 to 20. The loop iterates until this condition is true.

The PRINT statements on lines 25 and 26 display the table heading. The PRINT statements on line 28–31 display the first character in the variable AString, utilizing the ! control code in the PRINT USING statement. The program uses the FOR-NEXT loop on lines 33–45 to display portions of AString, using the \ \ control code with a variable number of spaces between the backslash characters. The statement on line 35 builds the format string and stores it in FrmtStr. The PRINT statements on lines 36–39 display the format string itself using the & control code. The PRINT statements on lines 41–44 display the characters in AString, utilizing the format in FrmtStr. The PRINT statements on lines 47–50 display the entire string in AString, using the & control code.

9

Formatting Integer Output

The PRINT USING statement offers a lot of formatting power for numbers. Table 9.3 shows the numeric control codes for the PRINT USING statement. The table also shows simple examples. The programs that I present in this subsection and in the next sections will give you a better idea of how these control codes work.

Table 9.3. The numeric control codes for the PRINT USING statement.

Control Code	Purpose
#	Displays a digit for every pound character. If there are fewer digits than # characters, the PRINT USING statement displays the number right justified with leading spaces. By contrast, if there are more digits than # characters, the PRINT USING statement displays one or two % characters (the % is a warning character) followed by the entire number. Here are a few examples:
	`PRINT USING "'##'"; 2 ' displays ' 2'`
	`PRINT USING "'###'"; 123 ' displays '123'`
	Places a decimal in the output, even if the number is an integer. The PRINT USING statement rounds the output number as required. Here are a few examples:
	`PRINT USING "'#.#'"; 2 ' displays '2.0'`
	`PRINT USING "'##.#'"; 1.23 ' displays ' 1.2'`
	`PRINT USING "'##.#'"; 1.26 ' displays ' 1.3'`
	`PRINT USING "'##.##'"; 1.23 ' displays ' 1.23'`

Control Code	Purpose

+	Displays a mandatory sign (+ or -) to appear before the number. You may place the + control code at the beginning or at the end of the format string. The `PRINT USING` statement displays the sign before or after the number, respectively. Here are a few examples:
	
	`PRINT USING "'+##'"; 2 ' displays ' +2'`
	
	`PRINT USING "'+###'"; -123 ' displays '-123'`

-	Displays a minus sign only for negative numbers. You may place the - control code at the beginning or at the end of the format string. The `PRINT USING` statement displays the minus sign before or after a negative number, respectively. Here are a few examples:
	
	`PRINT USING "'-##'"; 2 ' displays '  2'`
	
	`PRINT USING "'-###'"; -123 ' displays '-123'`
	
	`PRINT USING "'###-'"; -123 ' displays '123-'`
	
	`PRINT USING "'###-'"; 123 ' displays '123 '`

**	Displays asterisks to the left of the number. When the format string has more # control codes than actual digits to display, the ** control code fills the extra characters with asterisks. Here are a few examples:
	
	`PRINT USING "'**####'"; 2 ' displays '***2'`
	
	`PRINT USING "'**###'"; -123 ' displays '-123'`

continues

9

Table 9.3. continued

Control Code	Purpose
$$	Displays a floating dollar sign to the left of a number. Here is an example: `PRINT USING "'$$##.##'"; 2.45 ' displays ' $2.45'`

**$	Displays a dollar amount. This control code fills the leading characters with asterisks, followed by the dollar sign, and then the number. In the case of negative numbers, the control code makes the minus sign appear to the left of the dollar sign. Here are a few examples:
	
	`PRINT USING "'**$##.##'"; 2 ' displays '*$2.00'`
	
	`PRINT USING "'**$##.##'"; -12.35`
	
	`'displays '*-$12.35'`

	Displays two types of commas in an output. The first type places commas between every three digits in the integer part of a number (for example, 1,234,456.767). To display a number with this kind of comma, place the comma control code to the left of the decimal in the format string. The second kind of comma appears at the end of the number only when the number has a decimal point. Here is an example:
	
	`' displays 1,123,456.89`
	
	`PRINT USING "######,.##"; 1123456.89`
	
	`' display 1.20,`
	
	`PRINT USING "#.##,"; 1.2`

Control Code	Purpose

^^^^	Displays the number in scientific format with two digits in the exponent. Here is an example:
	
	`PRINT USING "#.##^^^^"; 12! ' displays`
	`0.12E+02`
	
	`PRINT USING "+#.##^^^^"; 12! ' displays`
	`+1.20E+01`

^^^^^	Displays the number in expanded scientific format with three digits in the exponent. Here is an example:
	
	`PRINT USING "#.##^^^^^"; 12! 'displays`
	`0.12E+002`
	
	`PRINT USING "+#.##^^^^^"; 12! 'displays`
	`+1.20E+001`

DO use the format +#.#####^^^^^ as the best general-purpose numeric output format.

DON'T limit testing the numeric format to a narrow range of values. Try a wide range of positive and negative values (if applicable) to ensure that your program is using a good output format.

Here's the PRINT USING statement at work, displaying integers using various control codes. Listing 9.6, USING2.BAS, displays formatted integers. The program prompts you to enter a single-digit integer and displays your input using various format strings. Then the program prompts you to enter an integer between –50,000 and +50,000. The program displays the number you enter using various format strings.

Listing 9.6. USING2.BAS, which displays formatted integers.

```
1: REM Program demonstrates the PRINT USING
2: REM statement with integers
3: REM
4: ' declare constants
5: CONST TAB1 = 10
6: CONST TAB2 = 40
7: ' declare the variables
8: DIM L AS LONG
9: DIM FrmtStr AS STRING
10: DIM Q AS STRING
11: DIM C AS STRING
12:
13: CLS
14: Q = CHR$(34)
15:
16: DO
17:    INPUT "Enter an integer between 0 and 9 "; L
18:    PRINT
19: LOOP UNTIL L >= 0 AND L < 10
20:
21: PRINT TAB(TAB1); "Format"; TAB(TAB2); "Output"
22: PRINT STRING$(60, "-")
23: FOR I = 1 TO 4
24:    FrmtStr = STRING$(I, "#")
25:    PRINT TAB(TAB1); FrmtStr;
26:    PRINT TAB(TAB2); Q;
27:    PRINT USING FrmtStr; L;
28:    PRINT Q
29: NEXT I
30:
31: PRINT
32: PRINT "Press any key to continue...";
33: C = INPUT$(1)
34: CLS
35:
36: DO
```

```
37:    INPUT "Enter an integer between -50000 and 50000 "; L
38:    PRINT
39: LOOP UNTIL L >= -50000 AND L <= 50000
40:
41: PRINT TAB(TAB1); "Format"; TAB(TAB2); "Output"
42: PRINT STRING$(60, "-")
43: FOR I = 1 TO 8
44:    FrmtStr = STRING$(I, "#")
45:    PRINT TAB(TAB1); FrmtStr;
46:    PRINT TAB(TAB2); Q;
47:    PRINT USING FrmtStr; L;
48:    PRINT Q
49: NEXT I
50:
51: FOR I = 1 TO 8
52:    FrmtStr = "+#." + STRING$(I - 1, "#") + "^^^^"
53:    PRINT TAB(TAB1); FrmtStr;
54:    PRINT TAB(TAB2); Q;
55:    PRINT USING FrmtStr; L;
56:    PRINT Q
57: NEXT I
58:
59: PRINT
60: PRINT "Press any key to continue...";
61: C = INPUT$(1)
62: CLS
63:
64: PRINT TAB(TAB1); "Format"; TAB(TAB2); "Output"
65: PRINT STRING$(60, "-")
66: FOR I = 1 TO 8
67:    FrmtStr = "**" + STRING$(I, "#")
68:    PRINT TAB(TAB1); FrmtStr;
69:    PRINT TAB(TAB2); Q;
70:    PRINT USING FrmtStr; L;
71:    PRINT Q
72: NEXT I
73:
74: END
```

9

Here is some sample output for the program in Listing 9.6:

```
Enter an integer between 0 and 9 ? 5

        Format                          Output
------------------------------------------------------------
        #                               "5"
        ##                              " 5"
        ###                             "  5"
        ####                            "   5"


Press any key to continue...
```

SCREEN CLEARS

```
Enter an integer between -50000 and 50000 ? -30000

        Format                          Output
------------------------------------------------------------
        #                               "%%-3E+00"
        ##                              "%-30000"
        ###                             "%-30000"
        ####                            "%-30000"
        #####                           "%-30000"
        ######                          "-30000"
        #######                         " -30000"
        ########                        "  -30000"
        +#.^^^^                         "-3.E+04"
        +#.#^^^^                         "-3.0E+04"
        +#.##^^^^                        "-3.00E+04"
        +#.###^^^^                       "-3.000E+04"
        +#.####^^^^                      "-3.0000E+04"
        +#.#####^^^^                     "-3.00000E+04"
        +#.######^^^^                    "-3.000000E+04"
        +#.#######^^^^                   "-3.0000000E+04"


Press any key to continue...
```

SCREEN CLEARS

Format	Output
**#	"%-30000"
**##	"%-30000"
**###	"%-30000"
**####	" -30000"
**#####	" *-30000"
**######	" **-30000"
**#######	" ***-30000"
**########	" ****-30000"

Analysis

Before I discuss the program lines, take a look at the output. The first screen contains the output of the number 5 using the "#", "##", "###", and "####" formats. The output, which is enclosed in double-quotes, shows that the extra # characters in the format string translate into leading spaces.

In the case of the second integer, the program shows the output for a negative number. The second screen contains two kinds of formats: the # character sequence and the scientific notation format. The output for the first five # character formats begins with at least one % character. This character is QBasic's way of telling you that the format string is inadequate for the number you are trying to display. In this case, the number -30000 needs a format string with at least six # characters. In the case of the scientific notation formats, the output is fine, except that it includes a decimal and gives the impression that the number is a floating-point. The third screen shows the number -30000 displayed using the ** and # control codes. The first three format strings are inadequate for the number—QBasic flags this problem by including the % character in the output. The other format strings are adequate. Notice that the last four format strings cause leading asterisks to appear before the number.

Now look at the statements in Listing 9.6. Lines 5 and 6 declare the constants used to align the two columns in the tables. Lines 8–11 declare the variables. The DO-UNTIL loop on lines 16 and 19 ensure that you enter a single-digit integer. The INPUT statement on line 17 prompts you for the integer and stores it in the variable L. The LOOP UNTIL clause on line 19 ensures that the DO-UNTIL loop iterates until you enter the required numeric input.

The program displays the first table using the statements on lines 21–29. The PRINT statements on lines 21 and 22 display the table heading. The FOR-NEXT loop on lines 23–29 display the contents of L using a format string

9

(stored in the variable FrmtStr) with a varying number of # control codes. Each loop iteration builds a format string with a number of # control codes equal to the value in the loop-control variable I. The PRINT statements on lines 25–28 display the format string and the formatted value of the variable L. Lines 32–34 enable the program to wait for you to press any key to resume.

On lines 36–39 the program prompts you to enter an integer in the range from –50000 to 50000. The program uses a DO-UNTIL loop that contains an INPUT statement, just like the loop on lines 16–19.

The program displays the table heading using the PRINT statements on lines 41 and 42. The FOR-NEXT loop on lines 43–49 contains statements that are very similar to those on lines 23–29. The only difference is that the FOR-NEXT loop on lines 43–49 iterates from 1 to 8, instead of from 1 to 4.

The FOR-NEXT loop on lines 51–57 generates the output for the second part of the table. This kind of output displays the value in the variable L using a scientific notation. Each loop iteration assigns a new format string to FrmtStr (line 52). The PRINT statements on lines 53–55 display the format string and the integer value. Lines 59–61 enable the program to wait for you to press any key to resume.

The program displays the table heading using the PRINT statements on lines 64 and 65. The FOR-NEXT loop on lines 66–72 contains statements that display the value of L using the ** and # control codes. Each loop iteration creates and uses a format string with a varying number of # characters.

Format Float Output

Let's apply a few format control codes to a floating-point number. Listing 9.7, USING3.BAS, displays formatted floating-point numbers. The program prompts you to enter a floating-point number and then displays several tables that show the output generated by various format strings.

 Listing 9.7. USING3.BAS, which displays formatted floating-point numbers.

```
1: REM Program demonstrates the PRINT USING
2: REM statement with floating-point numbers
3: REM
```

```
 4: ' declare constants
 5: CONST TAB1 = 10
 6: CONST TAB2 = 40
 7: ' declare the variables
 8: DIM X AS DOUBLE
 9: DIM FrmtStr AS STRING
10: DIM Q AS STRING
11: DIM C AS STRING
12:
13: CLS
14: Q = CHR$(34)
15:
16: INPUT "Enter a floating-point number "; X
17:
18: PRINT TAB(TAB1); "Format"; TAB(TAB2); "Output"
19: PRINT STRING$(60, "-")
20: FOR I = 1 TO 8
21:    FrmtStr = STRING$(I, "#")
22:    PRINT TAB(TAB1); FrmtStr;
23:    PRINT TAB(TAB2); Q;
24:    PRINT USING FrmtStr; X;
25:    PRINT Q
26: NEXT I
27:
28: FOR I = 1 TO 8
29:    FrmtStr = STRING$(I, "#") + "." + STRING$(I - 1, "#")
30:    PRINT TAB(TAB1); FrmtStr;
31:    PRINT TAB(TAB2); Q;
32:    PRINT USING FrmtStr; X;
33:    PRINT Q
34: NEXT I
35:
36: PRINT
37: PRINT "Press any key to continue...";
38: C = INPUT$(1)
39: CLS
40:
41: PRINT TAB(TAB1); "Format"; TAB(TAB2); "Output"
42: PRINT STRING$(60, "-")
43: FOR I = 1 TO 8
44:    FrmtStr = "+#." + STRING$(I - 1, "#") + "^^^^^"
```

continues

```
45:    PRINT TAB(TAB1); FrmtStr;
46:    PRINT TAB(TAB2); Q;
47:    PRINT USING FrmtStr; X;
48:    PRINT Q
49: NEXT I
50: FOR I = 1 TO 8
51:    FrmtStr = "#." + STRING$(I - 1, "#") + "^^^^^-"
52:    PRINT TAB(TAB1); FrmtStr;
53:    PRINT TAB(TAB2); Q;
54:    PRINT USING FrmtStr; X;
55:    PRINT Q
56: NEXT I
57:
58: PRINT
59: PRINT "Press any key to continue...";
60: C = INPUT$(1)
61: CLS
62:
63: PRINT TAB(TAB1); "Format"; TAB(TAB2); "Output"
64: PRINT STRING$(60, "-")
65: FOR I = 1 TO 4
66:    FrmtStr = "**$" + STRING$(I, "#") + ".##"
67:    PRINT TAB(TAB1); FrmtStr;
68:    PRINT TAB(TAB2); Q;
69:    PRINT USING FrmtStr; X;
70:    PRINT Q
71: NEXT I
72: FOR I = 1 TO 4
73:    FrmtStr = STRING$(4 + I, "#") + ",." + STRING$(I, "#")
74:    PRINT TAB(TAB1); FrmtStr;
75:    PRINT TAB(TAB2); Q;
76:    PRINT USING FrmtStr; X;
77:    PRINT Q
78: NEXT I
79: FOR I = 1 TO 4
80:    FrmtStr = STRING$(4 + I, "#") + "." + STRING$(I, "#") + ","
81:    PRINT TAB(TAB1); FrmtStr;
82:    PRINT TAB(TAB2); Q;
83:    PRINT USING FrmtStr; X;
```

```
84:   PRINT Q
85: NEXT I
86:
87: END
```

Here is some sample output for the program in Listing 9.7:

```
Enter a floating-point number ? 144000.12
        Format                          Output
-----------------------------------------------------------
        #                               "%1D+00"
        ##                              "%144000"
        ###                             "%144000"
        ####                            "%144000"
        #####                           "%144000"
        ######                          "144000"
        #######                         " 144000"
        ########                        "  144000"
        #.                              "%1.D+00"
        ##.#                            "%144000.1"
        ###.##                          "%144000.12"
        ####.###                        "%144000.120"
        #####.####                      "%144000.1200"
        ######.#####                    "144000.12000"
        #######.######                  " 144000.120000"
        ########.#######                "  144000.1200000"
```

```
Press any key to continue...
```

SCREEN CLEARS

```
        Format                          Output
-----------------------------------------------------------
        +#.^^^^^                        "+1.D+005"
        +#.#^^^^^                       "+1.4D+005"
        +#.##^^^^^                      "+1.44D+005"
        +#.###^^^^^                     "+1.440D+005"
        +#.####^^^^^                    "+1.4400D+005"
        +#.#####^^^^^                   "+1.44000D+005"
        +#.######^^^^^                  "+1.440001D+005"
        +#.#######^^^^^                 "+1.4400012D+005"
```

```
#.^^^^^-                        "1.D+005 "
#.#^^^^^-                       "1.4D+005 "
#.##^^^^^-                      "1.44D+005 "
#.###^^^^^-                     "1.440D+005 "
#.####^^^^^-                    "1.4400D+005 "
#.#####^^^^^-                   "1.44000D+005 "
#.######^^^^^-                  "1.440001D+005 "
#.#######^^^^^-                 "1.4400012D+005 "


Press any key to continue...
```

 ## SCREEN CLEARS

Format	Output
**$#.##	"%$144000.12"
**$##.##	"%$144000.12"
**$###.##	"%$144000.12"
**$####.##	"$144000.12"
####,.#	"%144,000.1"
#####,.##	"144,000.12"
######,.###	" 144,000.120"
#######,.####	" 144,000.1200"
#####.#,	"%144000.1,"
######.##,	"144000.12,"
#######.###,	" 144000.120,"
########.####,	" 144000.1200,"

 The program in Listing 9.7 is very similar to the one in Listing 9.6. Therefore, I only discuss the program output.

The first table contains two sets of format strings. The first set uses the # control code only to build the format string. Such a format displays a floating-point number as an integer. Notice that the first five lines in the table show an output that starts with the % character—this is QBasic signalling that the number of # characters is less than the number of digits to display. Line six in the table has the correct number of # characters in the format string. This line displays the integral part of the input value without any leading spaces. The next two lines display spaces, because the number of # characters in the format string exceeds the number of digits in the integral part of 144000.12.

The second kind of output in the first table uses the # and . control codes. Each line has a format with an increasing number of # characters on both sides of the decimal. Again, the first five format strings are inadequate for displaying all the digits in the input. The other lines contain more-than-adequate format strings. These strings have leading spaces and/or display trailing zeros.

The second table displays the input value using the scientific notation and a sign. The first set of formats use the leading + control code along with the #, ., and ^^^^^ control codes. Notice that the third through seventh lines in the table display the input value adequately. The eighth line displays all the digits of the input value.

The second set of format strings uses the trailing - control code to display a trailing minus sign (for negative numbers) or a space (for non-negative numbers). The output generated by this set of format strings resembles the one generated by the first set of format strings.

The third output table contains three sets of format strings. The first set uses the **$, #, and . control codes. Notice that only the last format string in the set adequately displays the input value.

The second set of format strings uses the , control code and places it to the left of the . control code. This set of format strings displays values with the comma grouping every three digits to the left of the decimal point.

The third set of format strings uses the , control code and puts it at the end of the format. This set of format strings displays values with trailing commas.

Tables with *PRINT USING*

QBasic allows the PRINT USING statement to use a format that displays multiple values. This feature makes the PRINT USING statement suitable for displaying tabulated values. To demonstrate this feature, I present program USING4.BAS in Listing 9.8. This program is a version of Listings 9.2, 9.3, and 9.4 that use the PRINT USING statement to display tabulated data.

9

Listing 9.8. USING4.BAS, which displays tabulated values by utilizing the PRINT USING statement.

```
 1: REM Program that displays a table using
 2: REM the PRINT USING statement
 3: REM
 4: CONST MARGIN = 30
 5: CONST TITLE1 = "Sample Table of Squares and Cubes"
 6: CONST TITLE2 = "(using the PRINT USING statement)"
 7: CONST FIRST = 10
 8: CONST LAST = 20
 9: ' declare the variables
10: DIM N AS INTEGER
11:
12: CLS
13: PRINT
14: PRINT TAB(40 - LEN(TITLE1) \ 2); TITLE1
15: PRINT TAB(40 - LEN(TITLE2) \ 2); TITLE2
16: PRINT
17: PRINT
18:
19: PRINT TAB(MARGIN); "N      N^2      N^3"
20: PRINT TAB(MARGIN); "------------------"
21: FOR N = FIRST TO LAST
22:   PRINT TAB(MARGIN);
23:   PRINT USING "##     ###      ####"; N; N * N; N * N * N
24: NEXT N
25:
26: END
```

Here is some sample output for the program in Listing 9.8:

```
Sample Table of Squares and Cubes
(using the PRINT USING statement)


N     N^2     N^3
------------------
10    100     1000
11    121     1331
```

12	144	1728
13	169	2197
14	196	2744
15	225	3375
16	256	4096
17	289	4913
18	324	5832
19	361	6859
20	400	8000

The lines in this fourth version of the numeric table program should look familiar. The highlight of the program is line 23, which contains the "## ### ####" format string. This string has three groups of # characters. The PRINT statement displays the values for N, N squared, and N cubed.

Printer Output

The PRINT and PRINT USING statements send the output to the screen. What about sending the output to the printer? QBasic offers the LPRINT and LPRINT USING statements as the printer versions of PRINT and PRINT USING. Everything you learned about PRINT and PRINT USING works in a similar way with LPRINT and LPRINT USING. This includes, for example, the TAB and SPC functions.

The LPRINT Statement

The general syntax for the LPRINT statement is

```
LPRINT [listOfValues] [{; ¦ ,}]
```

The listOfvalues is a list of expressions (string or numeric) separated by commas and/or semicolons. Each expression is either a literal constant, named constant, variable, function call, or any combination of these components. The LPRINT statement with no arguments advances the printer by one line.

Examples:

```
' prints two blank lines
LPRINT : LPRINT
```

9

```
FOR I = 1 TO 10
    LPRINT I, I * I, I * I * I
NEXT I


S$ = "List Of Names"
LPRINT SPC(40 - LEN(S2) \ 2); S$
```

The LPRINT USING Statement

The general syntax for the LPRINT USING statement is

```
LPRINT USING formatStr ; [listOfValues] [{; ¦ ,}]
```

The *formatStr* parameter is a string expression. The arguments for this parameter can be a string literal, string constant, string variable, string function, or any combination of these basic components. The *listOfvalues* is a list of expressions (string or numeric) separated by commas and/or semicolons. Each expression is either a literal constant, named constant, variable, function call, or any combination of these components.

Examples:

```
FOR I = 1 TO 10
    LPRINT USING "## ###  ####"; I, I * I, I * I * I
NEXT I


LPRINT "+#.#####^^^^^"; 355 / 113
```

DO use the form feed character CHR$(12) (and in some printers, CHR$(140)) to eject a page in the printer.

DON'T forget to turn on your printer and set it online.

Take a look at an example for using the LPRINT and LPRINT USING statements. Listing 9.9, LPRINT1.BAS, prints a financial table related to investing funds. The program prompts you to enter an amount and the period of investment (in years). The program then prints a table for the future values of your investment for every year in the period you specify. The table shows the future value at 3 percent, 5 percent, 7 percent, and 9 percent interest rates. The calculations use the financial equation

$$FV = PV (1 + i)N$$

where PV is the present value, FV is the future value, i is the interest rate in decimal, and N is the number of investment periods.

Listing 9.9. LPRINT1.BAS, which prints a financial table related to investing a fund.

```
 1: REM Program that uses the LPRINT statement
 2: REM to print financial tables
 3: REM
 4: ' declare the constant
 5: CONST TITLE = "Future Values Table"
 6: ' declare the variables
 7: DIM PV AS DOUBLE
 8: DIM FV AS DOUBLE
 9: DIM Interest AS DOUBLE
10: DIM N AS INTEGER
11: DIM I AS INTEGER
12:
13: CLS
14: INPUT "Enter present value "; PV
15: INPUT "Enter number of periods "; N
16: LPRINT TAB(40 - LEN(TITLE) \ 4); TITLE
17: LPRINT
18: LPRINT TAB(15);
19: LPRINT "Year         3%            5%            7%            9%"
20: LPRINT TAB(15);
21: LPRINT "----------------------------------------------------------"
22: FOR I = 1 TO N
23:    LPRINT TAB(15);
```

continues

Listing 9.9. continued

```
24:    LPRINT USING "####"; I;
25:    FOR Interest = 3 TO 9 STEP 2
26:      FV = PV * (1 + Interest / 100) ^ I
27:      LPRINT USING "  #######.##"; FV;
28:    NEXT Interest
29:    LPRINT
30: NEXT I
31: END
```

Here is some sample printer output for the program in Listing 9.9. The output shows the results for an initial value of $1000 invested for up to 10 years:

                         Future Values Table

Year	3%	5%	7%	9%
1	1030.00	1050.00	1070.00	1090.00
2	1060.90	1102.50	1144.90	1188.10
3	1092.73	1157.63	1225.04	1295.03
4	1125.51	1215.51	1310.80	1411.58
5	1159.27	1276.28	1402.55	1538.62
6	1194.05	1340.10	1500.73	1677.10
7	1229.87	1407.10	1605.78	1828.04
8	1266.77	1477.46	1718.19	1992.56
9	1304.77	1551.33	1838.46	2171.89
10	1343.92	1628.89	1967.15	2367.36

The program in Listing 9.9 declares the constant TITLE on line 5. The program declares its variables on lines 7–11. The INPUT statement on line 14 prompts you to enter the present investment value and stores it in the variable PV. The INPUT statement on line 15 prompts you to enter the number of periods and stores it in the variable N. The LPRINT statement on line 16 displays the centered title on the printer page.

The LPRINT statement on line 17 advances the printer by a line. The LPRINT statements on lines 18 and 21 print the table heading. The program uses the outer FOR-NEXT loop on lines 22–30 to print the results. The loop uses the control variable I and iterates from 1 to N (the number of investment periods).

The `LPRINT` statement on line 23 uses the `TAB` function to begin printing at column 23. The `LPRINT USING` statement on line 24 displays the value of the outer loop control variable I. Lines 25–28 contain the inner `FOR-NEXT` loop. This loop uses the control variable `Interest` and iterates from 3 to 9 in steps of 2.

The statement on line 26 calculates the future value for the year I and the interest rate `Interest`. The statement assigns the future value to the variable FV. The `LPRINT USING` statement on line 27 displays the future value. Notice that the statement ends with a semicolon to keep printing the future values for the various interest rates on the same line. The `LPRINT` statement on line 29 advances the printing to the next line.

Locating the Screen Cursor

QBasic enables you to locate the position of the screen cursor using the `CSRLIN` and `POS` functions.

The CSRLIN Function

The general syntax for the `CSRLIN` function is

```
CSRLIN
```

The function returns the current row position of the cursor. The values returned by the function range from 1 to 25.

Examples:

```
Y = CSRLIN
```

```
IF Y > 24 THEN CLS
```

The POS Function

The general syntax for the `POS` function is:

```
POS(dummyValue)
```

The parameter *dummyValue* is a dummy parameter. The typical value for this parameter is 0. The `POS` function returns the current column position of the cursor.

315

Examples:

```
X = POS(0)


IF POS(0) > 75 THEN CLS
```

Moving the Screen Cursor

The counterpart of the CSRLIN and POS functions is the LOCATE statement. This statement enables you to move the cursor to a new location.

The LOCATE Statement

The general syntax for the LOCATE statement is

```
LOCATE [row][,[column][,visible][,[scanStart][,scanStop]]]]
```

The parameter *row* is the number of the sought cursor row. The valid range of arguments for this parameter is from 1 to 25. The parameter *column* is the number of the sought cursor column. The valid range of arguments for this parameter is from 1 to 80. The parameter *visible* indicates whether or not the cursor is visible. A value of 1 makes the cursor visible, and a value of 0 hides the cursor. The cursor size is determined by the values passed to the optional parameters scanStart and scanStop.

Examples:

```
LOCATE 1, 1 ' top left corner of screen


' move cursor to lower right corner, or wrap around
Y = CSRLIN MOD 25 + 1
X = POS(0) MOD 80 + 1
LOCATE X, Y
```

Take a look at an example that uses the CSRLIN function, the POS function, and the LOCATE statement. Listing 9.10, LOCATE1.BAS, displays the letter o traversing the screen. The letter o traverses the screen moving down and to the right, and it wraps around when it reaches the right or bottom edge of the screen. To end the program, press the Escape key.

Listing 9.10. LOCATE1.BAS, which displays the letter o traversing the screen.

```
 1: REM Program that uses the LOCATE statement
 2: REM with the CSRLIN and POS functions
 3: REM to manipulate the cursor
 4: ' declare constants
 5: CONST CURSOR = "o"
 6: CONST INVISIBLE = 0
 7: CONST DELAY = .25
 8: ' declare variables
 9: DIM X AS INTEGER
10: DIM Y AS INTEGER
11: DIM TheTime AS SINGLE
12: DIM C AS STRING
13:
14: CLS
15: PRINT "Press the Esc key to stop the program"
16: PRINT
17: PRINT "Press any key to start the program... ";
18: C = INPUT$(1)
19: CLS
20: ' loop to move the cursor
21: DO
22:    ' get the current cursor coordinates
23:    Y = CSRLIN
24:    X = POS(0)
25:    ' increments the cursor coordinates
26:    Y = Y MOD 25 + 1
27:    X = X MOD 80 + 1
28:    ' display the cursor
29:    LOCATE Y, X, INVISIBLE
30:    PRINT CURSOR;
```

continues

Screen and Printer Output

Listing 9.10. continued

```
31:    ' wait for a short while
32:    TheTime = TIMER
33:    DO
34:    LOOP UNTIL (TIMER - TheTime) >= DELAY
35:    ' erase the cursor
36:    LOCATE Y, X, INVISIBLE
37:    PRINT " ";
38: LOOP UNTIL INKEY$ = CHR$(27)
39: END
```

Run the program in Listing 9.10 and observe the letter o as it traverses the screen. To end the program, press the Escape key.

Analysis

The program in Listing 9.10 declares three constants on lines 5–7. The constant CURSOR defines the moving cursor character as the letter o. The constant INVISIBLE has a value of 0 and is used to hide the cursor during the program execution. The constant DELAY specifies a delay of 0.25 seconds between cursor moves. The program declares its variables on lines 9–12. The PRINT statements on lines 15–17 display a message reminding you to press the Escape key to stop the program.

Lines 21–38 contain the DO-UNTIL loop that moves the cursor. The statement on line 23 calls the function CSRLIN and stores the row position of the cursor in the variable Y. The statement on line 24 calls the function POS and stores the column position of the cursor in the variable X. The statement on line 26 increments the value of Y. The statement uses the MOD function to ensure that the value of Y resets to 1 when it reaches 25 (the maximum number of screen rows). The statement on line 27 increments the value of X. The statement uses the MOD function to ensure that the value of X resets to 1 when it reaches 80 (the maximum number of screen columns). The LOCATE statement on line 29 moves the cursor to column X and row Y. The PRINT statement on line 30 displays the cursor character at the new cursor coordinates. Once the statement is executed, the cursor position moves to column X+1 and row Y.

The program uses lines 32 and 34 to implement a delay loop. After the loop stops iterating, the program moves the cursor back to column X and row Y. This time, the program uses the PRINT statement on line 37 to erase the cursor

character. This statement prepares the cursor to be drawn in the next iteration. The LOOP UNTIL clause compares the INKEY$ function with the escape character. If this condition is true, the loop stops iterating and the program ends.

Summary

This chapter presented you with QBasic functions and statements that enable you to format output to the screen and to the printer. In addition, the chapter discusses topics related to managing the screen cursor. Today you learned about the following topics:

☐ Tabbing output using commas to separate the displayed values in the PRINT statement. The commas cause each item to appear in the next display zone. Each display zone is 14 characters wide.

☐ Tabbing output using the TAB function, which enables you to specify the column position where the next output appears. If the specified column position is already beyond the current position, the output appears at the specified column position on the next line.

☐ Spacing output with the SPC function, which enables you to specify the relative difference in column positions between the last and next output values.

☐ Formatting output with the PRINT USING statement, which controls the output of string and numeric values. QBasic supports a variety of control codes that support flexible formatted output.

☐ Printer output that uses the LPRINT and LPRINT USING statements in a manner that parallels the PRINT and PRINT USING statements.

☐ Locating the screen cursor with the CSRLIN and POS functions, which enables you to query the current cursor location. You can use this information to move the cursor by a relative number of rows and/or columns. In addition, you also can store the cursor location, display information elsewhere on the screen, and then return back to the original location.

9

☐ Moving the screen cursor with the LOCATE statement, which enables you to direct output to any location on the screen. The LOCATE statement also enables you to specify the shape of the cursor and its visibility. You can use this statement to display fancy menus, input forms, output reports, and even support games.

Q&A

Q. How do I send the same output to the screen and to the printer?

A. You need to use two sets of similar statements, one with LPRINT and the other with PRINT. Here is an example of a program that displays and prints a small set of values:

```
FOR I = 1 TO 10
    LPRINT I, I * I
    PRINT I, I * I
NEXT I
```

Notice that the LPRINT and PRINT statements contain an identical list of values.

Q. How do I advance a page on the printer?

A. The form feed character is CHR$(12). On some printers, such as the Hewlett-Packard LaserJet printers, you need to add 128 to the ASCII code of 12. Consequently, the form feed character for such printers is CHR$(140).

Q. What kind of programs hide the cursor?

A. Typically, programs that play games look better if the cursor is invisible.

Q. Does QBasic support statements that manipulate the current output position for printers?

A. No. Many factors (mainly the different types of printers) make this task difficult.

Workshop

The Workshop provides quiz questions to help you solidify your understanding of the material covered and exercises to provide you with experience in using what you've learned. Try to understand the quiz and exercise answers before continuing on to the next chapter. Answers are provided in Appendix B, "Answers."

Quiz

1. What is the output of each of the following PRINT USING statements?

   a. `PRINT USING "'#.#####'"; 1.2`
   b. `PRINT USING "'+#.####^^^^^'"; 355 / 113`
   c. `PRINT USING "'+#.####^^^^^'"; 12`
   d. `PRINT USING "'#.####^^^^^'"; 12`
   e. `PRINT USING "'#.####^^^^^+'"; 12`
   f. `PRINT USING "'#.####^^^^^-'"; 12`
   g. `PRINT USING "'#.####^^^^^-'"; -12`
   h. `PRINT USING "'$$###.##'"; 98.55`
   i. `PRINT USING "'**$###.##'"; 98.55`
   j. `PRINT USING "'###########,.##'"; 1.2E+09`
   k. `PRINT USING "'###########.##,'"; 1.2E+09`

2. What is the output of each of the following PRINT USING statements?

   a. `PRINT USING "'!'"; "Hello"`
   b. `PRINT USING "'\\'"; "Hello"`
   c. `PRINT USING "'\   \'"; "Hello"`

3. True or false: The next two PRINT statements display the same output.

   ```
   S$ = "MAIN MENU"
   PRINT TAB(40 - LEN(S$) \ 2); S$
   PRINT SPC(40 - LEN(S$) \ 2); S$
   ```

4. True or false: The next two PRINT statements display the same output.

   ```
   PRINT TAB(10); 1; TAB(20); 2; TAB(30); 3
   PRINT SPC(10); 1; SPC(20); 2; SPC(30); 3
   ```

9

5. Replace the following PRINT USING statement with a PRINT statement:

   PRINT USING "!"; AString

6. Replace the following PRINT USING statement with a PRINT statement:

   PRINT USING "\ \"; AString

7. Replace the following PRINT USING statement with a PRINT statement:

   PRINT USING "&"; AString

Exercises

1. Create a version of the program LPRINT1.BAS (call it USING5.BAS) that displays the formatted output to the screen. Take into account that the number of years might exceed the number of screen rows. (Hint: use an IF statement to pause the program every 15 years, clear the screen, redisplay the table heading, and display the next set of values.)

2. Write a set of QBasic statements that clears the characters from the current cursor position to the end of the line. Make the statements restore the cursor to its original position before erasing the characters. Use the variables X and Y to store the current cursor position.

DAY
10

Subroutines
and Functions

QBasic is the first structured implementation of BASIC bundled with MS-DOS. This chapter introduces you to the aspects of QBasic that support structured programming. These language features include the ability to write semi-independent program components. On Day 16, "Advanced Subprograms," I discuss more advanced topics regarding such program components. Today, you will learn about the following topics:

☐ An overview of writing structured programs

☐ Writing subroutines with the GOSUB statement

☐ Writing and using your own functions with the DEF FN statement

☐ Writing and using SUB procedures

☐ The DECLARE statement

☐ Using the QBasic environment to manage procedures

☐ Value parameters

☐ Reference parameters

☐ Writing and using FUNCTION procedures

An Overview of Writing Structured Programs

Structured programming encourages you to plan your programs in terms of the tasks they carry out. The pseudocode you write should specify these tasks. In the case of complex programs, it is a good idea to write several versions of pseudocode, each revealing more details for the various tasks and their own subtasks.

Let me put this concept to work by presenting the pseudocode for a simple program that displays a table of squares and cubes:

1. Clear the screen.

2. Display the centered titles.

3. Display the table heading.

4. Display the contents of the table in a paginated fashion.

The first pseudocode gives you a general idea of what the program does. Here is the refined pseudocode, which reveals more details:

1. Clear the screen.

2. Display the centered titles.

3. Display the table heading.

4. Repeat the following steps for numbers 1 to 100:

    4.1.   Display the number, its squared value, and its cubed value.

    4.2.   Display a new screen page if the output is near the bottom of the screen.

This pseudocode reveals more of what the task in step 4 does. Here is another version of the refined pseudocode:

1. Clear the screen.

2. Display the centered titles.

3. Display the table heading.

4. Repeat the following steps for numbers 1 to 100:

    4.1.   Display the number, its squared value, and its cubed value.

    4.2.   If the cursor is at screen row 20, then do the following:

    4.2.1. Ask the user to press any key.

    4.2.2. Clear the screen.

    4.2.3. Display the centered titles.

    4.2.4. Display the table heading.

This version specifies more tasks and also reveals that the tasks in steps 1 and 4.2.2., in steps 2 and 4.2.3., and in steps 3 and 4.2.4. are identical. Moreover, these tasks are repeated in the same sequence. In the next section I show you how to use the same program lines for redundant tasks.

Listing 10.1, TABLE.BAS, displays a table of squares and cubes.

Listing 10.1. TABLE.BAS, which displays a table of squares and cubes.

```
 1: REM Program displays table of squares and cubes
 2: REM
 3: CONST TITLE1 = "Sample Table of Squares and Cubes"
 4: CONST TITLE2 = "(plain version)"
 5: ' declare the variables
 6: DIM A AS DOUBLE
 7: DIM C AS STRING
 8:
 9: CLS
10: PRINT
11: PRINT SPACE$(40 - LEN(TITLE1) \ 2) + TITLE1
12: PRINT SPACE$(40 - LEN(TITLE2) \ 2) + TITLE2
13: PRINT
14: PRINT
15: PRINT , "  X", "X ^ 2", "  X ^ 3"
16: PRINT , STRING$(35, "-")
17: FOR A = 1 TO 100
18:    PRINT , A, A * A, A * A * A
19:    IF CSRLIN = 20 THEN
20:      PRINT
21:      PRINT "Press any key to continue"
22:      C = INPUT$(1)
23:      CLS
24:      PRINT
25:      PRINT SPACE$(40 - LEN(TITLE1) \ 2) + TITLE1
26:      PRINT SPACE$(40 - LEN(TITLE2) \ 2) + TITLE2
27:      PRINT
28:      PRINT
29:      PRINT , "  X", "X ^ 2", "  X ^ 3"
30:      PRINT , STRING$(35, "-")
31:    END IF
32: NEXT A
33:
34: END
```

Here is a snapshot of the sample output for the program in Listing 10.1. The program continues printing squares and cubes until it reaches 100, but for the sake of brevity, I only show one screen (I also do this in other versions of this program later in the chapter):

```
Sample Table of Squares and Cubes
           (plain version)


      X              X ^ 2              X ^ 3
- - - - - - - - - - - - - - - - - - - - - - - - -

      1              1                  1
      2              4                  8
      3              9                  27
      4              16                 64
      5              25                 125
      6              36                 216
      7              49                 343
      8              64                 512
      9              81                 729
      10             100                1000
      11             121                1331
      12             144                1728


Press any key to continue
```

The program in Listing 10.1 declares the constants TITLE1 and TITLE2 on lines 3 and 4. The program declares the variables A and C on lines 6 and 7. The PRINT statements on lines 11–16 display the titles and the table heading. The FOR-NEXT loop on lines 17–32 displays the paginated output. The loop uses the control variable A and iterates from 1–100 (enough to fill a few screens). The PRINT statement on line 18 displays the value in A, its value squared, and its value cubed. The IF-THEN statement on line 19 determines whether the cursor is at screen row 20. If this condition is true, the program executes the THEN clause statements, found on lines 20–30. These statements prompt you to press any key, clear the screen, display the centered titles, and display the table heading.

10

The *GOSUB* Statement

The program in Listing 10.1 contains a set of statements that appear twice in the program and perform the same tasks. Structured programming promotes consolidating redundant statements into a single occurrence that can be invoked as many times as needed. QBasic offers two different methods to consolidate redundant statements. They are the GOSUB statement and the SUB procedure. In this section I present the GOSUB statement, which is the first mechanism and was part of the early BASIC implementations. The GOSUB statement enables your programs to jump to a program location, execute the sequence of statements in that location, and then return to the GOSUB statement. Figure 10.1 shows the mechanism of the GOSUB statement. When a program executes a GOSUB statement, it performs the following steps:

1. Obtain the label in the GOSUB statement.

2. Remember the location of the current GOSUB statement.

3. Jump to the subroutine label.

4. Execute the sequence statements that come after the label.

5. Return from the subroutine when the program encounters a RETURN statement.

6. Resume execution at the statement that immediately follows the GOSUB statement.

Figure 10.1 depicts some of these steps. The subroutine targeted by the GOSUB statement can be called many times and from various places in the program (including other subroutines). The RETURN statement sends the program execution back to the statement that follows the last GOSUB statement executed.

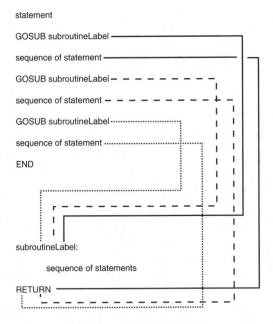

Figure 10.1. The mechanism of the GOSUB statement.

The GOSUB and RETURN Statements

The general syntax for the GOSUB and RETURN statements is

```
GOSUB label
[sequence of statements]
END


label:


    sequence of statements


RETURN [returnLabel]
```

The GOSUB statement contains the *label* name that specifies the program label that contains the subroutine's statements. The RETURN statement causes the program execution to return to the statement after the last GOSUB statement executed. The optional *returnLabel* enables the RETURN statement to specify where the program execution resumes.

All subroutines must be placed *after* the END statement. Otherwise, they will be executed as a normal set of statements. This kind of execution is not desired in the overwhelming majority of cases.

The subroutines invoked by GOSUB statements can contain other GOSUB statements.

Example:

```
DIM I AS INTEGER

I = 1
PRINT "I ="; I ' displays I = 1
GOSUB Incr.I
PRINT "I ="; I ' displays I = 2
GOSUB Incr.I
PRINT "I ="; I ' displays I = 3
END
' subroutine Incr.I
Incr.I:
    I = I + 1
RETURN
```

10

Let's apply the GOSUB statement to modify the program in Listing 10.1. Listing 10.2, GOSUB1.BAS, creates the table of squares and cubes using GOSUB statements.

Listing 10.2. GOSUB1.BAS, which creates the table of squares and cubes using GOSUB statements.

```
1: REM Program uses the GOSUB statement
2: REM
3: CONST TITLE1 = "Sample Table of Squares and Cubes"
4: CONST TITLE2 = "(GOSUB version)"
5: ' declare the variables
6: DIM A AS DOUBLE
7: DIM C AS STRING
8:
9: GOSUB Show.Centered.Titles
10: GOSUB Show.Table.Heading
11: FOR A = 1 TO 100
12:    PRINT , A, A * A, A * A * A
13:    IF CSRLIN = 20 THEN
14:      GOSUB Press.Any.Key
15:      GOSUB Show.Centered.Titles
16:      GOSUB Show.Table.Heading
17:    END IF
18: NEXT A
19:
20: END
21:
22: Show.Centered.Titles:
23:    CLS
24:    PRINT
25:    PRINT SPACE$(40 - LEN(TITLE1) \ 2) + TITLE1
26:    PRINT SPACE$(40 - LEN(TITLE2) \ 2) + TITLE2
27:    PRINT
28:    PRINT
29: RETURN
30:
31: Show.Table.Heading:
32:    PRINT , "  X", "X ^ 2", "  X ^ 3"
33:    PRINT , STRING$(35, "-")
34: RETURN
```

```
35:
36: Press.Any.Key:
37:   PRINT
38:   PRINT "Press any key to continue"
39:   C = INPUT$(1)
40: RETURN
```

Here is a snapshot of the sample output for the program in Listing 10.2:

```
Sample Table of Squares and Cubes
          (GOSUB version)


    X              X ^ 2              X ^ 3
    - - - - - - - - - - - - - - - - - - - - - - - -
    1              1                  1
    2              4                  8
    3              9                  27
    4              16                 64
    5              25                 125
    6              36                 216
    7              49                 343
    8              64                 512
    9              81                 729
   10              100                1000
   11              121                1331
   12              144                1728
```

```
Press any key to continue
```

The program in Listing 10.2 uses three subroutines, labeled Press.Any.Key, Show.Centered.Titles, and Show.Table.Heading. Lines 9 and 15 contain the GOSUB Show.Centered.Titles statement, which invokes the subroutine at label Show.Centered.Titles. The statements in this subroutine clear the screen and display centered labels. Lines 10 and 16 contain the GOSUB Show.Table.Heading statement, which invokes the subroutine at label Show.Table.Heading. The statements in this subroutine display the table heading. Line 14 contains the GOSUB Press.Any.Key statement which invokes subroutine at the label Press.Any.Key. This subroutine prompts you to press any key to resume the program.

10

Notice that the statements in the THEN clause contain three GOSUB statements. These statements use somewhat verbose labels to describe their tasks. Although using these labels requires a bit more typing, they help make your program easier to read.

The three subroutines are located after the END statement and use the RETURN statement with no return label. Most programs that use the RETURN statement don't use labels.

> **Note:** Looking at the program in Listing 10.2, you might have thought about combining the GOSUB statements on lines 9 and 10, and on lines 15 and 16. You can replace these two subroutines with a single one. Although this approach works, it contradicts structured programming disciplines. Such disciplines foster maintaining separate subroutines for different tasks. The solution that enables the program to use a single GOSUB call, while still maintaining the distinct subroutines, is shown in Listing 10.3. The GOSUB2.BAS program in this listing uses nested GOSUB statements. Lines 9 and 14 contain GOSUB statements that invoke the subroutine at the label Show.Titles.And.Heading. This subroutine contains two GOSUB statements that invoke the subroutines at labels Show.Centered.Titles and Show.Table.Heading.

 Listing 10.3. GOSUB2.BAS, which uses nested GOSUB statements.

```
1: REM Program uses nested GOSUB statements
2: REM
3: CONST TITLE1 = "Sample Table of Squares and Cubes"
4: CONST TITLE2 = "(nested GOSUB version)"
5: ' declare the variables
6: DIM A AS DOUBLE
7: DIM C AS STRING
8:
9: GOSUB Show.Titles.And.Heading
10: FOR A = 1 TO 100
11:   PRINT , A, A * A, A * A * A
```

```
12:    IF CSRLIN = 20 THEN
13:      GOSUB Press.Any.Key
14:      GOSUB Show.Titles.And.Heading
15:    END IF
16: NEXT A
17:
18: END
19:
20: Show.Titles.And.Heading:
21:    GOSUB Show.Centered.Titles
22:    GOSUB Show.Table.Heading:
23: RETURN
24:
25: Show.Centered.Titles:
26:    CLS
27:    PRINT
28:    PRINT SPACE$(40 - LEN(TITLE1) \ 2) + TITLE1
29:    PRINT SPACE$(40 - LEN(TITLE2) \ 2) + TITLE2
30:    PRINT
31:    PRINT
32: RETURN
33:
34: Show.Table.Heading:
35:    PRINT , "   X", "X ^ 2", "   X ^ 3"
36:    PRINT , STRING$(35, "-")
37: RETURN
38:
39: Press.Any.Key:
40:    PRINT
41:    PRINT "Press any key to continue"
42:    C = INPUT$(1)
43: RETURN
```

The *DEF FN* Statement

Another aspect of writing semi-independent program components involves the user-defined functions created with the DEF FN statement. The DEF FN function also is inherited from early BASIC implementations. QBasic also supports FUNCTION procedures, which implement more versatile user-defined functions. I present FUNCTION procedures later in this chapter.

Defining Functions

The DEF FN statement enables you to create your own string and numeric functions. Conceptually, such functions allow you to extend the QBasic language in the direction that suits your own programs.

The DEF FN Statement

The DEF FN statement has two forms:

```
DEF FNname(parameterList) = expression
```

and

```
DEF FNname(parameterList)
    sequence of statements
  ...
    FNname = expression
  ...
    sequence of statements
END DEF
```

FNname defines the name of the function, which cannot exceed 40 characters (not counting the letters FN). This name can include the data type suffixes to specify the nondefault data type of the function's result. The parameterList is a list of parameters, which have the following general syntax:

```
variable1 [AS type1] [, variable2 [AS type2], ...]
```

variable1, variable2, and so on, are the names of the function's parameters. These names can include data type suffixes to declare their data type. Alternatively, you can use the AS clause to declare the parameter's data type. If you use neither the type suffix nor the AS clause, QBasic uses the current association between the name of the variable and the default data type.

The expression assigned to the function's name (in either version of the DEF FN statement) must be compatible with the function's data type.

The parameters of a function are temporary variables that exist only when the program calls the function. Once the function has finished its tasks, the program removes the memory space occupied by the parameters.

Examples:

```
DEF FNSqr(X#) = X# * X#
DEF FNCube(X#) = X# * FNSqr(X#)
FNTrimmed$(S$) = LTRIM$(RTRIM$(S$))
FNFirstAndLastChars$(S$) = LEFT$(S$, 1) + RIGHT$(S$, 1)

DEF FNmin%(A%, B%)
  IF A% > B% THEN
    FNmin% = B%
  ELSE
    FNmin% = A%
  END IF
END DEF
```

Note: Indenting the statements in a user-defined function is not mandatory. However, if you do indent your statements, your programs will be easier to read.

Calling Functions

Calling user-defined functions is similar to calling built-in QBasic functions. Figure 10.2 depicts calling a user-defined function. The figure shows the function FNProcess with three parameters, N%, Z#, and T$. The figure also indicates that there are three variables: the integer variable A, the double-precision variable X, and the string variable S. There is also a PRINT statement in the figure that calls FNProcess. The function call has three arguments, A, X, and S. The number of arguments **must** match the number of parameters. In addition, the type of arguments at least must be compatible with the type of the parameters. QBasic will automatically perform any required numeric conversion. The function call causes the variables A, X, and S to pass a copy of their contents to parameters N%, Z#, and T$, respectively. This mapping process is the *positional association* between the arguments in a function call and the parameters of a function. The positional association is essentially a sequential, one-to-one mapping of the members in the argument list to the members in the parameter list. Once the parameters receive values from the arguments, the function starts executing and produces the sought result.

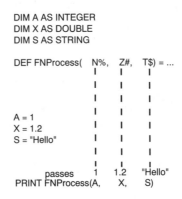

Figure 10.2. The mechanism of calling a user-defined function.

Let's look at an example. Listing 10.4, FN1.BAS, uses the DEF FN statement to create user-defined functions for the tables of squares and cubes. The program uses two numeric functions and one string function.

Listing 10.4. FN1.BAS, which uses the DEF FN statement to create user-defined functions for the tables of squares and cubes.

```
1: REM Program uses the DEF FN statement
2: REM
3: CONST TITLE1 = "Sample Table of Squares and Cubes"
4: CONST TITLE2 = "(DEF FN version)"
5: ' declare the variables
```

```
 6: DIM A AS DOUBLE
 7: DIM C AS STRING
 8:
 9: ' define functions
10: DEF FNSqr# (X#) = X# * X#
11: DEF FNCube# (X#) = X# * FNSqr#(X#)
12: DEF FNSpace$ (S$) = SPACE$(40 - LEN(S$) \ 2) + S$
13:
14: GOSUB Show.Centered.Titles
15: GOSUB Show.Table.Heading
16: FOR A = 1 TO 100
17:    PRINT , A, FNSqr#(A), FNCube#(A)
18:    IF CSRLIN = 20 THEN
19:      GOSUB Press.Any.Key
20:      GOSUB Show.Centered.Titles
21:      GOSUB Show.Table.Heading
22:    END IF
23: NEXT A
24:
25: END
26:
27: Show.Centered.Titles:
28:    CLS
29:    PRINT
30:    PRINT FNSpace$(TITLE1)
31:    PRINT FNSpace$(TITLE2)
32:    PRINT
33:    PRINT
34: RETURN
35:
36: Show.Table.Heading:
37:    PRINT , "  X", "X ^ 2", "  X ^ 3"
38:    PRINT , STRING$(35, "-")
39: RETURN
40:
41: Press.Any.Key:
42:    PRINT
43:    PRINT "Press any key to continue"
44:    C = INPUT$(1)
45: RETURN
```

Here is a snapshot of the sample output for the program in Listing 10.4:

```
Sample Table of Squares and Cubes
         (DEF FN version)


   X            X ^ 2            X ^ 3
   - - - - - - - - - - - - - - - - - - - - - - - -

   1            1                1
   2            4                8
   3            9                27
   4            16               64
   5            25               125
   6            36               216
   7            49               343
   8            64               512
   9            81               729
   10           100              1000
   11           121              1331
   12           144              1728
```

```
Press any key to continue
```

The program in Listing 10.4 declares the functions FNSqr#, FNCube#, and FNSpace$. The function FNSqr# returns the square of its parameter X#. The function FNCube# returns the cube of its parameter X#. Notice that I wrote this function to call the FNSqr# function. This example indicates that you can call a previously defined function in the expression of a currently defined function. The FNSpace$ function returns a string that provides the image of a centered string S$.

Line 17 contains the PRINT statement that calls both functions FNSqr# and FNCube#. The argument for both functions is the loop control variable A. This variable has the same data type as the parameter X in FNSqr# and FNCube#. If I declared A as an INTEGER, the program would automatically convert the integer argument to a double-precision number.

Lines 30 and 31 contain PRINT statements that call the FNSpace$ function. The argument for the first call is the string constant TITLE1. The second function call passes the string constant TITLE2.

The *SUB* Procedure

The GOSUB statement has a few shortcomings. First, it makes no provisions to pass arguments. Second, the program does not isolate the variables in the subroutine from the rest of the program and other subroutines. Likewise, the program does not isolate the variables in the main part of the program from the subroutines. More about the topic of isolating variables is provided on Day 16.

These remarks should make it clear to you that the GOSUB statement fails to create semi-independent subroutines. Fortunately, QBasic offers the SUB procedure to implement semi-independent subroutines with a parameter list. In addition, the SUB procedure enables you to control sharing variables with the main program.

Declaring *SUB* Procedures

QBasic automates declaring new SUB procedures. To create a new SUB procedure, select the Edit option in the main menu and then choose the New SUB selection. QBasic responds by popping up a dialog box that allows you to enter the name of the new SUB procedure. After you type the required input, QBasic displays a new window that contains an empty SUB procedure (the SUB name and the END SUB clause). The initial form of the SUB procedure contains no parameter list.

The **SUB** Procedure

The general syntax for the SUB procedure is

```
SUB subName[(parameterList)] [STATIC]
    sequence of statements
END SUB
```

subName defines the subroutine's name. This name must not contain a data type suffix, because a SUB procedure does not return a value. The parameterList is a list of parameters that have the following general syntax:

```
variable1 [AS type1] [, variable2 [AS type2], ...]
```

variable1, variable2, and so on, are the names of the procedure's parameters. These names can include data type suffixes to declare their data type. Alternatively, you can use the AS clause to declare the parameter's data type. If you use neither the type suffix nor the AS clause, QBasic uses the current association between the name of the variable and default data type.

The optional STATIC keyword specifies the status of the local variables inside the SUB procedure. More about this topic on Day 16.

Examples:

```
SUB CenterText (S AS STRING)
  PRINT TAB(40 - LEN(S$) \ 2); S$
END SUB


SUB DisplayString (S AS STRING, X%, Y%)
  LOCATE Y%, X%
  PRINT S
END SUB
```

Note: Indenting the statements in a SUB procedure is not mandatory. However, if you do indent the statements, you code will be easier to read.

Calling *SUB* Procedures

QBasic provides two syntaxes for calling a SUB procedure. The first one involves the keyword CALL. The second syntax enables you to invoke the name of the subroutine.

Syntax

Calling SUB Procedures

The general syntax for calling SUB procedures is:

```
[CALL] subName [(]argumentList[)]
```

The *subName* is the name of the called SUB procedure. If you use the
CALL keyword, you must enclose the *argumentList* in parentheses. By
contrast, if you omit the CALL keyword, you must not use the parentheses. The *argumentList* is a list of arguments, separated by commas, that
is supplied to the called subroutines. If the declaration of the subroutine contains no parameters, do not use empty parentheses after the
subroutine name, even if you use the CALL keyword.

Examples:

```
CALL CenterText("Hello")
CenterText "Howdee"
CALL DisplayString ("Hi Yall", 2, 1)
DisplayString "Hello Word!", 10, 10
```

DO use SUB procedures to implement subroutines.

DON'T use GOSUB statements to implement subroutines.

Let's look at an example. Listing 10.5 is a version of Listing 10.2 that uses
the SUB procedure instead of the GOSUB statement. If you type in the program, invoke the New SUB selection in the Edit menu option. Enter the name
of each subroutine in the prompting dialog box. When QBasic displays the
name of the subroutine, type in the parameter list when applicable, and then
enter the statements for each subroutine. There is no need to type in the DECLARE
statements on lines 1–3 of Listing 10.5. When you save the program, QBasic
automatically inserts the DECLARE statement for you.

10

> **Note:** QBasic separates the SUB procedures from the main pro-
> gram. That's why after you run the program in Listing 10.5, you
> will not find the subroutines by simply using the cursor keys.
> Don't be alarmed! QBasic has not erased these subroutines.
> Instead, QBasic stores and displays them separately. More about
> this topic in the next section.

Type   **Listing 10.5. SUB1.BAS, which uses the SUB
procedure.**

```
1: DECLARE SUB ShowCenteredTitles (T1 AS STRING, T2 AS STRING)
2: DECLARE SUB ShowTableHeading ()
3: DECLARE SUB PressAnyKey ()
4: REM Program uses SUB procedures
5: REM
6: CONST TITLE1 = "Sample Table of Squares and Cubes"
7: CONST TITLE2 = "(SUB procedure version 1)"
8: ' declare the variables
9: DIM A AS DOUBLE
10:
11: ' define functions
12: DEF FNSqr (X#) = X# * X#
13: DEF FNCube (X#) = X# * X# * X#
14:
15: ' program use CALL statements to invoke the
16: ' SUB ShowCenteredTitle and ShowTableHeading
17: CALL ShowCenteredTitles(TITLE1, TITLE2)
18: CALL ShowTableHeading
19: FOR A = 1 TO 100
20:    PRINT , A, FNSqr(A), FNCube(A)
21:    IF CSRLIN = 20 THEN
22:       ' program uses direct invocation of the
23:       ' procedures PressAnyKey, ShowCenteredTitles,
24:       ' and ShowTableHeading
25:       PressAnyKey
26:       ShowCenteredTitles TITLE1, TITLE2
27:       ShowTableHeading
```

```
28:    END IF
29: NEXT A
30:
31: END
32:
33: SUB PressAnyKey
34:    PRINT
35:    PRINT "Press any key to continue"
36:    C$ = INPUT$(1)
37: END SUB
38:
39: SUB ShowCenteredTitles (T1 AS STRING, T2 AS STRING)
40:    CLS
41:    PRINT
42:    PRINT TAB(40 - LEN(T1) \ 2); T1
43:    PRINT TAB(40 - LEN(T2) \ 2); T2
44:    PRINT
45:    PRINT
46: END SUB
47:
48: SUB ShowTableHeading
49:    PRINT , "  X", "X ^ 2", "  X ^ 3"
50:    PRINT , STRING$(35, "-")
51: END SUB
```

Here is a snapshot of the sample output for the program in Listing 10.5:

```
            Sample Table of Squares and Cubes
                 (SUB procedure version 1)



        X              X ^ 2            X ^ 3
        -----------------------------------
        1              1                1
        2              4                8
        3              9                27
        4              16               64
        5              25               125
        6              36               216
        7              49               343
```

8	64	512
9	81	729
10	100	1000
11	121	1331
12	144	1728

```
Press any key to continue
```

Analysis The program in Listing 10.5 declares three SUB procedures. ShowCenteredTitles displays centered titles. The subroutine has two string-typed parameters. ShowTableHeading, which has no parameters, displays the table heading. PressAnyKey (another subroutine without parameters) prompts you to press any key to continue program execution.

Lines 17 and 18 invoke the subroutines ShowCenteredTitle and ShowTableHeading using the CALL keyword. Notice the subroutine on line 17 encloses its argument list in parentheses. Lines 25–27 invoke the three subroutines without using the CALL keyword. Notice the call to ShowCenteredTitles does not enclose its argument list in parentheses. This type of subroutine call comes across as a more natural way of extending the QBasic language.

The *DECLARE* Statement

The first three lines in Listing 10.5 contain DECLARE statements. QBasic uses this statement to list the SUB and FUNCTION procedures (more about these later in the chapter) used in the program. The DECLARE statement tells the program about the names of the subroutines and their parameter lists. This information allows the program to determine the validity of the argument lists. Another advantage of the DECLARE statement is the ability to write subroutine invocations without having to use the CALL keyword. QBasic automatically generates the DECLARE statements when you save a program.

Warning: If you alter the parameter list of a SUB procedure, you are also responsible for altering the parameter list in the DECLARE statement.

The SUBs Options

The QBasic environment displays the SUB and FUNCTION procedures in separate windows. To view the list of the main program and procedures, choose the SUBs selection in the View menu option (or press the F2 key). Figure 10.3 shows the list of procedures generated by QBasic for the program in Listing 10.5. The list is part of a dialog box that has the following options:

1. The *Edit in Active* option enables you to edit the currently selected subroutine (or the main menu). You also can edit the currently selected program component by pressing the Return key.

2. The *Delete* option enables you to remove the currently selected subroutine from the program.

3. The *Cancel* option permits you to close the dialog box.

4. The *Help* option offers online help.

Figure 10.4 shows the window for SUB ShowCenteredTitles. Notice that the title of the currently edited window is SUB1.BAS:ShowCenteredTitles.

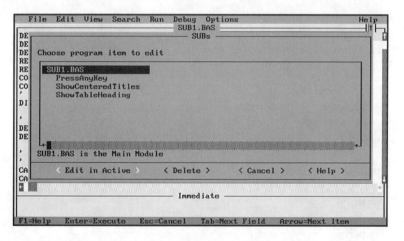

Figure 10.3. The list of procedures for the program in Listing 10.5.

```
 File  Edit  View  Search  Run  Debug  Options                    Help
                    SUB1.BAS:ShowCenteredTitles
 SUB ShowCenteredTitles (T1 AS STRING, T2 AS STRING)
   CLS
   PRINT
   PRINT TAB(40 - LEN(T1) \ 2); T1
   PRINT TAB(40 - LEN(T2) \ 2); T2
   PRINT
   PRINT
 END SUB




                             Immediate
 <Shift+F1=Help> <F6=Window> <F2=Subs> <F5=Run> <F8=Step>       N 00001:001
```

Figure 10.4. The window for SUB ShowCenteredTitles.

Value Parameters

The parameters of the DEF FN function pass copies of the values of their
arguments. This means you can alter the value of the parameter inside the
function without affecting the original source of data outside the function.
Here is an example:

```
DEF FNInc%(I%)
  I% = I% + 1
  FNInc% = I%
END DEF

DIM J AS INTEGER
J = 1
PRINT J
PRINT FNInc%(J)
PRINT J
END
```

The function FNInc% increments the value of its parameter I% and then
returns the incremented value. The first PRINT statement displays 1, the current

value in J. The second PRINT statement invokes the function FNInc%. This function call passes a *copy* of the value in J to the parameter I%. When the function alters the value in parameter I%, the contents of J remain intact. The second PRINT statement displays 2. The third PRINT statement displays 1, the value in J. This value is unaffected by incrementing the parameter I%.

Reference Parameters

In the last section I mentioned that the DEF FN functions pass their arguments by value. You might have noticed that I did not mention anything about parameter passing in the case of SUB procedures. Do they also pass arguments by value or do they support a different mechanism? The answer is the latter. Passing parameters in SUB procedures is not as clear-cut as in DEF FN functions. The reason for this complexity is the kind of argument passed. The SUB procedure reacts differently when you pass it a variable than when you pass it an expression. In the latter case, the SUB procedure passes the expression by value. In the case of a variable, the SUB procedure passes it by reference. This means that the parameter that corresponds to the variable becomes an alias to that variable. Another way of looking at this is as if the parameter is given some sort of power of attorney to represent the variable. Consequently, any changes made to the parameter inside the SUB procedure also affect the data in the variable outside the procedure.

DO enclose a variable in parentheses to ensures that it is passed by value.

DON'T pass a variable to a parameter by reference if that parameter is altered by its procedure.

Let me present two short examples. Listing 10.6, SUB2.BAS, passes a numeric parameter by reference in a SUB procedure. The program requires no input from you. It simply displays a set of strings centered on the screen.

10

Listing 10.6. SUB2.BAS, which passes a numeric parameter by reference in a SUB procedure.

```
1: DECLARE SUB CenterText (S AS STRING, L AS INTEGER)
2: DECLARE SUB INC (N AS INTEGER)
3: REM Program that passes a variable by reference
4: REM to a SUB procedure.
5: REM
6: ' declare variables
7: DIM Row AS INTEGER
8: DIM Text AS STRING
9: DIM N AS INTEGER
10: DIM I AS INTEGER
11:
12: CLS
13: Row = 2
14: READ N
15: FOR I = 1 TO N
16:    READ Text
17:    CenterText Text, Row
18: NEXT I
19:
20: ' ****************** DATA Statements ******************
21:
22: DATA 4
23: DATA Hello World, version 1.0,  by, Namir Clement Shammas
24: END
25:
26: SUB CenterText (S AS STRING, L AS INTEGER)
27:    LOCATE L, 1
28:    PRINT SPC(40 - LEN(S) \ 2); S
29:    INC L
30: END SUB
31:
32: SUB INC (N AS INTEGER)
33:    N = N + 1
34: END SUB
```

Here is sample output for the program in Listing 10.6:

```
        Hello World
        version 1.0
             by
   Namir Clement Shammas
```

The program in Listing 10.6 declares the CenterText and INC subroutines. The INC subroutine increments the value of its parameter N. The CenterText subroutine displays the string S centered at row L, and increments the row number by calling the subroutine INC. The program uses the FOR-NEXT loop on lines 15–18 to read the strings in the DATA statements and display them centered in successive screen rows. The main program only calls subroutine CenterText on line 17. This call passes the variables Text and Row to display the contents of Text on screen row number Row. The subroutine call passes both variables by reference. However, only variable Row is altered because the subroutine CenterText calls subroutine INC and supplies it with the argument L (which is a reference to variable Row). This means that parameter N of subroutine INC becomes an alias to the variable Row. The increment in parameter N simultaneously increments the number stored in Row.

The second example, which appears in Listing 10.7, shows how string parameters are passed by reference. In addition, this example shows how reference parameters also can supply the subroutine caller with multiple results. The program prompts you to enter a string. The program then calls a subroutine that returns the first and second half of your input, as well as the result of processing your input.

Listing 10.7. SUB3.BAS, which passes a string parameter by reference to a SUB procedure.

```
1: DECLARE SUB Process (S1 AS STRING, S2 AS STRING, S3 AS STRING)
2: REM Program that passes a string by
3: REM reference to a SUB procedure
4: REM
5: ' declare variables
6: DIM AString AS STRING
7: DIM FirstHalfStr AS STRING
8: DIM SecondHalfStr AS STRING
9: DIM Q AS STRING
```

continues

10

Listing 10.7. continued

```
10:
11: CLS
12: Q = CHR$(34)
13: LINE INPUT "Enter a string : "; AString
14: PRINT
15: PRINT "You entered "; Q; AString; Q
16: Process AString, FirstHalfStr, SecondHalfStr
17: PRINT "Processed string is "; Q; AString; Q
18: PRINT "The first half of your input is "; Q; FirstHalfStr; Q
19: PRINT "The second half of your input is "; Q; SecondHalfStr; Q
20: END
21:
22: SUB Process (S1 AS STRING, S2 AS STRING, S3 AS STRING)
23:    S2 = LEFT$(S1, LEN(S1) \ 2)
24:    S3 = RIGHT$(S1, LEN(S1) \ 2)
25:    S1 = UCASE$(LTRIM$(RTRIM$(S1)))
26: END SUB
```

Here is sample output for the program in Listing 10.7:

```
Enter a string :"    I like QBasic     "

You entered "    I like QBasic     "
Processed string is "I LIKE QBASIC"
The first half of your input is "    I like "
The second half of your input is "QBasic     "
```

The program in Listing 10.7 declares the subroutine Process. This subroutine has three string-typed parameters, S1, S2, and S3. S1 passes the string to and from the subroutine. The statement on line 23 extracts the first half of S1 and stores it in the parameter S2. The statement on line 23 extracts the second half of S1 and saves it in the parameter S3. Thus, S2 and S3 only return data to the subroutine caller. Line 25 manipulates the parameter S1 and assigns the modified string back to the same parameter. The call to Process on line 16 passes three string-typed variables.

The *FUNCTION* Procedure

QBasic also combines the features of the DEF FN function and the SUB procedure to offer the FUNCTION procedure. This kind of procedure is a version of the SUB procedure that returns a value.

Syntax

The FUNCTION Procedure

The general syntax for the FUNCTION procedure is

```
FUNCTION functionName[(parameterList)] [STATIC]
    sequence of statements
END FUNCTION
```

functionName defines the function's name. This name contains a data-type suffix because a FUNCTION procedure returns a value. The parameterList is a list of parameters that has the following general syntax:

```
variable1 [AS type1] [, variable2 [AS type2], ...]
```

variable1, variable2, and so on, are the names of the function's parameters. These names can include data-type suffixes to declare their data type. Alternatively, you can use the AS clause to declare the parameter's data type. If you use neither the type suffix nor the AS clause, QBasic uses the current association between the name of the variable and default data type.

The optional STATIC keyword specifies the status of the local variables inside the FUNCTION procedure. More about this topic on Day 16.

Examples

```
FUNCTION Square#(X#)
  Square# = X# * X#
END FUNCTION


FUNCTION ProperString$(S AS STRING)
  ProperString$ = UCASE$(LEFT$(S, 1)) + LCASE$(MID$(S, 2))
END FUNCTION
```

Note: Indenting the statements in a FUNCTION procedure is not mandatory. However, if you do indent the statements, your programs will be easier to read.

DO use FUNCTION procedures to implement functions.

DON'T use the DEF FN statement to implement functions.

Let's look at an example. Listing 10.8, FUNCT1.BAS, is a version of Listing 10.3 that uses FUNCTION procedures instead of DEF FN functions.

Listing 10.8. FUNCT1.BAS, which uses FUNCTION procedures to display the table of squares and cubes.

```
1: DECLARE FUNCTION Square# (X#)
2: DECLARE FUNCTION Cube# (X AS DOUBLE)
3: DECLARE FUNCTION Center$ (S AS STRING)
4: DECLARE SUB ShowCenteredTitles (T1 AS STRING, T2 AS STRING)
5: DECLARE SUB ShowTableHeading ()
6: DECLARE SUB PressAnyKey ()
7: REM Program uses SUB procedures
8: REM
9: CONST TITLE1 = "Sample Table of Squares and Cubes"
10: CONST TITLE2 = "(FUNCTION procedure version)"
11: ' declare the variables
12: DIM A AS DOUBLE
13:
14: CALL ShowCenteredTitles(TITLE1, TITLE2)
15: CALL ShowTableHeading
16: FOR A = 1 TO 100
17:   PRINT , A, Square#(A), Cube#(A)
18:   IF CSRLIN = 20 THEN
19:     PressAnyKey
```

```
20:    ShowCenteredTitles TITLE1, TITLE2
21:    ShowTableHeading
22:   END IF
23: NEXT A
24:
25: END
26:
27: FUNCTION Center$ (S AS STRING)
28:    Center$ = SPACE$(40 - LEN(S) \ 2) + S
29: END FUNCTION
30:
31: FUNCTION Cube# (X AS DOUBLE)
32:    Cube# = X * Square#(X)
33: END FUNCTION
34:
35: SUB PressAnyKey
36:    PRINT
37:    PRINT "Press any key to continue"
38:    C$ = INPUT$(1)
39: END SUB
40:
41: SUB ShowCenteredTitles (T1 AS STRING, T2 AS STRING)
42:    CLS
43:    PRINT
44:    PRINT Center$(T1)
45:    PRINT Center$(T2)
46:    PRINT
47:    PRINT
48: END SUB
49:
50: SUB ShowTableHeading
51:    PRINT , "  X", "X ^ 2", "  X ^ 3"
52:    PRINT , STRING$(35, "-")
53: END SUB
54:
55: FUNCTION Square# (X#)
56:    Square# = X# * X#
57: END FUNCTION
```

10

Here is some of the sample output for the program in Listing 10.8:

Output

```
Sample Table of Squares and Cubes
   (FUNCTION procedure version)


   X              X ^ 2            X ^ 3
- - - - - - - - - - - - - - - - - - - - - - - - - - -
   1              1                1
   2              4                8
   3              9                27
   4              16               64
   5              25               125
   6              36               216
   7              49               343
   8              64               512
   9              81               729
   10             100              1000
   11             121              1331
   12             144              1728


Press any key to continue
```

Analysis

The program in Listing 10.8 declares three FUNCTION procedures. The function Square# returns the squared value of its parameter X#. The Cube# function yields the cubed value of its parameter X. The function Center$ returns the image of a centered parameter S.

The PRINT statement on line 17 calls the functions Square# and Cube# and passes each function the argument A (the loop-control variable). The statement at line 32, inside function Cube#, invokes the function Square# as part of evaluating the cubed value. The PRINT statements on lines 44 and 45 (inside the subroutine ShowCenteredTitles) invoke the Center$ function.

Summary

This chapter introduced you to creating structured program components. You learned about the following topics:

☐ Writing structured program components involves creating semi-independent modules that perform specific tasks.

☐ The GOSUB statement enables you to write subroutines that can be called from different program locations. The GOSUB statement has a few shortcomings. First, it makes no provisions to pass arguments. Second, the program does not isolate the variables in the subroutine from the rest of the program and other subroutines. Similarly, the program does not isolate the variables in the main part of the program from the various subroutines.

☐ The DEF FN statement allows you to write single-line and multiple-line user-defined functions. Such functions have parameter lists and return a result.

☐ The SUB procedure enables you to write semi-independent program components. The SUB procedure offers more structured subroutine versions than the GOSUB statement. A SUB procedure is allowed to have a list of parameters and is able to isolate its variables from those of the main program (more about this on Day 16).

☐ The DECLARE statement informs QBasic of the SUB and FUNCTION procedures used in the program. This information enables QBasic to detect erroneous calls to SUB and FUNCTION procedures.

☐ The QBasic environment provides options to manage creating, deleting, and editing SUB and FUNCTION procedures.

☐ Value parameters obtain copies of the data in their corresponding arguments. Altering such parameters in a SUB or FUNCTION procedure does not affect the original source of data.

☐ Reference parameters are aliases of their corresponding arguments (which must be variables). Altering such parameters in a SUB or FUNCTION procedure also alters the original data in their sources.

☐ The FUNCTION procedure is very similar to the SUB procedure, except that FUNCTION returns a value.

Q&A

Q. What is the typical number of lines in a subroutine?

A. The number of lines in a subroutine depends on what the subroutine does. Many programmers recommend that the number of lines should not exceed a printed page. Otherwise, the numerous statements make the subroutine more difficult to read. In this case, you can most likely break down the task of a large subroutine and create new subroutines that contain smaller number of lines.

Q. How do I prevent a variable from being passed by reference to a SUB or FUNCTION procedure?

A. Enclose the variable in parentheses. The procedure call regards this argument as an expression and therefore passes it by value.

Q. Can I nest the declaration of procedures in a QBasic program?

A. No. QBasic does not support nested procedures. Other languages such as Pascal do support this feature.

Q. Can I specify that a parameter in a SUB or FUNCTION procedure be passed by value only?

A. No, not in QBasic. Other Microsoft BASIC dialects, however, such as Visual Basic, do support declaring by-value parameters.

Workshop

The Workshop provides quiz questions to help you solidify your understanding of the material covered and exercises to provide you with experience in using what you've learned. Try to understand the quiz and exercise answers before continuing on to the next chapter. Answers are provided in Appendix B, "Answers."

Quiz

1. What is wrong with the following set of statements?

```
DECLARE SUB INCR (N%)
DIM I AS INTEGER
I = 1
DO WHILE I < 10
    PRINT I
    INCR (I)
```

```
    LOOP
    END

    SUB INCR (N%)
      N% = N% + 1
    END SUB
```

2. What is the error in the following set of statements?

```
DECLARE SUB Process (I%, Y#, T$)
DIM N AS INTEGER
DIM X AS DOUBLE
DIM S AS STRING

N = 123
X = 3.14
S = "QBasic"

Process S, X, N
END

SUB Process (I%, Y#, T$)

    PRINT T$; Y# / I%
END
```

3. What is the error in the following set of statements?

```
DECLARE SUB Calc (I%, Y#, T$)
DIM N AS INTEGER
DIM X AS DOUBLE
DIM Y AS DOUBLE
DIM S AS STRING

N = 123
X = 3.14
S = "QBasic"

Calc S, X, Y, N
```

```
END

SUB Process (I%, Y#, T$)

    PRINT T$; Y# / I%
END
```

4. What is wrong with the following function?

```
DEFDBL A-Z
DEF FNCalc(X#, Y#)
  IF X# <> 0 AND Y# <> 0 THEN
    FNCalc = STR$(X# / Y# + Y# / X#)
  ELSE
    FNCalc = 1.0D+100
  END IF
END DEF
```

Exercises

1. Modify the program SUB1.BAS in Listing 10.5 to create the SUB procedure CheckCursor that calls the subroutines ShowCenteredTitles and ShowTableHeading. Call the new program SUB4.BAS.

2. Write subroutines that are shells (or wrappers) that rename the LOCATE statement, the POS function, and the CSRLIN function. Use the following names, which are easier to remember:

```
SUB GotoXY is a shell for the LOCATE statement
FUNCTION WhereX is a shell for function POS
FUNCTION WhereY is a shell for function CSRLIN
```

DAY
11

Handling
Program Errors

Programs, especially in the development stages, often contain logical errors or fail to handle certain data values properly. These errors and failures produce runtime errors that bring QBasic programs to an abrupt end. In this chapter I present the error-handling mechanism supported by QBasic. You will learn about the following topics:

- [ ] An overview of error-handling strategies

- [ ] Trapping errors with the `ON ERROR GOTO` statement

- [ ] Handling errors with the `RESUME` statement

- [ ] The `ERR` and `ERL` functions

- [ ] Raising user-defined errors with the `ERROR` statement

Error-Handling Strategy

There are two general error-handling strategies. The first one, called *defensive programming,* attempts to avoid creating runtime errors by detecting the conditions that cause these errors. Here is a simple example. If you are dividing two numbers, you may want to use an `IF` statement to guard against dividing by zero, as shown in the following code:

```
INPUT "Enter first number "; X
INPUT "Enter second number "; Y
IF Y <> 0 THEN
  PRINT X; "/"; Y; "="; X / Y
ELSE
  PRINT "Cannot divide by zero!"
END IF
```

These statements should give you a small taste of defensive programming. Imagine a more complex program filled with `IF` statements that guard against a variety of conditions that produce all kinds of runtime errors. This approach to error prevention (to be exact) requires an overhead of extra program statements.

The second error-handling strategy uses an *error trap*—a group of statements where the program automatically jumps to when a runtime error occurs. QBasic supports such error traps by providing the `ON ERROR` statement. This

approach to error handling reduces the overhead in the number of program statements.

In the next section I discuss the QBasic statements and functions for trapping and handling runtime errors. After explaining all these statements and functions, I present several examples. I am using this approach because the error-handling statements and functions are interdependent.

The *ON ERROR GOTO* Statement

QBasic offers the ON ERROR GOTO statement to set up and clear error traps.

The ON ERROR GOTO Statement

The general syntax for the ON ERROR GOTO is

```
ON ERROR GOTO {errorHandlerLabel ¦ 0}
```

The *errorHandlerLabel* is the name of a label that contains statements to handle the occurring error. The ON ERROR GOTO 0 statement turns off the error trap. Any runtime error that occurs after this statement and before another ON ERROR GOTO *errorHandlerLabel* statement causes the program to end.

The error-handling statements must be placed after the END statement.

Example:

The following program uses an ERROR GOTO statement to trap the division-by-zero error.

```
INPUT "Enter first number "; X
INPUT "Enter second number "; Y
ON ERROR GOTO Divide.By.Zero
PRINT X; "/"; Y; "="; X / Y
END
Divide.By.Zero:
    PRINT "Cannot divide by zero"
END
```

The RESUME Statement

The ON ERROR GOTO statement directs the program flow to an error-handling label. The statements after this label give you the chance to inspect the type of error and respond to it. If the error is not fatal, you can resume the program. QBasic offers the RESUME statement to allow you to specify where the program resumes execution. In addition, QBasic considers the error resolved when it executes a RESUME statement.

Syntax

The RESUME Statement

The general syntax for the RESUME statement is

```
RESUME [{0 ¦ NEXT ¦ label}]
```

The 0 value (which has the same effect as just using RESUME) causes the program to resume at the offending statement. The NEXT keyword makes the program resume at the statement following the offending one. The label parameter directs the program to resume execution at that label.

QBasic considers the error resolved when it executes a RESUME statement. Until then, any error that occurs in the error-handling statements will halt the program.

Examples:

```
' example 1
DEFDBL A-Z
INPUT "Enter first number "; X
INPUT "Enter second number "; Y
ON ERROR GOTO Divide.By.Zero
Z = X / Y
PRINT X; "/"; Y; "="; Z
END
Divide.By.Zero:
  DO
     INPUT "Enter second number "; Y
  LOOP UNTIL Y <> 0
  RESUME 0
' example 2
DEFDBL A-Z
```

```
INPUT "Enter first number "; X
INPUT "Enter second number "; Y
ON ERROR GOTO Divide.By.Zero
Z = 1D+100
Z = X / Y
PRINT X; "/"; Y; "="; Z
END
Divide.By.Zero:
    RESUME NEXT

' example 3
DEFDBL A-Z
INPUT "Enter first number "; X
INPUT "Enter second number "; Y
ON ERROR GOTO Divide.By.Zero
Retry:
Z = X / Y
PRINT X; "/"; Y; "="; Z
END
Divide.By.Zero:
    DO
        INPUT "Enter second number "; Y
    LOOP UNTIL Y <> 0
    RESUME Retry
```

DO resolve errors before resuming program execution.

DON'T end the program, unless you have a fatal error.

The *ERR* and *ERL* Functions

QBasic provides you with the ERR and ERL functions to identify the type and location of the statement that raises a runtime error. The ERR function returns the error number. The ERL function returns the last line number (that is, numeric label, such as 50:, 100:, etc.) before the offending line.

Syntax

The ERR Function

The general syntax for the ERR function is

```
ERR
```

The ERR function returns the error number. Table 11.1 shows the runtime error codes returned by this function.

Example:

```
ON ERROR GOTO HaveError
X = 1 / 0
END
HaveError:
      PRINT "Error number "; ERR
END
```

Syntax

The ERL Function

The general syntax for the ERL function is

```
ERL
```

The function returns the last label that appears before the offending number.

You can make your line number reflect the program line number that contains the offending statement. The following example illustrates this trick.

Example:

```
ON ERROR GOTO HaveError
3:
X = 1 / 0
END
HaveError:
      PRINT "Error number "; ERR; " at line "; ERL
END
```

 DO use a SELECT CASE with the ERR function to identify the type of runtime error and translate the error number into a more comprehensible message. Table 11.1 lists the runtime error codes and their descriptions.

DON'T bother the end-user with cryptic error messages. Such messages make your program less user-friendly and prone to be quickly abandoned.

11

Table 11.1. **The QBasic runtime error codes returned by the ERR function.**

Error Code	Error Description	Code	Description
1	NEXT without FOR	37	Argument-count mismatch
2	Syntax error	38	Array not defined
3	RETURN without GOSUB	40	Variable required
4	Out of DATA	50	FIELD overflow
5	Illegal function call	51	Internal error
6	Overflow	52	Bad file name or number
7	Out of memory	53	File not found
8	Label not defined	54	Bad file mode
9	Subscript out of range	55	File already open
10	Duplicate definition	56	FIELD statement active
11	Division by zero	57	Device I/O error
12	Illegal in direct mode	58	File already exists

continues

Table 11.1. **continued**

Error Code	Error Description	Code	Description
13	Type mismatch	59	Bad record length
14	Out of string space	61	Disk full
16	String formula too complex	62	Input past end of file
17	Cannot continue	63	Bad record number
18	Function not defined	64	Bad file name
19	No RESUME	67	Too many files
20	RESUME without error	68	Device unavailable
24	Device timeout	69	Communication-buffer overflow
25	Device fault	70	Permission denied
26	FOR without NEXT	71	Disk not ready
27	Out of paper	72	Disk-media error
29	WHILE without WEND	73	Feature unavailable
30	WEND without WHILE	74	Rename across disks
33	Duplicate label	75	Path/File access error
35	Subprogram not defined	76	Path not found

The *ERROR* Statement

QBasic enables you either to artificially raise a predefined runtime error or raise your own runtime error using the ERROR statement. In either case, QBasic uses the current error trap, or halts the program if no error trap is currently set. The ERROR statement is useful when you want to handle a condition or value that

represents a logical error. In addition, you might want to raise a predefined runtime error early on, because it is more suitable to handle the error this way. For example, you might have a complicated formatted output which contains an error-prone function call. In this case, it is better to handle the output separately for the offending arguments.

The ERROR Statement

The general syntax for the ERROR statement is

```
ERROR errorNumber
```

The errorNumber is the runtime error number. The values 1–76 refer to predefined errors (the same values returned by ERR when a runtime error occurs). The values 77–255 are available as user-defined errors.

Examples:

```
DIM A AS DOUBLE
ON ERROR GOTO Bad.Value
INPUT "Enter a nonzero number "; A
' create user defined error for zero-number input
IF A = 0 THEN ERROR 254
PRINT "1 /"; A; "="; 1 / A
END
Bad.Value
    PRINT "Cannot divide by zero"
END


DIM A AS DOUBLE
ON ERROR GOTO Bad.Value
INPUT "Enter a nonzero number "; A
' raise the divide-by-zero error BEFORE it actually occurs
IF A = 0 THEN ERROR 11
PRINT "1 /"; A; "="; 1 / A
END
Bad.Value
    PRINT "Cannot divide by zero"
END
```

Syntax

11

Examples

Let me present a series of examples that handle errors using the statements and functions I presented earlier in this chapter. The examples I present are variations of each other. The basic program displays a table of square roots (the QBasic SQR function returns the square root value) ranging from 5 to –5. The SQR function requires its arguments be non-negative. Negative arguments result in a runtime error because QBasic does not handle complex numbers. Mathematicians tell us that the square roots of negative numbers are complex numbers, made up of two components: the *real* part and the *imaginary* part. Complex numbers use the letter i (which represents the square root of –1) to indicate the imaginary part of a complex number. Thus, the complex number 1 + i2 contains the real part 1 and the imaginary part 2.

The examples that I present next offer a range of solutions to handle supplying the SQR function with negative values. Some solutions simply end the program, others ignore the generated runtime error, and still others produce complex numbers.

Fatal Error Example

The first example is shown in Listing 11.1, which contains the program ERR1.BAS. This program stops when the call to the SQR function generates a runtime error. The program uses the ERR and ERL functions to identify the error type and line number that contains the offending statement.

 Listing 11.1. ERR1.BAS, which uses the ERR and ERL functions.

```
1: REM Program that tests the ON ERROR statement
2: REM and the functions ERR and ERL
3: REM
4: ' declare constants
5: CONST TITLE = "Table of Square Roots"
6: CONST FIRST% = 5
7: CONST LAST% = -2
8: CONST INCR% = -1
9: ' declare variables
```

```
10: DIM I AS INTEGER
11:
12: CLS
13: PRINT
14: PRINT TAB(40 - LEN(TITLE) \ 2); TITLE
15: PRINT
16: PRINT
17: ' set error trap
18: ON ERROR GOTO Bad.Value
19:
20: PRINT , " X", "  SQR(X)"
21: PRINT , STRING$(35, "-")
22: FOR I = FIRST TO LAST STEP INCR
23: 24 :
24:    PRINT , I, SQR(I)
25: NEXT I
26:
27: END
28:
29: Bad.Value:
30:    PRINT
31:    SELECT CASE ERR
32:       CASE 5
33:          PRINT "Illegal function call in line"; ERL
34:       CASE 6
35:          PRINT "Numeric overflow in line"; ERL
36:       CASE 11
37:          PRINT "Divide-by-zero error in line"; ERL
38:       CASE ELSE
39:          PRINT "Runtime error in line"; ERL
40:    END SELECT
41: END
```

Here is a sample output for the program in Listing 11.1:

```
           Table of Square Roots


   X              SQR(X)
- - - - - - - - - - - - - - - - - - - - - - - - - - - - - - - - - -
   5              2.236068
   4              2
```

```
3            1.732051
2            1.414214
1            1
0            0
-1
Illegal function call in line 24
```

 The program in Listing 11.1 sets the error trap using the ON ERROR GOTO statement on line 18. The statement directs the program flow to the label Bad.Value when a runtime error occurs. Line 23 contains the label 24: which is actually the program line number that contains the SQR function. The Bad.Value label contains the SELECT CASE statement that identifies and displays the type of error and the line number that contains the offending statement.

Complex Number Output Example

The program in Listing 11.1 simply halted after displaying the error number and location. It made no effort to resume program execution. The other extreme solution is a program version that proceeds to display imaginary square root values. The new program version deals with the error internally and gives you the impression that everything is sailing smoothly! Listing 11.2, ERR2.BAS, uses the RESUME NEXT statement to display complex square root values.

 Listing 11.2. ERR2.BAS, which uses the RESUME NEXT statement.

```
 1: REM Program that tests the ON ERROR statement
 2: REM with the RESUME NEXT statement
 3: REM
 4: ' declare constants
 5: CONST TITLE = "Table of Square Roots"
 6: CONST FIRST% = 5
 7: CONST LAST% = -5
 8: CONST INCR% = -1
 9: ' declare variables
10: DIM I AS INTEGER
11:
12: CLS
13: PRINT
```

```
14: PRINT TAB(40 - LEN(TITLE) \ 2); TITLE
15: PRINT
16: PRINT
17: ' set error trap
18: ON ERROR GOTO Bad.Value
19:
20: PRINT , " X", "  SQR(X)"
21: PRINT , STRING$(35, "-")
22: FOR I = FIRST TO LAST STEP INCR
23:   PRINT , I, SQR(I)
24: NEXT I
25:
26: END
27:
28: Bad.Value:
29:   PRINT "i"; SQR(ABS(I))
30:   RESUME NEXT
```

11

Here is a sample output for the program in Listing 11.2 (the output shows
the complex numbers as i followed by the imaginary component):

```
        Table of Square Roots


   X              SQR(X)
- - - - - - - - - - - - - - - - - - - - - - - - - -
   5              2.236068
   4              2
   3              1.732051
   2              1.414214
   1              1
   0              0
  -1              i 1
  -2              i 1.414214
  -3              i 1.732051
  -4              i 2
  -5              i 2.236068
```

The program in Listing 11.2 sets the error trap using a ON GOTO ERROR
statement on line 18. The two error-handling statements are located after
the label Bad.Value. The first statement (on line 29), displays the letter i
followed by the square root of the absolute value of I (the loop control variable).

This PRINT statement displays the complex result of taking the square root of a negative number. The RESUME NEXT statement on line 30 tells the program to resume at the statement on line 24, which comes after the offending statement on line 23. Line 24 contains the NEXT clause that resumes another loop iteration.

Retry Example

There is another way to display the complex values of negative square root numbers. This solution uses the RESUME 0 to resume execution at the offending statement. ERR3.BAS, found in Listing 11.3, implements this method using two more variables and a few more statements to implement the scheme. I discuss these additional variables and statements after you examine the listing and the program output.

 Listing 11.3. ERR3.BAS, which uses the RESUME 0 statement.

```
 1: REM Program that tests the ON ERROR statement
 2: REM with the RESUME 0 statement
 3: REM
 4: ' declare constants
 5: CONST TITLE = "Table of Square Roots"
 6: CONST FIRST% = 5
 7: CONST LAST% = -5
 8: CONST INCR% = -1
 9: ' declare variables
10: DIM I AS INTEGER
11: DIM A AS DOUBLE
12: DIM S AS STRING
13:
14: CLS
15: PRINT
16: PRINT TAB(40 - LEN(TITLE) \ 2); TITLE
17: PRINT
18: PRINT
19: ' set error trap
20: ON ERROR GOTO Bad.Value
21: PRINT , " X", "  SQR(X)"
22: PRINT , STRING$(35, "-")
23: FOR I = FIRST TO LAST STEP INCR
```

```
24:    S = ""
25:    A = I
26:    A = SQR(A)
27:    PRINT , I, S; A
28: NEXT I
29:
30: END
31:
32: Bad.Value:
33:    A = -A
34:    S = "i"
35:    RESUME 0
```

Here is a sample output for the program in Listing 11.3:

```
        Table of Square Roots


     X              SQR(X)
     . . . . . . . . . . . . . . . . . . . . . . . . . . . .
     5              2.23606797749979
     4              2
     3              1.732050807568877
     2              1.414213562373095
     1              1
     0              0
    -1              i 1
    -2              i 1.414213562373095
    -3              i 1.732050807568877
    -4              i 2
    -5              i 2.23606797749979
```

The program in Listing 11.3 uses the additional variables A (a DOUBLE) and S (a STRING). The first statement in the FOR-NEXT loop assigns an empty string to S. The second statement in the loop copies the value of the loop-control variable I to A. The third statement takes the square root of A and stores it back in A. If this statement raises a runtime error, the error trap on line 20 directs the program flow to label Bad.Value. The first statement in the error-handler assigns -A to A, making sure that A is now positive. This step should make it clear why I have to use A and store in it a copy of I—tampering with the loop-control variable, I, disrupts the loop iteration. The statement on line 34 assigns the string "i" to S. The RESUME 0 statement on line 35 tells the program to resume execution at the offending statement on line 26. This time, A contains a positive value. The PRINT statement on line 27 ends up displaying the image of a complex number.

Directed Program Resumption Example

You also can write a version of the previous program that only displays the square root of non-negative numbers. The approach used in the new version is this: ignore the error and resume at the next loop iteration. In this version, I pretend that the next loop iteration might not generate a runtime error. Listing 11.4 contains the program ERR4.BAS which uses the RESUME label statement. The program jumps to the end of the FOR-NEXT loop when a runtime error occurs.

 Listing 11.4. ERR4.BAS, which uses the RESUME label statement.

```
1: REM Program that tests the ON ERROR statement
2: REM with the RESUME label statement
3: REM
4: ' declare constants
5: CONST TITLE = "Table of Square Roots"
6: CONST FIRST% = 5
7: CONST LAST% = -5
8: CONST INCR% = -1
9: ' declare variables
10: DIM I AS INTEGER
11: DIM A AS DOUBLE
12:
13: CLS
14: PRINT
15: PRINT TAB(40 - LEN(TITLE) \ 2); TITLE
16: PRINT
17: PRINT
18: ' set error trap
19: ON ERROR GOTO Bad.Value
20: PRINT , " X", "  SQR(X)"
21: PRINT , STRING$(35, "-")
22: FOR I = FIRST TO LAST STEP INCR
```

```
23:    A = SQR(I)
24:    PRINT , I, A
25: ResumeLoop:
26: NEXT I
27:
28: END
29:
30: Bad.Value:
31:    RESUME ResumeLoop
```

Here is a sample output for the program in Listing 11.4:

```
Table of Square Roots


X                  SQR(X)
- - - - - - - - - - - - - - - - - - - - - - - - - - - - - - - - - -
5                  2.23606797749979
4                  2
3                  1.732050807568877
2                  1.414213562373095
1                  1
0                  0
```

Analysis The program in Listing 11.4 sets the error trap on line 19. The ON ERROR GOTO statement in that line directs the program jump to label Bad.Value. When the SQR function on line 23 raises an error, program execution jumps to line 30. The RESUME statement on line 31 directs the program to resume at label ResumeLoop, on line 25, at the end of the FOR-NEXT loop. This type of resumption effectively skips the remaining loop statements and resumes at the NEXT clause. The program uses A to store the result of the SQR function. This approach prevents the partial output generated by a PRINT I, SQR(I) statement. Consequently, the runtime error does not produce incomplete output.

Raising Runtime Errors

The next example uses the ERROR statement to raise the illegal-function-call error *before it actually occurs*. I created ERR5.BAS in Listing 11.5 by modifying Listing 11.2. Both programs display complex values for the square roots of negative values. Each program uses a different route, however.

Listing 11.5. ERR5.BAS, which triggers a runtime error using the ERROR statement.

```
1: REM Program that tests the ON ERROR statement
2: REM with the ERROR statement
3: REM
4: ' declare constants
5: CONST ILLEGAL.CALL.ERROR = 5
6: CONST TITLE = "Table of Square Roots"
7: CONST FIRST% = 5
8: CONST LAST% = -5
9: CONST INCR% = -1
10: ' declare variables
11: DIM I AS INTEGER
12:
13: CLS
14: PRINT
15: PRINT TAB(40 - LEN(TITLE) \ 2); TITLE
16: PRINT
17: PRINT
18: ' set error trap
19: ON ERROR GOTO Bad.Value
20:
21: PRINT , " X", "  SQR(X)"
22: PRINT , STRING$(35, "-")
23: FOR I = FIRST TO LAST STEP INCR
24:    IF I < 0 THEN ERROR ILLEGAL.CALL.ERROR
25:    PRINT , I, SQR(I)
26: ResumeLoop:
27: NEXT I
28:
29: END
30:
31: Bad.Value:
32:    PRINT , I, "i"; SQR(ABS(I))
33:    RESUME ResumeLoop
```

Here is a sample output for the program in Listing 11.5:

```
Table of Square Roots


     X            SQR(X)
```

```
-------------------------------------
 5               2.236068
 4               2
 3               1.732051
 2               1.414214
 1               1
 0               0
-1               i 1
-2               i 1.414214
-3               i 1.732051
-4               i 2
-5               i 2.236068
```

The program in Listing 11.5 declares an additional constant on line 5. The constant ILLEGAL.CALL.ERROR is assigned the runtime error 5, associated with illegal function calls.

The new version handles the errors differently. Notice that line 24 contains an IF-THEN statement which determines if the loop control variable, I, is negative. If this condition is true, the THEN clause statement invokes the ERROR statement. This statement raises the runtime error number 5. The program handles the runtime error in the statements that appear after label Bad.Value. Notice that the PRINT statement on line 32 displays the value of I and SQR(ABS(I)). In other words, this PRINT statement is comparable to the one on line 25—it does not merely *clean up* the rest of the output, as is the case in Listing 11.2. The RESUME statement on line 33 directs the program resumption to label ResumeLoop on line 26. Thus, the RESUME statement allows the program to skip the PRINT statement on line 25 when an error occurs.

Summary

This chapter presented the mechanisms for trapping and handling errors in QBasic programs. You learned about the following topics:

☐ There are two basic error-handling strategies: defensive programming and error trapping. The first strategy detects the conditions that cause runtime errors and takes the necessary steps to avoid the errors. Error trapping is a bolder strategy that sets an error trap that is automatically used when a runtime error occurs.

☐ The ON ERROR GOTO statement enables you to set and clear error traps. The statement uses the name of a label to direct the program to the error-handling statement should a run error occur.

☐ The RESUME statement enables you to determine how the program continues executing. Typically, error-handling statements end with a RESUME statement.

☐ The ERR and ERL functions report the error number and the closest line number to the offending statement.

☐ The ERROR statement enables you to raise either a predefined error or a user-defined error.

Questions and Answers

Q. How close before an error-prone statement should I declare an ON ERROR GOTO statement?

A. Right before the error-prone statement, if appropriate. You might need to insert special statements between the ON ERROR GOTO statement and the error-prone statement. These special statements assist in preparing the response to the occurring error.

Q. What happens if there is a runtime error inside the statements which handle another runtime error?

A. QBasic will halt the program because it cannot deal with the new runtime error.

Q. Can I then use an ON ERROR GOTO statement inside the error-handing statements mentioned in the last question?

A. Yes, but you must first use a RESUME statement to declare the first error as handled. Here is the general form for a nested error-handler:

```
Error1.Label:
    sequence of statements
    RESUME Here.Label
Here.Label:
    ' set nested error handler
    ON ERROR GOTO Error2.Label
```

```
    sequence of statements
    GOTO Return.Label
Error2.Label:
    sequence of statements
    RESUME Return.Label
```

Notice that the first `RESUME` statement returns to the subsequent line. This programming trick satisfies QBasic's need to handle the first error. The `ON ERROR GOTO` statement then sets the internal error-handler.

Q. What happens if I use the `RESUME 0` statement and nothing else in the error handler?

A. The program enters into an endless error-handling cycle because the program is not actually resolving the runtime error.

Workshop

The Workshop provides quiz questions to help you solidify your understanding of the material covered and exercises to provide you with experience in using what you've learned. Try to understand the quiz and exercise answers before continuing on to the next chapter. Answers are provided in Appendix B, "Answers."

Quiz

1. What is the output of the following program?

```
DIM S AS STRING
DIM L AS INTEGER
CLS
ON ERROR GOTO RunTimeError
S = "Hello"
L = 0
MID$(S, L, 1) = "J"
PRINT S
END
RunTimeError:
  RESUME NEXT
```

2. What is the output of the following program?

```
DIM S AS STRING
DIM L AS INTEGER
CLS
ON ERROR GOTO RunTimeError
S = "Hello"
L = 0
MID$(S, L, 1) = "J"
PRINT S
END
RunTimeError:
  L = 1
  RESUME 0
```

3. What is the output of the following program? What does it tell you about the number of times the program calls the error-handling statements?

```
DIM S AS STRING
DIM L AS INTEGER
DIM Count AS INTEGER
CLS
Count = 0
ON ERROR GOTO RunTimeError
S = "Hello"
L = -10
MID$(S, L, 1) = "J"
PRINT S
PRINT Count
END
RunTimeError:
  Count = Count + 1
  L = L + 1
  RESUME 0
```

4. What is the output of the following program?

```
DIM S AS STRING
DIM L AS INTEGER
CLS
```

```
ON ERROR GOTO RunTimeError
S = "Hello"
L = 0
MID$(S, L, 1) = "J"
PRINT S
END
RunTimeError:
   PRINT "Runtime error number"; ERR
END
```

Exercises

1. Write ERR6.BAS, which traps the runtime error raised by supplying the MID$ function with invalid indices. Here is the pseudocode for the program:

```
1. Clear the screen.
2. Prompt the user to enter a string.  Save the input in
   string S1.
3. Prompt the user to enter the index of the first
   extracted character.
4. Prompt the user to enter the number of extracted
   characters.
5. Display a character ruler.
6. Display the input string.
7. Set the error trap.
8. Assign the extracted characters to string S2.
9. Display the string S2.
10. End the program.
```

The error handler has the following pseudocode.

```
1. Assign an empty string to the variable S2.
2. Store the current screen row position of the cursor.
3. Display an error message at the bottom of the screen.
4. Restore the previous cursor position.
5. Resume executing the program at the statement which
   follows the offending one.
```

2. Single-step through the programs in Listings 11.1 to 11.5. Use the F8 function key to execute these programs, one statement at a time. You may inspect the values in the variables. To do so click on the Immediate window which appears below the Editing window. Type in a PRINT statement (you can also type ? as shorthand for PRINT) followed by the name of a variable, or a list of variables (separated by commas). QBasic displays the contents of these variables in the output screen. Naturally, this process will disrupt the output from the program somewhat. When you are finished with inspecting the contents of the variables, click the Editing window.

DAY
12

Simple Arrays

This chapter looks at simple arrays—popular data structures supported by most programming languages. Today you will learn about the following topics:

- [ ] What's an array?
- [ ] The OPTION BASE statement
- [ ] Declaring arrays using the DIM statement
- [ ] Using arrays
- [ ] Obtaining the dimensions of an array using the LBOUND and UBOUND functions
- [ ] Redimensioning arrays using the REDIM statement
- [ ] Clearing and removing arrays using the ERASE statement
- [ ] Sorting arrays
- [ ] Searching arrays

 Note: The last two sections explain important array applications. However, the information presented in these sections is **not** vital for using QBasic arrays. You can read these sections later at your leisure.

What's an Array?

An array is a collection of variables that share the same name and separate themselves by a single integer index. An example of a real-world array is the days in a month. For example, Independence Day occurs on July 4th. In this case, the name of the month is the name of the array. The number 4 is the day number, or index, if you prefer.

Figure 12.1 shows a sample numeric array. The name of the array is A. You can use any valid QBasic name for arrays. The array in Figure 12.1 has 9 members and has the indices 1 to 9. The figure shows how the statement PRINT A(4) works. First, the statement searches for the array A in the program's memory. Once it finds the array A, it then accesses the element at index 4.

Finally, the PRINT statement obtains a copy of the contents of A(4) and displays it on the screen.

Arrays enable you to store similar data in the same array variable. You can think of each array element as a simple variable. One advantage of using arrays is they work well in loops. By combining arrays and loops (typically, the FOR-NEXT loop), you can write a few statements that process a large number of data. Performing the same tasks using single variables might generate a multiple-page listing.

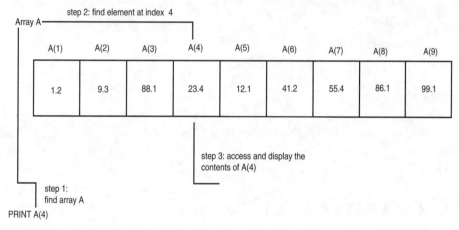

Figure 12.1. A sample numeric array.

The *OPTION BASE* Statement

Figure 12.1 shows the array A with indices that range from 1 to 9. You might ask "Who gets to decide the range of array indices?" The answer is essentially you do. As I explain in the next section, you can specify the first (or low) index of an array. If you don't, QBasic assigns the default value of 0 as the first index. QBasic also offers the OPTION BASE statement to enable you to specify this default lower index as 0 or 1. Which one should you use? The answer is whatever makes you comfortable. If it is more intuitive to make the first index of your arrays 1, use OPTION BASE 1. Otherwise, use the default of 0. You might want to insert the OPTION BASE 0 statement in your programs to specify explicitly the default first index of arrays.

The OPTION BASE Statement

The general syntax for the OPTION BASE is:

```
OPTION BASE {0 | 1}
```

The OPTION BASE statement enables you to specify 0 or 1 as the default first index of arrays. When you omit this statement, QBasic assumes OPTION BASE 0 is in effect.

If you want to use 1 as your default first index, place the OPTION BASE 1 before declaring any arrays. There can be only one OPTION BASE in a program.

Example:

```
' the default setting
OPTION BASE 0


OPTION BASE 1
```

Declaring Arrays

QBasic also uses the DIM statement to declare arrays. In fact, historically, the DIM statement was used for declaring arrays only. Microsoft has extended the use of the DIM statement to declare simple variable and user-defined variables (more about this on Day 15, "User-Defined Data Types").

Note: QBasic does not require you to declare arrays that have as many as 10 elements. This rule goes back to an early BASIC tradition that made programming in BASIC easy. Many programmers today feel that this rule is really very dangerous, because you can accidentally create such arrays by misspelling the names of existing ones. It is a good programming practice to declare ALL your arrays. Some new BASIC implementations use the OPTION TYPO statement to guard against misspelling the names of existing arrays.

Syntax

The DIM Statement

The general syntax for the DIM statement is

```
DIM [SHARED] arrayName([low TO] high) [AS type]
```

The SHARED clause indicates that the declared array can be shared with FUNCTION and SUB procedures without explicitly passing it as a parameter. The *arrayName* is the name of the array. You explicitly can declare the range of indices by specifying the *low* and *high* limits (separated by the keyword TO). If you omit the *low* index, QBasic uses the OPTION BASE value as the default lower index. The AS clause enables you to specify the data type associated with each array element. When omitted, you can use the data type suffixes with the array name. If you use neither, QBasic applies the default association between the array name and data types. You also can influence this default data type association by placing DEF*type* statements before declaring arrays. You can declare multiple arrays in a DIM statement. QBasic initializes the numeric arrays with zeros, and the string arrays with empty strings.

The number of elements in an array declared with the following form:

```
DIM [SHARED] arrayName(high) [AS type]
```

is equal to ($high + 1 - optionBaseSetting$). The number of elements in an array declared with the following form:

```
DIM [SHARED] arrayName(low TO high) [AS type]
```

is equal to $high - low + 1$. QBasic requires that the number of elements in an array not exceed 32767 elements.

Examples:

```
' declare string-typed array January
DIM January(1 TO 31) AS STRING


' declare string-typed array January
OPTION BASE 1
DIM January(31) AS STRING


' declare string-typed array January
OPTION BASE 1
DIM January$(31)
```

12

```
' declare string-typed array January
DEFSTR J
OPTION BASE 1
DIM January(31)


DIM January(31), February(28), March(31)
```

Using Arrays

Using arrays is simple. You state the name of the array and use a valid index enclosed in parentheses.

Accessing Array Elements

The general syntax for accessing an array element is

arrayName(validIndex)

The *arrayName* is the name of an array. The *validIndex* parameter is a valid index. Such an index must lie in the range of indices used to declare the array (or less than 11 if you do not declare the array).

Example:

```
DIM Factorial(0 TO 30) AS DOUBLE
Factorial(0) = 1
FOR I = 1 TO 30
    Factorial(I) = I * Factorial(I - 1)
NEXT I
```

Let's look at an example. Listing 12.1, ARRAY1.BAS, declares and uses a numeric array. The program prompts you to enter the number of values (which must be in the range of 3 to 15). Then, the program prompts you to enter the values, which are stored in an array. If you simply press the Return key, the program converts your lack of input into a value equal to the current value of the loop control variable. (For example, if you just hit return on the third prompt, the program will store a three in that element.) The program then

displays that value after the ? mark in the prompt. Once you finish entering the numbers, the program displays the values you typed and asks you to enter the valid indices that define a range of array elements to process. The program then calculates and displays the sum and mean values for the range of array elements you selected. Finally, the program prompts you whether you want to obtain another set of sum and mean values for a different range of array elements.

Listing 12.1. ARRAY1.BAS, which declares and uses a numeric array.

```
 1: DECLARE FUNCTION Pound$ (N AS INTEGER)
 2: DECLARE FUNCTION PoundNumber$ (Z AS DOUBLE)
 3: REM Program uses fixed arrays
 4: REM
 5: OPTION BASE 1
 6: ' declare constants
 7: CONST ARRAY.SIZE% = 15
 8: CONST FRMT = "Number of values to enter (3 TO ##) "
 9: ' declare variables
10: DIM X(ARRAY.SIZE) AS DOUBLE
11: DIM Sum AS DOUBLE
12: DIM I AS INTEGER
13: DIM N AS INTEGER
14: DIM I1 AS INTEGER
15: DIM I2 AS INTEGER
16: DIM Xcurs AS INTEGER
17: DIM Ycurs AS INTEGER
18: DIM C AS STRING
19:
20: CLS
21: ' prompt for number of values
22: DO
23:   PRINT USING FRMT; ARRAY.SIZE;
24:   INPUT N
25:   PRINT
26: LOOP UNTIL N >= 3 AND N <= ARRAY.SIZE
27:
28: ' enter values
29: FOR I = 1 TO N
30:   PRINT "Enter value #"; I; " ";
```

continues

Listing 12.1. continued

```
31:     Xcurs = POS(0)
32:     ' store each value in a member of array X
33:     INPUT ; X(I)
34:     ' if value is 0 assign X(I) the loop control variable
35:     IF X(I) = 0 THEN
36:       X(I) = I
37:       ' display the value after the ? mark
38:       LOCATE , Xcurs + 1
39:       PRINT X(I);
40:     END IF
41:     PRINT
42: NEXT I
43:
44: ' loop to display array and query range of members to sum
45: DO
46:    CLS
47:    ' display the elements of array X
48:    FOR I = 1 TO N
49:      PRINT USING "Value _# ## = "; I;
50:      PRINT X(I)
51:    NEXT I
52:
53:    PRINT
54:    ' get the indices of the elements to add
55:    DO
56:      INPUT "Enter index of first value to add (default=1) "; I1
57:      IF I1 = 0 THEN I1 = 1
58:      PRINT
59:    LOOP UNTIL I1 >= 1 AND I1 <= N
60:
61:    DO
62:      INPUT "Enter index of last value to add (default=last) "; I2
63:      IF I2 = 0 THEN I2 = N
64:      PRINT
65:    LOOP UNTIL I2 >= 1 AND I2 <= N AND I2 <> I1
66:    ' add the elements of X from X(I1) to X(I2)
67:    Sum = 0
```

```
68:    FOR I = I1 TO I2
69:      Sum = Sum + X(I)
70:    NEXT I
71:    ' display the results
72:    C = "Sum of X(" + Pound$(I1) + ") to X(" + Pound$(I2) + ") = "
73:    C = C + PoundNumber$(Sum)
74:    PRINT USING C; I1; I2; Sum
75:    C = "Mean of X(" + Pound$(I1) + ") to X(" + Pound$(I2) + ") = "
76:    C = C + PoundNumber$(Sum)
77:    PRINT USING C; I1; I2; Sum / (I2 - I1 + 1)
78:    PRINT
79:    ' prompt for a Y/N answer
80:    Xcurs = POS(0)
81:    Ycurs = CSRLIN
82:    DO
83:      LOCATE Ycurs, Xcurs
84:      PRINT SPACE$(80);
85:      LOCATE Ycurs, Xcurs
86:      PRINT "Add another set of values? (Y/N) ";
87:      C = INPUT$(1)
88:      PRINT C
89:      C = UCASE$(C)
90:    LOOP UNTIL C = "Y" OR C = "N"
91: LOOP UNTIL C = "N"
92: END
93:
94: FUNCTION Pound$ (N AS INTEGER)
95:    Pound$ = STRING$(1 + FIX(LOG(N) / LOG(10)), "#")
96: END FUNCTION
97:
98: FUNCTION PoundNumber$ (Z AS DOUBLE)
99:    IF Z >= 0 THEN
100:     IF Z > 1000 THEN
101:       PoundNumber$ = "+#.#####^^^^^"
102:     ELSE
103:       PoundNumber$ = "###.####"
104:     END IF
105:   ELSE
106:     IF ABS(Z) > 1000 THEN
```

continues

Listing 12.1. continued

```
107:        PoundNumber$ = "+#.#####^^^^^"
108:     ELSE
109:        PoundNumber$ = "-###.####"
110:     END IF
111:   END IF
112: END FUNCTION
```

Here is a sample output for the program in Listing 12.1:

```
Number of values to enter (3 TO 15) ? 5

Enter value # 1  ? 1.2
Enter value # 2  ? 2.5
Enter value # 3  ? 3.4
Enter value # 4  ? 4.1
Enter value # 5  ? 5.2
```

 SCREEN CLEARS

```
Value #  1 =  1.2
Value #  2 =  2.5
Value #  3 =  3.4
Value #  4 =  4.1
Value #  5 =  5.2

Enter index of first value to add (default = 1) ? 2

Enter index of last value to add (default = last) ? 4

Sum of X(2) to X(4) =  10.0000
Mean of X(2) to X(4) =   3.3333

Add another set of values? (Y/N) n
```

 The program in Listing 12.1 contains the OPTION BASE 1 statement on line
5, which explicitly sets the default first array index to 1. Line 7 contains
the declaration of the constant ARRAY.SIZE%, which defines the size of the

array used in the program. Line 8 defines the constant FRMT, which stores a format string. Line 10 declares the array X. Notice that this declaration only specifies the last array index. The AS DOUBLE clause indicates that X stores double-precision, floating-point numbers. Lines 11–18 declare simple variables.

The DO UNTIL loop on lines 22–26 prompts you to enter a number that lies in the range of 3 to ARRAY.SIZE. The loop stores your input in the variable N. The FOR-NEXT loop on lines 29–42 obtains the individual values and stores them in array X. The loop uses the control variable I and iterates from 1 to N. The PRINT statement on line 30 displays the prompt message. On line 31 the program stores the current column position of the screen cursor in the variable Xcurs. The INPUT statement on line 33 obtains a numeric input and stores it in X(I). Here and in other statements in the loop, the control variable supplies the index to select an element in X. The IF-THEN statement on line 35 compares the value in X(I) (element number I of array X) with 0. If this condition is true, the THEN clause statements assign I to X(I) and displays that value.

The second DO-UNTIL loop in the program is located on lines 45–91. This loop contains a FOR-NEXT loop on lines 48–51. The FOR-NEXT loop displays the values stored in X. The inner DO-UNTIL loops on lines 55–59 and 61–65 prompt you for a valid index for the first and last array elements to process. The first DO-UNTIL loop, which stores your input in I1, examines the condition I1 >= 1 AND I1 <= N. The second DO-UNTIL loop, which stores your input in I2, examines the condition I1 >= 1 AND I1 <= N AND I2 <> I1. The last relational term in the tested condition ensures that the indices in I1 and I2 are different. In addition, the DO-UNTIL loop assigns default values when you enter 0 or simply press the Return key. The first loop assigns 1 to I2, whereas the second loop assigns N to I2.

The statement on line 67 initializes the summation variable Sum. The FOR-NEXT loop on lines 68 and 69 accumulates the values of X in Sum. The loop uses the control variable I and iterates from I1 to I2. The statement on line 69 retrieves each element of X using X(I).

The statements on lines 72–77 display the sum and mean value for the specified range of elements in X. These statements call the functions Pound$ and PoundNumber$ to build the proper formatting string.

12

> **Note:** The statements on lines 80–91 ask you whether you want to process another set of array elements. Notice the statements use the POS function, the CSRLIN function, and the LOCATE statement to re-display the prompt at the same location if you do not press the Y or N keys.

Redimensioning Arrays

The DIM statement enables you to declare an array and specify its size. The size of the array should accommodate the number of values you want to store in the array. What if you cannot foretell the number of stored values? This unpredictable number causes two extreme problems. If the size of the array exceeds by far the number of stored values, then the array is wasting memory—perhaps a significant amount of memory. The other extreme is when the size of the array cannot accommodate all the stored values. This is a worse problem than the first one. In reading about the problem of sizing arrays, you might ask if the DIM statement fixes the size of an array? The answer is yes and no, with an explanation! The DIM statement that declares the array X in Listing 12.1 fixes the size of the array. Such an array is called a *static* array. QBasic arrays are, by default, static. In addition, QBasic supports dynamic arrays that you can resize (or redimension, to be a bit more accurate) during program execution. QBasic offers the REDIM statement to redimension dynamic arrays. How does QBasic distinguish between static and dynamic arrays? The answer lies in the special *metacommands* $STATIC and $DYNAMIC that must appear in comments.

Syntax

The Static and Dynamic Metacommands
The general syntax for the static and dynamic metacommands is

```
' $DYNAMIC
REM $DYNAMIC
```

```
' $STATIC
REM $STATIC
```

The $DYNAMIC metacommand tells QBasic that all subsequent DIM statements declare dynamic arrays. The $STATIC metacommand tells QBasic that all subsequent DIM statements declare static arrays. You can include both metacommands in a program to toggle the type of declared arrays.

Dynamic arrays occupy more memory than comparable static arrays. Therefore, make your arrays static unless you need to redimension them.

Examples:

```
'$DYNAMIC
' declare array X as dynamic
DIM X(10 TO 20) AS DOUBLE
'$STATIC
' declare array Y as static
DIM Y(10 TO 20) AS DOUBLE
'$DYNAMIC
' declare array Z as dynamic
DIM Z(10 TO 20) AS DOUBLE
'$STATIC
' declare array W as static
DIM W(10 TO 20) AS DOUBLE
```

12

The REDIM Statement

The general syntax for the REDIM statement is

```
REDIM [SHARED] arrayName([low TO] high) [AS type]
```

Examples:

```
'$DYNAMIC
DIM January(1 TO 31) AS STRING
' redimension array with difference indices
```

```
REDIM January(10 TO 15) AS STRING

' declare string-typed array January
OPTION BASE 1
'$DYNAMIC
DIM January(31) AS STRING
' redimension array with a different last index
REDIM January(5) AS STRING
```

Warning: The SHARED clause indicates the declare array can be shared with FUNCTION and SUB procedures without explicitly passing it as a parameter. The *arrayName* is the name of an array. You can declare the range of indices explicitly by specifying the *low* and *high* limits (separated by the keyword TO). If you omit the *low* index, QBasic uses the OPTION BASE value as the default lower index. The AS clause enables you to specify the data type associated with the array. When omitted, you can use a data type suffix with the array name. If you use neither, QBasic applies the default association between the array name and data types. You also can influence this default data type association by placing DEF*type* statements before declaring arrays. The REDIM statement can redimension multiple dynamic arrays. Please note: REDIM erases the contents of the redimensioned arrays.

Here is an example of a dynamic QBasic array. Listing 12.2, ARRAY2.BAS, declares and uses a dynamic array. I created this program by modifying ARRAY1.BAS in Listing 12.1. The new program prompts you to enter the number of values (which becomes the size of the array used in the program). The prompt reminds you that your input should be at least the number 3. The remaining program tasks are identical to those of ARRAY1.BAS.

Listing 12.2. ARRAY2.BAS, which declares and uses a dynamic array.

```
 1: DECLARE FUNCTION Pound$ (N AS INTEGER)
 2: DECLARE FUNCTION PoundNumber$ (Z AS DOUBLE)
 3: REM Program uses dynamic arrays
 4: REM
 5: OPTION BASE 1
 6: ' declare constants
 7: CONST MSG = "Number of values to enter (minimum 3) "
 8: ' declare variables
 9: '$DYNAMIC
10: DIM X(1) AS DOUBLE
11: DIM Sum AS DOUBLE
12: DIM I AS INTEGER
13: DIM N AS INTEGER
14: DIM I1 AS INTEGER
15: DIM I2 AS INTEGER
16: DIM Xcurs AS INTEGER
17: DIM Ycurs AS INTEGER
18: DIM C AS STRING
19:
20: CLS
21: ' prompt for number of values
22: DO
23:   PRINT MSG;
24:   INPUT N
25:   PRINT
26: LOOP UNTIL N >= 3
27:
28: REDIM X(N) AS DOUBLE
29:
30: ' enter values
31: FOR I = 1 TO N
32:   PRINT "Enter value #"; I; " ";
33:   Xcurs = POS(0)
34:   ' store each value in a member of array X
35:   INPUT ; X(I)
36:   ' if value is 0 assign X(I) the loop control variable
37:   IF X(I) = 0 THEN
38:     X(I) = I
39:     ' display the value after the ? mark
```

continues

Listing 12.2. continued

```
40:     LOCATE , Xcurs + 1
41:       PRINT X(I);
42:     END IF
43:     PRINT
44: NEXT I
45:
46: ' loop to display array and query range of members to sum
47: DO
48:   CLS
49:   ' display the elements of array X
50:   FOR I = 1 TO N
51:       PRINT USING "Value _# ## = "; I;
52:       PRINT X(I)
53:   NEXT I
54:
55:   PRINT
56:   ' get the indices of the elements to add
57:   DO
58:       INPUT "Enter index of first value to add (default=1) "; I1
59:       IF I1 = 0 THEN I1 = 1
60:       PRINT
61:   LOOP UNTIL I1 >= 1 AND I1 <= N
62:
63:   DO
64:       INPUT "Enter index of last value to add (default=last) "; I2
65:       IF I2 = 0 THEN I2 = N
66:       PRINT
67:   LOOP UNTIL I2 >= 1 AND I2 <= N AND I2 <> I1
68:   ' add the elements of X from X(I1) to X(I2)
69:   Sum = 0
70:   FOR I = I1 TO I2
71:       Sum = Sum + X(I)
72:   NEXT I
73:   ' display the results
74:   C = "Sum of X(" + Pound$(I1) + ") to X(" + Pound$(I2) + ") = "
75:   C = C + PoundNumber$(Sum)
76:   PRINT USING C; I1; I2; Sum
```

```
77:    C = "Mean of X(" + Pound$(I1) + ") to X(" + Pound$(I2) + ") = "
78:    C = C + PoundNumber$(Sum)
79:    PRINT USING C; I1; I2; Sum / (I2 - I1 + 1)
80:    PRINT
81:    ' prompt for a Y/N answer
82:    Xcurs = POS(0)
83:    Ycurs = CSRLIN
84:    DO
85:      LOCATE Ycurs, Xcurs
86:      PRINT SPACE$(80);
87:      LOCATE Ycurs, Xcurs
88:      PRINT "Add another set of values? (Y/N) ";
89:      C = INPUT$(1)
90:      PRINT C
91:      C = UCASE$(C)
92:    LOOP UNTIL C = "Y" OR C = "N"
93: LOOP UNTIL C = "N"
94: END
95:
96: REM $STATIC
97: FUNCTION Pound$ (N AS INTEGER)
98:    Pound$ = STRING$(1 + FIX(LOG(N) / LOG(10)), "#")
99: END FUNCTION
100:
101: FUNCTION PoundNumber$ (Z AS DOUBLE)
102:    IF Z >= 0 THEN
103:      IF Z > 1000 THEN
104:        PoundNumber$ = "+#.#####^^^^^"
105:      ELSE
106:        PoundNumber$ = "###.####"
107:      END IF
108:    ELSE
109:      IF ABS(Z) > 1000 THEN
110:        PoundNumber$ = "+#.#####^^^^^"
111:      ELSE
112:        PoundNumber$ = "-###.####"
113:      END IF
114:    END IF
115: END FUNCTION
116:
```

12

Here is a sample output for the program in Listing 12.2:

```
Number of values to enter (minimum 3) ? 5

Enter value # 1   ? 1
Enter value # 2   ? 2
Enter value # 3   ? 3
Enter value # 4   ? 4
Enter value # 5   ? 5
```

SCREEN CLEARS

```
Value #  1 =  1
Value #  2 =  2
Value #  3 =  3
Value #  4 =  4
Value #  5 =  5

Enter index of first value to add (default = 1) ? 2

Enter index of last value to add (default = last) ? 5

Sum of X(2) to X(5) =  14.0000
Mean of X(2) to X(5) =   3.5000

Add another set of values? (Y/N) n
```

Because the program in Listing 12.2 is very similar to the one in Listing 12.1, I only discuss the differences between them:

1. ARRAY2.BAS only declares the constant MSG, which replaces the constant FRMT in ARRAY1.BAS. There is no constant ARRAY.SIZE declared in ARRAY2.BAS.

2. Line 9 contains the $DYNAMIC metacommand.

3. Line 10 declares array X as having the last index of 1. Consequently, X stores one element. This dummy-size declaration is typical when you will redimension the array before using it.

4. Line 28 contains the REDIM statement that redimensions X using N. Consequently, the program uses X with a tailor-fit size.

5. Line 96 contains the $STATIC metacommand, which QBasic inserted when I saved the ARRAY2.BAS program.

The *LBOUND* and *UBOUND* Functions

To keep track of the sizes of static and dynamic arrays, you typically use sets of one or two variables to store the indices of these arrays. If you rely on such variables, you must ensure that they maintain accurate and updated values. Otherwise, your programs will not work correctly. Fortunately, QBasic supports the LBOUND and UBOUND functions that return the lower and upper array indices. The beauty of these functions is their reliability.

12

The LBOUND and UBOUND Functions

The general syntax for the LBOUND and UBOUND functions is

```
LBOUND(arrayName)
UBOUND(arrayName)
```

The LBOUND function returns the first index of *arrayName*. The UBOUND function returns the last index of *arrayName*. These two functions work with both static and dynamic arrays.

Example:

```
DIM S(3 TO 9) AS STRING

FOR I = LBOUND(S) TO UBOUND(S)
     S(I) = STRING$(10, 65 + I)
NEXT I
```

By praising the virtues of the LBOUND and UNBOUND, I have perhaps spoken hastily, especially in the case of the latter function. There are cases when you do not fully populate an array with meaningful data. The typical pattern is to start storing data at the first index and gradually use higher indices. Frequently, the index of the last element that stores meaningful data is less than the last index of the array (reported by UBOUND). Such a common use of arrays requires that you employ a variable to store the *highest working index* of an array. Figure 12.2 shows a sample array A and its working partition. The first 10 elements contain meaningful data, whereas the last five elements contain zeros or are empty strings. The figure suggests that a variable can be used to store the index 10.

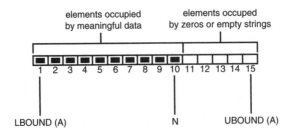

Note: The variable N stores highest index of array A that contains meaningful data.

Figure 12.2. The working partition of an array.

Note: The variable N stores the highest index of array A that contains meaningful data.

Let's look at an example that uses the LBOUND and UBOUND functions. Listing 12.3, LUBOUND1.BAS, uses the LBOUND and UBOUND functions to obtain the first and last indices of an array with an arbitrary range of indices. The program requires no input from you. Instead it creates and displays an array with random first and last indices.

Listing 12.3. LUBOUND1.BAS, which uses the LBOUND and UBOUND functions to obtain the first and last indices of an array.

```
 1: REM Program that uses the LBOUND and UBOUND
 2: REM functions to obtain the lower and upper
 3: REM indices of an arbitrarily sized array
 4: ' declare constant
 5: CONST FIRST = 10
 6: CONST LAST = 100
 7: CONST MAX.SIZE = 20
 8: CONST TITLE = "Arbitrary Array"
 9: ' declare variables
10: '$DYNAMIC
11: DIM A(1) AS INTEGER
```

```
12: DIM I AS INTEGER
13: DIM J AS INTEGER
14: DIM C AS STRING
15:
16: CLS
17: RANDOMIZE TIMER
18: ' use variables I and J to temporarily
19: ' store the lower and upper bounds of the
20: ' redimensioned array A
21: I = INT(RND * (LAST - FIRST + 1)) + FIRST
22: J = I + INT(RND * MAX.SIZE)
23: ' redimension array A
24: REDIM A(I TO J)
25:
26: ' assign values to the elements of array A
27: FOR I = LBOUND(A) TO UBOUND(A)
28:    A(I) = INT(RND * 1000)
29: NEXT I
30:
31: PRINT SPC(40 - LEN(TITLE) \ 2); TITLE
32: PRINT
33: ' display the values in array A
34: FOR J = LBOUND(A) TO UBOUND(A)
35:    ' this IF-THEN statement is useful when
36:    ' you increase the value of constant MAX.SIZE
37:    ' well beyond 20
38:    IF CSRLIN = 21 THEN
39:      PRINT
40:      PRINT "Press any key to continue";
41:      C = INPUT$(1)
42:      CLS
43:    END IF
44:    PRINT "A("; MID$(STR$(J), 2); ") = "; A(J)
45: NEXT J
46: END
```

Here is sample output for the program in Listing 12.3: Your output will be different because of the random-number generator.

```
Arbitrary Array

A(96)  =  578
A(97)  =  167
A(98)  =  42
A(99)  =  429
A(100) =  425
A(101) =  402
A(102) =  263
A(103) =  236
A(104) =  837
A(105) =  913
A(106) =  739
A(107) =  34
A(108) =  15
A(109) =  912
```

 The program in Listing 12.3 declares its constants on lines 5–8. The constants FIRST and LAST define the range of array indices. The constant MAX.SIZE specifies the maximum array size. Line 10 contains the $DYNAMIC metacommand to allow the declaration of a dynamic array on line 11. Line 11 declares the array A with a dummy value for the last index. Lines 12–14 declare the simple variables used in the program.

The process of determining the array size uses random numbers. The first step is to randomize the seed using the TIMER function on line 17. The statement on line 21 obtains a random number in the range of FIRST to LAST and stores it in the variable I. This number represents the first index of the redimensioned array A. The statement on line 22 calculates the last index of the redimensioned array A. The statement on line 24 redimensions A to have indices from I to J. At this point, the variables I and J maintain the same values returned by the function calls LBOUND(A) and UBOUND(A). However, as you will see in the next lines, I reuse the variables I and J as control variables in FOR-NEXT loops. By doing so, I forfeit the values for the first and last array indices stored in these variables.

The FOR-NEXT loop on lines 27–29 assigns random numbers to the elements of A. The loop uses the control variable I and iterates to access all the elements in A. The function calls LBOUND(A) and UBOUND(A) provide the correct iteration range for the loop.

The PRINT statement on line 31 displays the centered title of the program. The FOR-NEXT loop on lines 34–45 displays the values in A. The loop uses the control variable J and iterates from LBOUND(A) to UBOUND(A). The loop contains an IF-THEN statement that handles paginating the display of a longer array. This statement is useful should you decide to increase the value of MAX.SIZE.

Erasing Arrays

QBasic offers the ERASE statement to erase static arrays and remove dynamic arrays from memory.

12

Syntax

The ERASE Statement

The general syntax for the ERASE statement is

```
ERASE array1 [, array2, ...]
```

The ERASE statement erases *array1*, *array2*, and so on. In the case of static arrays, the ERASE statement assigns zeros to the elements of numeric arrays, and empty strings to the elements of string arrays. In the case of dynamic arrays, the ERASE statement removes them from memory.

Example:

```
'$STATIC
DIM X (1 TO 10) AS SINGLE
FOR I = LBOUND(X) TO UBOUND(X)
    X(I) = I * I
    PRINT X(I) ' displays the value of I squared
NEXT I
ERASE X
FOR I = LBOUND(X) TO UBOUND(X)
    PRINT X(I) ' displays zero
NEXT I
```

Let's look at an example. Listing 12.4, ERASE1.BAS, erases a static and a dynamic array. The program tests the static array as follows:

1. Assign values to the elements of the array.

2. Display the values in the array.

3. Erase the array.

4. Display the values in the array. This time, the output shows zeros.

The program tests the dynamic array as follows:

1. Assign values to the elements of the array.

2. Display the values in the array.

3. Erase the array.

4. Set an error trap.

5. Attempt to display the values in the array. This step generates a runtime error that is caught by the error trap. The trap displays an array-access error message.

Listing 12.4. **ERASE1.BAS, which erases a static and a dynamic array.**

```
 1: REM Program that tests the ERASE statement
 2: REM
 3: OPTION BASE 1
 4: ' declare constants
 5: CONST ARRAY.SIZE% = 9
 6: '$STATIC
 7: DIM X(ARRAY.SIZE) AS INTEGER
 8: '$DYNAMIC
 9: DIM Y(ARRAY.SIZE) AS INTEGER
10: DIM I AS INTEGER
11: DIM C AS STRING
12:
13: CLS
14: ' assign values to the elements of array X
15: FOR I = LBOUND(X) TO UBOUND(X)
16:    X(I) = I * I
17: NEXT I
18: ' display the elements of array X
19: PRINT "Array X contains:"
20: FOR I = LBOUND(X) TO UBOUND(X)
```

```
21:    PRINT USING "X(#) = ##"; I; X(I)
22: NEXT I
23:
24: PRINT
25: PRINT "Press any key to continue";
26: C$ = INPUT$(1)
27:
28: ' erase the array X
29: ERASE X
30:
31: CLS
32: ' display the elements in array X
33: PRINT "After erasing array X, the array elements contains:"
34: FOR I = LBOUND(X) TO UBOUND(X)
35:    PRINT USING "X(#) = ##"; I; X(I)
36: NEXT I
37:
38: PRINT
39: PRINT "Press any key to continue";
40: C$ = INPUT$(1)
41: CLS
42: ' assign values to the elements of array Y
43: FOR I = LBOUND(Y) TO UBOUND(Y)
44:    Y(I) = I * I
45: NEXT I
46: ' display the elements of array Y
47: PRINT "Array Y contains:";
48: FOR I = LBOUND(Y) TO UBOUND(Y)
49:    PRINT USING "Y(#) = ##"; I; Y(I)
50: NEXT I
51:
52: PRINT
53: PRINT "Press any key to continue";
54: C$ = INPUT$(1)
55:
56: ' remove the dynamic array Y from memory
57: ERASE Y
58:
59: ' set error trap
60: ON ERROR GOTO Bad.Index
61:
62: CLS
```

continues

Listing 12.4. continued

```
63: ' display (if possible?) the elements of array Y
64: PRINT "After erasing array Y, the array elements contains:"
65: FOR I = LBOUND(Y) TO UBOUND(Y)
66:   PRINT USING "Y(#) = ##"; I; Y(I)
67: NEXT I
68:
69: ' clear the error trap
70: ON ERROR GOTO 0
71:
72: END
73:
74: ' ********************* ERROR HANDLER *********************
75: Bad.Index:
76:   PRINT
77:   PRINT "Error: Cannot access the ERASEd dynamic array Y"
78: END
```

Here is sample output for the program in Listing 12.4:

```
Array X contains:
X(1) =  1
X(2) =  4
X(3) =  9
X(4) = 16
X(5) = 25
X(6) = 36
X(7) = 49
X(8) = 64
X(9) = 81

Press any key to continue
```

SCREEN CLEARS

```
After erasing array X, the array elements contains:
X(1) =  0
X(2) =  0
X(3) =  0
```

```
X(4) =  0
X(5) =  0
X(6) =  0
X(7) =  0
X(8) =  0
X(9) =  0

Press any key to continue
```

 SCREEN CLEARS

```
Array Y contains:
Y(1) =  1
Y(2) =  4
Y(3) =  9
Y(4) = 16
Y(5) = 25
Y(6) = 36
Y(7) = 49
Y(8) = 64
Y(9) = 81

Press any key to continue
```

SCREEN CLEARS

```
After erasing array Y, the array elements contains:

Error: Cannot access the ERASEd dynamic array Y
```

Analysis The program in Listing 12.4. contains the OPTION BASE 1 statement on line 3 and declares the ARRAY.SIZE constant on line 5. The comment on line 6 contains the metacommand $STATIC used to declare explicitly the array X (on line 7) as static. The comment on line 8 contains the metacommand $DYNAMIC used to declare explicitly the array Y (in line 9) as dynamic. Both arrays use the constant ARRAY.SIZE to specify their last indices. Lines 10 and 11 contain the declarations for the variables I and C.

The FOR-NEXT loop on lines 15–17 assigns values to the elements of static array X. The PRINT statement on line 19 displays a message that clarifies the output generated by the FOR-NEXT loop on lines 20–22. This loop uses the control variable I and iterates from LBOUND(X) to UBOUND(X). Each loop iteration displays the value in X(I). The statements on lines 25 and 26 prompt you to press any key to continue. Line 29 contains the ERASE X statement that resets the elements of X to 0. The FOR-NEXT loop on lines 34–36 display the values of the erased array X.

The FOR-NEXT loop on lines 43–45 assigns values to the elements of dynamic array Y. The PRINT statement on line 47 displays a message that clarifies the output generated by the FOR-NEXT loop on lines 48–50. This loop uses the control variable I and iterates from LBOUND(Y) to UBOUND(Y). Each loop iteration displays the value in Y(I). Line 57 contains the ERASE Y statement that removes Y from memory. Line 60 sets an error trap to handle the array-access error generated by calling the function LBOUND(Y) in the subsequent FOR-NEXT loop. The error trap sends the program execution to the label Bad.Index. There, the program displays an array-access error message and then ends the program. The sample output indicates that the program indeed experiences an array-access error, as suspected, and invokes the error-handler.

Sorting Arrays

Note: This section (and the one that follows) contains important applications of arrays. However, the information presented is *not* vital for using QBasic arrays. You can read these sections later.

The two most common non-numerical operations for arrays are sorting and searching. Sorting is a process that arranges the values in the array in either ascending or descending order. Such an order makes searching for data in arrays fast and efficient. Computer scientists have spent much time studying methods to sort arrays. In this section I present the simplest and, yes, the slowest sorting method, called the *bubblesort* method. Because you are a novice programmer, I want to avoid overwhelming you with a more advanced method. However, I still feel that you should know about sorting arrays. I present the bubblesort method because it is easy to understand.

The bubblesort method arranges the elements of an array by comparing neighboring elements. Here is the pseudocode for the bubblesort method:

Given an array A with indices from 1 to N.

1. FOR I = 1 to N - 1

1.1. FOR J = I + 1 to N

1.1.1. If A(I) > A(J) then swap A(I) and A(J)

The bubblesort causes the elements to slowly move (or bubble, if you prefer) toward their final location in the sorted array.

Rather that showing you a figure that shows a example of the bubblesort method, I present a QBasic program that demonstrates the sorting process visually. Listing 12.5, SORT1.BAS, performs the demonstration. The program requires no input from you. Instead, it creates an array, assigns random integers to its elements, and sorts it. The program displays pointers indicating the elements being compared and swapped. I added some sound effects to go along with the comparison and swapping operations.

12

 Listing 12.5. **SORT1.BAS, which visually demonstrates the bubblesort method.**

```
 1: DECLARE SUB WaitAWhile (Period AS SINGLE)
 2: DECLARE SUB ShowCompare (S1$, I%, S2$, J%)
 3: REM Program performs animated sorting of an array
 4: REM
 5: OPTION BASE 1
 6: ' declare constants
 7: CONST ARRAY.SIZE = 10
 8: CONST DELAY = 1
 9: CONST PTR.ROW = 29
10: CONST FRMT = "Value at element ## = ####"
11: CONST STR1 = "<---- compare this element"
12: CONST STR2 = "<---- with this element"
13: CONST STR3 = "<---- swap this element"
14:
15: ' declare variables
16: DIM IntArr(ARRAY.SIZE) AS INTEGER
17: DIM I AS INTEGER
18: DIM J AS INTEGER
19: DIM TheTime AS SINGLE
20:
```

continues

Listing 12.5. continued

```
21: CLS
22: ' reseed random number generator
23: RANDOMIZE TIMER
24:
25: ' assign random numbers to the elements of array IntArr
26: FOR I = 1 TO ARRAY.SIZE
27:   IntArr(I) = INT(RND * 1000)
28: NEXT I
29:
30: ' display the array elements
31: FOR I = 1 TO ARRAY.SIZE
32:   LOCATE 1 + 2 * (I - 1), 1
33:   PRINT USING FRMT; I; IntArr(I)
34: NEXT I
35:
36: ' start sorting the array
37: FOR I = 1 TO ARRAY.SIZE - 1
38:   FOR J = I + 1 TO ARRAY.SIZE
39:       SOUND 600, 1
40:       ' display arrows that indicate the
41:       ' elements being compared
42:       CALL ShowCompare(STR1, I, STR2, J)
43:
44:       IF IntArr(I) > IntArr(J) THEN
45:         SOUND 50, 1
46:         ' indicate that compared elements
47:         ' will be swapped
48:         CALL ShowCompare(STR3, I, STR2, J)
49:         ' swap elements at index I and J
50:         SWAP IntArr(I), IntArr(J)
51:         ' display the new positions of the
52:         ' swapped elements
53:         LOCATE 1 + 2 * (I - 1), 1
54:         PRINT USING FRMT; I; IntArr(I);
55:         LOCATE 1 + 2 * (J - 1), 1
56:         PRINT USING FRMT; J; IntArr(J);
57:       END IF
58:   NEXT J
```

```
59: NEXT I
60:
61: LOCATE 22, 1
62:
63: PRINT "Array is now sorted!"
64: END
65:
66: SUB ShowCompare (S1$, I1%, S2$, I2%)
67:    LOCATE 1 + 2 * (I1% - 1), PTR.ROW
68:    PRINT S1$;
69:    LOCATE 1 + 2 * (I2% - 1), PTR.ROW
70:    PRINT S2$;
71:    CALL WaitAWhile(DELAY)
72:    LOCATE 1 + 2 * (I1% - 1), PTR.ROW
73:    PRINT SPACE$(LEN(S1$));
74:    LOCATE 1 + 2 * (I2% - 1), PTR.ROW
75:    PRINT SPACE$(LEN(S2$));
76: END SUB
77:
78: SUB WaitAWhile (Period AS SINGLE)
79:    TheTime = TIMER
80:    DO
81:    LOOP UNTIL (TIMER - TheTime) >= Period
82: END SUB
```

Here is just a snapshot of a sample session with the program in Listing 12.5:

```
Value at element  1 =   21  <---- compare this element

Value at element  2 =  568

Value at element  3 =  188

Value at element  4 =  322

Value at element  5 =  123

Value at element  6 =  543

Value at element  7 =   3  <---- with this element
```

413

```
Value at element  8 =  901

Value at element  9 =   64

Value at element 10 =  942
```

Analysis   Because the program in Listing 12.5 is a bit advanced, I present the following pseudocode as a tool to explain the program:

1. Declare constants (lines 7 to 13).

2. Declare array IntArr (line 16).

3. Declare other variables (lines 17 to 19).

4. Assign random values to all elements in array IntArr (lines 23 to 28).

5. Display the elements of array IntArr, skipping every other screen   line (lines 31 to 34).

6. Start sorting the array IntArr (lines 37).

6.1. Make a sound for the comparison step (line 39).

6.2. Show the comparison-pointers (line 42).

6.3. Compare elements of IntArr (line 44). If these elements must be swapped, then carry out the following steps:

6.3.1. Make a special sound for the swapping step (line 45).

6.3.2. Show the swap-pointers (line 48).

6.3.3. Swap the elements of IntArr (line 50).

6.3.4. Update the screen location of the swapped elements (lines 53 to 56).

6.4. Display a message indicating that the array is sorted (lines 61 to 63).

The program uses the SOUND statement to generate the special sounds. On Day 21, "Music and Sound," I explain the SOUND statement. For now, just type the SOUND statements in.

The SUB WaitAWhile enables the program to pause for a specified period. The SUB ShowCompare displays various pointers and then erases them after a specified period.

Now that you have used SORT1.BAS, let me present SORT2.BAS in Listing 12.6. This program is the more practical version of SORT1.BAS. It executes the statements for the bubblesort at full speed.

Listing 12.6. SORT2.BAS, which sorts an array using the bubblesort method.

```
1: REM Program sorts of an array of integers
2: REM
3: OPTION BASE 1
4: ' declare constants
5: CONST ARRAY.SIZE = 10
6: CONST FRMT = "####"
7:
8: ' declare variables
9: DIM IntArr(ARRAY.SIZE) AS INTEGER
10: DIM I AS INTEGER
11: DIM J AS INTEGER
12: DIM C AS STRING
13:
14: CLS
15: ' reseed random-number generator
16: RANDOMIZE TIMER
17: FOR I = 1 TO ARRAY.SIZE
18:    IntArr(I) = INT(RND * 1000)
19: NEXT I
20:
21: FOR I = 1 TO ARRAY.SIZE
22:    PRINT USING FRMT; IntArr(I)
23: NEXT I
24:
25: PRINT
26: PRINT "Press any key to sort the array";
27: C = INPUT$(1)
```

continues

Listing 12.6. continued

```
28:
29: ' nested loops which implement the bubble sort method
30: FOR I = 1 TO ARRAY.SIZE - 1
31:   FOR J = I + 1 TO ARRAY.SIZE
32:       ' is element at index I greater than element
33:       ' at index J?
34:       IF IntArr(I) > IntArr(J) THEN
35:          ' swap the elements
36:          SWAP IntArr(I), IntArr(J)
37:       END IF
38:   NEXT J
39: NEXT I
40:
41: CLS
42:
43: FOR I = 1 TO ARRAY.SIZE
44:    PRINT USING FRMT; IntArr(I)
45: NEXT I
46: PRINT
47: PRINT "Array is now sorted!"
48: END
```

Here is a sample output for the program in Listing 12.6 (your output will be different because of the RND function):

```
 25
431
307
841
443
959
630
394
460
130
```

 SCREEN CLEARS

```
Press any key to sort the array
```

```
      25
     130
     307
     394
     431
     443
     460
     630
     841
     959
```

```
Array is now sorted!
```

 Analysis The program in Listing 12.6 is a no-frills version of the one in Listing 12.5.

Searching Arrays

Searching through arrays is another common non-numeric operation for arrays. There are two general methods for searching an array. These methods depend on the order of the searched array. When dealing with an unordered array you must use a *linear search* method (there are several variations of the basic linear search method). When handling a sorted array, use the *binary search* method (there is basically only one binary search method).

The basic linear search method is a very simple method that scans the array from its first to last elements. Here is the pseudocode for the linear search:

Given an array A, with indices from 1 to N. Search for the value X.

1. Set not-found-flag to true.

2. Set the search index I to 1, the first array index.

3. Repeat the next steps while I is less than or equal to N
    AND the not-found flag is true.

3.1 If A(I) is not equal to X, the search value, then:

3.1.1 Increment index I.

3.1.2 Otherwise set not-found flag to false.

The not-found flag indicates whether the linear search is successful. If it is, the matching array element is found in index I.

The binary search method is regarded by many programmers as the best general-purpose method for searching an ordered array. Rather than searching the ordered array from beginning to end, the binary method takes advantage of the array order. It treats the array elements as an interval and first examines the median array element. This examination tells the method if it needs to set the first or second half of the array as the next search interval. The method repeats this scheme with the smaller intervals. Eventually, the method either finds a match or runs out of sub-intervals to search.

The pseudocode for the binary search method is:

Given an array A, with indices from 1 to N. Search for the value X.

1. Set the low interval limit (call it Low) to 1.

2. Set the high interval limit (call it High) to N.

3. Repeat the following steps until A(Median) is equal to X
   or Low is greater than High:

3.1. Set Median as the median value of Lo and High.

3.2. If X is less than A(Median) then set Hi to Median - 1.
   Otherwise, Set Lo to Median + 1.

When the search is over, compare the values of X and A(Median) to determine whether the search was successful. If it was, the index of the matching array element is found in Median. Figure 12.3 shows a sample binary search.

DO use the linear method when you are not certain that the searched array is ordered.

DON'T apply the binary search method on an unsorted array. You will get erroneous results.

DON'T willingly apply the linear search method to a sorted array. Although such a search yields the correct result, it is not taking advantage of the array's order.

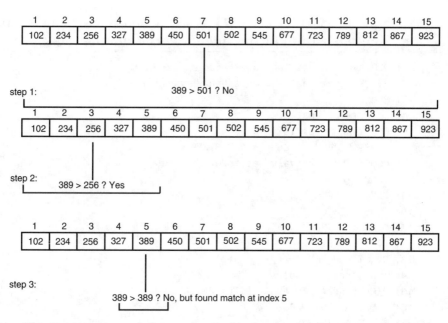

Figure 12.3. A sample binary search that locates the element containing the value 389.

Linear Search Program

Let's look at a program that visually demonstrates the linear search method on an array. Listing 12.7, SEARCH1.BAS, performs the demonstration. The program creates an array, assigns its elements with random numbers, and then searches for the elements in the array. To make the search more interesting, the program logically divides the array elements into two categories. The first category contains elements that appear on the screen. The display gives you the impression that these are all the array elements. The second category includes elements that are kept visually hidden. The program uses the *entire* array elements in searching the set of displayed elements. Consequently, the program is able to demonstrate both successful and unsuccessful searches (because the hidden elements do not match the displayed ones).

Listing 12.7. SEARCH1.BAS, which performs a visual demonstration of the linear search in an array.

```
1: DECLARE SUB WaitAWhile (Period AS SINGLE)
2: REM Program that searches unordered array
3: REM
4: ' declare constants
5: CONST ARRAY.SIZE% = 10
6: CONST SEARCH.SIZE% = ARRAY.SIZE% - 2
7: CONST FRMT$ = "Value at index # = ####"
8: CONST TRUE% = -1
9: CONST FALSE% = 0
10: CONST PTR.COL = 25
11: CONST MSG.ROW = 23
12: CONST SHORT.DELAY = 1
13: CONST LONG.DELAY = 3
14: ' declare variables
15: DIM IntArr(1 TO ARRAY.SIZE) AS INTEGER
16: DIM I AS INTEGER
17: DIM J AS INTEGER
18: DIM NotFound AS INTEGER
19:
20: CLS
21: RANDOMIZE TIMER
22:
23: ' assign random values to the array IntArr
24: FOR I = 1 TO ARRAY.SIZE
25:   IntArr(I) = INT(RND * 1000)
26: NEXT I
27:
28: ' display the first SEARCH.SIZE elements
29: FOR I = 1 TO SEARCH.SIZE
30:   PRINT USING FRMT; I; IntArr(I)
31:   PRINT
32: NEXT I
33:
34: ' search for the elements of IntArray
35: ' in the first SEARCH.SIZE elements
36: FOR I = 1 TO ARRAY.SIZE
37:   ' display the search status at the bottom of the screen
38:   LOCATE MSG.ROW, 1
```

```
39:    PRINT SPACE$(80);
40:    LOCATE MSG.ROW, 1
41:    PRINT "Searching for "; IntArr(I);
42:    ' start searching
43:    J = 1
44:    NotFound = TRUE
45:    DO
46:      ' display "?=?" near searched entry
47:      LOCATE 1 + 2 * (J - 1), PTR.COL
48:      PRINT "?=?"; IntArr(I)
49:      SOUND 50, 1
50:      CALL WaitAWhile(SHORT.DELAY)
51:      LOCATE 1 + 2 * (J - 1), PTR.COL
52:      PRINT SPACE$(80 - PTR.COL);
53:      ' no match found?
54:      IF IntArr(J) <> IntArr(I) THEN
55:        ' increment search index
56:        J = J + 1
57:      ELSE
58:        ' set not-found flag to FALSE
59:        NotFound = FALSE
60:      END IF
61:    LOOP UNTIL J > SEARCH.SIZE OR NotFound = FALSE
62:
63:    IF NotFound THEN
64:      ' display no-match found message
65:      LOCATE MSG.ROW, 1
66:      PRINT SPACE$(80);
67:      LOCATE MSG.ROW, 1
68:      PRINT "No match for "; IntArr(I)
69:      SOUND 100, 2
70:    ELSE
71:      ' display found-match message
72:      LOCATE MSG.ROW, 1
73:      PRINT SPACE$(80);
74:      LOCATE MSG.ROW, 1
75:      PRINT "Found "; IntArr(I); " at index "; J
76:      SOUND 400, .5
77:    END IF
78:    CALL WaitAWhile(LONG.DELAY)
79: NEXT I
```

continues

Listing 12.7. continued

```
80:
81: END
82:
83: SUB WaitAWhile (Period AS SINGLE)
84:   TheTime = TIMER
85:   DO
86:   LOOP UNTIL (TIMER - TheTime) >= Period
87: END SUB
```

Here is just a snapshot from a sample session with the program in Listing 12.7:

```
Value at index 1 =  969

Value at index 2 =  693

Value at index 3 =  239

Value at index 4 =  886 ?=? 886

Value at index 5 =  777

Value at index 6 =  551

Value at index 7 =   75

Value at index 8 =  405




Searching for  886
```

 Let me discuss the program in Listing 12.7 using the following pseudocode:

1. Declare program constants (lines 5 to 13).

2. Declare the array IntArr (line 15). Notice that the DIM statement specifies the first and last indices of the array.

3. Declare the program variables (in lines 16 to 18).

4. Assign random numbers to the elements of array IntArr (lines 21 to 26).

5. Display the first SEARCH.SIZE elements of array IntArr (lines 29 to 32).

6. Search in the set of displayed elements for the entire array elements (FOR-NEXT loop starts in line 36).

6.1. Display search status at the bottom of the screen (lines 38 to 41).

6.2. Start searching for IntArr(I) in the elements IntArr(1) to IntArr(SEARCH.SIZE). The search uses variable J. Set the not-found flag to false. Repeat the following steps until J > SEARCH.SIZE, or the not-found flag is false:

6.2.1. Display the "?=?" string and the sought value of IntArr(I) (lines 47 and 48).

6.2.2. Make a sound (line 49).

6.2.3. Wait for a while (line 50).

6.2.4. Erase comparative string (lines 51 and 52).

6.2.5. If IntArr(I) is not equal to IntArr(J), then increment variable J. Otherwise set no-match flag to false.

6.3. If not-found flag is true, then display no-match message (lines 65 to 69). Otherwise, display found-match message (72 to 76).

6.4. Wait for a while (line 78).

12

Binary Search Program

Let's look at a program that visually demonstrates the binary search method on a sorted array. Listing 12.8, SEARCH2.BAS, carries out the demonstration. The program performs the following tasks:

1. Create two integer arrays that have the same index ranges.

2. Assign random numbers to the elements of the first array.

3. Copy the elements of the first array to the second array.

4. Sort the first array.

5. Search for the elements of the second, unordered array in the first ordered array. To demonstrate unsuccessful searches, the program alters the values of the last two elements in the second array in a such a way that ensures search failure.

Type

Listing 12.8. SEARCH2.BAS, which performs a visual demonstration of the binary search in an array.

```
 1: DECLARE SUB WaitAWhile (Period AS SINGLE)
 2: REM Program that searches ordered array
 3: REM using the binary search method
 4: REM
 5: ' declare constants
 6: CONST ARRAY.SIZE% = 10
 7: CONST FRMT$ = "Value at index ## = ####"
 8: CONST PTR.COL = 27
 9: CONST MSG.ROW = 23
10: CONST SHORT.DELAY = 1
11: CONST LONG.DELAY = 3
12: ' declare variables
13: DIM IntArr1(1 TO ARRAY.SIZE) AS INTEGER
14: DIM IntArr2(1 TO ARRAY.SIZE) AS INTEGER
15: DIM I AS INTEGER
16: DIM J AS INTEGER
17: DIM Hi AS INTEGER
18: DIM Lo AS INTEGER
19: DIM Median AS INTEGER
20:
21: CLS
```

```
22: RANDOMIZE TIMER
23:
24: ' assign random values to the arrays IntArr1 and IntArr2
25: ' The IntArr2 copies the unordered values in array IntArr1
26: FOR I = 1 TO ARRAY.SIZE
27:   IntArr1(I) = INT(RND * 1000)
28:   IntArr2(I) = IntArr1(I)
29: NEXT I
30:
31: ' alter the values in the last two elements of IntArr2
32: ' to ensure that they do not match any element in array IntArr1
33: IntArr2(ARRAY.SIZE) = -1001
34: IntArr2(ARRAY.SIZE - 1) = 1001
35:
36: ' sort elements of array IntArr1
37: FOR I = 1 TO ARRAY.SIZE - 1
38:   FOR J = I + 1 TO ARRAY.SIZE
39:     IF IntArr1(I) > IntArr1(J) THEN
40:       SWAP IntArr1(I), IntArr1(J)
41:     END IF
42:   NEXT J
43: NEXT I
44:
45: ' display the elements of IntArr1
46: FOR I = 1 TO ARRAY.SIZE
47:   PRINT USING FRMT; I; IntArr1(I)
48:   PRINT
49: NEXT I
50:
51: ' search for the elements of IntArray2
52: ' in the elements of array IntArr1
53: FOR I = 1 TO ARRAY.SIZE
54:   ' display the search status at the bottom of the screen
55:   LOCATE MSG.ROW, 1
56:   PRINT SPACE$(80);
57:   LOCATE MSG.ROW, 1
58:   PRINT "Searching for "; IntArr2(I);
59:   ' start searching
60:   Lo = 1
61:   Hi = ARRAY.SIZE
```

continues

```
62:    DO
63:      Median = (Lo + Hi) \ 2
64:      ' display "?=?" near searched entry
65:      LOCATE 1 + 2 * (Median - 1), PTR.COL
66:      PRINT "?=?"; IntArr2(I)
67:      SOUND 50, 1
68:      CALL WaitAWhile(SHORT.DELAY)
69:      LOCATE 1 + 2 * (Median - 1), PTR.COL
70:      PRINT SPACE$(80 - PTR.COL);
71:      IF IntArr2(I) < IntArr1(Median) THEN
72:        Hi = Median - 1
73:      ELSE
74:        Lo = Median + 1
75:      END IF
76:    LOOP UNTIL IntArr2(I) = IntArr1(Median) OR Lo > Hi
77:
78:    ' found match
79:    IF IntArr2(I) = IntArr1(Median) THEN
80:      ' display found-match message
81:      LOCATE MSG.ROW, 1
82:      PRINT SPACE$(80);
83:      LOCATE MSG.ROW, 1
84:      PRINT "Found "; IntArr2(I); " at index "; Median
85:      SOUND 400, .5
86:    ELSE
87:      ' display no-match found message
88:      LOCATE MSG.ROW, 1
89:      PRINT SPACE$(80);
90:      LOCATE MSG.ROW, 1
91:      PRINT "No match for "; IntArr2(I)
92:      SOUND 100, 2
93:    END IF
94:    CALL WaitAWhile(LONG.DELAY)
95: NEXT I
96:
97: END
98:
99: SUB WaitAWhile (Period AS SINGLE)
```

```
100:   TheTime = TIMER
101:   DO
102:   LOOP UNTIL (TIMER - TheTime) >= Period
103: END SUB
```

Here is just a snapshot taken during a sample session with the program in Listing 12.8:

```
Value at index   1 =     52

Value at index   2 =    235

Value at index   3 =    265

Value at index   4 =    525

Value at index   5 =    527

Value at index   6 =    651

Value at index   7 =    667

Value at index   8 =    681   ?=? 681

Value at index   9 =    946

Value at index 10 =    984
```

```
Searching for   681
```

Let me discuss the program in Listing 12.8 using the following pseudocode:

1. Declare the constants (lines 6 to 11).

2. Declare the twin arrays IntArr1 and IntArr2 (lines 13 and 14).

3. Declare the variables (lines 15 to 19).

4. Assign random numbers to the elements of array IntArr1 and copy the same values in the corresponding elements of array IntArr2 (lines 22 to 29).

427

5. Alter the values in the last two elements of array `IntArr2` so that they do not match any value in array `IntArr1`.

6. Search for every `IntArr2` element in array `IntArr1`.

6.1. Display search status at the bottom of the screen (lines 55 to 58).

6.2. Initialize the variables `Lo` and `Hi` that store the current search interval (lines 60 and 61).

6.3. Repeat the following steps until `IntArr2(I)` is equal to `IntArr1(Median)` or `Lo` is greater than `Hi`.

6.3.1. Set `Median` to the median value of `Lo` and `Hi`.

6.3.2. Display search pointer (lines 65 to 66).

6.3.3. Sound a beep (line 67).

6.3.4. Wait for a while (line 68).

6.3.5. Clear the search pointer (lines 69 to 70).

6.3.6. If `IntArr2(I)` is less than `IntArr1(Median)`, assign `Median - 1` to `Hi`. Otherwise, assign `Median + 1` to `Lo`.

6.4. If `IntArr2(I)` is equal to `IntArr1(Median)`, then display a found-match message (lines 81 to 85). Otherwise, display a no-match-found message (lines 88 to 92).

6.5. Wait for a while (line 94).

Summary

This chapter introduced you to the arrays—the simplest and perhaps the most popular data structure in programming languages. You learned about the following topics:

☐ An array is a collection of variables that share the same name and separate themselves using a single integer index.

☐ The `OPTION BASE` statement enables you to set explicitly the default first index of arrays to either 0 or 1. By default, QBasic assumes an `OPTION BASE 0` is in effect.

☐ When you declare arrays with the DIM statement, you must state at least the name of the array and its last index. You can specify the first index and the data type of each array element. You can use the AS clause or the data type suffixes to indicate the data type of each array element.

☐ Using arrays simply involves stating the array name and a valid index, enclosed in parentheses.

☐ Redimensioning arrays enables you to resize dynamic arrays at runtime, using the REDIM statements.

☐ You can obtaining the dimensions of an array with the LBOUND and UBOUND functions. These functions return the first and last indices of an array.

☐ The ERASE statement enables you to clear static arrays and remove dynamic arrays from memory. The ERASE statement assigns zeros to numeric arrays and empty strings to string arrays.

☐ Sorting arrays is a popular non-numeric operation by which the values in an array are ordered either in ascending or (less commonly) descending order. Sorted arrays can be searched more efficiently.

☐ Searching arrays is another popular non-numeric operation. You search unordered arrays using a linear search method. If the array is ordered, you can use the efficient binary-search method to take advantage of the array's order.

Q&A

Q. Are there any side effects of not using OPTION BASE 1?

A. Yes, if you think 1 is the first array index. Then, in this case, you are wasting the array element at index 0. In addition, if you use the LBOUND function to obtain the lowest array index, you might experience logical problems in your programs.

Q. Can I alter the data types of array elements in a REDIM statement?

A. No, QBasic allows you to resize the array only.

Q. Can I alter the data type of a dynamic array in a REDIM statement after I erase it with an ERASE statement?

A. No. QBasic seems to remember the original data type of the array elements. This protection actually supports good programming practice, discouraging you from using the same array to store different types of data.

Q. How can I expand a simple array and still preserve its data?

A. There is a simple programming trick that involves the following steps:

1. Copy your array to another "twin" array (call it the backup array).

2. Expand the targeted array.

3. Copy the data from the elements of the backup array.

Here is an example for expanding the array X using the array Xcopy (call it XCOPY.BAS):

```
OPTION BASE 1
CONST OLD.SIZE = 10
CONST NEW.SIZE = 15
CONST FRMT = "### "
'$DYNAMIC
DIM X(OLD.SIZE) AS INTEGER
DIM Xcopy(1) AS INTEGER
DIM I AS INTEGER
CLS
' assign values to the elements of array X
FOR I = LBOUND(X) TO UBOUND(X)
  X(I) = I * I
NEXT I
' display the contents of array X
FOR I = LBOUND(X) TO UBOUND(X)
  PRINT USING FRMT; X(I);
NEXT I
PRINT
' redimension the array Xcopy to match array X
REDIM Xcopy(OLD.SIZE) AS INTEGER
' copy the data from array X to array Xcopy
```

```
FOR I = LBOUND(X) TO UBOUND(X)
  Xcopy(I) = X(I)
NEXT I
' redimension array X
REDIM X(NEW.SIZE) AS INTEGER
' copy the data from array Xcopy to the expanded array X
FOR I = LBOUND(X) TO OLD.SIZE
  X(I) = Xcopy(I)
NEXT I
' assign new data to the additional elements of array X
FOR I = OLD.SIZE + 1 TO UBOUND(X)
  X(I) = I
NEXT I
' display the array X
FOR I = LBOUND(X) TO UBOUND(X)
  PRINT USING FRMT; X(I);
NEXT I
END
```

12

Q. The bubblesort method is the slowest sorting method in the universe! What method do you recommend to speed up sorting arrays?

A. One of the best (and easiest to implement) methods to use is relatively new. It is called the Comb sort method and is based on refining the bubblesort method. Here is the listing for program COMBSORT.BAS, which is a version of SORT2.BAS:

```
REM Program sorts of an array of integers
REM
OPTION BASE 1
' declare constants
CONST ARRAY.SIZE = 10
CONST TRUE% = -1
CONST FALSE% = 0
CONST FRMT = "####"
' declare variables
DIM IntArr(ARRAY.SIZE) AS INTEGER
DIM I AS INTEGER
DIM J AS INTEGER
DIM C AS STRING
```

```
DIM InOrder AS INTEGER
DIM Offset AS INTEGER

CLS
' reseed random-number generator
RANDOMIZE TIMER
FOR I = 1 TO ARRAY.SIZE
  IntArr(I) = INT(RND * 1000)
NEXT I

FOR I = 1 TO ARRAY.SIZE
  PRINT USING FRMT; IntArr(I)
NEXT I

PRINT
PRINT "Press any key to sort the array";
C = INPUT$(1)

' use the Comb sort method
Offset = ARRAY.SIZE
DO
  Offset = INT(Offset * 8 / 11)
  IF Offset = 0 THEN Offset = 1
  InOrder = TRUE
  FOR I = 1 TO ARRAY.SIZE - Offset
    J = I + Offset
    IF IntArr(I) > IntArr(J) THEN
      SWAP IntArr(I), IntArr(J)
      InOrder = FALSE
    END IF
  NEXT I
LOOP UNTIL Offset = 1 AND InOrder = TRUE

CLS

FOR I = 1 TO ARRAY.SIZE
  PRINT USING FRMT; IntArr(I)
NEXT I
```

```
PRINT
PRINT "Array is now sorted!"
END
```

Workshop

The Workshop provides quiz questions to help you solidify your understanding of the material covered and exercises to provide you with experience in using what you've learned. Try to understand the quiz and exercise answers before continuing on to the next chapter. Answers are provided in Appendix B, "Answers."

Quiz

1. What are the values stored in the array A, shown in the following statements?

```
DIM A(1 TO 9) AS LONG
DIM I AS INTEGER
A(LBOUND(A)) = 2
FOR I = LBOUND(A) + 1 TO UBOUND(A)
    A(I) = 2 * A(I - 1) - 1
NEXT I
```

2. What is the problem with the following set of statements?

```
DIM ProjIncome(1995 TO 1999) AS DOUBLE
DIM I AS INTEGER
ProjIncome(1995) = 1000
FOR I = 1995 TO 2000
    ProjIncome(I) = 1.1 * ProjectIncome(I - 1)
NEXT I
```

3. What is the error in the following set of statements?

```
OPTION BASE 1
DIM X(100) AS DOUBLE
DIM I AS INTEGER
FOR I = 1 TO 100
    X(I) = I * I
```

433

```
NEXT I
FOR I = 1 TO 100
    PRINT I, X(I)
NEXT I
REDIM X(10) AS INTEGER
FOR I = 1 TO 10
    X(I) = I * I
NEXT I
FOR I = 1 TO 10
    PRINT I, X(I)
NEXT I
```

4. What is the error in the following statements?

```
OPTION BASE 2
DIM A(9) AS LONG
DIM I AS INTEGER
A(LBOUND(A)) = 2
FOR I = LBOUND(A) + 1 TO UBOUND(A)
    A(I) = 2 * A(I - 1) - 1
NEXT I
```

5. What is the error in the following statements?

```
OPTION BASE 1
DIM A(9) AS LONG
OPTION BASE 0
DIM B(9) AS LONG
DIM I AS INTEGER
A(LBOUND(A)) = 2
FOR I = LBOUND(A) + 1 TO UBOUND(A)
    A(I) = 2 * A(I - 1) - 1
    B(I) = 2 * A(I - 1)
NEXT I
```

6. What is the error in the following statements?

```
DIM A(9) AS LONG
OPTION BASE 0
DIM B(9) AS LONG
DIM I AS INTEGER
A(LBOUND(A)) = 2
```

```
FOR I = LBOUND(A) + 1 TO UBOUND(A)
   A(I) = 2 * A(I - 1) - 1
   B(I) = 2 * A(I - 1)
NEXT I
```

Exercises

1. Modify SORT2.BAS (in Listing 12.6) to sort strings.y. Use the following DATA statements to supply the data.y. Call the resulting program SORT3.BAS.

   ```
   DATA "California", "Virginia", "Washington", "Oregon"
   DATA "Michigan", "New York", "Ohio", "Indiana"
   DATA "Georgia", "Texas"
   ```

2. Modify SEARCH1.BAS (in Listing 12.7) to search unordered strings. Use the following DATA statements to supply the data. Call the resulting program SEARCH3.BAS.

   ```
   DATA "California", "Virginia", "Washington", "Oregon"
   DATA "Michigan", "New York", "Ohio", "Indiana"
   DATA "Georgia", "Texas"
   ```

3. Modify SEARCH2.BAS (in Listing 12.8) to search ordered strings. Use the following DATA statements to supply the data. The last two strings should be stored in the last two elements of the second array. Call the resulting program SEARCH4.BAS.

   ```
   DATA "California", "Virginia", "Washington", "Oregon"
   DATA "Michigan", "New York", "Ohio", "Indiana"
   DATA "Georgia", "Texas"
   DATA "Maine", "Florida"
   ```

12

DAY

13

Multidimensional
Arrays

This chapter looks at multidimensional arrays, which represent more evolved and more powerful arrays. Today, you learn about the following topics:

☐ What's a multidimensional array?

☐ Declaring multidimensional arrays using the DIM statement

☐ Using multidimensional arrays

☐ Obtaining the dimensions of a multidimensional array using the LBOUND and UBOUND functions

☐ Redimensioning multidimensional arrays using the REDIM statement

☐ Erasing multidimensional arrays using the ERASE statement

What's a Multidimensional Array?

On Day 12, "Simple Arrays," I presented the simple array and defined it as a collection of variables that share the same name but separate themselves using a single index. Thus, simple arrays are single-dimensional because they use a single index. Multidimensional arrays are variables that share the same name but separate themselves using multiple indices. Figure 13.1 shows a two-dimensional array, X, that resembles a numeric table or spreadsheet. Two-dimensional arrays are the most common multidimensional arrays and are called **matrices**. To access an element in matrix X, you need to specify row and column indices. For example, the element at row 2 and column 4 contains the value 11.

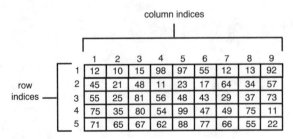

Figure 13.1. A sample two-dimensional array, X.

Declaring Multidimensional Arrays

In a manner that resembles declaring simple arrays, declaring multidimensional arrays also involves the DIM statement.

> **Note:** QBasic does not require you to declare multidimensional arrays that have as many as 10 elements in each dimension! You might remember this rule for simple arrays from Day 12. The same comments for simple arrays hold true for multidimensional arrays.

The DIM Statement

The general syntax for the DIM statement is

```
DIM [SHARED] arrayName([lo1 TO] hi1, [lo2 TO] hi2, ...) [AS type]
```

The SHARED clause indicates the declare array can be shared with FUNCTION and SUB procedures without explicitly passing it as a parameter. The *arrayName* is the name of a multidimensional array. You can declare the range of indices explicitly by specifying the low and high limits (separated by the keyword TO). If you omit the low indices, QBasic uses the OPTION BASE value as the default lower indices. The AS clause enables you to specify the data type associated with each array element. When omitted, you can use a data type suffix with the array name. If you use neither, QBasic applies the default association between the array name and data types. You also can influence this default data type association by placing DEF*type* statements before declaring arrays. You can declare more than one array in a DIM statement. QBasic initializes numeric multidimensional arrays with zeros, and string multidimensional arrays with empty strings.

QBasic requires that the number of elements in any dimension not exceed 32,767 elements.

Examples:

```
' declare string-typed multidimensional array January
DIM January(1 TO 31, 8 TO 18) AS STRING

' declare string-typed multidimensional array January
OPTION BASE 1
DIM January(31, 8 TO 18) AS STRING

' declare string-typed multidimensional array January
OPTION BASE 1
DIM January$(31, 8 TO 18)

' declare string-typed multidimensional array January
DEFSTR J
OPTION BASE 1
DIM January(31, 8 TO 18)

' declare three-dimensional integer array
OPTION BASE 1
DIM Cube(10, 4, 1 TO 3) AS INTEGER
```

Using Arrays

Using multidimensional arrays is simple. You state the name of the array and use valid indices enclosed in parentheses.

Accessing Multidimensional Array Elements

The general syntax for accessing a multidimensional array element is

```
arrayName(validIndex1, validIndex2, ...)
```

The `arrayName` is the name of an existing array. The parameters `validIndex1`, `validIndex2`, and so on, are valid indices. These indices must lie in the range of indices used to declare the multidimensional array, or must be less than 11 if the array is not declared in a DIM statement.

Example:

```
DIM X(1 TO 10, 1 TO 10) AS DOUBLE
' stores zeros in nondiagonal elements and stores
```

```
' ones in diagonal elements
FOR Row = 1 TO 10
    FOR Col = 1 TO 10
        X(Row, Col) = 0
    NEXT Col
    X(Row, Row) = 1
NEXT Row
```

Let's look at an example. Listing 13.1, MAT1.BAS, declares and uses a numeric array. The program prompts you to enter the number of rows (which must be in the range of 3 to 15) and the number of columns (which must be in the range of 3 to 5). Then the program prompts you to enter the values, which are stored in a matrix. If you simply press the Return key, the program converts your lack of input into a value equal to the current value of the row and column numbers. The program then displays that value after the question mark in the prompt. As soon as you finish entering the numbers, the program displays the matrix you typed and asks you to select a matrix column and a range for rows to process. The program then calculates and displays the sum and mean values for the range of rows you specified. Finally, the program prompts you whether you want to obtain another set of sum and mean values for a different range of matrix elements.

Listing 13.1. MAT1.BAS, which declares and uses a numeric matrix.

```
1: DECLARE FUNCTION Pound$ (R AS INTEGER)
2: DECLARE FUNCTION PoundNumber$ (Z AS DOUBLE)
3: REM Program uses a static matrix
4: REM
5: OPTION BASE 1
6: ' declare constants
7: CONST MAX.ROWS% = 15
8: CONST MAX.COLS% = 5
9: CONST FRMT1 = "Enter number of rows (3 TO ##) "
10: CONST FRMT2 = "Enter number of columns (2 to ##) "
11: ' declare variables
12: DIM X(MAX.ROWS, MAX.COLS) AS DOUBLE
13: DIM Sum AS DOUBLE
```

continues

> **Type**
>
> Listing 13.1. continued

```
14: DIM Rows AS INTEGER
15: DIM Cols AS INTEGER
16: DIM I AS INTEGER
17: DIM J AS INTEGER
18: DIM I1 AS INTEGER
19: DIM I2 AS INTEGER
20: DIM Xcurs AS INTEGER
21: DIM Ycurs AS INTEGER
22: DIM C AS STRING
23:
24: CLS
25: ' prompt for number of rows
26: DO
27:    PRINT USING FRMT1; MAX.ROWS;
28:    INPUT Rows
29:    PRINT
30: LOOP UNTIL Rows >= 3 AND Rows <= MAX.ROWS
31:
32: ' prompt for number of columns
33: DO
34:    PRINT USING FRMT2; MAX.COLS;
35:    INPUT Cols
36:    PRINT
37: LOOP UNTIL Cols >= 2 AND Cols <= MAX.COLS
38:
39: ' enter matrix values
40: FOR I = 1 TO Rows
41:    FOR J = 1 TO Cols
42:      PRINT "Enter value for row "; I; " and column"; J; " ";
43:      Xcurs = POS(0)
44:      ' store each value in a member of matrix X
45:      INPUT ; X(I, J)
46:      ' if value is 0 assign X(I, J) the loop control variable
47:      IF X(I, J) = 0 THEN
48:        X(I, J) = 10 * I + J
49:        ' display the value after the ? mark
50:        LOCATE , Xcurs + 1
51:        PRINT X(I, J);
52:      END IF
```

```
53:     PRINT
54:   NEXT J
55: NEXT I
56:
57: ' loop to display matrix and query range of members to sum
58: DO
59:   CLS
60:   ' display the elements of matrix X
61:   FOR I = 1 TO Rows
62:     FOR J = 1 TO Cols
63:       'PRINT USING "Value(##,##) = "; I; J;
64:       PRINT USING "####.### "; X(I, J);
65:     NEXT J
66:     PRINT
67:   NEXT I
68:
69:   PRINT
70:   ' get the indices of the elements to add
71:   DO
72:     INPUT "Select column by index (default=1) "; J
73:     IF J = 0 THEN J = 1
74:     PRINT
75:   LOOP UNTIL J >= 1 AND J <= Cols
76:
77:   ' get the indices of the elements to add
78:   DO
79:     INPUT "Enter index of first value to add (default=1) "; I1
80:     IF I1 = 0 THEN I1 = 1
81:     PRINT
82:   LOOP UNTIL I1 >= 1 AND I1 <= Rows
83:
84:   DO
85:     INPUT "Enter index of last value to add (default=last) ";
   ➡I2
86:     IF I2 = 0 THEN I2 = Rows
87:     PRINT
88:   LOOP UNTIL I2 >= 1 AND I2 <= Rows AND I2 <> I1
89:   ' add the elements of X from X(I1, J) to X(I2, J)
90:   Sum = 0
91:   FOR I = I1 TO I2
92:     Sum = Sum + X(I, J)
```

continues

Type **Listing 13.1. continued**

```
 93:    NEXT I
 94:    ' display the results
 95:    C = "Sum of X(" + Pound$(I1) + "_," + Pound$(J)
 96:    C = C + ") to X(" + Pound$(I2) + "_," + Pound$(J) + ") = "
 97:    C = C + PoundNumber$(Sum)
 98:    PRINT USING C; I1; J; I2; J; Sum
 99:    C = "Mean of X(" + Pound$(I1) + "_," + Pound$(J)
100:    C = C + ") to X(" + Pound$(I2) + "_," + Pound$(J) + ") = "
101:    C = C + PoundNumber$(Sum / (I2 - I1 + 1))
102:    PRINT USING C; I1; J; I2; J; Sum / (I2 - I1 + 1)
103:    PRINT
104:    ' prompt for a Y/N answer
105:    Xcurs = POS(0)
106:    Ycurs = CSRLIN
107:    DO
108:      LOCATE Ycurs, Xcurs
109:      PRINT SPACE$(80);
110:      LOCATE Ycurs, Xcurs
111:      PRINT "Add another set of values? (Y/N) ";
112:      C = INPUT$(1)
113:      PRINT C
114:      C = UCASE$(C)
115:    LOOP UNTIL C = "Y" OR C = "N"
116: LOOP UNTIL C = "N"
117: END
118:
119: FUNCTION Pound$ (R AS INTEGER)
120:    Pound$ = STRING$(1 + FIX(LOG(R) / LOG(10)), "#")
121: END FUNCTION
122:
123: FUNCTION PoundNumber$ (Z AS DOUBLE)
124:    IF Z >= 0 THEN
125:      IF Z > 1000 THEN
126:        PoundNumber$ = "+#.#####^^^^"
127:      ELSE
128:        PoundNumber$ = "###.####"
129:      END IF
130:    ELSE
131:      IF ABS(Z) > 1000 THEN
```

```
132:        PoundNumber$ = "+#.#####^^^^^"
133:     ELSE
134:        PoundNumber$ = "-###.####"
135:     END IF
136:   END IF
137: END FUNCTION
```

Here is a sample output for the program in Listing 13.1:

```
Enter number of rows (3 TO 15) ? 3

Enter number of columns (2 to  5) ? 3

Enter value for row  1  and column 1  ? 11
Enter value for row  1  and column 2  ? 12
Enter value for row  1  and column 3  ? 13
Enter value for row  2  and column 1  ? 21
Enter value for row  2  and column 2  ? 22
Enter value for row  2  and column 3  ? 23
Enter value for row  3  and column 1  ? 31
Enter value for row  3  and column 2  ? 32
Enter value for row  3  and column 3  ? 33
```

 SCREEN CLEARS

```
11.000    12.000    13.000
21.000    22.000    23.000
31.000    32.000    33.000
```

```
Select column by index (default=1) ? 2

Enter index of first value to add (default=1) ? 1

Enter index of last value to add (default=last) ? 2

Sum of X(1,2) to X(2,2) =  34.0000
Mean of X(1,2) to X(2,2) =  17.0000

Add another set of values? (Y/N) n
```

Analysis   The program in Listing 13.1 contains the OPTION BASE 1 statement, which explicitly sets the default first matrix indices to 1. Lines 7 and 8 contain the declarations of the constants MAX.ROWS% and MAX.COLS%, which define the number of rows and columns of the matrix, respectively. Lines 9 and 10 define the constants FRMT1 and FRMT2, which store format strings. Line 12 declares the matrix X. Notice this declaration only specifies the high matrix indices. The AS DOUBLE clause indicates that X stores double-precision, floating-point numbers. Lines 13–22 declare simple variables.

The DO UNTIL loop on lines 26–30 prompt you to enter the number of rows, which must be in the range of 3 to MAX.ROWS. The loop stores your input in the variable Rows. The DO UNTIL loop on lines 33–37 prompt you to enter the number of columns, which must be in the range of 2 to MAX.COLS. The loop stores your input in the variable Cols.

The nested FOR-NEXT loop on lines 40–55 obtains the individual values and stores them in X. The loops use the control variables I and J. The outer loop iterates from 1 to Rows, whereas the inner loop iterates from 1 to Cols. The PRINT statement on line 42 displays the prompt message (which includes the row and column number for the matrix element receiving input). On line 43 the program stores the current column position of the screen cursor in the variable Xcurs. The INPUT statement on line 45 obtains a numeric input and stores it in X(I, J). Here and in other statements in the loops, the control variables supply the indices for an element in X. The IF-THEN statement on line 47 compares the value in X(I, J) (the matrix element at row I and column J) with 0. If this condition is true, the THEN clause statements assign the value of 10 * I + J to X(I, J) and display that value.

The second DO-UNTIL loop in the program is located on lines 58–116. The loop contains a nested FOR-NEXT loop on lines 61–67. The FOR-NEXT loops display the values stored in X. The inner DO-UNTIL loops on lines 71–75, lines 78–82, and lines 84–88, prompt you for a valid column index and a range of rows. The second DO-UNTIL loop, which stores your input in the variable I1, examines the condition I1 >= 1 AND I1 <= Rows. The third DO-UNTIL loop, which stores your input in the variable I2, examines the condition I1 >= 1 AND I1 <= Rows AND I2 <> I1. The additional relational term in the tested condition ensures that the indices in I1 and I2 are different. In addition, the DO-UNTIL loop assigns default values when you enter 0 or simply press the Return key. The second loop assigns 1 to the I1, whereas the third loop assigns N to the variable I2.

The statement on line 90 initializes the summation variable Sum. The FOR-NEXT loop on lines 91–93 accumulates the values of X in Sum. The loop uses the control variable I and iterates from I1 to I2. The statement on line 92 retrieves each element of X using X(I, J).

The statements on lines 95–102 display the sum and mean value for the specified range of elements in X. These statements call the functions Pound$ and PoundNumber$ to build the proper formatting string. The statements on lines 105–116 ask you whether you want to process another set of matrix elements.

Redimensioning Arrays

QBasic enables you to redimension multidimensional arrays using the REDIM statement. As is the case with simple arrays, you need to use the $DYNAMIC metacommand to declare the arrays as dynamic.

13

The REDIM Statement

The general syntax for the REDIM statement is

```
REDIM [SHARED] arrName([lo1 TO] hi1, [lo2 TO] hi2,...) [AS
type]
```

The SHARED clause indicates the declared array can be shared with FUNCTION and SUB procedures without explicitly passing it as a parameter. The arrName is the name of an array. You can declare the range of indices explicitly by specifying the low and high limits (separated by the keyword TO). If you omit the low index, QBasic uses the OPTION BASE value as the default lower index. The AS clause enables you to specify the data type associated with the array. When omitted, you can use a data type suffix with the array name. If you use neither, QBasic applies the default association between the array name and data types. You also can influence this default data type association by placing DEFtype statements before declaring arrays. The REDIM statement can redimension multiple dynamic arrays. However, please note that REDIM erases the contents of the redimensioned arrays.

Examples:

```
'$DYNAMIC
DIM January(1 TO 31, 8 to 18) AS STRING
```

```
' redimension array with difference indices
REDIM January(10 TO 15, 7 TO 14) AS STRING

' declare string-typed array January
OPTION BASE 1
'$DYNAMIC
DIM January(31, 8 TO 18) AS STRING
' redimension array with difference indices
REDIM January(5, 8 TO 18) AS STRING
```

Here's an example of a dynamic QBasic array. Listing 13.2, MAT2.BAS, declares and uses a dynamic array. I created this program by modifying MAT1.BAS in Listing 13.1. The new program prompts you to enter the number of rows and columns (which define the size of the matrix used in the program). The prompt states that the number of rows and columns must be at least 3 and 2. The remaining program tasks are identical to MAT1.BAS.

 Listing 13.2. MAT2.BAS, which declares and uses a dynamic matrix.

```
 1: DECLARE FUNCTION Pound$ (R AS INTEGER)
 2: DECLARE FUNCTION PoundNumber$ (Z AS DOUBLE)
 3: REM Program uses a dynamic matrix
 4: REM
 5: OPTION BASE 1
 6: ' declare constants
 7: CONST MSG1 = "Enter number of rows (at least 3) "
 8: CONST MSG2 = "Enter number of columns (at least 2) "
 9: ' declare variables
10: '$DYNAMIC
11: DIM X(1, 1) AS DOUBLE
12: DIM Sum AS DOUBLE
13: DIM Rows AS INTEGER
14: DIM Cols AS INTEGER
15: DIM I AS INTEGER
16: DIM J AS INTEGER
17: DIM I1 AS INTEGER
18: DIM I2 AS INTEGER
19: DIM Xcurs AS INTEGER
```

```
20: DIM Ycurs AS INTEGER
21: DIM C AS STRING
22:
23: CLS
24: ' prompt for number of rows
25: DO
26:    PRINT MSG1;
27:    INPUT Rows
28:    PRINT
29: LOOP UNTIL Rows >= 3
30:
31: ' prompt for number of columns
32: DO
33:    PRINT MSG2;
34:    INPUT Cols
35:    PRINT
36: LOOP UNTIL Cols >= 2
37:
38: ' redimension the matrix X
39: REDIM X(Rows, Cols) AS DOUBLE
40:
41: ' enter matrix values
42: FOR I = 1 TO Rows
43:    FOR J = 1 TO Cols
44:       PRINT "Enter value for row "; I; " and column"; J; " ";
45:       Xcurs = POS(0)
46:       ' store each value in a member of matrix X
47:       INPUT ; X(I, J)
48:       ' if value is 0 assign X(I, J) the loop control variable
49:       IF X(I, J) = 0 THEN
50:          X(I, J) = 10 * I + J
51:          ' display the value after the ? mark
52:          LOCATE , Xcurs + 1
53:          PRINT X(I, J);
54:       END IF
55:       PRINT
56:    NEXT J
57: NEXT I
58:
59: ' loop to display matrix and query range of members to sum
60: DO
61:    CLS
```

continues

Listing 13.2. continued

```
62:     ' display the elements of matrix X
63:     FOR I = 1 TO Rows
64:       FOR J = 1 TO Cols
65:         'PRINT USING "Value(##,##) = "; I; J;
66:         PRINT USING "####.### "; X(I, J);
67:       NEXT J
68:       PRINT
69:     NEXT I
70:
71:     PRINT
72:     ' get the indices of the elements to add
73:     DO
74:       INPUT "Select column by index (default=1) "; J
75:       IF J = 0 THEN J = 1
76:       PRINT
77:     LOOP UNTIL J >= 1 AND J <= Cols
78:
79:     ' get the indices of the elements to add
80:     DO
81:       INPUT "Enter index of first value to add (default=1) "; I1
82:       IF I1 = 0 THEN I1 = 1
83:       PRINT
84:     LOOP UNTIL I1 >= 1 AND I1 <= Rows
85:
86:     DO
87:       INPUT "Enter index of last value to add (default=last) ";
   ➡I2
88:       IF I2 = 0 THEN I2 = Rows
89:       PRINT
90:     LOOP UNTIL I2 >= 1 AND I2 <= Rows AND I2 <> I1
91:     ' add the elements of X from X(I1, J) to X(I2, J)
92:     Sum = 0
93:     FOR I = I1 TO I2
94:       Sum = Sum + X(I, J)
95:     NEXT I
96:     ' display the results
97:     C = "Sum of X(" + Pound$(I1) + "_," + Pound$(J)
98:     C = C + ") to X(" + Pound$(I2) + "_," + Pound$(J) + ") = "
99:     C = C + PoundNumber$(Sum)
100:    PRINT USING C; I1; J; I2; J; Sum
101:    C = "Mean of X(" + Pound$(I1) + "_," + Pound$(J)
102:    C = C + ") to X(" + Pound$(I2) + "_," + Pound$(J) + ") = "
```

```
103:    C = C + PoundNumber$(Sum / (I2 - I1 + 1))
104:    PRINT USING C; I1; J; I2; J; Sum / (I2 - I1 + 1)
105:    PRINT
106:    ' prompt for a Y/N answer
107:    Xcurs = POS(0)
108:    Ycurs = CSRLIN
109:    DO
110:      LOCATE Ycurs, Xcurs
111:      PRINT SPACE$(80);
112:      LOCATE Ycurs, Xcurs
113:      PRINT "Add another set of values? (Y/N) ";
114:      C = INPUT$(1)
115:      PRINT C
116:      C = UCASE$(C)
117:    LOOP UNTIL C = "Y" OR C = "N"
118: LOOP UNTIL C = "N"
119: END
120:
121: REM $STATIC
122: FUNCTION Pound$ (R AS INTEGER)
123:    Pound$ = STRING$(1 + FIX(LOG(R) / LOG(10)), "#")
124: END FUNCTION
125:
126: FUNCTION PoundNumber$ (Z AS DOUBLE)
127:    IF Z >= 0 THEN
128:      IF Z > 1000 THEN
129:        PoundNumber$ = "+#.#####^^^^^"
130:      ELSE
131:        PoundNumber$ = "###.####"
132:      END IF
133:    ELSE
134:      IF ABS(Z) > 1000 THEN
135:        PoundNumber$ = "+#.#####^^^^^"
136:      ELSE
137:        PoundNumber$ = "-###.####"
138:      END IF
139:    END IF
140: END FUNCTION
```

13

Here is sample output for the program in Listing 13.2:

```
Enter number of rows (at least 3) ? 3

Enter number of columns (at least 2) ? 3

Enter value for row  1   and column 1  ? 11
Enter value for row  1   and column 2  ? 12
Enter value for row  1   and column 3  ? 13
Enter value for row  2   and column 1  ? 21
Enter value for row  2   and column 2  ? 22
Enter value for row  2   and column 3  ? 23
Enter value for row  3   and column 1  ? 31
Enter value for row  3   and column 2  ? 32
Enter value for row  3   and column 3  ? 33
```

 SCREEN CLEARS

```
11.000   12.000   13.000
21.000   22.000   23.000
31.000   32.000   33.000
```

```
Select column by index (default=1) ? 3

Enter index of first value to add (default=1) ? 1

Enter index of last value to add (default=last) ? 3

Sum of X(1,3) to X(3,3) =  69.0000
Mean of X(1,3) to X(3,3) =  23.0000

Add another set of values? (Y/N) n
```

Because the program in Listing 13.2 is very similar to the one in Listing 13.1, I discuss only the differences between them:

1. MAT2.BAS declares the constants MSG1 and MSG2, which replace the constants FRMT1 and FRMT2 in MAT1.BAS. There are no constants MAX.ROWS% and MAX.COLS% declared in MAT2.BAS.

2. Line 10 contains the $DYNAMIC metacommand.

3. Line 11 declares matrix X as having the last indices of 1. Consequently, X stores one element. This dummy-size declaration is typical when you will redimension the matrix before using it.

4. Line 39 contains the REDIM statement that redimensions X using the variables Rows and Cols. Consequently, the program uses X with a tailor-fit size.

5. Line 121 contains the $STATIC metacommand, which QBasic inserted when I saved the MAT2.BAS program.

The *LBOUND* and *UBOUND* Functions

On Day 12 I presented the LBOUND and UBOUND functions and showed you how to use them with simple arrays. QBasic enables these functions to work with multidimensional arrays. In this case, you need to include a second argument to the LBOUND and UBOUND functions. This additional argument selects the dimension of the array.

The LBOUND and UBOUND Functions

The general syntax for the LBOUND and UBOUND functions is

```
LBOUND(arrayName, dimensionNumber)
UBOUND(arrayName, dimensionNumber)
```

The parameter *dimensionNumber* specifies the dimension of the multidimensional array *arrayName*. LBOUND returns the first index of the selected dimension in *arrayName*. UBOUND returns the last index of the selected dimension in *arrayName*. These two functions work with both static and dynamic multidimensional arrays.

Example:

```
DIM S(3 TO 9, 2 TO 5) AS STRING

FOR I = LBOUND(S, 1) TO UBOUND(S, 1)
    FOR J = LBOUND(S, 2) TO UBOUND(S, 2)
```

453

```
            S(I, J) = STRING$(10, 55 + 10 * I + J)
        NEXT J
    NEXT I
```

Let's look at an example that uses the LBOUND and UBOUND functions. Listing 13.3, LUBOUND2.BAS, uses the LBOUND and UBOUND functions to obtain the first and last indices of a matrix with an arbitrary range of indices. The program requires no input from you. Instead, it creates and displays a matrix with random first and last indices.

Listing 13.3. LUBOUND2.BAS, which uses the LBOUND and UBOUND functions to obtain the first and last indices of a matrix.

```
1: REM Program that uses the LBOUND and UBOUND
2: REM functions to obtain the lower and upper
3: REM indices of an arbitrarily sized matrix
4: ' declare constant
5: CONST FIRST = 10
6: CONST LAST = 100
7: CONST MAX.ROWS = 20
8: CONST MAX.COLS = 5
9: CONST TITLE = "Arbitrary Matrix"
10: ' declare variables
11: '$DYNAMIC
12: DIM A(1, 1) AS INTEGER
13: DIM I AS INTEGER
14: DIM J AS INTEGER
15: DIM K AS INTEGER
16: DIM L AS INTEGER
17: DIM C AS STRING
18:
19: CLS
20: RANDOMIZE TIMER
21: ' use variables I, J, K, and L to temporarily
22: ' store the lower and upper bounds of the
23: ' redimensioned matrix A
24: I = INT(RND * (LAST - FIRST + 1)) + FIRST
```

```
25: J = I + INT(RND * MAX.ROWS)
26: K = INT(RND * (LAST - FIRST + 1)) + FIRST
27: L = K + INT(RND * MAX.COLS)
28:
29: ' redimension the matrix A
30: REDIM A(I TO J, K TO L)
31:
32: ' assign values to the elements of matrix A
33: FOR I = LBOUND(A, 1) TO UBOUND(A, 1)
34:   FOR J = LBOUND(A, 2) TO UBOUND(A, 2)
35:     A(I, J) = INT(RND * 1000)
36:   NEXT J
37: NEXT I
38:
39: PRINT SPC(40 - LEN(TITLE) \ 2); TITLE
40: PRINT
41: ' display the values in matrix A
42: FOR I = LBOUND(A, 1) TO UBOUND(A, 1)
43:    ' this IF-THEN statement is useful when
44:    ' you increase the value of constant MAX.ROWS
45:    ' well beyond 20
46:    IF CSRLIN = 21 THEN
47:      PRINT
48:      PRINT "Press any key to continue";
49:      C = INPUT$(1)
50:      CLS
51:    END IF
52:    FOR J = LBOUND(A, 2) TO UBOUND(A, 2)
53:      'PRINT "A("; MID$(STR$(I), 2);
54:      'PRINT ","; MID$(STR$(J), 2); ") = "; A(I, J); "  ";
55:      PRINT USING "#### "; A(I, J);
56:    NEXT J
57:    PRINT
58: NEXT I
59: END
```

Here is a sample output for the program in Listing 13.3 (keep in mind that since the program uses random numbers to create the array, you will most likely see a different output):

```
Arbitrary Matrix

593    72   605   532
857   501   902   139
794   667   726   950
765   795   466   610
393   333   839   781
260   843   220   150
866   143   220   698
826   697   512   218
328   252   911    77
835   735   703   231
 36   389   219   496
 51   165   669    56
886   364   216   236
130   524   305   514
916   564   242   784
```

 The program in Listing 13.3 declares its constants on lines 5–9. The constants FIRST and LAST define the range of matrix indices. The constants MAX.ROWS and MAX.COLS specify the maximum number of rows and columns of the arbitrarily sized matrix. Line 11 contains the $DYNAMIC metacommand to allow the declaration of a dynamic matrix on line 12. Line 12 declares the matrix A with a dummy value for the last indices. Lines 13–17 declare the simple variables used in the program.

The process of determining the matrix size uses random numbers. The first step is to randomize the seed using the TIMER function on line 20. The statement on line 24 obtains a random number in the range of FIRST to LAST and stores it in I. This number represents the first index of the rows in the redimensioned matrix A. The statement on line 25 calculates the last index of the rows in the redimensioned matrix A and stores it in J. The statements on lines 26 and 27 perform similar tasks. Lines 26 and 27 calculate the first and last indices for the columns of matrix A. The statement on line 20 redimensions the matrix A to have indices from I to J and K to L. At this point, I, J, K, and L maintain the same values returned by the function calls LBOUND(A, 1), UBOUND(A, 1), LBOUND(A, 2), and UBOUND(A, 2), respectively. However, as you will see in the next lines, I reuse the variables I and J as control variables in FOR-NEXT loops. By doing so, I forfeit the values for the first and last matrix row indices stored in these variables.

The nested FOR-NEXT loops on lines 33–37 assign random numbers to the elements of A. The loops use the control variables I and J, and iterate to access all the elements in A. The function calls LBOUND(A, 1), UBOUND(A, 1), LBOUND (A, 2), and UBOUND(A, 1) provide the correct iteration range for the nested loops.

The PRINT statement on line 39 displays the centered title of the program. The nested FOR-NEXT loops on lines 42–58 display the values in A. The outer loop uses the control variable I to iterate from LBOUND(A, 1) to UBOUND(A, 1). The inner loop uses the control variable J to iterate from LBOUND(A, 2) to UBOUND (A, 2). The inner loop contains an IF-THEN statement that handles paginating the display of a matrix with more rows. This statement is useful should you decide to increase the value of MAX.ROWS.

Erasing Arrays

QBasic offers the ERASE statement to erase multidimensional static arrays and remove dynamic arrays from memory.

13

The ERASE Statement

The general syntax for the ERASE statement is

```
ERASE array1 [, array2, ...]
```

The ERASE statement erases the multidimensional *array1*, *array2*, and so on. In the case of static arrays, the ERASE statement assigns zeros to the elements of numeric arrays and empty strings to the elements of string arrays. In the case of dynamic arrays, the ERASE statement removes them from memory. You can use the same ERASE statement to erase any combination of single-dimensional and multidimensional arrays.

Example:

```
'$STATIC
DIM X (1 TO 10, 3 TO 5) AS SINGLE
FOR I = LBOUND(X, 1) TO UBOUND(X, 1)
    FOR J = LBOUND(X, 2) TO UBOUND(X, 2)
        X(I, J) = I * I + J
        PRINT X(I, J)
    NEXT J
```

```
NEXT I
ERASE X
FOR I = LBOUND(X, 1) TO UBOUND(X, 1)
    FOR J = LBOUND(X, 2) TO UBOUND(X, 2)
        PRINT X(I, J) ' displays zeros
    NEXT J
NEXT I
```

Summary

This chapter introduced you to multidimensional arrays. You learned about the following topics:

☐ A multidimensional array is a collection of variables that share the same name and separate themselves using a multiple integer indices.

☐ To declare arrays with the DIM statement, you must state at least the name of the array and its last indices. You can specify the first indices and the data type of each array element. You can use the AS clause or the data type suffixes to indicate the data type of each array element.

☐ Using arrays involves stating the array name and a list of comma-separated valid indices, enclosed in parentheses.

☐ The REDIM statement enables you to resize dynamic arrays at runtime.

☐ You can use the LBOUND and UBOUND functions to obtain the dimensions of an array. These functions return the first and last indices of a specified dimension in a multidimensional array.

☐ The ERASE statement clears numeric multidimensional static arrays and erases multidimensional dynamic arrays from memory. The statement assigns zeros and empty strings to numeric and string multidimensional arrays.

Q&A

Q. Are there any side effects for not using OPTION BASE 1 with multi-dimensional arrays?

A. Yes, if you think the first array indices are 1. Then, in this case, you are wasting several multidimensional array elements at index 0. In addition, if you use LBOUND to obtain the lowest array indices, you might experience logical problems in your programs.

Q. How can I expand a simple matrix and still preserve its data?

A. There is a simple programming trick that involves the following steps:

1. Copy your matrix to another "twin" matrix (call it the backup matrix).

2. Expand the targeted matrix.

3. Copy the data from the elements of the backup matrix to the expanded matrix.

Here is an example for expanding the matrix X using the matrix Xcopy (call the program XCOPY2.BAS):

```
OPTION BASE 1
CONST OLD.ROWS = 2
CONST NEW.ROWS = 4
CONST OLD.COLS = 2
CONST NEW.COLS = 4
CONST FRMT = "### "
'$DYNAMIC
DIM X(OLD.ROWS, OLD.COLS) AS INTEGER
DIM Xcopy(1, 1) AS INTEGER
DIM I AS INTEGER
DIM J AS INTEGER
CLS
' assign values to the elements of matrix X
FOR I = LBOUND(X, 1) TO UBOUND(X, 1)
  FOR J = LBOUND(X, 2) TO UBOUND(X, 2)
    X(I, J) = I * I + 10 * J
  NEXT J
```

13

```
    PRINT
  NEXT I
  ' display the contents of matrix X
  FOR I = LBOUND(X, 1) TO UBOUND(X, 1)
    FOR J = LBOUND(X, 2) TO UBOUND(X, 2)
      PRINT USING FRMT; X(I, J);
    NEXT J
    PRINT
  NEXT I
  PRINT
  ' redimension the matrix Xcopy to match matrix X
  REDIM Xcopy(OLD.ROWS, OLD.COLS) AS INTEGER
  ' copy the data from matrix X to matrix Xcopy
  FOR I = LBOUND(X, 1) TO UBOUND(X, 1)
    FOR J = LBOUND(X, 2) TO UBOUND(X, 2)
      Xcopy(I, J) = X(I, J)
    NEXT J
  NEXT I
  ' redimension matrix X
  REDIM X(NEW.ROWS, NEW.COLS) AS INTEGER
  ' copy the data from matrix Xcopy to the expanded matrix X
  FOR I = LBOUND(X, 1) TO OLD.ROWS
    FOR J = LBOUND(X, 2) TO OLD.COLS
      X(I, J) = Xcopy(I, J)
    NEXT J
  NEXT I
  ' assign new data to the additional elements of matrix X
  FOR I = LBOUND(X, 1) TO UBOUND(X, 1)
    FOR J = LBOUND(X, 2) TO UBOUND(X, 2)
      IF I > OLD.ROWS OR J > OLD.COLS THEN
        X(I, J) = I * I + J
      END IF
    NEXT J
  NEXT I
  ' display the contents of matrix X
```

```
FOR I = LBOUND(X, 1) TO UBOUND(X, 1)
  FOR J = LBOUND(X, 2) TO UBOUND(X, 2)
    PRINT USING FRMT; X(I, J);
  NEXT J
  PRINT
NEXT I
END
```

Workshop

The Workshop provides quiz questions to help you solidify your understanding of the material covered and exercises to provide you with experience in using what you've learned. Try to understand the quiz and exercise answers before continuing on to the next chapter. Answers are provided in Appendix B, "Answers."

Quiz

1. How many array elements are in the following declaration?

   ```
   OPTION BASE 1
   DIM Cube(10, 2 TO 5, 5) AS INTEGER
   ```

2. What are the values returned by the function calls LBOUND(A, 1), LBOUND(A, 2), LBOUND(A, 3), UBOUND(A, 1), UBOUND(A, 2), and UBOUND(A, 3) for the following multidimensional array?

   ```
   OPTION BASE 1
   DIM A(1980 TO 1990, 10, 5 TO 9)
   ```

3. What is wrong with the following set of statements?

   ```
   OPTION BASE 1
   DIM X(10, 20) AS DOUBLE

   FOR I = 1 TO 10
       FOR J = 1 TO 20
           X(I, J) = INT(RND * 1000)
       NEXT J
   NEXT I
   ```

```
REDIM X(5, 10) AS SINGLE

FOR I = 1 TO 5
    FOR J = 1 TO 10
        X(I, J) = INT(RND * 1000)
    NEXT J
NEXT I
```

4. True or false: Inserting an ERASE X statement before the REDIM statement in the previous program will fix the problem.

Exercise

1. Write the program SORT4.BAS that sorts a numeric matrix (with 10 rows and 3 columns) using the data of the second column. Apply the bubblesort method and remember to swap entire rows of the matrix. Assign random numbers to the matrix elements.

DAY
14

Math Functions

This chapter looks at the various math functions QBasic supports. You can browse through this chapter if you do not intend to write number-crunching QBasic programs. In any case, the chapter focuses on QBasic functions and does not teach new programming techniques. If you have used a scientific pocket calculator, you should be familiar with most of the QBasic mathematical functions. Today, you learn about the following topics:

- [ ] Common functions
- [ ] The random-number generating function
- [ ] Integer functions
- [ ] Logarithmic functions
- [ ] Trigonometric functions
- [ ] The LEN function

The examples in this chapter are similar to each other and create tables that contain sample function values.

Common Functions

QBasic offers the SQR, ABS, and SGN functions to perform common mathematical operations. The SQR function returns the square root value. The ABS function yields the absolute value. The SGN function produces the sign value.

The *SQR* Function

The SQR function returns the square root of a numeric expression. This function is useful in scientific, statistical, engineering, and mathematical calculations.

The SQR Function

The general syntax for the SQR function is

```
SQR(numericExpression)
```

The parameter *numericExpression* is a non-negative numeric constant, named constant, numeric variable, numeric function, or any combination of these items. If you supply a negative value to the SQR function,

QBasic raises a runtime error.

Examples:

```
Radius = SQR(Area / Pi)


SquareShapeWidth = SQR(AreaOfSquareShape)


FOR I = 1 TO 100
    PRINT I, SQR(I)
NEXT I
```

DO verify the arguments of the SQR function when there could be negative values.

DON'T forget to use the ON ERROR GOTO error handler to deal with bad arguments for the SQR function.

Take a look at an example. Listing 14.1, SQR1.BAS, creates a table of square root values. The program requires no input and simply displays the table of square root values from 0 to 100 in increments of 10.

14

Listing 14.1. SQR1.BAS, which creates a table of square root values.

```
1: REM Program that tests the SQR function
2: REM
3: ' declare constants
4: CONST TAB1 = 30
5: CONST TAB2 = 40
6: CONST TITLE = "Table of SQR values"
7: CONST FIRST = 0
8: CONST LAST = 100
9: CONST INCR = 10
```

continues

465

Listing 14.1. continued

```
10: ' declare variable
11: DIM X AS DOUBLE
12:
13: CLS
14: PRINT
15: PRINT TAB(40 - LEN(TITLE) \ 2); TITLE
16: PRINT
17: PRINT TAB(TAB1); "  X"; TAB(TAB2); " SQR(X)"
18: PRINT TAB(TAB1 - 5); STRING$(40, "-")
19: FOR X = FIRST TO LAST STEP INCR
20:   PRINT TAB(TAB1);
21:   PRINT USING "###.#"; X;
22:   PRINT TAB(TAB2);
23:   PRINT USING "##.####"; SQR(X)
24: NEXT X
25:
26: END
```

Here is some sample output for the program in Listing 14.1:

```
        Table of SQR values

         X        SQR(X)
-----------------------------------------
         0.0       0.0000
        10.0       3.1623
        20.0       4.4721
        30.0       5.4772
        40.0       6.3246
        50.0       7.0711
        60.0       7.7460
        70.0       8.3666
        80.0       8.9443
        90.0       9.4868
       100.0      10.0000
```

The program in Listing 14.1 is typical of most programs in this chapter. Lines 4–9 declare the various constants. These constants fall into three groups. The constants TAB1 and TAB2 define the tab position for the columns in the table. The constant `TITLE` contains the program's title. The constants `FIRST`, `LAST`, and `INCR` define the range and step of the loop iteration used to create the table of values. Line 11 contains the declaration of the variable `X`.

The `PRINT` statements on lines 15–18 display the centered title and the table heading. The `FOR-NEXT` loop on lines 19–24 uses the control variable `X` and iterates from `FIRST` to `LAST` in steps of `INCR`. Each loop iteration displays the formatted values of `X` and `SQR(X)`. The `PRINT` statements on lines 20 and 22 use the `TAB` function to align the values of `X` and `SQR(X)`.

The *ABS* Function

The `ABS` function returns the absolute value of a numeric expression. You can use this function to ensure that the arguments of other functions, such as `SQR`, are never negative.

The ABS Function

The general syntax for the `ABS` function is

```
ABS(numericExpression)
```

The parameter `numericExpression` is a numeric constant, named constant, numeric variable, numeric function, or any combination of these items. The `ABS` function converts negative values into positive ones. The function does not alter non-negative values.

Examples:

```
IF X < 0 THEN X = ABS(X)

FOR I = -10 TO 10
    PRINT I, ABS(I)
NEXT I
```

14

Here is an example that utilizes the `ABS` function. Listing 14.2 shows the program ABS1.BAS, which creates a table of absolute values. The program requires no input. The program simply displays a table of absolute values for numbers in the range from –50 to 50, in increments of 10.

Listing 14.2. ABS1.BAS, which creates a table of absolute values.

```
1: REM Program that tests the ABS function
2: REM
3: ' declare constants
4: CONST TAB1 = 30
5: CONST TAB2 = 40
6: CONST TITLE = "Table of ABS values"
7: CONST FIRST = -50
8: CONST LAST = 50
9: CONST INCR = 10
10: ' declare variable
11: DIM X AS DOUBLE
12:
13: CLS
14: PRINT
15: PRINT TAB(40 - LEN(TITLE) \ 2); TITLE
16: PRINT
17: PRINT TAB(TAB1); "  X"; TAB(TAB2); " ABS(X)"
18: PRINT TAB(TAB1 - 5); STRING$(40, "-")
19: FOR X = FIRST TO LAST STEP INCR
20:   PRINT TAB(TAB1);
21:   PRINT USING "###.#"; X;
22:   PRINT TAB(TAB2);
23:   PRINT USING "##.####"; ABS(X)
24: NEXT X
25:
26: END
```

Here is some sample output for the program in Listing 14.2:

```
        Table of ABS values

        X        ABS(X)
- - - - - - - - - - - - - - - - - - - - - - - - - - - - - - - - -
      -50.0    50.0000
      -40.0    40.0000
      -30.0    30.0000
      -20.0    20.0000
      -10.0    10.0000
        0.0     0.0000
```

```
10.0      10.0000
20.0      20.0000
30.0      30.0000
40.0      40.0000
50.0      50.0000
```

The program output shows that the ABS function strips the minus sign from negative numbers. Non-negative numbers remain intact.

The program in Listing 14.2 is very similar to the program in Listing 14.1. The differences are:

1. The constants FIRST and LAST are defined by the values –50 and 50, respectively.

2. The constant TITLE mentions the ABS function.

3. The PRINT USING statement on line 23 calls the ABS function and passes it the value of X, the loop control variable.

The *SGN* Function

The sign function, SGN, is a function that might be new to you. This function returns +1, –1, and 0, for positive, negative, and zero values, respectively.

14

The SGN Function

The general syntax for the SGN function is

```
SGN(numericExpression)
```

The parameter *numericExpression* is a numeric constant, named constant, numeric variable, numeric function, or any combination of these items. The SGN function converts negative values into –1, positive values into +1, and returns 0 if the *numericExpression* is also 0.

Examples:

```
IF SGN(X) < 0 THEN X = ABS(X)


FOR I = -10 TO 10
    PRINT I, SGN(I)
NEXT I
```

Math Functions

Here is an example that utilizes the SGN function. Listing 14.3, SGN1.BAS, creates a table of sign function values. The program simply displays the table of sign values for numbers in the range from –50 to 50, in increments of 10.

Listing 14.3. SGN1.BAS, which creates a table of sign function values.

```
 1: REM Program that tests the SGN function
 2: REM
 3: ' declare constants
 4: CONST TAB1 = 30
 5: CONST TAB2 = 40
 6: CONST TITLE = "Table of SGN values"
 7: CONST FIRST = -50
 8: CONST LAST = 50
 9: CONST INCR = 10
10: ' declare variable
11: DIM X AS DOUBLE
12:
13: CLS
14: PRINT
15: PRINT TAB(40 - LEN(TITLE) \ 2); TITLE
16: PRINT
17: PRINT TAB(TAB1); "  X"; TAB(TAB2); " SGN(X)"
18: PRINT TAB(TAB1 - 5); STRING$(40, "-")
19: FOR X = FIRST TO LAST STEP INCR
20:    PRINT TAB(TAB1);
21:    PRINT USING "###.#"; X;
22:    PRINT TAB(TAB2);
23:    PRINT USING "##.####"; SGN(X)
24: NEXT X
25:
26: END
```

Here is some sample output for the program in Listing 14.3:

```
        Table of SGN values

         X          SGN(X)
-----------------------------------------
        -50.0      -1.0000
        -40.0      -1.0000
        -30.0      -1.0000
```

470

```
-20.0    -1.0000
-10.0    -1.0000
  0.0     0.0000
 10.0     1.0000
 20.0     1.0000
 30.0     1.0000
 40.0     1.0000
 50.0     1.0000
```

 Analysis The program in Listing 14.3 is very similar to the one in Listing 14.2. Only the title and the function call on line 23 are different.

Random-Number Generation

I have always been fascinated by computer games where you play against the computer. Some of these games, such as computer chess, use powerful methods to study your moves and enhance the chances of the computer winning. Other types of games employ random numbers to help the computer make its move. Such games are easier to win (my favorites, naturally!). QBasic supports the RANDOMIZE statement and RND function. Although the programs presented on Day 1, "Getting Started," used the RANDOMIZE statement and RND function, I make their formal introduction in this chapter. The RND function generates a sequence of random numbers. The RANDOMIZE statement helps the RND function generate a different sequence of random numbers. Otherwise, you get the same sequence of numbers, making the games that rely on them predictable and dull.

14

The *RANDOMIZE* Statement

The RANDOMIZE statement enables you to supply a new seed for the random number generator.

Syntax

The RANDOMIZE Statement

The general syntax for the RANDOMIZE statement is

RANDOMIZE [*numericExpression*]

The parameter *numericExpression* is a numeric constant, named constant, numeric variable, numeric function, or any combination of these items. When omitted, the RANDOMIZE statement prompts you for input.

A good way to supply a value to the RANDOMIZE statement is to use the TIMER function.

Examples:

```
RANDOMIZE ' prompt user

RANDOMIZE TIMER ' use computer clock

RANDOMIZE 13
```

The *RND* Function

The RND function returns a number between 0 and 1.

The RND Function

The general syntax for the RND function is

```
RND[(numericExpression)]
```

The optional parameter *numericExpression* is a numeric constant, named constant, numeric variable, numeric function, or any combination of these items. Positive *numericExpression* values make the RND function return the next random number. They have the same effect as omitting the *numericExpression* value. Negative *numericExpression* values make the RND function first reseed the random number and then return the next random number. When you supply 0 to the RND function, it returns the last random number it generated.

Examples:

```
' the next two statements are equivalent
X = RND * 100
X = RND(1.3) * 100

' store the random number in X
' only if it exceeds 0.5
IF RND > 0 .5 THEN X = RND(0)
```

```
' does RND produce a number below 0.1?
IF RND < 0.1 THEN
    X = RND(-1) ' reseed and generate another number
ELSE
    X = RND(0) ' store the last number
END IF
```

Here is a program that uses the RANDOMIZE statement and RND function. Listing 14.4, RND1.BAS, implements a number-guessing game. The program generates a secret number from 1 to 1000. You have seven chances to guess the secret number. The program will tell you after each incorrect guess if that guess was higher or lower than the secret number. To be a bit more friendly, the program also displays the new (and narrower) range of values that contains the secret number. To automatically select the mid-range value, press the Return key or enter 0. To quit the game, enter a negative number. If you fail to guess the secret number in seven attempts, you lose the game and the program displays the secret number.

Listing 14.4. RND1.BAS, which implements a number-guessing game.

```
 1: REM Program uses the RANDOMIZE statement
 2: REM with the RND function to implement
 3: REM a number-guessing game
 4: REM
 5: CONST MAX.GUESS% = 7
 6: CONST LO.NUM% = 1
 7: CONST HI.NUM% = 1000
 8: ' declare the variables
 9: DIM HI AS INTEGER
10: DIM LO AS INTEGER
11: DIM Number AS INTEGER
12: DIM NumGuess AS INTEGER
13: DIM Count AS INTEGER
14: DIM Guess AS INTEGER
15: DIM Answer AS STRING
16:
```

continues

Listing 14.4. continued

```
17: DO
18:   CLS
19:   ' randomize the random-number generator seed
20:   ' using the TIMER function
21:   RANDOMIZE TIMER
22:   HI = HI.NUM
23:   LO = LO.NUM
24:   NumGuess = 0
25:   Number = CINT(RND * HI.NUM) + LO.NUM
26:   PRINT "*******************************************************"
27:   PRINT "* Enter 0 to select the middle of the suggested range *"
28:   PRINT "* Enter a negative number to quit the game            *"
29:   PRINT "*******************************************************"
30:   PRINT
31:   ' game loop
32:   DO
33:     ' get the next guess
34:     PRINT "Enter a number between "; LO; " and "; HI;
35:     INPUT ; Guess
36:     IF Guess = 0 THEN Guess = (HI + LO) \ 2
37:     IF Guess < 0 THEN NumGuess = MAX.GUESS - 1
38:     PRINT
39:     ' compare guess with secret number
40:     IF Guess < Number THEN
41:       PRINT "Guess is low"
42:       LO = Guess
43:     ELSEIF Guess > Number THEN
44:       PRINT "Guess is high"
45:       HI = Guess
46:     ELSE
47:       BEEP
48:       PRINT "You guessed it in "; NumGuess; "attempts!"
49:     END IF
50:     NumGuess = NumGuess + 1
51:   LOOP UNTIL NumGuess = MAX.GUESS OR Guess = Number
52:
53:   ' display secret number if player did not guess it
54:   IF Guess <> Number THEN
55:     PRINT "The secret number is "; Number
```

```
56:    END IF
57:
58:    ' loop to ask player for another game
59:    DO
60:      PRINT "Want to play another game? (Y/N) ";
61:      Answer = INPUT$(1)
62:      PRINT Answer
63:      Answer = UCASE$(Answer)
64:    LOOP UNTIL Answer = "Y" OR Answer = "N"
65:
66: LOOP UNTIL Answer <> "Y"
67: END
```

Here is some sample output for the program in Listing 14.4 (remember that every time you run this program you get slightly different results):

```
**********************************************************
* Enter 0 to select the middle of the suggested range *
* Enter a negative number to quit the game            *
**********************************************************

Enter a number between  1   and  1000 ? 500
Guess is high
Enter a number between  1   and  500 ? 250
Guess is high
Enter a number between  1   and  250 ? 125
Guess is low
Enter a number between  125  and  250 ? 225
Guess is high
Enter a number between  125  and  225 ? 150
Guess is low
Enter a number between  150  and  225 ? 175
Guess is high
Enter a number between  150  and  175 ? 160
Guess is low
The secret number is  161
Want to play another game? (Y/N) n
```

The program in Listing 14.4 declares its constants on lines 5–7. The constant MAX.GUESS% defines the maximum number of trials. To make the game easier to play, increase the value of MAX.GUESS%. By contrast, to make the game harder, decrease the value assigned to the constant MAX.GUESS%. The constants LO.NUM% and HI.NUM% define the range that contains the secret number. The program declares its variables on lines 9–15.

The program contains an outer DO-UNTIL loop that spans lines 17–66. This loop contains most of the program statements and plays the game. The RANDOMIZE statement on line 21 reseeds the random-number generator by calling the TIMER function. The statements on lines 22 and 23 assign the constants HI.NUM and LO.NUM to the variables HI and LO, respectively. These variables store the current range. The statement on line 24 initializes the guess counter, stored in the variable NumGuess. Line 25 calls the RND function to assign the secret number in the range from LO.NUM to HI.NUM. The statement stores the secret number in the variable Number. The PRINT statements on lines 26–29 display a few instructions about special input values.

The inner DO-UNTIL loop on lines 32–51 obtains your guesses and responds to them. The PRINT statement on line 34 displays the input prompt message that specifies the current range containing the secret number. The INPUT statement on line 35 obtains your input and stores it in the variable Guess. The IF-THEN statement on line 36 compares the value in Guess with 0. If this condition is true, the program executes the THEN clause statement, which assigns the mid-range value to Guess. The IF-THEN statement on line 37 determines whether Guess stores a negative number. If this condition is true, the THEN clause statement assigns the value of MAX.GUESS - 1 to NumGess. This assignment ensures that the inner DO-UNTIL loop will not re-iterate.

The IF-THEN-ELSEIF statement on lines 40–49 compares the value in Guess with the secret number stored in the variable Number. If your guess is lower than the secret number, the statements on lines 41 and 42 display "Guess is low" and assign your guess to the variable LO. By contrast, if your guess is higher than the secret number, the statements in lines 44 and 45 display "Guess is high" and assign your guess to variable HI. If you guess the secret number, the statements on lines 47 and 48 beep and display a congratulatory message. The message also specifies the number of guesses you made. The statement on line 50 increments the value in the variable NumGuess. The LOOP UNTIL clause on line 51 examines the condition where the number of guesses has reached the maximum allowable (the relational expression NumGuess = MAX.GUESS), or you guessed the secret number (the relational expression Guess = Number).

The IF-THEN statement on lines 54–56 display the secret number, in case you couldn't guess it. The DO-UNTIL loop on lines 59–64 prompts you to play

another round. The LOOP UNTIL clause of the outer loop, found on line 66, examines the condition where the variable Answer does not contain the string "Y".

Integer Functions

In addition to the CINT and CLNG functions, which I introduced on Day 4, "Operators and Expressions," QBasic offers the INT and FIX functions to convert floating-point numbers to integers. The two functions convert the numbers differently. The FIX function chops off the decimal part, whereas the INT function rounds its number to the same or smaller integer.

The *INT* Function

The INT function converts a floating-point number into an integer by rounding the number to a value that is smaller or equal to the float-point argument.

Syntax

The INT Function

The general syntax for the INT function is

```
INT(numericExpression)
```

The parameter *numericExpression* is a numeric constant, named constant, numeric variable, numeric function, or any combination of these items. The INT function rounds the converted number to an integer that is equal to or less than the converted number. Only negative numbers are rounded down to a lesser value (remember that unlike positive numbers, negative numbers with higher magnitudes are smaller than the ones with smaller magnitudes. –5 is smaller that –2).

The INT function works with variables that are either INTEGER or LONG. The value returned by the INT function must be in the range of valid numbers for both INTEGER and LONG data types.

Examples:

```
I = INT(10.1) ' I stores 10
J = INT(10.9) ' J stores 10
K = INT(-10.9) ' K stores -11
L = INT(-10.1) ' L stores -10
```

14

Take a look at an example. Listing 14.5 shows the program INT1.BAS, which creates a table of integers produced by the INT function. The program requires no input and simply displays the table of integers values from –2 to 2 in increments of 0.25.

 Listing 14.5. INT1.BAS, which creates a table of integers produced by the INT function.

```
 1: REM Program that tests the INT function
 2: REM
 3: ' declare constants
 4: CONST TAB1 = 30
 5: CONST TAB2 = 40
 6: CONST TITLE = "Table of INT values"
 7: CONST FIRST = -2
 8: CONST LAST = 2
 9: CONST INCR = .25
10: ' declare variable
11: DIM X AS DOUBLE
12:
13: CLS
14: PRINT
15: PRINT TAB(40 - LEN(TITLE) \ 2); TITLE
16: PRINT
17: PRINT TAB(TAB1); "  X";
18: PRINT TAB(TAB2); "INT(X)"
19: PRINT TAB(TAB1 - 5); STRING$(40, "-")
20: FOR X = FIRST TO LAST STEP INCR
21:    PRINT TAB(TAB1);
22:    PRINT USING "+##.##"; X;
23:    PRINT TAB(TAB2);
24:    PRINT USING "+##.#"; INT(X)
25: NEXT X
26:
27: END
```

Here is some sample output for the program in Listing 14.5:

```
Table of INT values

    X       INT(X)
----------------------------------------
  -2.00     -2.0
```

```
-1.75    -2.0
-1.50    -2.0
-1.25    -2.0
-1.00    -1.0
-0.75    -1.0
-0.50    -1.0
-0.25    -1.0
+0.00    +0.0
+0.25    +0.0
+0.50    +0.0
+0.75    +0.0
+1.00    +1.0
+1.25    +1.0
+1.50    +1.0
+1.75    +1.0
+2.00    +2.0
```

 Looking at the output, you should notice that the INT function rounds the numbers between –1.75 and –1.25 to –2. Similarly, the function rounds the numbers between –0.75 and –0.25 to –1. As for the positive values, the INT function effectively chops off the fractional part.

The program in Listing 14.5 is very similar to the one in Listing 14.1. The differences are in the constants TITLE, FIRST, LAST, and INCR, and in the last PRINT statement inside the FOR-NEXT loop. The constants FIRST, LAST, and INCR specify that the table-generating FOR-NEXT loop iterates from –2 to 2, in steps of 0.25.

The *FIX* Function

The FIX function converts a floating-point number to an integer by truncating the fractional part of the number.

The FIX Function

The general syntax for the FIX function is

FIX(*numericExpression*)

The parameter *numericExpression* is a numeric constant, named constant, numeric variable, numeric function, or any combination of these items. The FIX function simply chops off the fractional part of the converted number.

14

479

The FIX function works with variables that are either INTEGER or LONG. The value returned by the FIX function must be in the range of valid numbers for both INTEGER and LONG data types.

Examples:

```
I = FIX(10.1) ' I stores 10
J = FIX(10.9) ' J stores 10
K = FIX(-10.9) ' K stores -10
L = FIX(-10.1) ' L stores -10
```

Now take a look at another example. Listing 14.6, FIX1.BAS, creates a table of integers produced by the FIX function. The program requires no input and simply displays the table of integers values from –2 to 2 in increments of 0.25.

Listing 14.6. FIX1.BAS, which creates a table of integers generated by the FIX function.

```
1: REM Program that tests the FIX function
2: REM
3: ' declare constants
4: CONST TAB1 = 30
5: CONST TAB2 = 40
6: CONST TITLE = "Table of FIX values"
7: CONST FIRST = -2
8: CONST LAST = 2
9: CONST INCR = .25
10: ' declare variable
11: DIM X AS DOUBLE
12:
13: CLS
14: PRINT
15: PRINT TAB(40 - LEN(TITLE) \ 2); TITLE
16: PRINT
17: PRINT TAB(TAB1); "  X";
18: PRINT TAB(TAB2); "FIX(X)"
19: PRINT TAB(TAB1 - 5); STRING$(40, "-")
20: FOR X = FIRST TO LAST STEP INCR
21:    PRINT TAB(TAB1);
```

```
22:    PRINT USING "+##.##"; X;
23:    PRINT TAB(TAB2);
24:    PRINT USING "+##.#"; FIX(X)
25: NEXT X
26:
27: END
```

Here is some sample output for the program in Listing 14.6:

```
      Table of FIX values

      X        FIX(X)
   ----------------------------------------
      -2.00    -2.0
      -1.75    -1.0
      -1.50    -1.0
      -1.25    -1.0
      -1.00    -1.0
      -0.75    +0.0
      -0.50    +0.0
      -0.25    +0.0
      +0.00    +0.0
      +0.25    +0.0
      +0.50    +0.0
      +0.75    +0.0
      +1.00    +1.0
      +1.25    +1.0
      +1.50    +1.0
      +1.75    +1.0
      +2.00    +2.0
```

The program in Listing 14.6 is very similar to the one in Listing 14.5. The differences are in the constant TITLE and the last PRINT statement in the FOR-NEXT loop.

Logarithmic Functions

Scientific, engineering, and statistical calculations often use the logarithm and exponential functions. QBasic supports the natural logarithm (base e), but not the common logarithm (base 10).

481

The *LOG* Function

The LOG function returns the natural logarithm of a positive numeric value.

The LOG Function

The general syntax for the LOG function is:

```
LOG(numericExpression)
```

The parameter *numericExpression* is a positive numeric constant, named constant, numeric variable, numeric function, or any combination of these items. If you supply a non-positive value to the LOG function, QBasic raises a runtime error.

Examples:

```
X = 12
PowerOfX = INT(LOG(X) / LOG(10))

FOR I = 1 TO 100
    PRINT I, LOG(I)
NEXT I
```

DO verify the arguments of the LOG function when there might be negative values.

DON'T forget to use the ON ERROR GOTO error handler to deal with bad arguments for the LOG function.

Here's another example for you. Listing 14.7, LOG1.BAS, creates a table of logarithm values. The program does not require any input and simply dis-plays the table of logarithm values from .0000001# to 10000000#, using a multiplicative factor of 10.

Listing 14.7. LOG1.BAS, which creates a table of logarithm values.

```
1: REM Program that tests the LOG function
2: REM
3: ' declare constants
4: CONST TAB1 = 30
5: CONST TAB2 = 50
6: CONST TITLE = "Table of LOG values"
7: CONST FIRST# = .0000001#
8: CONST LAST# = 10000000#
9: CONST SCALE = 10
10: ' declare variable
11: DIM X AS DOUBLE
12:
13: CLS
14: PRINT
15: PRINT TAB(40 - LEN(TITLE) \ 2); TITLE
16: PRINT
17: PRINT TAB(TAB1); "  X"; TAB(TAB2); " LOG(X)"
18: PRINT TAB(TAB1 - 5); STRING$(40, "-")
19: X = FIRST
20: DO WHILE X <= LAST
21:    PRINT TAB(TAB1);
22:    PRINT USING "+#.###^^^^^"; X;
23:    PRINT TAB(TAB2);
24:    PRINT USING "+##.####"; LOG(X)
25:    X = SCALE * X
26: LOOP
27:
28: END
```

Here is some sample output for the program in Listing 14.7:

```
             Table of LOG values

                X                  LOG(X)
         - - - - - - - - - - - - - - - - - - - - - - - - - - - - - - -
            +1.000D-007           -16.1181
            +1.000D-006           -13.8155
            +1.000D-005           -11.5129
            +1.000D-004            -9.2103
            +1.000D-003            -6.9078
            +1.000D-002            -4.6052
            +1.000D-001            -2.3026
            +1.000D+000            +0.0000
            +1.000D+001            +2.3026
            +1.000D+002            +4.6052
            +1.000D+003            +6.9078
            +1.000D+004            +9.2103
            +1.000D+005           +11.5129
            +1.000D+006           +13.8155
            +1.000D+007           +16.1181
```

The program in Listing 14.7 declares the various constants on lines 4–9. These constants fall into three groups. The constants TAB1 and TAB2 define the tab position for the columns in the table. The constant TITLE contains the program's title. The constants FIRST, LAST, and SCALE define the range and scaling factor of the loop iteration used to create the table of values. Line 11 contains the declaration of the variable X.

The PRINT statements on lines 15–18 display the centered title and the table heading. The statement on line 19 assigns the constant FIRST to the variable X. This statement prepares for the DO-WHILE loop on lines 20–26. This loop iterates as long as the value in X is less than or equal to the constant LAST. Each loop iteration displays the formatted values of X and LOG(X). The statement on line 25 multiplies the value in the variable X by the constant SCALE and assigns the result back to X.

The *EXP* Function

The counterpart of the LOG function is the EXP function (that is, X is equal to EXP(LOG(X)), within the numerical accuracy of QBasic). This function returns the exponential of its value.

Syntax

The EXP Function

The general syntax for the EXP function is

```
EXP(numericExpression)
```

The parameter *numericExpression* is a numeric constant, named constant, numeric variable, numeric function, or any combination of these items. The upper limit for the *numericExpression* is 88.713 (equal to LOG(3.3E+30)) and 709.709 (equal to LOG(1.67D+308)) for single-precision and double-precision floating-point numbers, respectively. As for the lower limit of *numericExpression*, EXP can handle much larger negative values because the exponential of a large negative value approaches zero.

Examples:

```
E = EXP(1)


FOR I = 1 TO 10
    PRINT I, EXP(I)
NEXT I
```

DO verify the arguments of the EXP function when they might cause numeric overflow.

DON'T forget to use the ON ERROR GOTO error handler to deal with bad arguments for the EXP function.

14

Here is an example. Listing 14.8, EXP1.BAS, creates a table of exponential values. The program does not require any input and simply displays the table of exponential values from −4 to 4, in steps of 0.5.

Math Functions

 Listing 14.8. EXP1.BAS, which creates a table of exponential values.

```
1: REM Program that tests the EXP function
2: REM
3: ' declare constants
4: CONST TAB1 = 30
5: CONST TAB2 = 40
6: CONST TITLE = "Table of EXP values"
7: CONST FIRST = -4
8: CONST LAST = 4
9: CONST INCR = .5
10: ' declare variable
11: DIM X AS DOUBLE
12:
13: CLS
14: PRINT
15: PRINT TAB(40 - LEN(TITLE) \ 2); TITLE
16: PRINT
17: PRINT TAB(TAB1); "  X"; TAB(TAB2); " EXP(X)"
18: PRINT TAB(TAB1 - 5); STRING$(40, "-")
19: FOR X = FIRST TO LAST STEP INCR
20:   PRINT TAB(TAB1);
21:   PRINT USING "###.#"; X;
22:   PRINT TAB(TAB2);
23:   PRINT USING "+#.####^^^^^"; EXP(X)
24: NEXT X
25:
26: END
```

Here is some sample output for the program in Listing 14.8:

```
        Table of EXP values

        X        EXP(X)
- - - - - - - - - - - - - - - - - - - - - - - - - - - - - - - -
        -4.0     +1.8316D-002
        -3.5     +3.0197D-002
        -3.0     +4.9787D-002
        -2.5     +8.2085D-002
        -2.0     +1.3534D-001
```

486

-1.5	+2.2313D-001
-1.0	+3.6788D-001
-0.5	+6.0653D-001
0.0	+1.0000D+000
0.5	+1.6487D+000
1.0	+2.7183D+000
1.5	+4.4817D+000
2.0	+7.3891D+000
2.5	+1.2182D+001
3.0	+2.0086D+001
3.5	+3.3115D+001
4.0	+5.4598D+001

 The program in Listing 14.8 is very similar to the one in Listing 14.1. The differences are in the values of the constants TITLE, FIRST, LAST, and INCR. These constants define a title, iterated range, and control variable increment that are customized to the EXP1.BAS program. In addition, the last PRINT statement inside the FOR-NEXT loop calls the EXP function instead of the SQR function.

Trigonometric Functions

QBasic supports four trigonometric functions. They are the SIN, COS, TAN, and ATN functions. These functions deal with angles in radians.

The *SIN* Function

The SIN function returns the sine of its values, taken as an angle in radians.

The SIN Function
The general syntax for the SIN function is

SIN(*numericExpression*)

The parameter *numericExpression* is a numeric constant, named constant, numeric variable, numeric function, or any combination of these items. The values for this parameter are considered angles in radians. The function returns the sine of *numericExpression*.

Math Functions

Examples:

```
IF SIN(X) < 0 THEN X = ABS(SIN(X))

FOR I = 1 TO 360
    PRINT I, SIN(Factor * I)
NEXT I
```

Here's an example. Listing 14.9 shows the program SIN1.BAS, which creates a table of sine values. The program does not require any input and simply displays a table of sine values from 0 to 360 degrees, in steps of 30 degrees.

Type Listing 14.9. **SIN1.BAS, which creates a table of sine values.**

```
 1: REM Program that tests the SIN function
 2: REM
 3: ' declare constants
 4: CONST TAB1 = 30
 5: CONST TAB2 = 40
 6: CONST TITLE = "Table of SIN values"
 7: CONST FIRST = 0
 8: CONST LAST = 360
 9: CONST INCR = 30
10: ' declare variable
11: DIM Angle AS DOUBLE
12: DIM Factor AS DOUBLE
13:
14: CLS
15: Factor = 4 * ATN(1) / 180
16: PRINT
17: PRINT TAB(40 - LEN(TITLE) \ 2); TITLE
18: PRINT
19: PRINT TAB(TAB1); "  Angle"; TAB(TAB2); " SIN(Angle)"
20: PRINT TAB(TAB1 - 5); STRING$(40, "-")
21: FOR Angle = FIRST TO LAST STEP INCR
22:    PRINT TAB(TAB1);
23:    PRINT USING "###.#"; Angle;
24:    PRINT TAB(TAB2);
```

```
25:    PRINT USING "+#.####"; SIN(Factor * Angle)
26: NEXT Angle
27:
28: END
```

Here is some sample output for the program in Listing 14.9:

```
Table of SIN values

    Angle    SIN(Angle)
---------------------------------------
      0.0    +0.0000
     30.0    +0.5000
     60.0    +0.8660
     90.0    +1.0000
    120.0    +0.8660
    150.0    +0.5000
    180.0    +0.0000
    210.0    -0.5000
    240.0    -0.8660
    270.0    -1.0000
    300.0    -0.8660
    330.0    -0.5000
    360.0    -0.0000
```

The program in Listing 14.9 declares the various constants on lines 4–9. These constants fall into three groups. The constants TAB1 and TAB2 define the tab position for the columns in the table. The constant TITLE contains the program's title. The constants FIRST, LAST, and INCR define the range and increment for the loop iteration used to create the table of values. Lines 11 and 12 contain the declarations for the variables Angle and Factor. The statement on line 15 assigns the conversion factor between degrees and radians.

The PRINT statements on lines 17–20 display the centered title and the table heading. The FOR-NEXT loop appears on lines 21–26. The loop uses the control variable Angle and iterates from FIRST to LAST in steps of INCR. The range of iteration represents the angles in degrees. Each loop iteration displays the formatted values of Angle (in degrees) and SIN(Angle). The call to the SIN function actually passes the expression Factor * Angle to perform the needed angle conversion.

The *COS* Function

The COS function returns the cosine of its values, taken as an angle in radians.

The COS Function

The general syntax for the COS function is

```
COS(numericExpression)
```

The parameter *numericExpression* is a numeric constant, named constant, numeric variable, numeric function, or any combination of these items. The values for this parameter are considered angles in radians. The function returns the cosine of *numericExpression*.

Examples:

```
IF COS(X) < 0 THEN X = ABS((X))


FOR I = 1 TO 360
    PRINT I, COS(Factor * I)
NEXT I
```

Now take a look at this example. Listing 14.9 shows the program COS1.BAS, which creates a table of cosine values. The program does not require any input and simply displays the table of cosine values from 0 to 360 degrees, in steps of 30 degrees.

Listing 14.10. COS1.BAS, which creates a table of cosine values.

```
 1: REM Program that tests the  function
 2: REM
 3: ' declare constants
 4: CONST TAB1 = 30
 5: CONST TAB2 = 40
 6: CONST TITLE = "Table of COS values"
 7: CONST FIRST = 0
 8: CONST LAST = 360
 9: CONST INCR = 30
10: ' declare variable
11: DIM Angle AS DOUBLE
```

```
12: DIM Factor AS DOUBLE
13:
14: CLS
15: Factor = 4 * ATN(1) / 180
16: PRINT
17: PRINT TAB(40 - LEN(TITLE) \ 2); TITLE
18: PRINT
19: PRINT TAB(TAB1); "  Angle"; TAB(TAB2); " COS(Angle)"
20: PRINT TAB(TAB1 - 5); STRING$(40, "-")
21: FOR Angle = FIRST TO LAST STEP INCR
22:    PRINT TAB(TAB1);
23:    PRINT USING "###.#"; Angle;
24:    PRINT TAB(TAB2);
25:    PRINT USING "+#.####"; COS(Factor * Angle)
26: NEXT Angle
27:
28: END
```

Here is some sample output for the program in Listing 14.10:

```
        Table of   values

        Angle    COS(Angle)
    ----------------------------------------
          0.0    +1.0000
         30.0    +0.8660
         60.0    +0.5000
         90.0    +0.0000
        120.0    -0.5000
        150.0    -0.8660
        180.0    -1.0000
        210.0    -0.8660
        240.0    -0.5000
        270.0    -0.0000
        300.0    +0.5000
        330.0    +0.8660
        360.0    +1.0000
```

The program in Listing 14.10 is very similar to the one in Listing 14.9. The differences between the two programs are in the constant TITLE and in the last PRINT statement, located in the FOR-NEXT loop.

The *TAN* Function

The TAN function returns the tangent of its values, taken as an angle in radians.

The TAN Function

The general syntax for the TAN function is

```
TAN(numericExpression)
```

The parameter *numericExpression* is a numeric constant, named constant, numeric variable, numeric function, or any combination of these items. The values for this parameter are considered angles in radians. The function returns the tangent of *numericExpression*.

Examples:

```
IF TAN(X) < 1 THEN X = 2 * TAN(X)


FOR I = 1 TO 360
    PRINT I, TAN(Factor * I)
NEXT I
```

Here's an example. Listing 14.11, TAN1.BAS, creates a table of tangent values. The program does not require any input and simply displays the table of tangent values from 0 to 360 degrees, in steps of 30 degrees.

 Listing 14.11. **TAN1.BAS, which creates a table of tangent values.**

```
 1: REM Program that tests the TAN function
 2: REM
 3: ' declare constants
 4: CONST TAB1 = 30
 5: CONST TAB2 = 40
 6: CONST TITLE = "Table of TAN values"
 7: CONST FIRST = 0
 8: CONST LAST = 360
 9: CONST INCR = 30
10: ' declare variable
11: DIM Angle AS DOUBLE
12: DIM Factor AS DOUBLE
```

```
13:
14: CLS
15: Factor = 4 * ATN(1) / 180
16: PRINT
17: PRINT TAB(40 - LEN(TITLE) \ 2); TITLE
18: PRINT
19: PRINT TAB(TAB1); "  Angle"; TAB(TAB2); " TAN(Angle)"
20: PRINT TAB(TAB1 - 5); STRING$(40, "-")
21: FOR Angle = FIRST TO LAST STEP INCR
22:    IF Angle <> 90 AND Angle <> 270 THEN
23:      PRINT TAB(TAB1);
24:      PRINT USING "###.#"; Angle;
25:      PRINT TAB(TAB2);
26:      PRINT USING "+#.####"; TAN(Factor * Angle)
27:    ELSE
28:      PRINT TAB(TAB1);
29:      PRINT USING "###.#"; Angle;
30:      PRINT TAB(TAB2); "infinity(?)"
31:    END IF
32: NEXT Angle
33:
34: END
```

Here is some sample output for the program in Listing 14.11:

```
          Table of TAN values

          Angle    TAN(Angle)
---------------------------------------
            0.0    +0.0000
           30.0    +0.5774
           60.0    +1.7321
           90.0    infinity(?)
          120.0    -1.7321
          150.0    -0.5774
          180.0    -0.0000
          210.0    +0.5774
          240.0    +1.7321
          270.0    infinity(?)
          300.0    -1.7321
          330.0    -0.5774
          360.0    -0.0000
```

14

The program in Listing 14.11 is very similar to the one in Listing 14.10. The differences between the two programs are

1. The constant TITLE has different values.

2. The FOR-NEXT loop in Listing 14.11 has an IF-THEN-ELSE statement that examines the condition when Angle is neither 90 nor 270. When Angle is 90 or 270 degrees, the value of the tangent function is, in theory, infinity. In reality, QBasic returns a very large number. I chose to detect these two critical angles and display the string "infinity(?)" for these if Angle is equal to either 90 or 270. I added the question mark because the QBasic TAN function does not overflow at these critical values.

The *ATN* Function

The inverse of the tangent function is the arctangent function. QBasic supports the ATN arctangent function.

The ATN Function

The general syntax for the ATN function is

```
ATN(numericExpression)
```

The parameter *numericExpression* is a numeric constant, named constant, numeric variable, numeric function, or any combination of these items. The values for this parameter are considered angles in radians. The function returns the arctangent of *numericExpression*, in radians.

Examples:

```
IF ATN(X) < 1 THEN X = 2 * ATN(X)


FOR I = 1 TO 80 STEP 5
    PRINT I, ATN(I)
NEXT I
```

Take a look at an example. Listing 14.12 shows the program ATN1.BAS, which creates a table of arctangent values. The program does not require any input and simply displays the table of arctangent values from 0 to 7, in steps of 0.5.

Listing 14.12. ATN1.BAS, which creates a table of arctangent values.

```
1: REM Program that tests the ATN function
2: REM
3: ' declare constants
4: CONST TAB1 = 30
5: CONST TAB2 = 40
6: CONST TITLE = "Table of ATN values"
7: CONST FIRST = 0
8: CONST LAST = 7
9: CONST INCR = .5
10: ' declare variable
11: DIM ArcTan AS DOUBLE
12: DIM Factor AS DOUBLE
13:
14: CLS
15: Factor = 180 / (4 * ATN(1))
16: PRINT
17: PRINT TAB(40 - LEN(TITLE) \ 2); TITLE
18: PRINT
19: PRINT TAB(TAB1); "  ArcTan"; TAB(TAB2); " ATN(ArcTan)"
20: PRINT TAB(TAB1 - 5); STRING$(40, "-")
21: FOR ArcTan = FIRST TO LAST STEP INCR
22:    PRINT TAB(TAB1);
23:    PRINT USING "###.#"; ArcTan;
24:    PRINT TAB(TAB2);
25:    PRINT USING "####.##"; Factor * ATN(ArcTan)
26: NEXT ArcTan
27:
28: END
```

14

Here is some sample output for the program in Listing 14.12:

```
Table of ATN values

ArcTan    ATN(ArcTan)
- - - - - - - - - - - - - - - - - - - - - - - - - - - - - -
   0.0         0.00
   0.5        26.57
   1.0        45.00
   1.5        56.31
   2.0        63.43
   2.5        68.20
   3.0        71.57
   3.5        74.05
   4.0        75.96
   4.5        77.47
   5.0        78.69
   5.5        79.70
   6.0        80.54
   6.5        81.25
   7.0        81.87
```

Looking at the output, you should notice that as the argument for the ATN function increases, the function returns an angle that approaches 90 degrees (actually, the ATN function produces the equivalent value in radians).

The program in Listing 4.12 resembles the one in Listing 4.10. The differences are found in the constants TITLE, LAST, and INCR. In addition, the ATN1.BAS program uses the variable ArcTan instead of the variable Angle. Moreover, the last PRINT statement in the FOR-NEXT loop displays the value Factor * ATN(ArcTan) to convert the output into degrees.

The *LEN* Function

The LEN function originally specialized in returning the length of a string. Microsoft expanded the role of the LEN function to include returning the size of predefined and user-defined types (more about the latter in Day 15, "User-Defined Data Types").

Syntax

The LEN Function

The general syntax for the LEN function is

```
LEN(variableName)
```

The *variableName* is the name of a variable that has a predefined data type or a user-defined data type. The LEN function returns the number of bytes occupied by *variableName*.

Examples:

```
DIM X as DOUBLE
DIM N AS INTEGER
DIM L AS LONG

PRINT "Size of DOUBLE = "; LEN(X); " bytes"
PRINT "Size of INTEGER = "; LEN(N); " bytes"
PRINT "Size of LONG = "; LEN(L); " bytes"
```

Summary

This chapter focused on the QBasic mathematical functions. Today you learned about the following topics:

14

☐ The common QBasic functions, which are SQR (the square root function), ABS (the absolute value function), and SGN (the sign function).

☐ The random-number generating RANDOMIZE statement and the RND function. The RANDOMIZE statement reseeds the QBasic random-number generator. The RND function generates random numbers from 0 to 1. The optional argument for the RND function influences the value and sequence of random-numbers produced by the function.

☐ The integer functions INT and FIX convert floating-point values into integers. The INT function rounds the argument to an integer that is equal to or less than (in the case of negative numbers) the function's argument. The FIX function chops off the fractional part of its argument.

The logarithmic functions LOG and EXP. The LOG function returns the natural logarithm. The EXP function returns the exponential value.

The trigonometric functions SIN (the sine function), COS (the cosine function), TAN (the tangent function), and ATN (the arctangent function). These functions deal with radians and not degrees.

The LEN function, which returns the number of bytes occupied by a variable.

Q&A

Q. How do I define a function for the common logarithm (base 10) in QBasic?

A. Here is the function for the common logarithm:

```
FUNCTION Log10#(X AS DOUBLE)
    IF X > 0 THEN
        Log10# = LOG(X) / LOG(10)
    ELSE
        ' return value to indicate bad argument
        Log10# = -1.0D+100
    END IF
END FUNCTION
```

Q. How do I define functions for the inverse sine and cosine?

A. Here are the QBasic functions for the inverse sine and cosine:

```
FUNCTION ArcSin#(X AS DOUBLE)
    IF X <> 1 THEN
        ArcSin# = ATN(1 / (SQR(1 - X * X)))
    ELSE
        ' return value to indicate bad argument
        ArcSin# = -1.0D+100
    END IF
END FUNCTION
```

```
FUNCTION ArcCos#(X AS DOUBLE)
    IF X <> 1 THEN
        ArcCos# = ATN(X / (SQR(1 - X * X))
    ELSE
            ' return value to indicate bad argument
        ArcCos# = -1.0D+100
    END IF
END FUNCTION
```

Q. How do I define functions for the hyperbolic functions?

A. Here are the QBasic functions for the hyperbolic sine, cosine, and tangent:

```
FUNCTION HypSin#(X AS DOUBLE)
    HypSin# = (EXP(X) - EXP(-X)) / 2
END FUNCTION


FUNCTION HypCos#(X AS DOUBLE)
    HypCos# = (EXP(X) + EXP(-X)) / 2
END FUNCTION


FUNCTION HypTan#(X AS DOUBLE)
    HypTan# = (EXP(X) - EXP(-X)) / (EXP(X) + EXP(-X))
END FUNCTION
```

Q. How do I define functions for the inverse hyperbolic functions?

A. Here are the QBasic functions for the inverse hyperbolic sine, cosine, and tangent:

```
FUNCTION ArcHypSin#(X AS DOUBLE)
    ArcHypSin# = LOG(X + SQR(X * X + 1))
END FUNCTION


FUNCTION ArcHypCos#(X AS DOUBLE)
    IF ABS(X) >= 1 THEN
        ArcHypCos# = LOG(X + SQR(X * X - 1))
    ELSE
```

14

```
            ' return value to indicate bad argument
            ArcHypCos# = -1.0D+100
      END IF
END FUNCTION


FUNCTION ArcHypTan#(X AS DOUBLE)
    IF ABS(X) < 1 THEN
        ArcHypTan# = LOG((1 + X) / (1 - X))
    ELSE
            ' return value to indicate bad argument
        ArcHypTan# = -1.0D+100
    END IF
END FUNCTION
```

Workshop

The Workshop provides quiz questions to help you solidify your understanding of the material covered and exercises to provide you with experience in using what you've learned. Try to understand the quiz and exercise answers before continuing on to the next chapter. Answers are provided in Appendix B, "Answers."

Quiz

1. What is the output of the following statements?

   ```
   DIM X AS DOUBLE
   X = EXP(EXP(EXP(1)))
   PRINT USING "X = +#.##^^^^"; X
   ```

2. What is the output of the following statements?

   ```
   DIM X AS DOUBLE
   X = EXP(EXP(EXP(2)))
   PRINT USING "X = +#.##^^^^"; X
   ```

3. What is the output of the following statements?

```
DIM X AS DOUBLE
X = SQR(EXP(1) - 3)
PRINT USING "X = #.##"; X
```

4. What QBasic function can emulate the SGN function?

Exercises

1. Write the program SIN2.BAS that offers numerical (and practical) proof that SIN(X)^2 + COS(X)^2 is equal to 1, for all values of X. Modify the program SIN1.BAS to create SIN2.BAS.

2. Write the program COS2.BAS that offers numerical (and practical) proof that SIN(2*X) is equal to 2 * SIN(X) * COS(X), for all values of X. Modify the program SIN1.BAS to create COS2.BAS.

14

Week 2
in Review

When I reviewed the first week, I presented a program that manages a to-do list. After learning more QBasic statements and language features, I present a new version that supports the following operations:

1. Add a new task

2. Automatically sort the tasks by date

3. Delete any task

4. Print the tasks

5. Quit

Printing the to-do list is now supported by the program. You no longer need to press the PrtScr key to print the list. You can delete any task, not just the last one on the list. Also, the program now sorts the tasks by date. In addition to these enhancements, the new program uses statements you've learned this past week to enhance the implementation.

 Listing 1. TODO2.BAS, which implements a to-do list program.

```
1: REM Program which manages a To-Do list
2: REM
3: REM   Version 2.0          1/20/93
4: REM
5: ' declare constants
6: CONST MARK = "◊ "
```

continues

Listing 1. continued

```
 7: CONST MENU = "A)dd, D)elete P)rint, Q)uit"
 8: CONST MAX.TODO = 20
 9: CONST TITLE = "TO DO LIST"
10: ' declare variables
11: DIM S(1 TO MAX.TODO) AS STRING
12: DIM Choice AS STRING
13: DIM DateStr AS STRING
14: DIM ToDo AS STRING
15: DIM I AS INTEGER
16: DIM J AS INTEGER
17: DIM K AS INTEGER
18: DIM ToDoCount AS INTEGER
19:
20: ToDoCount = 0
21: DO
22:    CLS
23:    ' sort to do list
24:    FOR I = 1 TO ToDoCount - 1
25:      FOR J = I TO ToDoCount
26:        IF S(I) > S(J) THEN SWAP S(I), S(J)
27:      NEXT J
28:    NEXT I
29:    FOR I = 1 TO ToDoCount
30:      PRINT S(I)
31:    NEXT I
32:    LOCATE 23, 1
33:    PRINT MENU
34:    INPUT ">", Choice
35:    Choice = UCASE$(LEFT$(Choice, 1))
36:    SELECT CASE Choice
37:      CASE "A"
38:        IF ToDoCount < MAX.TODO THEN
39:          PRINT
40:          DO
41:            INPUT "Enter date : ", DateStr
42:          LOOP UNTIL DateStr <> ""
```

```
43:          DO
44:             LINE INPUT "Enter task : ", ToDo
45:          LOOP UNTIL ToDo <> ""
46:          ToDoCount = ToDoCount + 1
47:          S(ToDoCount) = MARK + DateStr + SPACE$(12 - LEN(DateStr))
48:          S(ToDoCount) = S(ToDoCount) + ToDo
49:        END IF
50:
51:      CASE "D" ' delete a task
52:      IF ToDoCount > 0 THEN
53:         DO
54:            INPUT "Enter index of task to delete"; J
55:         LOOP UNTIL J > 0 AND J <= ToDoCount
56:         FOR K = J + 1 TO ToDoCount
57:            S(K - 1) = S(K)
58:         NEXT K
59:         S(ToDoCount) = ""
60:         ToDoCount = ToDoCount - 1
61:      END IF
62:
63:      CASE "P"
64:         IF ToDoCount > 0 THEN
65:            LPRINT SPC(40 - LEN(TITLE) \ 2); TITLE
66:            LPRINT
67:            FOR I = 1 TO ToDoCount
68:               LPRINT S(I)
69:            NEXT I
70:         END IF
71:    END SELECT
72: LOOP UNTIL Choice = "Q"
73: END
```

Here is some sample output for the program in Listing 1:

```
◊ 01/18/93     Deadline for QBasic book
◊ 02/02/93     Meeting with D. Jenkins in NY City
◊ 03/04/93     Nancy's birthday
◊ 05/03/93     QBasic conference in London
◊ 06/15/93     Regional sales meeting in Chicago
◊ 11/15/93     Comdex Fall 93 in Las Vegas
```

◊ 12/01/93   QBasic conference in Tokyo

```
A)dd, D)elete P)rint, Q)uit
>p
```

Notice that the output consistently shows dates with two-digit months and days. This consistent format enables the program to sort the dates in the same year properly. If the dates span different years, the sort might fail to order the array. If you want to sort by year also, use the date format yy/mm/dd to obtain a perfect sort across different years (at no extra programming cost!).

Because TODO2.BAS is similar to TODO1.BAS, I focus on the altered and new program features:

1. A different string defines the constant MENU.

2. The declaration of the string array S to store the to-do tasks. Using an array enables the new program version to sort the tasks by date.

3. The nested FOR-NEXT loops on lines 24–28 sort the elements of S before displaying them using the FOR-NEXT loop on lines 29–31.

4. The LOCATE statement on line 32 moves the cursor to row number 23 to display the one-line menu. The new version uses a more straightforward approach to displaying the tasks and menu.

5. The first CASE clause uses a LINE INPUT statement instead of a INPUT statement to enter the task. By using the LINE INPUT statement, you can include commas when you enter a task.

6. The statements that assign the date and task to the next available element of array S. This approach is easier than appending strings and newline characters.

7. The second CASE clause now prompts you to enter the index of the task to delete. The program uses the FOR-NEXT loop on lines 56–58 to overwrite the deleted task. Using arrays of strings proves to be very convenient in managing the list of tasks.

8. The new version contains a third CASE that is followed by statements that print the title and the elements of the array S.

The next version of the program will benefit from upcoming topics. Most likely, you will modify the final version for your own use.

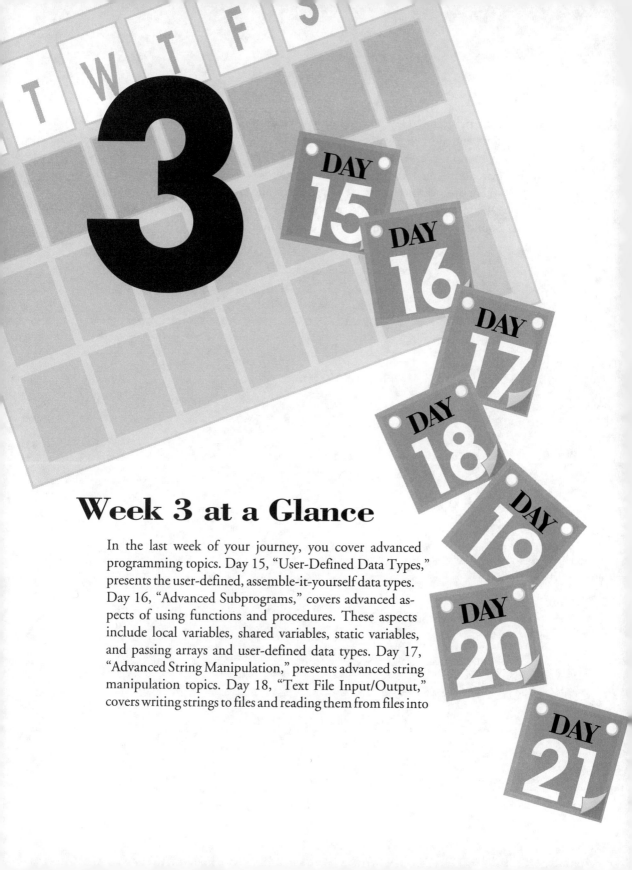

Week 3 at a Glance

In the last week of your journey, you cover advanced programming topics. Day 15, "User-Defined Data Types," presents the user-defined, assemble-it-yourself data types. Day 16, "Advanced Subprograms," covers advanced aspects of using functions and procedures. These aspects include local variables, shared variables, static variables, and passing arrays and user-defined data types. Day 17, "Advanced String Manipulation," presents advanced string manipulation topics. Day 18, "Text File Input/Output," covers writing strings to files and reading them from files into your programs. Day 19, "Random-Access and Binary File Input/Output," complements Day 18 and discusses the file input and output operations related to random-access and binary files. Day 20, "Drawing Graphics Shapes," introduces you to the graphics features of QBasic. You learn how to plot points and draw lines, boxes, circles, ellipses, arcs, and custom shapes. Your journey in QBasic programming ends on a light note, when on Day 21, "Music and Sound," you learn about the sound and music features of QBasic.

DAY
15

User-Defined
Data Types

QBasic supplies you with predefined data types. These data types represent the most common and basic information blocks. By contrast, the information we deal with in the real world is more complex than simple numbers and strings. QBasic provides a mechanism for declaring new data types that better represent real-world information, such as mailing lists and personnel information. This chapter discusses this QBasic mechanism, which enables you to create data molds, so to speak, and to build custom data types. Today you will learn about the following topics:

- Fixed strings
- Declaring user-defined data types using the TYPE statement
- Declaring variables that have the user-defined types using the DIM statement
- Arrays of user-defined data types
- Nested user-defined data types

Fixed Strings

The string variables that I have presented so far have varying lengths. QBasic also supports fixed-length strings. Such strings serve two main purposes. First, they are useful to save memory when you know the maximum number of characters you are going to store in a string variable. Second, fixed strings are the only type of strings that you can incorporate when defining your own data types. More about this capability in the next section.

Declaring Fixed Strings

The general syntax for declaring a fixed string is

```
DIM fixedStringVar AS STRING * count
```

The DIM statement declares the string variable *fixedStringVar* with a fixed size of *count* characters. The valid range of values for *count* is 1 to 32767. QBasic maintains *count* number of character at all times. If you assign a string with fewer than *count* characters to *fixedStringVar*, QBasic pads the variable with trailing spaces. By contrast, If you assign a string with more than *count* characters to *fixedStringVar*, QBasic truncates the extra characters.

Example:

```
DIM OneChar AS STRING * 1
DIM State AS STRING * 2
DIM Zip AS STRING * 14
DIM Phone AS STRING * 13
DIM Text AS STRING * 8000
DIM ScreenText AS STRING * 2000
```

DO use fixed strings when you know the maximum number of characters you want stored.

DON'T forget to use the RTRIM$ function with fixed strings to remove trailing spaces.

Let's look at a program to test fixed strings. Listing 15.1, FIXSTR1.BAS, assigns a varying number of characters to a fixed string and displays that string in a table. The program requires no input from you.

Listing 15.1. FIXSTR1.BAS, which tests a fixed string.

```
 1: REM Program that tests fixed strings
 2: REM
 3: ' declare constants
 4: CONST STR.SIZE = 10
 5: CONST TITLE = "Fixed String Test"
 6: CONST FILL.CHAR = "!"
 7: ' declare variables
 8: DIM FixedStr AS STRING * STR.SIZE
 9: DIM Q AS STRING * 1
10: DIM I AS INTEGER
11:
```

continues

15

Listing 15.1. **continued**

```
12: CLS
13: PRINT
14: PRINT TAB(40 - LEN(TITLE) \ 2); TITLE
15: PRINT
16: PRINT
17: PRINT , "    Number of "
18: PRINT , "assigned characters", "   String"
19: PRINT , STRING$(41, "-")
20: Q = CHR$(34)
21: FOR I = 1 TO STR.SIZE + 2
22:   FixedStr = STRING$(I, FILL.CHAR)
23:   PRINT , "         "; I, , Q; FixedStr; Q
24: NEXT I
25: END
```

Here is some sample output for the program in Listing 15.1:

```
                 Fixed String Test


          Number of
    assigned characters          String
    -----------------------------------------
             1              "!           "
             2              "!!          "
             3              "!!!         "
             4              "!!!!        "
             5              "!!!!!       "
             6              "!!!!!!      "
             7              "!!!!!!!     "
             8              "!!!!!!!!    "
             9              "!!!!!!!!!   "
            10              "!!!!!!!!!!"
            11              "!!!!!!!!!!"
            12              "!!!!!!!!!!"
```

 The program in Listing 15.1 declares its constants on lines 4–6. The program declares the fixed-string variable FixedStr on line 8. The declaration uses the constant STR.SIZE to set the size of the fixed-string variable.

 Note: The program also declares the variable Q as a single-character fixed string. Q stores the double-quotation mark character. In the previous programs I have declared Q as a flexible string. The declaration on line 9 is more efficient.

The PRINT statements on lines 14–19 display the title and table heading. The statement on line 20 assigns a single-character string to the single-character variable Q. The FOR-NEXT loop on lines 21–24 uses the control variable I and iterates from 1 TO STR.SIZE + 2. I purposely used this upper limit to exceed the length of the fixed-string variable, FixedStr. This excess demonstrates how QBasic truncates the extra characters assigned to a fixed-string variable. The statement on line 22 assigns a string created with the STRING$ function. The statement creates a string by duplicating I times the FILL.CHAR character. The statement assigns the result of STRING$ to FixedStr. The PRINT statement on line 23 displays the contents of FixedStr, enclosed in double-quotation marks. This display indicates the padding of trailing spaces performed by QBasic.

Declaring User-Defined Types

QBasic allows you to create you own data types. These **user-defined** types encapsulate or package multiple fields in a record. This packaging enables you to bind logically related data items. The collective data in a record present meaningful information. Consider a name in a mailing list. Such a data item typically contains the name, address, city, state, and zip code of an addressee. Together, these fields make up a meaningful record. Individually, these fields do not convey exact or even coherent meaning. QBasic offers the TYPE statement to create a user-defined data type.

The TYPE Statement

The general syntax for the TYPE statement is

```
TYPE userTypeName
    field1 AS type1
    field2 AS type2
    ...
END TYPE
```

The *userTypeName* defines the name of a new user-defined data type. *field1*, *field2*, and so on, declare the names of the fields that make up the user-defined type. The AS clauses specify the data type for each field. These data types can be the predefined numeric data types (INTEGER, LONG, SINGLE, and DOUBLE), a fixed string type, or a previously declared user-defined type.

QBasic does not allow you to:

1. Use data type suffixes with the fields of a records. The AS clause is **mandatory**.

2. Declare a field as an array.

3. Declare a field as a flexible string.

4. Declare multiple fields on the same line.

Examples:

```
TYPE TCoordinate
  X AS SINGLE
  Y AS SINGLE
END TYPE

TYPE TVelocity
  Speed AS DOUBLE
  Direction AS DOUBLE
END TYPE

TYPE TPerson
  LastName AS STRING * 15
```

```
      FirstName AS STRING * 10
      Age AS INTEGER
      Weight AS SINGLE
END TYPE
```

New Term In this book I use the terms *structure* and *structured type* as synonyms for user-defined data type. I also use the term *structured variable* as an abbreviation for a variable that has a user-defined data type.

DO start the name of a structure with the uppercase T. Then you can use the rest of the structure name to declare a related variable. For example, if you declare the structure TRectangle, you can declare the structured variable Rectangle.

DON'T use cryptic names for structures.

Declaring Variables with User-Defined Types

The DIM statement is the most common way to declare structured variables. You also can use the REDIM statement to redimension arrays of structured types.

Declaring User-Defined Variable

The general syntax for declaring variables that have user-defined types is

```
DIM varName AS userTypeName
```

The DIM statement declares the variable *varName*, which is associated with the user-defined data type *userTypeName*.

Example:

```
TYPE TCoordinate
  X AS SINGLE
  Y AS SINGLE
END TYPE
DIM Here AS TCoordinate
DIM There AS TCoordinate
DIM Origin AS TCoordinate, FocalPoint AS TCoordinate

TYPE TVelocity
  Speed AS DOUBLE
  Direction AS DOUBLE
END TYPE
DIM RocketVel AS TVelocity

TYPE TPerson
  LastName AS STRING * 15
  FirstName AS STRING * 10
  Age AS INTEGER
  Weight AS SINGLE
END TYPE
DIM Me as TPerson, You AS TPerson
```

Once you declare a structured variable. you can access the individual fields of that variable using the dot operator. This operator is called the *access operator* because it enables you to access the various fields in a structured variable.

Accessing Fields in Structured Variables

The general syntax for accessing a field in a structured variable is

```
structVar.field
```

The dot operator gives access to the *field* of the structured variable *structVar*. QBasic treats the field of a structured variable as a variable.

Example:

```
TYPE TCoordinate
  X AS SINGLE
  Y AS SINGLE
END TYPE
DIM Origin AS TCoordinate
Origin.X = 0 ' access field X
Origin.Y = 0 ' access field Y

TYPE TVelocity
  Speed AS DOUBLE
  Direction AS DOUBLE
END TYPE
DIM RocketVel AS TVelocity
RocketVel.Speed = 100 ' speed
RocketVel.Direction = 45 ' degrees

TYPE TPerson
  LastName AS STRING * 15
  FirstName AS STRING * 10
  Age AS INTEGER
  Weight AS SINGLE
END TYPE
DIM Me as TPerson
Me.LastName = "Shammas"
Me.FirstName = "Namir"
Me.Age = 38
Me.Weight = 190.5
```

15

Let's look at an example that illustrates declaring a user-defined type, declaring structured variables, and using these variables. Listing 15.2, TYPE1.BAS, offers such an example. The program requires no input from you. Instead, it displays a list of daily book orders for an unnamed book publisher. The program also lists the weekly total book orders. Random numbers are used to generate the number of daily book orders.

Listing 15.2. TYPE1.BAS, which uses several
variables of the same user-defined type.

```
 1: REM Program that declares user-defined data types
 2: REM using the TYPE statement
 3: REM
 4: ' declare the type TDay
 5: TYPE TDay
 6:    DayName AS STRING * 10
 7:    BookOrders AS LONG
 8: END TYPE
 9: ' declare constants
10: CONST MAX.ITER = 100
11: CONST MAX.BOOKS = 1000
12: CONST MIN.DAY = 2
13: CONST MAX.DAY = 6
14: CONST TITLE = "Weekly Book Orders"
15: CONST FRMT = "& : ###### copies"
16: ' declare variables
17: DIM Monday AS TDay
18: DIM Tuesday AS TDay
19: DIM Wednesday AS TDay
20: DIM Thursday AS TDay
21: DIM Friday AS TDay
22: DIM I AS INTEGER
23: DIM J AS INTEGER
24: DIM L AS LONG
25: DIM Total AS LONG
26:
27: ' initialize TDay-typed variables
28: Monday.DayName = "Monday"
29: Monday.BookOrders = 0
30: Tuesday.DayName = "Tuesday"
31: Tuesday.BookOrders = 0
32: Wednesday.DayName = "Wednesday"
33: Wednesday.BookOrders = 0
34: Thursday.DayName = "Thursday"
35: Thursday.BookOrders = 0
36: Friday.DayName = "Friday"
37: Friday.BookOrders = 0
38:
```

```
39: ' initialize the variable Total
40: Total = 0
41:
42: ' reseed random-number generator
43: RANDOMIZE TIMER
44:
45: FOR I = 1 TO MAX.ITER
46:   ' obtain the weekday index
47:   J = MIN.DAY + INT(RND * (MAX.DAY - MIN.DAY + 1))
48:   ' obtain the book order
49:   L = INT(RND * MAX.BOOKS)
50:   ' update the total book orders
51:   Total = Total + L
52:   ' update the book order for day J
53:   SELECT CASE J
54:     CASE 2
55:       Monday.BookOrders = Monday.BookOrders + L
56:     CASE 3
57:       Tuesday.BookOrders = Tuesday.BookOrders + L
58:     CASE 4
59:       Wednesday.BookOrders = Wednesday.BookOrders + L
60:     CASE 5
61:       Thursday.BookOrders = Thursday.BookOrders + L
62:     CASE 6
63:       Friday.BookOrders = Friday.BookOrders + L
64:   END SELECT
65: NEXT I
66:
67: CLS
68: PRINT
69: PRINT TAB(40 - LEN(TITLE) \ 2); TITLE
70: PRINT
71: PRINT
72: PRINT USING FRMT; Monday.DayName; Monday.BookOrders
73: PRINT USING FRMT; Tuesday.DayName; Tuesday.BookOrders
74: PRINT USING FRMT; Wednesday.DayName; Wednesday.BookOrders
75: PRINT USING FRMT; Thursday.DayName; Thursday.BookOrders
76: PRINT USING FRMT; Friday.DayName; Friday.BookOrders
77: PRINT STRING$(26, "-")
78: PRINT "Total      = "; Total; "copies"
79: END
```

15

Here is some sample output for the program in Listing 15.2 (Because the program generates random numbers, your output will be different):

```
Weekly Book Orders


Monday      :   8448 copies
Tuesday     :   8681 copies
Wednesday   :  10751 copies
Thursday    :   7592 copies
Friday      :  11461 copies
- - - - - - - - - - - - - - - - - - - - - - - - -
Total       =  46933 copies
```

The program in Listing 15.2 declares the user-defined type TDay. This type contains two fields: the DayName field is a 10-character string, and the BookOrders field is a long integer. DayName stores the name of the day as a string, whereas BookOrders stores the total orders for that day. Lines 10–15 contain the declaration of various constants that are used to generate the random book orders, specify the program title, and define the output format. Lines 17–25 contain the declaration of the program's variables. Lines 17–21 declare five structured variables, named after the working weekdays, Monday through Friday.

The program initializes the fields of the structured variables on lines 28–37. Notice that the program uses the access operator to assign strings and numbers to the individual fields of each structured variable. The statement on line 40 initializes the variable Total, which keeps track of the total weekly book orders.

The process of simulating book sales starts with reseeding the random-number generator, using the RANDOMIZE statement on line 43. The program uses a FOR-NEXT loop on lines 45–65 to select a weekday at random and increase its book orders by a random number. The loop uses the control variable I and iterates from 1 to MAX.ITER. The upper limit is rather arbitrary and serves to select the various weekdays several times. The statement on line 47 obtains the index, at random, of a selected weekday and stores that index in J. The statement on line 49 generates a random number of books ordered and stores that number in the variable L. The statement on line 51 adds the number of books ordered to the current value in Total.

The program uses the SELECT-CASE statement on lines 53–64 to update the number of books ordered for the selected weekday. The various CASE clauses update the BookOrders field of their respective structures variables.

The PRINT statements on lines 68–78 display the centered title, daily book orders, and the weekly total. The PRINT statements on lines 72–76 access the fields DayName and BookOrders for the structured variables Monday through Friday using the dot operator. The PRINT USING statement treats these fields as ordinary variables.

Arrays of User-Defined Types

To declare arrays of a structured type, you use the DIM statement just like declaring arrays of predefined data types. Accessing the fields of a structured array also uses one or more indices, depending on the number of array dimensions.

Let's look at an example that uses a structured array. The program in Listing 15.2 uses individual structured variables to represent the books ordered on Monday through Friday. Listing 15.3 uses an array instead of a set of several simple variables. The program basically performs the same tasks as TYPE1.BAS.

Listing 15.3. TYPE2.BAS, which uses an array of a user-defined type.

```
 1: REM Program that declares user-defined data type
 2: REM using the TYPE statement
 3: REM
 4: ' declare the type TDay
 5: TYPE TDay
 6:    DayName AS STRING * 10
 7:    BookOrders AS LONG
 8: END TYPE
 9: ' declare constants
10: CONST MAX.ITER = 100
11: CONST MAX.BOOKS = 1000
12: CONST MIN.DAY = 2
13: CONST MAX.DAY = 6
```

continues

```
14: CONST TITLE = "Weekly Book Orders"
15: CONST FRMT = "& : ###### copies"
16: ' declare variables
17: DIM Days(MIN.DAY TO MAX.DAY) AS TDay
18: DIM I AS INTEGER
19: DIM J AS INTEGER
20: DIM L AS LONG
21: DIM Total AS LONG
22:
23: ' initialize Day-typed array
24: FOR I = MIN.DAY TO MAX.DAY
25:   READ Days(I).DayName
26:   Days(I).BookOrders = 0
27: NEXT I
28:
29: ' initialize the variable Total
30: Total = 0
31:
32: ' reseed random-number generator
33: RANDOMIZE TIMER
34:
35: FOR I = 1 TO MAX.ITER
36:   J = MIN.DAY + INT(RND * (MAX.DAY - MIN.DAY + 1))
37:   L = INT(RND * MAX.BOOKS)
38:   Total = Total + L
39:   Days(J).BookOrders = Days(J).BookOrders + L
40: NEXT I
41:
42: CLS
43: PRINT
44: PRINT TAB(40 - LEN(TITLE) \ 2); TITLE
45: PRINT
46: PRINT
47: FOR I = MIN.DAY TO MAX.DAY
48:   PRINT USING FRMT; Days(I).DayName; Days(I).BookOrders
49: NEXT I
50: PRINT STRING$(26, "-")
51: PRINT "Total     = "; Total; "copies"
52:
```

```
53: ' *************** DATA Statements ***************
54:
55: DATA Monday, Tuesday, Wednesday, Thursday, Friday
56:
57: END
```

Here is some sample output for the program in Listing 15.3 (Once again, this program generates random numbers, so your input will be different):

```
        Weekly Book Orders


    Monday     :  10171 copies
    Tuesday    :  13694 copies
    Wednesday  :  12774 copies
    Thursday   :   5148 copies
    Friday     :  11013 copies
    ------------------------
    Total      =  52800 copies
```

The program in Listing 15.3 resembles the one in Listing 15.2. Therefore, I point out the differences between the two versions. Here are the aspects that are either new or modified in the new program:

1. The declaration of the structure array Days on line 17. The array has indices ranging from MIN.DAY to MAX.DAY.

2. The program uses a FOR-NEXT loop, on lines 24–27, to initialize the members of the array Days. The statement on line 25 obtains the weekday name by using a READ statement. The statement on line 26 assigns 0 to the BookOrders field of array element Days(I).

3. The program uses a short FOR-NEXT loop to add up the random number for book orders. By using the weekday index (stored in J), the program easily updates the BookOrders field in the array element Days(J).

4. A FOR-NEXT loop on lines 47–49 displays the daily book orders. The PRINT statement on line 48 displays the DayName and BookOrders fields for the array element Days(I).

5. DATA statements supply the names of the weekdays to the DayName fields of the elements of array Days.

15

Nested User-Defined Types

When I presented the general syntax of the TYPE statement, I indicated that the fields of a structure can be structured variables. The type of these structure fields must be previously defined. Declaring variables with nested structures is no different from declaring structured variables. Accessing variables with nested structures requires multiple dot operators to access the various fields of the nested structures. The number of dot operators is equal to the number of levels of nesting in the structured type.

Let me present an example. Listing 15.4, TYPE3.BAS, uses a nested structure. I wrote this program by modifying the one in Listing 15.2. I created a nested structure to contain the fields Monday through Friday, and the field Total. In other words, I encapsulated many of the segregated variables, in Listing 15.2, into a new structured type. The program in Listing 15.4 essentially performs the same tasks as the one in Listing 15.2.

 Listing 15.4. **TYPE3.BAS, which uses a nested structure.**

```
 1: REM Program that declares nested user-defined
 2: REM Data types using the TYPE statements
 3: REM
 4: ' declare the type TDay
 5: TYPE TDay
 6:    DayName AS STRING * 10
 7:    BookOrders AS LONG
 8: END TYPE
 9: ' declare the type TWeekDays
10: TYPE TWeekDays
11:     Monday AS TDay
12:     Tuesday AS TDay
13:     Wednesday AS TDay
14:     Thursday AS TDay
15:     Friday AS TDay
16:     Total AS LONG
17: END TYPE
18: ' declare constants
19: CONST MAX.ITER = 100
20: CONST MAX.BOOKS = 1000
```

```
21: CONST MIN.DAY = 2
22: CONST MAX.DAY = 6
23: CONST TITLE = "Weekly Book Orders"
24: CONST FRMT = ": ###### copies"
25: ' declare variables
26: DIM Days AS TWeekDays
27: DIM I AS INTEGER
28: DIM J AS INTEGER
29: DIM L AS LONG
30:
31: ' initialize TWeekDay-typed variable
32: Days.Total = 0
33: Days.Monday.DayName = "Monday"
34: Days.Monday.BookOrders = 0
35: Days.Tuesday.DayName = "Tuesday"
36: Days.Tuesday.BookOrders = 0
37: Days.Wednesday.DayName = "Wednesday"
38: Days.Wednesday.BookOrders = 0
39: Days.Thursday.DayName = "Thursday"
40: Days.Thursday.BookOrders = 0
41: Days.Friday.DayName = "Friday"
42: Days.Friday.BookOrders = 0
43:
44: ' reseed random-number generator
45: RANDOMIZE TIMER
46:
47: FOR I = 1 TO MAX.ITER
48:    J = MIN.DAY + INT(RND * (MAX.DAY - MIN.DAY + 1))
49:    L = INT(RND * MAX.BOOKS)
50:    Days.Total = Days.Total + L
51:    SELECT CASE J
52:      CASE 2
53:        Days.Monday.BookOrders = Days.Monday.BookOrders + L
54:      CASE 3
55:        Days.Tuesday.BookOrders = Days.Tuesday.BookOrders + L
56:      CASE 4
57:        Days.Wednesday.BookOrders = Days.Wednesday.BookOrders + L
58:      CASE 5
59:        Days.Thursday.BookOrders = Days.Thursday.BookOrders + L
60:      CASE 6
61:        Days.Friday.BookOrders = Days.Friday.BookOrders + L
```

continues

15

Listing 15.4. continued

```
62:   END SELECT
63: NEXT I
64:
65: CLS
66: PRINT
67: PRINT TAB(40 - LEN(TITLE) \ 2); TITLE
68: PRINT
69: PRINT
70: PRINT Days.Monday.DayName;
71: PRINT USING FRMT; Days.Monday.BookOrders
72: PRINT Days.Tuesday.DayName;
73: PRINT USING FRMT; Days.Tuesday.BookOrders
74: PRINT Days.Wednesday.DayName;
75: PRINT USING FRMT; Days.Wednesday.BookOrders
76: PRINT Days.Thursday.DayName;
77: PRINT USING FRMT; Days.Thursday.BookOrders
78: PRINT Days.Friday.DayName;
79: PRINT USING FRMT; Days.Friday.BookOrders
80: PRINT STRING$(26, "-")
81: PRINT "Total     = "; Days.Total; "copies"
82: END
```

Here is some sample output for the program in Listing 15.4 (these numbers are random, so your output won't match mine):

```
        Weekly Book Orders


    Monday     :  13380 copies
    Tuesday    :  11358 copies
    Wednesday  :   3912 copies
    Thursday   :  11460 copies
    Friday     :  11859 copies
    ------------------------
    Total      =  51969 copies
```

Analysis Because the programs in Listings 15.2 and 15.4 are similar, I focus on their differences. The new program is different in the following ways:

1. The declaration of the TWeekDays structured type. This type contains the fields Monday though Friday, and the field Total.

2. The declaration of the single structured variable (or nested structured variable, to be more accurate) Days, on line 26.

3. The initialization of the various fields and nested fields of the structure Days. The statements on lines 32–42 perform this task. Notice that the statements on lines 33–42 use two dot operators to assign values to nested fields.

4. The statements in the CASE clauses of the SELECT-CASE (which spans lines 51–62) use double dot operators to accumulate the number of book orders in the nested fields BookOrders.

5. The PRINT statements on lines 70–79 also use double dot operators to display the values in the nested fields DayName and BookOrders.

6. The program accesses and displays the total number of weekly book orders by using the Days.Total expression.

Summary

This chapter introduced you to creating user-defined data types. Such data types represent structures that combine logically related data fields. In this chapter you learned about the following topics:

☐ Fixed strings are strings declared with a fixed number of characters. QBasic truncates the extra characters assigned to a fixed string. In addition, QBasic pads the fixed strings with trailing spaces when these strings are assigned fewer characters than their capacity.

☐ The TYPE statement enables you to declare user-defined data types. The declaration lists the names and data types of the fields that make up the user-defined type. These fields can have predefined data types or previously declared user-defined types.

☐ The DIM statement enables you to declare structured variables and state the associated user-defined data type. QBasic allows you to access the fields of structured variables using the dot operator.

15

☐ The DIM statement also can be used to declare arrays of structured type. The declaration specifies the range of indices (at least the last index) and the associated user-defined data type.

☐ Nested user-defined data types contain fields that are themselves structured variables. Accessing the fields of the nested structures requires the use of multiple dot operators.

Q&A

Q. Should the fields in a structure be declared in any particular order?

A. The order of declaring the fields in a structure makes no difference for QBasic.

Q. Can the same field name be used in multiple TYPE declarations?

A. Yes, QBasic does not give one TYPE declaration a monopoly over the names of its fields. However, your program is easier to read if you minimize or eliminate duplicate field names.

Q. Does QBasic support nested declarations of user-defined types?

A. No. Each structure must be separately and completely declared. In addition, you must declare a structure before using it in declaring other structures.

Q. Does the REDIM statement work with dynamic arrays of structures?

A. Yes, the REDIM statement works with arrays of structures just like with arrays of predefined data types.

Workshop

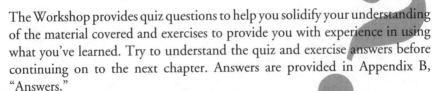

The Workshop provides quiz questions to help you solidify your understanding of the material covered and exercises to provide you with experience in using what you've learned. Try to understand the quiz and exercise answers before continuing on to the next chapter. Answers are provided in Appendix B, "Answers."

Quiz

1. Where is the error in the following statements?

```
TYPE TCoord
  X AS INTEGER
  Y AS INTEGER
END TYPE
CONST MAX.POINTS = 10
DIM Points(1 TO MAX.POINTS) AS TCoord
DIM I AS INTEGER
FOR I = 1 TO MAX.POINTS
  Points.X(I) = INT(RND * 1000)
  Points.Y(I) = INT(RND * 1000)
NEXT I
```

2. What is the output of the following statements?

```
DIM S AS STRING * 10
DIM Q AS STRING * 1
CLS
Q = CHR$(34)
S = "Hello" : PRINT Q; S; Q
S = "1234567890" : PRINT Q; S; Q
S = "1234567890!@#$%" : PRINT Q; S; Q
END
```

3. Where is the error in the following set of statements?

```
TYPE TCoord
  X AS INTEGER
  Y AS INTEGER
END TYPE

TYPE TPolygon
  Area AS DOUBLE
  NumVertices AS INTEGER
  Vertex (1 TO 10) AS DOUBLE
END TYPE
```

15

4. What is the output generated by the following statements?

```
CONST MAX.SIZE = 2000
DIM S AS STRING * MAX.SIZE
CLS
S = STRING$(MAX.SIZE, "A")
PRINT S;
END
```

Exercises

1. Write the program TYPE4.BAS that uses the following data type:

```
TYPE TMessage
   Text AS STRING * 80
   X AS INTEGER
   Y AS INTEGER
END TYPE
```

to store the text and location of a message. Use a TMessage array to read and display the text from the following DATA statements:

```
' format: message, Y, X
DATA Hello, 10, 10
DATA Bonjour, 12, 40
DATA Howdee, 20,1
DATA Greetings!, 3, 5
```

2. Write the program TYPE5.BAS that uses the following user-defined type to fill the screen with single characters:

```
CONST SCREENSIZE = 2000
TYPE TScreen
   Text AS STRING * SCREENSIZE
   FillChar AS STRING * 1
   Count AS INTEGER
END TYPE
```

Fill the screen with the characters A–F. Use the INPUT$ function to pause after filling the screen with each character.

DAY 16

Advanced Subprograms

On Day 10, "Subroutines and Functions," I introduced you to writing QBasic SUB and FUNCTION procedures. In this chapter I present more advanced aspects of programming these procedures. These aspects cover declaring and using local variables, sharing variables, and passing various kinds of parameters. Today you will learn about the following topics:

- [ ] Overview of scoping variables in a program
- [ ] Declaring local variables in SUB and FUNCTION procedures
- [ ] Sharing variables among the main program and procedures
- [ ] Static variables in SUB and FUNCTION procedures
- [ ] Passing arrays as parameters to SUB and FUNCTION procedures
- [ ] Passing matrices as parameters to SUB and FUNCTION procedures
- [ ] Passing structures to SUB and FUNCTION procedures
- [ ] Recursive FUNCTION procedures
- [ ] Exiting DEF FN functions, SUB procedures, and FUNCTION procedures

Scopes of Variables

The creation of semi-independent program components with SUB and FUNCTION procedures depends on the ability to limit the access of variables. In GW-BASIC, the precursor to QBasic, all variables were global. Consequently, all the subroutines (created with the GOSUB statement) in GW-BASIC had full access to all program variables. This means that if you accidentally used the same variable in nested subroutines, you corrupted the values of that variable in the higher-level subroutines. QBasic remedies this problem by supporting different *scopes* for variables.

☐New Term A variable's *scope* is its visibility and access in various program components.

Here are the default rules for scoping variables:

1. The SUB and FUNCTION procedures do not have automatic access to the variables declared in the main program.

2. By default, the variables inside a procedure exist only while that procedure is executing.

3. Constants are global. Any SUB and FUNCTION procedure has automatic access to all constants.

Figure 16.1 shows the default scoping of variables in a program. The main program, the procedure ProcA, and the procedure ProcB declare the variables I and S. The program stores three sets of these variables, one for the main program section, one for SUB ProcA, and one for SUB ProcB. The output of the sample program is:

```
2 In ProcA
3 In ProcB
1 In Main
```

16

The PRINT statement in the main section clearly indicates that the variables I and S inside the procedures ProcA and ProcB do not overwrite the variables I and S in the main program.

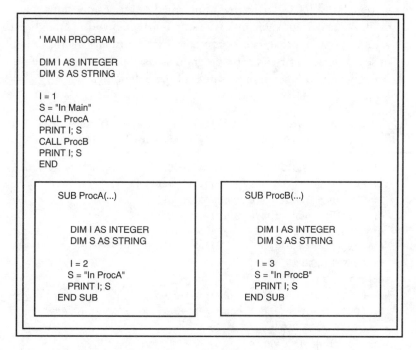

Figure 16.1. The default scoping of variables in a program.

Local Variables

Let me present a program that uses a numerical function with local variables. Listing 16.1, ADVSUB1.BAS, uses a FUNCTION procedure with local variables and arrays. I derived this program from the program FOR6.BAS (Listing 7.10) on Day 7, "Looping." The new version expands on FOR6.BAS by searching for the numerical roots of a general polynomial, not just a quadratic equation. The program contains DATA statements that supply the coefficients of the polynomial. The general form of a polynomial is:

$$f(X) = C_N X^N + C_{N-1} X^{N-1} + \ldots + C_2 X^2 + C_1 X + C_0$$

A polynomial of order N (the highest power of X) has N roots. Depending on the values of the polynomial coefficients, some of the roots might be complex.

The program searches for the real roots in the range of –10 to 10, in increments of 0.01. To keep you informed of the search status, the program displays the current value of X (the search variable) and f(X). When the program finds the approximate location of a root, it displays the root and proceeds to search for other roots. The program stops searching when the number of real roots found is equal to the order of the polynomial.

Listing 16.1. ADVSUB1.BAS, which uses a FUNCTION procedure with local variables and arrays.

```
1: DECLARE FUNCTION FofX! (X AS DOUBLE, PolyOrder AS INTEGER)
2: REM Program that uses local variables
3: REM in a FUNCTION procedure to get
4: REM the approximate roots a polynomial
5: CONST FIRST# = -10
6: CONST LAST# = 10
7: CONST INCREM# = .01
8: CONST MAX.COEFF = 10
9: CONST FRMT1 = "f(+##.####) = +#.######^^^^^"
10: CONST FRMT2 = "Root near X = +#.####   f(X) = +#.#####"
11: CONST VIEW.ROW = 3
12: ' declare the variables
13: DIM X AS DOUBLE
14: DIM Y1 AS DOUBLE
15: DIM Y2 AS DOUBLE
16: DIM Xroot AS DOUBLE
```

```
17: DIM Yroot AS DOUBLE
18: DIM Sum AS INTEGER
19: DIM N AS INTEGER
20: CLS
21: PRINT "Wait please..."
22: PRINT
23: ' initialize the number of roots found
24: Sum = 0
25: READ N
26: X = FIRST
27: Y1 = FofX(X, N)
28: ' loop t search for roots
29: FOR X = FIRST + INCREM TO LAST STEP INCREM
30:    Y2 = FofX(X, N)
31:    LOCATE VIEW.ROW, 1
32:    PRINT USING FRMT1; X; Y2
33:    IF Y2 * Y1 < 0 THEN
34:      Sum = Sum + 1
35:      Xroot = X - INCREM / 2
36:      Yroot = FofX(Xroot, N)
37:      LOCATE VIEW.ROW + Sum + 2, 1
38:      PRINT USING FRMT2; Xroot; Yroot
39:      ' found the last root?
40:      IF Sum = N THEN EXIT FOR ' exit loop
41:    END IF
42:    Y1 = Y2
43: NEXT X
44: LOCATE VIEW.ROW + Sum + 4, 1
45: PRINT
46: PRINT "Found"; Sum; "roots"
47:
48: ' ***************** DATA Statements *****************
49:
50: ' the polynomial order
51: DATA 3
52: CoeffLabel:
53: ' C(0), C(1), C(2), C(3), etc
54: DATA 6, -5, -1, 1
55:
56: END
57:
```

continues

Listing 16.1. continued

```
58: FUNCTION FofX (X AS DOUBLE, PolyOrder AS INTEGER)
59: ' Function calculates the value of the polynomial
60: ' at the value X
61:   DIM C(0 TO MAX.COEFF) AS DOUBLE
62:   DIM Sum AS DOUBLE
63:   DIM I  AS INTEGER
64:
65:   RESTORE CoeffLabel
66:   ' read the polynomial coefficients
67:   FOR I = 0 TO PolyOrder
68:     READ C(I)
69:   NEXT I
70:   ' calculate the value of the polynomial
71:   Sum = C(PolyOrder) * X
72:   FOR I = PolyOrder - 1 TO 1 STEP -1
73:     Sum = (Sum + C(I)) * X
74:   NEXT I
75:   Sum = Sum + C(0)
76:   FofX = Sum
77: END FUNCTION
```

Here is some sample output for the program in Listing 16.1:

```
Wait please...

f( +2.0100) = +3.050017D-002


Root near X = -2.3050   f(X) = -0.03455
Root near X = +1.3050   f(X) = -0.00558
Root near X = +2.0050   f(X) = +0.01512


Found 3 roots
```

The program in Listing 16.1 is similar to the one in Listing 7.10. The highlight of this program is the function FofX and its local variables. The function declares the local array C on line 61 and the local variables Sum and I on lines 62 and 63. Notice that the program section also declares the

variable Sum on line 18. I use this duplicate variable name (though with different data types) to illustrate that the program distinguishes between the local variables of a procedure and variables with the same name in the main program section.

The function FofX uses the parameter PolyOrder to pass the polynomial order. The function calculates the value of the polynomial using the variable Sum. The local array C receives its values using the READ statement on line 70. The FOR-NEXT loop on lines 67–69 reads the DATA statements to supply the coefficients with values. The FOR-NEXT loop on lines 72–74 and the statement on line 75 calculate the value of the polynomial. The statement on line 76 assigns the value in Sum to the function FofX.

The main program calls FofX on lines 27, 30, and 36. Sum maintains the number of roots found. This variable appears on lines 24, 34, and 40. These lines place Sum before and after the lines that call FofX. However, the variable Sum in the main program section is not affected by the use of the variable Sum in the function FofX. The integrity of the value in Sum in the main section indicates that QBasic isolates this instance of the variable Sum from the one in function FofX.

To find the roots of another polynomial, you need to alter the values in the DATA statements.

Static Variables

What happens to the local variables of a SUB or FUNCTION procedure between calls? The answer is that they are removed from memory. Therefore, the data stored by the local variable also is lost. QBasic enables you to declare local variables such that they retain their data between procedure calls. Such variables are called *static* variables. To declare a static variable, use the STATIC keyword instead of the DIM keyword. The STATIC declaration tells QBasic to store the declared variables in a special memory location that is maintained throughout the program's execution.

Take a look at a simple example. One of my favorite illustrations of a static variable is the following user-defined random-number generator:

```
seedi+1 = FRAC((p + seedi)3)
```

The above function generates numbers greater than or equal to 0 and less than 1. The function stores the last random number it generated as the seed for the next random number. Listing 16.2, ADVSUB2.BAS, uses a local static variable to implement the random-number generating function Rand#. The program, which does not require any external input, tests the random-number function. Statistical analysis states that a good uniform random-number function generates numbers with the mean of 0.5 and standard deviation of about 0.28. The program samples the random-number function and displays the mean and standard deviation values for the sampled values.

Listing 16.2. ADVSUB2.BAS, which uses a local static variable to implement a random-number generator.

```
1: DECLARE FUNCTION Rand# (Seed AS INTEGER)
2: DECLARE FUNCTION Frac# (X AS DOUBLE)
3: REM Program that uses static local variables
4: REM to store values between calls
5: REM
6: ' declare constants
7: CONST PI# = 3.14159
8: CONST MAX.ITER = 1000
9: ' declare variables
10: DIM X AS DOUBLE
11: DIM Sum AS DOUBLE
12: DIM SumX AS DOUBLE
13: DIM SumXX AS DOUBLE
14: DIM Mean AS DOUBLE
15: DIM Sdev AS DOUBLE
16: DIM I AS INTEGER
17:
18: CLS
19: PRINT "Please wait..."
20: PRINT
21: ' reseed the random-number generating function
22: X = Rand#(17)
23: ' initialize the summation variables
24: Sum = MAX.ITER
25: SumX = 0
26: SumXX = 0
27: ' loop to sample the values generated by function Rand#
28: FOR I = 1 TO MAX.ITER
29:    ' display a dot every 100th iteration
```

```
30:    IF (I MOD MAX.ITER / 10) = 0 THEN PRINT ".";
31:    ' get the random number
32:    X = Rand#(0)
33:    ' update the summation variables
34:    SumX = SumX + X
35:    SumXX = SumXX + X * X
36: NEXT I
37: ' calculate the mean and standard deviation
38: Mean = SumX / Sum
39: Sdev = SQR((SumXX - SumX * SumX / Sum) / (Sum - 1))
40: ' display the statistics of the random-number generator
41: PRINT
42: PRINT
43: PRINT "Number of iterations ="; Sum
44: PRINT USING "Mean = #.#####"; Mean
45: PRINT USING "Sdev = #.#####"; Sdev
46: END
47:
48: FUNCTION Frac# (X AS DOUBLE)
49: ' return the fractional part of X
50:    Frac# = X - FIX(X)
51: END FUNCTION
52:
53: FUNCTION Rand# (Seed AS INTEGER)
54: ' random-number generator.  The function uses the
55: ' local variable LclSeed to store the random number
56:    STATIC LclSeed AS DOUBLE
57:    IF Seed <> 0 THEN LclSeed = Seed
58:    LclSeed = Frac#((PI + LclSeed) ^ 3)
59:    Rand# = LclSeed
60: END FUNCTION
```

16

Here is some sample output for the program in Listing 16.2:

```
Please wait...

..........

Number of iterations = 1000
Mean = 0.50440
Sdev = 0.28671
```

Analysis The program in Listing 16.2 declares the functions Rand# and Frac#. The function Rand# returns random numbers. The function Frac# returns the fractional part of a floating-point number. The program declares the constants PI# and MAX.ITER on lines 7 and 8, respectively. The program also declares its variables on lines 10–16.

Lines 21–26 contain statements that prepare for the loop on line 28. The statement on line 22 calls Rand# and supplies it with a non-zero value to reseed the function. The function returns the first random number it generates and stores it in the variable X. This statement mainly serves to reseed the random number—the value in X is ignored.

The statements on lines 24–26 initialize the summation variables Sum, SumX, and SumXX. The FOR-NEXT loop on lines 28–36 uses the control variable I and iterates from 1 to MAX.ITER. The IF-THEN statement on line 30 displays a dot every 100 iterations. This output confirms the progress of the program. Otherwise, you might get the impression that the program has crashed your system!

The statement on line 32 calls Rand# and supplies it with an argument of 0. This argument tells the function to return the next random number. The statement stores the random number in X. The statements on lines 34 and 35 update the summation variables SumX and SumXX.

When the FOR-NEXT loop stops iterating, the statements on lines 38 and 39 calculate the mean and standard deviation statistics. The PRINT statements on lines 43–45 display the results. The sample session indicates that the statistics come close to the theoretical values. Therefore, it is safe to conclude that the Rand# function is a good uniform random-number generator.

Now take a look at the declarations and statements in the Rand# function. The function declares the local variable LclSeed as static. The declaration uses STATIC LclSeed AS DOUBLE instead of DIM LclSeed AS DOUBLE. The statement on line 57 determines whether the value of the parameter Seed is not 0. If this condition is true, the function assigns the value of Seed to the local variable LclSeed. Thus, supplying non-zero arguments to the Rand# function reseeds the function. The statement on line 58 calculates the next random number and stores it in the local static variable LclSeed. The statement on line 59 copies the value in the static variable to the function's returned value. By using a static variable, the Rand# function retains the last random-number and uses that number to generate the next random number (for a zero argument).

Sharing Variables

QBasic enables you to share variables between the main program section and the various procedures. This language feature seems to contradict the segregation of variables that I discussed earlier in this chapter. Indeed, many programmers do not favor sharing variables because it circumvents sound structured-programming techniques. To these programmers, sharing variables reminds them of the poor and rather barbaric programming techniques of GW-BASIC. So why talk about sharing variables? First, because you should know about this QBasic language feature. Second, sharing variables has one virtue that I can think of: it speeds program execution. I recommend it only when program speed becomes really critical. Otherwise, avoid sharing variables because it fosters sloppy programming.

16

To share a variable between the main program and the other procedures, declare that variable by placing the keyword SHARED after the DIM keyword. Here are some examples:

```
DIM SHARED ArraySize AS INTEGER
DIM SHARED AnArray(1 TO 100) AS DOUBLE
```

Here is an example of a program that shares an array and a variable with its procedures. The program performs the following tasks:

1. Creates an array of integers and fills it with random numbers

2. Displays the unordered array

3. Sorts the array

4. Displays the sorted array

Listing 16.3. ADVSUB3.BAS, which shares variables between the main program section and the various procedures.

```
1: DECLARE SUB DisplayArray ()
2: DECLARE SUB SortArray ()
3: DECLARE SUB WaitAWhile ()
4: DECLARE SUB InitializeArray ()
5: REM Program that uses SHARED variables
6: REM to initialize, sort, and display the
```

continues

Listing 16.3. continued

```
 7: REM elements of an array
 8: REM
 9: ' declare constants
10: CONST ARRAY.SIZE = 15
11: ' declare variables
12: DIM SHARED IntArr(1 TO ARRAY.SIZE) AS INTEGER
13: DIM SHARED N AS INTEGER
14: DIM I AS INTEGER
15:
16: N = ARRAY.SIZE
17: CALL InitializeArray
18: CALL DisplayArray
19: CALL WaitAWhile
20: CALL SortArray
21: CALL DisplayArray
22: END
23:
24: SUB DisplayArray
25: ' display the elements of array IntArr
26:    DIM I AS INTEGER
27:
28:    CLS
29:    FOR I = 1 TO N
30:      PRINT USING "IntArr(##) = ####"; I; IntArr(I)
31:    NEXT I
32: END SUB
33:
34: SUB InitializeArray
35: ' initialize the array IntArr with random values
36:    DIM I AS INTEGER
37:
38:    ' reseed the random number generator
39:    RANDOMIZE TIMER
40:    FOR I = 1 TO N
41:      IntArr(I) = INT(RND * 1000)
42:    NEXT I
43: END SUB
44:
45: SUB SortArray
```

```
46: ' sort the array
47:  DIM I AS INTEGER
48:  DIM J AS INTEGER
49:
50:  ' loops implement the bubblesort method
51:  FOR I = 1 TO N - 1
52:    FOR J = I + 1 TO N
53:      IF IntArr(I) > IntArr(J) THEN SWAP IntArr(I), IntArr(J)
54:    NEXT J
55:  NEXT I
56: END SUB
57:
58: SUB WaitAWhile
59: ' pauses with a message
60:  DIM Char AS STRING * 1
61:
62:  PRINT
63:  PRINT "Press any key to continue"
64:  Char = INPUT$(1)
65: END SUB
```

Here is some sample output for the program in Listing 16.3. (Remember, this program generates random numbers, so your output will be different):

```
IntArr( 1) =   466
IntArr( 2) =   579
IntArr( 3) =   458
IntArr( 4) =   606
IntArr( 5) =   490
IntArr( 6) =   786
IntArr( 7) =   244
IntArr( 8) =   272
IntArr( 9) =   669
IntArr(10) =   971
IntArr(11) =   772
IntArr(12) =   686
IntArr(13) =   684
IntArr(14) =   402
IntArr(15) =   303

Press any key to continue
```

16

545

SCREEN CLEARS

```
IntArr( 1) =   244
IntArr( 2) =   272
IntArr( 3) =   303
IntArr( 4) =   402
IntArr( 5) =   458
IntArr( 6) =   466
IntArr( 7) =   490
IntArr( 8) =   579
IntArr( 9) =   606
IntArr(10) =   669
IntArr(11) =   684
IntArr(12) =   686
IntArr(13) =   772
IntArr(14) =   786
IntArr(15) =   971
```

Analysis

The program in Listing 16.3 declares the shared array `IntArr` on line 12. The program also declares the shared variable N to store the number of manipulated elements in `IntArr`. The program also declares the SUB procedures `InitializeArray`, `DisplayArray`, `SortArray`, `InitializeArray`, and `WaitAWhile`. The first three procedures initialize, display, and sort the array `IntArr`, respectively. Notice that these procedures have no parameters. Therefore, they rely on the shared array `IntArr` and the variable N to manipulate the array. The price to pay for using shared arrays is that these procedures work exclusively for the array `IntArr`. If the program was manipulating another integer array in a similar fashion, the shared array method would require duplicate routines. This overhead violates good structured programming methods, which foster the creation of general-purpose procedures.

The statement on line 16 assigns the constant `ARRAY.SIZE` to the shared variable N. You can replace the constant with a smaller value to manipulate a portion of the array `IntArr`. Lines 17–21 contain calls to the various subroutines to manipulate the array.

The SUB procedure `DisplayArray`, on lines 24–32, displays the elements of the shared array `IntArr`. The procedure uses the FOR-NEXT loop on lines 29–31 to display the first N array elements of `IntArr`. The procedure uses the shared variable N as the upper iteration limit.

The SUB procedure InitializeArray, on lines 34–43, initializes the first N elements of the shared array IntArr. The procedure uses the FOR-NEXT loop on lines 40–42 to assign random numbers to the array elements. The procedure uses the shared variable N as the upper iteration limit.

The SUB procedure SortArray, on lines 45–56, sorts the first N elements of the shared array IntArr using the bubblesort method. The nested FOR-NEXT loops on lines 51–55 use the shared variable N in the expression of the upper iteration limits.

16

Passing Array Parameters

The ADVSUB3.BAS program in Listing 16.3 shares the array IntArr between the main program section and the procedures InitializeArray, DisplayArray, and SortArray. A sounder approach for writing ADVSUB3.BAS is to pass the array IntArr and the variable N as arguments. Indeed, QBasic enables you to declare arrays that are parameters of SUB and FUNCTION procedures. To indicate that the parameter is an array, put empty parentheses after the parameter's name. This syntax tells QBasic that the parameter is an array. What about the array limits? The beauty of the QBasic syntax is that it leaves the array limits open. Consequently, you can write procedures that handle arrays of various sizes. The predefined functions LBOUND and UBOUND come in handy in tracking the limits of the array arguments. When you call a procedure and supply it with a parameter that is an array, just use the name of the array followed by empty parentheses.

Listing 16.4, ADVSUB4.BAS, passes arrays as parameters. This new version of the program performs the same basic tasks as program ADVSUB3.BAS. The main difference is that ADVSUB4.BAS uses a much sounder structured-programming approach.

Listing 16.4. ADVSUB4.BAS, which passes arrays as parameters.

```
1: DECLARE SUB InitializeArray (A() AS INTEGER, Count AS INTEGER)
2: DECLARE SUB DisplayArray (S$, A() AS INTEGER, Count AS INTEGER)
3: DECLARE SUB SortArray (A() AS INTEGER, Count AS INTEGER)
4: DECLARE SUB WaitAWhile ()
```

continues

Listing 16.4. continued

```
 5: REM Program that passes arrays as arguments
 6: REM to SUB procedures.  These procedures
 7: REM initialize, sort, and display the elements
 8: REM of an array
 9: REM
10: ' declare constants
11: CONST ARRAY.SIZE = 15
12: ' declare variables
13: DIM IntArr(1 TO ARRAY.SIZE) AS INTEGER
14: DIM Num AS INTEGER
15:
16: Num = ARRAY.SIZE
17: InitializeArray IntArr(), Num
18: DisplayArray "IntArr", IntArr(), Num
19: WaitAWhile
20: SortArray IntArr(), Num
21: DisplayArray "IntArr", IntArr(), Num
22: END
23:
24: SUB DisplayArray (S$, A() AS INTEGER, Count AS INTEGER)
25: ' display the elements of array IntArr
26:    DIM I AS INTEGER
27:    DIM N AS INTEGER
28:
29:    CLS
30:    N = UBOUND(A) - LBOUND(A) + 1
31:    IF Count < 0 OR Count > N THEN Count = N
32:    FOR I = LBOUND(A) TO LBOUND(A) + Count - 1
33:      PRINT USING "&(##) = ####"; S$; I; A(I)
34:    NEXT I
35: END SUB
36:
37: SUB InitializeArray (A() AS INTEGER, Count AS INTEGER)
38:    DIM I AS INTEGER
39:    DIM N AS INTEGER
40:
41:    ' reseed the random-number generator
42:    RANDOMIZE TIMER
43:    N = UBOUND(A) - LBOUND(A) + 1
```

```
44:    IF Count < 0 OR Count > N THEN Count = N
45:    FOR I = LBOUND(A) TO LBOUND(A) + Count - 1
46:      A(I) = INT(RND * 1000)
47:    NEXT I
48: END SUB
49:
50: SUB SortArray (A() AS INTEGER, Count AS INTEGER)
51: ' sort the array using the bubblesort method
52:    DIM I AS INTEGER
53:    DIM J AS INTEGER
54:    DIM N AS INTEGER
55:
56:    N = UBOUND(A) - LBOUND(A) + 1
57:    IF Count < 0 OR Count > N THEN Count = N
58:    ' loops which implement the bubblesort method
59:    FOR I = LBOUND(A) TO LBOUND(A) + Count - 2
60:      FOR J = I + 1 TO LBOUND(A) + Count - 1
61:        IF A(I) > A(J) THEN SWAP A(I), A(J)
62:      NEXT J
63:    NEXT I
64: END SUB
65:
66: SUB WaitAWhile
67: ' pauses and displays a message
68:    DIM Char AS STRING * 1
69:
70:    PRINT
71:    PRINT "Press any key to continue"
72:    Char = INPUT$(1)
73: END SUB
```

Here is some sample output for the program in Listing 16.4:

```
IntArr( 1) =   365
IntArr( 2) =   162
IntArr( 3) =   863
IntArr( 4) =   922
IntArr( 5) =   950
IntArr( 6) =   187
IntArr( 7) =   699
IntArr( 8) =   939
```

```
IntArr( 9) =   573
IntArr(10) =   540
IntArr(11) =   221
IntArr(12) =   870
IntArr(13) =   540
IntArr(14) =   616
IntArr(15) =   317


Press any key to continue
```

 SCREEN CLEARS

```
IntArr( 1) =   162
IntArr( 2) =   187
IntArr( 3) =   221
IntArr( 4) =   317
IntArr( 5) =   365
IntArr( 6) =   540
IntArr( 7) =   540
IntArr( 8) =   573
IntArr( 9) =   616
IntArr(10) =   699
IntArr(11) =   863
IntArr(12) =   870
IntArr(13) =   922
IntArr(14) =   939
IntArr(15) =   950
```

The program in Listing 16.4 declares the SUB procedures InitializeArray and SortArray with two parameters. The first parameter is the array A(), an array of integers. The second parameter is the integer Count, the number of elements to process. The procedure DisplayArray contains the additional parameter S$, a commenting message that appears with the array. The array-manipulating procedures work with integer arrays of different sizes—not just IntArr.

The main program section invokes the various SUB procedures on lines 17–21. Notice that the array-manipulating procedures pass the array IntArr as an argument using the syntax IntArr(). This syntax tells QBasic that you are passing an array. You don't need to specify the number of dimensions for the array. QBasic determines that information on its own.

The procedure DisplayArray appears on lines 24–35. The procedure stores the total number of array elements in the local variable N. The number of array elements is obtained by calling the LBOUND and UBOUND functions. The procedure then ensures that the value for the parameter Count is in the range of 1 to N. If not, Count is assigned the value of N. The FOR-NEXT loop on lines 32–34 iterates from LBOUND(A) to UBOUND(A) + Count - 1. The procedures InitializeArray and SortArray perform similar range checking on the number of array elements to manipulate. These array-manipulating procedures can deal, in principle, with integer arrays of any size.

Passing Matrix Parameters

QBasic does not limit parameters to single-dimensional arrays. Instead, you can pass multidimensional arrays. The declaration and parameter passing of such arrays follows the same syntax as single-dimensional arrays.

Let me present a simple example. Listing 16.5, ADVSUB5.BAS, passes multidimensional arrays to procedures. The program essentially displays and adds numerical matrices. You don't need to supply input. The program performs the following tasks:

1. Creates matrices MatA, MatB, and MatC.

2. Initializes matrices MatA and MatB by assigning random numbers to their elements.

3. Adds matrices MatA and MatB to form matrix MatC.

4. Displays the matrices MatA, MatB, and MatC.

Listing 16.5. ADVSUB5.BAS, which passes multidimensional arrays to procedures.

```
1: DECLARE SUB InitializeMatrix (Mat#(), R%, C%)
2: DECLARE FUNCTION AddMatrix% (Mat1#(), Mat2#(), Mat3#(), R%, C%)
3: DECLARE SUB ShowMatrix (MatName$, Mat#(), R%, C%)
4: REM Program which passes matrices as
5: REM arguments to procedures
6: REM
7: ' declare constants
```

continues

Advanced Subprograms

Type

Listing 16.5. continued

```
 8: CONST ROWS = 3
 9: CONST COLS = 3
10: CONST TRUE = -1
11: CONST FALSE = 0
12: ' declare variables
13: DIM MatA(1 TO ROWS, 1 TO COLS) AS DOUBLE
14: DIM MatB(1 TO ROWS, 1 TO COLS) AS DOUBLE
15: DIM MatC(1 TO ROWS, 1 TO COLS) AS DOUBLE
16:
17: CLS
18: InitializeMatrix MatA(), ROWS, COLS
19: InitializeMatrix MatB(), ROWS, COLS
20: IF AddMatrix%(MatA(), MatB(), MatC(), ROWS, COLS) = TRUE THEN
21:   ShowMatrix "Matrix A", MatA(), ROWS, COLS
22:   PRINT
23:   ShowMatrix "Matrix B", MatB(), ROWS, COLS
24:   PRINT
25:   ShowMatrix "Matrix C", MatC(), ROWS, COLS
26: ELSE
27:   PRINT
28:   PRINT "Cannot add matrices of incompatible sizes"
29: END IF
30: END
31:
32: FUNCTION AddMatrix% (Mat1#(), Mat2#(), Mat3#(), R%, C%)
33: ' add the matrices Mat#1 and Mat#2 and store the
34: ' product in Mat#3
35:   DIM I AS INTEGER
36:   DIM J AS INTEGER
37:   DIM OK AS INTEGER
38:
39:   ' check that R% and C% are within the
40:   ' limits of the three matrices
41:   OK = R% <= UBOUND(Mat1#, 1)
42:   OK = OK AND C% <= UBOUND(Mat1#, 2)
43:   OK = OK AND R% <= UBOUND(Mat2#, 1)
44:   OK = OK AND C% <= UBOUND(Mat2#, 2)
45:   OK = OK AND R% <= UBOUND(Mat3#, 1)
46:   OK = OK AND C% <= UBOUND(Mat3#, 2)
```

```
47:
48:    ' add the compatible matrices?
49:    IF OK = TRUE THEN
50:      FOR I = 1 TO R%
51:        FOR J = 1 TO C%
52:          Mat3#(I, J) = Mat1#(I, J) + Mat2#(I, J)
53:        NEXT J
54:      NEXT I
55:    END IF
56:    AddMatrix% = OK
57: END FUNCTION
58:
59: SUB InitializeMatrix (Mat#(), R%, C%)
60: ' initialize the elements in matrix Mat with
61: ' random data
62:    DIM I AS INTEGER
63:    DIM J AS INTEGER
64:
65:    ' adjust the arguments for the rows and columns, if needed
66:    IF R% > UBOUND(Mat#, 1) THEN R% = UBOUND(Mat#, 1)
67:    IF C% > UBOUND(Mat#, 2) THEN C% = UBOUND(Mat#, 2)
68:    ' reseed the random-number generator
69:    RANDOMIZE TIMER
70:    ' fill the matrix with random values
71:    FOR I = 1 TO R%
72:      FOR J = 1 TO C%
73:        Mat#(I, J) = INT(RND * 1000)
74:      NEXT J
75:    NEXT I
76: END SUB
77:
78: SUB ShowMatrix (MatName$, Mat#(), R%, C%)
79: ' display the matrix Mat
80:    DIM I AS INTEGER
81:    DIM J AS INTEGER
82:
83:    ' adjust the arguments for the rows and columns, if needed
84:    IF R% > UBOUND(Mat#, 1) THEN R% = UBOUND(Mat#, 1)
85:    IF C% > UBOUND(Mat#, 2) THEN C% = UBOUND(Mat#, 2)
86:    ' display the matrix
```

continues

Advanced Subprograms

Listing 16.5. continued

```
87:   PRINT MatName$; " is:"
88:   PRINT
89:   FOR I = 1 TO R%
90:     FOR J = 1 TO C%
91:       PRINT USING "####  "; Mat#(I, J);
92:     NEXT J
93:     PRINT
94:   NEXT I
95: END SUB
```

Here is some sample output for the program in Listing 16.5:

```
Matrix A is:

 726    908    142
 536    747    875
 400    538    669


Matrix B is:

 114    265    440
 721    402    975
 842    166    358


Matrix C is:

 840   1173    582
1257   1149   1850
1242    704   1027
```

The program in Listing 16.5 declares constants on lines 8–11. The constants ROWS and COLS define the maximum number of rows and columns for the matrices created in the program. The constants TRUE and FALSE define the Boolean values used in the program. Lines 13–15 declare the matrices MatA, MatB, and MatC. All these floating-point matrices have ROWS number of rows and COLS number of columns.

The statements on lines 18 and 19 call the SUB procedure InitializeMatrix to initialize MatA and MatB. The procedure InitializeMatrix takes three

arguments: a floating-point matrix, the number of rows, and the number of columns. The procedure calls pass the constants ROWS and COLS as the last two arguments.

The program uses the IF-THEN-ELSE statement on lines 20–29 to add and display the matrices. The tested condition determines whether the function AddMatrix% returns TRUE. If this condition is true, the program executes the statements in the THEN clause. These statements invoke the SUB procedure ShowMatrix three times to display the three matrices. Otherwise, the program executes the ELSE clause statements, which display an error message.

16

AddMatrix% adds the matrix parameters Mat1# and Mat2# to yield the matrix returned by parameter Mat3#. The parameters R% and C% pass the number of rows and columns, which must be the same value for the three matrix parameters. The function AddMatrix% returns a Boolean value. If the arguments for the three matrix parameters have the same upper bound values (I am assuming that the matrices start at index 1), the function proceeds with the matrix addition. Otherwise, the function returns FALSE.

The statements on lines 41–46 conduct a series of tests to determine whether the number of rows and columns are within the upper bounds of the three matrices. Notice that the statements on lines 42–46 use the AND operator to update the previous Boolean value of the variable OK with the Boolean value of the tested condition. The IF-THEN statements on lines 49–55 perform the matrix addition when OK stores the value defined by the constant TRUE. The procedure uses nested FOR-NEXT loops on lines 50–54. The statement on line 56 assigns the Boolean value in OK to the function's result.

The SUB procedure InitializeMatrix initializes the R% rows and C% columns of matrix Mat#. The procedure adjusts the values of the parameters R% and C% if they exceed the upper bounds of their respective dimensions. The statements on lines 69–75 reseed the random-number generator and assign random values to the elements of Mat#. The procedure uses the nested FOR-NEXT loops on lines 71–75 to perform this assignment.

The SUB procedure ShowMatrix displays the R% rows and C% columns of matrix Mat#. The parameter MatName$ passes a matrix name to the procedure. The procedure adjusts the values of the parameters R% and C% if they exceed the upper bounds of their respective dimensions. The statements on lines 87–94 display the name and the elements of matrix Mat#.

Passing Structured Parameters

QBasic supports declaring and passing parameters that are structures. The syntax for declaring and using such parameters is no different from that of other parameters, including arrays. However, when QBasic creates the DECLARE statements at the beginning of the program, it uses the type ANY when referring to a structured parameter. Why use the type ANY, and what is it anyway? QBasic uses the type ANY as a variant to represent any structure. The use of ANY in declaring a structured parameter is needed because the DECLARE statement appears before any other statement, including the ones that actually declare the structures.

Let me present an example that passes both structured variables and structured arrays. Listing 16.6 shows the program ADVSUB6.BAS, which passes these kinds of parameters. The program prompts you to enter the x- and y-coordinates for three points. The program then prompts you to enter the x- and y-coordinates for a reference point. The program determines which point is closest to the reference point. The program displays the index of the closest point and the distance between that point and the reference point.

 Listing 16.6. ADVSUB6.BAS, which declares procedures with structured parameters.

```
 1: DECLARE FUNCTION GetIndex% (Pt() AS ANY, RfPt AS ANY, N%, Sml#)
 2: REM Program which passes arrays and single
 3: REM structured variables to a function
 4: REM
 5: ' declare constants
 6: CONST MAX.POINTS = 3
 7: ' declare structure
 8: TYPE TCoord
 9:    X AS DOUBLE
10:    Y AS DOUBLE
11: END TYPE
12: ' declare variables
13: DIM Points(1 TO MAX.POINTS) AS TCoord
14: DIM RefPoint AS TCoord
```

```
15: DIM Distance AS DOUBLE
16: DIM I AS INTEGER
17:
18: CLS
19: ' get the coordinates for the array of points
20: FOR I = 1 TO MAX.POINTS
21:     PRINT "Enter the X coordinate for point #"; I;
22:     INPUT ; Points(I).X
23:     PRINT
24:     PRINT "Enter the Y coordinate for point #"; I;
25:     INPUT ; Points(I).Y
26:     PRINT
27: NEXT I
28: ' get the coordinates for the reference point
29: INPUT "Enter the X coordinate for reference point "; RefPoint.X
30: INPUT "Enter the Y coordinate for reference point "; RefPoint.Y
31: ' obtain the index of the point closest to the reference point
32: I = GetIndex%(Points(), RefPoint, MAX.POINTS, Distance)
33: ' display the results
34: PRINT
35: PRINT "Point number"; I; "is the closest to the reference point"
36: PRINT
37: PRINT "The distance between the two points is ";
38: PRINT USING "+#.####^^^^^"; Distance
39: END
40:
41: FUNCTION GetIndex% (Pt() AS TCoord, RfPt AS TCoord, N%, Sml#)
42: ' return the index of the closest point in array
43: ' Pt to the reference point RfPt
44:     DIM Dist AS DOUBLE
45:     DIM I AS INTEGER
46:     DIM J AS INTEGER
47:
48:     ' initialize the smallest distance
49:     Sml# = SQR((Pt(1).X - RfPt.X) ^ 2 + (Pt(1).Y - RfPt.Y) ^ 2)
50:     J = 1
51:     FOR I = 2 TO N%
52:         Dist = SQR((Pt(I).X - RfPt.X) ^ 2 + (Pt(I).Y - RfPt.Y) ^ 2)
53:         IF Dist < Sml# THEN
```

continues

557

Listing 16.6. continued

```
54:        J = I
55:          Sml# = Dist
56:      END IF
57:    NEXT I
58:    GetIndex% = J
59: END FUNCTION
```

Here is some sample output for the program in Listing 16.6:

```
Enter the X coordinate for point # 1 ? 1
Enter the Y coordinate for point # 1 ? 1
Enter the X coordinate for point # 2 ? 2
Enter the Y coordinate for point # 2 ? 2
Enter the X coordinate for point # 3 ? 3
Enter the Y coordinate for point # 3 ? 3
Enter the X coordinate for reference point ? 2.5
Enter the Y coordinate for reference point ? 4.7


Point number 3 is the closest to the reference point

The distance between the two points is +1.7720D+000
```

The program in Listing 16.6 contains the DECLARE statement, which uses the special type ANY with the first two structured parameters. The program declares the constant MAX.POINTS on line 6. This constant specifies the size of the structured array. Lines 8–11 contain the declaration of the TCoord structure. This structure contains two floating-point fields, X and Y, and models the coordinates of a point. Line 13 declares the structured array Points. Line 14 declares the structured variable RefPoint, which represents the reference point. Lines 15 and 16 declare the variables Distance and I, respectively.

The program uses the FOR-NEXT loop on lines 20–27 to prompt you to enter the x- and y-coordinates for the elements of the array Points. The loop uses the control variable I and iterates from 1 to MAX.POINTS. The INPUT statements on lines 29 and 30 prompt you for the x- and y-coordinates of the reference point RefPoint, respectively.

The statement on line 32 calls the function GetIndex% to obtain the index of the element in array Points that is closest to the reference point. The function

call passes the arguments Points, RefPoint, MAX.POINTS, and Distance. The first three arguments supply the function with data. The last argument reports the distance between the reference point and the closest element of Points. The statement stores the result of the function call in the variable I. The PRINT statements on lines 35–38 display the contents of the variables I and Distance.

The program declares the FUNCTION procedure GetIndex% on lines 41–59. The first parameter, Pt, is an array of TCoord structures. The second parameter, RfPt, is a single TCoord structure. The third parameter, N%, specifies the number of elements in Pt to examine. The last parameter, Sml#, reports the distance between the reference point and the closest element in Pt.

The search for that point starts on line 49, where the procedure assigns the distance between Pt(1) and RfPt to the parameter Sml#. The statement on line 50 assigns 1, the index of the first point, to the local variable J. The FOR-NEXT loop on lines 51–57 examines the elements Pt(2) to Pt(N%) to determine the closest point to the reference point. The loop calculates the distance between Pt(I) and RfPt on line 52, and stores that distance in the variable Dist. If the value of Dist is less than the current value of parameter Sml#, the procedure assigns the value of I (the loop control variable) to J, and Dist to Sml#. The function returns the index of the closest point, stored in variable J.

Recursive Functions

Structured programming encourages you to implement tasks of different levels using SUB and FUNCTION procedures. In addition, it is a good programming practice to have multiple levels of procedures where high-level procedures call other low-level procedures. You may ask, "Can a procedure call itself?" The answer is yes. The technique of a procedure calling itself is called *recursion*. Programmers often compare recursion with a picture of a person looking at a smaller picture of himself, looking at an even smaller picture of himself, and so on. You can think of recursion as a kind of iteration that serves to perform a task (or return a function value) by simplifying the arguments with each recursive call.

Recursion has its rules and overhead. First, when you write a recursive procedure, you must include a tested condition that stops the procedure from calling itself further. Otherwise, you are guaranteed to overflow the QBasic resources. Every time you make a recursive call, you force QBasic to store the contents of the current call in an area of the memory called the *stack*. Because the stack has limited memory, you risk running out of stack space and raising a runtime error. Therefore, keep in mind that recursive calls do not have open-ended resources.

DO use recursive calls if they are relatively limited and significantly simplify the program.

DON'T use recursive calls when you can easily perform the same tasks using a fixed or conditional loop.

Here's a program that uses a recursive function to calculate factorials. A factorial of a number N is defined as:

```
N! = N * (N - 1) * (N - 2) * ... * 3 * 2 * 1
```

You can also write the factorial using the recursive equation

```
N! = N * (N - 1)!
```

because

```
(N - 1)! = (N - 1) * (N - 2)!
(N - 2)! = (N - 2) * (N - 3)!
```

and so on. Listing 16.7, ADVSUB7.BAS, uses a recursive factorial function. The program prompts you to enter an integer between 1 and 37. The program also asks you whether you want to display a list of function calls that identify the arguments of the recursive function. The function then displays the list of function calls (if you answered the last prompt affirmatively) and the factorial value.

Listing 16.7. **ADVSUB7.BAS, which uses a recursive factorial function.**

```
1: DECLARE FUNCTION Factorial# (I AS INTEGER)
2: REM Program which issues a recursive
3: REM call to a FUNCTION procedure to
4: REM calculate a factorial
```

```
 5: REM
 6: ' declare constant
 7: CONST MAX.VAL = 37
 8: CONST TRUE = -1
 9: CONST FALSE = NOT TRUE
10: ' declare variable
11: DIM N AS INTEGER
12: DIM FactorialVal AS DOUBLE
13: DIM SHARED Debug AS INTEGER
14: DIM C AS STRING * 1
15:
16: CLS
17: DO
18:    PRINT "Enter an integer between 1 and"; MAX.VAL;
19:    INPUT N
20: LOOP UNTIL N > 0 AND N <= MAX.VAL
21: PRINT
22: DO
23:    PRINT "Trace the calls to the recursive function? (Y/N) ";
24:    C = INPUT$(1)
25:    PRINT C
26:    C = UCASE$(C)
27: LOOP UNTIL C = "Y" OR C = "N"
28: ' set debug flag
29: Debug = C = "Y"
30: IF Debug = TRUE THEN PRINT
31: ' calculate factorial
32: FactorialVal = Factorial#(N)
33: PRINT
34: PRINT USING "##& = +#.######^^^^"; N; "!"; FactorialVal
35: END
36:
37: FUNCTION Factorial# (I AS INTEGER)
38: ' recursive function which calculates
39: ' the factorial value
40:
41:    ' display current argument
42:    IF Debug = TRUE THEN
43:      PRINT USING "In FUNCTION Factorial%(##)"; I
44:    END IF
```

continues

Listing 16.7. continued

```
45:
46:   IF I > 1 THEN
47:     ' make the recursive call
48:     Factorial# = I * Factorial#(I - 1)
49:   ELSE
50:     Factorial# = 1
51:   END IF
52: END FUNCTION
```

Here is some sample output for the program in Listing 16.7:

```
Enter an integer between 1 and 37 ? 5

Trace the calls to the recursive function? (Y/N) y

In FUNCTION Factorial%( 5)
In FUNCTION Factorial%( 4)
In FUNCTION Factorial%( 3)
In FUNCTION Factorial%( 2)
In FUNCTION Factorial%( 1)

  5! = +1.200000D+002
```

The program in Listing 16.7 declares three constants on lines 7–9. The program also declares variables on lines 11–14. Notice that line 13 declares the shared variable Debug. This type of declaration is ideal when you want the recursive function calls to access the same data in the main program section.

The DO-UNTIL loop on lines 17–20 prompts you to enter an integer between 1 and 37 (defined by the MAX.VAL constant). The DO-UNTIL loop on lines 22–27 asks you whether you want to trace the recursive calls. You need to press the Y or N key to answer this prompt. The statement on line 29 sets the Boolean value in the variable Debug.

The statement on line 32 calls the recursive function Factorial# and passes the argument N. The statement assigns the function result to the variable FactorialVal. The PRINT statement on line 34 displays the values in N and FactorialVal.

The program declares the recursive function Factorial# on lines 37–52. The function has the single integer-typed parameter I. The IF-THEN statement on line 42 determines whether the shared variable Debug contains TRUE. If this condition is true, the function displays the value of I.

The IF-THEN-ELSE statement on lines 46–51 plays an important role in returning the function's result. The tested condition determines whether the parameter I is greater than 1. If this condition is true, the function makes a recursive call, passing the argument I - 1. Otherwise, the function returns the value of 1. The statement in the ELSE clause ensures that the recursive calls to function Factorial# come to an end.

16

Now that I have discussed function Factorial#, let me present Figure 16.2, which shows a sample recursion for the Factorial#(3) function call.

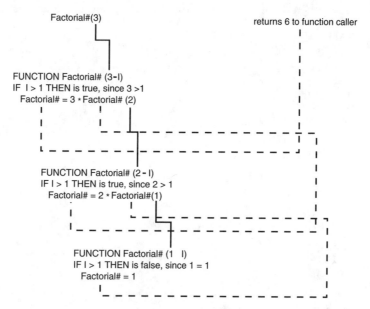

Figure 16.2. The recursive calls for Factorial#(3).

Exiting Procedures

QBasic enables you to exit functions and procedures using the EXIT statements. QBasic defines a special EXIT statement for each of the DEF FN function, SUB procedure, and FUNCTION procedure. The EXIT statements allows you to exit a function or procedure early in the following cases:

☐ The arguments are invalid.

☐ The arguments correspond to special or trivial conditions that do not require executing the bulk of the statements.

The EXIT Statement

The general syntax for the exiting functions and procedures is:

```
EXIT DEF        ' exit DEF FNname
EXIT SUB        ' EXIT SUB procedure
EXIT FUNCTION   ' EXIT FUNCTION procedure
```

Examples:

```
DEF FNSquare#(X#)
  FNSquare# = -1
  IF X# < 0 THEN EXIT DEF
  FNSquare# = SQR(X#)
END DEF


SUB INCR(I%)
  IF I% = 32767 THEN EXIT SUB
  I% = I% + 1
END SUB


FUNCTION Square#(X#)
  Square# = -1
  IF X# < 0 THEN EXIT FUNCTION
  Square# = SQR(X#)
END FUNCTION
```

<table>
<tr><td>
DO use the <code>EXIT</code> statement, when appropriate, to avoid nested <code>IF</code> statements.

DON'T forget to supply the function with a return value when leaving that function with an <code>EXIT</code> statement.
</td></tr>
</table>

Let me present an example that modifies a previous program in this chapter and uses the <code>EXIT</code> statement. Recall that ADVSUB5.BAS, in Listing 16.5, contains the following lines in function <code>AddMatrix%</code>:

```
41:    OK = R% <= UBOUND(Mat1#, 1)
42:    OK = OK AND C% <= UBOUND(Mat1#, 2)
43:    OK = OK AND R% <= UBOUND(Mat2#, 1)
44:    OK = OK AND C% <= UBOUND(Mat2#, 2)
45:    OK = OK AND R% <= UBOUND(Mat3#, 1)
46:    OK = OK AND C% <= UBOUND(Mat3#, 2)
```

These lines perform a series of logical tests and update the variable OK. Once a statement assigns 0 (that is, FALSE) to OK, the remaining statements in this list cannot alter that value. However, these statements do not take advantage of this fact and exit early. I modified the ADVSUB5.BAS program to create ADVSUB8.BAS, shown in Listing 16.8. The two programs perform the same basic tasks of creating, initializing, adding, and displaying matrices.

 Listing 16.8. ADVSUB8.BAS, which exits a function using the EXIT FUNCTION statement.

```
1: DECLARE SUB InitializeMatrix (Mat#(), R%, C%)
2: DECLARE FUNCTION AddMatrix% (Mat1#(), Mat2#(), Mat3#(), R%, C%)
3: DECLARE SUB ShowMatrix (MatName$, Mat#(), R%, C%)
4: REM Program which passes matrices as
5: REM arguments to procedures
6: REM
7: ' declare constants
8: CONST ROWS = 3
9: CONST COLS = 3
```

continues

Listing 16.8. continued

```
10: CONST TRUE = -1
11: CONST FALSE = 0
12: ' declare variables
13: DIM MatA(1 TO ROWS, 1 TO COLS) AS DOUBLE
14: DIM MatB(1 TO ROWS, 1 TO COLS) AS DOUBLE
15: DIM MatC(1 TO ROWS, 1 TO COLS) AS DOUBLE
16: DIM I AS INTEGER
17: DIM J AS INTEGER
18:
19: CLS
20: InitializeMatrix MatA(), ROWS, COLS
21: InitializeMatrix MatB(), ROWS, COLS
22: IF AddMatrix%(MatA(), MatB(), MatC(), ROWS, COLS) = TRUE THEN
23:    ShowMatrix "Matrix A", MatA(), ROWS, COLS
24:    PRINT
25:    ShowMatrix "Matrix B", MatB(), ROWS, COLS
26:    PRINT
27:    ShowMatrix "Matrix C", MatC(), ROWS, COLS
28: ELSE
29:    PRINT
30:    PRINT "Cannot add matrices of incompatible sizes"
31: END IF
32: END
33:
34: FUNCTION AddMatrix% (Mat1#(), Mat2#(), Mat3#(), R%, C%)
35: ' add the matrices Mat#1 and Mat#2 and store the
36: ' product in Mat#3
37:    DIM I AS INTEGER
38:    DIM J AS INTEGER
39:    DIM OK AS INTEGER
40:
41:    ' set default function result
42:    AddMatrix% = FALSE
43:    ' check that R% and C% are within the
44:    ' limits of the three matrices
45:    OK = R% <= UBOUND(Mat1#, 1)
46:    IF OK = FALSE THEN EXIT FUNCTION
47:    OK = OK AND C% <= UBOUND(Mat1#, 2)
```

```
48:    IF OK = FALSE THEN EXIT FUNCTION
49:    OK = OK AND R% <= UBOUND(Mat2#, 1)
50:    IF OK = FALSE THEN EXIT FUNCTION
51:    OK = OK AND C% <= UBOUND(Mat2#, 2)
52:    IF OK = FALSE THEN EXIT FUNCTION
53:    OK = OK AND R% <= UBOUND(Mat3#, 1)
54:    IF OK = FALSE THEN EXIT FUNCTION
55:    OK = OK AND C% <= UBOUND(Mat3#, 2)
56:    IF OK = FALSE THEN EXIT FUNCTION
57:
58:    ' loop to add the matrix elements
59:    FOR I = 1 TO R%
60:      FOR J = 1 TO C%
61:        Mat3#(I, J) = Mat1#(I, J) + Mat2#(I, J)
62:      NEXT J
63:    NEXT I
64:    ' return function value
65:    AddMatrix% = TRUE
66: END FUNCTION
67:
68: SUB InitializeMatrix (Mat#(), R%, C%)
69: ' initialize the elements in matrix Mat with
70: ' random data
71:    DIM I AS INTEGER
72:    DIM J AS INTEGER
73:
74:    ' adjust the arguments for the rows and columns, if needed
75:    IF R% > UBOUND(Mat#, 1) THEN R% = UBOUND(Mat#, 1)
76:    IF C% > UBOUND(Mat#, 2) THEN C% = UBOUND(Mat#, 2)
77:    ' reseed the random-number generator
78:    RANDOMIZE TIMER
79:    ' fill the matrix with random values
80:    FOR I = 1 TO R%
81:      FOR J = 1 TO C%
82:        Mat#(I, J) = INT(RND * 1000)
83:      NEXT J
84:    NEXT I
85: END SUB
86:
87: SUB ShowMatrix (MatName$, Mat#(), R%, C%)
88: ' display the matrix Mat
```

continues

Listing 16.8. continued

```
89:    DIM I AS INTEGER
90:    DIM J AS INTEGER
91:
92:    ' adjust the arguments for the rows and columns, if needed
93:    IF R% > UBOUND(Mat#, 1) THEN R% = UBOUND(Mat#, 1)
94:    IF C% > UBOUND(Mat#, 2) THEN C% = UBOUND(Mat#, 2)
95:    ' display the matrix
96:    PRINT MatName$; " is:"
97:    PRINT
98:    FOR I = 1 TO R%
99:      FOR J = 1 TO C%
100:       PRINT USING "####  "; Mat#(I, J);
101:     NEXT J
102:     PRINT
103:   NEXT I
104: END SUB
```

Here is some sample output for the program in Listing 16.8:

```
Matrix A is:

437    477    326
313    431    775
840    797    158

Matrix B is:

 29    615    109
557    363    686
929    250     76

Matrix C is:

 466   1092    435
 870    794   1461
1769   1047    234
```

The highlight of the program in Listing 16.8 is lines 45–56. These lines intermittently update the Boolean value in the variable OK and then test to exit the function if OK is FALSE. Therefore, if the function determines that a row or column value is out-of-range, it does not test the remaining conditions. Notice that the function assigns the pessimistic default value of FALSE to the function's name on line 42. If the row and column values are valid, the function performs the matrix addition and assigns TRUE to the function's name on line 65.

16

Summary

This chapter discussed advanced topics concerning SUB and FUNCTION procedures. Today you learned the following:

☐ The explicit declaration of local variables in SUB and FUNCTION procedures involves using the DIM statement. The local variables exist only while the procedure is executing.

☐ Sharing variables among the main program and procedures requires declaring these variables with the DIM SHARED statement. All procedures have access to shared variables.

☐ Declaring static variables in SUB and FUNCTION procedures involves using the STATIC declaration statement. This statement declares variables that retain their data between procedure calls.

☐ Passing an array as a parameter to SUB and FUNCTION procedures requires that you declare the array parameter by enclosing empty parentheses after the array's name. Passing an array argument also requires enclosing empty parentheses after the array's name. The LBOUND and UBOUND functions allow the procedure to determine the bounds of the array arguments.

☐ Passing a matrix as a parameter to SUB and FUNCTION procedures requires that you declare the matrix parameter by placing empty parentheses after the name of the matrix. Passing a matrix argument also requires placing empty parentheses after the name of the matrix. The LBOUND and UBOUND functions allow the procedure to determine the bounds of the matrix arguments.

☐ Passing structures to SUB and FUNCTION procedures is very similar to passing predefined single or array parameters.

☐ Recursive SUB and FUNCTION procedures call themselves. Such calls must be limited and controlled by conditions that end the recursive calls.

☐ Exiting DEF FN functions, SUB procedures, and FUNCTION procedures involves using the EXIT DEF, EXIT SUB, and EXIT FUNCTION statements, respectively. These EXIT statements enable you to leave a function or procedure because of invalid data or (by contrast) special effort-saving values.

Q&A

Q. Can a procedure redimension an array?

A. Yes it can. However, you can only redimension a dynamic array.

Q. How could I improve the function FofX in program ADVSUB1.BAS (Listing 16.1)?

A. The function can be improved by replacing the local array C with the array parameter C. This parameter passes the coefficients of the polynomial to the function FofX. Consequently, the program reads these coefficients into a main-program-level array and passes these coefficients as arguments to the new version of the function FofX. Here is the new version of the function:

```
FUNCTION FofX(X AS DOUBLE, PolyOrder AS INTEGER, C#())
' Function calculates the value of the polynomial
' at the value X
  DIM Sum AS DOUBLE
  DIM I  AS INTEGER

  ' calculate the value of the polynomial
  Sum = C(PolyOrder) * X
  FOR I = PolyOrder - 1 TO 1 STEP -1
    Sum = (Sum + C(I)) * X
  NEXT I
  Sum = Sum + C(0)
  FofX = Sum
END FUNCTION
```

Workshop

The Workshop provides quiz questions to help you solidify your understanding of the material covered and exercises to provide you with experience in using what you've learned. Try to understand the quiz and exercise answers before continuing on to the next chapter. Answers are provided in Appendix B, "Answers."

16

Quiz

1. Where is the error in the following FUNCTION procedure?

```
FUNCTION Factorial#(N%)
  DIM I AS INTEGER
  DIM Product AS DOUBLE

  IF N% < 0 THEN EXIT FUNCTION
  Product = 1
  FOR I = 2 TO N%
    Product = I * Product
  NEXT I
  Factorial# = Product
END FUNCTION
```

2. Where is the error in the following function?

```
FUNCTION Factorial# (I AS INTEGER)
' recursive function which calculates
' the factorial value
  IF I > 1 THEN
    ' make the recursive call
    Factorial# = I * Factorial#(I)
  ELSE
    Factorial# = 1
  END IF
END FUNCTION
```

3. True or false: The function `Factorial1#` is better than `Factorial2#`.

```
FUNCTION Factorial1# (I AS INTEGER)
' recursive function which calculates
' the factorial value
 DIM Product AS DOUBLE
 DIM J AS INTEGER
 Product = 1
 FOR J = 1 TO I
     Product = J * Product
 NEXT J
  Factorial1# = Product
END FUNCTION

FUNCTION Factorial2# (I AS INTEGER)
' recursive function which calculates
' the factorial value
  IF I > 1 THEN
    ' make the recursive call
    Factorial2# = I * Factorial2#(I - 1)
  ELSE
    Factorial2# = 1
  END IF
END FUNCTION
```

Exercises

1. Write the program ADVSUB9.BAS, which implements a recursive integer-power function. The pseudocode for the function is:

Function `PowerOf` has the parameters `Base` (a float) and `Exponent` (an integer).
   1. If `Exponent` is 0, then `PowerOf` returns 1.
   2. Otherwise, if `Exponent` is 1, then `PowerOf` returns `Base`.
   3. Otherwise, if `Exponent` is an even number, then `PowerOf` returns the square of `PowerOf(Base, Exponent \ 2)`.
   4. Otherwise, `PowerOf` returns the square of `Base` * `PowerOf(Base, Exponent \ 2)`.

You will need to declare a function that returns the square of floating-point numbers. The main program should prompt you to enter a non-zero base number and an exponent of at least 2.

2. Write the program ADVSUB10.BAS, which essentially sorts an array of points according to their distances from the origin (0, 0). The following data type represents the individual point:

```
TYPE TCoord
   X AS SINGLE        ' X coordinate
   Y AS SINGLE        ' Y coordinate
   OrgDist AS SINGLE  ' distance from origin
END TYPE
```

16

The program should perform the following tasks:
   1. Prompt you to enter 5 points
   2. Display the points you entered
   3. Sort the points according to the field `OrgDist`
   4. Display the sorted points

DAY
17

Advanced String Manipulation

On Day 5, "String Manipulation," I introduced you to the basic string manipulating functions. In this chapter I cover more advanced string functions and topics. The latter includes deleting and replacing characters in strings using the MID$ function because QBasic does not have predefined functions for these tasks. Today you learn about the following topics:

☐ Deleting substrings using the MID$ function

☐ Replacing substrings using the MID$ function

☐ Creating strings from smaller strings using the SPACE$ and STRING$ functions

☐ Removing leading and trailing spaces in a string using the LTRIM$ and RTRIM$ functions

☐ Getting and setting the date and time using the DATE$ and TIME$ functions and commands

Deleting Substrings

Although QBasic provides you with various functions to manipulate strings, it does not offer a function to delete parts of a string. However, the missing character deletion function can be emulated using the MID$ function. Consider the string variable StrVar, which contains N characters. To delete M characters from StrVar, starting at the character number I, use the following general statement:

```
StrVar = MID$(StrVar, 1, I - 1) + MID$(StrVar, I + M)
```

Figure 17.1 shows the MID$ function deleting 3 characters inside the string S, which contains "QuickBasic", starting at character 4.

The general form works by extracting the undeleted leading and trailing characters of StrVar. The statement assigns the updated contents back to variable StrVar.

You might ask, "what if the values of I and M end up either deleting the first or last character of StrVar? Would the statement not work?" The answer is no; the MID$ function works in such a way that it succeeds in providing the correct string even for these two special cases. Consider the case when I is 1. This value transforms the call to the first MID$ function into MID$(StrVar, 1, 0), which returns an empty string. The call to the second MID$ function becomes

MID$(StrVar, 1 + M). This function call returns the trailing string characters of StrVar, starting with the character at index 1 + M. Figure 17.2 illustrates deleting 3 characters from the string S, which contains "QuickBasic", starting with the first character.

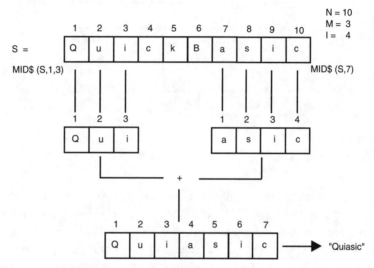

Figure 17.1. Deleting 3 characters inside the string S, which contains "QuickBasic", starting with character 4.

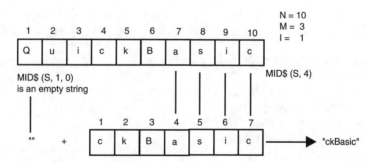

Figure 17.2. Deleting 3 characters inside the string S, which contains "QuickBasic", starting with the first character.

Now consider the other extreme case, where you end up deleting to the end of a string. If the value of M is equal to or greater than N, the number of characters in StrVar, the second call to MID$ returns an empty string. Consequently, the first call to MID$ assigns the first I - 1 characters to StrVar. Figure 17.3 illustrates deleting 3 characters inside the string S, which contains "QuickBasic", starting with the character 8.

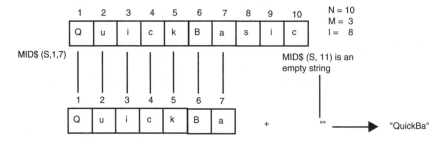

Figure 17.3. Deleting 3 characters inside the string S, which contains "QuickBasic", starting with the character 8.

Let's look at an example that uses the MID$ function to delete characters in a string. Listing 17.1, STRING12.BAS, illustrates the method in question. The program prompts you to enter a string, the index of the first deleted character, and the number of deleted characters. The program then displays a character ruler, and the string you entered before and after the program removes its characters.

Listing 17.1. STRING12.BAS, which deletes the characters in a string using the MID$ function.

```
 1: REM Program that deletes strings
 2: REM
 3: ' declare the program variables
 4: DIM AStr AS STRING
 5: DIM Start AS INTEGER
 6: DIM Count AS INTEGER
 7: DIM Q AS STRING
 8:
 9: CLS
10: ' assign the double-quote character to variable Q
11: Q = CHR$(34)
12: INPUT "Enter a string : ", AStr
13: INPUT "Enter the index of the first deleted character"; Start
```

```
14: INPUT "Enter the number of characters to delete"; Count
15: PRINT
16: PRINT "          1         2         3         4         5"
17: PRINT " 12345678901234567890123456789012345678901234567890"
18: PRINT
19: PRINT "String before deletion is:"
20: PRINT Q; AStr; Q
21: AStr = MID$(AStr, 1, Start - 1) + MID$(AStr, Start + Count)
22: PRINT "String after deletion is:"
23: PRINT Q; AStr; Q
24: END
```

Here is a sample output for the program in Listing 17.1:

```
Enter a string : He said he saw it there
Enter the index of the first deleted character? 3
Enter the number of characters to delete? 19


          1         2         3         4         5
 12345678901234567890123456789012345678901234567890

String before deletion is:
"He said he saw it there"
String after deletion is:
"Here"
```

The program in Listing 17.1 declares its variables on lines 4–7. The INPUT statement on line 12 prompts you to enter a string and saves your input in the variable AStr. The INPUT statements on lines 13 and 14 prompt you to enter the index of the first deleted character and the number of deleted characters. The program saves the input of lines 13 and 14 in the variables Start and Count. The PRINT statements on lines 16 and 17 display the character ruler. On line 19 the program displays text that indicates the subsequent output represents the input string with its characters intact. The PRINT statement on line 20 displays the contents of AStr. On line 21 the program calls MID$ twice to delete the substring. The line also assigns the updated string to AStr. On line 22 the program displays text that indicates the subsequent output represents the input string after the removal of some of its characters. The PRINT statement on line 23 displays the new contents of AStr.

17

Replacing Substrings

Essentially, QBasic provides the MID$ statement to overwrite the characters of a string. However, the MID$ statement does not alter the size of the string it works on. This inflexibility makes the straightforward use of the MID$ statement unsuitable for operations that find and replace text in a string. Such operations often alter the size of the processed string because the sizes of the search and replacement strings are not equal.

Consider the string variable StrVar, which contains N characters. To replace the characters defined by FindStr (which is M characters long) with the characters defined by ReplStr, use the following general statements:

```
M = LEN(FindStr)
I = INSTR(StrVar, FindStr)
StrVar = MID$(StrVar, 1, I - 1) + ReplStr + MID$(StrVar, I + M)
```

These general statements expand on the method of deleting characters in a string by inserting the characters of the replacement string. Keep in mind that the above method replaces only the first occurrence of FindStr in StrVar. To replace all other possible occurrences you need to repeat the process using a loop.

Let's look at a demonstration program. Listing 17.2, STRING13.BAS, replaces characters in a string by using the QBasic functions MID$ and INSTR. The program prompts you to enter the main string, the search string, and the replacement string. The program displays the main string before and after changing its characters.

Listing 17.2. STRING13.BAS, which replaces characters in a string by using the QBasic functions MID$ and INSTR.

```
1: REM Program that replaces strings by using
2: REM the INSTR function with the MID$ statement
3: ' declare the program variables
4: DIM S AS STRING
5: DIM Find AS STRING
6: DIM Replace AS STRING
7: DIM Start AS INTEGER
8: DIM Count AS INTEGER
9: DIM Q AS STRING
```

```
10:
11: CLS
12: ' assign the double-quote character to variable Q
13: Q = CHR$(34)
14: INPUT "Enter the main string : ", S
15: INPUT "Enter string to find in the main string : ", Find
16: INPUT "Enter string to replace in the main string : ", Replace
17: Start = INSTR(S, Find)
18: '****************** NOTICE *******************************
19: '* This statement prevents a runtime error if the string  *
20: '* in variable Find has no match in variable S.  The      *
21: '* price to pay for eliminating the runtime error is      *
22: '* that the program produces the wrong text change!       *
23: '*******************************************************
24: ' assign 1 to Start if function INSTR assigned 0 to Start
25: Start = Start - (Start = 0)
26: Count = LEN(Find)
27: PRINT
28: PRINT "          1         2         3         4         5"
29: PRINT " 12345678901234567890123456789012345678901234567890"
30: PRINT
31: PRINT "String before change is:"
32: PRINT Q; S; Q
33: S = MID$(S, 1, Start - 1) + Replace + MID$(S, Start + Count)
34: PRINT "String after change is:"
35: PRINT Q; S; Q
36: END
```

17

Here is a sample output for the program in Listing 17.2:

```
Enter the main string : I program with QuickBasic at work
Enter string to find in the main string : QuickBasic
Enter string to replace in the main string : QBasic


          1         2         3         4         5
 12345678901234567890123456789012345678901234567890

String before change is:
"I program with QuickBasic at work"
String after change is:
"I program with QBasic at work"
```

The program in Listing 17.2 declares its variable on lines 4–9. The INPUT statement on line 14 prompts you to enter the main string and stores your input in the variable S. The INPUT statement on line 15 prompts you to enter the search string and stores your input in the variable Find. The INPUT statement on line 16 prompts you to enter the replacement string and stores your input in the variable Replace. On line 17 the program uses INSTR to locate Find in variable S.

 Note: To ensure that Start does not contain 0 (the value returned by INSTR when it does not find the search string in the main string), I included the assignment statement of line 25. This statement uses a simple programing trick that ensures assigning a positive value to Start. Here is how it works. If line 17 already assigns a positive value to Start, the expression (Start = 0) is false and yields 0. Consequently, the value in Start is reassigned to itself. However, if line 17 assigns 0 to Start, the expression (Start = 0) is true and yields −1. Consequently, the mathematical term -(Start = 0) produces the value 1, which is assigned to Start.

The assignment statement on line 26 assigns the size of the search string to the variable Count. The PRINT statements on lines 28 and 29 display the character ruler. On line 31 the program displays text that indicates the subsequent output represents the main string, as you entered it. The PRINT statement on line 32 displays the contents of variable S. On line 33 the program makes the replacement using two MID$ function calls and the replacement string, Replace, to change the characters in string variable S. On line 34 the program displays text that indicates the subsequent output represents the new main string after replacing some of its characters. The PRINT statement on line 35 displays the new contents of the main string.

Creating Strings from Smaller Strings

As you advance in using strings in your own QBasic programs, you often will find the need to create strings that either contain multiple spaces or other characters. QBasic provides the functions SPACE$ and STRING$ for this purpose.

The *SPACE$* Function

The SPACE$ function permits you to create a string that is made up of multiple spaces. This function is useful when you need to pad strings or create a string that centers text.

The **SPACE$** Function

The general syntax for the SPACE$ function is

```
SPACE$(count)
```

The *count* parameter specifies the number of spaces in the string created by SPACE$. The values for *count* can range from 0 to 32,767. Supplying 0 to SPACE$ produces an empty string.

Examples:

```
S$ = SPACE$(10) ' S$ = "          "

T$ = "Hello World"
' padding with leading spaces to display centered string
PRINT SPACE$(40 - LEN(T$) / 2); T$
```

17

Take a look at an example. Listing 17.3, STRING16.BAS, illustrates using SPACE$. I modified STRING13.BAS, shown in Listing 5.12, to use the SPACE$ function. The program requires no input from you. It displays the following items:

☐ The centered title "SPACE$ Demo Program".

☐ A character ruler.

☐ The string "Here, there, and everywhere".

☐ The "ere" search string.

☐ The carat character (the ^ symbol), which appears below the first character of the scanned string that matches the search string.

Listing 17.3. **STRING16.BAS, which illustrates using SPACE$.**

```
 1: REM Program that tests the SPACE$ function
 2: REM
 3: CONST TITLE = "SPACE$ Demo Program"
 4: ' declare the program variables
 5: DIM AString AS STRING
 6: DIM SearchString AS STRING
 7: DIM Start AS INTEGER
 8: DIM I AS INTEGER
 9: DIM J AS INTEGER
10: DIM Q AS STRING
11:
12: CLS
13: ' assign the double-quote character to variable Q
14: Q = CHR$(34)
15: AString = "Here, there, and everywhere"
16: SearchString = "ere"
17: PRINT SPACE$(40 - LEN(TITLE) / 2); TITLE
18: PRINT
19: PRINT "          1         2         3         4         5"
20: PRINT "12345678901234567890123456789012345678901234567890"
21: ' search from the beginning of string AString
22: I = INSTR(AString, SearchString)
23: PRINT AString; " <-- Main string"
24: PRINT SPACE$(I - 1); "^";
25: ' save the old value of I in J
26: J = I
27: Start = 3
28: I = INSTR(Start, AString, SearchString)
29: PRINT SPACE$(I - J - 1); "^";
30: ' save the old value of I in J
31: J = I
32: Start = 10
33: I = INSTR(Start, AString, SearchString)
34: PRINT SPACE$(I - J - 1); "^"
35: PRINT Q; SearchString; Q; " <--- Search string"
36: END
```

Here is a sample output for the program in Listing 17.3:

```
                          SPACE$ Demo Program

            1         2         3         4         5
   12345678901234567890123456789012345678901234567890
   Here, there, and everywhere <-- Main string
   ^       ^                  ^

   "ere" <--- Search string
```

The program in Listing 17.3 declares the constant TITLE on line 3. Lines 4–10 contain the declarations of the program variables. On line 15 the program assigns the string literal "Here, there, and everywhere" to AString. On line 16 the program assigns the string literal "ere" to SearchString. Line 17 contains a PRINT statement that displays the centered title. Lines 19 and 20 display the character ruler.

The string search begins after line 21. The statement on line 22 invokes INSTR and passes the strings AString and SearchString. Consequently, this call to INSTR begins searching for SearchString at the first character of AString. The statement assigns the result of INSTR to I. Line 23 contains a PRINT statement that displays the variable AString. On Line 24 the program uses a PRINT statement with the SPACE$ function to place the carat under character 2 in AString. Line 26 assigns the value in variable I to variable J. On line 27 the program assigns the value 3 (which is greater than 2, the current value in I) to Start. The statement on line 28 calls INSTR and passes the values in Start, AString, and SearchString. This function call causes the search to begin at the third character in AString. The function INSTR returns 9, the index where the second occurrence of SearchString in AString begins. The PRINT statement displays the carat under character number 9 in AString. Notice that the call to function SPACE$ uses the values in I and J to append the correct number of spaces to the current line.

The rest of the program repeats the steps on lines 26–29. On line 32 the program assigns 10 (one value higher than the result returned by the last call to INSTR) to the variable Start. This time, the function INSTR returns 25. Consequently, the PRINT statement on line 34 displays the carat under the character number 25 in AString.

The *STRING$* Function

The STRING$ function represents a more general and slightly more versatile version of the SPACE$ function. STRING$ enables you to create a string that repeats a single-character pattern.

Syntax

The STRING$ Function

There are two forms of the STRING$ function:

```
STRING$(count, stringExpression)
```

and

```
STRING$(count, numericExpression)
```

The *count* parameter specifies the size of the string created by the STRING$ function. The values for the *count* parameter range from 0 to 32767. Supplying a value of 0 to the STRING$ function produces an empty string. The *stringExpression* parameter is either a string literal, string constant, string variable, string function, or an expression that contains these different components. The STRING$ function uses only the first character in the *stringExpression*. The *numericExpression* parameter is either a numeric constant, a named constant, a variable with a numeric type, a numeric function, or a numeric expression. The STRING$ uses the integer part of the *numericExpression* as the ASCII code for the character to duplicate.

Figure 17.4 shows the STRING$("QBasic", 3) function call, which creates the string "QQQ". Figure 17.5 shows the STRING$(81, 3) function call, which creates the string "QQQ".

Examples:

```
S$ = STRING$(10, " ") ' S$ = "          "
V$ = STRING$(10, " +") ' V$ = "          "
T$ = STRING$(3, 65) ' T$ stores "AAA"
```

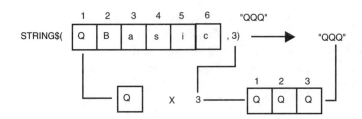

Figure 17.4. The STRING$("QBasic",3) function call creates the string "QQQ."

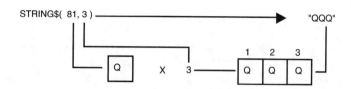

Figure 17.5. The STRING$(81, 3) function call creates the string "QQQ".

Listing 17.4, STRING17.BAS, uses the STRING$ function to create character patterns. The program prompts you for the following information:

☐ The basic character-pattern string.

☐ The number of times to duplicate the character-pattern string.

☐ The ASCII code for the character pattern.

☐ The number of times to duplicate the ASCII code-based character-pattern.

The program displays a character ruler and the strings created using the two forms of STRING$.

 Listing 17.4. STRING17.BAS, which uses the STRING$ function to create character patterns.

```
1: REM Program that tests the STRING$ function
2: REM
3: ' declare the program variables
4: DIM CharPattern AS STRING
5: DIM Ascii AS INTEGER
6: DIM Count1 AS INTEGER
7: DIM Count2 AS INTEGER
8: DIM Q AS STRING
9:
10: CLS
11: ' assign the double-quote character to variable Q
12: Q = CHR$(34)
13: INPUT "Enter a character : ", CharPattern
14: INPUT "Enter number of times to repeat the above pattern"; Count1
```

continues

Listing 17.4. continued

```
15: INPUT "Enter an ASCII code : ", Ascii
16: INPUT "Enter number of times to repeat the code"; Count2
17: PRINT
18: PRINT "         1         2         3         4         5"
19: PRINT " 12345678901234567890123456789012345678901234567890"
20: ' use the first form of the STRING$ function
21: PRINT Q; STRING$(Count1, CharPattern); Q
22: ' use the second form of the STRING$ function
23: PRINT Q; STRING$(Count2, Ascii); Q
24: END
```

Here is a sample output for the program in Listing 17.4:

```
Enter a character : +
Enter number of times to repeat the above pattern? 10
Enter an ASCII code : 65
Enter number of times to repeat the code? 5

         1         2         3         4         5
 12345678901234567890123456789012345678901234567890
"++++++++++"
"AAAAA"
```

The program in Listing 17.4 declares its variables on lines 4–8. Lines 13–16 contain the four INPUT statements that prompt you for data. The INPUT statement on line 13 prompts you to enter the character pattern and stores it in the variable CharPattern. The INPUT statement on the next line prompts you to enter the number of times to duplicate the character pattern. The statement stores your numeric input in Count1. The INPUT statement on line 15 prompts you to enter the ASCII code for a character pattern and stores it in the variable Ascii. The INPUT statement on the next line prompts you to enter the number of times to duplicate the latter character pattern. The statement stores your numeric input in Count2.

Lines 18 and 19 contain PRINT statements that display the character ruler. Line 21 has a PRINT statement that uses the first form of the STRING$ function to duplicate the first character in CharPattern. Line 23 has a PRINT statement that uses the second form of the STRING$ function to duplicate the character specified by the ASCII code in Ascii.

Removing Leading and Trailing Spaces

Frequently, programs obtain text input that contains leading spaces, trailing spaces, or both. QBasic offers the LTRIM$ and RTRIM$ functions to remove the leading and trailing spaces, respectively.

The *LTRIM$* Function

The LTRIM$ function removes the leading spaces from a string. The trailing and internal spaces in the string are not affected.

The LTRIM$ Function

The general syntax for the LTRIM$ function is

```
LTRIM$(stringExpression)
```

The *stringExpression* parameter is either a string literal, string constant, string variable, string function, or an expression that contains these different components. If the first character in the *stringExpression* is not a space, the function returns the *stringExpression* intact.

Figure 17.6 shows the LTRIM$ function removing the leading spaces from the string " ABC ".

Examples:

```
S$ = LTRIM$("   Hello World ") ' S$ = "Hello World "
V$ = LTRIM$("  New York") ' V$ stores "New York"
T$ = LTRIM$("QBasic") ' T$ stores "QBasic"
```

Listing 17.5, STRING18.BAS, trims the leading spaces in an input string using the LTRIM$ function. The program prompts you to enter a string. To enter leading spaces with the INPUT statement, you must begin your input by entering the double-quotation mark character. Otherwise, the INPUT statement ignores the leading spaces. The program displays your original input and the one without the leading spaces (if you typed leading spaces after the double-quotation mark).

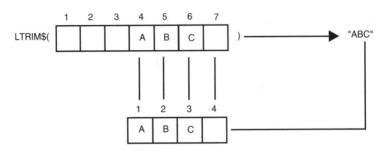

Figure 17.6. The LTRIM$ function removing the leading spaces from the string " ABC ".

Listing 17.5. STRING18.BAS, which trims the leading spaces in an input string using the LTRIM$ function.

```
 1: REM Program that demonstrates the LTRIM$ function
 2: REM
 3: ' declare program variables
 4: DIM S AS STRING
 5: DIM Q AS STRING
 6:
 7: CLS
 8: Q = CHR$(34)
 9: INPUT "Enter a string : ", S
10: PRINT "Input string is "; Q; S; Q
11: S = LTRIM$(S)
12: PRINT "Trimmed string is "; Q; S; Q
13: END
```

Here is a sample output for the program in Listing 17.5:

```
Enter a string : "     Howdy World!
Input string is "     Howdy World!"
Trimmed string is "Howdy World!"
```

The program in Listing 17.5 declares the variables S and Q on lines 4 and 5. Line 9 has an INPUT statement that prompts you for a string and stores the input in S. The PRINT statement on line 10 displays your input. Line 11 applies LTRIM$ to S and assigns the result back to S. Line 12 contains a PRINT statement that displays the trimmed string.

The *RTRIM$* Function

The RTRIM$ function removes the trailing spaces from a string. The leading and internal spaces in that string are not affected.

The RTRIM$ Function

The general syntax for the RTRIM$ function is

```
RTRIM$(stringExpression)
```

The *stringExpression* parameter is either a string literal, string constant, string variable, string function, or an expression that contains these different components. If the last character in *stringExpression* is not a space, the function returns *stringExpression* intact.

Figure 17.7 shows the RTRIM$ function removing the trailing spaces from the string " ABC ".

Examples:

```
S$ = RTRIM$(" Hello World   ") ' S$ = " Hello World"
V$ = RTRIM$("New York   ") ' V$ stores "New York"
T$ = RTRIM$("QBasic") ' T$ stores "QBasic"
```

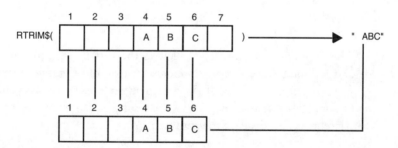

Figure 17.7. The RTRIM$ function removing the leading spaces from the string " ABC ".

Listing 17.6, STRING19.BAS, trims the trailing spaces in an input string using the RTRIM$ function. The program prompts you to enter a string. To enter trailing strings with the INPUT statement, you must enclose your input in double-quotation marks. Otherwise, the INPUT statement ignores the trailing spaces.

The program displays your original input and the one without the trailing spaces (if you typed leading spaces after the double-quotation mark).

Listing 17.6. STRING19.BAS, which trims the trailing spaces in an input string using the RTRIM$ function.

```
 1: REM Program that demonstrates the RTRIM$ function
 2: REM
 3: ' declare program variables
 4: DIM S AS STRING
 5: DIM Q AS STRING
 6:
 7: CLS
 8: Q = CHR$(34)
 9: INPUT "Enter a string : ", S
10: PRINT "Input string is "; Q; S; Q
11: S = RTRIM$(S)
12: PRINT "Trimmed string is "; Q; S; Q
13: END
```

Here is a sample output for the program in Listing 17.6:

```
Enter a string : "Hello World      "
Input string is "Hello World      "
Trimmed string is "Hello World"
```

The program in Listing 17.6 declares the variables S and Q on lines 4 and 5. Line 9 has an INPUT statement that prompts you for a string and stores the input in S. The PRINT statement on line 10 displays your input. Line 11 applies RTRIM$ to S and assigns the result back to S. Line 12 contains a PRINT statement that displays the trimmed string.

Getting and Setting the Date and Time

QBasic provides the functions DATE$ and TIME$ to yield a string image of the computer's date and time. In addition, QBasic offers the DATE$ and TIME$ statements that enable you to set your computer's date and time. QBasic also supplies the TIMER function, which returns the number of seconds since midnight.

The *TIME$* Function

The TIME$ function reads the current time from your computer's clock.

Syntax

The TIME$ Function

The general syntax for the TIME$ function is

```
TIME$
```

The TIME$ function returns a string with the general format "*hh*:*mm*:*ss*", where *hh* is the hour, *mm* is the minute, and *ss* is the second.

Examples:

```
CurrentTime$ = TIME$
PRINT "The time now is "; TIME$
```

17

The *TIMER* Function

The TIMER function produces the number of seconds since midnight. This function is useful in timing operations.

Syntax

The TIMER Function

The general syntax for the TIMER function is

```
TIMER
```

The TIMER function produces a number that represents the number of seconds since midnight.

Examples:

```
DIM TimeVar AS DOUBLE
DIM S AS STRING
TimeVar = TIMER
INPUT "Enter a string "; S
TimeVar = TIMER - TimeVar
PRINT "The input operation took "; TimeVar; " seconds"
```

The *DATE$* Function

The DATE$ function obtains the current date from your computer's clock.

The DATE$ Function

The general syntax for the DATE$ function is:

```
DATE$
```

The DATE$ function returns a string with the general format
"*mm-dd-yyyy*". *mm* is the month, *dd* is the day, and *yyyy* is the year.

Example:

```
PRINT "Today is "; DATE$
```

Let's look at a program that uses the TIME$, DATE$, and TIMER functions. Listing 17.7, TIME1.BAS, displays the date, time, and the number of seconds you take typing in a string.

Listing 17.7. TIME1.BAS, which displays the date, time, and the number of seconds for an input statement.

```
1: REM Program that tests the TIME$, TIMER, and DATE functions
2: REM
3: ' declare program variables
4: DIM TheTime AS SINGLE
5: DIM S AS STRING
6: CLS
7: PRINT "The date is "; DATE$
8: PRINT "The time is "; TIME$
9: PRINT
10: ' read system timer and store in TheTime
11: TheTime = TIMER
12: INPUT "Enter a string : ", S
13: ' Calculate the elapsed time and save it in TheTime
14: TheTime = TIMER - TheTime
15: PRINT
16: PRINT "It took about"; CINT(TheTime + .5);
17: PRINT "second(s) for the prompt and your input"
18: END
```

Here is a sample output for the program in Listing 17.7:

```
The date is 12-23-1992
The time is 22:20:55

Enter a string : My name is Jack

It took about 7 second(s) for the prompt and your input
```

The program in Listing 17.7 declares its variables `TheTime` and `S` on lines 4 and 5. Line 7 contains a `PRINT` statement that displays the current date by calling the `DATE$` function. Line 8 contains a `PRINT` statement that displays the current time by calling the `TIME$` function. To time an input operation (or any other operation) a QBasic program needs to call the function `TIMER` just before and right after the operation. Line 11 has an assignment statement that stores the initial reading of `TIMER` in the variable `TheTime`. Line 12 contains the `INPUT` statement that prompts you to enter a string and stores it in the variable `S`. On line 14 the program calculates the elapsed time by calling the `TIMER` function again and subtracting `TheTime` from the function's result. The statement assigns the calculated elapsed time back to the variable `TheTime`. The `PRINT` statement on line 16 displays the elapsed time. Notice that the statement uses the `CINT` function to obtain the integral value of the number of seconds. The call to `CINT` uses the math expression `TheTime + .5` to round up the value in `TheTime` to the next integer.

The *TIME$* Statement

The `TIME$` statement enables you to set the time in your computer's clock.

The TIME$ Statement

The general syntax for the `TIME$` statement is

```
TIME$ = stringTime
```

The *stringTime* is a string expression that has the formats `"hh"`, `"hh:mm"`, or `"hh:mm:ss"`, where *hh* is the hour (with values ranging from 0–23), *mm* is the minute (with values ranging from 0–59), and *ss* is the seconds (with values ranging from 0–59). The `"hh"` string format sets

continues

595

the minutes and seconds to zeros. The `"hh:mm"` string format sets the
seconds to zeros.

Examples:

```
TIME$ = "14" ' set time to 14:00:00
TIME$ = "14:10" ' set time to 14:10:00
TIME$ = "14:10:20" ' set time to 14:10:20
```

The *DATE$* Statement

The DATE$ statement enables your QBasic programs to set the date in your
computer's clock

The **DATE$** Statement

The general syntax for the DATE$ statement is

```
DATE$ = stringDate
```

The *stringDate* is a string expression that has the formats `"mm-dd-yy"`,
`"mm-dd-yyyy"`, `"mm/dd/yy"`, or `"mm/dd/yyyy"`, where *mm* is the month
(with values ranging from 1–12), *dd* is the day (with values ranging
from 1–31), *yyyy* is the year (with values ranging from 1980–2099),
and *yy* is the an abbreviated form of the year (with values ranging
from 80–99).

Examples:

```
DATE$ = "5-11-1988" ' set date to May 11, 1988
DATE$ = "5-11-88" '  set date to May 11, 1988
DATE$ = "5/11/1988" ' set date to May 11, 1988
DATE$ = "5/11/88" '  set date to May 11, 1988
```

Summary

This chapter introduced you to advanced string manipulation functions and
techniques. Some methods, such as deleting and replacing characters, are not

directly supported by QBasic functions. The chapter presented the following topics:

- ☐ To delete substrings, use the MID$ function to extract the undeleted leading and trailing portion of a string.

- ☐ Replacing substrings is an operation that is similar to deleting a string, except the replacement string is inserted between the unchanged leading and trailing portion of a string.

- ☐ Creating strings from smaller strings involves the SPACE$ and STRING$ functions. The SPACE$ function creates a string that contains a specified number of space characters. The STRING$ function creates a string that is made up of a specified number of the same character.

- ☐ To remove leading and trailing spaces in a string, use the LTRIM$ and RTRIM$ functions.

- ☐ You can get the date and time with the DATE$ and TIME$ functions. To set the time, use the DATE$ and TIME$ statements. QBasic also offers the TIMER function, which returns the number of seconds since midnight.

Q&A

Q. If I have a string that contains a special character marker, how can I extract a certain number of characters from that string, beginning at or right after the location of the character marker?

A. The solution involves using the INSTR function, which I presented on Day 5, to locate the character marker. Here is a general statement that extracts N characters including the character marker itself:

```
ExtString = MID$(AString, INSTR(AString, CharMarker), N)
```

Here is a general statement that extracts N characters **after** the character marker:

```
ExtString = MID$(AString, INSTR(AString, CharMarker) + 1, N)
```

Both solutions assume that the marker is in the scanned string.

Q. What are the two most common errors in the arguments for the string functions?

A. The two most common errors are supplying nonpositive starting indices and negative character counts.

Workshop

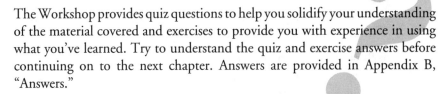

The Workshop provides quiz questions to help you solidify your understanding of the material covered and exercises to provide you with experience in using what you've learned. Try to understand the quiz and exercise answers before continuing on to the next chapter. Answers are provided in Appendix B, "Answers."

Quiz

1. True or false: the following statement displays the string "+-+-+-":

```
PRINT STRING$(3, "+-")
```

2. What is the output of the following program?

```
DIM S AS STRING
S = "The rain in Spain"
MID$(S, 5, 3) = STRING$(7, "!")
```

3. Simplify the following statement by replacing the MID$ function with another string function that uses fewer arguments:

```
PRINT "I'm going to "; MID$("Spain", 1, 3)
```

Exercises

1. Write a program (call it ALIGN1.BAS) that aligns at column 40 the last characters of three input strings.

2. Write a program (call it DATE1.BAS) that extracts and displays the year, month number, and day number of the date string produced by function DATE$.

DAY
18

Text File Input/Output

This chapter presents file input and output (I/O, for short) operations that involve text. These operations are similar to the keyboard input and screen output operations in that they handle characters and text lines. On Day 19, "Random-Access and Binary File Input/Output," I present more advanced forms of file input and output. File I/O has the advantage of providing storage for information that you can retrieve later. Today you will learn about the following topics:

- [ ] Renaming a file with the NAME statement

- [ ] Deleting one or more files with the KILL statement

- [ ] Displaying a list of files using the FILES statement

- [ ] Opening a file for input and output using the OPEN statement

- [ ] Closing a file using the CLOSE statement

- [ ] Text file output operations

- [ ] Text file input operations

Overview

This chapter assumes that you are familiar with DOS filenames, directories, and drive names. My guess is that you employ your PC to use a word processor, a spreadsheet, or a database. Each of these applications uses drive names, directory names, and filenames.

Why use files? The end-user applications I just mentioned would be of little or no use if they failed to store data. What's the use of typing part of a letter, for example, if you cannot store it to complete it later? Files are disk storage locations that save information for later retrieval. MS-DOS uses filenames to tag these storage locations. An MS-DOS filename is made up of two parts. The first part contains from one to eight characters and is called the *primary* filename or the *main* filename. The second part, called the *file extension*, is optional and may contain as many as three characters. Typically, files use the extension part as a way to identify the type of file. The .EXE and .COM file extensions identify executable programs. The .BAS file extension identifies BASIC programs. The .BAT extension identifies MS-DOS batch files.

Renaming Files

Before I introduce you to the file I/O statements and functions, I present three statements that enable you to manipulate files. These statements support the file I/O operations, but do not themselves perform file I/O. In this section I introduce the NAME statement, which enables you to rename a file.

The NAME Statement

The general syntax for the NAME statement is

```
NAME oldName$ AS newName$
```

The `oldName$` parameter is the name of the existing file. This name may include a drive name and a directory name. The `newName$` parameter is the name of the new file. This parameter may include a directory name. Both parameters are string expressions.

You can use the NAME statement to move a file to another directory on the same disk. To move a file, preserve the same filename and use a different directory name.

Examples:

```
' rename the MYDATA.DAT file to MYDATA.OLD
NAME "MYDATA.DAT" AS "MYDATA.OLD"


' move the file MYDATA.DAT from the root directory to
' the \DOS directory
NAME "\MYDATA.DAT" AS "\DOS\MYDATA.DAT"
```

18

DO supply valid drive names, directory names, and filenames to the NAME statement. Otherwise, QBasic raises a runtime error.

DON'T use the NAME statement to rename or move critical .BAT batch files, .EXE program files, and .SYS system files.

Deleting Files

QBasic enables you to remove files once they are no longer useful. The KILL statement deletes one or more files.

Syntax

The KILL Statement

The general syntax for the KILL statement is

```
KILL {filename$ ¦ fileWildcard$}
```

The *filename$* parameter specifies the complete name of a file. This parameter may include a drive name and a directory name. The *fileWildcard$* parameter is the name of one or more files that include the MS-DOS wildcards * and ?. If you attempt to delete a nonexistent or invalid file, QBasic raises a runtime error. Both parameters are string expressions.

Examples:

```
' delete .BAK backup files in the current directory
KILL "*.BAK"


' delete the backup file MYDATA.BAK
KILL "MYDATA.BAK"


' delete the backup file that start with MYDATA
' and have one other letter
KILL "MYDATA?.BAK"
```

DO remove unwanted files, especially data files, to minimize the clutter on your disk drives.

DON'T delete critical .BAT batch files, .EXE program files, and .SYS system files.

Listing Files

The MS-DOS DIR command is perhaps the most frequently used command. Using DIR enables you to list the files in a specific drive and directory. QBasic offers the FILES statement to partially emulate the DIR command. I say *partially* because the FILES statement only displays the names of the files, as if you typed DIR /W.

The FILES Statement

The general syntax for the FILES statement is

```
FILES [{filename$ ¦ fileWildcard$}]
```

The parameter `filename$` specifies the complete name of a file. This parameter may include a drive name and a directory name. The `fileWildCard$` parameter is the name of one or more files that include the MS-DOS wildcards * and ?. Issuing the FILES statement without any arguments displays all of the files in the current directory. Both optional parameters are string expressions.

Examples:

```
' list all files in current directory
FILES

' list all of .BAS files in current directory
FILES ".BAS"

' list all files in the current directory of drive A:
FILES "A:"
```

Opening Files

The first step in performing any file I/O operation is to open the file. What does this step accomplish? Opening a file is an important process in which you specify the name of the file involved, the type of I/O operation, the file handle, and any other optional parameters. QBasic sets up the file for input or output, associates it with a numeric handle (a kind of social security number for files), and establishes a special memory area called the *buffer* or *file buffer*. This buffer serves as a holding area where information flows to a file (in the case of file output) or flows to the program (in the case of file input). Most of the file I/O operations use the file handle instead of the filename. Figure 18.1 shows the role of a buffer in file output. Figure 18.2 shows the role of a buffer in file input.

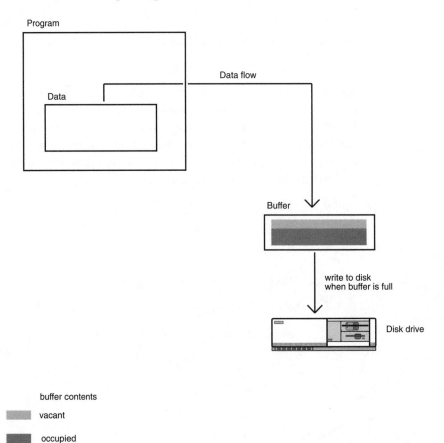

Figure 18.1. The role of a buffer in file output.

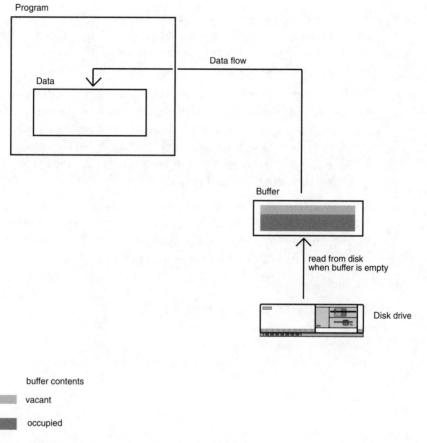

Figure 18.2. The role of a buffer in file input.

The OPEN Statement

The general syntax for the two forms of the OPEN statement is

```
OPEN filename [FOR accessMode] AS [#]fileHandle [LEN=recLen]
OPEN accessModeChar, [#]fileHandle, filename [, recLen]
```

The *filename* parameter specifies the name of the file to open. The *filename* parameter may include a drive name and a directory name. If you supply an invalid filename, QBasic raises a runtime error.

continues

The *accessMode* parameter specifies the I/O mode. The *accessModeChar* parameter is a single-character abbreviation for the access mode. Table 18.1 lists the various access mode keywords and their access mode characters.

The *fileHandle* parameter is an integer expression that specifies the file handle. The file handle must not be in use already. Otherwise, QBasic raises a runtime error. You can use the predefined parameterless function FREEFILE to obtain the next available file handle number. I highly recommend this approach to avoid conflict among file handles. The smallest file handle number is 1.

The *recLen* parameter specifies the size of the buffer used in the file I/O. When omitted, QBasic uses a buffer with 512 bytes for the INPUT, OUTPUT, and APPEND modes. In the case of the BINARY and RANDOM file I/O modes, QBasic uses a default of 128 bytes.

Examples:

```
OPEN "\AUTOEXEC.BAT" FOR INPUT AS #1


FileNum% = FREEFILE
OPEN Filename$ FOR OUTPUT AS #FileNum% LEN = 1024


FileNum% = FREEFILE
OPEN Filename$ FOR APPEND AS #FileNum%


OPEN "I", #1, "\AUTOEXEC.BAT"
```

DO use the FREEFILE function to obtain the next available file handle.

DON'T assume that the file handle number 1 is always available, especially when you open a file in a procedure.

Table 18.1. **The various file I/O access modes.**

Access Mode	Access Mode Char	Purpose
INPUT	I	The file is opened for text input.
OUTPUT	O	The file is opened for text output.
APPEND	A	The file is opened to append text.
BINARY	B	The file is opened to read and write single bytes.
RANDOM	R	The file is opened to read and write structured variables. This is the default file I/O access mode.

Closing Files

I mentioned in the last section that you must open a file before you can use it. Likewise, when you finish reading or writing data to a file, you should close that file. This is especially true when you are writing data in the OUTPUT, APPEND, BINARY, and RANDOM modes. Closing a file in these modes ensures that all the transient data in the file buffer is flushed to its associated files. Otherwise, your output operation may not be complete. QBasic offers the CLOSE and RESET statements to close files. The CLOSE statement enables you to close one or more files. The RESET statement simultaneously closes all file buffers.

The RESET Statement

The general syntax for the RESET statement is

RESET

The statement closes all of the opened files and flushes their buffers.

Example:

```
InFile = FREEFILE
OPEN InFile$ FOR INPUT AS #InFile
```

Syntax

18

```
OutFile = FREEFILE
OPEN OutFile$ FOR INPUT AS #OutFile
RESET
```

The CLOSE Statement

The general syntax for the CLOSE statement is

```
CLOSE [[#]fileHandle1 [, [#]fileHandle2]]...
```

The statement closes the specified file handles. If none are specified, the CLOSE statement closes all the file buffers, behaving like the RESET statement.

Example:

```
InFile = FREEFILE
OPEN InFile$ FOR INPUT AS #InFile
OutFile = FREEFILE
OPEN OutFile$ FOR INPUT AS #OutFile
CLOSE #InFile
CLOSE #OutFile
```

Text File Output

You might recall that QBasic offers various statements for screen output. These statements include PRINT and PRINT USING. The good news is that QBasic supports similar statements for text file input. In addition, QBasic provides the WRITE statement to generate a list of output that is separated by commas.

The File-Oriented PRINT Statement

The general syntax for the file-oriented PRINT statement is

```
PRINT #fileHandle [USING formatStr$] [, variableList] [{; |,}]
```

The *fileHandle* parameter represents the handle of an output file. The optional USING clause enables you to format the output using the format string *formatStr$*. The *variableList* is a list of variables separated by commas. The PRINT statement outputs the string image of numeric variables. When omitted, the PRINT statement writes an empty line in the output text file. The trailing comma and semicolon work only in the screen output.

Example:

```
CONST FILENAME = "SAMPLE.DAT"
DIM S AS STRING
DIM I AS INTEGER
DIM FileNum AS INTEGER
FileNum = FREEFILE
OPEN FILENAME FOR OUTPUT AS #FileNum
S = "Hello"
I = 51
PRINT #FileNum, S
PRINT #FileNum, I
CLOSE #FileNum
END
```

18

The WRITE Statement

The general syntax for the WRITE statement is

```
WRITE #fileHandle [, variableList]
```

The *fileHandle* parameter represents the handle of an output file. The *variableList* is a list of variables separated by commas. The WRITE statement outputs the string image of numeric variables and separates all items in the same WRITE statement by commas.

Example:

```
CONST FILENAME = "SAMPLE.DAT"
DIM S AS STRING
DIM I AS INTEGER
DIM FileNum AS INTEGER
FileNum = FREEFILE
OPEN FILENAME FOR OUTPUT AS #FileNum
```

```
WRITE #FileNum, S
WRITE #FileNum, I
CLOSE #FileNum
END
```

> **DO** use the WRITE statement to write multiple data items on the same text line.
>
> **DON'T** use the PRINT statement to write multiple data items on the same text line.

Take a look at an example of a program that writes strings to a text file. Listing 18.1, SQFILE1.BAS, writes the strings in an array to a text file. The program obtains its data from DATA statements and performs the following tasks:

1. Displays the unordered elements of the array.

2. Writes the unordered elements of the array to the file ARR.DAT.

3. Sorts the elements of the array.

4. Displays the sorted elements of the array.

5. Writes the sorted elements of the array to the file SORTARR.DAT.

Listing 18.1. **SQFILE1.BAS, which writes the strings in an array to a text file.**

```
1: DECLARE SUB WriteArray (Filename$, S$(), N%)
2: DECLARE SUB ShowArray (Title$, S$(), N%)
3: DECLARE SUB SortArray (S$(), N%)
4: DECLARE SUB WaitAWhile ()
5: DECLARE SUB ReadArray (S$(), N%)
6: REM Program that writes two arrays of strings
```

```
 7: REM to two files.
 8: REM
 9: OPTION BASE 1
10: ' declare constants
11: CONST FILE1 = "ARR.DAT"
12: CONST FILE2 = "SORTARR.DAT"
13: CONST TITLE1 = "Unordered Array"
14: CONST TITLE2 = "Sorted Array"
15: ' declare variables
16: '$DYNAMIC
17: DIM StrArr(1) AS STRING
18: DIM N AS INTEGER
19:
20: ' read the number of strings
21: READ N
22: REDIM StrArr(N) AS STRING
23:
24: ReadArray StrArr(), N
25: ShowArray TITLE1, StrArr(), N
26: WaitAWhile
27: WriteArray FILE1, StrArr(), N
28: PRINT
29: PRINT "Wrote array to file "; FILE1
30: PRINT
31: WaitAWhile
32: SortArray StrArr(), N
33: ShowArray TITLE2, StrArr(), N
34: WaitAWhile
35: WriteArray FILE2, StrArr(), N
36: PRINT
37: PRINT "Wrote array to file "; FILE2
38:
39:
40: '****************** DATA Statements ******************
41:
42: DATA 15
43:
44: DATA Washington, Virginia, Maryland, California, Nevada
```

continues

Listing 18.1. continued

```
45: DATA Alabama, Alaska, Michigan, Indiana, Illinois
46: DATA Oregon, Arizona, New Mexico, New York, Ohio
47:
48: END
49:
50: REM $STATIC
51: SUB ReadArray (S$(), N%)
52: ' read the DATA statements to supply
53: ' the array S$ with values
54:    DIM I AS INTEGER
55:
56:    FOR I = 1 TO N%
57:       READ S$(I)
58:    NEXT I
59: END SUB
60:
61: SUB ShowArray (Title$, S$(), N%)
62: ' display the N% elements of array S$
63:    DIM I AS INTEGER
64:
65:    CLS
66:    PRINT
67:    PRINT TAB(40 - LEN(Title$) \ 2); Title$
68:    PRINT
69:    FOR I = 1 TO N%
70:       PRINT S$(I)
71:    NEXT I
72:    PRINT
73: END SUB
74:
75: SUB SortArray (S$(), N%)
76: ' sort the elements of array S$
77:    DIM I AS INTEGER
78:    DIM J AS INTEGER
79:
80:    FOR I = 1 TO N% - 1
```

```
 81:      FOR J = I TO N%
 82:        IF S$(I) > S$(J) THEN SWAP S$(I), S$(J)
 83:      NEXT J
 84:    NEXT I
 85: END SUB
 86:
 87: SUB WaitAWhile
 88: ' pause the program
 89:    DIM C AS STRING * 1
 90:
 91:    PRINT "Press any key to continue"
 92:    C = INPUT$(1)
 93: END SUB
 94:
 95: SUB WriteArray (Filename$, S$(), N%)
 96: ' writes the first N% elements of array S$
 97: ' to file Filename$
 98:    DIM FileNum  AS INTEGER
 99:
100:    ' get the next available file handle
101:    FileNum = FREEFILE
102:    OPEN Filename$ FOR OUTPUT AS FileNum
103:    ' write the number of strings
104:    PRINT #FileNum, N%
105:    ' write the elements of array S$
106:    FOR I = 1 TO N%
107:      PRINT #FileNum, S$(I)
108:    NEXT I
109:    ' close the file
110:    CLOSE FileNum
111: END SUB
```

Here is some sample output for the program in Listing 18.1:

```
Unordered Array

Washington
Virginia
```

```
Maryland
California
Nevada
Alabama
Alaska
Michigan
Indiana
Illinois
Oregon
Arizona
New Mexico
New York
Ohio


Press any key to continue


Wrote array to file ARR.DAT


Press any key to continue
```

 SCREEN CLEARS

```
Sorted Array

Alabama
Alaska
Arizona
California
Illinois
Indiana
Maryland
Michigan
Nevada
New Mexico
New York
Ohio
Oregon
Virginia
Washington


Press any key to continue


Wrote array to file SORTARR.DAT
```

 The highlight of the program in Listing 18.1 is the procedure `WriteArray`. The other procedures should look familiar because I presented similar ones in previous chapters.

The procedure `WriteArray` has three parameters. The parameter `Filename$` specifies the name of the output file. The parameter `S$()` designates the array of strings to be written to the output file. The parameter `N%` indicates the number of array elements to write to the file.

The procedure declares the local variable `FileNum`, which stores the handle number for the output file. The statement on line 101 assigns the result of function `FREEFILE` to the variable `FileNum`. The statement on line 102 contains the `OPEN` statement, which opens the file `Filename$` for output and specifies the file handle `FileNum`. The procedure first writes the number of strings to the output file. The `PRINT` statement on line 104 writes the string image of the value in parameter `N%` to the output file. This value is useful when I present the next program, which reads the array from the files ARR.DAT and SORTARR.DAT.

The `FOR-NEXT` loop on lines 106–108 writes the elements of the string array `S$`. The loop uses the control variable `I` and iterates from 1 to `N%`. The `PRINT` statement on line 107 writes each array element on a separate line. This approach makes it easier to read the individual array elements later. The statement on line 110 closes the file buffer before exiting the subroutine.

The main program section calls the `WriteArray` procedure twice, on lines 27 and 35. The program uses the first procedure call to write the elements of the unordered array to file ARR.DAT. The second function call writes the elements of the sorted array to file SORTARR.DAT.

Text File Input

You might recall that QBasic offers various statements for keyboard input. These statements include `INPUT`, `LINE INPUT`, and `INPUT$`. The good news is that QBasic supports similar statements for text file input.

Syntax

The File-Oriented INPUT Statement

The general syntax for the file-oriented INPUT statement is

```
INPUT #fileHandle, variableList
```

The *fileHandle* parameter represents the handle of an input file. The *variableList* parameter is a list of string variables separated by commas.

Example:

```
CONST FILENAME = "SAMPLE.DAT"
DIM S AS STRING
DIM SI AS STRING
DIM I AS INTEGER
DIM FileNum AS INTEGER
FileNum = FREEFILE
OPEN FILENAME FOR INPUT AS #FileNum
INPUT #FileNum, S
INPUT #FileNum, SI
I = VAL(SI)
PRINT S, I
CLOSE #FileNum
END
```

Syntax

The File-Oriented LINE INPUT Statement

The general syntax for the file-oriented LINE INPUT statement is

```
LINE INPUT #fileHandle, stringVariable
```

The *fileHandle* parameter represents the handle of an input file. The *stringVariable* parameter is a string variable. The LINE INPUT statement reads an entire line from the input text file.

Example:

```
CONST FILENAME = "SAMPLE.DAT"
DIM S AS STRING
DIM SI AS STRING
DIM I AS INTEGER
DIM FileNum AS INTEGER
FileNum = FREEFILE
```

```
OPEN FILENAME FOR INPUT AS #FileNum
LINE INPUT #FileNum, S
LINE INPUT #FileNum, SI
I = VAL(SI)
PRINT S, I
CLOSE #FileNum
END
```

The INPUT$ Statement

The general syntax for the file-oriented INPUT$ statement is

```
INPUT$(count, [#] fileHandle)
```

The *count* parameter specifies the number of characters to read from the file with the handle `fileHandle`.

Example:

```
CONST FILENAME = "SAMPLE.DAT"
DIM S AS STRING
DIM SI AS STRING
DIM I AS INTEGER
DIM FileNum AS INTEGER
FileNum = FREEFILE
OPEN FILENAME FOR INPUT AS #FileNum
S = INPUT$(1, #FileNum)
PRINT "The first character is "; S
CLOSE #FileNum
END
```

DO use the WRITE and INPUT statements to write and read multiple items on the same line. Also use the PRINT and LINE INPUT statements to write and read single items from the same line.

> **DON'T** make it harder for your programs by writing multiple items using the WRITE statement and then reading them with a LINE INPUT statement. In this case, you must extract the individual data items that are separated by commas.

What happens if a program attempts to read beyond the end of a file? QBasic raises a runtime error. Fortunately, QBasic offers the Boolean function EOF, which returns –1 (True) if the input operation has reached the end of file, and 0 (False) if there is more data to read.

Syntax

The EOF Function

The general syntax for the EOF function is

```
EOF(fileHandle)
```

The *fileHandle* is a handle for an input file being read. Typically, a program uses the EOF function in a DO-WHILE loop when reading the lines of text file.

Example:

```
CONST FILENAME = "\AUTOEXEC.BAT"
DIM Text AS STRING
DIM FileNum AS INTEGER
CLS
FileNum = FREEFILE
OPEN FILENAME FOR INPUT AS #FileNum
DO WHILE EOF(FileNum)
  LINE INPUT #FileNum, Text
  PRINT Text
LOOP
CLOSE
END
```

Listing 18.2, SQFILE2.BAS, reads the array elements in the two files created by the program SQFILE1.BAS. The program performs the following tasks:

1. Reads the elements of the unordered array from file ARR.DAT

2. Displays the elements of the unordered array

3. Reads the elements of the sorted array from file SORTARR.DAT

4. Displays the elements of the sorted array

 Listing 18.2. SQFILE2.BAS, which reads the strings in a array from a text file.

```
 1: DECLARE SUB InputArray (Filename$, S$(), N%)
 2: DECLARE SUB ShowArray (Title$, S$(), N%)
 3: DECLARE SUB WaitAWhile ()
 4: REM Program that reads two arrays of strings
 5: REM from two files.
 6: REM
 7: OPTION BASE 1
 8: ' declare constants
 9: CONST FILE1 = "ARR.DAT"
10: CONST FILE2 = "SORTARR.DAT"
11: CONST TITLE1 = "Unordered Array"
12: CONST TITLE2 = "Sorted Array"
13: ' declare variables
14: '$DYNAMIC
15: DIM StrArr(1) AS STRING
16: DIM N AS INTEGER
17:
18: InputArray FILE1, StrArr(), N
19: ShowArray TITLE1, StrArr(), N
20: WaitAWhile
21: InputArray FILE2, StrArr(), N
22: ShowArray TITLE2, StrArr(), N
23: WaitAWhile
24: END
```

continues

```
25:
26: REM $STATIC
27: SUB InputArray (Filename$, S$(), N%)
28: ' reads the first N% elements of array S$
29: ' from file Filename$
30:   DIM FileNum  AS INTEGER
31:   DIM AString AS STRING
32:
33:   ' get the next available file handle
34:   FileNum = FREEFILE
35:   OPEN Filename$ FOR INPUT AS FileNum
36:   LINE INPUT #FileNum, AString
37:   N% = VAL(AString)
38:   REDIM S$(N%)
39:   ' read the elements of array S$
40:   FOR I = 1 TO N%
41:     LINE INPUT #FileNum, S$(I)
42:   NEXT I
43:   ' close the file
44:   CLOSE FileNum
45: END SUB
46:
47: SUB ShowArray (Title$, S$(), N%)
48: ' display the N% elements of array S$
49:   DIM I AS INTEGER
50:
51:   CLS
52:   PRINT
53:   PRINT TAB(40 - LEN(Title$) \ 2); Title$
54:   PRINT
55:   FOR I = 1 TO N%
56:     PRINT S$(I)
57:   NEXT I
58:   PRINT
59: END SUB
60:
61: SUB WaitAWhile
62: ' pause the program
63:   DIM C AS STRING * 1
```

```
64:
65:    PRINT "Press any key to continue"
66:    C = INPUT$(1)
67: END SUB
```

Here is some sample output for the program in Listing 18.2:

```
Unordered Array

Washington
Virginia
Maryland
California
Nevada
Alabama
Alaska
Michigan
Indiana
Illinois
Oregon
Arizona
New Mexico
New York
Ohio


Press any key to continue
```

 SCREEN CLEARS

```
Sorted Array

Alabama
Alaska
Arizona
California
Illinois
Indiana
Maryland
Michigan
Nevada
New Mexico
New York
```

```
Ohio
Oregon
Virginia
Washington
```

The highlight of the program in Listing 18.2 is the procedure `InputArray`. The procedure `InputArray` has three parameters. The parameter `Filename$` specifies the name of the input file. The parameter `S$()` designates the array of strings to be read from the input file. The parameter `N%` indicates the number of array elements read from the file.

The procedure declares the local variable `FileNum`, which stores the handle number for the input file. The statement on line 34 assigns the result of the function `FREEFILE` to the variable `FileNum`. The statement on line 35 contains the `OPEN` statement, which opens the file `Filename$` for input and specifies the file handle `FileNum`. The procedure first reads the number of strings from the input file. The `LINE INPUT` statement on line 36 reads the string image of the number of array elements into the local variable `AString`. Then the procedure converts the string into an integer and stores it in the parameter `N%`. The statement on line 38 redimensions the array `S$` to accommodate `N%` elements. The `FOR-NEXT` loop on lines 40–42 reads the elements of the string array `S$`. The loop uses the control variable `I` and iterates from 1 to `N%`. The `LINE INPUT` statement on line 41 reads each array element from a separate line. The statement on line 44 closes the file buffer before exiting the subroutine.

The main program section calls the `InputArray` procedure twice: on lines 18 and 21. The first call reads the elements of the unordered array from file ARR.DAT. The second call retrieves the elements of the sorted array from file SORTARR.DAT.

Text File Input and Output

Now take a look at a program that reads and writes strings from and to text files. Listing 18.3, SQFILE3.BAS, reads the lines in a file, replaces certain text, and writes the output to another file. The program performs the tasks described by the following pseudocode:

1. Prompt you for an input file

2. Prompt you for the output file

3. Prompt you for the search string

4. Prompt you for the replacement string

5. Open the input file

6. Open the output file

7. Repeat the following steps while there are more lines to read in the input file:

   7.1. Read a line

   7.2. Locate the search string in the line read

   7.3. While there is a search string in the line read, repeat the following steps:

      7.3.1. Replace the search string
      7.3.2. Locate the next search string in the line read

   7.4. Write the line to the output file

   7.5. Close the input file buffer

   7.6. Close the output file buffer

The program also uses error-handling routines to manage various kinds of runtime errors.

Listing 18.3. SQFILE3.BAS, which reads the lines in a file, replaces certain text, and writes the output to another file.

```
 1: REM Program which translates text in a file
 2: REM
 3: ' declare variables
 4: DIM InFilename AS STRING
 5: DIM OutFilename AS STRING
 6: DIM InFile AS INTEGER
 7: DIM OutFile AS INTEGER
 8: DIM S AS STRING
 9: DIM FindStr AS STRING
10: DIM ReplStr AS STRING
11: DIM I AS INTEGER
```

continues

Type Listing 18.3. continued

```
12: DIM FindLen AS INTEGER
13: DIM ReplLen AS INTEGER
14:
15: CLS
16: DO
17:   INPUT "Enter input filename : ", InFilename
18:   PRINT
19: LOOP UNTIL InFilename <> ""
20:
21: DO
22:   INPUT "Enter output filename : ", OutFilename
23:   PRINT
24: LOOP UNTIL OutFilename <> ""
25:
26: DO
27:   INPUT "Enter search string : ", FindStr
28:   PRINT
29: LOOP UNTIL FindStr <> ""
30: FindLen = LEN(FindStr)
31:
32: INPUT "Enter replacement string : ", ReplStr
33: ReplLen = LEN(ReplStr)
34: PRINT
35:
36: ' handle the case when both input and output
37: ' files have the same name
38: IF UCASE$(InFilename) = UCASE$(OutFilename) THEN
39:   ' find the . in the filename
40:   I = INSTR(InFilename, ".")
41:   ' make the InFilename a .BAK file
42:   IF I > 0 THEN
43:     InFilename = LEFT$(InFilename, I) + "BAK"
44:   ELSE
45:     ' append .BAK if filename has no extension
46:     InFilename = InFilename + ".BAK"
47:   END IF
48:   ' delete any current .BAK file
49:   ON ERROR GOTO Bad.DeleteBAK
50:   KILL InFilename
51:   ON ERROR GOTO 0
```

```
52:    ' rename input file to .BAK file
53:    NAME OutFilename AS InFilename
54: END IF
55:
56: ON ERROR GOTO Bad.InFilename
57: InFile = FREEFILE
58: OPEN InFilename FOR INPUT AS InFile
59: ON ERROR GOTO 0
60:
61: ON ERROR GOTO Bad.OutFilename
62: OutFile = FREEFILE
63: OPEN OutFilename FOR OUTPUT AS OutFile
64: ON ERROR GOTO 0
65:
66: DO WHILE NOT EOF(InFile)
67:    LINE INPUT #InFile, S
68:    I = INSTR(S, FindStr)
69:    DO WHILE I > 0
70:      S = LEFT$(S, I - 1) + ReplStr + MID$(S, I + FindLen)
71:      I = INSTR(I + ReplLen - FindLen + 1, S, FindStr)
72:    LOOP
73:     PRINT #OutFile, S
74: LOOP
75:
76: ' close files
77: CLOSE
78: PRINT
79: PRINT "Done!"
80: EndPrgm:
81: END
82:
83: Bad.InFilename:
84:    PRINT
85:    PRINT "Cannot open file "; InFilename
86:    RESUME EndPrgm
87:
88: Bad.OutFilename:
89:    PRINT
90:    PRINT "Cannot open file "; OutFilename
91:    RESUME EndPrgm
92:
93: Bad.DeleteBAK:
94:    RESUME NEXT
```

18

Here is some sample output for the program in Listing 18.3:

```
Enter input filename : \config.sys

Enter output filename : \config.new

Enter search string : DOS

Enter replacement string : dos


Done!
```

The following shows the contents of my CONFIG.SYS file and the resulting CONFIG.NEW file:

CONFIG.SYS

```
files=40
buffers=50
break=on
rem uncomment next command to use SETVER utility
rem DEVICE=C:\DOS\SETVER.EXE
device=C:\himem.sys
rem DEVICE=C:\DOS\EMM386.EXE auto 2784
DEVICE=C:\DOS\EMM386.EXE auto 1776 RAM
rem device=C:\WIN386\smartdrv.sys 512 512
device=C:\DOS\ramdrive.sys 1424 /e
DEVICE=C:\DOS\ANSI.SYS
DEVICE=C:\DOS\MOUSE.SYS
DEVICE=C:\POPDROP.SYS
rem SHARE.EXE is not needed for DOS 5.0
rem INSTALL=C:\DOS\share.exe
lastdrive=z
SHELL=C:\COMMAND.COM C:\ /e:512 /p
stacks=0,0
DOS=HIGH,UMB
```

The contents of the CONFIG.NEW file:

```
files=40
buffers=50
break=on
rem uncomment next command to use SETVER utility
```

```
rem DEVICE=C:\dos\SETVER.EXE
device=C:\himem.sys
rem DEVICE=C:\dos\EMM386.EXE auto 2784
DEVICE=C:\dos\EMM386.EXE auto 1776 RAM
rem device=C:\WIN386\smartdrv.sys 512 512
device=C:\dos\ramdrive.sys 1424 /e
DEVICE=C:\dos\ANSI.SYS
DEVICE=C:\dos\MOUSE.SYS
DEVICE=C:\POPDROP.SYS
rem SHARE.EXE is not needed for dos 5.0
rem INSTALL=C:\dos\share.exe
lastdrive=z
SHELL=C:\COMMAND.COM C:\ /e:512 /p
stacks=0,0
dos=HIGH,UMB
```

The program in Listing 18.3 declares its variables on lines 4–13. The DO-UNTIL loop on lines 16–19 prompts you for an input filename. The loop iterates until you enter a nonempty filename. The DO-UNTIL loop on lines 21–24 prompts you for an output filename. The loop iterates until you enter a nonempty filename. The DO-UNTIL loop on lines 26–29 prompts you for a search string. The loop iterates until you enter a nonempty search string. The statement on line 30 assigns the length of the search string to the variable FindLen. The INPUT statement on line 32 prompts you to enter the replacement string (which may be an empty string). The statement stores your input in the variable ReplStr. The statement on line 33 stores the length of the replacement string in the variable ReplLen.

The statements on lines 38–54 handle the case where both input and output filenames are the same (based on a noncase-sensitive comparison of filenames.) The basic solution involves renaming the input file with a .BAK extension while the output file retains the name you entered. To accomplish this task, the statement on line 40 scans for the dot in the variable InFilename. If the string in that variable contains a dot, the program executes the statement on line 43 to adjust the name of the file in variable InFilename. If the input filename has no dot, the program executes the statement on line 46, which appends the string ".BAK" to the input filename.

The next step involves deleting any file with a name that matches the string in variable InFilename. The statement on line 49 sets an error trap to handle the possibility that the targeted .BAK file does not exist. The KILL statement on

627

line 50 deletes the existing .BAK filename. If this statement generates a runtime error, the program jumps to the label Bad.DeleteBAK. That label is followed by a RESUME NEXT statement. Consequently, the program resumes at line 51, which turns off the error trap. The statement on line 53 renames the input file using the name with the .BAK extension. Had I not used the KILL statement, line 53 would generate a runtime error if the .BAK file already existed.

Lines 56–59 open the input file and use an error trap to handle the runtime error raised by an invalid filename or a nonexistent file. Lines 61–64 perform similar tasks for the output file, protecting against an invalid filename.

The DO-WHILE loop uses the EOF function to read the lines from the input file. The LINE INPUT statement on line 67 reads a line from the input file and stores it in the variable S. The statement on line 68, together with the DO-WHILE loop on lines 69 through 72, replaces all of the occurrences of the search string. The PRINT statement on line 73 writes the updated string in variable S to the output file. The statement on line 77 closes the input and output file buffers.

Summary

This chapter introduced you to text file I/O operations. Such operations enable you to read and write readable text from files. Today you learned the following:

- ☐ Renaming a file with the NAME statement involves stating the current and new names of the files. You can use the NAME statement to actually move a file to another directory on the same drive.

- ☐ Deleting one or more files with the KILL statement involves stating the name of the targeted file or files. The KILL statement accepts the ? and * filename wildcards. You also can specify a drive and directory name.

- ☐ You can display a list of files using the FILES statement. The FILES statement accepts the ? and * filename wildcards. You can also specify a drive and directory name.

- ☐ You can open a file for input and output using the OPEN statement. This statement specifies the name of the file, the I/O mode, the associated file handle, and the optional buffer size.

- ☐ You can close a file using the CLOSE statement to close the buffer of one or more files. If no file handles are specified, the CLOSE statement closes all of the file buffers. The RESET statement performs the same task.

☐ Text file output operations involve special versions of the PRINT, PRINT USING, and WRITE statements.

☐ Text file input operations involve special versions of the INPUT statement, LINE INPUT function, and INPUT$ function. QBasic also provides the Boolean EOF function to detect the end of a file and to avoid a runtime error.

Q&A

Q. Can a program store the output of the FILES function in an array?

A. No. Unfortunately, the FILES function only displays the list of files.

Q. Can I rename a file across a drive using the NAME statement?

A. No, QBasic will raise a runtime error.

Q. Should a program always use the LINE INPUT statement, instead of the INPUT statement, to read an entire text line?

A. Yes. As with the keyboard version, the file-oriented LINE INPUT statement reads an entire line, including commas.

Q. How does the APPEND access mode affect the file output?

A. The APPEND mode causes any output to the targeted file to be added to the original contents of the output file.

Q. What happens if an OPEN statement opens an existing file for output?

A. The existing file is first automatically deleted and then re-created to receive the new batch of input.

Q. What happens if an OPEN statement opens a nonexistent file for output?

A. QBasic creates the file first and then sets it to receive input from the program.

Q. What happens if an OPEN statement opens a nonexistent file for input?

A. QBasic raises a runtime error.

Q. Does the KILL "*.*" statement prompt you to confirm the deletion of all files in the current directory (like the DEL command in DOS)?

18

A. No. That's probably why Microsoft gave the name `KILL` to the file deletion statement!

Workshop

The Workshop provides quiz questions to help you solidify your understanding of the material covered and exercises to provide you with experience in using what you've learned. Try to understand the quiz and exercise answers before continuing on to the next chapter. Answers are provided in Appendix B, "Answers."

Quiz

1. Where is the error in the following statements?

```
DIM oldFile AS STRING
DIM newFile AS STRING

oldFile = "DATA>DAT"
newFile = "MYDATA.DAT"
NAME oldFile AS newFile
END
```

2. Where is the error in the following statements?

```
DIM InFilename AS STRING
DIM OutFilename AS STRING
DIM S AS STRING
InFilename = "\AUTOEXEC.BAT"
OutFilename = "\AUTOEXEC.NEW"
OPEN InFilename FOR INPUT AS #1
OPEN OutFilename FOR INPUT AS #1
DO WHILE NOT EOF(1)
  LINE INPUT#1, S
  PRINT #1, S
LOOP
CLOSE
```

3. Where is the error in the following statements?

```
DIM InFilename AS STRING
DIM OutFilename AS STRING
DIM S AS STRING
InFilename = "\AUTOEXEC.BAT"
OutFilename = "\AUTOEXEC.BAT"
OPEN InFilename FOR INPUT AS #1
OPEN OutFilename FOR INPUT AS #2
DO WHILE NOT EOF(1)
   LINE INPUT#1, S
   PRINT #2, S
LOOP
CLOSE
```

4. Where is the likely error in the following statements?

```
DIM InFilename AS STRING
DIM OutFilename AS STRING
DIM S AS STRING
InFilename = "\AUTOEXEC.BAT"
OutFilename = "\AUTOEXEC.NEW"
OPEN InFilename FOR INPUT AS #1
OPEN OutFilename FOR INPUT AS #2
DO WHILE NOT EOF(1)
   INPUT#1, S
   PRINT #2, S
LOOP
CLOSE
```

18

Exercise

1. Write a program (call it SQFILE4.BAS) that copies the contents of one text file to another.

DAY 19

Random-Access and Binary File I/O

On Day 18 I presented text file I/O. This chapter presents the two other types of file I/O—random-access and binary—that are supported by QBasic. Today you learn about the following topics:

- [ ] What is a random-access file?

- [ ] Selecting and locating a record in a random-access file using the SEEK statement and SEEK function.

- [ ] Reading and writing random-access records using the GET and PUT statements.

- [ ] What is a binary file?

- [ ] Locating a byte in a binary file using the SEEK statement.

- [ ] Reading and writing bytes using the GET and PUT statements.

What is a Random-Access File?

The text files that I presented on Day 18 store text lines with varied lengths. If you think of each line as a *record*, then you can think of a text file as a file that stores variable-length records. The lack of a uniform length forces you to process the records by sequentially reading and/or writing the records in text files.

QBasic supports another type of file, one that stores records with the same length. Therefore, it is very easy to calculate the location of each uniform-length record. QBasic supports the random-access file mode, which enables a program to read and write data, in random records, without having to read and/or write all the other records. To open a file for random-access, specify the RANDOM access mode in the FOR clause of the OPEN statement. The CLOSE statement and EOF function also work with random-access files.

What kind of *uniform* data does the random-access files store and recall? The BASIC implementations prior to QBasic (which had no user-defined data types) assembled a group of fields with predefined data types in the FIELD statement. QBasic still supports the FIELD statement for backward compatibility. However, QBasic offers a better random-access I/O using predefined types (except variable-length strings) or user-defined data types. I focus on this QBasic mechanism for random-access file I/O, because it is much simpler than the old mechanism. You can store simple numbers or fixed strings (one item per record) in a random-access file. In the case where you want to store more than one item per record, you must use a user-defined data type. Structures are ideal for storage in random-access files, because they do not have any variable-length fields, such as flexible strings. Consequently, you can store and recall records in a random-access file by writing and reading structures.

The *SEEK* Statement

QBasic offers the SEEK statement to move the internal file pointer to a specific record in a random-access file. QBasic also provides the SEEK function to return the current record number.

The SEEK Statement

The general syntax for the SEEK statement is

```
SEEK [#]fileHandle, recordNumber
```

The *fileHandle* parameter is the file handle for the random-access file. The *recordNumber* parameter is the sought record number in the random-access file. The range of values for this parameter is from 1 to the number of actual records plus one. The maximum value for the *recordNumber* parameter is 2,147,483,647. When *recordNumber* parameter has the latter value, the SEEK statement expands the file by one (empty) record.

Example:

```
FileNum = FREEFILE
OPEN "SALES.DAT" FOR RANDOM AS #FileNum
SEEK #FileNum, 10
```

19

The SEEK Function

The general syntax for the SEEK function is

```
SEEK(fileHandle)
```

The *fileHandle* parameter is the file handle for the random-access file. The SEEK function returns the current record number.

Example:

```
FileNum = FREEFILE
OPEN "SALES.DAT" FOR RANDOM AS #FileNum
SEEK #FileNum, 10
PRINT "At record number "; SEEK(FileNum)
```

The *PUT* and *GET* Statements

QBasic provides the PUT and GET statements to write and read records to and from a random-access file.

The PUT Statement

The general syntax for the PUT statement is

```
PUT [#]fileHandle, [recordNumber], varName
```

The *fileHandle* parameter is the file handle for the random-access file. The *recordNumber* parameter is the sought record number in the random-access file. The range of values for this parameter is from 1 to the number of actual records plus one. The maximum value for the *recordNumber* parameter is 2,147,483,647. When the *recordNumber* parameter has the latter value, the PUT statement expands the file by writing a new record. If you omit the *recordNumber* parameter, the PUT statement writes to the next record. This language feature allows the PUT statement to sequentially write records. The *varName* parameter is the name of a simple or structured variable with fields that are written to the file. The *varName* parameter cannot be a variable-length string.

Example:

```
TYPE TCoord
  X AS INTEGER
```

```
   Y AS INTEGER
END TYPE
DIM Point AS TCoord
FileNum = FREEFILE
OPEN "NUMBERS.DAT" FOR RANDOM AS #FileNum
FOR I = 1 TO 100
  Point.X = INT(RND * 1000)
  Point.Y = INT(RND * 1000)
  PUT #FileNum, , Point
NEXT I
CLOSE #FileNum
```

The GET Statement

The general syntax for the GET statement is

```
GET [#]fileHandle, [recordNumber], varName
```

The *fileHandle* parameter is the file handle for the random-access file. The *recordNumber* parameter is the sought record number in the random-access file. The range of values for this parameter is from 1 to the number of actual records plus one. The maximum value for the *recordNumber* parameter is 2,147,483,647. If you omit the *recordNumber* parameter, the GET statement reads the next record. This language feature allows the GET statement to read records sequentially. The *varName* parameter is the name of a simple or structured variable that receives the data from the record read. The *varName* parameter cannot be a variable-length string.

Example:

```
TYPE TCoord
   X AS INTEGER
   Y AS INTEGER
END TYPE
DIM Point AS TCoord
FileNum = FREEFILE
OPEN "NUMBERS.DAT" FOR RANDOM AS #FileNum
FOR I = 1 TO 100
```

19

```
    GET #FileNum, , Point
    PRINT "("; Point.X; ", "; Point.Y; ")"
  NEXT I
  CLOSE #FileNum
```

Let me present two programs that illustrate the use of random-access files. Listing 19.1, RAFILE1.BAS, sequentially writes records to a random-access file. The program displays the names of various states dispersed on the screen, and then writes the names of these states and their screen location to a random-access file.

Listing 19.1. RAFILE1.BAS, which sequentially writes records to a random-access file.

```
 1: DECLARE SUB ShowMessage (Msg AS ANY)
 2: DECLARE SUB Delay (T AS SINGLE)
 3: REM Program that writes structures to a file
 4: REM
 5: ' declare the data type TMessage
 6: TYPE TMessage
 7:    Text AS STRING * 80
 8:    X AS INTEGER
 9:    Y AS INTEGER
10: END TYPE
11: ' declare constants
12: CONST FILENAME = "MESSAGE.DAT"
13: CONST PERIOD = 1
14: ' declare variables
15: DIM Message AS TMessage
16: DIM FileNum AS INTEGER
17:
18: CLS
19: FileNum = FREEFILE
20: OPEN FILENAME FOR RANDOM AS FileNum
21: DO
22:    READ Message.Text
23:    ' read the last data item?
```

```
24:    IF UCASE$(RTRIM$(Message.Text)) = "EOD" THEN EXIT DO
25:    READ Message.Y
26:    READ Message.X
27:    ' display message
28:    ShowMessage Message
29:    Delay PERIOD
30:    ' write message to the random-access file
31:    PUT #FileNum, , Message
32: LOOP
33:
34: CLOSE #FileNum
35:
36: ' ****************** DATA Statements **************
37:
38: DATA California, 1, 3
39: DATA Virginia, 4, 18
40: DATA Maryland, 15, 10
41: DATA Colorado, 5, 40
42: DATA Maine, 17, 34
43: DATA Michigan, 10, 10
44: DATA Alabama, 20, 40
45: DATA Oregon, 7, 50
46:
47: DATA EOD, 0, 0
48:
49: END
50:
51: SUB Delay (T AS SINGLE)
52:    DIM DT AS SINGLE
53:    DT = TIMER
54:    DO
55:    LOOP UNTIL (TIMER - DT) >= T
56: END SUB
57:
58: SUB ShowMessage (Msg AS TMessage)
59: ' display message
60:    LOCATE Msg.Y, Msg.X
61:    PRINT RTRIM$(Msg.Text)
62: END SUB
```

19

Here is some sample output for the program in Listing 19.1:

```
California


Virginia
Colorado

Oregon



Michigan




Maryland

Maine



Alabama
```

The program in Listing 19.1 declares the user-defined type TMessage on lines 6–10. The structure has three fields: the fixed-string field Text, the integer field X, and the integer field Y. These fields store the text and location of a state (which I call a message) that appears on the screen. Lines 12 and 13 declare the constants FILENAME and PERIOD, respectively. Lines 15 and 16 declare the variables Message (of type TMessage) and FileNum, respectively.

The statement on line 19 assigns the next available file handle number to the variable FileNum. The OPEN statement on line 20 opens the file FILENAME for random-access I/O and specifies the file handle FileNum. The DO-LOOP on lines 21–32 reads the messages from the DATA statements, displays them, and then writes them to the random-access file.

Take a look at these tasks in more detail. The READ statement on line 22 obtains the next string from the DATA statements. The IF-THEN statement on line 24 determines if the uppercase version of the trimmed variable Message.Text matches the string literal "EOD". If this condition is true, the loop has read the last data item. The program then executes the EXIT DO in the THEN clause and exits the open DO-LOOP. Otherwise, the program proceeds to read the values for the

Y and X fields from the DATA statements. The statement on line 28 calls the subroutine ShowMessage to display the message in the structure Message. The statement on line 29 calls the subroutine Delay to delay the program for PERIOD seconds. Finally, the PUT statement on line 31 writes the Message structure to the next record in the random-access file. The CLOSE statement on line 34 closes the file buffer.

The file MESSAGE.DAT now contains a set of random-access records. Listing 19.2 shows the program RAFILE2.BAS, which reads and updates the records in the random-access file MESSAGE.DAT. The program performs the following tasks:

1. Opens the file MESSAGE.DAT for random-access.

2. Repeats the following tasks until you press any key:

   2.1. Reads a record at random in the data file.

   2.2. Displays the message in the record.

   2.3. Waits for a second.

   2.4. Erases the message.

   2.5. Assigns new random values to the coordinates of the message.

   2.6. Updates the record with the new coordinates.

3. Closes the random-access file.

 Listing 19.2. RAFILE2.BAS, which reads and updates the records in the random-access file MESSAGE.DAT.

```
1: DECLARE SUB EraseMessage (Msg AS ANY)
2: DECLARE SUB ShowMessage (Msg AS ANY)
3: DECLARE SUB Delay (T AS SINGLE)
4: REM Program that reads structures from a file
5: REM
6: ' declare the data type TMessage
7: TYPE TMessage
8:   Text AS STRING * 80
9:   X AS INTEGER
10:   Y AS INTEGER
11: END TYPE
```

continues

Listing 19.2. continued

```
12: ' declare constants
13: CONST FILENAME = "MESSAGE.DAT"
14: CONST PERIOD = 1
15: ' declare variables
16: DIM Message AS TMessage
17: DIM FileNum AS INTEGER
18: DIM N AS INTEGER
19: DIM I AS INTEGER
20:
21: CLS
22: FileNum = FREEFILE
23: OPEN FILENAME FOR RANDOM AS FileNum
24:
25: N = 0
26: ' loop to count the number of records
27: DO WHILE NOT EOF(FileNum)
28:   GET #FileNum, , Message
29:   N = N + 1
30: LOOP
31:
32: PRINT "Press any key to stop random messages"
33: Delay 2
34:
35: CLS
36: ' reseed the random-number generator
37: RANDOMIZE TIMER
38:
39: ' loop to display messages at random
40: DO
41:   ' get index
42:   I = INT(RND * (N - 1)) + 1
43:   ' seek record number I
44:   SEEK #FileNum, I
45:   ' get the record number I
46:   GET #FileNum, , Message
47:   ' display message
48:   ShowMessage Message
49:   Delay PERIOD
50:   ' erase the message
```

```
51:    EraseMessage Message
52:    SOUND 100, 1
53:    ' see record I again
54:    SEEK #FileNum, I
55:    ' update the X and Y fields of structure Message
56:    Message.X = 1 + INT(RND * 80)
57:    Message.Y = 1 + INT(RND * 25)
58:    ' write the updated structure to record number I
59:    PUT #FileNum, , Message
60: LOOP UNTIL INKEY$ <> ""
61:
62: CLOSE #FileNum
63: END
64:
65: SUB Delay (T AS SINGLE)
66:    DIM DT AS SINGLE
67:    DT = TIMER
68:    DO
69:    LOOP UNTIL (TIMER - DT) >= T
70: END SUB
71:
72: SUB EraseMessage (Msg AS TMessage)
73: ' erase the message Msg
74:    LOCATE Msg.Y, Msg.X
75:    PRINT SPACE$(LEN(RTRIM$(Msg.Text)));
76: END SUB
77:
78: SUB ShowMessage (Msg AS TMessage)
79: ' display message
80:    LOCATE Msg.Y, Msg.X
81:    PRINT RTRIM$(Msg.Text);
82: END SUB
```

Run the program in Listing 19.2 and observe the randomness of the names of states as each appears on the screen and then quickly disappears.

The program in Listing 19.2 declares the same TMessage structure as in Listing 19.1. The program also declares the same constants that appear in Listing 19.1. Lines 16–19 declare the program's variables, including the structure Message.

The statement on line 22 assigns the next available file handle number to the variable FileNum. The OPEN statement on line 23 opens the file FILENAME for random-access I/O and specifies the file handle FileNum.

To count the current number of records in the random-access file, the program uses the variable N. The statement on line 25 initializes that variable. The program uses the DO-WHILE loop on lines 27–30 to traverse and count the records in the file. Notice that the condition of the WHILE clause uses the EOF function. Also notice that the record traversal uses the GET statement on line 28. This statement does not specify the record number parameter, allowing it to read the records sequentially. When the loop stops iterating, the file pointer is at the end of the file. Any additional input must follow a SEEK statement or a GET statement that specifies a valid record number.

The DO-UNTIL loop on lines 40–60 displays, hides, and updates the messages (the names of the states, to be more exact). The statement on line 42 obtains a random index for a record and stores the index in variable I. The SEEK statement on line 44 moves the file pointer to record number I. The GET statement on line 46 obtains the data of the targeted record and saves it in the structured variable Message. I can eliminate the SEEK statement from the program by stating the record number in the GET statement.

The statement on line 48 calls the subroutine ShowMessage to display the Text field of the structure Message at the Message.X and Message.Y screen coordinates. The statement on lines 49 calls the subroutine Delay to pause the program for a PERIOD number of seconds. The statement on line 51 erases the current message by calling subroutine EraseMessage. The SOUND statement (more about this statement in Day 21, "Music and Sound") sounds a short low-tone beep.

The SEEK statement on line 54 moves the file pointer back one record, to record number I. The statements on lines 56 and 57 assign random values to the X and Y fields of structure Message. The PUT statement on line 59 writes the structure Message to record number I. The CLOSE statement on line 62 closes the buffer of the random-access file.

What is a Binary File?

A binary file is merely a single-byte, random-access file. Because a byte is the smallest unit of storage, binary files offer the ability to read and manipulate the

lowest units of data. When you become very proficient in file I/O operation, you will find that binary files offer more control than text or random-access files. For now, I offer a simple introduction to binary files.

To open a file for binary I/O, use the BINARY keyword in the FOR clause of an OPEN statement. The EOF function and the CLOSE statement also work for binary files and perform the same tasks as for the other two types of file I/O.

The SEEK statement and SEEK function also work with binary files in a manner very similar to that of random-access files. The main difference is that with binary files you must regard the record number as a byte location in the file.

The PUT and GET statements also work with binary files in a manner very similar to that of random-access files. The main difference is that you need to use a string variable as a buffer that receives bytes from the file or supplies bytes to the file.

The PUT Statement

The general syntax for the PUT statement is

```
PUT [#]fileHandle, [byteNumber], varName
```

The *fileHandle* parameter is the file handle for the random-access file. The *byteNumber* parameter is the sought byte number in the random-access file. The range of values for this parameter is from 1 to the number of actual bytes plus one. The maximum value for the *byteNumber* parameter is 2,147,483,647. When the *byteNumber* parameter has the latter value, the PUT statement expands the file by writing new bytes. If you omit the *byteNumber* parameter, the PUT statement writes the next bytes. This language feature allows the PUT statement to write bytes sequentially. The *varName* parameter is the name of a variable (typically a string variable) that contains the bytes written to the file.

Example:

```
DIM S AS STRING
FileNum = FREEFILE
OPEN "NUMBERS.DAT" FOR RANDOM AS #FileNum

S = ""
```

19

```
FOR I = 1 TO 100
  S = S + CHR$(I + 65)
NEXT I
PUT #FileNum, 1, S
CLOSE #FileNum
```

The GET Statement

The general syntax for the GET statement is

```
GET [#]fileHandle, [byteNumber], varName
```

The *fileHandle* parameter is the file handle for the random-access file. The *byteNumber* parameter is the sought byte number in the random-access file. The range of values for this parameter is from 1 to the number of actual bytes plus one. The maximum value for the *byteNumber* parameter is 2,147,483,647. If you omit the *byteNumber* parameter, the GET statement reads the next bytes. This language feature allows the GET statement to read bytes sequentially. The *varName* parameter is the variable (typically a string variable) that receives the bytes read from the file. The number of bytes read is equal to or less than the current size of the parameter *varName*.

Example:

```
DIM S AS STRING
FileNum = FREEFILE
OPEN "NUMBERS.DAT" FOR RANDOM AS #FileNum
S = SPACE$(100)
PUT #FileNum, 1, S
CLOSE #FileNum
```

Let me present a simple and practical example of binary file I/O. Listing 19.3 shows the program BNFILE1.BAS, which copies files. The program is able to copy any kind of file, not just text files. To copy files, the program prompts you for the source and destination filenames. The program then displays a message that it is copying the files. Once the program is finished, it displays the message "Done!".

 Listing 19.3. BNFILE1.BAS, which copies files.

```
 1: REM Program which copies a file
 2: REM
 3: ' declare constant
 4: CONST BUFFER% = 8192
 5: ' declare variables
 6: DIM InFilename AS STRING
 7: DIM OutFilename AS STRING
 8: DIM InFile AS INTEGER
 9: DIM OutFile AS INTEGER
10: DIM BuffVar AS STRING
11:
12: CLS
13: DO
14:    INPUT "Enter input filename : ", InFilename
15:    InFilename = UCASE$(InFilename)
16:    PRINT
17: LOOP UNTIL InFilename <> ""
18:
19: DO
20:    INPUT "Enter output filename : ", OutFilename
21:    OutFilename = UCASE$(OutFilename)
22:    PRINT
23: LOOP UNTIL OutFilename <> "" AND InFilename <> OutFilename
24:
25: ON ERROR GOTO Bad.InFilename
26: InFile = FREEFILE
27: OPEN InFilename FOR BINARY AS InFile
28: ON ERROR GOTO 0
29:
30: ON ERROR GOTO Bad.OutFilename
31: OutFile = FREEFILE
32: OPEN OutFilename FOR BINARY AS OutFile
33: ON ERROR GOTO 0
34:
35: PRINT "Copying file "; InFilename; " to file "; OutFilename
36: PRINT
37: ' loop to copy the files
38: DO WHILE NOT EOF(InFile)
```

continues

Listing 19.3. continued

```
39:    ' prepare the buffer
40:    BuffVar = SPACE$(BUFFER)
41:    GET #InFile, , BuffVar
42:    PUT #OutFile, , BuffVar
43: LOOP
44:
45: ' close files
46: CLOSE
47: PRINT : PRINT "Done!"
48: EndPrgm:
49: END
50:
51: Bad.InFilename:
52:    PRINT
53:    PRINT "Cannot open file "; InFilename
54:    RESUME EndPrgm
55:
56: Bad.OutFilename:
57:    PRINT
58:    PRINT "Cannot open file "; OutFilename
59:    RESUME EndPrgm
```

Here is some sample output for the program in Listing 19.3:

```
Enter input filename : \command.com

Enter output filename : a:\c.com

Copying file \COMMAND.COM to file A:\C.COM


Done!
```

The program in Listing 19.3 declares the constant BUFFER% on line 4. Lines 6–10 contain the declarations of the variables. The DO-UNTIL loop on lines 13–17 prompts you to enter an input filename and stores it in the variable InFilename. The statement on line 15 converts your input into uppercase characters. The loop iterates until you enter a nonempty string. The DO-UNTIL loop on lines 19–23 prompts you to enter an output filename and stores it in the variable OutFilename. The statement on line 21 converts your input into uppercase. The loop iterates until the variable OutFile contains a nonempty string that differs from the contents of variable InFilename.

The statement on line 25 sets up an error trap for opening the input file. The statement on line 26 calls the function FREEFILE to return the next available file handle number and store it in the variable InFile. The OPEN statement on line 27 opens the input file in BINARY access mode and specifies the InFile file handle. The statement on line 28 turns off the error trap. The program performs similar steps for the output files on lines 30–33.

The PRINT statement on line 35 displays a message that the program is copying the source file to the destination file. The actual copy process occurs in the DO-WHILE loop on lines 38–43. The WHILE clause uses the EOF function to detect the end of the source file. The statement on line 40 assigns a BUFFER number of spaces to the variable BuffVar. This variable acts as a holding area for the transient bytes. The GET statement on line 41 reads characters from the file and stores then in the variable BuffVar. The statement reads at most BUFFER number of bytes. The PUT statement on line 42 writes the contents of the variable BuffVar to the output file. The CLOSE statement on line 46 closes the file buffers.

Summary

This chapter introduced you to the more advanced random-access and binary file I/O operations. Today you learned the following:

□ A random-access file contains equal-length records. Such records make it easy to navigate through the file to read and/or write records at random. To open a file in random-access mode, specify the RANDOM keyword in the FOR clause of the OPEN statement.

□ The SEEK statement enables you to select a record in the random-access file. You can then read data to or write data from that record. The SEEK function returns the current record number in a random-access file.

□ The GET and PUT statements enable you to read and write simple or structured variables from a random-access file.

□ A binary file is a single-byte, random-access file. To open a file in random-access mode, specify the BINARY keyword in the FOR clause of the OPEN statement.

19

☐ The SEEK statement enables you to select a byte location in the binary file. You can then read or write data starting at that byte location. The SEEK function returns the current byte location in a binary file.

☐ The GET and PUT statements enable you to read and write variables (typically string variables) from a binary file.

Q&A

Q. Does specifying a large buffer size in the LEN clause of the OPEN statement speed up file I/O operations?

A. Yes. In addition, it is helpful to declare matching buffer sizes for the input and output files. This approach really speeds up file I/O.

Q. What happens if the statement on line 40 in Listing 19.3 is removed?

A. The program hangs! The reason is that when the variable BuffVar reaches the GET statement inside the DO-WHILE loop, it contains an empty string. Consequently, it blocks the actual transfer of bytes and prevents the file pointer from advancing. The program is then stuck in the loop.

Q. Can a procedure pass a handle number of an open file?

A. Yes. In fact, this approach is better than passing the filename associated with the handle because it is easier to check the validity of the filename in the main program section.

Workshop

The Workshop provides quiz questions to help you solidify your understanding of the material covered and exercises to provide you with experience in using what you've learned. Try to understand the quiz and exercise answers before continuing on to the next chapter. Answers are provided in Appendix B, "Answers."

Quiz

1. Where is the error in the following statements (assuming that the file DATA.DAT does not exist when the program starts running)?

```
DIM N AS INTEGER
N = 12
OPEN "DATA.DAT" FOR RANDOM AS #1
PUT #1, 4, N
CLOSE #1
END
```

2. Where is the error in the following statements (assuming that the file DATA.DAT does not exist when the program starts running)?

```
DIM N AS INTEGER
DIM X AS DOUBLE
N = 12
X = 1.2
OPEN "DATA.DAT" FOR RANDOM AS #1
PUT #1, 1, N, X
CLOSE #1
END
```

3. How can you correct the preceding code?

19

Exercise

1. Modify the program BNFILE1.BAS (in Listing 19.3) to create the program BNFILE2.BAS. The new program should display the number of bytes copied in the DO-WHILE loop. Use the variable FileSize to maintain the number of bytes transferred.

DAY
20

Drawing
Graphics Shapes

This chapter introduces you to drawing graphics shapes in QBasic. The topic of graphics in QBasic is worthy of its own book. Therefore, in this chapter I touch on the most common aspects of QBasic graphics. Today, you learn about the following topics:

☐ The screen modes supported by QBasic

☐ The QBasic colors

☐ Selecting a screen mode using the SCREEN statement

☐ Selecting colors using the COLOR statement

☐ Changing default color values using the PALETTE statement

☐ An overview of the graphics-mode coordinates

☐ Setting the portion of the screen for graphics output (called the *viewport*) using the VIEW statement

☐ Setting the coordinates of the viewport with the WINDOW statement

☐ Drawing points and curves using the PSET statement

☐ Drawing lines and boxes using the LINE statement

☐ Drawing circles, ellipses, and arcs using the CIRCLE statement

☐ Drawing custom shapes using the DRAW statement

The first two sections offer you background information related to the graphics capability of various display adapters, and the colors supported by QBasic.

The Screen Modes

Until now, all the programs that I presented were in text mode. QBasic supports graphics screens in modes that take advantage of the various kinds of graphics adapters, such as CGA, EGA, VGA, MCGA, Hercules, Olivetti, and AT&T 6300. The text or graphics that you see on your screen is also stored in a special memory location used by the display adapter. A screen full of text requires 4000 bytes of storage: 2000 bytes for the characters and another 2000 bytes for their display attributes. Consequently, each 4K of display memory is called a **video page**. Although the screen in text mode uses 4K of display memory, high resolution graphics require more memory. The amount of memory required for graphics depends on the resolution and the number of colors supported. The higher the resolution and/or the number of colors supported, the more memory is needed. In this chapter I assume that you have a computer with a EGA or VGA display adapter. Unless you are using an old PC, your display adapter is most likely EGA or VGA. Table 20.1 summarizes the various screen modes supported by QBasic.

Table 20.1. The various screen modes for the different popular display adapters.

Screen Mode Value	Screen Mode	Adapters
0	Text	CGA, EGA, VGA, MCGA, and monochrome
1	320 x 200 graphics	CGA, EGA, VGA, and MCGA
2	640 x 200 graphics	EGA and VGA
3	720 x 384 graphics	Hercules
4	640 x 400 graphics	Olivetti, AT&T 6300
7	320 x 200 graphics	EGA and VGA
8	640 x 200 graphics	EGA and VGA
9	640 x 350 graphics	EGA and VGA
10	640 x 350 graphics	EGA and VGA
11	640 x 480 graphics	VGA and MCGA
12	640 x 480 graphics	VGA
13	320 x 200 graphics	VGA and MCGA

20

The QBasic Colors

QBasic supports as many as 16 colors, depending on the display adapter and the current screen mode setting. Table 20.2 shows the color attributes and default color values supported by QBasic. QBasic allows you to change the default color values using the PALETTE statement (more about PALETTE later in this chapter).

Table 20.2. The color attributes and default values supported by QBasic.

Color Attribute	Default Color Value[1]	Displayed Color	Screen Modes
0	0	Black	0, 7, 8, 9[2], 12,
1	1	Blue	and 13
2	2	Green	
3	3	Cyan	
4	4	Red	
5	5	Magenta	
6	6	Brown	
7	7	White	
8	8	Gray	
9	9	Light blue	
10	10	Light green	
11	11	Light cyan	
12	12	Light red	
13	13	Light magenta	
14	14	Yellow	
15	15	High-intensity white	

0	0	Black	1 and 9[3]
1	11	Light cyan	
2	13	Light magenta	
3	15	High-intensity white	
0	0	Black	2 and 11
1	15	High-intensity white	

Notes:

1. EGA color numbers. VGA and MCGA use display-color values that yield visually comparable colors.
2. For VGA or EGA with video memory in excess of 64K.
3. EGA with video memory 64K or less.

The *SCREEN* Statement

QBasic offers the SCREEN statement to enable you to select the screen mode and set other display characteristics listed in Table 20.1.

Syntax

The SCREEN Statement

The general syntax for the SCREEN statement is

```
SCREEN mode% [,[colorSwitch%] [,[activePage%] [,visualPage%]]]
```

The parameter *mode%* specifies the screen mode. The parameter *colorSwitch%* is a value (either 0 or 1) that shifts between color and monocolor display (modes 0 and 1 only). In screen mode 0, the value of 0 disables color. Any other value enables color. In screen mode 1, a value of 0 enables color. Any other value disables color. The parameter *activepage%* specifies the screen page that receives output text or graphics. The parameter *visualPage%* specifies the screen page that is currently displayed on the screen.

20

Examples:

```
' select screen mode 1 to view and write to page 0
SCREEN 1, , 0, 0


' select screen mode 8 to view page 0 and write to page 1
SCREEN 8, , 0, 1
```

The *COLOR* Statement

QBasic offers the COLOR statement to set the foreground and background colors on your screen.

Syntax

The **COLOR** Statement

The general syntax for the COLOR statement is for screen mode 0 (text only):

COLOR [*foreground%*] [,[*background%*] [,*border%*]]

For screen mode 1, the syntax is

COLOR [*background%*] [,*palette%*]

For screen modes 4, 12, and 13 the syntax is

COLOR [*foreground%*]

For screen modes 7–10 the syntax is

COLOR [*foreground%*] [,*background&*]

The parameter *foreground%* is a number that sets the foreground screen color. When the argument for parameter *foreground&* selects screen mode 0, the parameter *foreground%* is a color attribute that specifies the text color. In other screen modes, parameter *foreground%* sets a color attribute or 4-bit color value (only screen mode 4) that sets the text and line-drawing color. The parameter *background%* specifies a number that sets the background screen color. When the argument for parameter *background&* sets screen mode 0, *background%* is a color attribute. In screen mode 1, *background%* is a 4-bit color value. In screen modes 7-10, parameter *background&* is a color value. The parameter *border%* sets the color attribute that defines the screen border color. The parameter *palette%* sets a number (either 0 or 1) that selects one of the following two sets of color attributes to use

palette%	Attribute 1	Attribute 2	Attribute 3
0	Green	Red	Brown
1	Cyan	Magenta	Bright white

The accessible color attributes and values depend on your graphics adapter and the screen mode established by the last SCREEN statement. If your system has an EGA, VGA, or MCGA adapter, use the PALETTE statement to alter the color assignments of the color attributes.

Example:

```
DIM aColor AS INTEGER
SCREEN 8
FOR aColor = 0 TO 15
  COLOR aColor
  PRINT "Hello"
NEXT aColor
```

The *PALETTE* Statement

QBasic supports the PALETTE statement to change the color assignments of color attributes in the current screen mode. QBasic also offers the PALETTE USING statement to perform a similar task. I discuss the PALETTE statement because it offers adequate operations. The PALETTE and PALETTE USING statements work only on systems with EGA, VGA, or MCGA graphics display adapters.

20

Syntax

The PALETTE Statement

The general syntax for the PALETTE is

```
PALETTE [attribute%, color&]
```

The parameter *attribute%* specifies the color attribute to change. The parameter *color&* is a color value to assign to an attribute. If you don't specify any arguments, the PALETTE statement restores the default colors. The accessible color attributes and values depend on your graphics adapter and the screen mode established by the last SCREEN statement.

Examples:

```
PALETTE 0, 1
```

```
' restore default colors
PALETTE
```

The Graphics-Mode Coordinates

As shown in Table 20.1, the various graphics screen modes have different resolutions. Each screen mode resolution specifies the maximum number of **pixels** (short for picture elements) in the X and Y direction.

Note: The X screen coordinates for the graphics mode increase from the left to right. The Y screen coordinates for the graphics mode increase from the top to bottom. Thus, the Y coordinates run in the reverse order of the Cartesian coordinates (where they increase from bottom to top). Fortunately, QBasic allows you to specify the Cartesian-style Y coordinates. In addition, QBasic enables you to specify your own coordinate scale. QBasic performs automatic mapping between your custom coordinates scale and the actual coordinates of the graphics screen. This graphics feature greatly simplifies how you plan and write graphics programs in QBasic.

The *VIEW* Statement

The QBasic VIEW statement defines the size and location of a viewport where graphics can be displayed on the screen.

Syntax

The VIEW Statement

The general syntax for the VIEW statement is

VIEW [[SCREEN] *(x1!,y1!)-(x2!,y2!)* [,[*color%*] [,*border%*]]]

The keyword SCREEN indicates that the coordinates are relative to the screen rather than the viewport. The points *(x1!,y1!)-(x2!,y2!)* are the coordinates of diagonally opposite corners of the viewport. The parameter *color%* specifies the color attribute that sets the viewport fill color. The parameter *border%* sets the viewport border color. When all arguments are omitted, the entire screen is the viewport. The accessible color attributes and values depend on your graphics adapter and the screen mode established by the last SCREEN statement.

Example:

```
SCREEN 1
VIEW (10, 10)-(200, 150), , 1
LOCATE 1, 5: PRINT "A big hello!";
VIEW SCREEN (80, 80)-(200, 125), , 1
LOCATE 9, 5: PRINT "A small hello!";
```

The *WINDOW* Statement

The WINDOW statement defines logical dimensions for the current graphics viewport. Use the WINDOW statement to define your custom viewport coordinates scales.

Syntax

The WINDOW Statement

The general syntax for the WINDOW statement is

WINDOW [[SCREEN] *(x1!,y1!)-(x2!,y2!)*]

The keyword SCREEN inverts the normal Cartesian direction of the Y screen coordinates such that the y values decrease from the bottom of the screen to its top. The point *(x1!,y1!)* specifies the lower-left screen coordinates (upper-left when keyword SCREEN is used) of the

20

viewport. The point *(x2!,y2!)* specifies the upper-right screen coordinates (lower-right when keyword SCREEN is used) of the viewport. Without any arguments, the WINDOW statement disables the logical coordinate system.

Example:

```
SCREEN 8
' screen has (0, 0) at the lower-left corner and
' (1000, 1000) at the upper-right corner.
WINDOW (0, 0)-(1000, 1000)
Factor = 4 * ATN(1) / 180
FOR I = 0 TO 180
    PSET I, 1000 * ABS(SIN(I * Factor)
NEXT I
```

Plotting Points with the *PSET* Statement

QBasic offers the PSET statement to plot a point on the graphics screen. This statement is suitable for plotting individual points, curves of mathematical functions, and shapes with curved edges. QBasic also provides the PRESET statement to erase a point using reverse colors.

The **PSET** and **PRESET** Statements

The general syntax for the PSET and PRESET statements is

```
PSET [STEP] (x!, y!) [,color%]
PRESET [STEP] (x!, y!) [,color%]
```

The keyword STEP specifies that the parameters *x!* and *y!* represent values that are relative to the current graphics cursor position. The point (x!, y!) specifies the screen coordinates of the drawn pixel. The optional parameter *color%* sets the pixel color. If you omit this parameter, PRESET uses the current background color, whereas PSET uses the current foreground color.

The available color attributes depend on your graphics adapter and screen mode. The coordinate values depend on the graphics adapter, screen mode, and last VIEW and WINDOW statements.

Example:

```
' plot random points
CONST MAX.POINTS = 100
DIM I AS INTEGER
SCREEN 8
WINDOW (0, 0)-(1000, 1000)
FOR I = 1 TO MAX.POINTS
    PSET INT(RND * 1000) + 1, INT(RND * 1000) + 1
NEXT I
```

Let's look at an example. Listing 20.1, GRAF1.BAS, plots the sine function using the PSET statement. The program draws the X and Y axes and then plots three cycles of the sine function (the angle values run from -3 * 180 degrees to 3 * 180 degrees).

Listing 20.1. GRAF1.BAS, which plots the sine function using the PSET statement.

```
 1: REM Program which plots the SIN(X) function
 2: REM
 3: ' declare constants
 4: CONST CYCLES = 3
 5: CONST MAX.Y = 1.5
 6: CONST MIN.Y = -1.5
 7: CONST MAX.X = CYCLES * 180
 8: CONST MIN.X = CYCLES * -180
 9: CONST INCR = .1
10: ' declare variables
11: DIM X AS SINGLE
12: DIM Y AS SINGLE
13: DIM Factor AS DOUBLE
14:
15: ' obtain the angle conversion factor
```

continues

Type **Listing 20.1. continued**

```
16: Factor = 4 * ATN(1) / 180
17: SCREEN 2
18: WINDOW (MIN.X, MIN.Y)-(MAX.X, MAX.Y)
19: CLS
20: ' draw X-axis
21: LINE (MIN.X, 0)-(MAX.X, 0)
22: ' draw Y-axis
23: LINE (0, MIN.Y)-(0, MAX.Y)
24: ' draw the SIN(X) function
25: FOR X = MIN.X TO MAX.X STEP INCR
26:   Y = SIN(X * Factor)
27:   ' plot the point
28:   PSET (X, Y)
29: NEXT X
30: LOCATE 1, 1
31: PRINT "SIN(X) Plot"
32: END
```

A sample output for the program in Listing 20.1 appears in Figure 20.1:

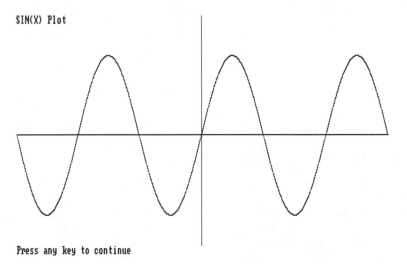

Figure 20.1. A sample session with the GRAF1.BAS program.

The program in Listing 20.1 declares its constants on lines 4–9. The program also declares its variables on lines 11–13. The statement on line 16 assigns the degrees-to-radians conversion factor to the variable Factor. The SCREEN statement in line 17 selects screen mode 2 to support high-resolution monocolor graphics. The WINDOW statement on line 18 defines the Cartesian coordinates used in plotting the sine function. The program uses the LINE statements (more about this statement in the next section) on lines 21 and 23 to draw the X-axis and the Y-axis, respectively. The program also uses the FOR-NEXT loop on lines 25–29 to draw the sine function. The loop utilizes the control variable X and iterates from MIN.X to MAX.X, in steps of INCR. The smaller the value assigned to constant INCR, the finer the plot. The statement on line 26 assigns the value of the sine function to the variable Y. Line 28 plots the point (X, Y) using the PSET statement. The statements on lines 30 and 31 display a title in the upper-left corner of the screen.

Plotting Lines with the *LINE* Statement

QBasic provides the dual-purpose LINE statement to draw lines and rectangles (also called *boxes*). In this section I present an example of drawing lines using the LINE statement.

The LINE Statment

The general syntax for the LINE statement is

```
LINE [[STEP](x1!, y1!)]-[STEP](x2!, y2!) [,[color%]
     [,[B ¦ BF] [,style%]]]
```

The keyword STEP indicates that the coordinates are relative to the current graphics cursor location. The parameters (x1!, y1!) and (x2!, y2!) are the screen coordinates that define the beginning and end of the drawn line. The parameter color% sets the color of the line or box. The available color attributes depend on your graphics adapter and the screen mode established by the last SCREEN statement. The optional parameter B causes the statement to draw a rectangle instead of a line. The optional parameter BF makes the statement draw a filled

20

box. The parameter *style%* specifies a 16-bit value whose bits set whether pixels are drawn. This parameter enables you to draw dashed or dotted lines.

Examples:

```
SCREEN 8
WINDOW (0, 0)-(1000, 1000)
' draw a line from (100, 100) to (200, 200)
LINE (100, 100)-(200, 200)
' draw a line from (200, 200) to (200, 100)
LINE (200, 200)-(200, 100)
' draw a line from (200, 100) to (100, 100)
LINE (200, 100)-(100, 100)
```

Let me present an example that builds on the last program. Listing 20.2, GRAF2.BAS, fills the area between the sine function and the X-axis with lines drawn with the LINE statement. In fact, the program uses a different color for each section (a section spans over each 90 degrees) of the sine function.

Listing 20.2. GRAF2.BAS, which fills the sine function plot using lines drawn with the LINE statement.

```
 1: REM Program which plots the SIN(X) function
 2: REM
 3: ' declare constants
 4: CONST CYCLES = 3
 5: CONST MAX.Y = 1.5
 6: CONST MIN.Y = -1.5
 7: CONST MAX.X = CYCLES * 180
 8: CONST MIN.X = CYCLES * -180
 9: CONST INCR = 1!
10: ' declare variables
11: DIM X AS SINGLE
12: DIM Y AS SINGLE
13: DIM LastY AS SINGLE
14: DIM Factor AS DOUBLE
15: DIM C AS STRING * 1
16: DIM aColor AS INTEGER
```

```
17:
18: ' get the angle conversion factor
19: Factor = 4 * ATN(1) / 180
20: SCREEN 8
21: WINDOW (MIN.X, MIN.Y)-(MAX.X, MAX.Y)
22: CLS
23: ' draw X-axis
24: LINE (MIN.X, 0)-(MAX.X, 0)
25: ' draw Y-axis
26: LINE (0, MIN.Y)-(0, MAX.Y)
27: ' draw the SIN(X) function
28: Y = SIN((MIN.X - INCR) * Factor)
29: aColor = 0
30: FOR X = MIN.X TO MAX.X STEP INCR
31:    Y = SIN(X * Factor)
32:    IF (Y * LastY) <= 0 THEN aColor = aColor + 1
33:    PSET (X, Y)
34:    ' fill in the area under the curve
35:    LINE (X, Y)-(X, 0), aColor
36:    LastY = Y
37: NEXT X
38: ' draw X-axis again
39: LINE (MIN.X, 0)-(MAX.X, 0)
40: LOCATE 1, 1
41: PRINT "SIN(X) Plot (filled)"
42: END
```

A sample output for the program in Listing 20.2 appears in Figure 20.2:

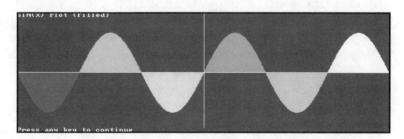

Figure 20.2. A sample session with the GRAF2.BAS program.

Because the program in Listing 20.2 is similar to Listing 20.1, I focus on the new features of program GRAF2.BAS:

1. The SCREEN statement on line 20 selects screen mode 8 to enable the use of colors. This screen mode has a lower graphics resolution than screen mode 2.

2. The program uses the variable aColor to specify the color of the lines filling in the area between the sine function and the X-axis. The statement on line 29 initializes aColor to 0.

3. The program uses the variable LastY to detect a change in the sign of the function values. The IF-THEN statement on line 32 increments the value aColor every time the sine curve crosses the X-axis.

4. The LINE statement on line 35 draws the line between the sine function value and the X-axis at the current value of the X coordinate.

5. The statement on line 36 copies the current value of Y to LastY. This assignment enables the program to keep track of the change in the sign of the function.

6. The LINE statement on line 39 redraws the X-axis. The program uses this statement to restore the white color of the X-axis.

Drawing Boxes with the *LINE* Statement

In this section I present the program GRAF3.BAS (Listing 20.3), which draws five empty and filled boxes. Using random numbers, the program obtains the random sizes of the boxes. In addition, using random numbers, the program determines whether to make the boxes filled or empty. A typical sample session with the program should produce both filled and empty boxes.

Type

Listing 20.3. **GRAF3.BAS, which draws a random combination of filled and empty boxes.**

```
1: REM Program which draws boxes
2: REM
3: ' declare constants
4: CONST MAX.Y! = 1000
5: CONST MAX.X! = 1000
6: CONST MAX.BOXES = 5
7: ' declare variables
8: DIM X1 AS SINGLE
9: DIM Y1 AS SINGLE
10: DIM X2 AS SINGLE
11: DIM Y2 AS SINGLE
12: DIM I AS INTEGER
13:
14: RANDOMIZE TIMER
15: SCREEN 8
16: WINDOW (0, 0)-(MAX.X, MAX.Y)
17: CLS
18: ' draw the empty or filled boxes
19: FOR I = 1 TO MAX.BOXES
20:    X1 = INT(RND * MAX.X)
21:    Y1 = INT(RND * MAX.Y)
22:    X2 = INT(RND * MAX.X)
23:    Y2 = INT(RND * MAX.Y)
24:    ' set foreground and background colors
25:    COLOR 1 + INT(RND * 15), 1 + INT(RND * 15)
26:    IF RND > .5 THEN
27:      ' draw a filled box
28:      LINE (X1, Y1)-(X2, Y2), , BF
29:    ELSE
30:      ' draw an empty box
31:      LINE (X1, Y1)-(X2, Y2), , B
32:    END IF
33: NEXT I
34: END
```

20

A sample output for the program in Listing 20.3 appears in Figure 20.3:

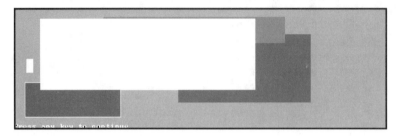

Figure 20.3. A sample session with the GRAF3.BAS program.

Analysis

The program in Listing 20.3 declares its constants on lines 4–6 and its variables on lines 8–12. The statement on line 14 reseeds the random-number generator. The SCREEN statement on line 15 selects the screen mode 8 for color graphics output. The WINDOW statement on line 16 defines the Cartesian coordinates used in drawing the boxes. The FOR-NEXT loop on lines 19–33 draws the boxes. The loop uses the control variable I and iterates from 1 to MAX.BOXES. The statements on lines 20–23 assign random values to the coordinates that define a box. The COLOR statement on line 25 sets the foreground and background colors using random numbers. On line 26 the program decides whether to draw a filled or empty box. The decision is based on comparing the result of the function RND with 0.5. When RND generates a number greater than 0.5, the program draws a filled box using the LINE statement on line 28. Notice that the statement on line 28 uses the parameter BF to draw the filled box. Otherwise, the program generates an empty box using the LINE statement on line 31. Notice that the statement in line 31 uses the parameter B to draw the empty box.

Drawing Circular Shapes Using the CIRCLE Statement

QBasic provides the versatile CIRCLE statement to draw circles, ellipses, and arcs.

The CIRCLE Statement

The general syntax for the CIRCLE statement is

```
CIRCLE [STEP] (x!, y!), radius! [, [color%]
    [,[start!] [,[end!] [,aspect!]]]]
```

The keyword STEP indicates that the coordinates are relative to the current graphics cursor location. The point *(x!,y!)* represents the center of the circle or ellipse. The parameter *radius!* is the radius of the circle or ellipse, expressed in units of the current coordinate scale. The last SCREEN, VIEW, and WINDOW statements establish the latter coordinate scale. The parameter *color%* defines the circle's color. The available color attributes depend on your graphics adapter and the screen mode set by the last SCREEN statement. The parameters *start!* and *end!* define the starting and ending angles (in radians) for the arc. The parameter *aspect!* specifies the ratio of the length of the Y-axis to the length of the X-axis, which is used to draw an ellipse.

Examples:

```
SCREEN 8
WINDOW (0, 0)-(1000, 1000)
Factor = 4 * ATN(1) / 180
' draw a circle
CICRLE (500, 500), 100
' draw an ellipse
CIRCLE (100, 100), 50, , , , 1.2
' draw an arc
CIRCLE (700, 700), 50, , 30 * Factor, 90 * Factor
```

20

Let me present a program that uses the CIRCLE statement. Listing 20.4, GRAF4.BAS, draws circles, ellipses, and arcs using the CIRCLE statement. The program uses random numbers to obtain the center, radius, and other parameters of the drawn circles, ellipses, and arcs.

Listing 20.4. GRAF4.BAS, which draws circles, ellipses, and arcs using the CIRCLE statement.

```
1: REM Program which draws circles
2: REM
3: ' declare constants
4: CONST MIN.X! = 0
5: CONST MIN.Y! = 0
6: CONST MAX.Y! = 200
7: CONST MAX.X! = 640
8: CONST MAX.SHAPES = 10
9: ' declare variables
10: DIM X AS SINGLE
11: DIM Y AS SINGLE
12: DIM Radius AS SINGLE
13: DIM AspectRatio AS SINGLE
14: DIM StartAngle AS SINGLE
15: DIM EndAngle AS SINGLE
16: DIM Factor AS SINGLE
17: DIM R AS SINGLE
18: DIM I AS INTEGER
19:
20: Factor = 4 * ATN(1) / 180
21: RANDOMIZE TIMER
22: SCREEN 8
23: WINDOW (MIN.X, MIN.Y)-(MAX.X, MAX.Y)
24: CLS
25: ' set foreground and background colors
26: COLOR 1 + INT(RND * 15), 1 + INT(RND * 15)
27: ' draw circles, ellipses, and arcs
28: FOR I = 1 TO MAX.SHAPES
29:   X = INT(RND * .75 * (MAX.X - MIN.X)) + .2 * (MAX.X - MIN.X)
30:   Y = INT(RND * .75 * (MAX.Y - MIN.Y)) + .2 * (MAX.Y - MIN.Y)
31:   Radius = INT(RND * (MAX.Y - MIN.Y) / 4)
32:   R = RND
33:   IF R > .667 THEN
34:     ' draw a circle
35:     CIRCLE (X, Y), Radius, 1 + INT(RND * 15)
36:   ELSEIF R > .334 THEN
37:     ' draw an ellipse
38:     AspectRatio = 1 + (RND - .5) / 2
39:     CIRCLE (X, Y), Radius, 1 + INT(RND * 15), , , AspectRatio
```

```
40:   ELSE
41:      ' draw an arc
42:      StartAngle = INT(RND * 90) * Factor
43:      EndAngle = StartAngle + (INT(RND * 145) + 30) * Factor
44:      CIRCLE (X, Y), Radius, , StartAngle, EndAngle
45:   END IF
46: NEXT I
47: END
```

A sample output for the program in Listing 20.4 appears in Figure 20.4:

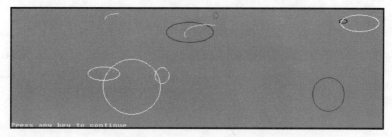

Figure 20.4. A sample session with the GRAF4.BAS program.

The program in Listing 20.4 declares its constants on lines 4–8 and its variables on lines 10–18. The statement on line 21 reseeds the random-number generator. The SCREEN statement on line 22 selects the screen mode 8 for color graphics output. The WINDOW statement on line 23 defines the Cartesian coordinates used in drawing the circular shapes. The COLOR statement on line 26 selects the foreground and background colors using random numbers. The FOR-NEXT loop on lines 28–46 draws the circular shapes. The loop uses the control variable I and iterates from 1 to MAX.SHAPES. The statements on lines 29–31 assigns random numbers to the variables X, Y, and Radius, respectively. The program uses these variables to specify the center and radius of a circular shape. The statement on line 32 assigns the value of RND to R. The program uses the value in this variable to determine what type of circular shape to draw. The IF-THEN-ELSEIF statement on lines 33–45 is instrumental in selecting the shape to draw. The condition on line 33 executes the statements in the THEN clause when the variable R stores a number greater than 0.667. The THEN clause executes the CIRCLE statement on line 35 to draw a circle. The condition on line 36 executes the statements in the second THEN clause when R stores a number greater than 0.334 (and less than 0.667). The THEN clause executes the CIRCLE statement on line 39 to draw an ellipse. The statement on line 38 calculates the aspect ratio using a random number. The program uses the ELSE clause to draw an arc. The statements on lines 42 and 43 obtain the starting and ending arc angles using random numbers. The CIRCLE statement on line 44 draws the arc.

Notice that the three CIRCLE statements in the IF-THEN-ELSEIF statement use different combinations of parameters to draw the desired circular shape.

Drawing Custom Shapes with the *DRAW* Statement

Most real-world shapes are not rectangles, circles, ellipses, or arcs. You can draw some complex shapes by combining the above simple shapes. To draw other custom shapes, such as triangles and polygonals, QBasic offers the DRAW statement.

The DRAW Statement

The general syntax for the DRAW statement is

```
DRAW commandString$
```

The parameter commandString$ is a string expression that encloses one or more of the DRAW commands shown in Tables 20.3 and 20.4. The DRAW statement only uses the graphics coordinate system of the selected screen mode. To execute a DRAW command substring from a DRAW command string, use the "X" command, as shown below:

```
DRAW "X"+ VARPTR$(commandString$)
```

The function VARPTR$ returns the pointer to the string variable commandString$.

Examples:

```
' draw box
DRAW "U100 L200 D100 R200 U100"

' draw triangle
DRAW "M+50,+50 M+0,-50 M-50,-0"
```

Table 20.3. The line-drawing and cursor-movement commands for the DRAW statement.

Command	Purpose
D[$n\%$]	Moves cursor down $n\%$ units.
E[$n\%$]	Moves cursor up and right $n\%$ units.
F[$n\%$]	Moves cursor down and right $n\%$ units.
G[$n\%$]	Moves cursor down and left $n\%$ units.
H[$n\%$]	Moves cursor up and left $n\%$ units.
L[$n\%$]	Moves cursor left $n\%$ units.
M[{+¦-}]$x\%,y\%$	Moves cursor to point $x\%$, $y\%$. If x% is preceded by + or -, the command makes a move that is relative to the current point.
R[$n\%$]	Moves cursor right $n\%$ units.
U[$n\%$]	Moves cursor up $n\%$ units.
[B]	Optional prefix that moves cursor without drawing.
[N]	Optional prefix that draws and then returns the cursor to its original position.

Table 20.4. The color, rotation, and scale commands for the DRAW statement.

Command	Purpose
A$n\%$	Rotates a shape $n\% * 90$ degrees ($n\%$ can be 0, 1, 2, or 3).
C$n\%$	Sets the drawing color ($n\%$ is a color attribute).
P$n1\%,n2\%$	Sets the paint fill colors and the border colors of a shape ($n1\%$ is the fill-color attribute, $n2\%$ is the border-color attribute).

continues

Table 20.4. **continued**

Command	Purpose
Sn%	Specifies the drawing scale by establishing the length of a unit of cursor movement. The default n% is 4, which is equal to 1 pixel.
TAn%	Turns an angle n% degrees (–360 through 360).

Here is an example that uses the DRAW statement. Listing 20.5, GRAF5.BAS, draws an empty rectangle, a filled rectangle, and two triangles.

Listing 20.5. **GRAF5.BAS, which draws shapes using the DRAW statement.**

```
 1: REM Program which draws shapes with the DRAW statement
 2: REM
 3: ' declare constants
 4: CONST RED = 4
 5: CONST YELLOW = 14
 6: SCREEN 8
 7: CLS
 8:
 9: COLOR YELLOW, RED
10: ' draw the first rectangle
11: DRAW "U50 R100 D50 L100 U50 P15,15"
12: ' move inside the rectangle
13: DRAW "BF20"
14: ' fill the rectangle with white color
15: DRAW "P15,15"
16: ' draw the second rectangle
17: DRAW "BM250,180"
18: DRAW "U50 R100 D50 L100 U50 P15,15"
19: ' draw first triangle
20: DRAW "BM100,100"
21: DRAW "M+50,+50 M+0,-50 M-50,-0"
22: ' draw second triangle
```

```
23: DRAW "BM550,150"
24: DRAW "M-75,-75"
25: DRAW "M+0,+75 M+75,-0"
26: END
```

A sample output for the program in Listing 20.5 appears in Figure 20.5:

Figure 20.5. A sample session with the GRAF5.BAS program.

The program in Listing 20.5 declares the constants RED and YELLOW on lines 4 and 5, respectively. The SCREEN statement on line 6 switches to screen mode 8. The COLOR statement on line 9 selects a yellow foreground color and a red background color. The DRAW statement on line 11 draws a rectangle. To fill this rectangle, the program uses the DRAW statement on line 13 to move inside the rectangle. The DRAW statement on line 15 uses the P command string to paint the rectangle. The program draws the second rectangle by using the DRAW statements on lines 17 and 18. The statement on line 17 moves the graphics cursor to coordinate (250, 180). The statement on line 18 draws the empty rectangle. The statements on lines 20 and 21 draw the first triangle. The statements on lines 23–25 draw the second triangle. These statements use relative moves to draw the triangles.

20

Summary

This chapter introduced to you to the common graphics operations supported by QBasic. You learned how to draw curves, lines, rectangles, circles, ellipses, arcs, and triangles. The chapter covered the following topics:

☐ QBasic supports various graphics screen modes depending on the display adapter you have in your computer. The different screen modes also offer separate combinations of screen resolutions and colors.

☐ QBasic supports as many as 16 color values. Each color value has a default color. You can alter this default color using the PALETTE statement.

☐ Selecting a screen mode involves using the SCREEN statement to specify the screen mode, the screen color, the number of the current output screen page, and the number of the currently viewed screen page.

☐ Selecting colors involves using the COLOR statement to set the foreground and background colors. The values for these colors depend on the display adapter in a computer and the currently selected screen mode.

☐ Changing default color values involves using the PALETTE statement. This statement enables you to specify the current and new color values. You also can use the PALETTE statement to restore the default color values.

☐ The graphics-mode coordinates in QBasic increase the X coordinate values from left of the screen to its right, and the Y coordinates from the screen top to its bottom.

☐ Setting the portion of the screen for graphics output (called the **viewport**) requires using the VIEW statement. This statement enables you to specify which part of the screen can be used for graphics output.

☐ Setting the coordinates of the viewport entails using the WINDOW statement to define the coordinate scales. You can select to use the Cartesian system for the Y coordinate values. The Cartesian system increases the values of Y from the bottom of the screen to its top.

☐ Drawing points and curves involves using the PSET statement to specify the location and color of the plotted point.

☐ Drawing lines and boxes entails using the LINE statement. This statement specifies the coordinates that define the limits of the line or box, and the shape's color. In addition, the LINE statement has special options to create boxes that are filled with the the specified color.

☐ Drawing circles, ellipses, and arcs involves using the CIRCLE statement. This statement enables you to specify the center and radius of a circle; center, radius, and aspect ratio of an ellipse; center, radius, starting angle, and ending angle of an arc.

☐ Drawing custom shapes entails using the DRAW statement and supplying special command strings. These strings enable you to draw and move in the four directions, rotate the drawn shape, draw at an angle, paint the shape, and specify the color.

Q&A

Q. Does QBasic generate a runtime error if any part of a point, line, or shape lies outside the valid range graphics coordinates?

A. No. QBasic simply clips the parts that are outside the valid range graphics coordinates. This feature eliminates the need to ensure that all the points, lines, and shapes are completely within the range of graphics coordinates.

Q. Why are the sine curves in Figures 20.1 and 20.2 not perfectly smooth?

A. The smoothness of a curve depends on the resolution of the screen mode. When a program draws a curve, such as the sine function, some of the Y values are too close to each other and end up appearing on pixels with the same **physical** Y coordinates.

Q. How can a text file be used to save instructions to draw multiple shapes?

A. Using text files allows you to store and recall an array of different shapes. This approach enables you to use the same set of statements to retrieve different sets of shapes. The statements used should have the following general syntax:

```
DO WHILE NOT EOF(FileNum)
    LINE INPUT #FileNum, ShapeName
    SELECT CASE UCASE$(ShapeName)
        CASE "POINT"
            ' read location and color
            PSET (X, Y), aColor
```

20

```
            CASE "LINE"
                    ' read parameters for a line
                    ' draw a line
            CASE "BOX"
                    ' read parameters for a box
                    ' draw a box
            ' other CASE clauses here
        END SELECT
    LOOP
```

Q. What is a good way to manage colors in a QBasic program?

A. Assign constants to the color values. These constants make writing, reading, and updating your programs much easier than constantly dealing with cryptic color values.

Workshop

The Workshop provides quiz questions to help you solidify your understanding of the material covered and exercises to provide you with experience in using what you've learned. Try to understand the quiz and exercise answers before continuing on to the next chapter. Answers are provided in Appendix B, "Answers."

Quiz

1. True or false: the following set of statements generates a runtime error.

```
SCREEN 2
WINDOW (0, 0) - (100, 100)
LINE (10, 10) - (40, 60)
LINE (110, 100) - (1000, 1000)
END
```

2. What happens to the sine function plotted in programs GRAF1.BAS and GRAF2.BAS if the WINDOW statement included the SCREEN keyword?

3. True or false: the following statements draw a box and then hide it
   (assume that the procedure WaitaWhile is available):

```
CONST WHITE = 15
CONST BLACK = 0
SCREEN 8 ' supports only black and white
WINDOW (0, 0) - (500, 500)
LINE (100, 100) - (200, 200), WHITE, BF
WaitaWhile 1
LINE (100, 100) - (200, 200), BLACK, BF
```

Exercise

1. Write the program GRAF6.BAS that plots the function SIN(X) /
   EXP(0.04 * X) from 0 to 1800 (ten 180-degree cycles).

20

DAY

21

Music and Sound

Congratulations! This is the last day of your 21-day course of learning to program in QBasic. I salute your patience and commitment to this project. I had asked my publisher to include a gadget in the book that would sound a trumpet when you turned to this page. Alas, the cost was monumentally prohibitive! However, the next best thing is to have you toot your own horn (with a little help from QBasic, naturally). Indeed, this last chapter presents the QBasic statements that play music and make sounds. Today, you learn about the following topics:

☐ The BEEP statement

☐ The SOUND statement

☐ The PLAY statement

The *BEEP* Statement

The BEEP statement simply sounds an **alarm** beep. Programs use the BEEP to emit an audible warning. We all have learned to dread hearing this eerie sound because it usually means that there is something wrong with an application.

The BEEP Statement

The general syntax for the BEEP statement is

```
BEEP
```

Example:

```
DO
  INPUT "Enter a positive number "; X
  IF X <= 0 THEN
    BEEP
    PRINT "You entered 0 or a negative number!"
  END IF
LOOP UNTIL X > 0
```

The *SOUND* Statement

The SOUND statement enables you to customize the frequency and duration of a beep. You also can execute several SOUND statements in a loop to create special effects, such as siren sounds.

The SOUND Statement

The general syntax for the SOUND statement is

```
SOUND frequency, duration
```

The parameter *frequency* specifies the frequency in hertz. The values for this parameter range from 37–32767. The parameter *duration* specifies the duration of the sound in clock ticks (a clock tick occurs 18.2 times per second). The values for this parameter range from 0–65535.

Example:

```
FOR Freq = 40 TO 100 STEP 10
    SOUND Freq, 1
NEXT Freq
```

Listing 21.1, SOUND1.BAS, uses the SOUND statement to sound sirens. The program displays the duration used in the SOUND statements to create a particular sound. Press any key to double the duration of the sound and obtain a different sound effect. The program doubles the duration, which is initially at 0.05. The program stops when the duration exceeds 1.

Listing 21.1. SOUND1.BAS, which uses the SOUND statement to sound sirens.

```
1: DECLARE SUB PulseSound (Duration AS SINGLE)
2: REM Program that uses the SOUND statement
3: REM
4: ' declare constants
5: CONST MIN.FREQ = 50
6: CONST MAX.FREQ = 500
```

continues

Listing 21.1. continued

```
 7: CONST INC.FREQ = 25
 8: CONST MIN.DUR = .05
 9: CONST MAX.DUR = 1
10: CONST SCALE.DUR = 2
11: ' declare variable
12: DIM Dur AS SINGLE
13:
14: CLS
15: Dur = MIN.DUR
16: DO WHILE Dur <= MAX.DUR
17:    PulseSound Dur
18:    Dur = SCALE.DUR * Dur
19: LOOP
20: END
21:
22: SUB PulseSound (Duration AS SINGLE)
23: ' make pulsating sound
24:    DIM Freq AS SINGLE
25:
26:    PRINT "Duration ="; Duration
27:    DO
28:      FOR Freq = MIN.FREQ TO MAX.FREQ STEP INC.FREQ
29:        SOUND Freq, Duration
30:      NEXT Freq
31:      FOR Freq = MAX.FREQ TO MIN.FREQ STEP -INC.FREQ
32:        SOUND Freq, Duration
33:      NEXT Freq
34:    LOOP UNTIL INKEY$ <> ""
35: END SUB
```

Here is some sample output for the program in Listing 21.1:

```
Duration = .05
Duration = .1
Duration = .2
```

```
Duration = .4
Duration = .8
```

 The highlight of the program in Listing 21.1 is the procedure PulseSound. This procedure has one parameter, Duration. The procedure uses two FOR-NEXT loops to supply the SOUND statements in lines 29 and 32 with increasing and then decreasing frequencies. The argument for Duration determines the speed of the pulsating sound. Small values produce the siren sound effect.

The *PLAY* Statement

QBasic offers the PLAY statement to allow programs to play tunes.

21

The PLAY Statement

The general syntax for the PLAY statement is

PLAY *commandString$*

The parameter *commandString$* is a string expression that contains one or more PLAY commands. Table 21.1 lists the octave and tone commands. Table 21.2 lists the duration and tempo commands. Table 21.3 lists the mode and suffix commands. To execute a PLAY command substring from a PLAY command string, use the following "X" command:

PLAY "X"+ VARPTR$(*commandString$*)

Example:

```
Scale$ = "ABDGFABA"
PLAY "L15"
FOR I = 0 TO 6
  PLAY "O" + MID$(STR$(I), 2)
  PLAY "X" + VARPTR$(Scale$)
NEXT I
```

Table 21.1. The octave and tone commands for the PLAY statement.

Command	Purpose
Ooctave	Sets the current octave (0–6).
< or >	Moves up or down one octave.
A–G	Plays the specified note in the current octave.
Nnote	Plays a specified note (0–84) in the seven-octave range (0 is a rest).

Table 21.2. The duration and tempo commands for the PLAY statement.

Command	Purpose
Llength	Sets the length of every note (1–64). L1 is whole note, L2 is a half note, and so on.
ML	Sets music legato.
MN	Sets music normal.
MS	Sets music staccato.
Ppause	Specifies a pause (1–64). P1 is a whole-note pause, P2 is a half-note pause, and so on.
Ttempo	Sets the tempo in quarter notes per minute (32–255).

Table 21.3. The mode and suffix commands for the PLAY statement.

Command	Purpose
MF	Plays music in foreground.
MB	Plays music in background.

Command	Purpose
# or +	Turns preceding note into a sharp.
-	Turns preceding note into a flat.
.	Plays the preceding note 3/2 as long as designated.

Let's look at an example. Listing 21.2, PLAY1.BAS, plays arbitrary music notes using the PLAY statement.

Listing 21.2. The program PLAY1.BAS which plays arbitrary music notes using the PLAY statement.

```
 1: DECLARE SUB PlayItSam (Scl$, LLen%, First%, Last%)
 2: REM Program that uses the PLAY statement
 3: REM
 4: CLS
 5: PRINT "Listen..."
 6: PlayItSam "CDCDC", 20, 1, 2
 7: PlayItSam "ABDCBA", 10, 1, 3
 8: PlayItSam "ABABA", 30, 1, 2
 9: PlayItSam "FGDBAF", 5, 1, 1
10: END
11:
12: SUB PlayItSam (Scl$, LLen%, First%, Last%)
13: ' play part of a tune
14:    DIM I AS INTEGER
15:    PLAY "L" + MID$(STR$(LLen%), 2)
16:    FOR I = First% TO Last%
17:      PLAY "O" + MID$(STR$(I), 2)
18:      PLAY "X" + VARPTR$(Scl$)
19:    NEXT I
21: END SUB
```

Here is some sample output for the program in Listing 21.2:

```
Listen...
```

Analysis The highlight of the program in Listing 21.2 is the procedure PlayItSam. This procedure has parameters that pass the scale string, the note's length, the tempo, the first octave, and the last octave. The PLAY statement on line 15 sets the note's length. The procedure uses the FOR-NEXT loop on lines 16–19 to play the notes in the octaves ranging from First% to Last%. The PLAY statement on line 17 sets the octave. The PLAY statement on line 18 plays the notes in string Scl$.

Summary

This chapter presented the QBasic statements that generate sound and play music. You learned about the following topics:

☐ The BEEP statement sounds the familiar alarming beep.

☐ The SOUND statement enables you to create a custom sound by specifying frequency and duration.

☐ The versatile PLAY statement enables you to play music in QBasic programs. The PLAY statement uses a string command that can contain octave, tone, duration, tempo, and other sound-related commands.

Q&A

Q. Does QBasic have a command to turn off the sound?

A. No.

Q. Am I done learning QBasic?

A. Yes. Congratulations!

Workshop

It's the last day of school, so instead of homework, you get one fun exercise.

Exercise

1. Modify the calls to the procedure PlayItSam by altering the scale strings as well as the other arguments.

Week 3 in Review

Recall that when reviewing the first two weeks, I presented a program that manages a to-do list. Now that the third week has ended, I present a final version that supports the following operations:

1. Add a new task.

2. Automatically sort the tasks by date.

3. Delete any task.

4. Print the tasks.

5. Read the tasks from the random-access file TODO.DAT.

6. Write the tasks to the random-access file TODO.DAT.

7. Quit.

Not only does the new version add file I/O operations, but the statements in the program reflect a radical reorganization. The new program version is more structured than its predecessors.

Listing 1. **The program TODO3.BAS which manages a to-do list.**

```
1: DECLARE SUB Confirm (C$)
2: DECLARE SUB SortTasks (A() AS ANY, N%)
3: DECLARE SUB ShowTasks (A() AS ANY, N%)
4: DECLARE SUB AddTask (A() AS ANY, N%)
5: DECLARE SUB DeleteTask (A() AS ANY, N%)
```

continues

Listing 1. **continued**

```basic
 6: DECLARE SUB PrintTasks (A() AS ANY, N%)
 7: DECLARE SUB SaveTasks (A() AS ANY, N%)
 8: DECLARE SUB LoadTasks (A() AS ANY, N%)
 9: REM Program which manages a To-Do list
10: REM
11: REM   Version 3.0            1/20/93
12: REM
13: OPTION BASE 1
14: ' declare type TToDo
15: TYPE TToDo
16:    DateStr AS STRING * 15
17:    ToDo AS STRING * 60
18: END TYPE
19: ' declare constants
20: CONST MARK = "◊ "
21: CONST MENU = "A)dd, D)elete P)rint, S)ave, L)oad, Q)uit"
22: CONST MAX.TODO = 20
23: CONST TITLE = "TO DO LIST"
24: CONST FILENAME = "TODO.DAT"
25: ' declare variables
26: DIM S(1 TO MAX.TODO) AS TToDo
27: DIM Choice AS STRING
28: DIM ToDoCount AS INTEGER
29:
30: ToDoCount = 0
31: DO
32:    CLS
33:    SortTasks S(), ToDoCount ' sort tasks
34:    ShowTasks S(), ToDoCount ' show tasks
35:    LOCATE 23, 1
36:    PRINT MENU
37:    INPUT ">", Choice
38:    Choice = UCASE$(LEFT$(Choice, 1))
39:    SELECT CASE Choice
40:      CASE "A"
41:        AddTask S(), ToDoCount
42:      CASE "D"
43:        DeleteTask S(), ToDoCount
44:      CASE "P"
```

```
45:        PrintTasks S(), ToDoCount
46:     CASE "S"
47:        SaveTasks S(), ToDoCount
48:     CASE "L"
49:        LoadTasks S(), ToDoCount
50:     CASE "Q"
51:        IF ToDoCount > 0 THEN Confirm Choice
52:   END SELECT
53: LOOP UNTIL Choice = "Q"
54: END
55:
56: Bad.Delete:
57:   RESUME NEXT
58:
59: SUB AddTask (A() AS TToDo, N%)
60: ' add a task
61:
62:   IF N% < MAX.TODO THEN
63:     PRINT
64:     N% = N% + 1
65:     DO
66:       LINE INPUT "Enter date : ", A(N%).DateStr
67:     LOOP UNTIL A(N%).DateStr <> ""
68:     DO
69:       LINE INPUT "Enter task : ", A(N%).ToDo
70:     LOOP UNTIL A(N%).ToDo <> ""
71:   ELSE
72:     SOUND 100, 1
73:   END IF
74: END SUB
75:
76: SUB Confirm (C$)
77: ' confirm choice
78:   PRINT
79:   PRINT "Really want to exit? (Y/N) ";
80:   C$ = INPUT$(1)
81:   PRINT C$
82:   C$ = UCASE$(C$)
83:   IF C$ = "Y" THEN C$ = "Q"
84: END SUB
85:
```

continues

```
86: SUB DeleteTask (A() AS TToDo, N%)
87: ' delete a task
88:    DIM I AS INTEGER
89:    DIM J AS INTEGER
90:
91:    IF N% > 0 THEN
92:      INPUT "Enter index of task to delete"; J
93:      FOR I = J + 1 TO N%
94:        A(I - 1) = A(I)
95:      NEXT I
96:      N% = N% - 1
97:    ELSE
98:      SOUND 1000, .5
99:    END IF
100: END SUB
101:
102: SUB LoadTasks (A() AS TToDo, N%)
103: ' read tasks from a file
104:    DIM I AS INTEGER
105:    DIM FileNum AS INTEGER
106:
107:    N% = 0
108:    FileNum = FREEFILE
109:    OPEN FILENAME FOR RANDOM AS FileNum LEN = LEN(A(1))
110:    DO WHILE NOT EOF(FileNum)
111:      N% = N% + 1
112:      GET #FileNum, , A(N%)
113:    LOOP
114:    N% = N% - 1
115:    CLOSE
116: END SUB
117:
118: SUB PrintTasks (A() AS TToDo, N%)
119: ' print the tasks
120:    DIM I AS INTEGER
121:
122:    IF N% > 0 THEN
123:      LPRINT SPC(40 - LEN(TITLE) \ 2); TITLE
124:      LPRINT
```

```
125:      FOR I = 1 TO N%
126:        LPRINT A(I).DateStr; RTRIM$(A(I).ToDo)
127:      NEXT I
128:    END IF
129: END SUB
130:
131: SUB SaveTasks (A() AS TToDo, N%)
132: ' write tasks to a file
133:    DIM I AS INTEGER
134:    DIM FileNum AS INTEGER
135:
136:    IF N% < 1 THEN EXIT SUB
137:    FileNum = FREEFILE
138:    ' set error trap
139:    ON ERROR GOTO Bad.Delete
140:    ' delete the file
141:    KILL FILENAME
142:    ON ERROR GOTO 0
143:    ' open the file
144:    OPEN FILENAME FOR RANDOM AS FileNum LEN = LEN(A(1))
145:    FOR I = 1 TO N%
146:      PUT #FileNum, , A(I)
147:    NEXT I
148:    CLOSE
149: END SUB
150:
151: SUB ShowTasks (A() AS TToDo, N%)
152: ' display tasks
153:    DIM I AS INTEGER
154:
155:    FOR I = 1 TO N%
156:      PRINT MARK; A(I).DateStr; RTRIM$(A(I).ToDo)
157:    NEXT I
158: END SUB
159:
160: SUB SortTasks (A() AS TToDo, N%)
161: ' sort the array A() by the DatStr fields
162:    DIM I AS INTEGER
163:    DIM J AS INTEGER
164:
165:    FOR I = 1 TO N% - 1
```

continues

Listing 1. **continued**

```
166:    FOR J = I TO N%
167:       IF A(I).DateStr > A(J).DateStr THEN SWAP A(I), A(J)
168:    NEXT J
169:  NEXT I
170: END SUB
```

Here is a sample output for the program in Listing 1:

```
◊ 01/18/93        Deadline for QBasic book
◊ 02/02/93        Meeting with D. Jenkins in NY City
◊ 03/04/93        Nancy's birthday
◊ 05/03/93        QBasic conference in London
◊ 06/15/93        Regional sales meeting in Chicago
◊ 11/15/93        Comdex Fall 93 in Las Vegas
◊ 12/01/93        QBasic conference in Tokyo
```

```
A)dd, D)elete P)rint, S)ave, L)oad, Q)uit
>S
```

 Let me discuss TODO3.BAS by comparing it with the TODO2.BAS version. Here are the changes and new program features:

1. The declaration of the structure TToDo to model the strings for the date and task wording. The structure declares two fixed-string fields, DateStr and ToDo. In the previous version, I used variables by the same names.

2. The constant MENU is defined by a new menu string. This new string reflects the new file I/O operations.

3. The use of the constant FILENAME specifies the name of the data file that stores the tasks.

4. The declaration of the structured array S with TToDo data type elements.

5. The program is highly structured and uses the following procedures:

Procedure	Purpose
Confirm	Confirm exit.
SortTasks	Sort array S using the field DateStr.
ShowTasks	Display tasks.
AddTask	Add a new task.
DeleteTask	Delete a task.
PrintTasks	Print the tasks.
SaveTasks	Store the tasks in TODO.DAT.
LoadTasks	Load tasks from TODO.DAT.

As a result of using procedures, the number of statements in the main DO-UNTIL loop has shrunk. Also, each CASE clause in the SELECT-CASE statement invokes a procedure to perform a specific task. The tasks performed by the procedures Confirm, SaveTasks, and LoadTasks are new.

6. The Confirm procedure prevents you from accidentally exiting the program, especially without saving the list of tasks.

7. SaveTasks writes the current list of to-do tasks to the random-access file TODO.DAT. The procedure uses the elements of the parameter A (this parameter is an array of TToDo elements) to write the tasks. The procedure first deletes the existing copy of TODO.DAT. This deletion ensures that the new file version receives exactly the number of current tasks. The KILL statement effectively removes the extra records.

8. The LoadTasks procedure reads the tasks from the random-access file TODO.DAT. The procedure overwrites the current list of tasks in memory.

9. The SortTasks procedure sorts the tasks using the strings in the DateStr field of each element in array A.

10. AddTask and DeleteTask use the SOUND statement to generate a low-tone beep if you cannot add or delete a task.

You can modify the TODO3.BAS program by making it automatically load and save the to-do list. As an exercise, I suggest that you remove the Load and Save options from the menu. Instead, systematically load the tasks from the file when the program start running, and save the tasks before exiting.

ASCII Table

Dec X_{10}	Hex X_{16}	Binary X_2	ASCII Character
000	00	0000 0000	null
001	01	0000 0001	☺
002	02	0000 0010	☻
003	03	0000 0011	♥
004	04	0000 0100	◆
005	05	0000 0101	♣
006	06	0000 0110	♠
007	07	0000 0111	●
008	08	0000 1000	■
009	09	0000 1001	○
010	0A	0000 1010	■
011	0B	0000 1011	♂
012	0C	0000 1100	♀
013	0D	0000 1101	♪
014	0E	0000 1110	♪♪
015	0F	0000 1111	☼
016	10	0001 0000	►
017	11	0001 0001	◄
018	12	0001 0010	↕
019	13	0001 0011	‼
020	14	0001 0100	¶
021	15	0001 0101	§
022	16	0001 0110	▬
023	17	0001 0111	↨
024	18	0001 1000	↑
025	19	0001 1001	↓
026	1A	0001 1010	→
027	1B	0001 1011	←
028	1C	0001 1100	FS
029	1D	0001 1101	GS
030	1E	0001 1110	RS

Dec X_{10}	Hex X_{16}	Binary X_2	ASCII Character
031	1F	0001 1111	US
032	20	0010 0000	SP
033	21	0010 0001	!
034	22	0010 0010	"
035	23	0010 0011	#
036	24	0010 0100	$
037	25	0010 0101	%
038	26	0010 0110	&
039	27	0010 0111	'
040	28	0010 1000	(
041	29	0010 1001	)
042	2A	0010 1010	*
043	2B	0010 1011	+
044	2C	0010 1100	,
045	2D	0010 1101	-
046	2E	0010 1110	.
047	2F	0010 1111	/
048	30	0011 0000	0
049	31	0011 0001	1
050	32	0011 0010	2
051	33	0011 0011	3
052	34	0011 0100	4
053	35	0011 0101	5
054	36	0011 0110	6
055	37	0011 0111	7
056	38	0011 1000	8
057	39	0011 1001	9
058	3A	0011 1010	:
059	3B	0011 1011	;

A

A ASCII Table

Dec X_{10}	Hex X_{16}	Binary X_2	ASCII Character
060	3C	0011 1100	<
061	3D	0011 1101	=
062	3E	0011 1110	>
063	3F	0011 1111	?
064	40	0100 0000	@
065	41	0100 0001	A
066	42	0100 0010	B
067	43	0100 0011	C
068	44	0100 0100	D
069	45	0100 0101	E
070	46	0100 0110	F
071	47	0100 0111	G
072	48	0100 1000	H
073	49	0100 1001	I
074	4A	0100 1010	J
075	4B	0100 1011	K
076	4C	0100 1100	L
077	4D	0100 1101	M
078	4E	0100 1110	N
079	4F	0100 1111	O
080	50	0101 0000	P
081	51	0101 0001	Q
082	52	0101 0010	R
083	53	0101 0011	S
084	54	0101 0100	T
085	55	0101 0101	U
086	56	0101 0110	V
087	57	0101 0111	W
088	58	0101 1000	X
089	59	0101 1001	Y
090	5A	0101 1010	Z

Dec X_{10}	Hex X_{16}	Binary X_2	ASCII Character
091	5B	0101 1011	[
092	5C	0101 1100	\
093	5D	0101 1101	]
094	5E	0101 1110	^
095	5F	0101 1111	–
096	60	0110 0000	`
097	61	0110 0001	a
098	62	0110 0010	b
099	63	0110 0011	c
100	64	0110 0100	d
101	65	0110 0101	e
102	66	0110 0110	f
103	67	0110 0111	g
104	68	0110 1000	h
105	69	0110 1001	i
106	6A	0110 1010	j
107	6B	0110 1011	k
108	6C	0110 1100	l
109	6D	0110 1101	m
110	6E	0110 1110	n
111	6F	0110 1111	o
112	70	0111 0000	p
113	71	0111 0001	q
114	72	0111 0010	r
115	73	0111 0011	s
116	74	0111 0100	t
117	75	0111 0101	u
118	76	0111 0110	v
119	77	0111 0111	w
120	78	0111 1000	x
121	79	0111 1001	y

A

Dec X_{10}	Hex X_{16}	Binary X_2	ASCII Character
122	7A	0111 1010	z
123	7B	0111 1011	{
124	7C	0111 1100	¦
125	7D	0111 1101	}
126	7E	0111 1110	~
127	7F	0111 1111	DEL
128	80	1000 0000	Ç
129	81	1000 0001	ü
130	82	1000 0010	é
131	83	1000 0011	â
132	84	1000 0100	ä
133	85	1000 0101	à
134	86	1000 0110	å
135	87	1000 0111	ç
136	88	1000 1000	ê
137	89	1000 1001	ë
138	8A	1000 1010	è
139	8B	1000 1011	ï
140	8C	1000 1100	î
141	8D	1000 1101	ì
142	8E	1000 1110	Ä
143	8F	1000 1111	Å
144	90	1001 0000	É
145	91	1001 0001	æ
146	92	1001 0010	Æ
147	93	1001 0011	ô
148	94	1001 0100	ö
149	95	1001 0101	ò
150	96	1001 0110	û
151	97	1001 0111	ù
152	98	1001 1000	ÿ

Dec X_{10}	Hex X_{16}	Binary X_2	ASCII Character
153	99	1001 1001	Ö
154	9A	1001 1010	Ü
155	9B	1001 1011	¢
156	9C	1001 1100	£
157	9D	1001 1101	¥
158	9E	1001 1110	Pt
159	9F	1001 1111	ƒ
160	A0	1010 0000	á
161	A1	1010 0001	í
162	A2	1010 0010	ó
163	A3	1010 0011	ú
164	A4	1010 0100	ñ
165	A5	1010 0101	Ñ
166	A6	1010 0110	a
167	A7	1010 0111	o
168	A8	1010 1000	¿
169	A9	1010 1001	⌐
170	AA	1010 1010	¬
171	AB	1010 1011	½
172	AC	1010 1100	¼
173	AD	1010 1101	¡
174	AE	1010 1110	«
175	AF	1010 1111	»
176	B0	1011 0000	░
177	B1	1011 0001	▒
178	B2	1011 0010	▓
179	B3	1011 0011	│
180	B4	1011 0100	┤
181	B5	1011 0101	╡
182	B6	1011 0110	╢
183	B7	1011 0111	╖
184	B8	1011 1000	╕

A

Dec X_{10}	Hex X_{16}	Binary X_2	ASCII Character
185	B9	1011 1001	╣
186	BA	1011 1010	║
187	BB	1011 1011	╗
188	BC	1011 1100	╝
189	BD	1011 1101	╜
190	BE	1011 1110	╛
191	BF	1011 1111	┐
192	C0	1100 0000	└
193	C1	1100 0001	┴
194	C2	1100 0010	┬
195	C3	1100 0011	├
196	C4	1100 0100	─
197	C5	1100 0101	+
198	C6	1100 0110	╞
199	C7	1100 0111	╟
200	C8	1100 1000	╚
201	C9	1100 1001	╔
202	CA	1100 1010	╩
203	CB	1100 1011	╦
204	CC	1100 1100	╠
205	CD	1100 1101	=
206	CE	1100 1110	╬
207	CF	1100 1111	╧
208	D0	1101 0000	╨
209	D1	1101 0001	╤
210	D2	1101 0010	╥
211	D3	1101 0011	╙
212	D4	1101 0100	╘
213	D5	1101 0101	╒
214	D6	1101 0110	╓

Dec X_{10}	Hex X_{16}	Binary X_2	ASCII Character
215	D7	1101 0111	╫
216	D8	1101 1000	╪
217	D9	1101 1001	┘
218	DA	1101 1010	┌
219	DB	1101 1011	█
220	DC	1101 1100	▄
221	DD	1101 1101	▌
222	DE	1101 1110	▐
223	DF	1101 1111	▀
224	E0	1110 0000	α
225	E1	1110 0001	β
226	E2	1110 0010	Γ
227	E3	1110 0011	π
228	E4	1110 0100	Σ
229	E5	1110 0101	σ
230	E6	1110 0110	μ
231	E7	1110 0111	τ
232	E8	1110 1000	Φ
233	E9	1110 1001	θ
234	EA	1110 1010	Ω
235	EB	1110 1011	δ
236	EC	1110 1100	∞
237	ED	1110 1101	$\emptyset$
238	EE	1110 1110	$\in$
239	EF	1110 1111	$\cap$
240	F0	1111 0000	$\equiv$
241	F1	1111 0001	$\pm$
242	F2	1111 0010	$\geq$
243	F3	1111 0011	$\leq$
244	F4	1111 0100	$\lceil$

A

Dec X_{10}	Hex X_{16}	Binary X_2	ASCII Character
245	F5	1111 0101	∫
246	F6	1111 0110	÷
247	F7	1111 0111	≈
248	F8	1111 1000	°
249	F9	1111 1001	●
250	FA	1111 1010	·
251	FB	1111 1011	√
252	FC	1111 1100	η
253	FD	1111 1101	2
254	FE	1111 1110	■
255	FF	1111 1111	

B

Answers

Answers to Day 1, "Getting Started"

Quiz

1. The program generates no output because the PRINT statement appears after the REM keyword. This leads QBasic to consider the PRINT statement part of a comment, not executing it.

2. By swapping the statements on lines 5 and 6, the CLS statement clears the screen after you type in a random-number seed. Therefore, the final output screen only shows the output of the PRINT statement. This is an example where swapping statements is not detrimental to the program.

Exercises

1. Here is a sample listing that includes a comment and the END statement:

```
' program that prints the message I am a QBasic Programmer
PRINT "I am a QBasic Programmer"
END
```

2. Here is a sample listing:

```
REM Program that selects a random month day number
REM Version 1.0
REM Created 12/16/1992   Last Update 12/18/1992
REM
RANDOMIZE ' randomize the seed
CLS ' clear the screen
' output number between 1 and 31
PRINT "Day number is "; INT(RND * 31) + 1
END
```

Answers to Day 2, "The QBasic Environment"

Quiz

1. False. Although many applications do use Alt+X for exiting back to DOS, QBasic requires you to press Alt+F and then X.

2. False. The F5 function key resumes the execution of a QBasic program. However, in practical use, you still can start a QBasic program by pressing the F5 function key.

3. True.

4. True.

5. False.

Answers to Day 3, "Data Types, Constants, and Variables"

Quiz

1. False. QBasic names are not case-sensitive,

2. True. The variable `Index%` stores an integer, whereas the variable `INDEX!` stores a single-precision, floating-point number.

3. False. The name `Input` is a really the reserved QBasic keyword `INPUT`.

4. False. The statement assigns the value of `index` to itself. The statement is wasteful but harmless.

5. The program displays `Number is 12` because the assignment statement on line 2 overwrites the value you enter on line 1.

6. The value of `33000` is outside the range of values for the integer type.

7. By changing the suffix to make the data type variable index either long, single, or double, as shown in the following code snippet:

```
index& = 33000 ' index stores long integers
index! = 33000 ' index stores single-precision floats
index# = 3000  ' index stores double-precision floats
```

8. The program displays 10 because the variable N (which is declared as DOUBLE) and N# are synonymous.

Exercises

1. Here is what the resulting program (call it VOLUME5.BAS) might look like:

```
REM Program that calculates the volume of a sphere
REM
CLS
DIM Radius AS DOUBLE
DIM Pi AS DOUBLE
DIM Volume AS DOUBLE
INPUT "Enter the sphere radius (ft.) "; Radius
PRINT
Pi = 4 * ATN(1) ' calculate pi
' calculate the sphere volume
Volume = Pi * Radius * Radius * Radius / 3
PRINT "Volume of sphere = "; Volume; " cuft"
END
```

2. Here is what the resulting program (call it PI1.BAS) might look like:

```
REM Program that calculates an accurate and
REM an approximate value of pi
REM
CLS
' declare the variables
DIM Pi1 AS DOUBLE ' accurate pi
DIM Pi2 AS DOUBLE ' approximate pi
DIM PiErr AS DOUBLE ' error (per billion)
' calculate both versions of pi
Pi1 = 4 * ATN(1)
Pi2 = 355# / 113#
' calculate the error
PiErr = (Pi2 - Pi1) / Pi1 * 1000000000#
' display the results
PRINT "Accurate Pi    = "; Pi1
PRINT "Approximate Pi = "; Pi2
PRINT "Error = "; INT(PiErr); "in a billion"
END
```

3. Here is what the resulting program (call it TEMP2.BAS) might look like:

```
REM Program that convert Fahrenheit Temperatures to Celsius
REM
' declare the constants SHIFT# and SCALE#
CONST SHIFT# = 32#   ' explicit type association
CONST SCALE = 1.8#   ' implicit type association
CONST TFChar = "F "  ' implicit type association
CONST TCchar = "C "  ' implicit type association
CONST Message = "Enter a Fahrenheit temperature "
' declare the program variables as double-precision floats
DIM TF AS DOUBLE
DIM TC AS DOUBLE
CLS
' obtain input temperature
PRINT Message;
INPUT TF
' convert the temperature to Celsius
TC = (TF - SHIFT) / SCALE
' display the result
PRINT TF; TFChar; "="; TC; TCchar
END
```

B

Answers to Day 4, "Operators and Expressions"

Quiz

1. The expression J% = 10 contains the relational operator =. Because the value in J% is 10, the relational operator yields –1 (True). Consequently, the second statement assigns –1 to the variable I%.

2. The answers are:

   a. 64
   b. 512
   c. 1.5
   d. 5

3. False. The number 32768 is just one number higher than the upper range of the integer data type.

4. The string expression in the PRINT statement cannot concatenate the contents of the numeric variable Area#. Another way of looking at the error is the attempt to add strings and numbers. Either way, QBasic displays an error message when you want to run the program that contains the PRINT statement in question.

5. The Boolean expression is always true, regardless of the value in J%. Judging from the PRINT statement, the correct version follows:

```
INPUT "Enter a number ";J%
I% = J% > 0 AND J% < 10
PRINT "Condition : "; J%; " is in range of 1 to 9 is "; I%
```

6. The Boolean expression is always false because a variable cannot have two different values at the same time. Judging from the PRINT statement, the correct version follows:

```
INPUT "Enter a number ";J%
I% = J% = 0 OR J% = 10
PRINT "Condition : "; J%; " = 0 or 10 is "; I%
```

7. The proposed solution works, although using XOR is rather unusual in this case.

8. Here are the simplified versions of the mathematical expressions:

```
a. I% = 1
b. J% = 2 * 3 + 1
c. K% = 4 * 5 + 6 * 7 + 1
d. M% = (1 + 4) / (5 + 9)
```

9. There is a missing close parenthesis. The correct statement should be:

```
D# = (2 + 3) * (47 - 12)
```

Exercises

1. The statement is

```
Flag% = NOT Flag%
```

2. The expression is

```
(N% MOD 2) = 0
```

3. The program might like the following listing (ASSIGN4.BAS):

```
REM Program demonstrates safe data conversion
REM between a single and an integer
REM
' declare the program variables
DIM IntVar AS INTEGER
DIM SingleVar AS SINGLE
DIM Ok AS INTEGER
'
CLS
' input value to variable SingleVar
INPUT "Enter a number "; SingleVar
PRINT "SingleVar = "; SingleVar
Ok = -1 * (SingleVar >= -32768 AND SingleVar <= 32767)
IntVar = Ok * SingleVar
PRINT "IntVar = "; IntVar
END
```

The variable Ok acts as a safety switch. When the value in SingleVar is also a valid integer value, line 13 assigns 1 to Ok. Otherwise, line 13 assigns 0. Consequently, line 14 assigns 0 to IntVar when the value in SingleVar is out of range. Otherwise, the program safely copies and converts the value in SingleVar to IntVar.

B

4. The simpler equivalent Boolean expressions are:

    a. A > 10
    b. X <= 0 OR X >= 10
    c. X >= 0 AND X <= 4

5. The ASSIGN5.BAS program might look like this:

```
REM Program demonstrates assigning a long integer to
REM the other numeric data types
REM
' declare the program variables
DIM IntVar AS INTEGER
DIM LongVar AS LONG
DIM SingleVar AS SINGLE
DIM DoubleVar AS DOUBLE
'
```

```
CLS
' Assign values to the long integer variable
LongVar = 45
PRINT "LongVar = "; LongVar
' copy long integer value to integer variable
IntVar = LongVar
PRINT "IntVar = "; IntVar
' copy long integer value to single variable
SingleVar = LongVar
PRINT "SingleVar = "; SingleVar
' copy long integer value to double variable
DoubleVar = LongVar
PRINT "DoubleVar = "; DoubleVar
END
```

6. The ASSIGN6.BAS program might look like this:

```
REM Program demonstrates assigning a double to
REM the other numeric data types
REM
' declare the program variables
DIM IntVar AS INTEGER
DIM LongVar AS LONG
DIM SingleVar AS SINGLE
DIM DoubleVar AS DOUBLE
'
CLS
' assign value to the double variable
DoubleVar = 1000.123456789#
PRINT "DoubleVar = "; DoubleVar
IntVar = DoubleVar
PRINT "IntVar = "; IntVar
' copy double value to long variable
LongVar = DoubleVar
PRINT "LongVar = "; LongVar
' copy double  value to single variable
SingleVar = DoubleVar
PRINT "SingleVar = "; SingleVar
```

Answers to Day 5, "String Manipulation"

Quiz

1. The extracted strings are:

   a. `""` (0 causes the LEFT$ to return an empty string.)
   b. `"QuickBasic"` (40 is greater than the length of the string "QuickBasic". Therefore, LEFT$ returns the string itself.)

2. False. The LEFT$ function does not pad its result.

3. True. The function call MID$(S, 2) extracts the second to last characters of S. MID$(S, 2, L - 1) extracts the same characters.

4. True. Although the last argument, L, in the function call MID$(S, 2, L) exceeds the actual number of available characters, the function call returns the same string as MID$(S, 2).

5. True. The function call RIGHT$(S, L) actually returns the entire string S. The same is true for the function call LEFT$(S, L). Both function calls produce an equal result. Therefore, the last statement assigns –1 (true) to areEqual.

6. The simpler, equivalent function calls are shown:

   a. `MID$(AString, 2)`
   b. `AString`
   c. `LEFT$(AString, LEN(AString) / 2)`
   d. `RIGHT$(AString, 1)`

Exercises

1. The following statements use the MID$ function to emulate the LEFT$ function:

```
DIM Str1 AS STRING
DIM Str2 AS STRING
DIM N AS INTEGER
N = 5
Str1 = "QuickBasic"
Str2 = MID$(Str1, 1, N)
```

B

2. The following statements use the MID$ function to emulate the RIGHT$ function:

```
DIM Str1 AS STRING
DIM Str2 AS STRING
DIM N AS INTEGER
N = 5
Str1 = "QuickBasic"
Str2 = MID$(Str1, LEN(Str1) - N, N)
```

3. There are two similar solutions. The first one uses the UCASE$ function with the strings passed to INSTR. This approach eliminates lowercase letters and thus makes the search case-insensitive:

```
DIM MainString AS STRING
DIM SearchStr AS STRING
DIM I AS INTEGER
MainString = "I still use DOS"
SearchStr = "Dos"
I = INSTR(UCASE$(MainString), UCASE$(SearchStr))
PRINT "Matching "; SearchStr; " @ "; I
END
```

The second similar solution uses LCASE$ instead of function UCASE$ when calling INSTR, as shown in the following line.

```
I = INSTR(LCASE$(MainString), LCASE$(SearchStr))
```

4. One possible solution follows:

```
DIM First AS STRING
DIM Last AS STRING
CLS
INPUT "Enter your first name : ", First
INPUT "Enter your last name : ", Last
First = UCASE$(LEFT$(First, 1)) + LCASE$(MID$(First, 2))
Last = UCASE$(LEFT$(Last, 1)) + LCASE$(MID$(Last, 2))
PRINT "Hello "; First; " "; Last
END
```

Answers to Day 6, "Making Decisions"

Quiz

1. The simpler version is

```
IF I > 0 AND I < 10 THEN
    PRINT "I = "; I
END IF
```

2. The simpler version is

```
IF I > 0 THEN
    J = I * I
    PRINT "J = "; J
ELSEIF I < 0 THEN
    J = 4 * I
    PRINT "J = "; J
ELSE
    J = 10 + I
    PRINT "J = "; J
END IF
```

B

3. False. When the variable I stores values between –10 and –1, the statements in the THEN clauses of the two IF-THEN statements execute. In this case all the assignment statements are executed. By contrast, it is impossible to execute the statements in both the THEN and ELSE clause of the supposedly equivalent IF-THEN-ELSE statement.

4. The simplified version is

```
IF I > 0 AND I < 100 THEN
    J = I * I
ELSEIF I >= 100 THEN
    J = I
ELSE
    J = 1
END IF
```

Notice that I eliminated the original first ELSEIF clause because the tested condition is a subset of the first tested condition. Consequently, the condition in the first ELSEIF never gets examined and its associated statement never gets executed. This is an example of what is called *dead code*.

5. The tested condition is always false. Consequently, the statements in the THEN clause are never executed. This is another example of dead code.

Exercises

1. IF6.BAS follows:

```
REM Program tests the multiple-alternative
REM IF-THEN-ELSE statement
REM
' declare the program variables
DIM A AS DOUBLE
DIM B AS DOUBLE
DIM C AS DOUBLE
DIM Discrim AS DOUBLE
DIM D AS DOUBLE
DIM TwoA AS DOUBLE
DIM Root1 AS DOUBLE
DIM Root2 AS DOUBLE

CLS
PRINT "For the quadratic equation:"
PRINT
PRINT "     A X^2 + BX + C = 0"
PRINT
INPUT "Enter non-zero value for A "; A
' handle the case when A is zero
IF A = 0 THEN
  PRINT
  PRINT "Error: Value for A must not be zero!"
  PRINT
  END
END IF
INPUT "Enter value for B "; B
```

```
INPUT "Enter value for C "; C
PRINT
Discrim = B * B - 4 * A * C
TwoA = A + A
IF Discrim > 0 THEN
  Root1 = (-B + SQR(Discrim)) / TwoA
  Root2 = (-B - SQR(Discrim)) / TwoA
  PRINT "Root #1 = "; Root1
  PRINT "Root #2 = "; Root2
ELSEIF Discrim < 0 THEN
  Discrim = -Discrim
  PRINT "Root #1 ="; (-B / TwoA); "+i("; SQR(Discrim) /
  ➥TwoA; ")"
  PRINT "Root #2 ="; (-B / TwoA); "-i("; SQR(Discrim) /
  ➥TwoA; ")"
ELSE
  Root1 = -B / TwoA
  Root2 = Root1
  PRINT "Root #1 = "; Root1
  PRINT "Root #2 = "; Root2
END IF
END
```

2. Here is my version of the pseudocode for CASE3.BAS:

```
1.        Clear the screen.
2.        Input the first operand.
3.        Input the operator.
4.        Input the second operand.
5.        Set the error flag to false.
6.        Process the operator
6.1.      when operator is "+" add operands
6.2.      when operator is "-" subtract operands
6.3.      when operator is "*" multiply operands
6.4.      when operator is "/" do the following
6.4.1     if second operand is not zero
6.4.1.1.  then divide operands
6.4.1.2.  else set error flag to true
6.5       set the error flag to true for all other operators
```

```
7.        If there is no error
7.1       then display operands, operator and the result
7.2       else display error message
```

Answers to Day 7, "Looping"

Quiz

1. The statements inside the loop fail to alter the value of I. Consequently, the tested condition is always true and the loop iterates endlessly.

2. The output of the program consists of the numbers 3, 5, and 7.

3. The output of the program is an endless sequence of lines that display the number 3. You need to press the Ctrl+Break keys to stop the program. The reason for the indefinite looping is the value of 0 in the STEP clause.

4. The nested FOR-NEXT loops use the same loop control variable. This program will not run.

5. The NEXT clauses of the nested FOR-NEXT loop overlap. This program will not run. You need to swap the loop-control variables in the NEXT clauses to make the program work.

6. The NEXT clause used with nested FOR-NEXT loop requires that you list the loop-control variable in the correct sequence.

7. The condition of the WHILE loop is always true. Therefore, the loop iterates endlessly.

8. The call to INSTR in the loop needs to use a character offset argument to prevent the program from being stuck in the loop. This problem occurs when FindString appears at least once in MainString. Here is the corrected listing:

```
I = INSTR(MainString, FindString)
DO WHILE I > 0
    PRINT "Found match at character "; I
    I = INSTR(I + 1, MainString, FindString)
LOOP
```

9. The program lacks a statement that explicitly initializes the variable Factorial to 1. Without this statement, the program automatically initializes the Factorial to 0—the wrong value. Consequently, the FOR-NEXT loop ends up assigning 0 to Factorial in every iteration. Here is the correct version of the program:

```
DIM I AS INTEGER
DIM N AS INTEGER
DIM Factorial AS DOUBLE
CLS
INPUT "Enter a positive integer "; N
Factorial = 1
FOR I = 1 TO N
    Factorial = Factorial * I
NEXT I
PRINT N; "! = "; Factorial
END
```

Exercises

1. The listing for GOTO3.BAS follows:

```
REM Program tests the GOTO statement
REM
' declare the program variables
DIM MainString AS STRING
DIM FindString AS STRING
DIM I AS INTEGER

CLS
INPUT "Enter the main string : ", MainString
IF MainString = "" THEN GOTO BAD.INPUT
INPUT "Enter the search string : ", FindString
IF FindString = "" THEN GOTO BAD.INPUT
I = INSTR(MainString, FindString)
PRINT
IF I > 0 THEN
  PRINT "Found search string at character "; I
ELSE
  PRINT "No match for search string"
END IF
```

B

```
GOTO PROGRAM.END

BAD.INPUT:
PRINT
PRINT "You must enter at least one character!"
PRINT
PRINT "End of program"
PRINT
PROGRAM.END
END
```

2. Here is my version of FOR7.BAS:

```
REM Program that sums up the odd integers
REM in the range of 11 to 121
REM
' declare the constants that define
' the range of integers
CONST LO.VAL% = 11
CONST HI.VAL% = 121
' declare the variables
DIM I AS INTEGER
DIM Sum AS SINGLE

CLS
' initialize the sum of integers
Sum = 0
' accumulate the sum of odd integers
FOR I = LO.VAL TO HI.VAL STEP 2
  Sum = Sum + I
NEXT I
' displays the result
PRINT "Sum of odd integers in the range of ";
PRINT LO.VAL; " to "; HI.VAL; " = "; Sum
END
```

3. Here is my version of WHILE2.BAS:

```
REM Program that sums up the squares of odd integers
REM in the range of 11 to 121
REM
```

```
' declare the constants that define
' the range of integers
CONST LO.VAL% = 11
CONST HI.VAL% = 121
' declare the variables
DIM I AS INTEGER
DIM Sum AS SINGLE

CLS
' initialize the sum of integers
Sum = 0
I = LO.VAL
' accumulate the sum of odd integers
DO WHILE I <= HI.VAL
  Sum = Sum + I * I
  I = I + 2
LOOP
' displays the result
PRINT "Sum of squared odd integers in the range of ";
PRINT LO.VAL; " to "; HI.VAL; " = "; Sum
END
```

4. Here is my version of UNTIL2.BAS:

```
REM Program that sums up the squares of odd integers
REM in the range of 11 to 121
REM
' declare the constants that define
' the range of integers
CONST LO.VAL% = 11
CONST HI.VAL% = 121
' declare the variables
DIM I AS INTEGER
DIM Sum AS SINGLE

CLS
' initialize the sum of integers
Sum = 0
I = LO.VAL
' accumulate the sum of odd integers
```

B

```
DO
  Sum = Sum + I * I
  I = I + 2
LOOP UNTIL I > HI.VAL
' displays the result
PRINT "Sum of squared odd integers in the range of ";
PRINT LO.VAL; " to "; HI.VAL; " = "; Sum
END
```

Answers to Day 8, "Keyboard and Program Input"

Quiz

1. The output of the program is:

   ```
   1.23E+08
   8
   ```

2. There are only two values in the DATA statement. The program needs three values.

3. The second value in the DATA statement must be an integer and not a string.

4. The LINE INPUT statement only works with a single string variable.

5. There are no DATA statements after the label MoreData.

Exercises

1. Here is my version of DATA3.BAS:

   ```
   REM Program uses the READ and DATA statements
   REM
   ' declare variables
   DIM C AS STRING
   DIM Title AS STRING
   DIM DateStr AS STRING
   DIM X AS DOUBLE
   DIM Sum AS DOUBLE
   ```

```
DIM SumX AS DOUBLE
DIM SumXX AS DOUBLE
DIM Mean AS DOUBLE
DIM Sdev AS DOUBLE
DIM N AS INTEGER
DIM I AS INTEGER

CLS
DO
  PRINT "Enter set number (1, 2, or 3) ? ";
  C = INPUT$(1)
  PRINT C
  PRINT
LOOP UNTIL INSTR("123", C) > 0

SELECT CASE C
  CASE "1"
    RESTORE DataSet1
  CASE "2"
    RESTORE DataSet2
  CASE ELSE
    RESTORE DataSet3
END SELECT

CLS
READ Title
READ DateStr
PRINT SPACE$(40 - LEN(Title) \ 2); Title
PRINT
PRINT "Date collected " + DateStr

PRINT
' initialize the summations variables
SumX = 0
SumXX = 0
' read the number of observations
READ N
Sum = N
```

B

```
FOR I = 1 TO N
  ' read the next observation
  READ X
  SumX = SumX + X
  SumXX = SumXX + X * X
NEXT I

Mean = SumX / Sum
Sdev = SQR((SumXX - SumX * SumX / Sum) / (Sum - 1))
PRINT "Number of observations = "; N
PRINT "Mean value = "; CINT(Mean * 100) / 100
PRINT "Standard deviation = "; CINT(Sdev * 100) / 100

DataSet1:
DATA Sample Steel Bar Thickness Data
DATA 1/23/93
DATA 10
DATA 3.4, 5.6, 9.8, 1.2, 6.5, 3.4
DATA 5.6, 8.1, 2.3, 4.5

DataSet2:
DATA Sample Steel Bar Thickness Data
DATA 2/13/93
DATA 10
DATA 2.4, 7.6, 8.8, 2.2, 3.5, 8.4
DATA 3.6, 7.9, 2.8, 3.9

DataSet3:
DATA Sample Steel Bar Thickness Data
DATA 3/3/93
DATA 10
DATA 4.1, 6.1, 9.1, 1.1, 5.9, 4.5
DATA 3.5, 9.1, 3.7, 3.2
```

2. Here is my version of DATA4.BAS:

```
REM Program uses the READ, DATA and
REM RESTORE statements
' declare constants
CONST TRUE% = -1
```

```
CONST FALSE% = 0
CONST EOD = "!"
' declare variables
DIM aName AS STRING
DIM FirstName AS STRING
DIM LastName AS STRING
DIM Phone AS STRING
DIM C AS STRING
DIM I AS INTEGER
DIM Found AS INTEGER

CLS
DO
  ' input search name
  LINE INPUT "Enter name : "; aName
  PRINT
  ' set search flag to false
  Found = FALSE
  ' use loop to search
  DO
    ' read the next data set
    READ FirstName, LastName, Phone
    ' find a match?
    IF INSTR(UCASE$(LastName), UCASE$(aName)) > 0 THEN
      Found = TRUE
    END IF
  LOOP UNTIL LastName = EOD OR Found = TRUE

  ' reset DATA statement pointer
  RESTORE DataList

  ' was a match found?
  IF Found = TRUE THEN
    PRINT "The phone number of "; FirstName; " "; astName;
    PRINT " is "; Phone
  ELSE
    PRINT aName; " is not in the database"
  END IF
```

B

```
    ' prompt user for more search
    DO
      PRINT
      PRINT "Search for another name? (Y/N) ";
      C = INPUT$(1)
      PRINT C
      C = UCASE$(C)
      PRINT
    LOOP UNTIL C = "Y" OR C = "N"


LOOP UNTIL C <> "Y"


'***************** DATA Statements Section *********

DataList:
DATA "Paul", "Hammer", "555-3232"
DATA "Jim", "Chataway", "555-9987"
DATA "Richard", "Lynch", "555-5432"
DATA "Kim", "Chin", "555-8765"
DATA "Darryl", "Lanz", "555-9263"
DATA "Jean", "Jarre", "555-2222"
DATA "Paul", "Jarvis", "555-9283"
' note: the next DATA statement marks the
' end of the miniature database
DATA "!", "!", "!"
END
```

3. Here is my version of INKEY3.BAS:

```
REM Program that tests the INKEY$ function
REM with the TIMER function to create
REM loops that exit after a certain
REM number of seconds
REM
' declare loop timeout
CONST MAX.TIME = 3
' declare variables
DIM AString AS STRING
DIM K AS STRING
DIM Q AS STRING
DIM TheTime AS DOUBLE
```

```
CLS
Q = CHR$(34)
DO
   LINE INPUT "Enter a string : "; AString
   PRINT
   PRINT "The uppercase of string "; Q; AString; Q;
   PRINT " is "; Q; UCASE$(AString); Q
   ' prompt for another input
   DO
      PRINT
      PRINT "Input another string? (Y/N) ";
      ' wait for keyboard input
      TheTime = TIMER
      DO
         K = INKEY$
      LOOP UNTIL K <> "" OR (TIMER - TheTime) > MAX.TIME
      IF K = "" THEN K = "N"
      PRINT K
      K = UCASE$(K)
      PRINT
   LOOP UNTIL K = "Y" OR K = "N"
LOOP UNTIL K = "N"
END
```

B

Answers to Day 9, "Screen and Printer Output"

Quiz

1. Here is the output of each of the PRINT USING statements:

   a. '1.20000'
   b. '+3.1416E+000'
   c. '+1.2000E+001'
   d. '0.1200E+002'
   e. '1.2000E+001+'
   f. '1.2000E+001 '
   g. '1.2000E+001-'

h. `'  $98.55'`
i. `'***$98.55'`
j. `'1,200,000,000.00'`
k. `'  1200000000.00,'`

2. Here is the output of each of the PRINT USING statement:

   a. `'H'`
   b. `'He'`
   c. `'Hello'`

3. True. The call to the function SPC produces the same effect as the call to the TAB function.

4. False. The first PRINT statement displays the numbers 1, 2, and 3 at column positions 10, 20, and 30. By contrast, the second PRINT statement displays the same numbers at column positions 10, 31, and 62.

5. Here is the equivalent PRINT statement:

   ```
   PRINT LEFT$(AString, 1)
   ```

6. Here is the equivalent PRINT statement:

   ```
   PRINT LEFT$(AString, 4)
   ```

7. Here is the equivalent PRINT statement:

   ```
   PRINT AString
   ```

Exercises

1. Here is my version of USING5.BAS:

   ```
   REM Program that uses the PRINT USING statement
   REM to print financial tables
   REM
   ' declare the constant
   CONST TITLE = "Future Values Table"
   CONST HDR1 = "Year         3%           5%           7%
   ➥9%"
   CONST HDR2 = 55
   ' declare the variables
   DIM PV AS DOUBLE
   ```

```
DIM FV AS DOUBLE
DIM Interest AS DOUBLE
DIM N AS INTEGER
DIM I AS INTEGER
DIM C AS STRING

CLS
INPUT "Enter present value "; PV
INPUT "Enter number of periods "; N
CLS
PRINT
PRINT TAB(40 - LEN(TITLE) \ 4); TITLE
PRINT
PRINT TAB(15); HDR1
PRINT TAB(15); STRING$(HDR2, "_")
PRINT
FOR I = 1 TO N
  IF (I MOD 15) = 0 THEN
    PRINT
    PRINT "Press any key to continue";
    C = INPUT$(1)
    CLS
    PRINT
    PRINT TAB(40 - LEN(TITLE) \ 4); TITLE
    PRINT
    PRINT TAB(15); HDR1
    PRINT TAB(15); STRING$(HDR2, "_")
    PRINT
  END IF
  PRINT TAB(15);
  PRINT USING "####"; I;
  FOR Interest = 3 TO 9 STEP 2
    FV = PV * (1 + Interest / 100) ^ I
    PRINT USING "  #######.##"; FV;
  NEXT Interest
  PRINT
NEXT I
```

2. Here are the statements that clear to the end of the current line:

```
Y = CSRLIN
X = POS(0)
PRINT SPACE$(81 - X);
LOCATE Y, X
```

Answers to Day 10, "Subroutines and Functions"

Quiz

1. The call to INCR passes a copy of the variable I to the subroutine INCR. The contents of the variable I are not affected by the subroutine call. Therefore, the DO-WHILE loop iterates indefinitely.

2. The function call uses the wrong type of parameters.

3. The function call has more arguments than the number of parameters in the SUB procedure.

4. The use of the STR$ function converts the numeric result into a string. You cannot, however, assign a string to the numeric function FNCalc.

Exercises

1. Here is my version of SUB4.BAS:

```
DECLARE SUB CheckCursor ()
DECLARE SUB ShowCenteredTitles (T1 AS STRING, T2 AS STRING)
DECLARE SUB ShowTableHeading ()
DECLARE SUB PressAnyKey ()
REM Program uses SUB procedures
REM
CONST TITLE1 = "Sample Table of Squares and Cubes"
CONST TITLE2 = "(SUB procedure version 2)"
' declare the variables
DIM A AS DOUBLE
```

```
' define functions
DEF FNSqr (X#) = X# * X#
DEF FNCube (X#) = X# * X# * X#

' program use CALL statements to invoke the
' SUB ShowCenteredTitle and ShowTableHeading
CALL ShowCenteredTitles(TITLE1, TITLE2)
CALL ShowTableHeading
FOR A = 1 TO 100
  PRINT , A, FNSqr(A), FNCube(A)
  CheckCursor
NEXT A

END

SUB CheckCursor
  IF CSRLIN = 20 THEN
    ' program uses direct invocation of the
    ' procedures PressAnyKey, ShowCenteredTitles,
    ' and ShowTableHeading
    PressAnyKey
    ShowCenteredTitles TITLE1, TITLE2
    ShowTableHeading
  END IF
END SUB

SUB PressAnyKey
  PRINT
  PRINT "Press any key to continue"
  C$ = INPUT$(1)
END SUB

SUB ShowCenteredTitles (T1 AS STRING, T2 AS STRING)
  CLS
  PRINT
  PRINT TAB(40 - LEN(T1) \ 2); T1
  PRINT TAB(40 - LEN(T2) \ 2); T2
```

```
    PRINT
    PRINT
  END SUB

  SUB ShowTableHeading
    PRINT , "  X", "X ^ 2", "   X ^ 3"
    PRINT , STRING$(35, "-")
  END SUB
```

2. Here are my versions of the SUB and FUNCTION procedures:

```
  SUB GotoXY(X%, Y%)
    IF X% > 0 AND X% < 81 AND Y% > 0 AND Y% < 25 THEN
      LOCATE Y%, X%
    END IF
  END SUB

  FUNCTION WhereX%
    WhereX% = POS(0)
  END FUNCTION

  FUNCTION WhereY%
    WhereY% = CSRLIN
  END FUNCTION
```

Answers to Day 11, "Handling Program Errors"

Quiz

1. The program displays the string Hello.

2. The program displays the string Jello.

3. The program displays the following:

```
Jello
 11
```

The number 11 indicates that the MID$ statement causes runtime error eleven times.

4. The program displays the following:

   Runtime error number 5

Exercise

1. Here is my version of ERR6.BAS:

```
REM Program that tests the ON ERROR statement
REM to handle bad arguments for the MID$ function
REM
' declare constants
CONST ERR.MSG = "Invalid indices in the MID$ function"
CONST ERR.ROW = 22
' declare variables
DIM S1 AS STRING
DIM S2 AS STRING
DIM Start AS INTEGER
DIM Count AS INTEGER
DIM Q AS STRING
DIM Y AS INTEGER

CLS
Q = CHR$(34)
LINE INPUT "Enter a string : "; S1
PRINT
INPUT "Enter the index of the first extracted character ";
➥Start
PRINT
INPUT "Enter the number of characters to extract "; Count
PRINT
PRINT "          1         2         3         4"
PRINT " 12345678901234567890123456789012345678901234567890"
PRINT
PRINT Q; S1; Q
ON ERROR GOTO Bad.Index
S2 = MID$(S1, Start, Count)
PRINT Q; S2; Q
END
```

```
Bad.Index:
  S2 = " "
  Y = CSRLIN
  LOCATE ERR.ROW, 1
  PRINT ERR.MSG
  LOCATE Y, 1
  RESUME NEXT
```

Answers to Day 12, "Simple Arrays"

Quiz

1. The array A contains the following values:

I	A(I)
1	2
2	3
3	5
4	9
5	17
6	33
7	65
8	129
9	257

2. The first loop iteration causes a runtime error because the element ProjIncome(I-1) is not valid for I = 1995.

3. The array X is static and cannot be redimensioned. The REDIM statement causes an error.

4. OPTION BASE cannot take a value other than 0 or 1.

5. There can be only one OPTION BASE statement in a program.

6. The OPTION BASE statement must appear before any array is declared.

Exercises

1. Here is my version of SORT3.BAS:

```
REM Program sorts of an array of strings
REM
OPTION BASE 1
' declare constants
CONST ARRAY.SIZE = 10

' declare variables
DIM StrArr(ARRAY.SIZE) AS STRING
DIM I AS INTEGER
DIM J AS INTEGER
DIM C AS STRING

CLS
' reseed random-number generator
RANDOMIZE TIMER
FOR I = 1 TO ARRAY.SIZE
   READ StrArr(I)
NEXT I

FOR I = 1 TO ARRAY.SIZE
   PRINT StrArr(I)
NEXT I

PRINT
PRINT "Press any key to sort the array";
C = INPUT$(1)

' nested loops which implement the bubble sort method
FOR I = 1 TO ARRAY.SIZE - 1
   FOR J = I + 1 TO ARRAY.SIZE
       ' is element at index I greater than element
       ' at index J?
```

B

741

```
        IF StrArr(I) > StrArr(J) THEN
          ' swap the elements
          SWAP StrArr(I), StrArr(J)
        END IF
    NEXT J
  NEXT I

  CLS

  FOR I = 1 TO ARRAY.SIZE
    PRINT StrArr(I)
  NEXT I
  PRINT
  PRINT "Array is now sorted!"

  '******************* DATA Statements ******************

  DATA "California", "Virginia", "Washington", "Oregon"
  DATA "Michigan", "New York", "Ohio", "Indiana"
  DATA "Georgia", "Texas"

  END
```

2. Here is my version of SEARCH3.BAS:

```
DECLARE SUB WaitAWhile (Period AS SINGLE)
REM Program that searches unordered array
REM
' declare constants
CONST ARRAY.SIZE% = 10
CONST SEARCH.SIZE% = ARRAY.SIZE% - 2
CONST FRMT$ = "String at index # = &"
CONST TRUE% = -1
CONST FALSE% = 0
CONST PTR.COL = 35
CONST MSG.ROW = 23
CONST SHORT.DELAY = 1
CONST LONG.DELAY = 3
' declare variables
DIM StrArr(1 TO ARRAY.SIZE) AS STRING
```

```
DIM I AS INTEGER
DIM J AS INTEGER
DIM NotFound AS INTEGER

CLS
' assign values to the array StrArr
FOR I = 1 TO ARRAY.SIZE
  READ StrArr(I)
NEXT I

' display the first SEARCH.SIZE elements
FOR I = 1 TO SEARCH.SIZE
  PRINT USING FRMT; I; StrArr(I)
  PRINT
NEXT I

' search for the elements of IntArray
' in the first SEARCH.SIZE elements
FOR I = 1 TO ARRAY.SIZE
  ' display the search status at the bottom of the screen
  LOCATE MSG.ROW, 1
  PRINT SPACE$(80);
  LOCATE MSG.ROW, 1
  PRINT "Searching for "; StrArr(I);
  ' start searching
  J = 1
  NotFound = TRUE
  DO
    ' display "?=?" near searched entry
    LOCATE 1 + 2 * (J - 1), PTR.COL
    PRINT "?=? "; StrArr(I)
    SOUND 50, 1
    CALL WaitAWhile(SHORT.DELAY)
    LOCATE 1 + 2 * (J - 1), PTR.COL
    PRINT SPACE$(80 - PTR.COL);
    ' no match found?
    IF StrArr(J) <> StrArr(I) THEN
      ' increment search index
      J = J + 1
```

```
      ELSE
        ' set not-found flag to FALSE
        NotFound = FALSE
      END IF
    LOOP UNTIL J > SEARCH.SIZE OR NotFound = FALSE

    IF NotFound THEN
      ' display no-match found message
      LOCATE MSG.ROW, 1
      PRINT SPACE$(80);
      LOCATE MSG.ROW, 1
      PRINT "No match for "; StrArr(I)
      SOUND 100, 2
    ELSE
      ' display found-match message
      LOCATE MSG.ROW, 1
      PRINT SPACE$(80);
      LOCATE MSG.ROW, 1
      PRINT "Found "; StrArr(I); " at index "; J
      SOUND 400, .5
    END IF
    CALL WaitAWhile(LONG.DELAY)
  NEXT I

  '******************** DATA Statements ******************

  DATA "California", "Virginia", "Washington", "Oregon"
  DATA "Michigan", "New York", "Ohio", "Indiana"
  DATA "Georgia", "Texas"


END

SUB WaitAWhile (Period AS SINGLE)
  TheTime = TIMER
  DO
  LOOP UNTIL (TIMER - TheTime) >= Period
END SUB
```

3. Here is my version of SEARCH4.BAS:

```
DECLARE SUB WaitAWhile (Period AS SINGLE)
REM Program that searches ordered array
REM using the binary search method
REM
' declare constants
CONST ARRAY.SIZE% = 10
CONST FRMT$ = "Value at index ## = &"
CONST PTR.COL = 35
CONST MSG.ROW = 23
CONST SHORT.DELAY = 1
CONST LONG.DELAY = 3
' declare variables
DIM StrArr1(1 TO ARRAY.SIZE) AS STRING
DIM StrArr2(1 TO ARRAY.SIZE) AS STRING
DIM I AS INTEGER
DIM J AS INTEGER
DIM Hi AS INTEGER
DIM Lo AS INTEGER
DIM Median AS INTEGER

CLS

' assign values to the arrays StrArr1 and StrArr2
' The StrArr2 copies the unordered values in array StrArr1
FOR I = 1 TO ARRAY.SIZE
  READ StrArr1(I)
  StrArr2(I) = StrArr1(I)
NEXT I

' alter the last two strings in array StrArr2
READ StrArr2(ARRAY.SIZE - 1)
READ StrArr2(ARRAY.SIZE)

' sort elements of array StrArr1
FOR I = 1 TO ARRAY.SIZE - 1
  FOR J = I + 1 TO ARRAY.SIZE
```

745

```
        IF StrArr1(I) > StrArr1(J) THEN
          SWAP StrArr1(I), StrArr1(J)
        END IF
      NEXT J
  NEXT I

  ' display the elements of StrArr1
  FOR I = 1 TO ARRAY.SIZE
    PRINT USING FRMT; I; StrArr1(I)
    PRINT
  NEXT I

  ' search for the elements of StrArray2
  ' in the elements of array StrArr1
  FOR I = 1 TO ARRAY.SIZE
    ' display the search status at the bottom of the screen
    LOCATE MSG.ROW, 1
    PRINT SPACE$(80);
    LOCATE MSG.ROW, 1
    PRINT "Searching for "; StrArr2(I);
    ' start searching
    Lo = 1
    Hi = ARRAY.SIZE
    NotFound = TRUE
    DO
      Median = (Lo + Hi) \ 2
      ' display "?=?" near searched entry
      LOCATE 1 + 2 * (Median - 1), PTR.COL
      PRINT "?=? "; StrArr2(I)
      SOUND 50, 1
      CALL WaitAWhile(SHORT.DELAY)
      LOCATE 1 + 2 * (Median - 1), PTR.COL
      PRINT SPACE$(80 - PTR.COL);
      IF StrArr2(I) < StrArr1(Median) THEN
        Hi = Median - 1
      ELSE
        Lo = Median + 1
      END IF
```

```
     LOOP UNTIL StrArr2(I) = StrArr1(Median) OR Lo > Hi


   ' found match
   IF StrArr2(I) = StrArr1(Median) THEN
     ' display found-match message
     LOCATE MSG.ROW, 1
     PRINT SPACE$(80);
     LOCATE MSG.ROW, 1
     PRINT "Found "; StrArr2(I); " at index "; Median
     SOUND 400, .5
   ELSE
     ' display no-match found message
     LOCATE MSG.ROW, 1
     PRINT SPACE$(80);
     LOCATE MSG.ROW, 1
     PRINT "No match for "; StrArr2(I)
     SOUND 100, 2
   END IF
   CALL WaitAWhile(LONG.DELAY)
NEXT I


'******************* DATA Statements **************

DATA "California", "Virginia", "Washington", "Oregon"
DATA "Michigan", "New York", "Ohio", "Indiana"
DATA "Georgia", "Texas"

DATA "Maine", "Florida"



END


SUB WaitAWhile (Period AS SINGLE)
  TheTime = TIMER
  DO
  LOOP UNTIL (TIMER - TheTime) >= Period
END SUB
```

B

Answers to Day 13, "Multidimensional Arrays"

Quiz

1. The array `Cube` has 150 elements.

2. The values for the various function calls are:

Function Call	Value Returned
LBOUND(A, 1)	1980
LBOUND(A, 2)	1990
LBOUND(A, 3)	1
UBOUND(A, 1)	10
UBOUND(A, 2)	5
UBOUND(A, 3)	9

3. The `REDIM` statement cannot alter the data type of the matrix elements.

4. False. Not even using the `ERASE` statement will let you alter the data type of the matrix elements.

Exercise

1. Here is my version of SORT4.BAS:

```
REM Program sorts of a matrix of integers
REM
OPTION BASE 1
' declare constants
CONST MAX.ROWS = 10
CONST MAX.COLS = 3
CONST SORT.COL = 2
CONST FRMT = "####   "

' declare variables
DIM IntMat(MAX.ROWS, MAX.COLS) AS INTEGER
DIM I AS INTEGER
```

```
DIM J AS INTEGER
DIM K AS INTEGER
DIM C AS STRING

CLS
' reseed random-number generator
RANDOMIZE TIMER
FOR I = 1 TO MAX.ROWS
  FOR J = 1 TO MAX.COLS
    IntMat(I, J) = INT(RND * 1000)
  NEXT J
NEXT I

FOR I = 1 TO MAX.ROWS
  FOR J = 1 TO MAX.COLS
    PRINT USING FRMT; IntMat(I, J);
  NEXT J
  PRINT
NEXT I

PRINT
PRINT "Press any key to sort the array";
C = INPUT$(1)

' nested loops which implement the bubble sort method
FOR I = 1 TO MAX.ROWS - 1
  FOR K = I + 1 TO MAX.ROWS
      ' is element at index I greater than element
      ' at index K?
      IF IntMat(I, SORT.COL) > IntMat(K, SORT.COL) THEN
        ' swap the elements
        FOR J = 1 TO MAX.COLS
          SWAP IntMat(I, J), IntMat(K, J)
        NEXT J
      END IF
  NEXT K
NEXT I
```

B

```
CLS

FOR I = 1 TO MAX.ROWS
  FOR J = 1 TO MAX.COLS
    PRINT USING FRMT; IntMat(I, J);
  NEXT J
  PRINT
NEXT I
PRINT
PRINT "Matrix is now sorted!"
END
```

Answers to Day 14, "Math Functions"

Quiz

1. The output is:

   ```
   X = +3.81E+06
   ```

2. The call to the outer EXP function causes an numeric overflow.

3. The value passed to the SQR function is negative. Consequently, the last statement raises a runtime error.

4. The QBasic function that emulates the SGN function is:

   ```
   FUNCTION Sign%(X AS DOUBLE)
       IF X > 0 THEN
           Sign% = 1
       ELSEIF X < 0 THEN
           Sign% = -1
       ELSE
           Sign% = 1
       END IF
   END FUNCTION
   ```

Exercises

1. Here is my version of SIN2.BAS:

```
REM Program that offers numerical proof
REM that SIN(X)^2 + COS(X)^2 = 1
REM for all X
REM
' declare constants
CONST TAB1 = 20
CONST TAB2 = 30
CONST TAB3 = 40
CONST TITLE = "Table of SIN^2 + COS^2 values"
CONST FIRST = 0
CONST LAST = 360
CONST INCR = 30
' declare variable
DIM Angle AS DOUBLE
DIM Factor AS DOUBLE
DIM Y AS DOUBLE

CLS
Factor = 4 * ATN(1) / 180
PRINT
PRINT TAB(40 - LEN(TITLE) \ 2); TITLE
PRINT
PRINT TAB(TAB1); "  Angle";
PRINT TAB(TAB2); " SIN(Angle)^2 + COS(Angle)^2"
PRINT TAB(TAB1 - 5); STRING$(40, "-")
FOR Angle = FIRST TO LAST STEP INCR
  PRINT TAB(TAB1);
  PRINT USING "###.#"; Angle;
  PRINT TAB(TAB3);
  Y = SIN(Factor * Angle) ^ 2 + COS(Factor * Angle) ^ 2
  PRINT USING "+#.####"; Y
NEXT Angle

END
```

Here is the output generated by the SIN2.BAS:

```
            Table of SIN^2 + COS^2 values


      Angle     SIN(Angle)^2 + COS(Angle)^2
- - - - - - - - - - - - - - - - - - - - - - -

        0.0           +1.0000
       30.0           +1.0000
       60.0           +1.0000
       90.0           +1.0000
      120.0           +1.0000
      150.0           +1.0000
      180.0           +1.0000
      210.0           +1.0000
      240.0           +1.0000
      270.0           +1.0000
      300.0           +1.0000
      330.0           +1.0000
      360.0           +1.0000
```

Notice that all the entries in the second column are equal to 1. These values offer the numerical (and practical) proof that, for all angles, the sum of the sine squared plus the cosine squared is equal to one.

2. Here is my version of COS2.BAS:

```
REM Program that gives a numeric
REM proof that SIN(2X) = 2 * SIN(X) * COS(X)
REM
' declare constants
CONST TAB1 = 20
CONST TAB2 = 30
CONST TAB3 = 40
CONST TITLE = "Table of SIN(2 * Angle) values"
CONST FIRST = 0
CONST LAST = 90
CONST INCR = 10
' declare variable
DIM Angle AS DOUBLE
DIM Factor AS DOUBLE
DIM Y AS DOUBLE
```

```
CLS
Factor = 4 * ATN(1) / 180
PRINT
PRINT TAB(40 - LEN(TITLE) \ 2); TITLE
PRINT
PRINT TAB(TAB1); "  A";
PRINT TAB(TAB2); " SIN(2*A)";
PRINT TAB(TAB3); "2*SIN(A)*COS(A)"
PRINT TAB(TAB1 - 5); STRING$(40, "-")
FOR Angle = FIRST TO LAST STEP INCR
  PRINT TAB(TAB1);
  PRINT USING "###.#"; Angle;
  PRINT TAB(TAB2);
  PRINT USING "+#.####"; SIN(2 * Factor * Angle);
  Y = 2 * SIN(Factor * Angle) * COS(Factor * Angle)
  PRINT TAB(TAB3);
  PRINT USING "+#.####"; Y
NEXT Angle

END
```

Here is the output generated by COS2.BAS:

```
            Table of SIN(2 * Angle) values

       A        SIN(2*A) 2*SIN(A)*COS(A)
    - - - - - - - - - - - - - - - - - - - - - - - - -
       0.0      +0.0000   +0.0000
      10.0      +0.3420   +0.3420
      20.0      +0.6428   +0.6428
      30.0      +0.8660   +0.8660
      40.0      +0.9848   +0.9848
      50.0      +0.9848   +0.9848
      60.0      +0.8660   +0.8660
      70.0      +0.6428   +0.6428
      80.0      +0.3420   +0.3420
      90.0      +0.0000   +0.0000
```

The values in the second and third columns are equal for each value of
A. These matching values offer the numerical (and practical) proof that
SIN(2*X) is equal to 2 * SIN(X) * COS(X).

Answers to Day 15, "User-Defined Data Types"

Quiz

1. The index should appear after the array name `Point` and before the dot access operator. Here are the correct statements in the `FOR_NEXT` loop:

```
FOR I = 1 TO MAX.POINTS
  Points(I).X = INT(RND * 1000)
  Points(I).Y = INT(RND * 1000)
NEXT I
```

2. The program output is

```
"Hello     "
"1234567890"
"1234567890"
```

3. The `TPolygon` structure cannot have the field `Vertex` as an array.

4. The program fills the screen with the letter A.

Exercises

1. Here is my version of TYPE4.BAS:

```
REM Program displays messages on the screen
REM
TYPE TMessage
  Text AS STRING * 80
  X AS INTEGER
  Y AS INTEGER
END TYPE

'$DYNAMIC
' declare variables
DIM Message(1) AS TMessage
DIM I AS INTEGER
DIM N AS INTEGER
```

```
CLS
' read the number of messages
READ N
' redimension the dynamic array
REDIM Message(1 TO N) AS TMessage
' read the data
FOR I = 1 TO N
  READ Message(I).Text
  READ Message(I).Y
  READ Message(I).X
NEXT I
' display the messages
FOR I = N TO 1 STEP -1
  LOCATE Message(I).Y, Message(I).X
  PRINT RTRIM$(Message(I).Text);
NEXT I

' ****************** DATA Statements **************

DATA 4
DATA Hello, 10, 10
DATA Bonjour, 12, 40
DATA Howdee, 20,1
DATA Greetings!, 3, 5

END
```

2. Here is my version of TYPE5.BAS:

```
REM Program that fills a screen with characters
REM
' declare constants
CONST SCREENSIZE = 2000
' declare the TScreen structure
TYPE TScreen
  Text AS STRING * SCREENSIZE
  FillChar AS STRING * 1
  Count AS INTEGER
END TYPE
' declare variables
DIM S AS TScreen
```

```
DIM C AS STRING * 1
DIM I AS INTEGER

CLS
S.Count = SCREENSIZE
FOR I = ASC("A") TO ASC("F")
  S.FillChar = CHR$(I)
  S.Text = STRING$(S.Count, S.FillChar)
  PRINT S.Text;
  C = INPUT$(1)
NEXT I
S.Text = STRING$(S.Count, " ")
PRINT S.Text;
END
```

Answers to Day 16, "Advanced Subprograms"

Quiz

1. The function makes no provision to return a value if it exits through the EXIT FUNCTION statement.

2. The recursive call to the function passes the argument I, which is also the argument for the current function call. This version of Factorial# is guaranteed to overflow!

3. True. Using the FOR-NEXT loop is more efficient than using recursive calls.

Exercises

1. Here is my version of ADVSUB9.BAS:

```
DECLARE FUNCTION PowerOf# (B AS DOUBLE, E AS INTEGER)
DECLARE FUNCTION Square# (X#)
REM Program which calculates the integer
REM power using a recursive function
REM
' declare constants
```

```
      DIM BaseNum AS DOUBLE
      DIM Exponent AS INTEGER
      DIM Power AS DOUBLE

      CLS
      DO
        INPUT "Enter a non-zero number "; BaseNum
        PRINT
      LOOP UNTIL BaseNum <> 0

      DO
        INPUT "Enter an exponent (>= 2) "; Exponent
        PRINT
      LOOP UNTIL Exponent >= 2
      Power = PowerOf(BaseNum, Exponent)
      PRINT BaseNum; "^"; Exponent; " = "; Power
      END

      FUNCTION PowerOf# (B AS DOUBLE, E AS INTEGER)
      ' recursive function to calculate the power function
        IF E = 0 THEN
          PowerOf# = 1
        ELSEIF E = 1 THEN
          PowerOf# = B
        ELSEIF (E MOD 2) = 0 THEN
          PowerOf# = Square(PowerOf#(B, E \ 2))
        ELSE
          PowerOf# = Square(PowerOf#(B, E \ 2)) * B
        END IF
      END FUNCTION

      FUNCTION Square# (X#)
        Square# = X# * X#
      END FUNCTION
```

B

2. Here is my version of ADVSUB10.BAS:

```
DECLARE SUB DisplayPoints (Pts() AS ANY, N%)
DECLARE SUB SortPoints (Pts() AS ANY, N%)
DECLARE SUB WaitAWhile ()
```

```
DECLARE SUB InputPoints (Pts() AS ANY, N%)
REM Program which sorts an array of
REM points according to their distances
REM from the origin (0,0)
REM
OPTION BASE 1
' declare the TCoord type
TYPE TCoord
  X AS SINGLE
  Y AS SINGLE
  OrgDist AS SINGLE
END TYPE

' declare constant
CONST MAX.POINTS = 5
' declare variable
DIM Points(MAX.POINTS) AS TCoord

CLS
InputPoints Points(), MAX.POINTS
DisplayPoints Points(), MAX.POINTS
WaitAWhile
SortPoints Points(), MAX.POINTS
DisplayPoints Points(), MAX.POINTS
END

SUB DisplayPoints (Pts() AS TCoord, N%)
' display points in array Pts
  DIM I AS INTEGER

  CLS
  FOR I = 1 TO N%
    PRINT USING "Point number ## is (##.##"; I;
    Pts(I).X;
    PRINT ",";
    PRINT USING "##.##)"; Pts(I).Y
  NEXT I
END SUB
```

```
SUB InputPoints (Pts() AS TCoord, N%)
' input N% points
  DIM I AS INTEGER

  FOR I = 1 TO N%
    PRINT "Enter coordinates for point #"; I
    INPUT "                 X"; Pts(I).X
    INPUT "                 Y"; Pts(I).Y
    PRINT
    Pts(I).OrgDist = SQR(Pts(I).X ^ 2 + Pts(I).Y ^ 2)
  NEXT I
END SUB

SUB SortPoints (Pts() AS TCoord, N%)
' sort the elements of array Pts

  DIM I AS INTEGER
  DIM J AS INTEGER

  FOR I = 1 TO N% - 1
    FOR J = I TO N%
      IF Pts(I).OrgDist > Pts(J).OrgDist THEN
        SWAP Pts(I), Pts(J)
      END IF
    NEXT J
  NEXT I
END SUB

SUB WaitAWhile
' pause the program
  DIM C AS STRING * 1

  PRINT "press any key to continue"
  C = INPUT$(1)
END SUB
```

Answers to Day 17, "Advanced String Manipulation"

Quiz

1. False. The STRING$ function uses only the first character in its second argument. The output is the string "+++".

2. The program displays the string "The !!! in Spain". The number of ! characters is controlled by the third argument of the MID$ statement.

3. When MID$ has the second argument of 1, you can substitute it with the LEFT$ function. The call to LEFT$ can use the first and third arguments of the MID$ function. Therefore the simpler form is:

```
PRINT "I'm going to "; LEFT$("Spain", 3)
```

Exercises

1. Here is my version of ALIGN1.BAS:

```
REM Program which aligns the last characters
REM of three strings at column 40
REM
' declare constant
CONST ALIGN.COL = 40
' declare variables
DIM S1 AS STRING
DIM S2 AS STRING
DIM S3 AS STRING

CLS
' enter strings
INPUT "Enter first string : ", S1
INPUT "Enter second string : ", S2
INPUT "Enter third string : ", S3
PRINT
' display strings with last characters
' aligned at column 40
PRINT SPACE$(ALIGN.COL - LEN(S1)); S1
```

```
PRINT SPACE$(ALIGN.COL - LEN(S2)); S2
PRINT SPACE$(ALIGN.COL - LEN(S3)); S3
END
```

2. Here is my version of DATE1.BAS:

```
REM Program extracts the year, month, and day numbers
REM from the result of the DATE$ function
REM
' declare variable
DIM DateStr AS STRING

CLS
DateStr = DATE$
PRINT "Year is : "; MID$(DateStr, 7)
PRINT "Month number is "; LEFT$(DateStr, 2)
PRINT "Day number is "; MID$(DateStr, 4, 2)
END
```

Answers to Day 18, "Text File I/O"

Quiz

1. The variable `oldFile` contains an invalid filename. DOS filenames must not contain the > character.

2. Both files use the same file handle number. To correct the program, use different file handle numbers. Better yet, use the FREEFILE function to eliminate the accidental duplicate use of file handles.

3. Both input and output filenames are the same. They must be different.

4. The program uses the INPUT statement to read the strings from the input line. When a text line in the input file contains one or more commas, it will cause that line to be read in chunks. Consequently, the output file will likely contain more (and smaller) lines than the input file.

Exercise

1. Here is my version of SQFILE4.BAS:

```
REM Program which copies a text file
REM
' declare variables
DIM InFilename AS STRING
DIM OutFilename AS STRING
DIM InFile AS INTEGER
DIM OutFile AS INTEGER
DIM TextLine AS STRING


CLS
DO
  INPUT "Enter input filename : ", InFilename
  InFilename = UCASE$(InFilename)
  PRINT
LOOP UNTIL InFilename <> ""


DO
  INPUT "Enter output filename : ", OutFilename
  OutFilename = UCASE$(OutFilename)
  PRINT
LOOP UNTIL OutFilename <> "" AND InFilename <> OutFilename


ON ERROR GOTO Bad.InFilename
InFile = FREEFILE
OPEN InFilename FOR INPUT AS InFile
ON ERROR GOTO 0


ON ERROR GOTO Bad.OutFilename
OutFile = FREEFILE
OPEN OutFilename FOR OUTPUT AS OutFile
ON ERROR GOTO 0


PRINT "Copying file "; InFilename; " to file "; OutFilename
PRINT
```

```
DO WHILE NOT EOF(InFile)
  LINE INPUT #InFile, TextLine
  PRINT #OutFile, TextLine
LOOP

' close files
CLOSE
PRINT : PRINT "Done!"
EndPrgm:
END

Bad.InFilename:
  PRINT
  PRINT "Cannot open file "; InFilename
  RESUME EndPrgm

Bad.OutFilename:
  PRINT
  PRINT "Cannot open file "; OutFilename
  RESUME EndPrgm
```

B

Answers to Day 19, "Random-Access and Binary File I/O"

Quiz

1. The record number in the PUT statement must be 1 because the OPEN statement creates a new file.

2. The PUT statement only takes three arguments. The last argument must be removed.

3. Convert the variables N and X into the fields of a structure, called TRec. Here is the working program version:

```
TYPE TRec
  N AS INTEGER
  X AS DOUBLE
END TYPE
```

```
DIM Rec AS TRec
Rec.N = 12
Rec.X = 1.2
OPEN "DATA.DAT" FOR RANDOM AS #1
PUT #1, 1, Rec
CLOSE #1
END
```

Exercise

1. Here is my version of BNFILE2.BAS:

```
REM Program which copies a file
REM
' declare constant
CONST BUFFER% = 8192
' declare variables
DIM InFilename AS STRING
DIM OutFilename AS STRING
DIM InFile AS INTEGER
DIM OutFile AS INTEGER
DIM BuffVar AS STRING
DIM FileSize AS LONG

CLS
DO
  INPUT "Enter input filename : ", InFilename
  InFilename = UCASE$(InFilename)
  PRINT
LOOP UNTIL InFilename <> ""

DO
  INPUT "Enter output filename : ", OutFilename
  OutFilename = UCASE$(OutFilename)
  PRINT
LOOP UNTIL OutFilename <> "" AND InFilename <> OutFilename

ON ERROR GOTO Bad.InFilename
InFile = FREEFILE
```

```
OPEN InFilename FOR BINARY AS InFile
ON ERROR GOTO 0

ON ERROR GOTO Bad.OutFilename
OutFile = FREEFILE
OPEN OutFilename FOR BINARY AS OutFile
ON ERROR GOTO 0

PRINT "Copying file "; InFilename; " to file "; OutFilename
PRINT
' initialize the file size
FileSize = 0
' loop to copy the files
DO WHILE NOT EOF(InFile)
  ' prepare the buffer
  BuffVar = SPACE$(BUFFER)
  GET #InFile, , BuffVar
  ' update the number of bytes copied
  FileSize = FileSize + LEN(BuffVar)
  PUT #OutFile, , BuffVar
LOOP

' close files
CLOSE
PRINT
PRINT "Copied"; FileSize; "bytes"
EndPrgm:
END

Bad.InFilename:
  PRINT
  PRINT "Cannot open file "; InFilename
  RESUME EndPrgm

Bad.OutFilename:
  PRINT
  PRINT "Cannot open file "; OutFilename
  RESUME EndPrgm
```

B

Answers to Day 20, "Drawing Graphics Shapes"

Quiz

1. False. Although the second LINE statement uses out-of-range coordinates, QBasic does not generate a runtime error. QBasic draws only the line in the first LINE statement.

2. Including the SCREEN keywords inverts the Y-coordinates. Consequently, the plot is reflected around the middle of the screen. You get the same figure if the GRAF1.BAS and GRAF2.BAS programs were plotting the -SIN(X) function.

3. True. The program shows one method to erase a shape. In general, to erase a shape, redraw it using the foreground color.

Exercise

1. Here is my version of GRAF6.BAS:

```
REM Program that plots the function SIN(X) / EXP(0.04 * X)
REM
' declare constants
CONST CYCLES = 10
CONST MAX.Y = 1.5
CONST MIN.Y = -1.5
CONST MAX.X = CYCLES * 180
CONST MIN.X = 0
CONST INCR = 1!
' declare variables
DIM X AS SINGLE
DIM Y AS SINGLE
DIM X2 AS SINGLE
DIM LastY AS SINGLE
DIM Factor AS DOUBLE
DIM C AS STRING * 1
DIM aColor AS INTEGER

' get the angle conversion factor
Factor = 4 * ATN(1) / 180
```

```
SCREEN 8
WINDOW (MIN.X, MIN.Y)-(MAX.X, MAX.Y)
CLS
' draw X-axis
LINE (MIN.X, 0)-(MAX.X, 0)
' draw Y-axis
LINE (0, MIN.Y)-(0, MAX.Y)
' draw the SIN(X) function
Y = SIN((MIN.X - INCR) * Factor)
aColor = 0
FOR X = MIN.X TO MAX.X STEP INCR
  X2 = X * Factor
  Y = SIN(X2) / EXP(.04 * X2)
  IF (Y * LastY) <= 0 THEN aColor = aColor + 1
  PSET (X, Y)
  ' fill in the area under the curve
  LINE (X, Y)-(X, 0), aColor
  LastY = Y
NEXT X
' draw X-axis again
LINE (MIN.X, 0)-(MAX.X, 0)
END
```

B

Glossary

address: The location of each byte in the computer's memory. The lowest memory address is 0. The highest memory address depends on the amount of memory in a computer.

argument: The value passed to a parameter of a function or a procedure.

array: A collection of variables that share the same name and use one or more indices to access an individual member.

ASCII: The acronym for American Standard Code for Information Interchange.

ASCII file: A file that contains readable text. ASCII files are called text files also.

AUTOEXEC.BAT: A special batch file that the computer automatically executes if it finds it in the root directory of the boot disk.

backup file: A duplicate copy of a file that protects your work in case you damage the text or data in the main file.

.BAK: The common file extension for backup files.

.BAS: The common file extension for BASIC programs.

batch file: An executable file that contains MS-DOS commands and other special commands. Batch files assist in automating various tasks.

binary: A two-digit numbering system (0 and 1).

bit: Short for **binary digit**. Bits are the smallest units of data storage. Programs commonly use groups of 8, 16, 32, and 64 bits to represent different kinds of data.

bubblesort: The slowest and simplest method for ordering the elements of an array in ascending or descending order.

buffer: A memory location where transient data flows in and out.

bug: A common name for a logical program error.

byte: A unit of data storage that contains 8 bits.

CGA: Short for Color Graphics Adapter. CGA screens have a resolution of 640-by-200 pixels.

clipboard: A special memory area in the QBasic environment that holds text you copied or deleted.

clock tick: The duration based on the CPU's internal clock. One second has 18.2 clock ticks.

Comb sort: A new and efficient method for sorting the elements of an array. This method is based on improving the bubblesort method.

CONFIG.SYS: The name of the system configuration file. When a machine boots, it reads the CONFIG.SYS file in the root directory of the boot disk.

concatenation: Joining two or more strings by chaining their characters.

conditional loop: A loop that iterates until or while a tested condition is true.

constant: Information that remains fixed during the execution of a program.

CPU: Short for Central Processing Unit, the computer's brain.

crash: The state in which a computer seems to freeze and does not respond to the keyboard, mouse, or any other input device.

cursor: The blinking underline or block that appears on the screen to indicate where the next character insertion will occur.

data processing: Manipulating or managing information.

data record: A collection of data items that conveys meaningful information. Your mailing address, for example, is a data record.

debug: To detect and remove logical errors in the program.

debugger: A tool that assists you in debugging the program. The QBasic environment contains a simple debugger.

default: A preselected action or value used when no other action or value is offered.

dialog box: A special pop-up screen that prompts you for input.

directory: A section or compartment of a hard, floppy, or electronic disk that contains files.

disk: The magnetic medium that stores data.

disk drive: The device that reads and loads data and programs on a disk.

diskette: A removable thin disk, also called floppy disk.

display: The screen, console, or monitor in a computer.

G

display adapter: The board inside a computer that assists in displaying text and graphics.

DOS: Acronym for Disk Operating System.

drag: The act of holding a mouse button down while moving the mouse. This action moves a window from one location in the screen to another.

EGA: Short for Enhanced Graphics Adapter. The resolution of an EGA display is 640-by-350 pixels.

element (of an array):   The member of an array, accessed by specifying one or more indices.

file: The name of a location on a disk that contains a program, text, or other data.

file extension: The three letters used by DOS files to identify the type of file. Programs have file extensions of .COM or .EXE.

file I/O: File input and/or output.

filename: The name of a DOS file.

fixed-length string variables: Variables that store a fixed number of characters. If you assign a string with fewer characters than the variable's capacity, QBasic pads the contents of that variable with spaces. By contrast, if you assign a string with more characters than the variable's capacity, QBasic throws away the extra characters.

fixed-length records: Data records with the same length.

floppy disk: *See* **diskette**

format: The image or map used to output data.

function: A subprogram that executes one or more statements and returns a single value.

function key: The keys labeled F1–F10 on a keyboard. Some keyboards also have keys labeled F11 and F12.

global variable: A variable that is accessible to all functions and procedures in a program.

graphics monitor: A monitor that is able to display high-resolution graphics.

hertz: The unit of measuring frequency. One hertz is one cycle per second.

HGA: Short for Hercules Graphics Adapter.

input: The data that a program obtains from the keyboard, disk drive, communication port, or any other input device.

I/O: Short for Input/Output.

integer variable: A variable that stores integers. QBasic has two types of integer variables. The first kind occupies two bytes and stores numbers between –32768 and 32767. The second kind, called the long integer, occupies four bytes and stores numbers between minus and plus two billions.

kilobyte (K): A unit of measuring memory. 1K is 1024 bytes.

least significant bit: The right-most bit in a byte, word, or any other unit of memory.

local variable: A variable that is declared inside a function or procedure.

loop: A set of statements that are repeatedly executed.

main module: The main program section.

main program: The main program section.

math operator: A symbol that performs a mathematical operation, such as addition, subtraction, multiplication, division, and raising to powers.

matrix: A two-dimensional array. The elements of a matrix are accessed by specifying the row and column indices.

MCGA: Short for Multi-Color Graphics Adapter.

MDA: Short for Monochrome Display Adapter.

megabyte (M): A unit of memory. 1M is approximately one million bytes.

memory: The part of the computer that retains programs and data while the computer is on.

menu: A display that offers a set of options to select from.

menu-driven: A program that depends on one or more menus to perform its tasks, as guided by the user.

modulus: The integer remainder of a division.

monitor: Screen, console, or display.

G

monochrome: Single color. Monochrome monitors can't display colors or high-resolution graphics.

most-significant bit: The leftmost bit in a byte, word, or other unit of memory.

MS-DOS: The Microsoft Disk Operator System.

multidimensional arrays: Arrays that have multiple subscripts.

nested loop: A loop inside another loop.

null string: An empty string.

numeric function: A function that returns a numerical value.

open loop: A loop that (in principle) iterates indefinitely. In practice, the majority of open loops use an exit mechanism located in a statement inside the loop.

order of operators: The priority of executing operations in an expression.

output device: A device that receives output. Common output devices are the screen, the printer, the disk drive, and the communication port. Some output devices also support input, such as the communication port and the disk drive.

palette: A set of possible colors.

parameter: A special variable that appears after the declaration of a function or procedure. Parameters fine-tune the operations of the function or procedure.

passing by reference: The task of passing an argument to a function or procedure by providing its reference. Consequently, the parameter receiving the reference becomes an alias to the argument. Changes made to the parameter inside the function or procedure also affect the argument.

passing by value: The task of passing an argument to a function or procedure by providing a copy of its value. Consequently, any changes made to the parameter inside the function or procedure do not affect the argument.

pixel: Picture element.

precedence of operators: *See* **order of operators.**

procedure: A QBasic subprogram. QBasic supports the SUB procedure and the FUNCTION procedure. The latter procedure returns a value.

program: A collection of executable statements or instructions.

programming language: The high-level human interface for communicating with a machine.

pseudocode: A text outline that describes in English the tasks of a program.

RAM: Acronym for Random-Access Memory.

random-access file: A file that permits you to access its fixed-length records for input and output by specifying the record number. Random-access files are suitable for databases.

random-access memory (RAM): Memory that can be accessed by specifying an address.

read-only memory (ROM): A class of memory that contains fixed data.

record: A unit of storing information in a data file. Typically, text files have variable-length records. Random-access files contain fixed-length records.

relational operators: Symbols that compare two compatible data items and return a logical value.

resolution: The sharpness of an image that appears on a screen.

ROM: *See* **read-only memory.**

scientific notation: A special form for representing numbers by specifying the mantissa and the exponent. In a number such as 1.23E+44, the 1.23 is the mantissa and +44 is the exponent (the power of ten). Therefore, 1.23E+44 is a more convenient way of writing $1.23 \times 10^{+44}$.

sequential file: A file that stores readable text using variable-length records.

single-dimensional arrays: An array that requires a single subscript to access its elements.

sorting: The task of arranging the elements of an array in either ascending or descending order. The array is ordered using part or all of the value in each element.

string constant: A constant associated with a string literal.

string literal: A set of characters enclosed in a pair of double-quotation marks.

string variable: A variable that stores a string of characters.

structure: A user-defined data type. QBasic enables you to define a structure using the TYPE statement.

G

structured variable: A variable whose type is a user-defined data type.

structured array: An array that contains user-defined data-type elements.

subdirectory: A directory that is connected to a parent directory.

subroutine: A set of statements that can be called by other program statements to perform the a basic task.

subscript: The index of an array.

SVGA: Short for Super VGA.

syntax error: An error in writing a statement.

system hang: *See* **crash**

text file: *See* **ASCII file**

unary operator: Symbols that require only one operand.

user-defined data type: *See* **structure.**

user-defined functions: A function defined by a programmer to conceptually extend the QBasic language by accomplishing a specific task.

variable: A tagged memory location that stores data.

variable-length string variables: A string variable that can accommodate a varying number of characters.

variable-length record: A record that can store a varying number of bytes or characters.

variable scope: The visibility of a variable in the different components of a program.

VGA: Short for Vector Graphics Array. The resolution of VGA is 640-by-480 pixels.

word: A unit of data storage that contains 2 bytes or 16 bits.

Index

binary
  files, I/O, 644-649
  math, 40
  searches, 417-419, 424-428
BINARY keyword, 645
BINARY mode, 607
bits, 40
  least significant, 41
  most significant, 41
BNFILE1.BAS program, 647-648
Boolean truth table, 85-86
border% parameter, 659-661
boxes, drawing, 668-670
bubblesorts, 410
buffers, 604
byteNumber parameter, 645-646
bytes, 40

C

CALL keyword, 341
calling
  functions, 104, 335-336
  SUB procedures, 340-344
case
  conversion, 138
    LCASE$ function, 141-143
    UCASE$ function, 138-140
  insensitivity, 105
  sensitivity, 105
CASE ELSE clause, 171
CASE1.BAS program, 172-173
CASE2.BAS program
  matching expressions, 176-177
  output, 176
  source code, 174-176
CASE3.BAS program, 180-181
CDBL function, 80-82

Center$ function, 354
CenterText subroutine, 349
Change (Search menu) option, 25
Change dialog box, 25-26
characters, 42
  converting from ASCII code, 111-114
  converting to ASCII code, 108-111
CHR$ function, 111-112
CINT function, 80-82
CIRCLE statement, 670-674
circles, drawing, 670-674
clauses
  AS, 516
  AS DOUBLE, 393
  CASE ELSE, 171
  ELSE, 165
  NEXT, consolidating, 207
  SHARED, 387, 396, 439, 447
  STEP, 198
Clear (Edit menu) option, 23
clipboard, 23
CLNG function, 80
CLOSE statement, 607-608
closing files, 607-608
CLS command, 12
codes
  ASCII, 42
  control
    !, 292
    #, 296
    $$, 298
    &, 292
    (,), 298
    **, 297
    **$, 298
    +, 297

L

N

O

Disk Offer

The programs in this book are available on disk from the author. Fill out this form and enclose a check for only $6.00. Outside the U.S. and Canada, please enclose a check for $10.00 in U.S. currency, drawn on a U.S. bank. Please make the check payable to **Namir C. Shammas**. Sorry, no credit card orders. Mail this form to:

Namir C. Shammas
3928 Margate Drive
Richmond, VA 23235

Name_____

Company (for company address) _____

Street _____

City _____

State/Province _____

ZIP or Postal Code _____

Country (outside USA) _____

Disk format (check one):

5.25 inch _____   3.5 inch _____